THE STORMRIDER GUIDE EUROPE

A LOW PRESSURE PUBLICATION

LOW PRESSURE LTD
Unit 2 Efford Farm Business Park
Bude Cornwall EX23 8LP
Tel/Fax +44 (0)1288 359867
E-mail enquiries@lowpressure.co.uk
Web www.lowpressure.co.uk

LOW PRESSURE – Europe
Tel/Fax +33 05 58 77 76 85

First published in 1992 by Low Pressure Publishing Ltd
Second edition 1995
Third edition 1998 (third impression 2000)

A catalogue record for this book can be obtained from the British Library
ISBN Softback 0 9519275 5 8

THE STORMRIDER GUIDE
EUROPE

A LOW PRESSURE PUBLICATION

ALEX WILLIAMS

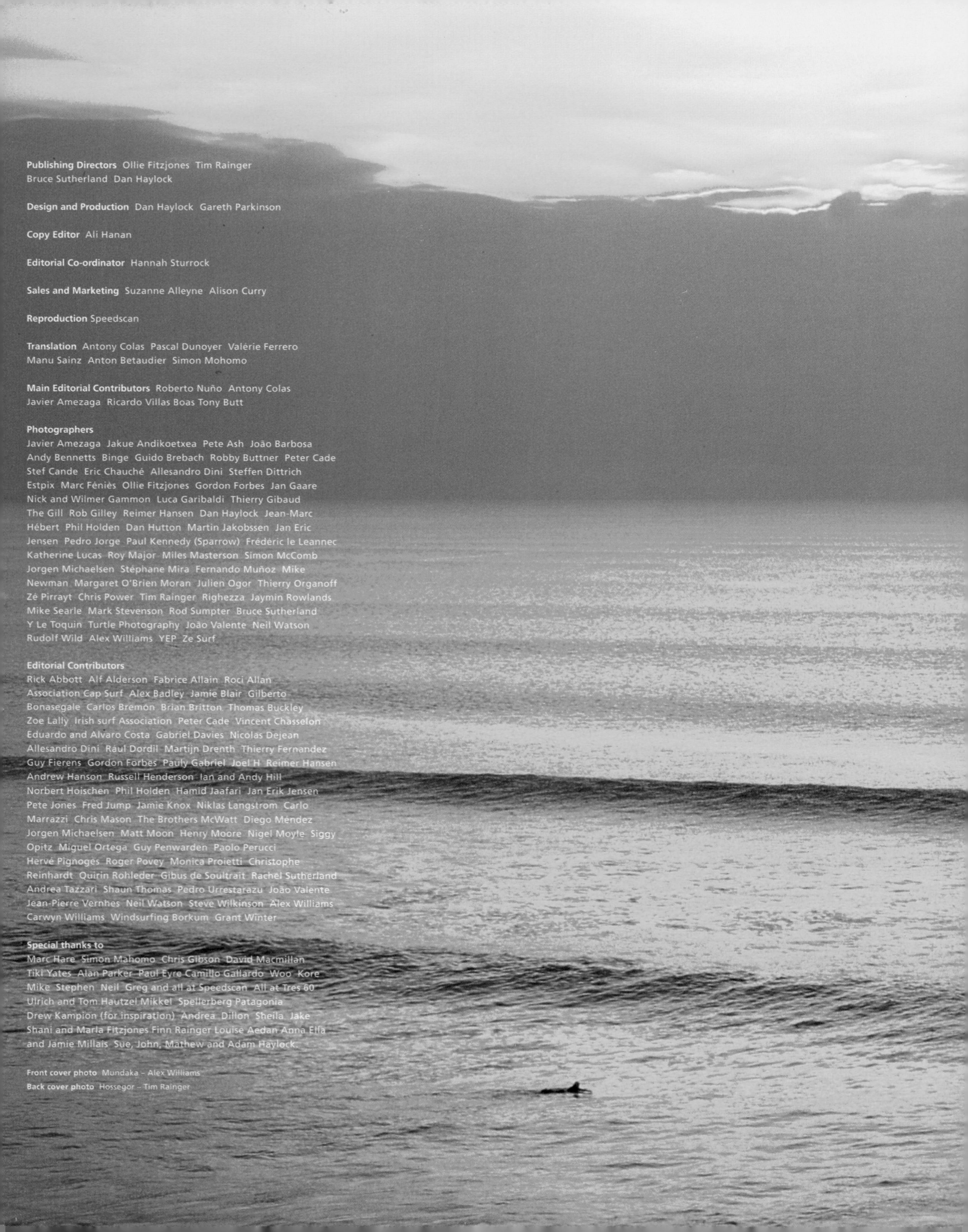

Publishing Directors Ollie Fitzjones Tim Rainger Bruce Sutherland Dan Haylock

Design and Production Dan Haylock Gareth Parkinson

Copy Editor Ali Hanan

Editorial Co-ordinator Hannah Sturrock

Sales and Marketing Suzanne Alleyne Alison Curry

Reproduction Speedscan

Translation Antony Colas Pascal Dunoyer Valérie Ferrero Manu Sainz Anton Betaudier Simon Mohomo

Main Editorial Contributors Roberto Nuño Antony Colas Javier Amezaga Ricardo Villas Boas Tony Butt

Photographers
Javier Amezaga Jakue Andikoetxea Pete Ash João Barbosa Andy Bennetts Binge Guido Brebach Robby Buttner Peter Cade Stef Cande Eric Chauché Allesandro Dini Steffen Dittrich Estpix Marc Fèniès Ollie Fitzjones Gordon Forbes Jan Gaare Nick and Wilmer Gammon Luca Garibaldi Thierry Gibaud The Gill Rob Gilley Reimer Hansen Dan Haylock Jean-Marc Hébert Phil Holden Dan Hutton Martin Jakobssen Jan Eric Jensen Pedro Jorge Paul Kennedy (Sparrow) Frédéric le Leannec Katherine Lucas Roy Major Miles Masterson Simon McComb Jorgen Michaelsen Stéphane Mira Fernando Muñoz Mike Newman Margaret O'Brien Moran Julien Ogor Thierry Organoff Zé Pirrayt Chris Power Tim Rainger Righezza Jaymin Rowlands Mike Searle Mark Stevenson Rod Sumpter Bruce Sutherland Y Le Toquin Turtle Photography João Valente Neil Watson Rudolf Wild Alex Williams YEP Ze Surf

Editorial Contributors
Rick Abbott Alf Alderson Fabrice Allain Roci Allan Association Cap Surf Alex Badley Jamie Blair Gilberto Bonasegale Carlos Bremón Brian Britton Thomas Buckley Zoe Lally Irish surf Association Peter Cade Vincent Chasselon Eduardo and Alvaro Costa Gabriel Davies Nicolas Dejean Allesandro Dini Raul Dordil Martijn Drenth Thierry Fernandez Guy Fierens Gordon Forbes Pauly Gabriel Joel H Reimer Hansen Andrew Hanson Russell Henderson Ian and Andy Hill Norbert Hoischen Phil Holden Hamid Jaafari Jan Erik Jensen Pete Jones Fred Jump Jamie Knox Niklas Langstrom Carlo Marrazzi Chris Mason The Brothers McWatt Diego Mendez Jorgen Michaelsen Matt Moon Henry Moore Nigel Moyle Siggy Opitz Miguel Ortega Guy Penwarden Paolo Perucci Hervé Pignoges Roger Povey Monica Proietti Christophe Reinhardt Quirin Rohleder Gibus de Soultrait Rachel Sutherland Andrea Tazzari Shaun Thomas Pedro Urrestarazu João Valente Jean-Pierre Vernhes Neil Watson Steve Wilkinson Alex Williams Carwyn Williams Windsurfing Borkum Grant Winter

Special thanks to
Marc Hare Simon Mahomo Chris Gibson David Macmillan Tiki Yates Alan Parker Paul Eyre Camillo Gallardo Woo Kore Mike Stephen Neil Greg and all at Speedscan All at Tres 60 Ulrich and Tom Hautzel Mikkel Spellerberg Patagonia Drew Kampion (for inspiration) Andrea Dillon Sheila Jake Shani and Marla Fitzjones Finn Rainger Louise Aedan Anna Ella and Jamie Millais Sue, John, Mathew and Adam Haylock.

Front cover photo Mundaka – Alex Williams
Back cover photo Hossegor – Tim Rainger

Surfing feeds the human body and spirit.
Discovery is just one joyous part of this
strangely indescribable experience.
For every break noted in this book there
are many more to find. It provides a
platform from which exploration springs.
Use the knowledge wisely.
DAN HAYLOCK

Contents

HARD 8

TAHITI

silvina

TIME IS WHAT YOU MAK OF IT

PHOTO BY TOM SERVAIS

swatch®
CONAN HAYES, MEMBER OF THE SWATCH PROTEAM

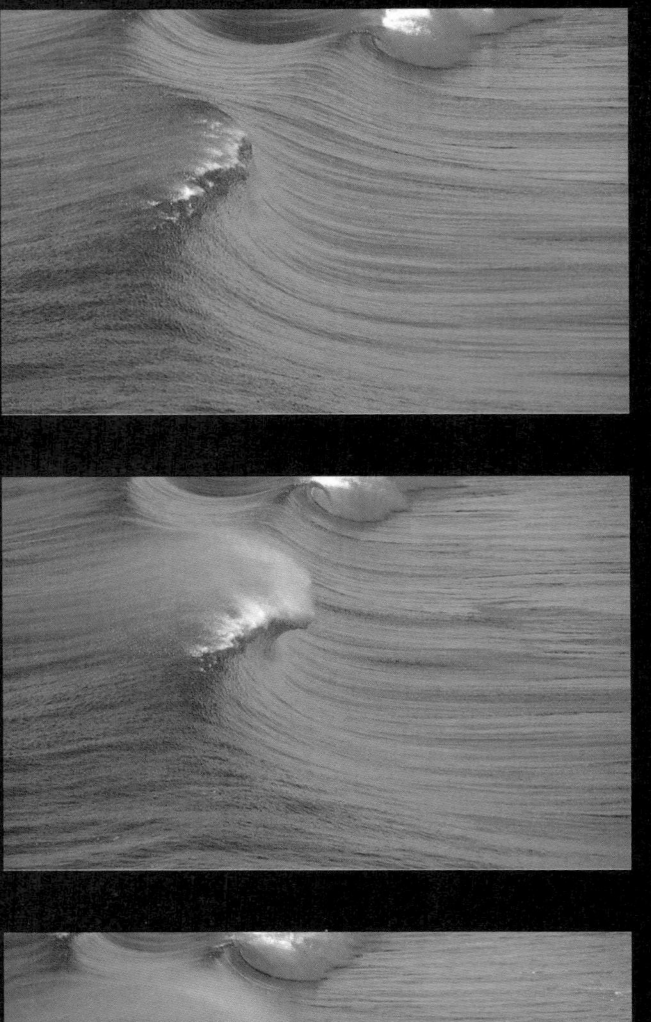

London is Europe's largest city.

It also has the biggest airports in Europe and it's here that most travelling surfers begin their European missions. Three main things will keep you in this expensive, surfless zone: the first is a job, the second is looking for a vehicle and lastly just trying to get the hell out of here and go surfing.

Work

Obtaining work is fine for EC nationals, Australians, Kiwis and other Commonwealth peoples who can obtain casual permits, with the easiest options finding employment in the building or catering trades. Keep an eye out for jobs in *TNT* and *Southern Cross* mags (both free outside many tube stations) and the *Evening Standard*. Australians and New Zealanders have a good reputation for hard work. As with everywhere else, use your imagination. London offers countless money-making opportunities.

Buying a vehicle

There are several options. Look in *TNT* and *Southern Cross*, or *Loot* and *What Car* magazines. *TNT* and *Southern Cross* often have the best deals as people selling vehicles are often about to leave the country and have to sell fast. Impromptu Antipodean used-van lots appear at various semi-permanent park-and-sell locations, including: Market Rd N7 (Caledonian tube) and Vestry Street (near Old Street). People often live here till they sell their vans! Car wreckers are spread all over the M25 area. A good one is: A1 Metro, Hendon: (0181) 205 2100.

Leaving

By air If you're looking for a cheap flight, and you're prepared to leave at the drop of a hat, look no further than the *Evening Standard*. The travel pages offer by far the cheapest flights to some excellent surfing destinations. Also look at *Time Out*, *TNT*, *Southern Cross* or in the travel sections of the Sunday newspapers. Here you'll find a selection of European and worldwide destinations at the best available prices.

Low Pressure offer a specialised surf and snowboard travel company that can solve many problems in one phone call. We book flights and accommodation at many primo European and international locations. Low Pressure Surf Travel: (0181) 960 1916

By bus The cheapest form of transport anywhere within Europe is the bus. They leave from Victoria Coach station (right by Victoria Tube). National Express have a 'no surfboards' policy, which renders them useless to the surfing community.

By train This form of travel offers no real advantages; prices are no cheaper than flights and you could be asked to pay a full fare for your surfboard. Still, if you're a student or if you plan to travel extensively on the rail networks of Europe, you can get worthwhile deals.

Y LE TOQUIN

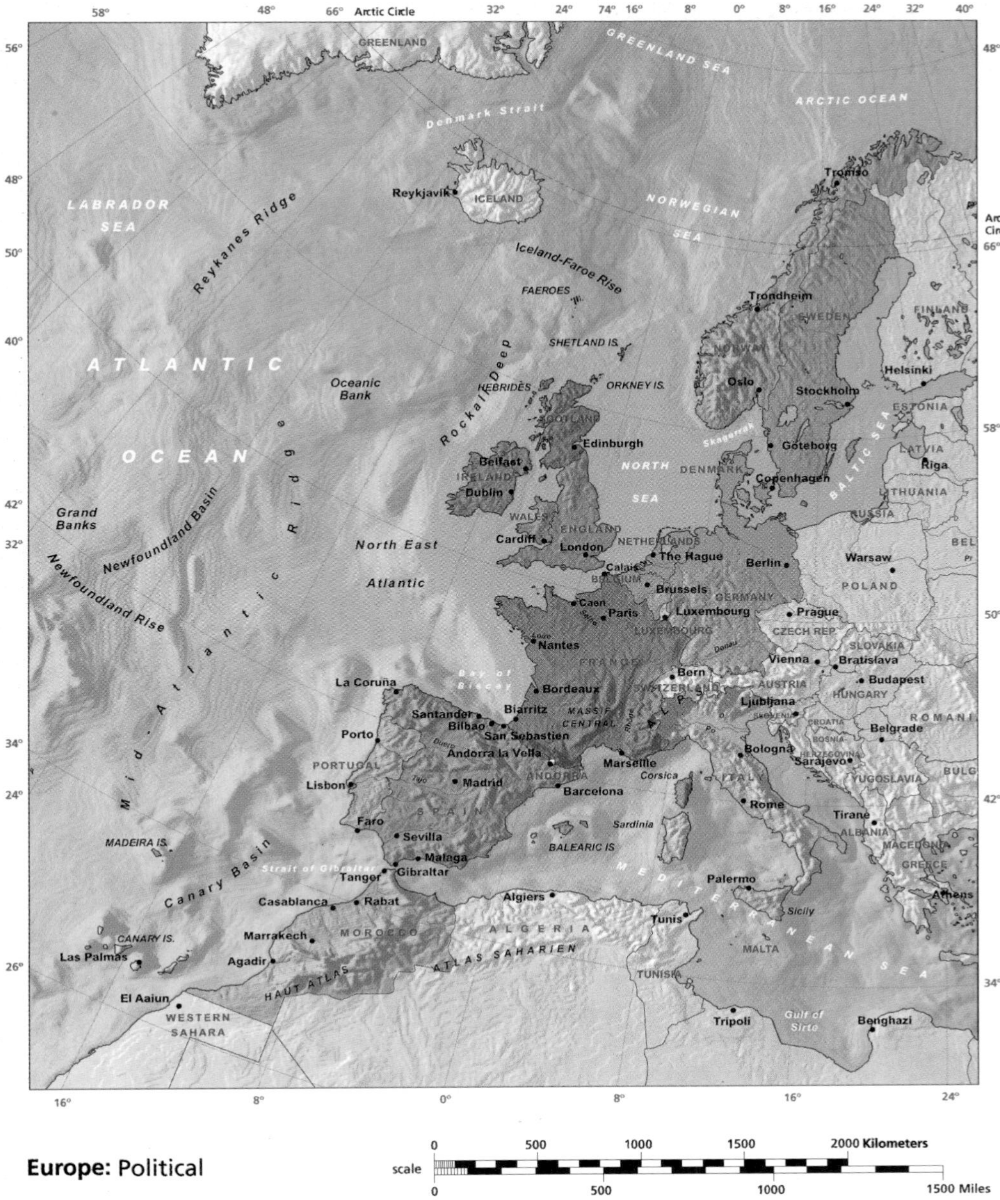

Europe: Political

scale 0 500 1000 1500 2000 Kilometers / 0 500 1000 1500 Miles

THE STORMRIDER GUIDE EUROPE

Introduction

Land Area

Europe	10,498,000 sqkm (4,052,000sqmi)

Population of Major Cities

Mexico City (highest in world)	18,749,000
London	9,092,044
Paris	9,060,000
Berlin	3,400,000
Rome	3,051,000
Madrid	2,991,253
Manchester	2,590,550
Barcelona	1,677,699
Stockholm	1,665,000
Munich	1,633,000
Lisbon	1,603,000
Hamburg	1,600,000
Copenhagen	1,338,214
Amsterdam	1,063,000
Brussels	970,401
Oslo	458,622

Mountains

Mont Blanc, France-Italy	4,808m (15,774ft)
Monte Rosa, Italy-Switzerland	4,634m (15,203ft)
Dom (Mischabel Group), Switzerland	4,545m (14,910ft)
Matterhorn, Italy-Switzerland	4,477m (14,688ft)
Toubkal, Morocco	4,165m (13,644ft)
Teide, Canary Islands	3,718m (12,198ft)
Etna, Sicily, Italy	3,323m (10,902ft)

River Length

Nile, Africa (longest in world)	6,695km (4,160mi)
Danube	2,850km (1,770mi)
Dneper	2,285km (1,420mi)
Kama	2,032km (1,270mi)
Don	1,870km (1,162mi)
Pechora	1,809km (1,124mi)
Oka	1,480km (925mi)
Rhine	1,320km (820mi)
Elbe	1,159km (720mi)
Loire	1,012km (629mi)
Tagus	1,006km (625mi)
Seine	761km (473mi)
Severn	354km (220mi)
Thames	346km (215mi)
Trent	300km (186mi)

Ocean Facts and Figures

The area of the earth covered by sea is estimated to be 361,740,000sqkm (139,670,000sqmi) or 70.92% of the total surface. The mean depth is estimated to be 3554m (11,660ft) and the volume of the oceans to be 1,285,600,000cukm (308,400,000cumi)

Atlantic Ocean

Commonly divided into North Atlantic (36,000,000sqkm) and South Atlantic (26,000,000sqkm). The greatest breadth in the North is 7200km (Morocco to Florida) and in the South 9600km (Guinea to Brazil). Average depth is 3600m; the greatest depths are the Puerto Rico Trench (9220m), Sandwich Trench (8264m) and Romansh Trench (7728m).

Area

Atlantic Ocean	82,217,000sqkm (31,736,000sqmi)
Mediterranean Sea	2,505,000sqkm (967,000sqmi)
Black Sea	461,000sqkm (178,000sqmi)
North Sea	575,000sqkm (222,000sqmi)
Baltic Sea	422,000sqkm (163,000sqmi)

The Birth of a Low

The most important phenomenon which produces rideable waves in Europe is the **low pressure**, or **mid-latitude depression**.

Uneven heating of the planet causes hot air to rise over the equator, which is replaced by colder polar air. These areas of different air are measured in barometric pressure and called 'lows' or 'highs'.

A low pressure is a pocket of cooler air, which sucks in air from surrounding areas of high pressure, creating winds. Because of the rotation of the earth, these winds will circulate around the low in an anti-clockwise direction in the Northern Hemisphere due to an effect called the Coriolis force.

For lows to form, they need something to make the pressure go down, and/or something to help them spin. One of many processes which does this is when a warm and cold air mass meet. The warm mass will tend to 'slide' over the top of the cold one, which not only lowers the pressure, but creates instability to make the air start spinning. These weather systems become more energetic in winter due to the temperature difference between the poles and the equator.

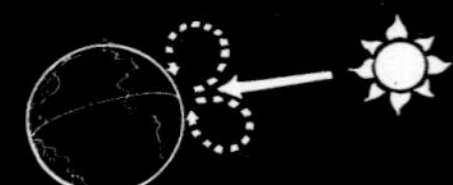

Hot air rises and is replaced by cool air

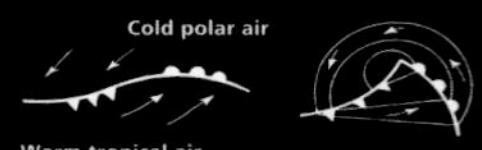

The anatomy of a depression

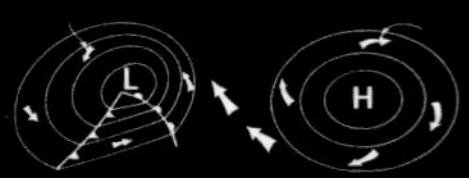

Flow of air from a high to a low

A primary influence on the movements of weather systems is the flow of air at high levels in the atmosphere, called **the jet-stream**. The jet-stream goes much faster than the air closer to the planet's surface, and blows more or less from west to east around the world. It dictates both the path and intensity of surface weather systems. In the Atlantic, its most consistent path is from Florida to Scotland, but it can deviate north towards Iceland or south towards Portugal. It may split, going north and south, and it can also change in intensity with strong or weak sections.

The details are usually reflected in the state of the surface charts. A jet which goes diagonally from south west to north east will favour the deepening of 'lows', while one which goes diagonally the other way (north west to south east) will tend to make the lows fizzle out.

Systèmes dépressionnaires

Le réchauffement inégal à la surface de la terre fait que l'air chaud qui s'élève au niveau de l'Equateur est remplacé par de l'air froid descendu du pôle. Ces masses d'air différent sont mesurées par leur pression barométrique, qu'on appelle des dépressions (Déps) et des anticyclones.

Une Dép est une masse d'air froid, qui aspire l'air des zones environnantes de pressions plus hautes, créant ainsi le vent. En raison de la rotation de la terre (force de Coriolis), ce vent va tourner autour du centre dépressionnaire dans un sens inverse des aiguilles d'une montre dans l'hémisphère nord et vice-versa dans l'hémisphère sud.

Pour qu'une Dép se forme, il faut que la pression puisse s'abaisser et que la rotation de la dép puisse être accélérée. Un des nombreux processus qui mènent à ça est la rencontre de masses d'air chaud et froid. La masse d'air chaud tend à glisser sur le dessus de la masse d'air froid, ce qui fait non seulement tomber la pression mais rend l'air instable, qui a tendance à tourbillonner. Ce système climatique devient plus énergique en hiver car l'écart se creuse entre le pôle et l'équateur. Une influence majeure sur ces mouvements est celle des flux d'air dans les couches élevées de l'atmosphère : le jet-stream. Le jet-stream circule beaucoup plus vite en altitude que les vents à la surface de l'eau, généralement d'ouest en est autour du globe. Il détermine la trajectoire et l'intensité des systèmes climatiques en surface. En Atlantique, son trajet le plus fréquent va de la Floride à l'Ecosse, mais il peut dévier vers le nord en Islande ou vers le sud au Portugal. Il peut aussi se scinder en deux courants sud et nord, comme changer en intensité avec des sections molles et rapides. Ces détails se reflètent souvent dans les cartes isobariques. Quand le jetstream va du sud-ouest au nord-est, il favorise la formation de bonnes Déps tandis qu'un jetstream sur l'autre diagonale (nord-ouest à sud-est) aura tendance à former de mauvaises Déps.

Naissance d'un swell

Le phénomène le plus important, qui produit des vagues surfables en Europe, est ce qu'on appelle une Dépression (Dép) de latitudes moyennes. D'autres phénomènes peuvent aussi créer des vagues comme les dépressions tropicales (ouragans, cyclones, typhons), les alizés de très hautes pressions et même les moussons (méga-brise de mer) mais ces systèmes sont rares en Atlantique nord. L'action du vent à la surface de l'eau est ce qui produit des vagues. La façon dont l'air transmet son énergie à l'eau n'est pas encore bien clair ; c'est probablement la combinaison de deux mécanismes. Le premier crée de petites vagues à partir d'une mer complètement plane, le deuxième accroît les ridules existantes. Le vent souffle non seulement horizontalement mais aussi verticalement. Ceci crée des bosses à la surface de l'eau. Une fois que la surface s'est ridée, le second processus provoque à la fois des crêtes et des creux qui croissent aussi lontemps que le vent continue à souffler. Comme les crêtes finissent toujours par mousser, cette croissance finit par s'éroder.

Birth of Swell

Various phenomena can produce sea waves, including tropical storms (hurricanes, cyclones, typhoons), strong high pressure trade winds, and even monsoons (giant sea breezes), but these other systems are rare in the Atlantic. Europe's single most important source of swell are **low pressure systems.** The action of the wind blowing over the sea surface is what produces waves. Just how the air transmits its energy to the water is still not entirely clear, however, it's probably a combination of two mechanisms: the first produces small waves from a completely flat sea, the second increases the existing ripples. The wind doesn't just blow horizontally, it can blow vertically too. This produces bumps in the water surface. Once the surface has become rippled, the second process causes both crests and troughs to grow for as long as the wind keeps blowing. Owing to things like whitecapping, they won't grow forever.

Concave refraction

ERIC CHAUCHE

Once a storm has produced swell, it will begin to travel (**propagate**) out into the ocean. As the swell propagates away from the generating area, two main things will happen to it. Firstly the waves will spread out and get smaller, a process called **circumferential dispersion**. In other words, the further a swell travels, the more it will spread out. The width it spreads is directly proportional to the distance it has travelled. For every doubling of the propagation distance, the height reduces by about one-third and it's something to watch out for if you're trying to predict the swell from a low that's thousands of kilometres away.

Secondly, the swell will clean up and organise itself, an event known as **radial dispersion**. Wave size is affected by three major factors: the strength of the wind, its duration and the fetch (the distance over which the wind blows). Wave speed is governed by how far apart the crests are (their wavelength). The longer the **wavelength**, the faster they go. When a swell is first generated, many different wavelengths are produced at the same time and the sea looks a mess. When the swell starts to propagate away, the faster, longer wavelengths progressively out-distance the shorter, slower ones. The waves in front are the clean swell lines, and the ones at the back are the short choppy ones with less power. So, if the low is a long distance offshore, when swell arrives it will be more lined up and will break with more speed and power.

When waves hit the coast

If swell comes in square-on to the coast, and there's not much of a continental shelf, it will 'jack up' when it suddenly hits shallow water. This effect is most noticeable on volcanic islands which rise rapidly from deep water, eg: The Canaries. As waves come into contact with the bottom, friction causes them to slow down, although strangely enough, they don't really lose any of their energy. As they slow, they squash closer together. The time between the passing of one wave and the next (known as **the period**) must remain constant throughout the swell. When they slow down they must get closer together, just like a traffic queue coming into a bottle-neck, which is termed **shoaling**. It increases wave size and the effect is greater the steeper the shelf.

Refraction is the word used to describe the way waves bend when they encounter obstacles. Think of a reef sticking out from a headland, with a deep-water bay next to the headland. When a swell line comes straight in towards the coast and strikes the reef, one half of the swell-line will start to slow down as it hits. The section which is still travelling faster in deep-water therefore must bend towards the reef. The energy gets concentrated towards the breaking point making the wave bigger, more sucky and faster. This is known as **concave refraction** and often makes the wave shorter, with all the power concentrated in the peak.

The second main example of refraction is the typical point break where the breaking area faces almost the opposite direction to the main swell direction. In this example the swell lines have to wrap around a headland before they break and have that 'fanned out' appearance. This is called **convex refraction** and spreads the wave over a wider area, producing smaller, less powerful waves, which are usually longer and more lined up.

Convex refraction

JOHN FRANK

Une fois qu'une Dép a créé un swell, celui-ci commence à se propager sur l'océan. Alors qu'il s'éloigne de sa zone d'origine, deux choses se produisent. D'abord, les vagues s'étalent et diminuent, c'est la dispersion circonférentielle. Plus une houle voyage, plus elle s'étale. A chaque fois qu'elle double, sa hauteur se réduit d'environ un tiers. C'est une donnée à intégrer si vous essayez de prévoir un swell qui provient d'une Dép qui se trouve à des milliers de kilomètres. Deuxièmement, la houle va s'organiser et devenir plus propre, ce qu'on appelle la dispersion radiale.

La taille des vagues dépend de 3 facteurs principaux: la force du vent, sa durée et le fetch, c'est à dire la distance sur laquelle le vent souffle. La vitesse de la vague dépend de l'écartement des crêtes de vagues (la longueur d'onde). Plus la longueur d'onde est élevée, plus elle va vite. Quand une houle vient de se créer, plein de longueurs d'onde coexistent. Quand la houle commence à se propager, les longueurs d'onde les plus longues, donc les plus rapides, distancent les longueurs d'onde les plus courtes, donc plus lentes. Les vagues à l'avant sont donc les plus propres et celles à l'arrière sont des vagues hachées avec moins de puissance. Si la Dép se trouve loin des côtes, la houle qui arrive sera bien en ligne avec de la vitesse et de la puissance.

Quand les vagues déferlent

Si les lignes de houle arrivent parallèles la côte et que le plateau continental est réduit, les vagues vont se lever d'un coup en sentant le fond remonter. Cette effet est notoire sur les îles volcaniques qui jaillissent des profondeurs (ex : Canaries). Comme il existe une friction de la vague sur le fond, la vitesse de propagation se ralentit et bizarrement, la perte d'énergie est faible. Dans ce ralentissement, les vagues se compriment. Le temps entre chaque vague (la période) devant rester le même, les vagues doivent se rapprocher, un peu comme un cortège de voiture qui arrivent dans une rue étroite. C'est ce qu'on appelle le "shoaling" (principe des haut-fonds). Cela augmente la taille des vagues et l'effet est d'autant plus grand que la pente du fond est forte.

La réfraction est le terme utilisé pour décrire la façon dont les lignes de houle se courbent quand elles rencontrent un obstacle. Imaginez un récif qui se détache d'un promontoire, qui jouxte une baie en eau profonde. Quand la houle arrive droit sur la côte et touche ce reef, la partie de la houle qui atteint le reef va se ralentir tandis que la partie en eau profonde continue sur sa lancée, la ligne se courbe donc autour du point de ralentissement. L'énergie se concentre vers le point de déferlement, rendant la section de vague plus grosse, plus creuse et plus rapide. C'est donc la réfraction concave, qui rend la vague plus courte, avec la puissance concentrée sur le pic.

Le deuxième cas de réfraction est le pointbreak typique où l'exposition de la zone de déferlement fait presque un angle droit avec la direction de la houle. Dans ce cas, la houle doit s'enrouler autour du cap pour déferler. C'est la réfraction convexe qui étale l'onde sur une zone plus large, qui crée des vagues moins puissantes, souvent plus longues, bien en ligne.

Tides and Currents

Types of tides

The moon's gravitational force produces a 'bulge' in the sea exactly in line with the moon itself, which is why oceans experience tides. What is not so well known is that there's an equal bulge on the opposite side of the earth. The two bulges are the high waters and the areas in between the bulges are the low waters. The earth spins around on its own axis underneath these two bulges and every point on the ocean's surface will experience at least one of these bulges every day.

JOÃO VALENTE

Throughout the time it takes for the earth and moon to go round each other (a lunar month), the moon has four 'phases': opposition, quadrature, conjunction and quadrature (again). The sun has a smaller influence on the tides, but it does produce bulges in the ocean just as the moon does. So when the sun and moon are lined up (in opposition or conjunction), their tidal effects are added together, which makes for big bulges in the same place, the cause of **spring tides**. When the sun is at an angle of 90 degrees to the moon (ie: in quadrature), they create bulges at right angles. The water is evened out all over the earth's oceans, producing **neap tides**.

Instead of just going in and out, tides tend to swirl around imaginary points called **amphidromes**. This is due to the rotation of the earth, and the Coriolis factor (yet again!). The greater the distance from the nearest amphidrome, the greater the tidal range.

Right: Springs and Neaps – the orange bulge is the moon-tide and the red bulge is the sun-tide. Quadrature will also occur when the moon is on the opposite side of the Earth than shown in the diagram

There are no rules, although most areas have a normal, **semi-diurnal** (two tides a day) regime and the surf is always effected by them. Europe experiences many tidal extremes particularly around the UK and in the North Sea. Shallow, narrow straits of water can greatly increase tidal ranges. The 12.6m (38ft) tidal range at the top of the Bristol Channel is the third largest in the world.

Most surf spots only work on certain heights of tide: too low and the wave may close out, too high and it barely breaks. Some breaks might be twice the size at high tide, while the adjacent beach breaks are more powerful at low tide. A lot of spots get bigger on the push of the tide possibly due to the incoming tide superimposing its motion on the swells, making them move faster. Many rivermouth waves can be impossible to surf on the outgoing tide, which will drag you past the take-off zone.

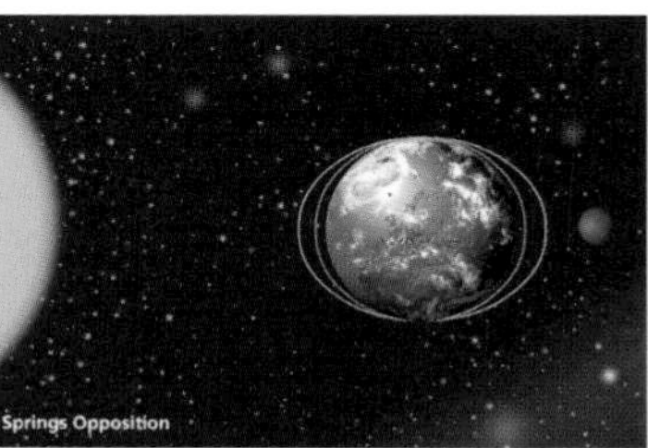

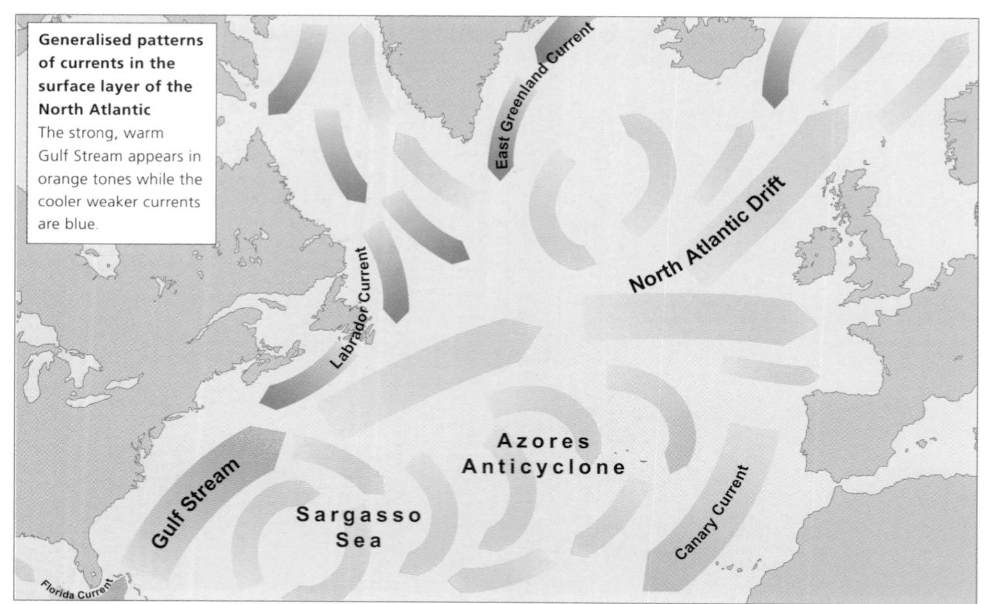

Generalised patterns of currents in the surface layer of the North Atlantic
The strong, warm Gulf Stream appears in orange tones while the cooler weaker currents are blue.

Currents

The water in north-west Scotland can actually be warmer than it is over a thousand kilometres south, in the Dover Straits. Surfing in the Canary Islands and Morocco is uncharacteristically cold for the latitude. Anomalies such as these are related to ocean currents and, to a lesser extent, a secondary effect called **upwelling**.

The Gulf Stream and its branches, plus the Canary Current, are the primary north Atlantic water flows. Their constant circulation brings annual water temperatures, with small seasonal variances, which sometimes seem completely out of character for the time of year. The Gulf Stream originates near Florida and heads towards Norway, with branches breaking off southwards along the way.

Some parts of the seas around Europe are fairly stagnant, being a long way away from where the ocean currents flow, such as the south-east corner of the Bay of Biscay, and the southern North Sea. Here the water has a chance to heat up in the summer and cool down in the winter, correctly reflecting the seasons. Ocean water temperatures change slowly, so there's always a delay of a couple of months before the sea temperature 'catches up' with the land. However it then holds its heat for a while after the land has cooled down.

Marées et courants

Types de marées

La force gravitationnelle de la lune tire la surface de l'eau dans sa direction. C'est pour cela que les marées existent. Ce qu'on sait moins est que ce renflement d'eau à la surface se fait à deux endroits diamétralement opposés. Ces points sont les marées hautes tandis que les lignes médianes sont les marées basses. Comme la terre tourne sur son axe, ces deux points vont passer par tous les points de la surface chaque jour.

Le temps d'un cycle lunaire, on dit que la lune connait 4 phases : opposition et conjonction sont séparées par deux quadratures. Le soleil exerce aussi un petite influence sur ces marées, qui renforce ou diminue celle de la lune selon leur position relative. Quand la lune et le soleil sont en ligne (opposition ou conjonction), les effets de marées s'ajoutent. L' attraction est d'autant plus forte en une même ligne. Pensez aux équinoxes. Quand le soleil est à la perpendiculaire de la lune, les points d'attraction sont à angle droit. La surface est étirée en deux lignes, ce qui provoquent des marées de faible amplitude (morte-eaux).

Au lieu de faire de simples flux et reflux, les marées tourbillonnnent autour de points imaginaires appelées amphidromes. Ceci est dû à la rotation de la Terre et à la force de Coriolis. Plus la distance est grande de l'amphidrome le plus proche, plus l'amplitude de marée est forte.

Il n'existe aucuns règle fixe bien que la plupart des endroits subissent un régime semi-diurne de 2 marées par jour. La qualité du surf en est toujours dépendant. L'Europe connaît beaucoup de marnages (amplitudes) extrêmes surtout autour de la Grande-Bretagne.

La plupart des spots de surf ne marchent qu'avec une certaine hauteur d'eau. Pas assez d'eau et ça ferme, trop d'eau et ça ne casse que rarement. Certains spots vont doubler leur taille à marée haute, alors que le beachbreak d'à côté va devenir plus puissant à marée basse.

Courants

Le Gulf Stream et ses dérivés, en plus du Courant des Canaries, sont les principaux mouvements d'eau. Leur circulation perpétuelle détermine une température annuelle qui varie peu et qui rend certaines eaux en décalage avec la saison. Le Gulf Stream naît au large de la Floride pour rejoindre la Norvège, avec des dérivés qui partent vers le sud en chemin.

Certains endroits de la mer en Europe sont particulièrement stables. Le coin sud-ouest du Golfe de Gascogne et le Sud de la Mer du Nord en sont des exemples. Dans ces endroits, l'eau peut bien chauffer en été mais aussi bien refroidir en hiver, suivant les températures de saison. La température des océans change doucement c'est pourquoi il y a toujours un décalage d'environ deux mois avant que la température de l'eau ne rejoigne celle de la terre.

Swell Forecasting

How to read a weather map

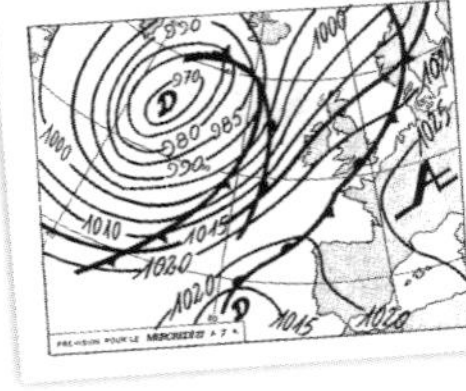

Our weather and swell conditions can appear random, though with a consistent eye, regular patterns can be perceived, in much the same way as when you watch the ocean for sets. Experienced surfers live by the weather charts. They give you up-to-the-minute information and can even predict the future. The lines on a weather chart are known as **isobars** and represent areas of equal pressure. Air pressure is measured in millibars (mb). The lower the air pressure and the closer the isobars are on a map, the faster the winds will rotate and the resulting waves will be larger. Lows in the Atlantic have been known to go down to around 900mb (see page 37). Swell comes off at similar angles to the orientation of the isobar lines, and can travel 300 to 400 kilometres in a day. The duration of a swell is related to the speed with which a low travels past a particular swell window, and unlike highs, lows tend to move rapidly.

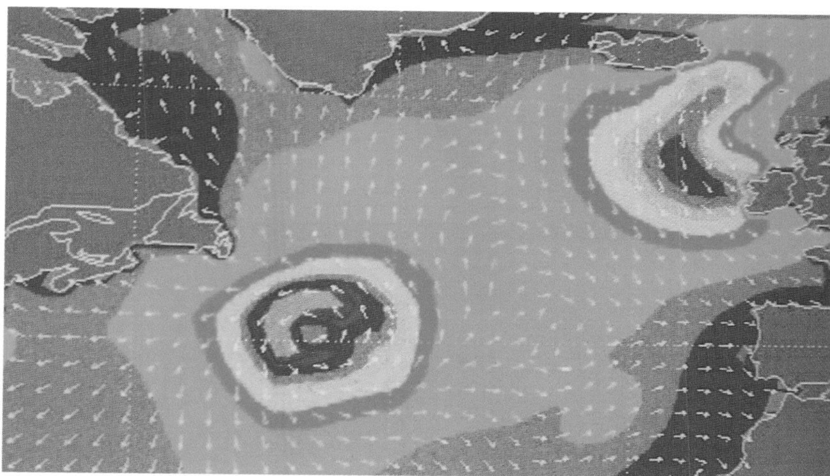

The WAM

The Atlantic

Lows can appear anywhere in the North Atlantic, typically deepening as they pass north and eastwards. In summer lows tend to skirt high above Great Britain, often developing over Greenland and then tracking north-east. Winter is a whole different ball game, when the oceans all come alive with lows, which roar over western Europe from all directions.

A low which deepens just north of the Azores will produce good surf for the Canary Islands, Morocco, south-west Spain and all of Portugal, but nothing for north Spain and south-west France. On the other hand, a low that's sitting right next to Ireland will produce classic surf for north Spain, yet Ireland itself will probably be huge and blown out. England and Wales have a problem with the swell shadow cast by Ireland, thus prefer a low which sits west of Land's End.

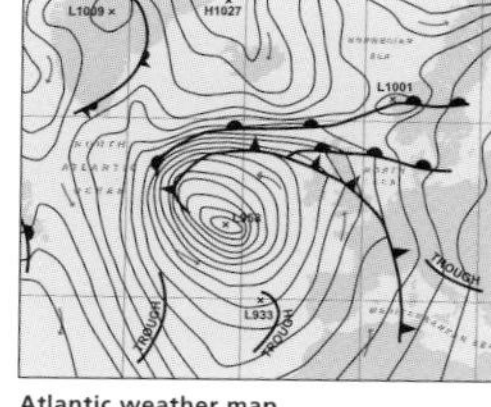

Atlantic weather map

The North Sea

Winter is the period of violent weather in this narrow, shallow sea. Deep lows are a regular part of the weather news and swell is highly consistent. A good North Sea summer scenario occurs when the Atlantic fills with a huge high called a **blocking anticyclone**. These may stay for weeks on end, forcing lows towards Scandinavia. This results in a squeeze of isobars running north to south, sending classic surf to the east coast of the UK, Norway, Holland and other North Sea spots. The north shore of Scotland may also crank, but could be blighted by onshores. A winter low forming around the English Channel will also produce surf from Norway to Belgium, but swells tend to appear, then disappear quickly as the wind swings. Occasional winter gales can bring cold east or north-east winds from the continent, which can produce sizeable surf for Britain.

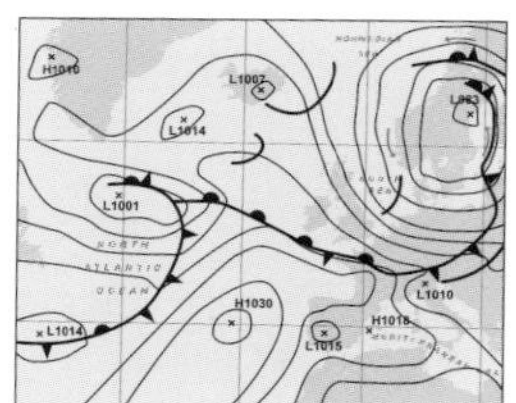

North Sea weather map

Mediterranean

The Med is like a large deep lake that's too small for the formation of deep depressions. Those that do occur tend to be on the periphery of large Atlantic systems. Local trade winds such as the 'mistral' are also regular swell producers, and if it blows onshore for a day, you might get a day of good short snappy waves as it cleans up. There are no tides in this sea which is surprisingly deep, allowing swells to travel quickly, but you've got to be on the lookout otherwise you'll miss swells when they do come.

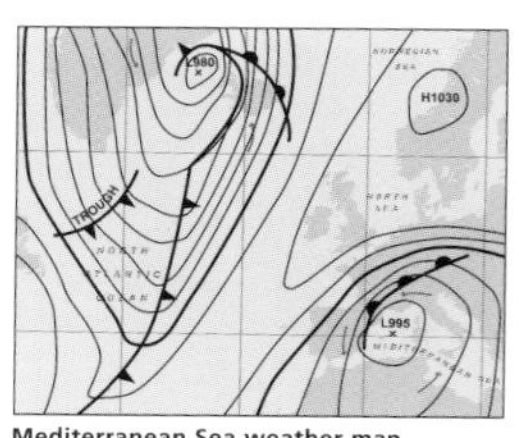

Mediterranean Sea weather map

Helpful swell prediction resources

The Met Fax is the most accurate surface barometric chart available, issued by the *Met office* in the UK (0336 400 445). Their 0336 calls are charged at 50p/min at all time, while 0331 calls are £1/min. Helpline (01344 854435).

Six Day Surface Charts off the net are sometimes accurate, but no guarantees – *www.ecmwf.int/charts/charts.html*

The WAM is a five-day swell prediction model worked off the six day surface chart. It predicts swell size, direction and dissipation for the globe – *www.fnoc.navy.mill/wam*

Interactive Marine Observations is data from buoys around the North Atlantic and North Sea, which monitor wave heights and period, air and sea temps, wind speed, visibility, etc. – *www.nws.fsu.edu/buoy*

TV weather forecasts are different for each country, but the national channel usually has the best reports. The *BBC* in Britain is excellent.

Newspaper charts can vary enormously in quality. You can usually look at a weather page of a paper without buying it

There are dozens of **surf report telephone lines** across Europe ranging from national coverage to local surf shop reports. A growing number of video cameras are being installed at major breaks around Europe that download images throughout the day onto the internet.

Mike Fish, BBC Television

CHRIS POWER

La carte isobarique

Les différents types de temps semblent arriver par hasard mais si on y prête attention, des séries régulières, de même que les séries de vagues, peuvent être perçues. Les surfers hardcore vivent au rythme des cartes isobariques. Ces cartes vous racontent ce que l'atmosphère raconte le jour-même et pour les jours à venir. Les isobares sont ces lignes de même pression qui définissent les masses d'air. La pression s'exprime en millibar ou hectopascal. Plus basse est la pression et plus les isobares sont rapprochés, plus les vents vont tourner vite et plus grosses seront les vagues. On a déjà vu des Déps en Atlantique descendre à 900 mb. La houle est toujours générée avec le même angle par rapport à l'orientation des isobares et peut parcourir jusqu'à 500 km/h. La durée d'une houle est liée à la vitesse de déplacement de la Dép dans une "fenêtre de swell" donnée. A l'inverse des anticyclones, les Déps ont tendance à bouger vite.

Les prévisions de houle en Europe

L' Atlantique Les Déps peuvent apparaître n'importe où dans l'Atlantique nord, elles se creusent en allant plus ou moins vers le nord-est. En été, les Déps passent très haut en latitude, au-dessus de la Grande-Bretagne, se développant vers le Groënland. L'hiver est une autre paire de manches : l'océan est secouée par de fréquentes et violentes Déps, qui balayent l'Europe de l'ouest dans tous les sens.

Une Dép qui se creuse juste au nord des Açores produira un bon surf pour les Canaries, le Maroc, le sud-ouest de l'Espagne et tout le Portugal mais rien pour le nord de l'Espagne et le sud-ouest de la France. D'un autre côté, une Dép qui se positionne au large de l'Irlande créera une houle idéale pour le nord de l'Espagne et la France, alors que l'Irlande subira une mer démontée. L'Angleterre et le Pays de Galles ont ce problème d'être dans l'ombre du swell à cause de l'Irlande. Mieux vaut donc une Dép qui arrive plein ouest à la parallèle du Cornwall.

La Méditerranée C'est une Mer trop restreinte pour la formation de Déps creuses. Celles qui se creusent là sont des résidus de grosses Déps atlantiques. Les vents locaux comme le Mistral générent souvent uen houle dite "de vent" quand ça souffle fort pendant quelques jours. Quand le vent se calme, des vagues rapprochées peu puissantes déferlent sur une courte période. Oubliez les marées dans cette mer, dont la profondeur est phénoménale à certains endroits. Ce qui permet aux houles de voyager très vite. Il faut donc être constamment aux aguets, autrement vous passerez souvent à côté.

The Ocean Environment

Europe is obviously one of the most densely developed continents on our planet, and as such has been the first to really suffer as a result of entrenched pollution problems. At the beginning of the 90s it seemed that environmentalists were knocking their heads against a brick wall, but thankfully things seem to be getting better as a result of increased pressure from the EC. Surfing has been at the forefront of lobbying in Brussels by marine environmentalists, with SAS and The Surfrider Foundation and national surf associations showing that while surfing may be considered a counter culture, it's a strong, universal voice with an ingrained environmental ethic.

'As a surfer you get a lot of pleasure from the sea – it is essential that you put something back. Please read this and then (if you haven't already) join **SAS** or **The Surfrider Foundation** – you'd sure as hell miss us if we weren't here!' *SAS*

The European Dimension

The main legislation driving a clean up of our seas comes from the EC. Having recognised that standards were painfully inadequate, SAS instigated and co-ordinated a lobby of the European Parliament in July 1996, which included representation from SAS (UK), the Dutch Surfing Association, the Belgian Surfing Association, the German Surfing Association and Surfrider Association France, who also represented Spain. This was repeated in December 1996 though this time with the inclusion of the Irish Surfing Association. Delegates from the surfers met with the European president before parliament voted to adopt the newer, tighter revision of the EC Bathing Water Directive. This still needs enforcing: we call on all surfers from all member states of Europe to write to their environment ministers, urging them to support the adoption of this vital piece of legislation. Importantly, the revised directive recognises the needs of water sports enthusiasts such as surfers.

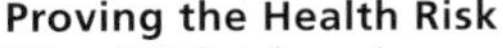

Proving the Health Risk

When SAS first formed no one knew about the health risks of untreated sewage, apart from the surfers who were used to having a dose of the shits or a raw throat. Members of SAS have taken part in two key pieces of scientific research that added significant weight to the call for full sewage treatment. The first analysed blood samples and looked for the antibodies to a particular sewage borne virus and they found that 93% of surfers' blood contained the traces of the virus compared to only 22% of the general public. The other piece of significant research looked at mouth swabs and the incidence of Hepatitis A; again the results were serious. SAS concluded: 'Surfers are three times more likely to contract Hepatitis A than the general public.' And the reason for contraction? In the search for waves, surfers often have to head into polluted areas. Wipe outs force water into nearly every orifice and infections result.

Principal Pollutants

Lead: from petrol, chemical industry, refineries, mines.
Cadmium: from batteries, cathode tubes, chemical fertilizers. Very toxic.
Mercury: from manufacturing of PVC, glue, agriculture, mineral industries, pharmaceutical and chemical waste. Very toxic.
Chromium: papermills, chemical, petrochemical, tannery, textile, fertilizers. Responsible for respiratory and colonic cancers.
Arsenic: from insecticides, electric components, colourants and chemical industry. Very toxic.
Hydrocarbons: from sea traffic, oil spills, industrial waste. Carcinogen.
Pesticides and Insecticides: agricultural waste.
Nitrates: fertilizer, domestic outflow, manure. Carcinogenic and algae supporting.
Phosphates: from sewage, detergents, fertilizers, chemical industries.
Human waste

Year-round Treatment

Another key role played by SAS is forcing the issue that people use the sea all year round. Some water companies dispute this and have argued that they don't need to treat the sewage all year. Publications such as *The Stormrider Guide* have proved invaluable in proving the opposite!

Your Ocean Needs You!

The Stormrider Guide is an excellent publication that has in many ways helped mature the position and role of surfers in this continent. At SAS we need your support not only to ensure that the seas around the UK and Europe are cleaned up but also to protect all of the world's oceans. As surfers we must establish the need for protection of breaks and surfing locations around the world. We've all heard of too many former paradises becoming marred by pollution.

Specificités du littoral

L'Europe est sans doute un des endroits les plus développés de cette planète, elle a donc été en première ligne face à la pollution. Au début des années 90, il semblait que les environnementalistes prêchaient dans le désert. Aujourd'hui, les choses commencent à s'améliorer suite à une pression croissante exercée par la CEE. Le surf a été mis en ligne de tir des Lobbies du littoral à Brusselles. SAS et Surfrider Foundation ainsi que d'autres associations nationales ont montré que bien que le surf soit considéré comme une contre-culture, c'est aussi une voix unie et résolue pour la protection de l'environnement.

Une dimension Europeenne La législation la plus importante qui pilote la salubrité de nos océans vient de la CEE. En ayant reconnu que la situation existante était parfaitement inacceptable, SAS fit des recherches et se joignit à un lobby parlementaire en juillet 1996, qui représentait SAS (UK), la Dutch Surfing Association, la Belgian Surfing Association, la German Surfing Association et Surfrider Foundation, qui couvre aussi l'Espagne. Cette initiative fut rééditée en décembre 1996 avec la venue supplémentaire de l'Irish Surfing Association. Une délégation de surfers ont rencontré le président Européen avant que le parlement ne votent des directives plus sèvères sur la qualité des eaux de baignade. Encore faut il que la loi soit respectée : on appelle tous les surfers des Etats-membres en Europe à écrire à leurs ministres de l'environnement, leur demandant de s'activer à faire respecter cet article de loi crucial. La nouvelle directive européenne reconnait les besoins des adeptes des sports nautiques, comme les surfers : cà, c'est un pas en avant.

Relevé des risques sanitaires Quand SAS se forma au départ, personne ne connaissait les risques sanitaires liés aux eaux usées non traitées, à part les surfers qui avaient déjà eu leur dose de merde à travers la gorge. Les membres de SAS se sont impliqués dans 2 études-clé de recherches scientifiques qui ont apporté des éléments essentiels justifier un retraitement à 100%.

Les premières analyses de sang faites pour dénicher la présence d'anticorps spécifiques à un virus issu d'eaux souillées ont montré que 93% des surfers avaient un sang contenant des traces du virus contre 22% seulement chez des non-surfers. L' autre partie intéressante de l'étude concerne les zones polluées de rivière avec un risque d'hépatite A. Là encore, les résultats sont probants. Les surfers sont trois fois plus exposés à la maladie que les non-surfers. Pourquoi ? Dans sa quête des vagues, les surfers ont souvent à pêtre confrontés à des zones polluées. Les wipeouts permettent à l'eau de s'infiltrer dans tous les orifices, ce qui provoque des infections.

Un traitement permanent Un des chevaux de bataille de SAS est de faire comprendre que des gens utilisent l'océan 12 mois sur 12. Certaines compagnies des eaux réfutent ce fait pour justifier la saisonnalité de leurs efforts.

It's on! I rounded up everything we had talked about: plane tickets,
film, journals, maps, a little pocket cash. Take ph
FEEL
GREAT NOW
VANS "OFF THE WALL"
STRIKES AGAIN
THE MOMENT IS RIGHT FOR IT
VANS
VANS WORLD TOUR
Vans, the young and restless since 19
Elijah Young
Kalani Robb
Megan Abubo
VANS
VANS
VANS

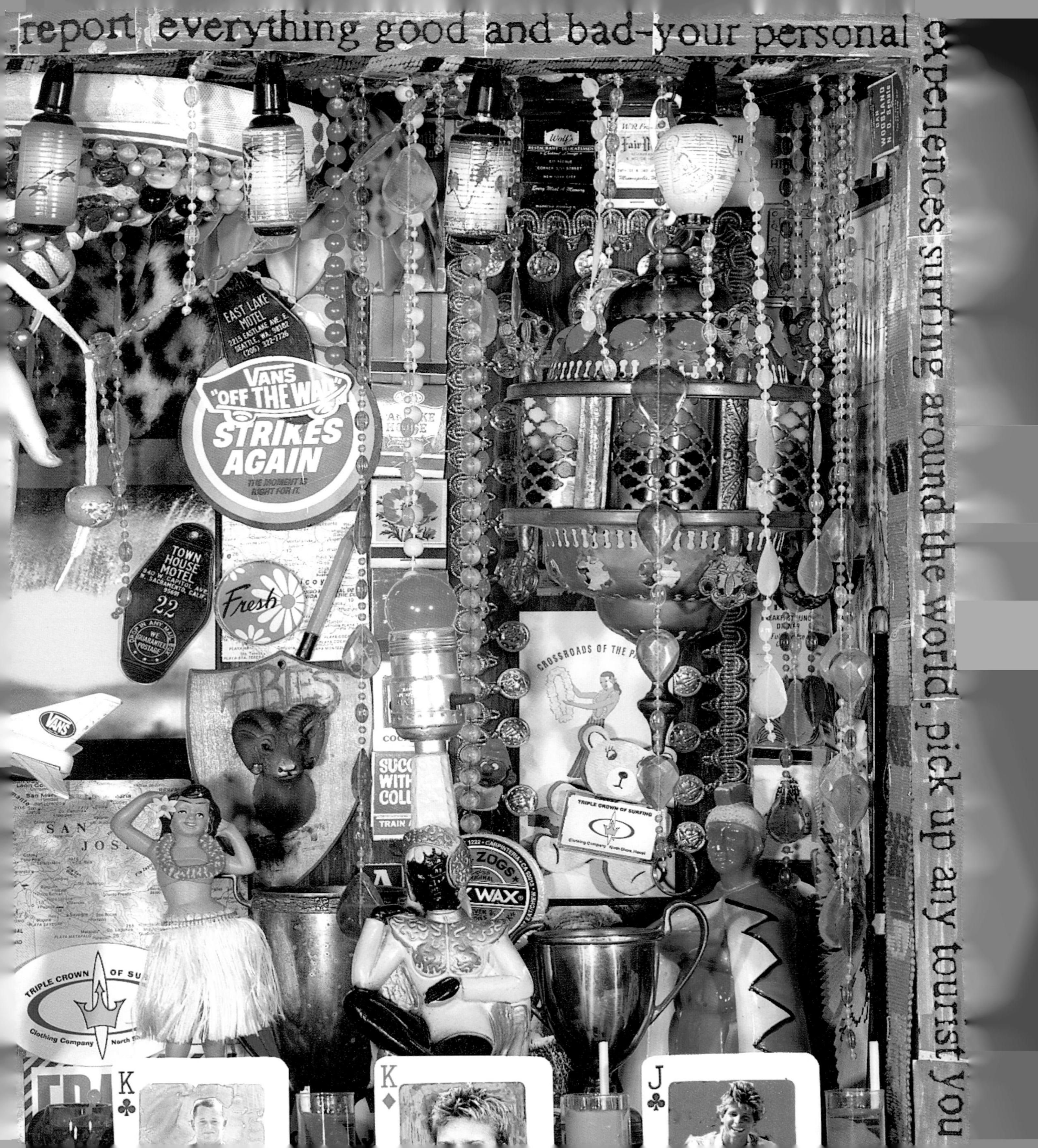
report everything good and bad-your personal experiences surfing around the world, pick up any tourist you
EAST LAKE MOTEL
VANS "OFF THE WALL" STRIKES AGAIN
TOWN HOUSE MOTEL
22
Fresh
TRIPLE CROWN OF SURFING
WAX

19 19

CAT®
12.20 HRS. JJ SOREN. STORYBOARD ARTIST. LAKE MEAD, NV

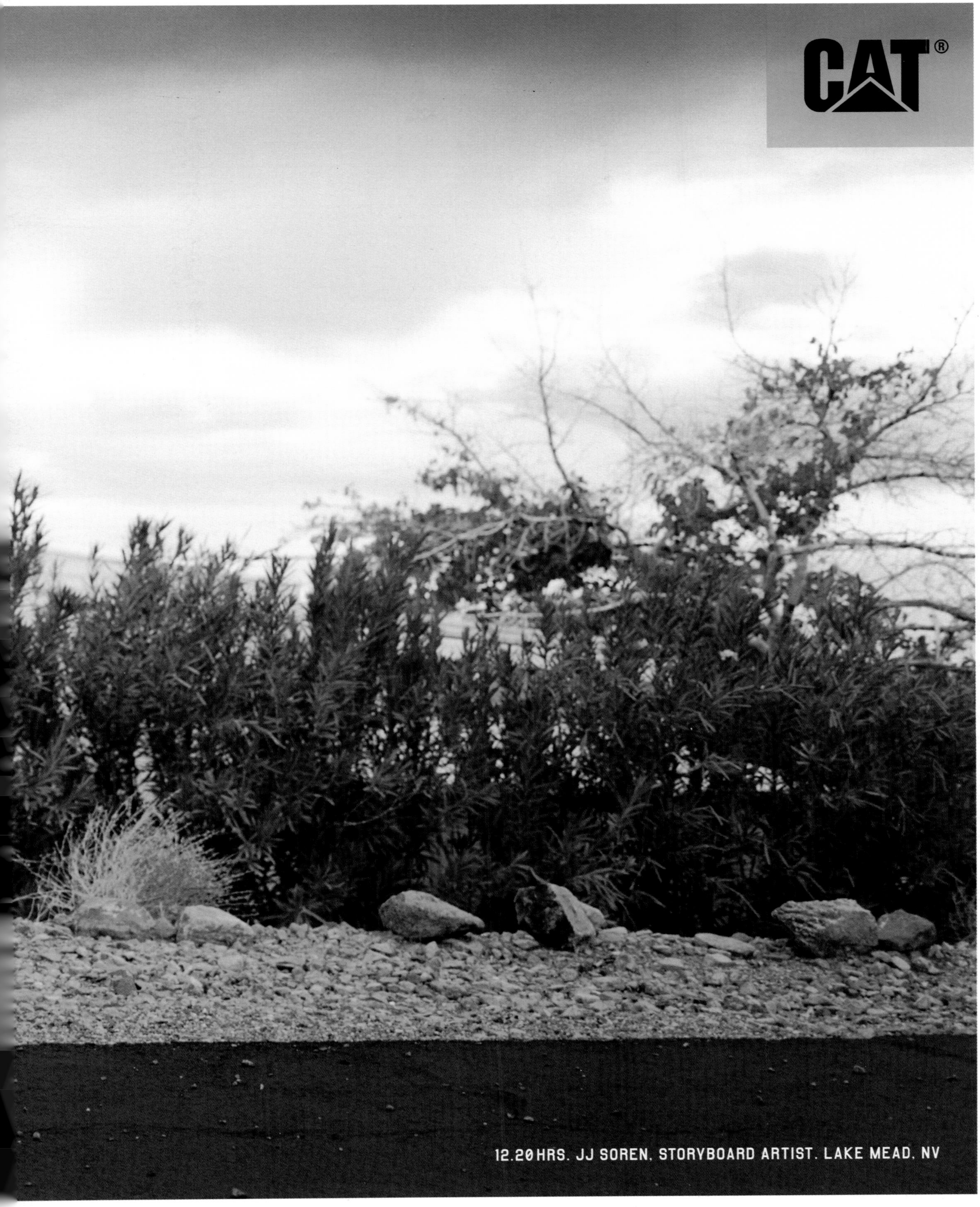

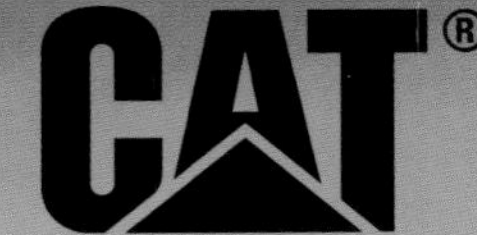

Few places in Europe share
Ireland's magical qualities

Ireland

The 'emerald isle' is a glistening gem in an already star-studded European line up, a sublime, cool nation with a calibre of surf equal to anywhere. Ireland's shimmering green waters bear the brunt of some of the Atlantic's most thunderous moods and its shoreline presents a series of headlands and flat rock reefs that face directly into nearly constant swell. This most mystical of Celtic lands holds a trove of the highest quality waves on jade-coloured shores, but while it's not the tropics, when it pumps, there're few places you'd rather be. All praise be to Finnbar McCool and the gods of Eire!

Irlande

L'île Emeraude est un joyau dans une Europe déjà gavée de bonnes destinations. C'est aussi un pays tranquille et merveilleux dont la qualité des reefs atteint des standards internationaux. Ses eaux verts chatoyantes supportent le chaos des tempêtes atlantiques les plsu féroces tandis que le littoral offre une palette de caps et de platiers rocheux qui font face à une houle quasi-constante. La plus mythique des terres celtiques détient le plus grand nombre de spots de qualité dans cette eau de jade si caractéristique. Bien que ce ne soit pas les Tropiques, comme en témoignent les pluies et vents impétueux, il y a peu d'endroits qui rivalisent avec l'Irlande quand ça marche ! Dieu bénisse Finnbar Mc Cool et les dieux de l' Eire !

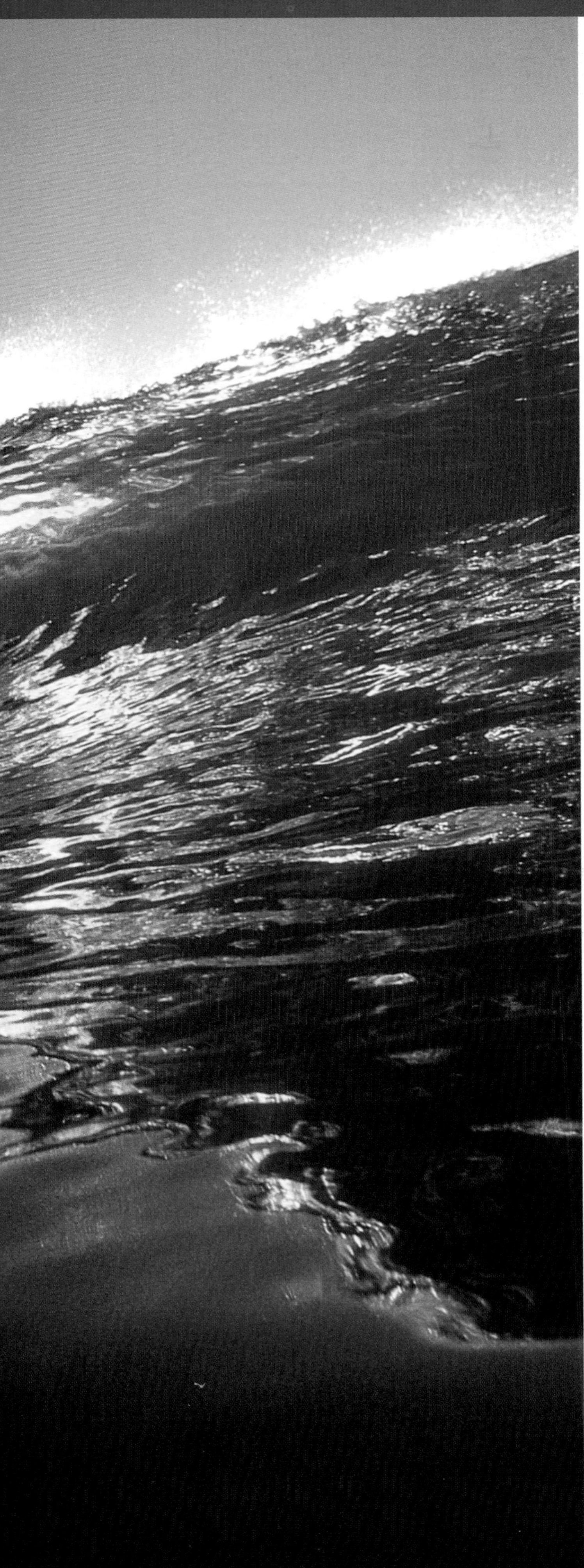

ALEX WILLIAMS

Introduction

The People

The island of Ireland was inhabited around 6,000BC by clans from north-east Scotland. Considered not worth invading by the Romans, the original Celtic tribes fought among themselves. Wars continued and the Vikings were followed by Norman and British invaders. Henry VIII broke with the Catholic church and declared himself the head of the Protestant Church of Ireland. Half a century later, Oliver Cromwell marched through the land with a bloodied sword, strengthening the English hold. In 1660 laws were enforced forbidding Catholics to hold mass or to buy or inherit land. The failure of the potato crops in 1845, 1846 and then 1848 threw the people into appaling famine. In less than 10 years the population was reduced by four million. Half died, the other half emigrated.

Population: 5 million
Area: 83 632sqkm/32 593sqmi
Time: GMT
Language: English and Irish
Currency: Republic – Irish Pound (IR£)
Northern Ireland – Stirling (GB£)

TIM RAINGER

Long-standing resentment deepened in Easter 1916 when a group of Fenians took control of public buildings in Dublin. They were overrun and executed, but this only strengthened sympathy for the Republicans. In 1921 the Anglo-Irish treaty was signed which did little but plunge the country deeper into civil war. A new constitution came into effect in 1938, finally declaring Ireland's complete independence and renouncing British sovereignty. This free state became known as Eire but even though a truce exists today, the troubles in Ireland remain its most reported topic. On Good Friday, 1998, political parties in Northern Ireland signed a new peace settlement, supported by the vast majority of the people, both north and south. This new settlement offers an opportunity of permanent peace for the first time and an end to the troubles in Northern Ireland, although events, like the August 1998 bombing of Omarh by the 'Real' IRA, which killed 28 innocent people, leave the process in a tenuous state.

OLLIE FITZJONES

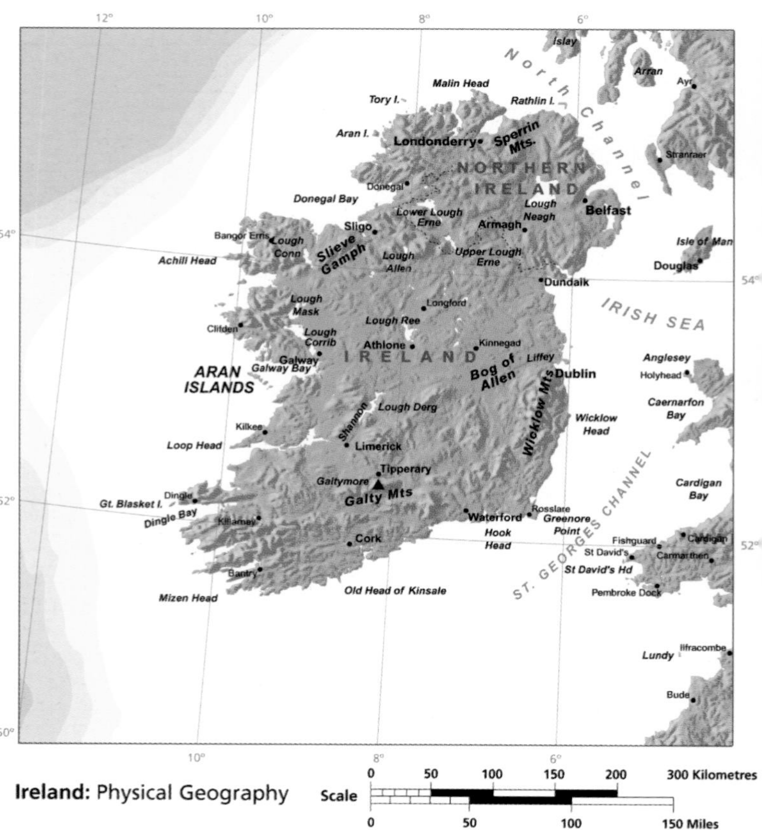

Ireland: Physical Geography

MARK STEVENSON

Introduction

La population

L'Irlande est l'île à l'ouest de l'Angleterre. L'Irlande du nord comprend les 6 comtès qui font partie intégrante du Royaume-uni depuis le traité anglo-irlandais de 1921. La république d'Irelande (Eire) comprend les 26 comtès gouvernés par Dublin. Dans le cadre de ce guide, l'Irelande est traitée comme un seul pays. Les premiers habitants arrivèrent il y a environ 8000 ans du nord-est de l'Ecosse. Ls suivants provenaient de tribus celtiques originaires d'Europe. Les Romains ne trouvaient pas intéressant de les envahir, alors les tribus se contentaient de s'entre-tuer sur place! Des siecles plus tard, le christianisme appparut. Les affrontements continuèrent et les Vikings précèdèrent les Normands et les envahisseurs venus d'Angleterre. Le temps passa et Olivier Cromwell défila avec une épée pleine de sang, renforçant la mainmise anglaise. Les lois interdirent aux catholiques de se réunir, d'acheter ou d'hériter. Les mauvaises récoltes de pommes de terre de 1845, 1846 et 1848 plongèrent la population dans une famine épouvantable. En moins de 10 ans, l'Irlande ne comptait plus que 2 millions d'habitants. Parmi ces deux millions, la moitiè mourrut, l'autre moitiè quitta le pays à jamais.

Le profond ressentiment s'accentua quand lors du lundi de Pâques 1916, un groupe prit le contrôle d'un nombre d'édifices publiques à Dublin. Ils furent maîtrisés et exécutés mais cela renforça la sympathie envers les Républicains et leur cause. Le 6 décembre 1921, le traité anglo-irlandais fut signé qui, l'air de rien, plongea encore plus pronfondément le pays dans la guerre civile. En 1938, une nouvelle constitution prit effet, déclarant la totale indépendance de l'Irlande et la renonciation à la souveraineté anglaise. Cet état libre porta le nom d'Eire et à ce jour, même s'il existe une trêve, les troubles en Irlande restent d'actualité.

PHIL HOLDEN

Giant's Causeway

ALEX WILLIAMS

Ben Bulben

The Land

Ireland's topography is wild and rolling. There are few high mountain ranges and most of the centre is covered by a flat, boggy plain. The country used to be covered in great forests, but intensive pressure on the land leading up to the famine of 1845 left it bare. The forests have been replaced by a patchwork of grass fields divided by hedgerows, though other natural ecosystems such as peat bogs and wetlands remain.

The Climate

Ireland escapes the extremes of temperature that its latitude would suggest, with the enveloping Gulf stream producing a mild, damp climate. It stands the closest in Europe to the general path of the north Atlantic depressions and consequently its weather is influenced heavily by their near permanent presence. Summers are rarely hot, winters rarely cold, but in parts of the west it rains two days out of three and coastal areas are pounded by big swells and strong winds. This mild, rainy climate is good for the growth of grass and moss and it's this phenomenon that led writer William Drennan to name it 'the emerald isle' in the 18th century.

Belfast Averages	Jan	Apr	Jul	Oct
rain (mm)	80	48	94	83
sun (hrs)	1	5	4	3
max temp°C	6	12	18	13
max temp°C	2	4	11	7

Cork Averages	Jan	Apr	Jul	Oct
rain (mm)	119	57	70	99
sun (hrs)	1	5	4	3
max temp°C	6	12	18	13
max temp°C	2	4	11	7

Le pays

Sa topographie est sauvage et variée. On y trouve quelques massifs montagneux et l'essentiel du centre est recouvert d'une plaine marécageuse. Jadis, le pays était recouvert d'immenses forêts mais une pression intense a été exercée sur les terres suite à la grande famine de 1845 et la déforestation a été massive. Les forêts ont été remplacées par un mélange de pâturages divisées par des haies. Il existe encore d'autres écosystèmes comme les bocages et marécages.

Le climat

L'Irlande échappe aux températures extrêmes que supposerait sa latitude et cela grâce au Gulf Stream qui provoque un climat doux et humide. C'est le pays qui s'approche le plus des dépressions atlantiques, ce qui conditionne sa climatologie de façon quasi-permanente. Les étés sont rarement chauds, les hivers rarement froids et sur certains endroits de la côte ouest, il pleut deux jours sur trois. La côte y est souvent martelée de bons swells et de vents violents. Ce climat doux océanique fait pousser une herbe verdoyante, ce qui incita William Drennan à la nommer " L'île Emeraude" au XVIIIème siècle.

MARK STEVENSON

Cottage, Dingle

Jersey, the Surf Club of Ireland at Eurosurf, 1970

Surf Culture

History

The first surfer on the emerald isle was a customs officer from Britain named Ian Hill, who had seen surfers in Devon during the summer of 1962. Hill entered the water at Castlerock in Easter 1963, and surfed Tullan and Bundoran alone the following summer, before returning to England where he stayed till 1969. Surfing emerged in the south almost simultaneously. When reading *The Readers' Digest*, Kevin Cavey saw a story on surfing. Having tried to ride an adapted skimboard with dismal results, he progressed onto a sophisticated craft constructed of marine ply with insulation plastic on the bottom. On this interesting device, Cavey became Ireland's first kneeboarder. The Mark Two was similarly shitty so he ordered a balsa kit from English board maker Tiki then left for Hawaii and California where he surfed Rincon and a few other spots. He returned stoked after a year on the road; the Tiki kit had arrived, and the rest evolved from there.

The Surf Club of Ireland was founded in 1966 at Bray, County Wicklow. That same year Cavey represented Ireland at the World Surfing Championships in California. In 1967 the first National Championships were held and naturally Kevin Cavey took the title

Ian Hill, Bundoran, 1964
COURTESY HILL FAMILY ALBUM

Culture surf

Histoire

Le premier surfer de l'île Emeraude fut un dounaier anglais nommé Ian Hill, qui avait vu des surfers dans le Devon pendant l'été 1962. Il se mit à l'eau à Castlerock à Paques 1963 et surfa Tullan et Bundoran tout seul pendant tout l'été, avant de retourner en Angleterre où il s' installa jusqu'en 1969. Le surf fit son apparition dans le sud du pays presqu'au même moment. Kevin Cavey lisait le Reders Digest en 1962 où il tomba sur une histoire de surf. Ayant déjà essayé de s'amuser sur une sorte de skimboard avec des résultats pitoyables, il fit une avancée technologique vers un engin en contreplaqué recouvert de plastique thermoformé sur le dessous. Sur ce modèle avant-gardiste, il devint le premier kneeboarder irlandais. Ses matériaux étant de mauvaise qualité, il commanda donc un kit en balsa de chez Tiki puis partit pour Hawaii et la Californie où il surfa Rincon et bien d'autres spots. Il en revint avec une passion dévorante et après une année de trips, le kit de chez Tiki arriva, le reste devait en découlait.

Le Surf Club d'Irelande fut fondé en 1966 à Bray dans le comté de Wicklow. La même année, Cavey représenta le pays aux Championnats du monde à San Diego. En 1967, les premiers Championnats nationaux eurent lieu. Kevin remporta logiquement l'épreuve suivi de Eamon Mathews et de Ted Alexander. Les premiers championnats inter-régionaux se déroulèrent à Rossnowlagh en 1968, où le comté de Down battit en finale le comté de Wicklow. Bizarrement, aucun de ces deux côtés n'a fait de finale depuis lors. A la fin des années 60, les membres du S.C.I se mirent à fonder d'autres club laissant le S.C.I représenter la zone de Dublin. Au début de 1970, cinq groupes évoluaient : le South Coast SC à Tramore (maintenant T-Bay SC), le West Coast SC (Lahinch), le Rossnowlagh SC (Donegal), le North Shore SC à Portrush et le Fastnet SC de Cork. La même année, ils se rejoignirent pour fonder la Fédération de Surf, qui devint et reste encore l'organisme officiel du sport dans le pays.

Second Eurosurf 1970
ISA

Kevin Cavey, Tigger Newling, Nick Kavanagh and James Trout at the 1969 Irish champs

ISA

with Eamon Mathews second and Ted Alexander third. The first Intercounties' Championships were held in Rossnowlagh in 1968, where County Down beat County Wicklow in the final. Ironically neither county has featured in a final since. By the end of the 60s members of the Surf Club of Ireland began to form other clubs leaving the Surf Club of Ireland to represent the Dublin area. Five local groups had evolved by early 1970 including the South Coast, in Tramore (now known as the T-Bay Surf Club), the West Coast (Lahinch), the Rossnowlagh (Donegal), the North Shore (Portrush) and the Fastnet (Cork) Surf Clubs. The same year they combined to establish the Irish Surfing Association, which became and remains the governing body of surfing in Ireland.

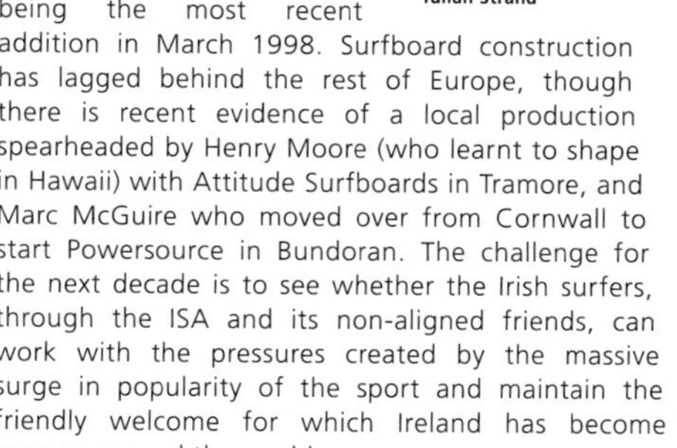

From left to right: Conor and Brian Britton, Kevin Cavey, Ted Alexander and in front Barry Britton

ISA

Surfing on the north coast was reinvigorated in 1966 when a group of youngsters led by Alan Duke (to be many times Irish champion) started surfing the Portrush/Portstewart area and began travelling to the west coast where they met up with other surfers. For 20 years the number of Northern Irish surfers stuck at around 40, but the advent of bodyboarding opened up the sport to a wider age group and a proportion of the youngsters progressed to stand-up surfing. Today the north coast is probably the most surfed in Ireland.

The national association has hosted the European Amateur Championships on three separate occasions: 1972, 1985 and 1997. Rossnowleigh surfer Grant Robinson has been the most successful Irish Surfer at international level taking the European Masters title in France in 1987 and again in Ireland, a decade later, in 1997. Andy Hill has been the most prolific, already representing all Ireland for 11 years, winning the Irish Championships six times and achieving a personal best result of 32nd in the 1992 World Amateurs in France.

Today

Tullan Strand

MIKE SEARLE

In recent years there has been a massive growth in the surf population: numbers currently stand at 1,500 hard-core and possibly 2,500 fair-weather surfers, with shops and surf schools dotted all along the coast. There are now 12 surf clubs attached to the Irish Surfing Association; the East Coast Surf Club in the Dublin area being the most recent addition in March 1998. Surfboard construction has lagged behind the rest of Europe, though there is recent evidence of a local production spearheaded by Henry Moore (who learnt to shape in Hawaii) with Attitude Surfboards in Tramore, and Marc McGuire who moved over from Cornwall to start Powersource in Bundoran. The challenge for the next decade is to see whether the Irish surfers, through the ISA and its non-aligned friends, can work with the pressures created by the massive surge in popularity of the sport and maintain the friendly welcome for which Ireland has become renown around the world.

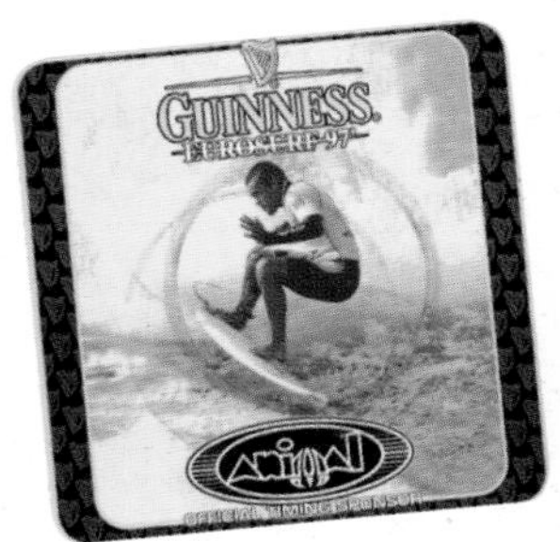

Further Info

Irish Surfing Association President: Brian Britton
3 Jocelyn Place, Dundalk, Co Louth
Tel:042 32700 Fax:042 37512

Barry Britton

Le vrius du surf sur la côte nord fut inoculé en 1966 quand un groupe de kids dont le meneur était Alan Duke (qui fut champion Irlandais à plusieurs reprises) se mit au surf dans la zone de Portrush/Portstewart avant de commencer à voyager sur la côte ouest pour rencontrer d'autres surfers. Pendant 20 ans, le nombre de surfers d'Irlande du nord stagna autour de 40 représentants. Ce n'est que depuis l'arrivée du bodyboard que la pratique des vagues s'est élargie à une classe d'âge plus large. A noter aussi que bon nombre de ces bodyboarders se mettent au surf maintenant. C'est ainsi que l'Irlande du Nord est devenue de loin la zone la plus surfée.

La fédération a organisé les championnats d'Europe Amateurs à 3 reprises : 1972, 1985 et 1997. Grant Robinson, le surfer de Rossnowlagh, obtint les meilleurs résultats sur le plan international, en remportant par deux fois la catégorie Masters en 1987 et en 1997. Andy Hill, lui, a été le surfer le plus titré en remportant les championnats nationaux par 6 fois et en décrochant une 32ème place aux championnats de monde amateur de 1992 à Lacanau.

Ian Hill, still charging today

TROGGS

Aujourd'hui

On observe depuis ces dernières années une croissance massive du nombre des surfers qu'on estime à envrion 1500 chevronnés et 2500 débutants, qui passent par les écoles de surf le long de la côte en été. Il existe aujourd'hui 12 clubs reconnus par la fédération, le dernier en date étant l'East Coast SC de Dublin. La fabrication de planches reste à la traîne par rapport aux autres pays. Signalons quand même l'émergence d'une bonne petite production locale supervisée par Henry Moore qui a appris à shaper à Hawaii, avec la marque Attitude Surfboards à Tramore et ensuite Merc Mc Guire qui a quitté le Cornwall pour lancer Powersource à Bundoran. La question d'avenir reste à résoudre : les surfers irlandais, à travers l'ISA et ses détracteurs, pourront-ils canaliser de façon positive la popularité du surf en conservant l'hospitalité qui a fait la renommée de l'Irlande à travers le monde ?

Donegal Bay

Kye Fitzgerald discovering his roots

Where to go

Surf Areas

The most easily accessible stretch of Northern Ireland's **Causeway Coast** stretches from Ballycastle to Magilligan Point and has, since 1963, remained the focus of the north's surfers. The 40 kilometres (26 miles) of outstanding natural beauty is dominated by fast, French-style beach breaks and the odd reef which are all offshore in prevailing south-west winds.

East Strand, Portrush

Despite the fame of the west coast spots, the north coast is the most surfed, drawing visitors from all over the north. The Belfast crew arrive in abundance at weekends, attracted by both the surf and the night life. Kelly's in Portrush is the biggest night club in Ireland, featuring guest DJs and crowds of up to 2,000 people. Accommodation is easy to find.

Donegal Bay in the north west might seem an unusual choice of location, but in Europe it's one of the few places to warrant the title 'a surfer's paradise'. A large portion of its coast faces north, so is offshore in the prevailing south-west airstream. It presents numerous reefs, points and beaches to the wrath of the north Atlantic and picks up swell from the west, north-west and north. Counties Donegal and Sligo are wet and windy, but it's a small price to pay.

A number of focal points have emerged: Rossnowlagh and Bundoran in south Donegal, Strandhill and Easky in Sligo. Rossnowlagh is home to one of the biggest surf clubs in Ireland as well as the Surfer's Bar, a shrine to Irish surf history. Bundoran is equally central to the surf culture, regularly hosting competitions at all levels, including the European Championships in 1997. The waves at Bundoran and Tullen are excellent and the surroundings are beautiful, but it's the two breaks at Easkey that have become the best known and it's not uncommon to find people of six nationalities camped on the point.

County Clare is exposed to the full influence of the Atlantic and would be one of Europe's most popular surf destinations if the weather was more hospitable. It offers a huge selection of surf spots ranging from mellow beaches to the big, gnarly tubes. Offshores, being south-east, aren't consistent so this area may be perfect less often than many north-facing areas, but when it's on, it's right on. To stand above Lahinch and see the points break is a magnificent experience and though Lahinch is only one of many superb spots, it's the surf centre for good reasons: it's situated next to a long, white beach with three excellent left reefs at its northern end. You'll find a variety of accommodation in town, a hostel at Spanish Point, many more in Doolin and two between Lahinch and the cliffs of Moher. There are other breaks along the coast but access is a problem. If you insist on trying to find them you could antagonise the local farmers, which wouldn't endear you to the local community.

The Dingle Peninsula is one of the most beautiful areas of Ireland. The surf can be excellent but is notoriously fickle. Brandon Bay is the most consistent, drawing swell from the widest angle, but is often blown out. The reefs without exception need very specific swell angles to work at all, though given the array of other things to do in the area, you needn't suffer when it's flat. A rule of the thumb is that if there's no surf in Brandon, there's no surf anywhere. From deep sea angling to surf casting for Atlantic bass, spinning for sea trout or trying to catch their wild

Ou Aller

Les zones de surf

La Causeway Coast Elle s'étend de Ballycastle à Magilligan Point et c'est depuis 1963 la Mecque des surfers du nord. Les 60 kilomètres de beauté naturelle sont dominés par des beachbreaks type "Les Landes" et quelques super reefs qui sont tous off-shore avec les vents dominants de sud-ouest. Malgré la renommée des spots de la côte ouest, la côte nord est, spot pour spot, la plus surfée, attirant les surfers de tout le nord. Les gens de Belfast débarquent en masse le week-end, attirés à la fois par les vagues et l'ambiance nocturne. "Kelly's" à Portrush est la plus grosse boîte d'Irlande, avec des DJ's de toutes provenances et jusqu'à 2000 personnes. Se loger est un jeu d'enfant.

Donegal Bay pourait donner l'impression d'être une destination peu habituelle, mais en Europe, c'est un des rares

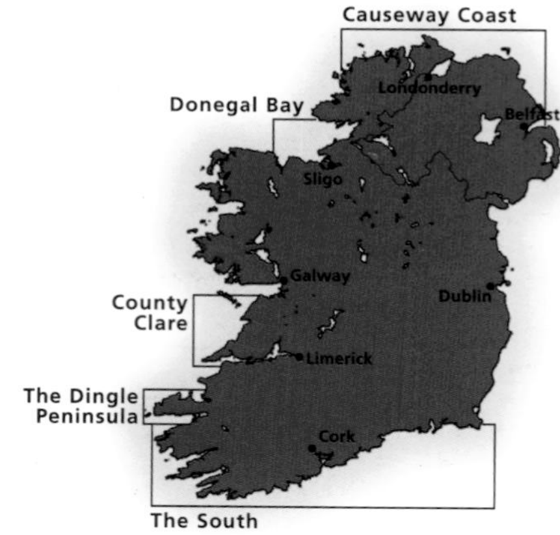

endroits à mériter le titre de "paradis des surfeurs". Une grande partie de cette côte est orientée nord, ainsi les vents favorables sont oriientés sud-ouest. On y trouve de nombreux reefs,caps et plages exposés aux tourmentes de l'Atlantique Nord en recevant la houle d'ouest, nord-ouest et nord.

Quelques spots sortent du lot: Rossnowlagh et Bundoran à S. Donegal & Strandhill et Easky à Sligo. Rossnowlagh est le lieu du plus grand surf club d'Irlande. Bundoran est le berceau de la surf culture, et l'on trouve de nombreux surf-shops. Les vagues à Bundoran et Tullen sont excellentes et la nature y est belle, mais ce sont les deux spots de Easky qui sont devenus les plus connus et il est courant de trouver 6 nationalités différentes à l'eau. La ville est petite et sympathique. Le logement n'est pas difficile à trouver.

County Clare est exposée à l'influence de l'Atlantique et serait une des destinations d'Europe les plus en vue si le temps était plus clément. Cette région offre une imposante brochette

County Clare

Clare lines

Ballydavid

lake cousins, there's fishing for everyone. Accommodation is no problem with camping and caravan parks of varying standards, a hostel in Dingle and many B&B establishments. It is also possible to rent holiday cottages by the day or week. A few pubs specialise in sea food such as Spillanes (in Castlegregory) and in Dingle there are some excellent if expensive restaurants.

Ireland's less visited **south**-facing portion of coastline is nonetheless home to a large variety of beach and reef breaks with small to medium and occasionally large surf. County Cork and the Ring of Kerry offer unusually special coastal areas with occasionally exceptional waves. Prevailing winds are onshore as for Wales, but the surf is uncrowded with plenty of undiscovered potential. Tramore is the centre for the south-east, Cork for the west. The surfing community is very relaxed and here the emphasis is on having fun rather than getting every wave, so be prepared to share, and throw your watches away.

When to go

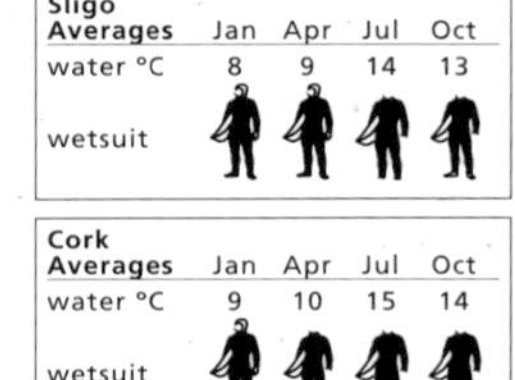

Sligo Averages	Jan	Apr	Jul	Oct
water °C	8	9	14	13
wetsuit				

Cork Averages	Jan	Apr	Jul	Oct
water °C	9	10	15	14
wetsuit				

The majority of waves come from lows tracking from the US to Iceland, deepening as they go. Surf comes from the south-west to north, as the lows approach, with winds from the lows generally blowing south-west to west. This means that the north and north-west facing breaks, angled to catch the swell, enjoy frequent cross/offshore winds. The best times to visit the west coast are spring and autumn. During summer the swells are sporadic and it has been known for flat periods to last as long as two weeks. Wintertime sees almost continuous surf conditions but the water is cold (3-4°C/36-38°F) and the winds can be very strong. April and May are often blessed with the best weather; the water is still quite cool but the winter swells have started to settle, while September to November is prime time. The winter swells begin to roll in and the water is still warm. If you are used to wearing a wetsuit you'll find temperatures totally acceptable up until late November. The main season on the north coast is also from mid August to mid May though in summer months the smaller systems high in the Atlantic can produce surprisingly consistent swell. Ironically, some of the deeper winter lows can be too far south, when Malin Head can stop swell getting round to the Causeway Coast.

Catching waves on the south coast is usually a wintertime experience, with good conditions in the north-west airstream that follows the passage of a big low.

---

de spots allant des récifs et plages offerts sur un plateau aux tubes les plus gros dans lesquels on puisse s'engouffrer!

Les vents offshores étant sud-est, ils ne sont pas fréquents; ainsi les vagues parfaites sont plus rares que dans la plupart des régions orientées au nord, mais quand c'est bon, c'est vraiment bon. Le point de vue est merveilleux lorsque l'on peut admirer les vagues au-dessus de Lahinch, et pourtant Lahinch n'est qu'un des nombreux superbes spots. Ce spot est digne de sa réputation de berceau du surf: il est situé à côté d'une longue plage de sable blanc avec trois excellents reefs qui partent en gauche du côté nord de la plage. La ville est très accueillante, il y a aussi une auberge à Spanish Point, plusieurs à Doolin et deux entre Lahinch et les falaises de Moher.

La Dingle Peninsula Rassurez-vous les spots aussi valent le détour. Tous les types de pêche sont possibles: de la pêche à la ligne à la pêche au gros (bar), en passant par la pêche à la truite (de mer ou d'eau douce) à la cuiller.

Le sud Cette partie moins fréquentée du pays est malgré tout le repère de bon nombre de beachbreaks et reefbreaks avec des vagues de taille allant du petit au moyen avec des pointes de gros à l'occasion. Les comtés de Cork et de Ring of Kerry offrent un littoral vraiment différent avec des vagues exceptionnelles de temps à autre. Les vents dominants sont onshore comme au Pays de Galles mais le surf est presque vierge avec un potentiel terrible de spots non découverts. Tramore s'affiche comme l'épicentre du phénomène surf au sud-est ; quant à l'ouest, c'est Cork. L' ambiance est détendue sur les vagues comme nulle part ailleurs : personne ne regarde sa montre au lineup !

Quand aller

La majorité des vagues provient de dépressions naissant entre Terre-Neuve et l' Islande, en se creusant à l'approche de l'Europe. La houle arrose la côte sud-ouest au nord alors que les fronts approchent, produisant des vents de sud-ouest à ouest. Ceci implique que les spots exposés nord/nord-ouest, chopent bien la houle tout en étant cross/offshore. La meilleure période pour zoner sur la côte orientale est le printemps ou l'automne. En été, les houles ont tendance à être rares et on a déjà vu des "flats" de deux semaines. En hiver, le surf déferle sans cesse mais l'eau descend jusqu'à 3-4°C avec des vents à décorner les boeufs. Les mois d'avril et mai sont statistiquement les mieux lotis pour un temps stable mais l'eau reste encore bien fraîche (10-12°c); les tempêtes ont commencé à se calmer un peu. Septembre et octobre sont les mois d'exception. Les houles hivernales débutent leurs trasnhumances et l'eau conserve une température presque agréable. Si vous êtes habitué à surfer en combinaison épaisse , vous trouverez l'eau franchement supportable jusqu'à la fin novembre.

Cead mile failte

A hundred thousand welcomes

JOHN FRANK

The Ocean Environment

Water Quality

By and large Ireland is blessed with some of the cleanest, most alive oceans in Europe. The Atlantic's integrity and biodiversity remain pristine in many areas, especially on her exposed western and northern fringes where the population hasn't traditionally congregated. Not so, however, are its tortured eastern shores that share the Irish sea with British Nuclear and the British Navy, both of whom have been responsible for a tragic history of toxic dumping into this important waterway, reportedly rendering it the most hazardous sea on earth. Other problems exist on all coasts, though as expected, are worst near the major population centres: in particular, Doughmore and Budoran are bad. Last year's competitors in the European championship were disgusted at the filthy water.

On Localism – by the County Kerry Surf Club

The good thing about *The Stormrider Guide* is that it has enabled people to discover spots that in the normal way they would never know about. Part of the ethos of surfing is travelling: we all want to pack a bag and surf somewhere new, it's in your bones. In the past three years, there has been a build up of tension between locals and visitors. This is a shame and totally unnecessary. The locals' only attitude stinks, but readers of this guide should remember that it is just as bad to travel to someone else's break and piss everybody off. The problems in Ireland stem for the fact the local surfing populations are small, and there are 50,000 people who claim to surf in Britain. Irish surfers are generally friendly and are pleased to see outsiders on their breaks. Being friendly is rule number one: you sit at the edge of the pack, you don't hassle anybody, you hoot at any good waves you see other people take, you take the scraps, and nine times out of ten they'll started calling you into set waves. Don't arrive in a big group. If there are more than two or three of you definitely don't surf reef breaks. And don't be aggressive in the water. If you've paddled inside the pack, don't assume that any wave is yours.

MIKE SEALE

Bundoran

Burning Issue

In response to the growing problem of pollution, an issue at some recent competitions, the Irish Surfing Association has set up an Environmental Committee in 1996 to monitor water quality and campaign for secondary treatment plants in surfing areas like Easkey where waste was pumped straight into the ocean.

Additionally, the recent growth in surfing reflects a new, vibrant Ireland, with tourism at the core, yet has led to increased tensions at some of the more popular spots, at times to alarming levels. This is completely unnecessary of course. If you use your initiative and a good dose of humility you are bound to befriend locals, and thus reap the benefits of years of accumulated experience.

Spécificités du littoral

Qualité de l'eau

L'Irlande est de loin le pays dont les eaux sont les plus propres et les plus oxygénées d'Europe. Surtout dans leurs parties nord et ouest, où les populations côtières ont toujours été faibles, la biodiversité de l'écosystème côtier est restée quasi-intacte dans plein d'endroits. Bien moins propres sont en revanche les rivages orientaux défigurés par le British Nuclear et la British Navy, les deux organismes ayant été responsables d'une histoire tragique de rejets dans cette zone maritime aux antécédents historiques, stratégiques et culturels des plus importants. Ce qui fait de la Mer d'Irlande une des plus toxiques dans le monde. D'autres problèmes apparaissent un peu partout, les plus aigus étant bien sûr localisés dans les grands bassins de population. En particulier à Easky, Doughmore, Bundoran où les compétiteurs des Championnats d'Europe l'année dernière eurent à se plaindre d'une eau gerbique. En réponse à ce problème croissant, l'ISA s'est doté d'un Comité Environnemental pour contrôler la qualité de l'eau et militer pour des bassins de retraitement autour des spots de surf comme Easky où des déchets ont été déversées tout droit dans l'océan.

Le localisme

La plupart des surfers vont sur les spots bien connus et une large majorité de locaux vous donneront la liste des spots à checker, si vous devez lancer ce genre de conversation. Cette générosité innée doit être appréciée à sa juste valeur sinon cette tendance amicale pourraît se dissiper envers des surfers étrangers perturbant la quiétude du lineup. A chaque fois que l'ISA se rencontre, de plus en plus de clubs enregistrent des plaintes concernant des comportements stupides, surtout à Easky, dans le Comté Kerry et le Comté Clare. Soyez respectueux, conduisez avec prudence et restez cools. Les choses vont lentement ici, soyez patient. Si ça marche, vous vous amuserez vraiment.

Points chauds

En 1996, l'ISA institua un Comité Environnemental pour faire état des préoccupations les plus vives de surfers, provoquées par la double menace du surdéveloppement et de la pollution sur un nombre croissant de spots sur la côte irlandaise. Cette prise de conscience relativement rapide reflète une Irlande plus ouverte, soucieuse de ses attraits touristiques. Cela a donné lieu à certaines tensions sur les spots les plus fréquentés, atteignant parfois un niveau intolérable. Ceci est bien sûr complètement superflu parce qu'il existe des tonnes de spots pour surfer, qui ne sont pas listées dans ce bouquin pour des raisons évidentes. Si vous avez un peu d'esprit d'initiative et une bonne dose d'humilité, vous êtes destiné à devenir un local amical et recueillir les fruits de nombreuses années de camaraderie déjà accumulées par les "vieux".

Travelling

Getting There

By air International carriers fly to Dublin, Belfast, Cork and Shannon and from these airports it's easy to catch a connecting flight to Ireland's many regional airports. Competition between airlines and ferry companies keep prices fluctuating and it's advised to shop around if you want to get the best deal. If you're heading to the north-west, Knock or Sligo are convenient places to end up, flights sometimes costing as low as £69 from London and other European Airports. Airlines flying to Ireland include: Air Lingus, Air UK, Britannia Airways, Ryanair, Dan Air, British Airways, British Midlands and Capital Airlines.

By ferry Ireland is serviced by a number of different ferry companies which sail from Britain and France. Prices vary considerably depending on which season you travel in and outside of the summer period they can be good value. The main advantage of travelling by ferry is that you can bring your car, which is vital if you're going to get the best out of Ireland's swell-pounded coasts.

MIKE NEWMAN

Camp with a view

Infos voyage

Y aller

Par avion Les vols internationaux arrivent à Dublin, Belfast, Cork et Shannon. De là, on peut atteindre n'importe quel aéroport régional. La concurrence entre les compagnies aériennes et les compagnies de ferrys rend les prix très changeants, il faut donc comparer pour dégoter le tarif le moins cher. Si vous allez vers le nord-ouest, Knock et Sligo sont des points de chute parfaits, qu'on atteint parfois pour 700 ff A/R depuis Londres voire d'autres villes européennes. Compagnies : Aer Lingus, Air UK, Britannia Airways, Ryanair, Dan Air, British Airways, British Midlands et Capital Airlines.

Par Ferry Le pays est desservi par un grand nombre de lignes de ferry venant du Royaume-Uni ou de France. Les prix varient considérablement selon la saison. Si vous pouvez éviter la saison estivale, les prix dégringolent. Le gros avantage de ce type de transport est bien sûr de pouvoir amener votre véhicule, outil indispensable pour rejoindre la côte la mieux exposée selon le type de houle.

Se déplacer

Rouler Il est bon de se rappeler que les routes irlandaises sont destinées à ceux qui savent prendre le temps. Il est difficile de tracer la route à toute bringue et mieux vaut l'éviter surtout quand le panneau "Accident Black Spot" apparaît. Profitez de ce rythme de vie plus cool en n'essayant pas de traverser le pays dans un laps de temps trop court. L'essence est un peu plus chère qu'en Angleterre, (IR£2.80 par gallon) qu'il est d'ailleurs pas toujours aisé de trouver dans certains coins paumés. Malgré cela, la tournée des spots reste un des grands plaisirs de ce pays parce que le panorama ne laisse jamais indifférent. Comme en Angleterre, on roule à gauche avec une signalisation routière semblable.

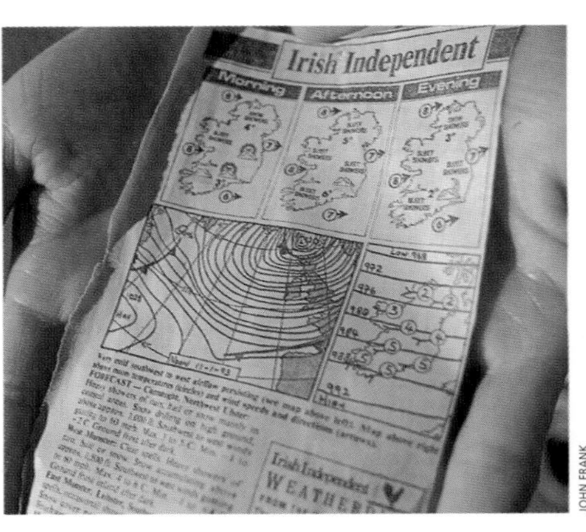

JOHN FRANK

Travel

Airports
Dublin (01) 844 4900
Belfast (01232) 422 888
Knock (094) 67222
Sligo (071) 68280

Airlines
British Midland
Dublin (01) 283 8833
Belfast (01232) 325 151
British Airways
Belfast (01232) 899 121
Aer Lingus
Dublin (01) 705 3333
Belfast (01232) 232 270

Trains
Irish Rail
Dublin (01) 836 6222
Northern Ireland Railways
Belfast (01232) 899 411

Ferries
Irish Ferries
UK 0990 17 17 17
Dublin (01) 661 0511
Holyhead - Dublin
Pembroke - Rosslare
Stena Line
UK 0990 17 17 1
Dublin (01) 204 7700
Fishguard - Rosslare
Holyhead - Dun Laoghaire
Swansea-Cork Ferries
Swansea (01792) 456 116
Cork (021) 271 166
Swansea - Cork
Isle of Man Steam
UK (0345) 523 523
Dublin (01) 874 1231
Isle of Man - Dubin
Liverpool - Dublin
Isle of Man - Belfast

Sea Cat Scotland
UK (0345) 523 523
Belfast (01232) 313 543
Stranraer - Belfast
Norse Irish Ferries
Belfast (01232) 779 090
Liverpool (0151) 944 1010
Liverpool - Belfast
P&O European Ferries
Ireland 0990 980 777
UK 0990 980 666
Cairnryan - Larne

By Bus
Irish Bus
Dublin (01) 836 6111
Ulsterbus
(01232) 320 011

Driving

Petrol prices
Leaded 66.9p per litre
Diesel 56.9p per litre
Super Unleaded 66.9p per litre
Regular Unleaded 60.9p per litre

Services
Irish Automobile Association:
(01) 677 9481
Breakdown Service:
(800) 667 788
Budget Rent-a-car
Dublin (01) 837 9611
Belfast (01232) 230 700

Speed Limits
Open 55mph (90kph)
Built up 30mph or 40mph

Other Info

Tourist Information
Dublin (1550) 112233
N. Ireland (1800) 230 230

Telephone
The Republic
From the Republic:
Operator: 190
Directory Inquiries
(for Republic and North) 1190
Directory Inquiries
(for Britain) 1197
Directory Assistance
(1800) 330 330
International operator 114
International access code 00
Northern Ireland
From Northern Ireland: 00
Operator: 100
Directory inquiries: 192
Other inquiries: 191
International operator: 155
International directory assistance: 153
International access code: 00
Emergency: 999

MIKE SEARLE

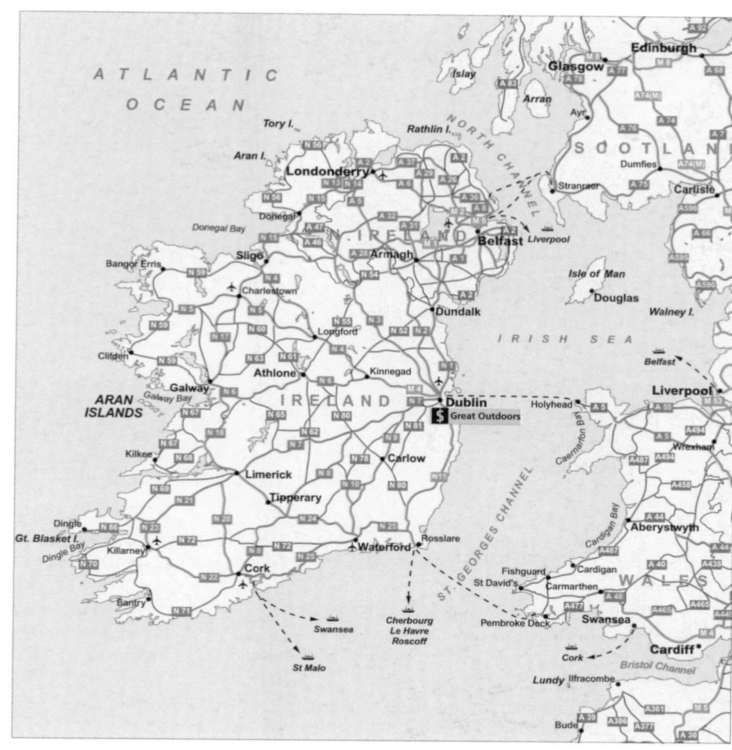

Ireland: Travelling Map

Scale 0 50 100 150 200 300 Kilometres
0 50 100 150 Miles

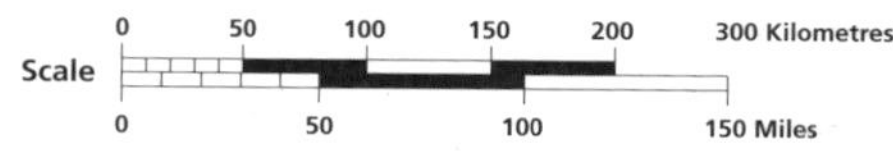

Getting Around

Driving It's well worth remembering that Ireland's roads cater for drivers who are prepared to take their time. You can't get anywhere very fast, so it's best not to try. Savour the slower pace of life and don't try to cover too large an area in too short a time. Another thing worth remembering is that petrol is expensive (IR£2.80 per gallon) and petrol stations in some of the more remote areas are few and far between. Still, driving around Ireland from one great reef break to the next is enjoyable and is one of Ireland's greatest delights.

Accommodation Ireland is not a cheap place to travel. It's hard to live cheaply owing to petrol and heating requirements, but it can be done by renting a cottage with a few friends and cooking your own food. Camping is easy and the bargain option, though due to Ireland's wet climate it's not for everyone. Farm cottages and B&Bs are numerous. No visit to Ireland is complete without a visit to a pub. The pub, especially in rural areas, is far more than just a place to drink: it's the heart of the Irish village and often the political centre too. For food, advice and conversation, head for your nearest inn – very often the pubs double up as venues for live entertainment and music.

ALEX WILLIAMS

Money In Ireland, you spends the Irish punt, which is divided into 100 pence as in Britain. One pound sterling stands at £1.16 at time of press. Change your money either in banks or 'bureaux de change' as normal.

Visas British nationals do not need a passport to enter the Republic or the North, but it is useful to carry one in case you use the medical services or cash travellers' cheques. If you don't take a passport, be sure to have some other form of convincing ID. Other EC nationals, travellers from the USA, Canada, Australia, New Zealand and Commonwealth countries simply need a passport and can stay for up to three months.

Coût de la vie L' Irlande n'est pas une destination bon marché, voire un plus chère qu'en Grande-Bretagne. C'est dur de ne pas dépenser d'argent car on roule beaucoup et il faut se réchauffer. On peut faire de grosses économies en louant un "cottage" entre amis et en faisant la cuisine. Camper est chose facile ; c'est sans doute la façon la moins chère de subsister mais gare à l'humidité ambiante, tout le monde ne la supportera pas. Les gites ruraux et les Bed&breakfast sont légion, avec un niveau de confort très au-dessus de la moyenne. Pas question de ne pas rentrer dans un pub ! Dans les patelins, le pub est plus qu'un bar ; c'est le centre du village voire le noyau politique ! Pour manger, se renseigner et tchatcher avec des locaux, le pub est toujours le meilleur spot sans oublier la présence systématique de musiciens amateurs toujours prêts à pousser la chansonnette typique qui ne vous laissera pas insensible.

Argent En Irlande, on compte en livre irlandaise, dite Punt, divisées en 100 pence comme au Royaume-Uni. Au change, £1 varie entre IR£1.05 ou IR£1,15 depuis les dix dernières années. Allez dans les banques ou aux bureaux de change.

Visas Les ressortissants de la CEE n'ont besoin que d'une carte d'identité et peuvent rester aussi longtemps qu'ils le désirent alors que les étrangers doivent avoir un passeport pour obtenir 90 jours sur place.

JOHN FRANK

You might find an empty line-up like this

Causeway Coast

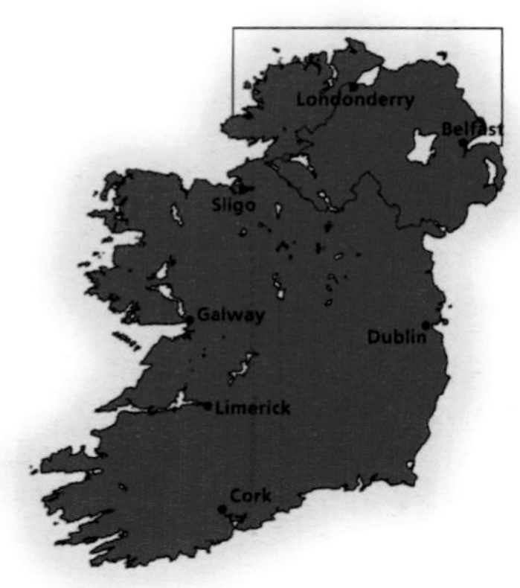

TROGGS

White Rocks

North and West Donegal

There are only a few coastal areas left in Europe where the possibility of finding perfect, empty waves still exists, however north and west Donegal are a few of these rarities. It receives so much swell that more often than not your only real concern will be the winds, which can blow hard from the south and the west. The relentless forces of nature have slowly carved up the desolate coastline around Donegal and consequently little protected bays and islands have become abundant. Such places offer unlimited potential, all they need is time and energy to explore. Donegal is sparsely populated due its harsh climate and inhospitable landscape and accessibility is therefore limited. Bloody Foreland, Magheroaty, Dunfanaghy, Gweebarra and Loughros Beg have been surfed in the past: beyond these breaks you'll probably be surfing alone.

Il existe peu de zones côtières en Europe où la possibilité de trouver des vagues vierges et parfaites existe encore. La partie ouest et nord du Donegal en est une! Cela chope tellement de houles que la plupart du temps le seul souci sera les conditions de vent. Ces vents peuvent souvent être trés forts en soufflant plus souvent du nord ou de l'ouest. Les forces infatigables de la nature ont lentement découpé les côtes sauvages autour du Donegal, c'est pourquoi des petites baies protégées et des îles se sont multipliées. Ces endroits offrent un potentiel illimité, tout ce qu'il faut est du temps et de l'énergie pour les explorer. Le Donegal est peu habité à cause de son climat difficle et de son paysage inhospitalier, son accessibilté est donc limitée. Bloody Foreland, Magheroaty, Dunfanaghy, Gweebarra et Loughros Beg ont été surfés par le passé, au-delà de ces spots vous trouverez certainement des territoires de vagues plutôt vierges.

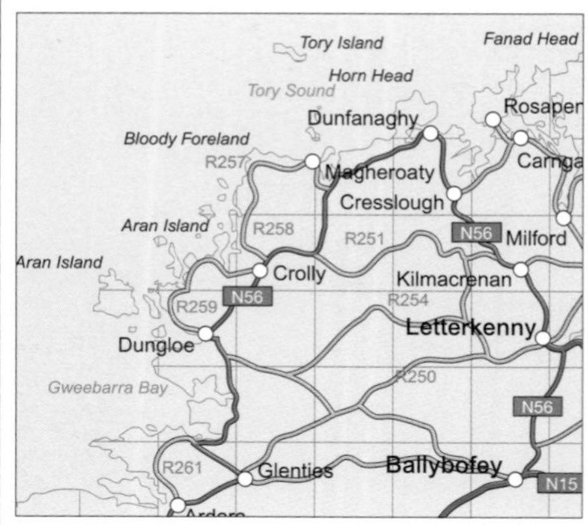

1. Benowe/Magilligan    

The longest beach in Ireland, with over 12km (8mi) of peaks, accessed via Downhills and Benowe. There's a superb view from Bishop's Road above the beach at Donegal and Londonderry.

La plage la plus longue d'Irlande...12kms de pics. L'accés se fait par Downhills et Benowe. Une vue superbe de Bishop's Road au-dessus la plage jusqu'à Donegal et Londonderry.

2. Castlerock    

A little way E of Castlerock is a long stone jetty, the presence of which has helped to create a consistent sandbank. This bank is best surfed around mid tide when it produces an excellent, long right-hander, best from 1-2m (3-6ft) – any bigger and it will close out. From low to mid tide the sands are wide, firm and are safe for most vehicles to drive on. You can either drive from Castlerock or, alternatively, drive along the beach from Portstewart and paddle out through the river, around the jetty, to the wave.

Un peu à l'est de Castlerock, y'a une grosse jetée de cailloux dont la présence a aidé à créer des bancs réguliers qui marchent mieux à mi-marée quand ça peut envoyer une droite longue et excellente, mieux de 1 à 2 mètres.

3. Portstewart Strand

Portstewart is a busy seaside resort that becomes crowded during summer months. The beach here can provide some of Northern Ireland's gentler waves with good rights and lefts surfable up to around 2.5m (8ft). Park above the beach or on the sands.

Portstewart en soi est une station plutôt animée où il y a foule l'été. La plage ici peut envoyer parmi les vagues les plus faciles d'Irlande du Nord avce des bonnes droites et gauches jusqu'à 2,5m. Soit vous vous garez au-dessus de la plage, ou comme les locaux directement sur le sable.

4. Portrush – West Strand

This area faces NW and catches swell when East Strand is small. Waves increase in size from E to W. It's one of the most surfed spots in the N.

Exposé NO et reçoit la houle quand East Strand est trop petit. Les vagues augmentent en taille d'est en ouest. Un des spots les plus surfés dans le nord.

East Strand   

Portrush, like Portstewart, is a popular holiday resort for people living in Northern Ireland. On the E side of the peninsula, you'll find an amping beach break which is also a good spot to check out on a large swell when the other nearby beaches are closing out.

Sur la partie Est de la peninsule, on trouve un bon beach-break qui est aussi un bon spot à checker en cas de gros swell, quand les plages d'à côté ferment.

Black Rocks/Dhu Varren

Located at the W end of West Strand, this is a left-hand reef that holds surf to 2.5m (8ft). Drive under the railway bridge to the car park.

Situé à l'ouest de West Strand, cette gauche de reef tient jusqu'à 2,5m. Roulez sous la vois ferrée jusqu'au parking.

5. White Rocks

Beach break waves here become crowded in summer with tourists, not surfers.

Beach break moyen qui se peuple en été de touristes, pas de surfers.

6. Portballintrae   

Just to E of Portballintrae lies a consistent bay that's often half a metre bigger and more powerful than other nearby beaches. The quality of the waves will depend on the state of the sandbanks and wind direction – too much W will mess up the swell. Park in Portballintrae, next to the SW corner of the beach. From here it's just a short walk.

Juste à l'Est de Portballintrae se trouve une baie consitente qui est souvent un à deux pieds plus gros et plus puissant que les plages environnantes. La qualité dépendra de l'état des bancs et de la direction du vent: s'il est trop à l'ouest, il désorganisera la houle. Bon jusqu'à 2,5m. SE garer à Portballintrae, au SO de la plage. Depuis là, y'a peu à marcher.

PHIL HOLDEN

Andy Hill, Portballintrae

7. White Park Bay   

An attractive 2km (1.2mi) beach, which can make surfing here that more worthwhile if the waves are good. The car park above the beach is five minutes' walk.

Une plage sympa de 2kms qui peut rendre le surf d'autant plus agréable les conditions y sont. Le parking au-dessus de la plage est à 5 minutes à pied du sable.

TROGGS

Portrush, East Strand

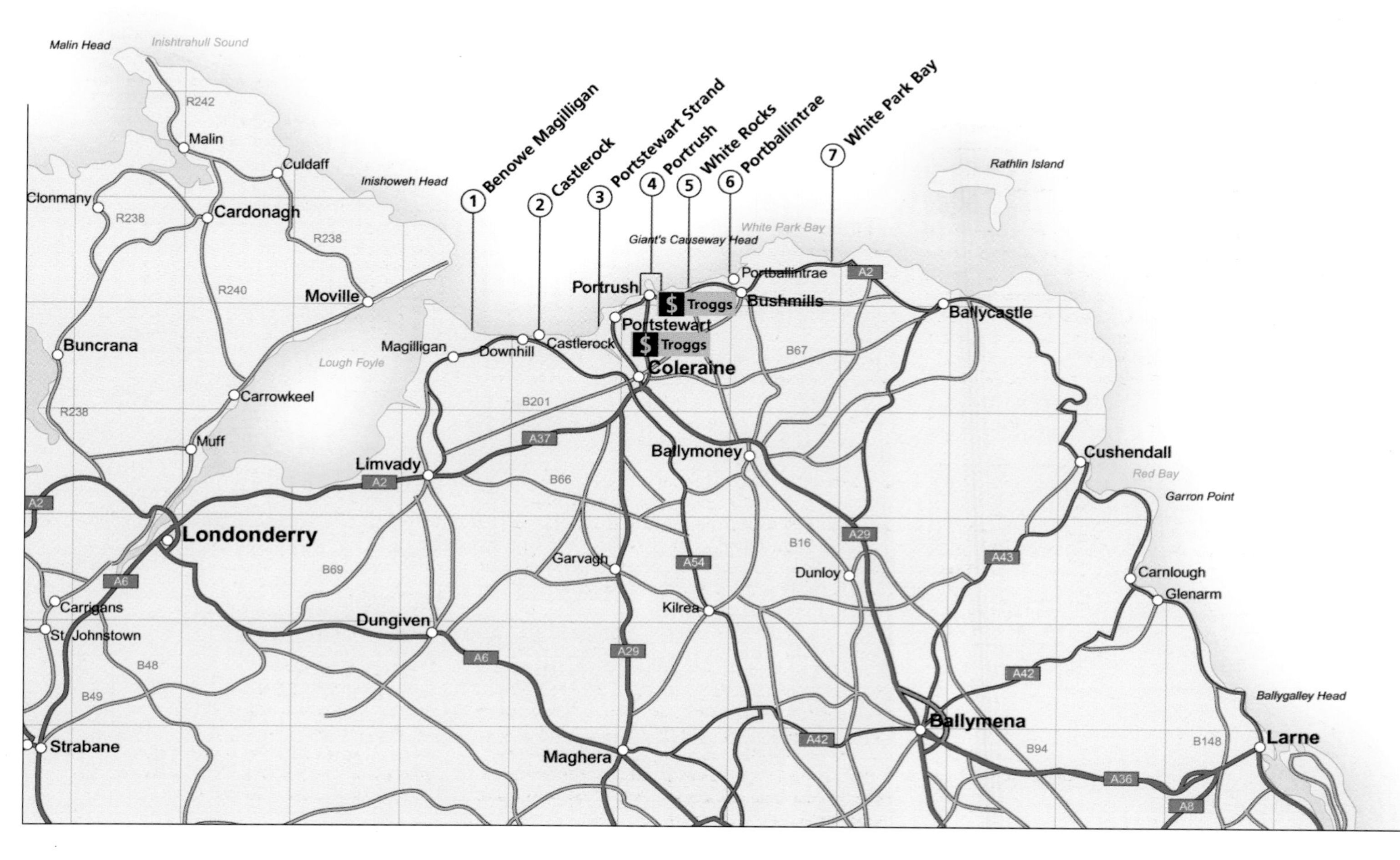

Donegal Bay

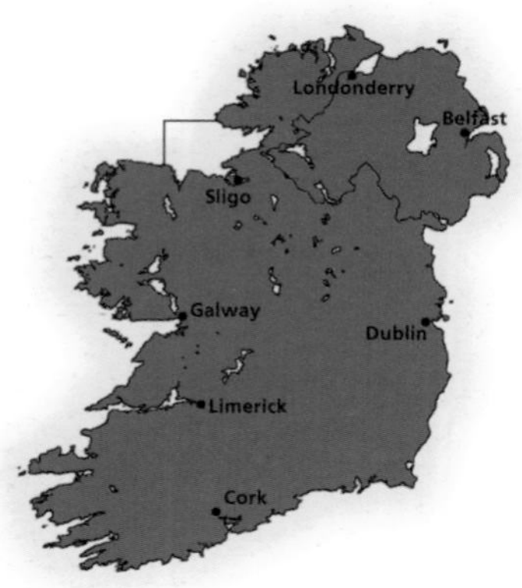

Ha ha ha he he he ho ho ho

JOHN FRANK

1. Bunatrahir Bay

A little way outside of Ballycastle is a road leading to a small, unmarked harbour. A nice left breaks at the W side of Bunatrahir Bay, but it needs a fair N swell to get going and a S wind to clean it up.

Un petit chemin en dehors de Ballycastle est en fait la route menant à un petit port non répertorié. Une jolie gauche déroule du côtè ouest de Bunatrahir Bay. Elle exige un swell de nord conséquent pour s'épanouir et un vent du sud pour être belle et propre!

2. Lackan Bay

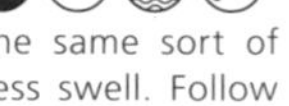

A secluded bay that works under the same sort of conditions as Kilcummin but needs less swell. Follow the road from Kilcummin.

C'est une baie isolée dont la vague marche dans les mêmes conditions qu'à Kilcummin, mais elle réclame moins de houle. Possibilité de se garer.

3. Kilcummin Harbour

In a big swell, an excellent long left breaks in front of the harbour wall. It peaks with a W wind, and when it does, it's crowded.

Lors d'un gros swell, on pourra trouver une gauche longue excellente qui casse devant le mur du port. Bien que le vent de sud ou sud-est permettent les meilleures conditions, abritée comme elle est, cette vague supporte les vents d'ouest. Kilcummin est indiqué sur la route principale.

Kilcummin

ALEX WILLIAMS

4. Inishcrone

At the E end, near the harbour, an excellent right will start to break when the swell is big enough. There's also a beach break with mellow peaks.

A l'extrème est, près du port se trouve une excellente droite qui commence à péter quand la houle est assez grosse. Il y a aussi un beach break qui forme de jolis pics prêts à être consommés!

5. Pollacheeny Harbour

A right-hander tube breaks down the rock point at the mouth of Pollacheeny Harbour giving fast rides up to 150m (130yd) in length. Don't get too excited, however, it only happens about twice a year.

Des tubes pour les normal foot. Il faut prendre le chemin pour descendre la pointe rocheuse à la sortie du port de Pollacheeny pour atteindre une vague qui peut faire 150 m de long. Comme la plupart des vagues irlandaises, elle est rarement surfée, alors que si elle était située dans le Cornwall ou dans le sud-ouest de la France, elle serait bondée! Parking près du chantier.

6. Easkey Left

The left breaking W of the harbour is an excellent reason for spending time in Easkey. It works under similar conditions as the right but breaks in a smaller swell. Paddle out off the harbour wall. Owing to Easkey's popularity the council and the ISA have erected toilets and changing facilities beside the castle overlooking the waves.

La gauche qui casse à l'ouest du port est une autre très bonne raison pour rester à Easkey. Elle marche avec les mêmes conditions que la droite mais se contente d'un plus petit swell. Il faut ramer au-delà du mur du port. En raison de la fréquentation, le conseil municipal, en accord avec la I.S.A, a fait construire des toilettes et fait changer les installations à côté du château, surplombant les vagues.

Easkey Right

A world-class right breaks on a flat rock reef at low tide. One of the major pluses for this break is its consistency and the amount of offshore winds you get here. These conditions provide perfect tubes and long fast walls up to 3m (10ft). It doesn't take a genius to work out that it's popular. Pollution problems have been recently resolved with the completion of a secondary sewage treatment plant.

Droite de réputation mondiale déferlant sur un récif de rochers plats. Meilleure à marée basse. Cette vague est remarquable par sa consistance et la fréquence de ses vents offshore.

7. Dunmoran Strand

An out-of-the-way place, this can have good waves up to 2m (6ft) and is particularly suitable for beginners.

Un endroit hors des sentiers battus, qui peut révèler de bonnes vagues jusqu'à 2 m, convient aux débutants.

8. Strandhill

Either surf the main beach or the sandbar (which involves a long paddle). If you enjoy surfing long rights, try Bluerock, an unforgiving 200m (180yd) wave breaking at the end of the beach.

Soit on surfe la plage principale soit le banc de sable (qui exige une longue rame). Si on aime surfer de longues droites, on peut surfer Bluerock, une incroyable vague de 200 m cassant à l'extrémité de la plage.

Easkey Rights

TIM RAINGER

9. Streedagh Strand

A fair-sized swell is needed to produce worthwhile waves, however, if the sandbanks aren't producing the goods, then your time spent getting here might not necessarily be wasted. Beyond Streedagh, all the way down to Ballyconnell, are numerous unmarked roads leading to various coves and inlets. The possibility of finding an unmarked reef or point break is high.

Exige une taille honorable de la houle pour former des vagues valables; cependant si les bancs de sable ne produisent pas de bonnes vagues, la journée n'est pas pour autant foutue. Après Streedagh, de nombreuses routes non balisées allant vers Ballyconnell ménent à divers criques et bras de mer. La probabilité de trouver un reef ou un point break non répertoriés est réelle.

10. Mullaghmore

With a SW wind and a big NW swell, clean lines push into the bay. It can also be worth taking a drive around Mullaghmore Head as there's reputedly a left-hander breaking over shallow rocks which can hold a 6.5m (20ft) swell!

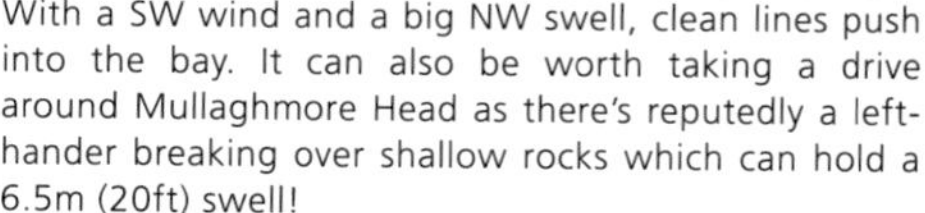

Avec un vent de sud-ouest et un gros swell de nord-ouest, on profite de lignes propres arrivant dans la baie. Mullaghmore peut valoir le détour. Une vague de goofy foot au-dessus de rochers à fleur d'eau; elle tient la houle jusqu'à 6 m!

11. Bundoran

One of Europe's premier reefs breaks best at low tide. 'The Peak' gives a short and snappy right with a longer left peeling and tubing its way across the rocks on the N side of the bay. When it's big, another more sheltered left starts to work. It's under threat from a proposed marina development.

Une des vagues les plus surfées d'Irlande; un spot de marée basse qui jette particulièrement entre 1,50 et 2m. Le pic donne une courte droite qui a du punch avec une gauche plus longue se soulevant et tubant sur des rochers du côtè nord de la baie. Quand c'est gros, une gauche plus abritée commence à marcher.

MIKE SEARLE

Tullan Strand

12. Tullan Strand

Considered to have some of the most consistent beach waves in Ireland, Tullan has become a fairly crowded spot. The S end has the best-shaped peaks. If it's flat along the rest of the coast, there can still be a wave here. Take the first left N of Bundoran (it isn't signposted). You will come to a parking area above the beach.

Un joli spot considéré comme un des meilleurs et des plus consistants en Irlande. La partie sud possèdent les pics les mieux formés. S'il n'y a rien sur le reste de la côte, alors il se peut qu'il y ait une vague ici. Il faut prendre la première à gauche à Bundoran (ce n'est pas indiqué). Un parking est disponible au-dessus de la plage.

13. Rossnowlagh

Home to Ireland's biggest surf club, the Surfer's Bar has been around since the 60s. Down a pint of well-earned Guiness with Irish surfing crew. The waves can be good but will be smaller and less powerful than those at Tullan.

Lieu du plus important club de surf d'Irlande, situé au "Surfer's Bar. Ici, avec les surfeurs irlandais et une pinte de Guiness, on peut trouver toute l'anthologie du surf depuis les années 60. Les vagues peuvent y être bonnes mais seront plus petites et moins puissantes que celles de Tullen.

ALEX WILLIAMS

Bundoran

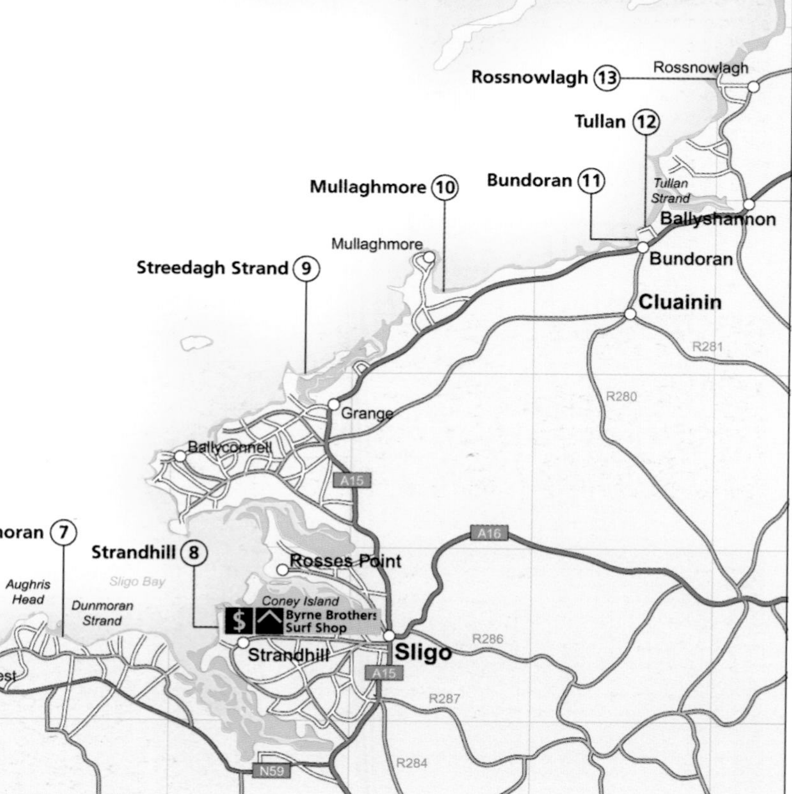

County Clare

PHIL HOLDEN

Lahinch

1. Crab Island

Not to be taken lightly because of its distance from Doolin Pier (a long paddle) and mostly because of its size, this break jacks up suddenly from deep water and can form very frightening tubes. Check your leash carefully. A great wave but few are capable of handling it!

La vague ne doit pas être prise à la légère la première fois, d'une part en raison de la distance qui la sépare de la jetée de Doolin (qui demande un bon coup de rame) mais surtout en raison de sa taille. C'est une grosse droite qui se soulève d'un seul coup et peut engendrer des tubes effrayants si le vent vient d'est. Avant de partir à l'eau, vérifiez votre leash!

CHRIS POWER

2. Doolin Point

A fast wave that can section, but with a clean swell long, walling rides are possible. There are other waves further inside the bay if this point isn't to your liking. Doolin is well signposted and there is a car park in front of the wave.

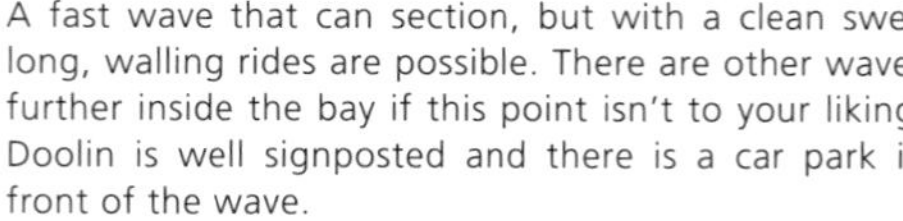

Après le parking, on peut voir une droite rapide qui déroule sur du récif. Souvent des sections cassent sans prévenir, ce qui gâche la vague. Mais quand le swell est assez clean, on peut surfer de longs murs. Doolin est bien indiqué e t il y a un parking devant la vague.

3. Lahinch Area

Beach

About the closest thing to a surf town in Ireland, with a great beginner's wave. Locals usually frequent the peak directly in front of the surf shop while beginners tend to surf more mellow peaks further N past O'Looneys bar. You pay to park in summer months.

Lahinch est la ville la plus 'surf' de toute l'Irlande. Il y a un surf shop, pas mal de surfeurs et un large évantail de bonnes vagues. Les meilleurs surfent généralement le reef break alors que les nombreux débutants s'entrainent sur de lentes et excellentes vagues de beach break. Il y a un parking facile d'accés.

Left

The most popular wave among the more experienced locals is an easy wave to ride, with a simple take-off and long walls up to 400m (360yd). On a big swell the high tide is surfable, otherwise low to mid is best.

C'est de loin la vague la plus connue des locaux de Lahinch. C'est une vague très facile à surfer, avec un take-off tranquille et de longs murs surfables sur 400m et jusqu'à 3m.

Cornish Left

This works under the same conditions as the left but it's a faster, more tubey wave. It doesn't get as crowded and there's a fairly easy paddle out between Cornish and Lahinch Left.

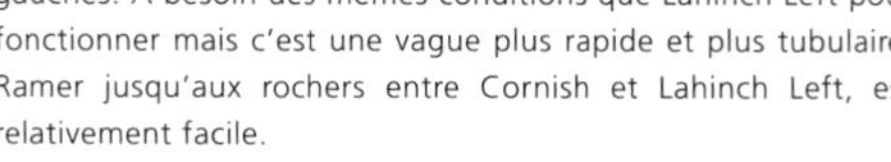

Cornish Reef peut donner de bonnes, voire d'excellentes gauches. A besoin des mêmes conditions que Lahinch Left pour fonctionner mais c'est une vague plus rapide et plus tubulaire. Ramer jusqu'aux rochers entre Cornish et Lahinch Left, est relativement facile.

LAHINCH SURF SHOP

Brendy, Lahinch Beach

Shit Creek

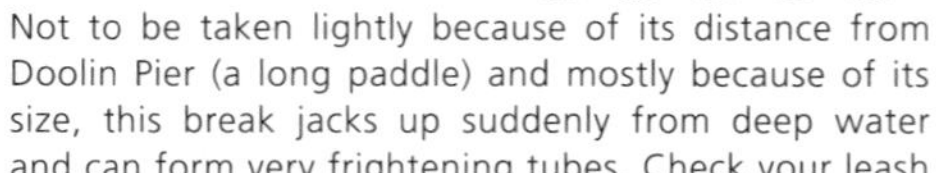

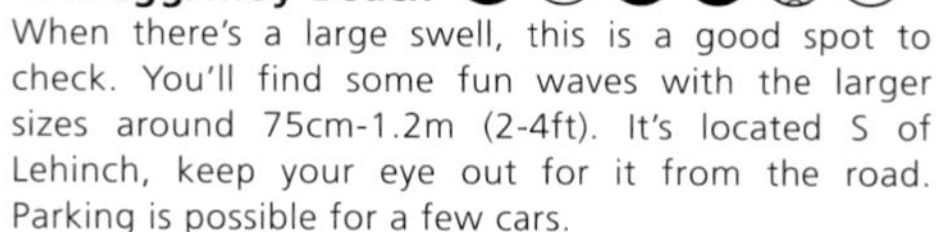

Don't be put off by the name: Shit Creek is so called because of murky river water discolouring the sea. Still, it's the least surfed and most demanding of Lahinch's reefs. The main ride is a left but the right is also good.

C'est le reef de Lahinch le moins surfé et le plus exigeant. On y surfe surtout la gauche mais il y a aussi une bonne droite. Enfin, ne soyez pas rebuté par le nom, Shit Creek est appelé ainsi en raison des eaux troubles de la rivière et pas en raison de la pollution!

4. Cregg/Moy Beach

When there's a large swell, this is a good spot to check. You'll find some fun waves with the larger sizes around 75cm-1.2m (2-4ft). It's located S of Lehinch, keep your eye out for it from the road. Parking is possible for a few cars.

Cette petite plage de galets peut être un bon spot à bien considérer quand il y a une grosse houle. Vous pourrez alors profiter de gauches et de droites particulièrement sympathiques entre 50cm et 1m. Située au sud de Lahinch, vous pourrez la voir de la route.

MIKE NEWMAN

Doolin Point and Crab Island

5. Green Point

This break picks up any swell and is by far the most challenging wave in the area. A maverick-like peak bowls out of deep water and throws a house-sized tube. It's a long walk out to the point; look for it as you cross the bridge on your way to Spanish Point.

Le premier vague pour maverick-esque barrels trés spectaculaire mais trés dangereuse.

6. Spanish Point

So named because it was here that survivors from wrecked Armada ships swam ashore. Unfortunately for them, the high Sheriff of Clare had them all executed. Today these hazardous rocky reefs provide some excellent rights. There's also a mellow beach break.

Ce spot s'appelle ainsi car on y a recueilli des survivants du naufrage des bateaux de l'Armada. Malheureusement pour eux, le Sheriff de Clare les avait fait tous exécuter. Maintenant, ces dangereux récifs de rochers peuvent générer d'excellentes droites!

Inside Point

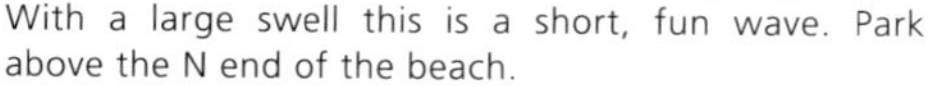

With a large swell this is a short, fun wave. Park above the N end of the beach.

Inside Point réclame une grosse houle avec un vent de sud-est, est ou nord-est pour produire de bonnes vagues. Pour l'Inside Point, il faut se garer au-dessus de l'extrémité nord de la plage.

Middle Point

This is usually the best of the reefs, giving fast walls and do-able tubes.

Middle Point est normalement le meilleur des trois reefs, offrant des murs rapides avec des tubes exploitables!

Outside Point

This receives the brunt of most swells and is rarely surfed due to its ferocity: it holds a 5-7m (15-21ft) swell. For Middle and Outside Point, take a small unmarked road about half a mile N.

Outside Point prend la plupart des houles et est rarement surfé car la vague est méchante. Peut tenir une houle de 5-6m. Pour Middle et Outside Point, prendre une petite route non répertoriée à environ1km au nord du parking.

7. Doughmore

When every other break is too small this one still works. If it's big it closes out right across the beach even in offshore winds. Access is a real problem – check with the local surf club before crossing anybody's land or you could find yourself in trouble.

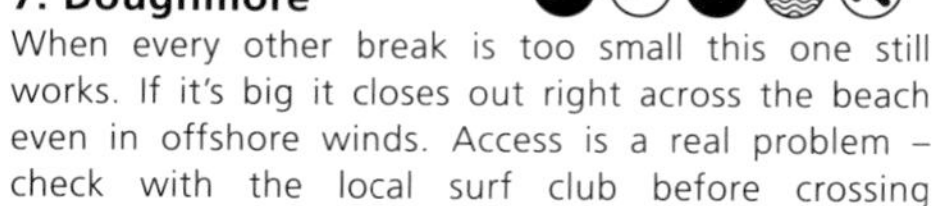

Beach break avec un reef outside. Lorsque c'est tout petit sur les autres spots, cela marche ici. Quand le swell est gros, cela arrive droit sur la plage même par vent offshore. Mais l'accès est un problème épineux. Demandez auprès du surf club local si la traversée des propriétés privées a été reglé. Sinon, vous pourriez vous retrouver en situation très délicate.

8. Doonbeg Castle

In a huge swell a nice wave can be found near the old ruined castle by the jetty in Doonbeg. Head here when all other breaks in Clare are closing out. Access is off the main coast road by the church.

Quand il y a un swell énorme avec un vent de sud-ouest, une très jolie gauche peut déferler près du vieux château en ruines au niveau de la jetée de Doonbeg. Cela casse sur un fond de rochers et c'est meilleur de la mi-marée à la marée haute. Cela vaut le coup lorsque tous les autres spots sont saturés. Il faut prendre la route côtière au niveau de l'église.

9. Killard

Works under the same conditions as Doonbeg, with waves surfable to 1.2m (4ft). There's easy parking by the beach.

Cette petite baie de sable marche dans les mêmes conditions que Doonbeg. Les vagues ici sont meilleures de marée basse à mi-marée et sont surfables jusqu'à 1,5 m. Il y a un parking facile d'accès au niveau de la plage.

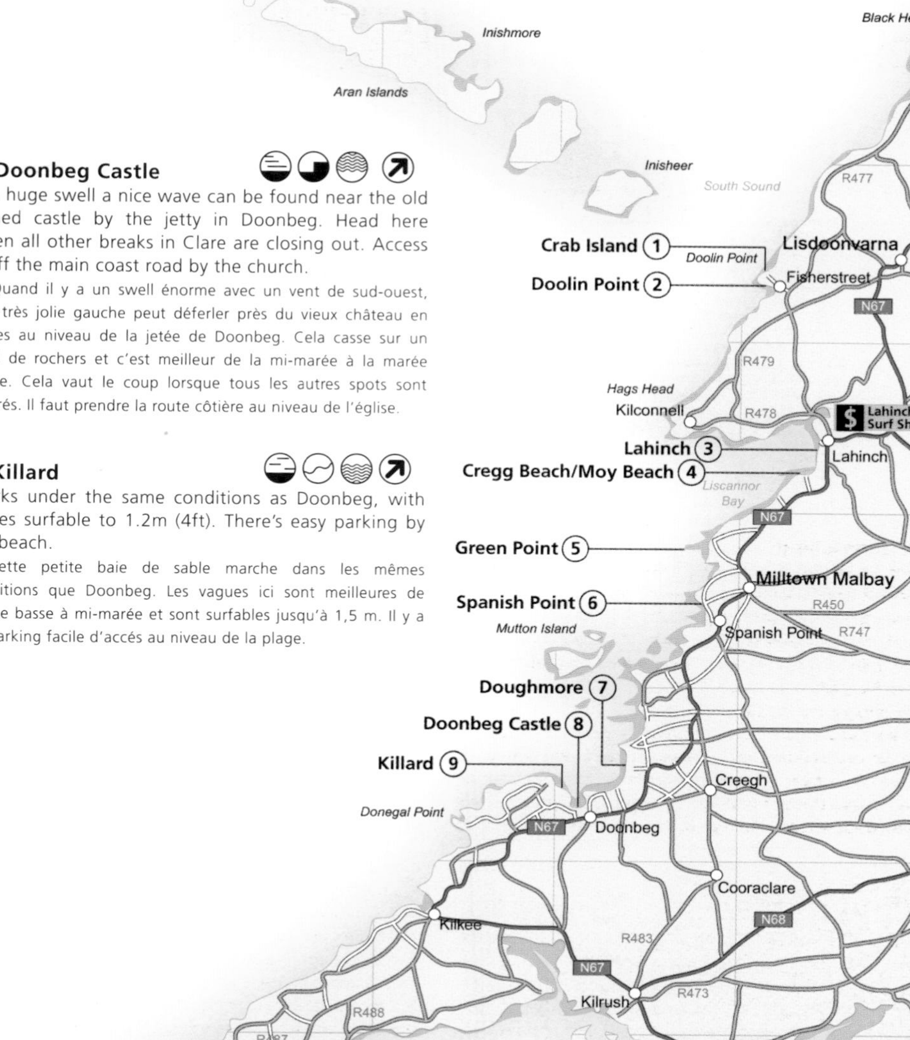

CHRIS POWER

Another Clare left

10. Ballybunion

Right

Locals who know this break will sit and wait for the waves just inches away from the cliffs. The take-off is fast and wedgy but otherwise it's an easy wave to ride. Located at the beach's N end.

Les locaux qui connaissent ce spot s'assoient et attendent les vagues qui sont à deux pas des falaises. Le take-off est rapide et raide mais sinon c'est une vague facile, c'est meilleur à marée haute.

Beach

The beach break can give good waves. Easy parking at the north end and by the ruin in the middle of the beach.

Le beach break peut aussi créer de bonnes vagues. Il y a un parking facile d'accès (sauf en été) au nord et également près de la ruine au milieu de la plage.

Left

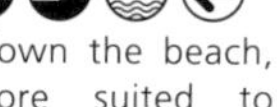

This breaks over the rocks further down the beach, providing fast hollow waves more suited to experienced surfers.

Breaking over the rocks further down the beach providing some fast hollow waves more suited to experienced surfers.

The Dingle Peninsula

SIMON McCOMB

Mossies

1. Garywilliam Point

This classy wave makes the most of a small swell (rather than being rated as a a bona fide big wave spot). It breaks over a shallow reef giving fast and hollow rides but maxes out easily. Access is by walking N from Mossies. Go to the end of the point and paddle round to the break. Only recommended for experienced surfers.

Une vague classieuse qui maximise le moindre swell plutôt qu'un spot de grosses vagues automatiques. Casse sur très peu d'eau en donnant des vagues rapides et creuses mais sature vite. On y va en marchant vers le nord depuis Mossie's. Allez jusqu'au bout de la pointe et ramez autour du cap. Uniquement pour surfers avertis.

2. Mossies

A mellow reef break, nicknamed after the farmer who first saw surfers at this spot. Unless you like a long paddle out, access is easiest from Garywilliam Point: drive to the end of the road, walk between the houses and head down the cliff. Respect the locals.

Reef tranquille d'excellente qualité, ainsi nommé après qu'un paysan ait vu pour la première fois des surfers sur ce spot. A moins que vous ne préfériez ramer pendant 2 plombes, mieux vaut y aller depuis Garywilliam en roulant jusqu'au bout de la route et en marchant entre les maisons puis en bas de la falaise.

3. Brandon Bay

From the top of Conner Pass you'll see the horseshoe sweep of Brandon Bay facing NW. It picks up most swell except S and SW and even then some swell pulls around Brandon Head. It's popular with windsurfers and longboarders.

En haut de Conner Pass, on peut voir l'étendue en fer à cheval de la baie de Brandon exposée nord-ouest. Elle prend presque toutes les houles sauf sud et sud-ouest même s'il y a alors quelques vagues à Brandon Head. Très prisé des winsurfers et des longboarders.

JULIEN OGOR

4. Ballydavid

A big wave spot that works infrequently. There's a sucky take-off, an almighty drop, then a fast, peeling wall, which sucks harder down the line the bigger it gets. It needs to be 2m (6ft) to break, gets good at 2.5m (8ft) and at 3-4m (10-12ft) it just gets better: the Admiralty charts show 90 fathoms just off the harbour. When you're in the water, line yourself up the old coast guard lookout post and the radio mast at all stages of tide (and all swell sizes) and just move up and down the line according to conditions.

Un point-break avec un take-off qui suce où il faut au moins 2 mètres pour que ça marche. Ca devient une bonne vague à 2,5m et à 3-4m, c'est carrément le pied avec un drop de tous les diables et un mur rapide qui aspire d'autant plus que c'est gros. Les cartes marines montrent 90 brasses de profondeur juste hors du port, ce qui explique ce topo. Ramez au line-up au niveau de l'ancien poste des garde-côtes avec la grosse antenne radio à toutes les périodes de marée et de tailles de houle. Il suffit de bouger le long de ce repère selon les conditions.

5. Coumeenole

Exposed beach break with intensely powerful peaks work best at low tide. As the tide pushes in, a heavy right breaks in front of the shipwreck (note well!) and rocky reef. There's a strong rip, so fools rush in where angels fear to tread.

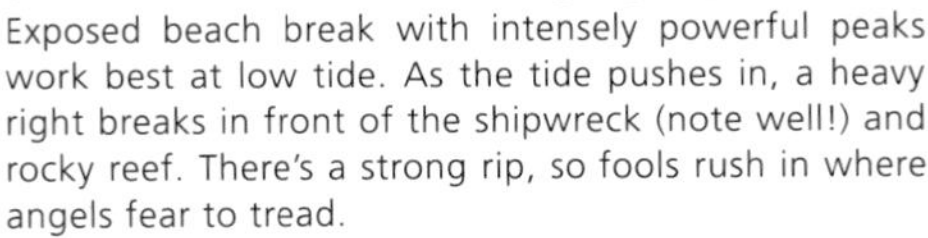

Trois pics qui marchent à marée basse avec les bancs de gauche qui marchent le mieux. Quand la marée remonte, des droites craignos cassent devant l'épave (Prenez en note) et une avancée rocheuse. Les idiots s'y précipitent alors que les anges ont peur d'y marcher. De puissants courants.

PHIL HOLDEN

Garywilliam Point

NICK GAMMON

Coumeenole

MARK STEVENSON

Garywilliam Point (1)
Mossies (2)
Brandon Bay (3)
The Seven Hogs
Magharee Islands
Jamie Knox
Brandon Point
Brandon Head
Brandon Bay
Brandon
Castle Gregory
Ballydavid (4)
Kilcummin
Kiliney
Stradbally
Aughacasla
Derrymore
R560
R559
Glashabeg
Ballinloghig
Smerwick
Ballydavid
Sybil Point
Ballyferriter
Teeravane
R559
Milltown
Annascaul
Inch
Aughils
Dunquin
Ventry
R559
Dingle
Lispole
Coumeenole
Parkmore Point
Bull's Head
Great Blasket Island
Slea Head
Inch Reefs (6)
Inch Strand (7)
Inishnabro
Inishvickillane
(5) Coumeenole

6. Inch Reefs

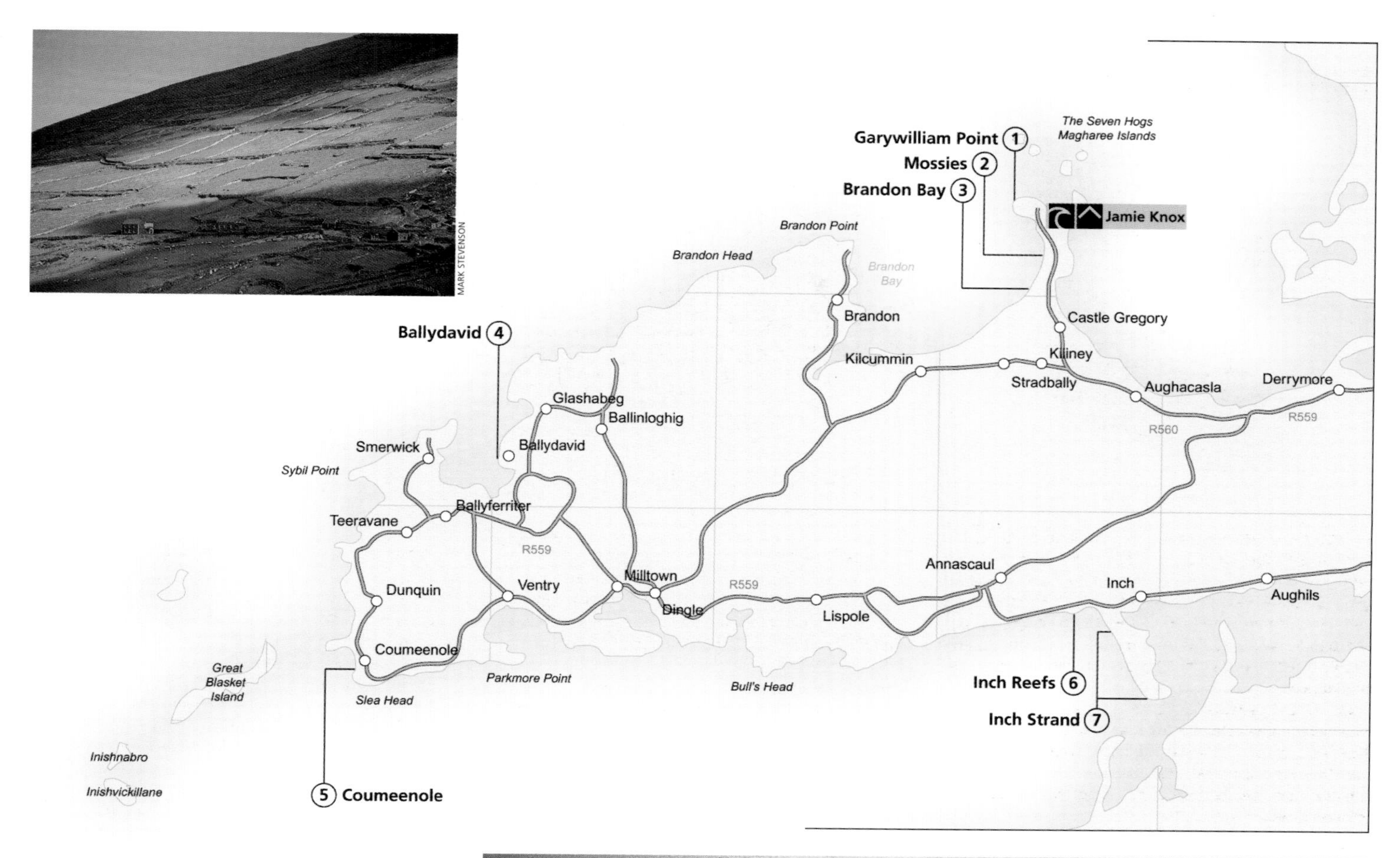

Inch is one of Ireland's sleeping beauties.Half-a-dozen times a year it reveals a stacked line up of rifling rights, which can peel for 400m (360yd) or more. Unfortunately the spots that's hurting the most from Ireland's recent crowd problems.

Staying in position is killer with a 0.5 knot rip pulling against you. Low tide is best – the bigger the swell the better. Take care getting in and out of the water and make sure you have a suitable exit point figured out before coming in. There's no clear access: park beside the road and find a way down the cliff.

Quand PJ vint habiter ici, il dit qu'il y avait un Jeffreys Bay en Irlande quelque part. Cet automne, je l'ai trouvé à Inch Reef. En deux heures, je pris 4 vagues mais je surfai tout le temps ou je ramai. Le jour d'après, je pouvais à peine marcher. Je mesurai la distance avec un appareil (la route suit le bord de la falaise au-dessus): presque 2 kms! La rame est carrément pénible à cause d'un contre-courant d'un demi-noeud. La marée basse est meilleure et plus c'est gros, mieux c'est. Attention à la mise et à la sortie de l'eau en vous assurant que vous connaissez une portie de sortie avant de prendre une vague. L'accès se fait où vous voulez. Garez-vous sur le bord de la route et trouvez un chemin pour descendre.

Inch Reefs

TIM RAINGER

7. Inch Strand

A beautiful spot providing some good quality surf. It's more of a longboarder's or beginner's wave, best at mid tide. The N end is the best part of the beach.

Un spot superbe qui peut fournir des vagues de bonne qualité. Plutôt un spot de longboards ou pour les débutants, mieux à mi-marée. L'extrémité nord de la baie est souvent le meilleur endroit de la plage.

Inch Strand

TIM RAINGER

Southern Ireland

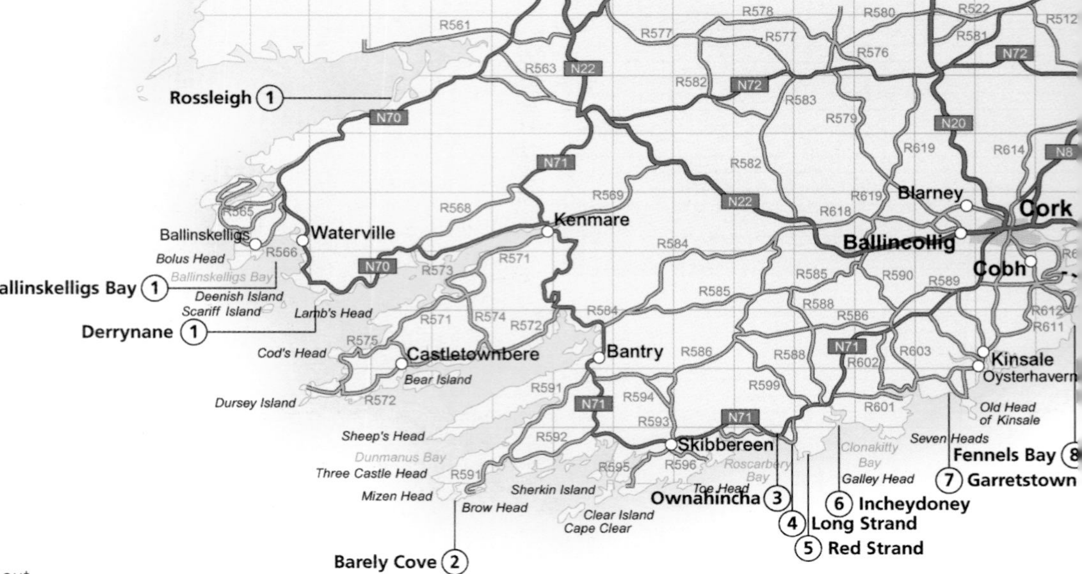

1. Ring of Kerry

Rossleigh is 6km (4mi) of solid beach break: seek out a hollow left, which requires a long paddle. Your next port of call should definitely be Ballinskelligs Bay: this sheltered bay contains a number of breaks ranging from gentle beaches to excellent reefs and points. With a SW swell, or a big W swell, waves will show up. Different breaks work on alternate tides with a variety of winds so something will nearly always be working here. Past Waterville is Derrnane where there's a lovely beach with crystal clear waters that can, when the swell is big enough, provide some pristine little waves. Even if there is no swell, then a trip around the Ring of Kerry should be considered a must for anyone who appreciates great countryside.

Rossleigh est 6 kms de beach break. De plus une gauche creuse qui exige un bon coup de rame. Votre prochaine escale devrait être sans aucun doute Ballinskelligs Bay. Cette baie protégée possède de nombreux spots allant des gentilles plages de sable aux excellents reefs et autres pointbreaks. Avec une houle de sud-ouest, ou un gros swell d'ouest, les vagues atteindront leur maximum. Chaque spot a ses propres exigences de marée et de vents, ainsi il y aura toujours quelque chose qui marchera dans la région. Après Waterville,c'est Derrnane; ici, il y a une jolie plage avec des eaux cristallines qui peuvent être le théâtre, lorsque le le swell est suffisament gros, de charmantes? Petites vagues. S'il n'y a pas de houle, alors un voyage dans le Kerry s'impose pour quiconque apprécie les paysages grandioses.

2. Barley Cove

A sandbar creates nice lefts in a small swell. There's breath-taking scenery.

Un banc de sable provoque de belles gauches par petit swell. Paysage à vous couper le souffle.

3. Ownahincha

Two beaches are separated by a rocky outcrop and have some nice waves created by sandbars.

Deux plages séparées par des rochers à fleur d'eau, quelques vagues sympathiques peuvent être prises essentiellement sur des bancs de sable.

4. Long Strand (Castlefreake)

This takes its name from a local castle and has some of the best surfing in Munster. Both ends of the beach have waves breaking off rocks and hold large swells. There are also several sandbars along the beach.

Tiens son nom d'un château des environs et est un des meilleurs endroits pour surfer de tout le Munster. Les deux extrémités de la plage ont des vagues cassant au-delà de rochers pouvant tenir de grosses vagues. Il y a aussi plusieurs bancs de sable le long de la plage.

5. Red Strand (Dirk Bay)

When every other place is blown out and the swell is big, Red Strand really works. A big reef in the middle of the bay breaks the large swells of winter (not surfable) and lets waves through on the reform, where some nice 1m (2-3ft) lefts and 1-2m (3-6ft) hollow rights break against cliffs.

Quand tous les autres spots sont hors-contrôle et que le swell est gros, Red Strand se révèle. Un méga récif au milieu de la baie interrompt les larges houles d'hiver (insurfable) et filtrent les vagues à la reforme pour offrir de jolies gauches de 0.5-1 m et des droites creuses de 1-1.5 m cassant près des falaises.

6. Inchedoney

An attractive beach greets you: there's a headland in the middle and a river at each end. Waves can be excellent depending on swell size and direction.

Une plage attrayante avec un promontoire au milieu et une rivière à chaque bout. Les vagues peuvent être excellentes selon la taille du swell et sa direction.

7. Garretstown

Two beaches are separated by a rocky point: the E beach has a nice right on large SW swell, which also gives good beach breaks that are ideal for beginners, while the W beach (Coakley's) works on any swell from E to W, with mainly beach breaks on an excellent right at the W end. There are two groynes in centre of beach that are dangerous when covered with high water.

Deux plages séparées par une pointe rocheuse. Sur la partie ouest de l'île, on peut découvrir une droite intéressante lors d'un swell sud-ouest conséquent. De bons beach breaks, idéals pour les débutants. La plage située à l'ouest (Coakleys) marche avec n'importe qu'elle houle d'est à d'ouest. Principalement des beachs breaks avec une excellente droite à l'extrémité ouest. Deux aines au centre de la plage risquent d'être négligées et se révèler dangereuses quand la marée les recouvrent.

8. Fennels Bay

A left reef that works on a SSE swell. Good hollow wave from 1-1.5m (2-4ft). Exiting from the water can be difficult.

Un reef qui déroule en gauche et qui fonctionne avec un swell de sud/sud-est. Sortir de l'eau peut être difficile. Agréable vague creuse de 50 cm à plus d'1 m.

IRISH SURF FEDERATION

Bunmahon

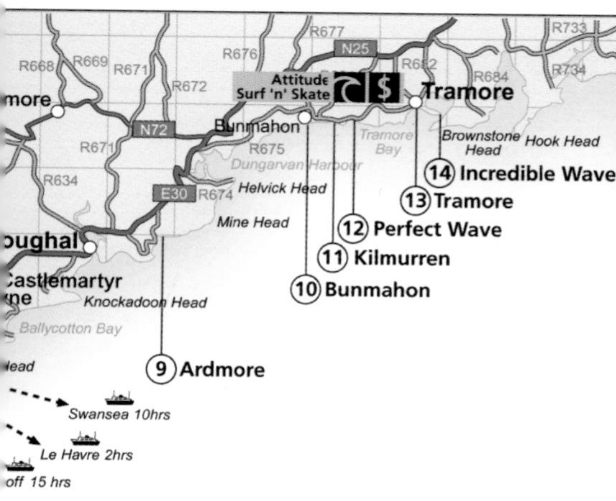

9. Ardmore

This is a sheltered bay with waves generally half the size of a prevailing swell. It's good in storm surf with N winds (very rare). Enjoy the picturesque seaside village.

Baie protégée, où les vagues font génèralement la moitié de la houle; bon dans des conditions de tempête avec du vent du nord (très rare). Pittoresque village de bord de mer.

10. Bunmahon

A beach break with rips (caused by a small rivermouth in the bay). It's one of the few waves in the SE that's good for bodyboarders and is always an option at the end of SW storms.

Beach break avec du courant dû à la présence, dans la baie, de l'embouchure d'une petite rivière. Une des rares vagues du sud-est du pays qui vale le déplacement pour les bodyboarders. Toujours une possibilité de se mettre à l'eau en fin de période de tempête de sud-ouest.

11. Kilmurren

This is the last resort when storm surf is closing out elsewhere. It has a big drop with little else. The wave breaks at the mouth of the cove – don't venture out beyond it.

L'endroit où il faut aler lorsque ça sature ailleurs. Posséde un bon drop mais pas grand-chose après. La vague casse à l'entrée d'une crique; ne pas s'aventurer au-delà.

12. The Perfect Wave

This beach offers good surf from 1-2m (2-6ft) and has a good left breaking outside on storm surf. The Perfect Wave is a small left reef to the left of the beach with access through a gap in the rocks – surf good, barreling surf from 1-2m (3-6ft). It's not for beginners due to the proximity of exposed rocks, but still rates as the most consistent quality wave on this coastline.

La plage offre un bon surf de 0.5 à 2 m et posséde une bonne droite déroulant outside lors des tempêtes. La 'vague parfaite' est une petite gauche de récif à gauche de la plage que l'on atteint par une ouverture parmi les rochers. Bonne vague tubulaire de 1 à 2 m. Pas conseillé aux débutants en raison des rochers qui attendent patiemment leur proie! Belle vague qui est, en plus, la plus consistante de la côte.

13. Tramore

The surf centre of SE Ireland which boasts 5km (3mi) of beach break waves. Lessons and surfboard hire are available from the surf shop on the beach.

Le point central du surf du sud-est irlandais avec 5 km de vagues de beach break. On peut prendre des leçons et louer une planche au surf shop de la plage.

14. Incredible Wave

A long left at E end of Tramore beach verifies this name. Cars are parked at end of paved road. It works on a medium to large swell, often occurring in February when the winds are particularly biting, so a good wetsuit is necessary. When it's on, it's top to bottom for as long as you can make it, but it's quite fickle due to swell direction and tide height. There are good relations between local farmers and surfers as long as consideration and courtesy for their property is given.

Longue gauche qui se trouve à l'extrémité est de Tramore Beach. On peut garer les voitures à l'issue d'une route pavée. Les fermiers locaux et les surfeurs entretiennent de bonnes relations (respect des propriétés). Marche par moyen et gros swell, ce qui corrrespond souvent au mois de février quand les vents sont particulièrement cinglants; une bonne combinaison est nécessaire. C'est alors vraiment bien du début jusqu'à la fin aussi longtemps que vous pouvez suivre la vague mais un peu inconstant car trop dépendant de la direction de la houle et des variations de profondeur duent aux marées.

East Coast

The E coast of Ireland can occasionally have rideable waves. During the winter, strong S winds will generate some swell. These winds then need to swing round to a more W direction to make the swell clean. If you are in the area and these conditions are present, Jack's Hole is worth a look. The Irish Sea is reputedly one of the most radioactive seas in the world: even if looks clean, it's not!

La côte est de l'Irlande peut avoir des vagues surfables. Pendant l'hiver des vents forts du sud peuvent engendrer de la houle. Ces vents doivent pivoter vers l'ouest pour créer un swell propre. Si vous êtes dans les parages et si les conditions sont réunies, Jack's Hole vaut le détour. La mer d'Irlande a la réputation d'être la mer la plus radioactive du monde, alors même si cela paraît clean, non!

MARGARET O'BRIEN MORAN

Henry Moore, a local shaper, tests his equipment in County Wexford

Winter brings challenging waves and weather to the rocky coasts of Great Britain.
'Unmaxibles', Cornwall, England

Great Britain

To this day, people the world over wil knowingly tell you: 'There're no waves in Britain!' Next time you hear it, politely offer them this picture as proof to the contrary. The British are an instinctively seafaring nation who equally share the wider world's intense passion for surfing. People ride waves on virtually every mile of her rich, varied coastline. A massive selection of beaches, points and reefs are home to a busy but friendly surf population who've been the most pervasive of European surf travellers from the beginnings of the sport.

Grande Bretagne

A ce jour les gens en connaissance de cause vous le diront bien : il n'y a pas de vagues en Grande-Bretagne! La prochaine fois que vous entendrez une telle phrase, offrez leur poliment cette photo comme preuve du contraire. Les Britanniques sont naturellement une nation de marins et partagent avec le reste du monde une intense passion pour le surf. La population surfe de fait sur chaque kilomètre d'une côte riche en histoire et variée . Les pointes et reefs est le lieu de rencontre d'une population de surfers très speed mais sympa qui est celle qui a le plus essaimée dans le monde parmi les surfers européens au tout début de ce sport. Croyez le ou pas, la Grande Bretagne est une zone de surf d'enfer.

TIM RAINGER

Introduction

The People

Scotland Gaelic tribes and Norse raiders from the north, Picts from the east, and Anglo-Saxon marauders from England have all left their cultural fingerprints over this northern partner in the current political union. There still remains a strong feeling of separation and animosity between the Scots and English, a legacy of a bloody history. The catalyst began with the Stuart Kings' ascendancy of the English throne in 1603. Within 150 years the English had regained a firm grip on the Scottish throne, outlawing clans, declaring bagpipes and kilts illegal and ruthlessly suppressing other aspects of highland culture in retaliation.

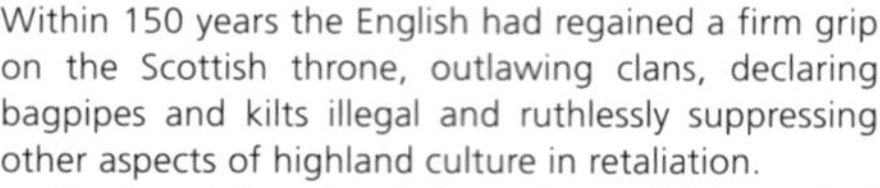

Capital: London
Population: 55,514,000
Area: 24,755sqkm/94,475sqmi
Time: GMT
Language: English, Gaelic, Welsh
Currency: British Pound

The Scots' lingering independent spirit is marked by distinctive accents, judicial system and currency, and since 1998, a greater degree of executive power as a result of the Labour Government's referendum. The predominant language is English, though Gaelic is widely spoken. Scottish accents differ widely, and some are hard to understand, but don't be afraid to make non-comprehension clear as they know people have problems with their vernacular.

ANDY BENNETTS

England's earliest immigrants were often refugees from tribal warfare and unrest (the Belgic tribesmen escaping from Imperial Rome, the Romans themselves, the Angles, Saxons, Jutes, Danes and Normans), who have all in turn brought genetic variety. Under Roman rule the population of the British Isles numbered about half a million. By the time of the Doomsday Census (1086) it had doubled and over the next 900 years it became, and remains, one of the most densely populated countries in the world.

The British Empire was, for over 200 years, all powerful and it wasn't until the end of the WWII that its strongholds began to disintegrate. In 1947 India and Pakistan became independent and by 1970 nearly most other Commonwealth countries had done the same. Today it retains its place among the world's leading nations. English culture continues to permeate global affairs, and its rich colonial history has created one of the world's most multi-cultural societies. Further integration with Europe should increase its cosmopolitan nature.

Wales Another nation of Celtic origins, the Welsh continually fought off the Romans and then the English until 1282, when Edward 1 defeated the last native Welsh prince Llewyn ap Gruffyd; Wales passed into English rule. Trouble flared in the 15th century when the Welsh Prince Henry Tudor defeated Richard III at the Battle of Bosworth. Tudor paved the way for the 1536 Act of Union that tied the Welsh and English in an uneasy but lasting relationship.

Once one of the great mining areas in the world, Wales' income has been replaced by tourism, farming and light industry. The passing centuries have watered down Welsh culture but the language is still widely used. Bi-lingual road signs all over the country display the longest words on the planet, especially in north and central Wales. Like the Scots, the Welsh also voted 'yes' to a greater degree of autonomy in early 1998.

EST PIX

The Land

Great Britain is the biggest of the British Isles, an island of surprisingly rich contrasts. Scotland is known for its highlands and plateaus and its storm-battered coast. The Scottish mainland divides into the highlands in the north west, the lowlands in central Scotland and the southern uplands on the English border. It's also home to the highest peak in the British Isles, Ben Nevis, which stands at 1,344 metres (4,408 feet). The Cheviot Hills to the far south form a natural border with England.

England is memorable for its rolling hills and gentle, green landscape of intensively farmed pastures, separated by hedgerows and stone walls. In the north, the Pennine chain, the Cheviot Hills and the Cumbrian Mountains provide a more rugged, dramatic contrast to the mostly flat east country.

Wales is Britain's smallest country and while it's mountainous it is bounded by water on three sides: the Irish Sea to the north, St George's Channel to the west and the Bristol Channel to the south. The Cambrian Mountains fill most of the interior.

The Climate

PETER CADE

Despite the UK's position relative to the Arctic, it enjoys a mild, favourable climate. Other countries lying at similar latitudes such as Eastern Siberia and Southern Alaska are much cooler with longer, harsher winters and ice-bound coasts.

'The Gulf Stream' is the main reason for the UK's comparatively temperate weather and most of the UK receives damp, maritime air from the Atlantic Ocean for much of the year, providing a background of mild summers and moderate winters. Other influential climatic changes are brought about by rapidly shifting air masses coming from the continent and the Arctic, which head over the freezing North Sea adding another element to an already dynamic climate.

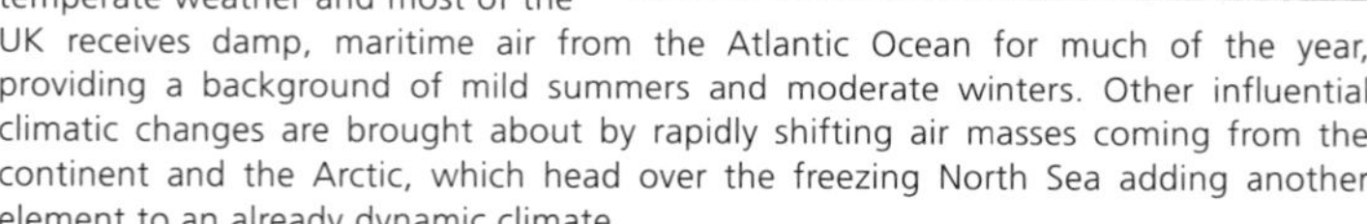

Scotland, like Ireland, sits closest to the lows that storm through the Atlantic all year round, often sweeping over the country with strong winds and rain. Combine this with lower sunshine hours and temperatures than the remainder of the UK and you'll understand the term 'land of the brave' better.

Like the rest of Britain, Wales also has a mild, damp climate. The high regions are cooler than the lowlands and have a heavy rainfall (over 200 days a year).

Introduction

La population

Ecosse La nation est un mélange de tribus gaéligues du nord, de Picts de l'est, d'aventuriers Viking ou Norse et de conquérants anglo-saxons. Il en reste un vif sentiment de séparation et d'animosité entre les écossais et les anglais, surtout depuis que la dynastie des Stuart accéda au trône, déclarèrent les clans hors-la-loi, les cornemuses et les kilts illégaux et réprimèrent sévèrement les autres aspects de la culture écossaise. Les écossais en gardèrent quand même certaines différences comme l'accent, les écoles, le système juridique et la monnaie. La langue dominante est l'anglais, bien que le Gaëlique soit souvent parlé. Les accents écossais varient drôlement, bien que tous soient un délice à attendre pour l'oreille inexpérimentée. N'hésitez pas à vous faire répéter si vous n'y comprenez rien, ils savent que plein de gens ont des problèmes à les comprendre mais ça ne les dérange pas pour autant.

Angleterre Les premiers immigrants furent souvent des réfugiés des guerres tribales et des invasions, comme les Belgres échappant à l'Empire romain, les Romains eux-mêmes, les Angles, les Saxons, les Jutes, les Danois et les Normands qui contribuèrent done à cette variété génétique des Anglais. Sous i'empire romain, on comptait environ un demi-million d'habitants. Au recensement de 1086, cette population avait doublé et en 900 ans, elle devint une des nations les plus importantes du monde.

L'Empire britannique fut pour plus de 200 ans le plus puissant au monde en ne se désagrégeant qu'à partir de la deuzième guerre mondiale. En 1947, l'Inde et le Pakistan devinrent independant et en 1970, presque tous les pays de la Couronne britannique s'étaient émancipés. Aujourd'hui, l'Angleterre garde sa place parmi les nations en pointe. Sa littérature, sa musique, sa mode et d'autres influences culturelles continuent à pénétrer les cultures du monde, son héritage colonial lui laissant une des sociétés multi-raciales les plus colorées. L'intégration croissante avec l'Europe devrait accroitre cette touche cosmopolitaine.

Pays de Galles Encore une nation aux origines celtiques, les Gallois ont continuellement lutté contre les Romains et les Angalis jusqu'en 1282, lorsqu'Edouard I battit le dernier prince gallois Llewyn ap Gruffyd et c'est alors que le pays tomba sous la loi anglaise. Des troubles sont apparus au XV siècle quand le prince gallois Henry Tudor infligea une défaite à Richard III à la bataille de Bosworth, il préfigurait alors l'acte d'Union de 1536 qui scella les relations anglo-galloises d'une façon difficile mais durable.

C'était alors une des grandes nations minières dans le monde, activité qui a maintenant beaucoup perdu au profit du

TURTLE PHOTOGRAPHY

Forecasting in Great Britain

Pressure systems pass over the islands almost daily, bringing the familiar variations of cloud, rain and sunshine that give the UK its fame for climatic changeability. Surfing conditions naturally share this fickleness, making sound knowledge of weather forecasting more necessary.

The British reputation for being preoccupied with the weather is well-deserved and they're amply supplied with accurate meteorological information. BBC Television has excellent forecasts (after news broadcasts), while *The Shipping Forecast* on BBC radio has detailed reports for every region as well as the crucial, accurate, Sunday lunchtime all-week forecasts. *Ceefax page 420* also contains surf information and of course major national broadsheet newspapers carry detailed weather maps.

Various commercial surf report numbers and those run by surf shops across the country are updated daily. These will tell you about the waves on the day of your call but will not help if you are trying to predict a few days in advance. For that, personal knowledge of weather maps is your best bet.

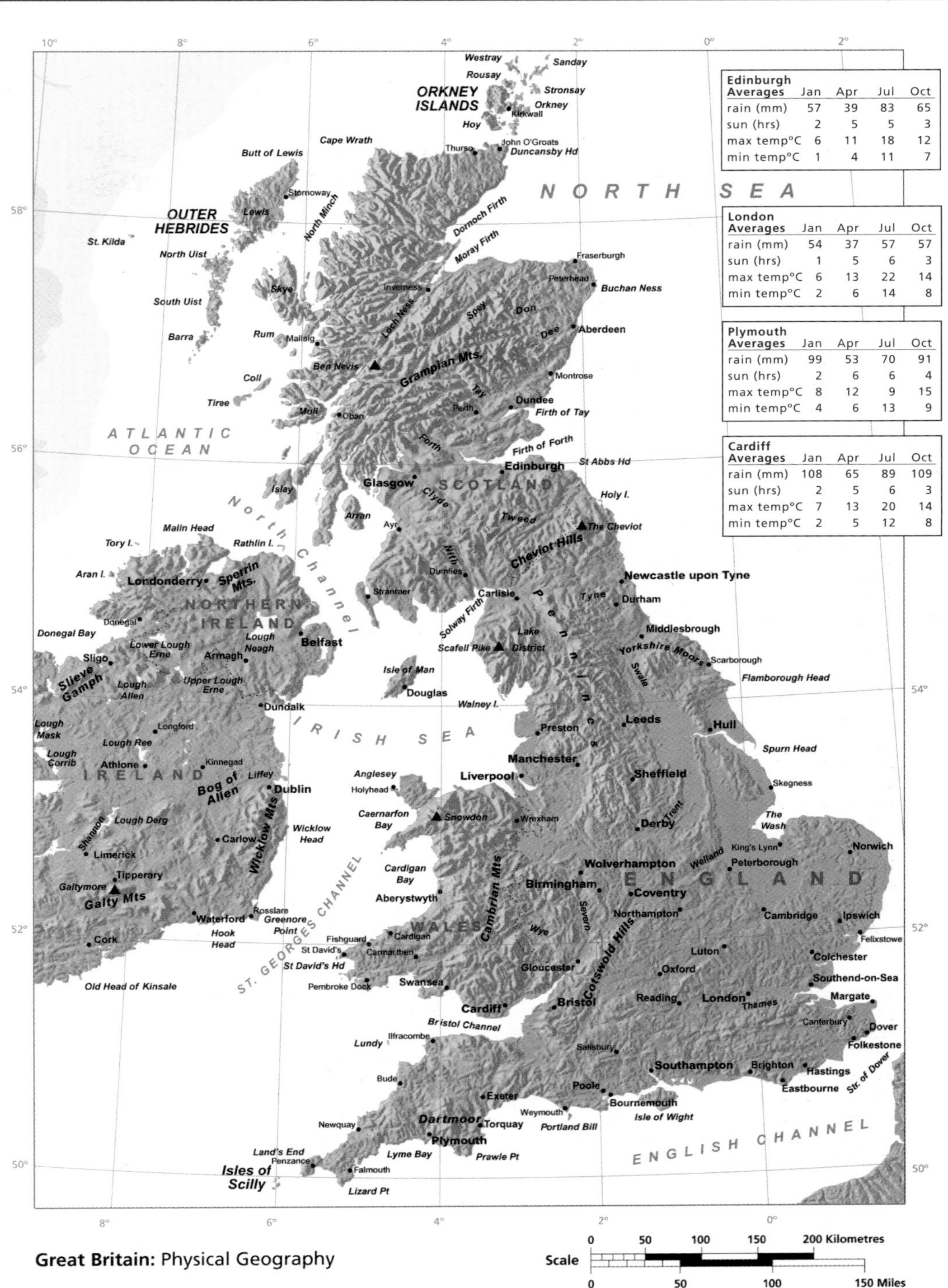

Edinburgh Averages	Jan	Apr	Jul	Oct
rain (mm)	57	39	83	65
sun (hrs)	2	5	5	3
max temp°C	6	11	18	12
min temp°C	1	4	11	7

London Averages	Jan	Apr	Jul	Oct
rain (mm)	54	37	57	57
sun (hrs)	1	5	6	3
max temp°C	6	13	22	14
min temp°C	2	6	14	8

Plymouth Averages	Jan	Apr	Jul	Oct
rain (mm)	99	53	70	91
sun (hrs)	2	6	6	4
max temp°C	8	12	9	15
min temp°C	4	6	13	9

Cardiff Averages	Jan	Apr	Jul	Oct
rain (mm)	108	65	89	109
sun (hrs)	2	5	6	3
max temp°C	7	13	20	14
min temp°C	2	5	12	8

Great Britain: Physical Geography

Scale: 0 50 100 150 200 Kilometres; 0 50 100 150 Miles

tourisme, l'agriculture et de l'élevage de l'industrie légère. Les siècles passant ont dilué quelque peu la culture galloise sauf la langue qui est toujours largement parlée surtout dans le nord et au centre du pays. Pour exemple, les panneaux sur la route sont bilingues dans tout le pays.

Le pays

La Grande Bretagne est la plus grande des îles britanniques, une terre de contrastes frappants. L' Ecosse est connue pour ses Highlands et ses plateaux, avec une côte façonnée par les tempêtes. L' Ecosse se partage entre les highlands au nord ouest, les Lowlands au centre et les southern Uplands au sud. Le point culminant des Iles Britanniques est le Ben Nevis dans les montagnes Cairngorn à 1344 metres(4408 pieds). Les collines Cheviot à l'extrême sud forment une frontière naturelle avec l'Angleterre.

L'Angleterre est célèbre pour ses collines en pente douce et ses paysages verts composés de pâturages travaillés intensivement séparée par des haies et des murs de pierre. Dans le nord, la chaîne Pennine, les collines de Cheviot, et les montagnes Cumbrian escarpées fournissent un contraste saisissant avec l'est du pays en gande partie plat.

Le Pays de Galles est le plus petit pays du Royaume-Uni et bien qu' il soit très montagneux, il est entouré d'eaux sur ses trois façades -la mer d'Irlande au Nord, le détroit de St-George à l' ouest et le détroit de Bristol au sud. Les montagnes Cambrian dominent presque tout le centre du pays.

Le climat

Malgré sa latitude élevée par rapport à l'Arctique, la Grande Bretagne jouit d' un climat privilégié. Les régions qui sse trouvent sur la même latitude comme la Sibérie orientale et l'Alaska septentrionale sont beaucoup plus froides avec des hivers longs et des côtes prises par la glace. La principale raison du climat relativement tempéré de la GB est le Gulf Stream qui explique en grande partie l'humidité et la douceur, l'air maritime de l'océan Atlantique donnant des étés agréables et des hivers doux. D'autres changements influençant le climat sont le résultat de masses d'air se déplaçant du continent et de l'Arctique, refroidissant la mer du Nord ce qui ajoute un autre élément à un climat déja dynamique.

L'Ecosse, comme l'Irlande, se trouve, toute l'année, sur le passage de la plupart des dépressions de l'Atlantique nord, ce qui amène à chaque fois vents forts et pluies. Ajoutez à cela un ensoleillement et des températures minima et vous comprendrez mieux l' appellation "Terre des Braves"

Comme ailleurs en Angleterre, le Pays de Galles a un climat doux et humide. Les régions hautes sont plus fraîches que les plaines avec de fortes précipitations (plus de 200 jours par an).

Jersey Surf Club – circa 1957

Surf Culture

GB Surf History

The UK's first surfer was quite possibly a lad called Nigel Oxendew, who learnt the sublime art in Waikiki in 1919 under the tutelage of the legend Duke Kahanamoku.

His Royal Majesty, Edward Prince of Wales, was hot on his heels. In 1920 he also spent three days in Hawaii, canoeing and surfing madly, initially in tandem, later alone. Joseph Brennan recounts in his biography *The Duke*: 'For several hours the Duke worked patiently, explaining and demonstrating. By later that afternoon the Prince had become quite adept, falling only occasionally.

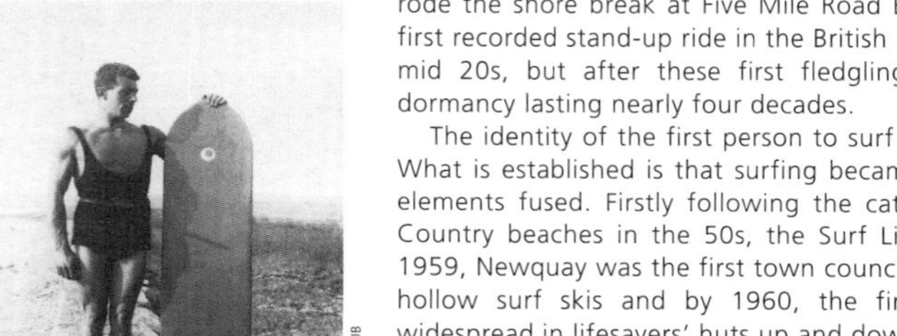

JERSEY SURF CLUB

Watersplash Jersey, Nigel Oxendew in the 20s. Note the natty woollen swimsuit

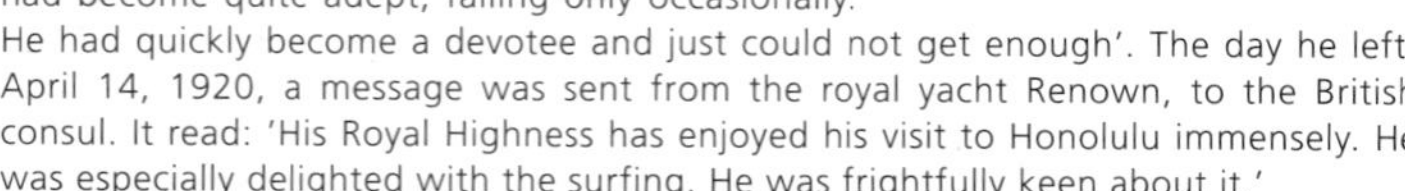

He had quickly become a devotee and just could not get enough'. The day he left, April 14, 1920, a message was sent from the royal yacht Renown, to the British consul. It read: 'His Royal Highness has enjoyed his visit to Honolulu immensely. He was especially delighted with the surfing. He was frightfully keen about it.'

After Nigel Oxendew returned, he told some friends about his experiences and the 'Island surf club' was formed in Jersey in 1923. Oxendew, Martin and Gordon rode the shore break at Five Mile Road Beach that year on short bodyboards. The first recorded stand-up ride in the British Isles was by Archie Mayne sometime in the mid 20s, but after these first fledgling efforts there appears to have been a dormancy lasting nearly four decades.

The identity of the first person to surf in Great Britain is shrouded in conjecture. What is established is that surfing became popular in Cornwall when two cultural elements fused. Firstly following the catastrophic number of drownings on West Country beaches in the 50s, the Surf Life Saving Association was established. In 1959, Newquay was the first town council to take on full-time life guards with their hollow surf skis and by 1960, the first wooden paddle boards had become widespread in lifesavers' huts up and down the coast.

Enter the Aussies, 1961. Bob Head, Ian Tilley, John Campbell and Warren Mitchell were four lifeguards from Sydney's Avalon surf club, in Britain for the holiday season. One chilly April morning not long after arriving, they paddled out on the first fiberglass and foam boards and gave a few enthralled onlookers a surfing display of style, power and grace. Clearly Great Western Beach had witnessed a departure from anything previously seen in Britain.

The SLSA kept growing while the Aussie lifeguards kept carving when in came Gidget, surf music and a greater awareness of the growing Californian 'surf culture.' As Doug Wilson says in his excellent book on the history of British surfing, *You Should Have Been Here Yesterday*: 'It was around this time that a clean-cut, surf-riding band, the *Beach Boys* were taking surf to the suburbs. Suddenly, every

Culture Surf

L'histoire du surf en GB

Le premier surfer de GB était probablement un gars répondant au nom de Nigel Oxendew qui apprit cet art sublime à Waikiki en 1919 sous la tutelle de Duke Kahanamoku. Son altesse royale, le prince de Galles était littéralement à ses genoux. En 1920 il passa trois jours à Hawaii, à faire du canöe et à surfer, au début en tandem puis seul sur une planche. Joseph Brennan relate l'anecdote suivante dans la biographie qu'il lui a consacré "Pendant des heures il s'est evertué patiemment à lui apprendre à surfer lors d'une session mémorable, plus tard au cours de l'après midi le prince était devenu un fervent pratiquant de ce sport, ne tombant qu'occasionnellement.Il etait devenu vite un mordu et ne voulait plus en décrocher. Le jour où il quitta l'île, le 14 avril 1920. Un message fut envoyé au consul de la Grande-Bretagne:"son altesse royale a été enthousiasmé par sa visite à Honolulu. Notamment il a apprécié le surf. Il a trouvé ça très excitant.

Après son retour Nigel Oxendew raconta ses aventures à ses amis et le "Island Surf Club" était créé en 1923. La première tentative de surf sur l' île fut l'oeuvre de messieurs Oxendew, Martin et Gordon qui surfèrent le shorebreak de"Five Mile Road Beach" cette année sur des Bodyboards vêtus de pimpantes tenues de bains en laine.Waouh le style ! Une légende douteuse dans les années 1920 fit d'Archie Mayne le premier a se mettre debout sur une planche dans les îles Britanniques mais après ces premiers efforts de moineau il semble qu'il y eut une période de ralentissement de l'activité surf.

Sur l'identité de la première personne qui surfa en grande Bretagne, on se perd en conjectures. Ce qui est établi est que le surf est devenu populaire dans les Cornouailles quand deux éléments culturels furent combinés. Avant tout, à la suite d'un nombre dramatique de personnes noyées sur les plages de West Country dans les années 50, l'association "Surf Life Saving"fut créée. En 1959, Newquay était la première ville à engager à plein temps des maîtres nageurs avec leurs wave-skis et en 1960 on trouvait les premiers paddle-boards dans les cabanes des maîtres nageurs tout au long de la côte. Arrivent ensuite les Australiens. Bob Head, Ian tilley, John Campbell et Warren Mitchell étaient quatre lifeguards de l'Avalon Surf Club de Sydney durant la saison des vacances de 1961. Un matin frigorifique d'avril peu après être arrivés, ils ramérent sur les premières planches en fibre de verre et en Clarkfoam et donnèrent à quelque "happy few" captivés une leçon de style, puissance et grâce. De manière claire, la plage du Great western avait été le témoin de quelque chose qui n'avait pas eu d'antécédents dans le pays jusqu'alors.

Pendant ce temps, la Surf Life Saving Association continua à se développer et les lifeguards australiens continuèrent à aligner les rollers, puis survint la série américaine Gidget, la musique surf et une plus grande conscience de l'avénement de la surf culture californienne. Comme le dit Doug Wilson dans son excellent livre sur l'histoire du surf Britannique, vous auriez du être là hier. C'était à cette époque qu'un groupe de surf musique propre sur lui, s'appelant les Beach Boys amena le surf dans les banlieues. Brutalement chaque gosse de la ville qui n'avait pas une vague à se mettre sous la dent se livra a un culte juvénile qui s'abattait sur la Californie et se répandait à travers le monde à la vitesse grand V. Une nouvelle époque arrivait , le flower power était au coin de la rue et être un surfer signifiait qu'on se préparait à se fendre la gueule.

ALEX WILLIAMS

Tigger Newlyn

city kid without a wave to his name tuned into a youth cult that stormed out of California and rushed around the world. A new era had arrived, flower power was around the corner, and being a surfer meant plugging into a happening of indescribable fun.'

As soon as people realised that it was possible to surf in Cornwall, surfing was here for good. By 1965, young entrepreneurs had set about the task of satisfying a demand for wetsuits, surfboards and equipment. Bilbo Surfboards, and later Tiki became the first manufacturers in the country, growing into a part of the European surf scene, which was also booming.

Surfing in **Wales** began in the early 60s, but it wasn't until 1967 that it took off when Australian surf champion Keith Paul came to the Gower during a summer swell at Langland, ripping up the shore break in his silver baggies while the locals gawked in amazement. During the 60s surfing was mainly confined to the beaches at Langland, Caswell and Llangennith. Heavy boards and the risk of damage to board and body (leashes only came into use in late 1972) meant the more inaccessible reefs and points were only surfed by the most hardcore. Keith Paul, Howard Davies and John Goss were the first to surf Crab Island and other pioneers include Viv Ganz, Dave Friar, Robin Hansen, Paul Connibear and Pete Jones.

By the mid 70s, most of the Gower reefs had been surfed but during the early 80s, a few 'secret' spots were added to the map by Carwyn Williams, and Rob and Phil Poutney. The South Pembrokeshire Surf Club has been running since then.

The first board factory in Wales was Crab Island Surfboards, spearheaded by 'technical-guru' Pete Phillips. By the late 70s Crab Island boards were used by most of Wales' top surfers. During this time, Kiwi airbrusher and shaper Craig Hughes worked there. Hughes, who later founded Wave Graffitti surfboards, provided the catalyst needed to enhance the talents of young Langland surfer Carwyn Williams, who became Britain's most successful competitive surfer of the 80s. By then, locally made boards were able to match the imports from Newquay and abroad and surfing in Wales had come of age.

ALEX WILLIAMS

In the early 60s, Andy Bennetts was a teenager at school in Edinburgh, **Scotland**. Every summer his family would make the three-day drive to visit his grandparents in Falmouth. In the summer of 1965, he ventured to Newquay where he saw some guys surfing on Towan beach. Boards became available the following year. The following year Bennetts bought a three-metre (nine foot, six inch) Bilbo Pop-Out for £26 and took it home. One day In early summer of 1968 he and a few friends headed off to Aberdeen with the board on the roof, nothing serious, just a look. On the beach that day was novice George Law: between them they share the honours of being Scotland's first surfers.

Small groups of enthusiasts have subsequently sprung up in Aberdeen, Edinburgh and Glasgow. Bill Batten was one of them. On the way to a relative's wedding up north in Armadale Bay, he had to drive along the north coast, where he happened to see huge surf. The North Shore was discovered after the tales Batten told.

In the early days, the surfing crew didn't know how to read a weather map so the 12-hour drive from Edinburgh was a lottery, but with the formation of the Surf Federation, Scotland has been active at European and World Amateur events.

ALEX WILLIAMS

Left to right – Paul Bassford, Nigel Semmens, Clive Rohdell, Denny Ingram

Dès que les gens se rendirent compte qu'il était possible de surfer dans les Cornouailles et que les conditions n'étaient pas trop pourries, les gens ne quittèrent plus leurs planches. En 1965, des jeunes entrepreneurs s'étaient mis en tête qu'ils allaient satisfaire la demande en combis, planches et équipement. Bilbo Surfboards et plus tard Tiki devinrent les premiers ateliers de fabrication dans le pays et sur la scène européenne du surf qui était elle aussi en plein boom.

Le surf au **Pays de Galles** commença au début des années 60 mais ce n'est pas avant 1967 qu il démarra vraiment. Le champion de surf australien Keith Paul vint sur le Gower durant un swell classique d'été à Langland et déchira le shorebreak avec son short couleur argent pendant que les locaux le mataient les yeux ébahis. Le surf international avait débarqué. pendant les années 60, le surf était principalement confiné aux seules plages de Langland, Caswell et Llangennith. Des lourdes planches avec le risque de les endommager voire de se blesser (les leashes arrivèrent seulement à la fin de 1972) ont fait que les reefs et pointbreaks les plus inaccessibles furent seulement surfés par les plus vaillants. Keith Paul, Howard Davies, et John Gosh furent les premiers à surfer Crab Island et d'autres pionniers dont Viv Ganz, Dave Friar, Robin Hansen, Paul Connibear et Pete Jones.

Le premier atelier de shape au pays de Galles fut Crab Island Surfboards dirigé par le maître de la technique Pete Phillips. A la fin des années 70 les planches Islands étaient utilisées par la majorité des meilleurs surfers gallois. Durant cette période le pilote et shaper nèo zélandais Craig Hughes travailla à Islands Factory. Craig, qui plus tard, fonda Wave Grafitti surfboards fut celui qui révéla au grand jour le talent d'un jeune surfer de Langland : Carwyn Williams, celui la même qui devint le surfer britannique le plus compétitif des années 80. A partir de cette époque les planches fabriquées localement égalaient celles qui étaient importées de Newquay et de l'étranger et le surf au Pays de Galles était devenu adulte.

Ecosse Au début des années 60, Andy Bennetts était un adolescent scolarisé à Edimbourg. Chaque été sa famille prenait la route pour trois jours afin de rendre visite à ses grands parents à Falmouth. Pendant l'été 65 il s'aventura à Newquay où il vit des gars surfer sur Towan Beach. En 1966 on pouvait louer des planches à Newquay aussi il saisit l'occasion. L'année suivante il acheta une 9'6 de la marque Bilbo Pop-Out pour 26 livres Sterlings et la rapporta en Ecosse. Un jour au début de l'été 68 avec quelques potes il alla jeter un coup d'oeil pour voir les vagues à Aberdeen avec la planche sur le toit de la voiture. Il y avait sur la plage ce jour là George Law avec qui il partage l'honneur d'être le premier surfer en Ecosse. Des petits groupes de passionnés commencèrent alors à se former à Aberdeen, Edinbourg et Glasgow. Bill Batten qui était de ceux-là avait un ami au nord à Armadale Bay. En allant à son mariage il fit la route le long de la côte nord, où il eut la surprise de voir de très grosses conditions. Le North Shore écossais fut découvert d'après les récits qu'il fit. Malheureusement, l'équipe de surfers qui partit à la conquête de ce territoire surfistique vierge ne savait pas lire une carte météo et le voyage de douze heures d'Edinbourg était toujours une partie de loterie. Robin Salmon et Pat Kiernan furent les premiers à surfer Thurso East. La fédération de surf fut créée en 1973 et depuis l'Ecosse a toujours été présente lors des compétitions européennes et mondiales.

Surf Culture

Today

Since the 60s, continual contact with foreign surfers, films, and magazines have kept the vibe strong. Wetsuit refinements in particular have produced quantum leaps in the surfing population of the UK. The British Surfing Association estimates there are currently around 100,000 surfers in the UK and that number grows every summer. Surfing has penetrated British society to a wide extent. A high number of style, lifestyle and fashion magazines have been paying attention to the rapid growth of this vivid sub-culture. Surf shops are springing up seemingly everywhere, from small coastal towns to inland cities, currently numbering around 150.

British surfers like Rod Sumptor, Ted Deerhurst, Nigel Semmens, Nigel Veitch, Carwyn Williams, Spencer Hargreaves and, most recently, Russell Winter have unquestionably led European surfing into the world arena. Britain is also home to Europe's highest output board factory (Nigel Semens, Newquay). Surprisingly the history of competitive surfing in the UK has been severely impeded by Britain's legendary summer flatness. The ASP events have come and gone, but the dismal reality of holding an expensive media-inspired operation in Newquay in mid-summer isn't an attractive prospect. Consequently there hasn't been an ASP event in Britain for four or five years.

What Britain lacks in pro events, it more than makes up for in balls-on-the-line surf environmentalism. Surfers Against Sewage began life in the badlands of west Cornwall as a small group of hard core activists, subsequently growing into the most vocal environmental group promoting clean water and have a current membership of 10,000. Their impassioned protests have galvanised the attention of health and environment ministers Europe-wide and created positive karma for the whole European surf community (see page 19 for more info).

EST PIX

English womens squad

Culture Surf

Aujourd'hui

Depuis les années 60, les contacts permanents avec les surfers étrangers, les films et magazines ont fait que l'engouement n'a pas faibli. L'amélioration de la qualité des combinaisons a permis l'agrandissement de la population surfistique en GB. Selon les chiffres de l'association Britannique de surf (British surfing association) il y a environ 100 000 surfers licenciés en Grande Bretagne et ce nombre augmente chaque été. Le surf a largement pénétré la société britannique avec une bonne couverture médiatique et des évènements d'envergure. Un grand nombre de magazines de mode et de société ont consacré leurs pages à la crossance rapide de cette bouillonnante sous-culture. Des surf-shops ont égalemement bourgeonné un peu partout. Ollie Fitzjones raconte: "il devait y avoir 80 shops à travers le pays quand nous avons écrit notre premier livre et ouvert notre magasin à Londres il y a une dizaine d'années de çà. Il y en a maintenant 150-200. C'est ce qu' on appelle une explosion. "

Des surfers britanniques comme Rod Sumpter, Ted Deerhurst, Nigel Semmens, Nigel Veitch, Carwyn Williams, Spencer Hargreaves et plus récemment, Russel Winter ont sans conteste lancé le surf européen dans le grand bain. GB est aussi le siège du plus gros atelier de shape d'Europe (Nigel Semens, Newquay). Aussi étonnant que cela puisse paraître, l'histoire du surf en GB a été sérieusement entravée par la légende selon laquelle les étés étaient flats chez les buveurs de thé. Les compets de l'ASP sont parties aussi vite qu'elles étaient venues, mais la perspective d'organiser une opération d'envergure à grand renforts de médias en plein été à Newquay n'est pas si attrayante que ça. Par conséquent, il n'y a pas eu de compets en GB depuis quatre ou cinq ans mais si le Royaume-Uni souffre de ne pas accueillir de tels événements, il se rattrape en étant en première ligne sur le front de la défense de l'environnement. L'association des Surfers contre la pollution marine (Surfers Against Sewage) est née dans les Cornouailles occidentales au sein d'un noyeau d'activistes purs et durs, se faisant la voix de groupes de pressions souhaitant une eau propre avec à l'heure actuelle plus de 10 000 membres ayant payé leurs cotisations. Leurs protestations vigoureuses ont mobilisé l'attention des ministres de l'environnement et de la santé à travers l'Europe et ont créé un karma positif pour toute la communauté du surf européen, même si certaines parties d'entre elles ne l'ont peut être pas mérité.

PHIL HOLDEN

Severn Bore madness

Travelling

Travel

By Air
London – Heathrow: (0181) 759 4321
London – Gatwick: (01293) 535 353
Stanstead: (01279) 680 500
Manchester: (0161) 489 3000
Bristol: (01275) 474 444
Cardiff: (01446) 711 111
Swansea: (01792) 204 063
Edinburgh: (0131) 333 1000
Glasgow: (0141) 887 1111

By Sea
P&O: 0990 980 9 80
Stena Sealink: (01233) 64 70 47
Hoverspeed: (01304) 240 241
Brittany Ferries: 0990 360 360
North Sea Ferries – Hull: (01482) 377 177
Color Line – Newcastle: (0191) 296 1313
Scandinavian Seaways: (0171) 616 1414

By Train
British Rail Information: (0345) 484 950
Also deals with ferry crossings to Ireland
London Transport Info: (0171) 222 1234
Gatwick Express: 0990 30 15 30
Heathrow-Paddington fast: 0845 600 1515
Eurostar: (01233) 61 75 75

By Bus and Coach
National Express (Victoria): 0990 80 80 80
Eurolines (Victoria): (0171) 730 8235

Rentals and Services
Budget Car and Van Rental: 0541 56 56 56
AA: 0990 500 600

STEPHEN HIRD

Driving

Speed Limits
Built up: 48 kmh (30mph)
B Roads: 96 kmh (60mph)
Motorways: 112 kmh (70mph)

Petrol Prices
Unleaded: 67p/l
4 Star: 73p/l
Diesel: 66p/l

Tolls
There are no tolls on British Motorways. Some bridges require a toll to be paid such as the Tamar Bridge on the Border of Devon and Cornwall.

Other Info

Embassies
Australia: The Strand WC2B 4LA
(0171) 379 4334
New Zealand: 80 Haymarket, SW1Y 4TQ
(0171)930 8422
South Africa: Trafalgar Square, WC2N 5DO
(0171) 930 4488
United States: 24 Grosvenor St, W1A 1AE
(0171) 499 9000
British Home Office (Immigration)
(0181) 686 0688

Tourist Authority
British Tourist Authority: (0181) 846 9000

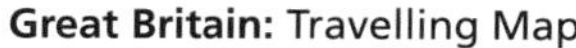

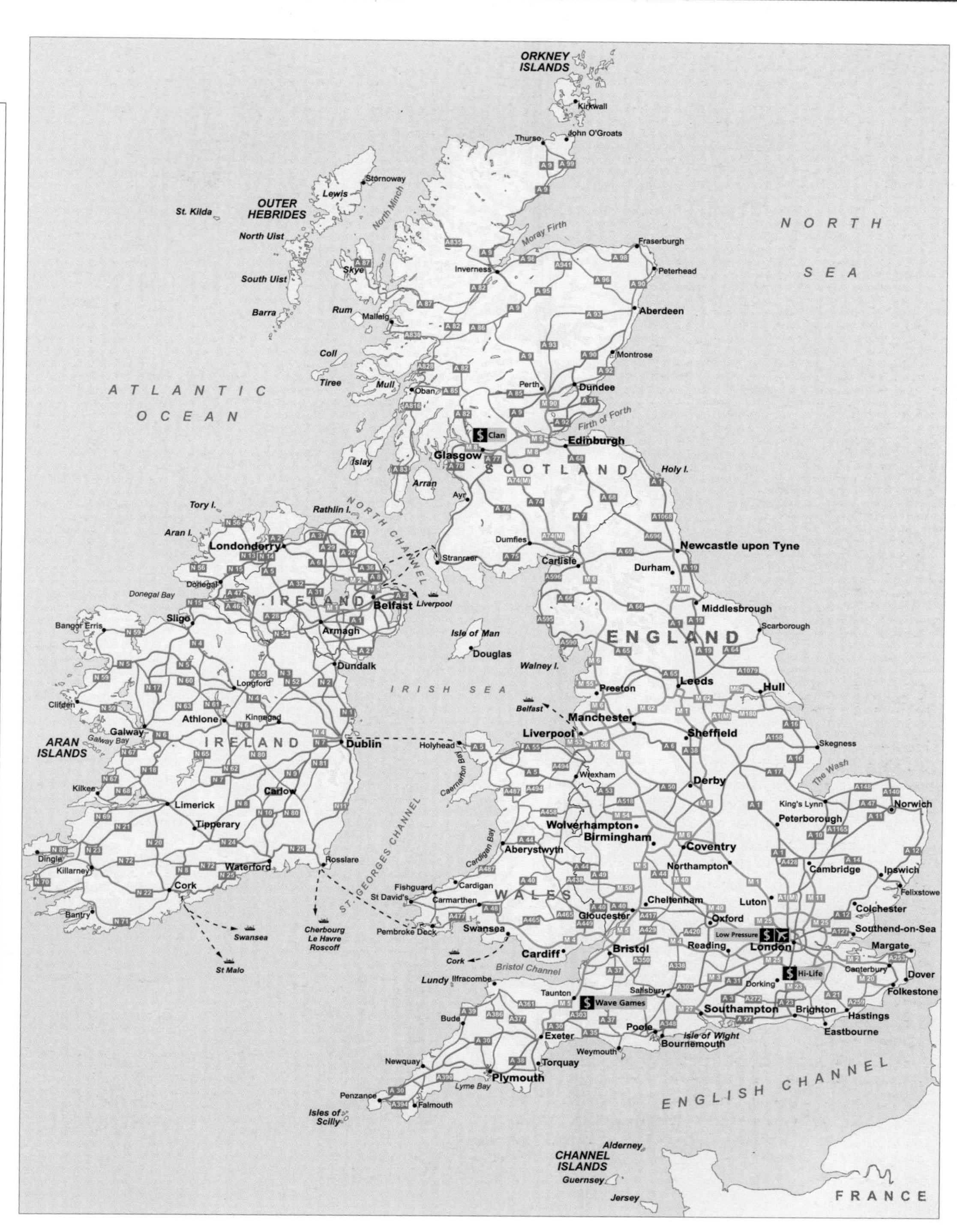

Great Britain: Travelling Map

Scale: 0 50 100 150 200 Kilometres; 0 50 100 150 Miles

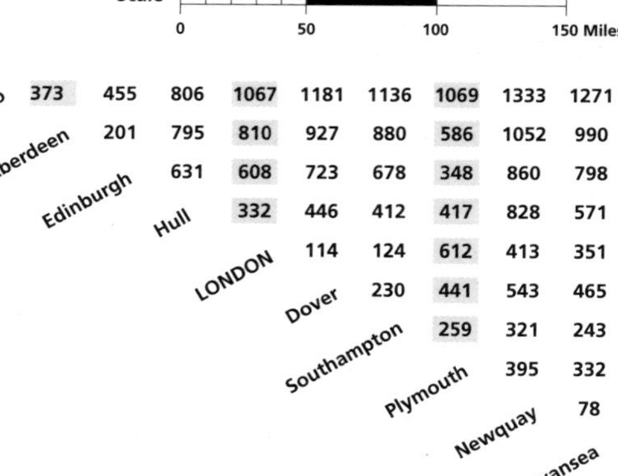

	Aberdeen	Edinburgh	Hull	LONDON	Dover	Southampton	Plymouth	Newquay	Swansea
Thurso	373	455	806	1067	1181	1136	1069	1333	1271
Aberdeen		201	795	810	927	880	586	1052	990
Edinburgh			631	608	723	678	348	860	798
Hull				332	446	412	417	828	571
LONDON					114	124	612	413	351
Dover						230	441	543	465
Southampton							259	321	243
Plymouth								395	332
Newquay									78

TIM RAINGER

Free camping by the beach is often an option - be discreet and tidy and you won't get rumbled

Scotland

Relentlessly pounded by huge swells from three sides, Scotland is a heavy place to go surfing. The wind blows hard from the Hebrides to the East Coast over a dramatic, beautiful landscape inhabited by a rugged, genuinely warm people. Friendly welcomes aside, Scotland remains one of Europe's wildest frontiers with a plethora of legendary, untapped waves. However, surfing in green-black water on a latitude comparable to Alaska can be pretty spooky – the big seals in the line ups, the reefs, the currents, the lack of surfers and the whiskey give it a unique presence that demands respect.

Ecosse

Matraquée sans cesse par de giga-houles d'ouest en est, l'Ecosse est un endroit sévère pour surfer. Le vent souffle fort des Hébrides à la Côte est, dans un décor fabuleux, habité par des gens authentiques dont l'hospitalité fait chaud au cœur. Mis à part ce message de bienvenu, l'Ecosse demeure une des frontières d'Europe les plus sauvages, dotée d'un potentiel de vagues illimité et presque inexploité. Cependant, surfer dans une eau vert sombre à des latitudes semblables à celles de l'Alaska peut donner quelques frissons...Les gros phoques qui sillonnent le line-up, les reefs, les courants, le manque de surfers et le whiskey local lui confèrent une atmosphère unique, qui force le respect !

Joe Curren, The Bowl

R. GILLEY

Where to go

Surf Areas

The surf breaks fall into four groups, with surf coming in from most compass points, depending on the location of the lows. With a good wetsuit and a big heart, you'll find Scotland a superb surf destination.

The Wild West The Western Isles feature 240 kilometres (150 miles) of exposed coast angling north-west into the wrath of all Atlantic depressions, presenting an almost limitless variety of wave breaking surfaces. Both The Outer and Inner Hebrides present the largest undiscovered coasts in Europe and their isolation makes them an explorer's dream. Clean, clear waters, white sands and desolate rocky points are three outstanding drawcards along with little chance of drop-ins. The Mull O'Kintyre's beauty is legendary and it picks up west swell from the Atlantic and south swell from the Irish Sea.

The North Shore Divided between the counties of **Caithness** and **Sutherland**, the North Shore stretches from John O'Groats to Cape Wrath on a coastline as beautiful as it is varied.

Caithness is flat and lies on beds of hard grey stone. These same stones, jutting into the Atlantic in huge flat slabs, are the breaking surface for some of Europe's hairiest waves. There are beautiful beaches in Caithness, however it is the reefs that make this such an intense surfing area. Travelling west from Melvich you enter the district of Sutherland and the Caithness flagstones disappear. Great glacial river valleys rake down into the ocean and their remains form boulder reefs and sandy beaches. Much of the coastline consequently offers empty surf.

In June, you can surf all day and most of the night, as it's only briefly dark around 3am. Several of the breaks, Brimms Ness in particular, experience strong currents and tidal water movements as the Atlantic charges along the coast to meet the North Sea. The tidal reach is vast, especially on full moons and spring tides. Often it's the tide and current pushing into a swell which gives the waves their extra power. It pays to exercise extreme caution, as there are few people around to help if you encounter difficulties, which are compounded by cold water conditions.

Sango Bay

Thurso is the main town and source of facilities including good supermarkets, hotels, garages, pubs, B&Bs and a heated public pool. Going west, human sightings thin considerably. It's a spooky experience – the knowledge that you're on a latitude comparable to Alaska: big seals in the line up, the lack of surfers, the reefs. The North Shore has a spirit all of its own that demands respect.

East Coast The North Sea coast of Scotland receives roughly the same north, and north east swells plus the consistent offshore winds that are experienced on the north coast. Conditions are similar to those of the English and other North Sea coastlines and the water temperature is always two to six degrees cooler than the North Atlantic so don't forget your boots and a wee dram for afters. Occasionally, the east coast will be huge when Thurso is flat. This is due to a swell window that ranges from north to south east. The Moray Firth receives the lion's share of North Sea swells occurring frequently in deepest winter. Despite cooler conditions, an abundance of reefs and points break swell and predominant winds blow offshore.

Europie

The south east is more heavily populated, and less spectacular than other parts, but conditions are similar to those on the Moray Firth and there is good surf.

The Orkney Islands These islands have a huge, steaming potential for surf. Large portions of the coastline consist of cliffs, but often they flatten out, creating rock reefs and sandy beaches. For substantial parts of the year, the islands are relentlessly battered by winds and the tidal range consequently rises an extra few metres. In general the surf seems to be at its best with a mid to high tide rolling in. There are a few local surfers and only on very rare occasions do surfers visiting Thurso take the ferry across – an oversight, as there really are wicked spots on most of the islands.

The most popular spot is the Bay of Skail, and further north is Outshore Point that works when Skail is too small. Further north is a short but powerful reef break. At Mar Wick there's a fast right that needs a large swell to be any good. On the north east of mainland, numerous lefts and reefs catch north swell: Fisk Hellia is one of these. If the swell is clean, it can break sectionless for more than 100m (90yd). There are many other spots which, if you go up there and meet the local crew, you'll be introduced to.

Ou aller

Les zones de surf

Il y a 4 grandes régions de surf avec des vagues venant de 3 directions différentes, suivant l'endroit où se situent les deps. Avec une bonne combi et un coeur bien accroché vous trouverez des conditions idéales pour pratiquer votre sport favori.

Le Wild West Les îles de l'ouest comprennent 240 kilomètres de côtes exposées sur leur versant nord-est à la fureur des dépressions de l'Atlantique, qui font d'elles le continuel réceptacle d'une grande variété de vagues. Les Outer et Inner Hebrides constituent les plus grandes côtes vierges de l'Europe et leur isolement fait d'elles un endroit de rêve pour qui veut partir à leur découverte.

Avec une eau cristalline, du sable blanc et des pointes rocheuses sans personne à l'eau vous avez peu de chances de vous planter si vous appréciez ce genre de destination carte postale. La beauté du Mull O'Kintyre est légendaire et elle prend les swells ouest de l'Atlantique et sud de la mer d'Irlande.

La côte nord est divisée entre les comtés de **Caithness** et de **Sutherland** et s'étend de John o'Groats à Sandwood bay, tout au long d'une côte superbe et variée. Caithness est plat et repose sur des lits de pierres grises. Ces mêmes cailloux qui font saillie dans l'Atlantique avec des plaques énormes sont le point de déferlement des vagues les plus velues d'Europe. Il y'a des plages magnifiques à Caithness, bien que ses reefs en font une région de surf intensif. Si vous allez à l'ouest de Melvich, vous entrez dans le district de Sutherland et les rochers de Caithness disparaissent.

Une grande rivière glaciale se déverse dans l'océan charriant des grosses pierres qui permettent la formation de récifs et de plages ensablées et presque toute la côte offre du grand surf. Les locaux d'Orkney surfent même à des endroits exposées aux latitudes nord.

Caithness

Thurso East

R.GILLEY

The East Coast

Sinclairs Bay

ALEX WILLIAMS

When to go

Scotland can have bonnie waves at any time of the year. Summer should see some lows cruise past Iceland, which send small to medium-sized swells to the north shore and the islands. In June and July, it's possible to sqeeze a session in after the pubs shut at 11pm. Autumn and winter cranks up the size, especially on the west and east coasts, which receive swells that the north coast doesn't get a sniff of. Only six hours of daylight in December means getting the right tide for a particular break can be tricky. Spring is usually cold and windy, but there will definitely be a few substantial swells. Like anywhere, Scotland suffers from long flat spells, compounded by rapid changes in weather conditions, but its versatility will reward the amateur surf forecaster.

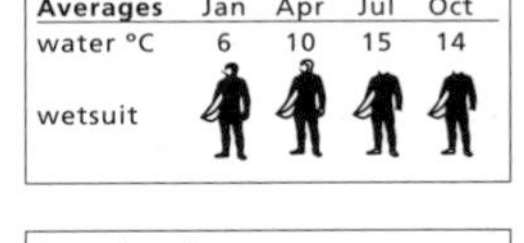

The Outer Hebrides Averages	Jan	Apr	Jul	Oct
water °C	6	10	15	14
wetsuit				

Fraserburgh Averages	Jan	Apr	Jul	Oct
water °C	4	6	12	12
wetsuit				

En été vous pouvez surfer toute la journée et la grande majorité de la nuit puisqu'il commence à faire nuit à 3 heures du matin. Sur beaucoup de spots, Brimms Ness en particulier, il y a beaucoup de courant et des mouvements de marée car l'Atlantique rencontre la mer du Nord sur la côte. L'étendue de la marée est grande, surtout en période de pleine lune et aux equinoxes de printemps. Souvent c'est la marée et le courant qui en amenant la houle donnent aux vagues leur si grande puissance. C'est pourquoi la pratique du surf nécessite à cet endroit la plus grande précaution car si vous rencontrez des difficultés il risque de n'y avoir personne pour vous aider à vous en sortir et les choses seront rendues d'autant plus difficiles que l'eau est très froide.

Thurso est la plus grosse ville de la region et dispose des multiples services dont vous aurez besoin: supermarchés, hôtels, garages, pubs, Beds & Breakfasts et une piscine publique chauffée. C'est vraiment une expérience à vivre : il faut savoir que vous serez à la même latitude que l'Alaska avec des phoques géants au line-up, peu ou prou de surfers au pic, et du reef. La côte Nord possède un esprit propre, qui demande à être respecté.

La côte est La côte donnant sur la mer du nord reçoit rigoureusement les mêmes swells du nord, de l'est et du sud ainsi que les forts vents offshore bien que les différentes régions ont des conditions de surf différentes selon leur orientation. Les conditions sont similaires à celles de l'Angleterre et à celles des côtes de la mer du nord et la température de l'eau est à toujours 1 ou 2 degrés de moins que dans l'Atlantique Nord aussi n'oubliez pas vos chaussons et une boisson chaude pour l'après-surf. Le Moray Firth reçoit les plus gros swells de la mer du Nord qui arrivent régulièremrent au coeur de l'hiver. Malgré des conditions glaciales, une abondance de récifs et de pointes, des vents dominants qui soufflent offshore rendent le surf excellent. Le sud est est plus peuplé et les conditions y sont moins spectaculaires mais elles ressemblent à celles du Moray Firth et il y a matière à taquiner la vague.

Quand Aller

L'Ecosse peut topper de super vagues à n'importe quel moment de l'année. L'été voit passer quelques déps vers l'Islande qui envoient des houles petites à moyennes sur la côte nord et sur les îles. En juin et juillet, il est possible de se caler une session après la fermeture des pubs à 23 heures. Automne et hiver garantissent le gros surtout sur la côte ouest et est, qui reçoivent la houle que la côte nord manque totalement. Avec seulement 6 heures de jour en décembre, il est difficile de viser la bonne marée. Le printemps est souvent froid et venté mais il restera encore sûrement de bons swells à se mettre sous la planche. Comme partout, l'Ecosse subit de longues accalmies, composées par les changements rapides du temps. C'est là que certaines notions de météo deviennent cruciales.

LOW PRESSURE
If you don't go, you don't know
www.lowpressure.co.uk

ANDY BENNETS

This break is called 'Shit Pipe' because of the tea-coloured water washing down from the peat bogs

The Ocean Environment

Water Quality

Somewhere between heaven and hell would be an accurate summation of where Scotland's environmentalists find themselves today. On one hand they have access to some of the cleanest waters in the western Atlantic, yet accompanying that privilege they have inherited Britain's biggest environmental nightmare: Dounreay.

Scotland has a huge coastline: it's so large that SEPA (Scottish Environmental Protection Agency) can't physically monitor it. Therefore SEPA have said that they will set discharge licences to achieve guideline water quality, SAS approved, at all designated beaches. This will also apply wherever people have access to the coast. In addition they will require discharges to guarantee at least mandatory standards at all areas of water recreation. While SAS will continue to push this, we welcome SEPA's recognition of these areas. The treatment will also be year round.

Burning issue

The Dounreay experimental nuclear reactor and processing plant was the first in Europe, constructed in the early 50s. Statistics show that the leukemia incidence in Caithness began to rise almost immediately. For years the British government has covered up a series of dangerous leaks and losses with a pile of fudge so thick it wouldn't wipe the dirt off a potato. Nuggets of radioactive waste have been found on beaches and surf breaks around the plant. Apparently they dumped 'intermediate' radioactive waste (nobody kept a list) in a disused shaft and plugged it with a 12-tonne concrete cork. Sea water leached into it, fizzed up the concoction, which then promptly blew its top with a violent explosion in 1977. Ten years later, admissions from the staff were finally extracted, but nobody knows the extent of the fall out. They also have an underground 'low level' discharge pipe pumping waste directly into the ocean. While there is an exclusion zone for fishing, no one has tackled the thorny issue of the risks faced by surfers and swimmers in the area. The plant has now been condemned to the scrap heap but as with all radioactive issues, this means a long, dangerous decommissioning process. SAS will keep its website updated as Dounreay is pulled apart.

On Localism

While not the ultimate surf travel destination, should you stray up to Scotland, the fact you're sure to find surf and a wave to yourself is very much a thing of the present. No guide to Europe would be complete without noting the lashing given to this coast by deep lows, and the dedication and hardiness of Scotland's locals, who surf in conditions as extreme as any. The folk here come from a long seafaring tradition, so it's not surprising that the sport is gaining newcomers every year. For many the idea is inconceivable, but humans being what they are, cold climates can be adapted to. For the young folk taking up surfing, there has been little precedent for their sport and we urge respect and encouragement, both in and out of the water.

Specificités du littoral

Qualité de l'eau

Quelque chose entre le paradis et l'enfer, voila une formule qui résume bien la situation des défenseurs de l'environnement écossais. D'un côté ils ont accès aux océans les plus propres de l'Atlantique ouest mais ils ont aussi "le privilége" d'avoir hérité du plus grand cauchemar environnemental de la GB (Dounreay).

L'Ecosse possède une grande étendue de côtes-tellement large que la SEPA (Agence de protection de l'environnement écossaise) ne peut pas physiquement tout contrôler. Donc la SEPA a décrété qu'elle mettrait en place des licences pour mener à bien les directives en matière de qualité de l'eau (avec l'approbation de la SAS) sur toutes les plages désignées. Ceci s'appliquera partout où les gens auront accès à la côte. En outre ils auront besoin de décharges pour garantir au moins des pavillons obligatoires dans toutes les zones balnéaires. Pendant ce temps La SAS continue à appuyer ce type de démarche, nous encourageons la reconnaissance par la SEPA de ces zones. Le traitement durera toute l'année.

Un problème épineux

Le réacteur nucléaire expérimental de Dounreay fut le premier à être construit en Europe au début des années 50 et les statistiques montrent son incidence sur l'augmentation immédiate des cas de leucémie à Caithness. Pendant des années le gouvernement britannique a tenu au secret une série de fuites et de pertes avec une telle dose d'irresponsabilité qu'elle frise le ridicule. Des morceaux de déchets radioactifs ont été trouvés sur les plages et les spots de surf à proximité de la centrale. Alors qu'il y a une zone d'exclusion pour la pêche, personne n'a mesuré les risques que courent les surfers et les nageurs à cet endroit. Devrait-il y avoir une zone d'exclusion ? La centrale a été jetée à la trappe mais comme avec tous les problèmes nucléaires, cela risque d'avoir des conséquences à long terme.

MIKE SEARLE

Localisme

Bien que ce ne soit pas une destinations idéale, si vous écumez aux alentours, vous trouverez certainement du surf et avoir une vague à soi reste encore tout à fait possible. Aucun guide en Europe ne pourrait être complet sans parler du défilé des perturbations qui circulent incessamment pendant les longs mois d'hiver et du courage des locaux qui surfent dans des conditions extrêmes. Les gens ici ont une longue tradition maritime et il n'est donc pas surprenant que ce sport attire des passionés de la mer.

The Wild West

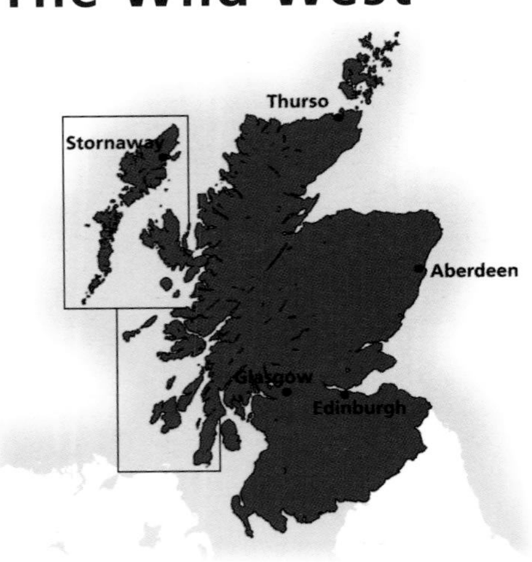

ALEX WILLIAMS

Eoropie

The Outer Hebrides

1. Eoropie

Steep and barrelling beach and reef waves. The locals at Barvas speak of this area in hushed tones and with a degree of awe.

Plage en pente avec des tubes et des vagues de reef. Les locaux de Barvas parlent de cette zone à demi-mot avec une certaine frayeur.

2. Carloway to Bragar

Dalmore, Dalbeg, Loch Shawbost and Port Mhor Bragar are all protected coves with small sand beaches and waves of unconfirmed quality. They're located off the A858 N of Carloway.

Toutes ces sorties depuis l'A858 au nord de Carloway. Ce sont toutes des petites anses avec un peu de sable et des vagues de qualité variable.

3. Cliff

This works with any swell to produce long walls. A rip to the right can sometimes be the only way out and, while it can be a handy conveyer belt, respect its strength. There's parking near some sheep pens. If it looks small from here, suit up – chances are it's overhead.

Marche avec n'importe quel swell, de longs murs en perspective. Un courant, sur la droite peut être la seule façon de sortir mais si ça peut être un tapis roulant pratique, attention au timing. On trouve un parking prés d'un enclos à moutons. Si; ça paraît petit de là, y'a des chances que ça fasse un bon mètre.

The Inner Hebrides

1. Balephetrish

A large pebble and sand beach with good sandbars.

Une grande plage de sable et de galets avec des bars animés.

2. The Hough

Facing W/NW, this beach receives some protection from 'the hough skerries'. A left reef break warrants further investigation.

Ces vagues sont protégées par les 'Hough Skerries'. Une gauche de reef d'abord qui vous assure le déplacement si vous cherchez.

3. The Maze

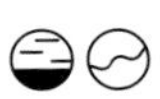   

This rates as the most popular spot on the island for windsurfing and subsequently is the scene of the British Nationals. There's a long sandy beach here open to all W swell. Long, fast peaks break on the beach and off the point. If you climb the remnants of a World War II radar station at Ben Hough, the secrets of The Maze will be revealed.

Maze est une longue plage sableuse ouverte à tous les swells d'Ouest. De longs murs cassent sur une plage à partir du 'point'. Si vous escaladez les ruines du poste d'observation de la deuxième guerre mondiale à Ben Hough, vous verrez tout le panorama.

4. Port Bharrapol

A magnificent rock and sand bay at the bottom of high cliffs. It faces W and catches heaps of swell. From The Glassery (a restaurant between Bharrapol and Middleton), you'll see the coastline.

Une baie splendide de roches et de sable, au pied de hautes falaises. Regarde L'ouest et chope un max de houle. Depuis The Glassery (un restaurant avec une vue imprenable entre Bharrapol et Middleton) on peut voir la côte de haut en bas.

5. Balephuil

A 2km (1.2mi) shell and sand beach picks up good amounts of swell; there are peaks on the beach. Kenavara Point could also hold secrets.

Plus de 2 kms de sable blanc qui fait face au Sud Sud-Ouest en récupérant bizarrement pas mal de houle. Gauches et droites cassent sur la plage et Kenavara Point peut aussi cacher quelques spots secrets. Plein d'autres endroits à voir mais on les laisse tranquilles.

The West Coast

6. Ardnave Bay

   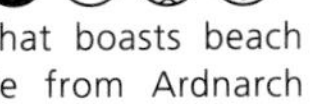

There's a sheltered N-facing bay that boasts beach and point waves and is accessible from Ardnarch House and Loch. It needs a good swell to go off.

Baie abritée exposée nord avec des plages et des points, accessibles depuis Ardnarch House. Il faut que ça rentre bien pour fonctionner.

7. Saligo Bay

A W-facing bay with strong currents produces thick, sucky, waves. There's left-handers to the S and rights to the N. Size it up before paddling out.

Baie impressionante exposée ouest avec des panneaux de mise en garde pour les courants. Les vagues sont d' épaisses et insidieuses gauches au sud et droites au nord.

8. Machir Bay

The N break works well with rights off the point. To the S the beach shelves more steeply, forming powerful lefts. It's good for camping.

4kms de sable divisé du nord au sud par une rivière. La partie nord marche bien avec des droites depuis le 'point'. Au sud, la plage se creuse pour former de puissantes gauches.

9. Lossit Bay

The bay lies at the bottom of high cliffs and here you'll find good waves – if you can get down. Take the track to Lossit Farm: it's likely you'll have to park there, so be courteous. It's a 5km (3mi) walk around and down the cliffs.

Se situe au pied de hautes falaises et vous pouvez choper de bonnes vagues si vous arrivez à descendre. Prendre le chemin de la ferme Lossit où il faudra probablement se garer, soyez polis. Pas moins de 5 kms de marche pour descendre à moins que vous ne sautiez.

10. Laggan Bay

The biggest beach on the island stretches for kilometres and works on all tides. Access is from S of the golf course. Park outside the Machrie Hotel and follow the stream to the beach.

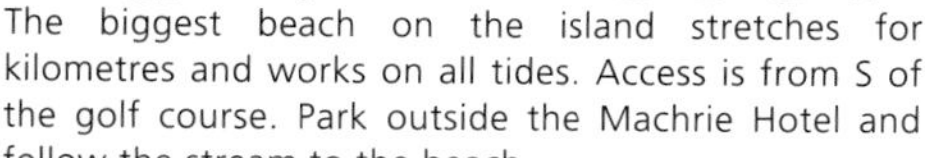

La plus grande plage de l'île qui s'étend sur plusieurs kms et comme c'est orienté sud-ouest avec les vents dominants, ça marche par toutes les marées. L'accés se fait au sud par le terrain de golf. Se garer à l'extérieur de l'hôtel Machrie et suivre le ruisseau jusqu'à la plage.

11. Caravans

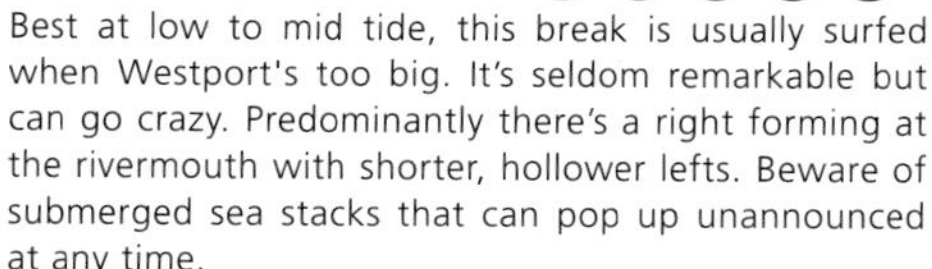

Best at low to mid tide, this break is usually surfed when Westport's too big. It's seldom remarkable but can go crazy. Predominantly there's a right forming at the rivermouth with shorter, hollower lefts. Beware of submerged sea stacks that can pop up unannounced at any time.

Mieux de marée basse à mi-marée, souvent surfé quand Westport est trop gros. Rarement transcendant mais peut être correct. Souvent une droite en sortie de rivière, avec des gauches plus courtes mais plus creuses. Attention aux cailloux immergés qui peuvent apparaître soudainement à n'importe quel moment.

12. Graveyards

The next access down from Caravans also shares similar waves but has more intense rocks in the line up, so it's not for beginners. There are numerous other peaks along this stretch of coast that get smaller the closer you get to the pub at Bellochanty. It's best above mid tide.

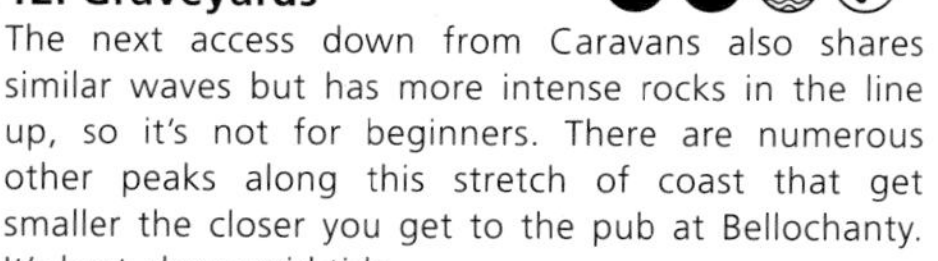

L'accés suivant aprés Caravans qui partage les mêmes caractéristiques de vagues mais avec encore plus de cailloux au line-up. Débutants s'abstenir. On trouve plein d'autres spots sur cette côte dont les vagues se rapetissent quand on se rapproche du pub de Bellochanty. Mieux au-dessus de la mi-marée.

13. Middle Beach

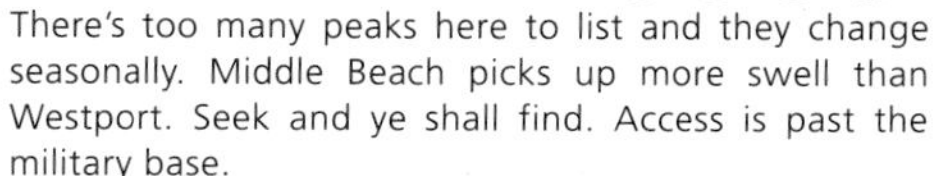

There's too many peaks here to list and they change seasonally. Middle Beach picks up more swell than Westport. Seek and ye shall find. Access is past the military base.

Trop de pics à référencer et ça change sans arrêt. Plus de houle qu'à Westport. Cherchez et vous trouverez. Accés aprés la base militaire.

14. Westport

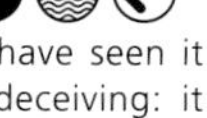

Another good spot, though recent years have seen it working low to mid tide. It's extremely deceiving: it can be a 1m (3ft) mush and only an hour later it can have 1.2m (4-6ft) jacking barrels. Rips by the rocks can be handy on big days.

Un autre bon spot bien que sur les dernières années ça ne marche plus à marée haute. Un spot trés trompeur en tous cas, qui peut passer d'une miose d'un mètre à des tubes explosifs d'1,5m-2m. Un courant prés des rochers à utiliser quand c'est gros.

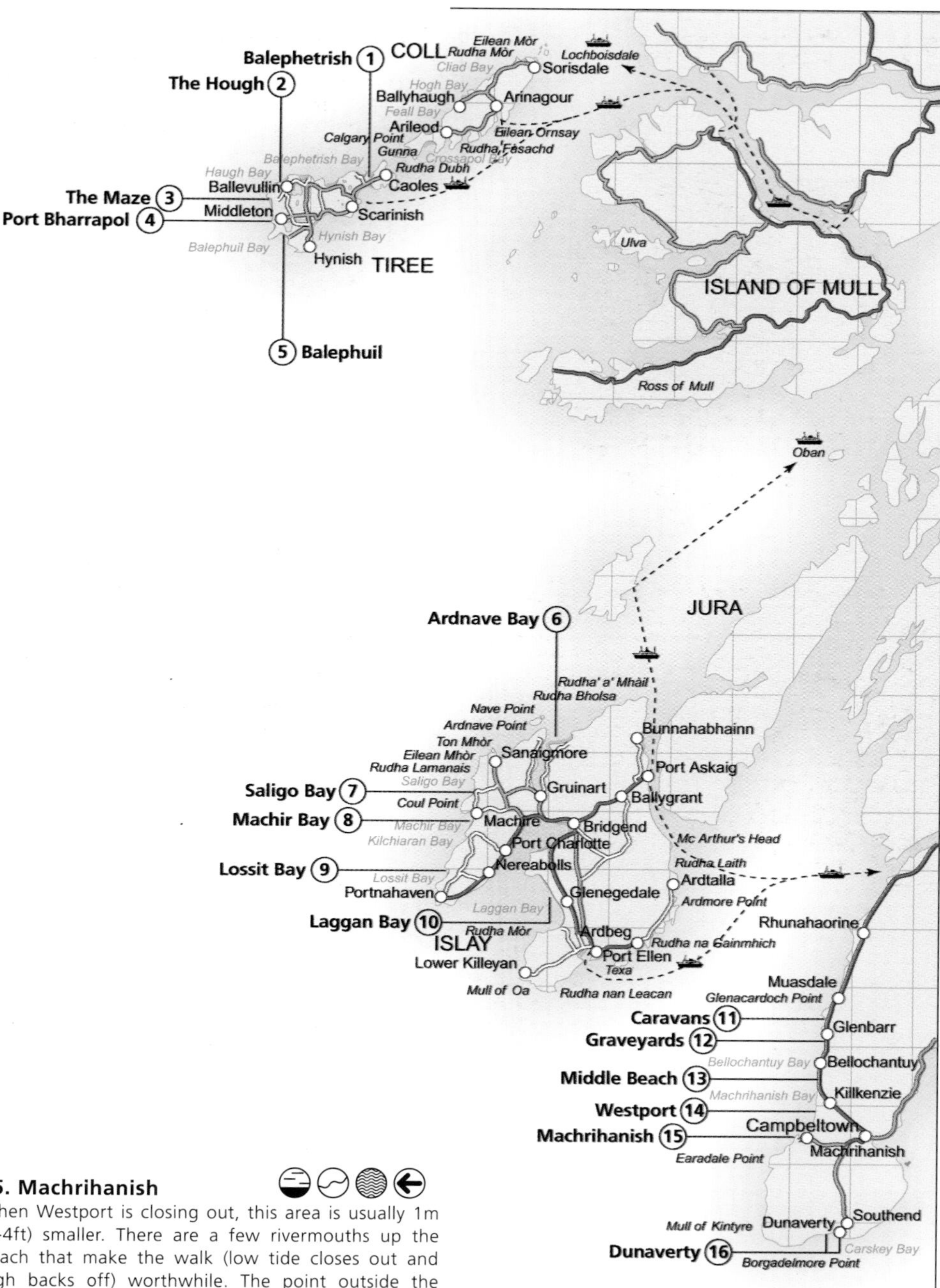

15. Machrihanish

When Westport is closing out, this area is usually 1m (3-4ft) smaller. There are a few rivermouths up the beach that make the walk (low tide closes out and high backs off) worthwhile. The point outside the Beachcomber Pub can hold clean waves in a howling SW wind.

Quand ça ferme sur Westport, cette zone est souvent surfable avec un bon mètre en moins. Quelques sorties de rivières à checker. Mieux vaut essayer à mi-marée. Zonez du côté du Beachcomber pub, qui peut encore être clean même par un vent et une houle furieuse de sud-ouest.

16. Dunaverty Beach

It has to be really large on the W coast before Dunaverty starts to crank. Low tide offers shifty close outs with the odd makeable barrel while working better as the tide pushes through. The wave size can drop dramatically as the tide fills in. The occasional swell up the Irish Sea can create waves here when the W coast is flat.

Il faut que ça soit énorme sur la côte ouest avant que Dunaverty commence à marcher. A marée basse, ça ferme sauf quelques ouvertures tubulaires à l'occasion mais ça s'améliore au montant même si la taille diminue au fur et à mesure que ça se remplit.

Point

A classic reef that needs S swells, which are unfortunately rare. There's a long paddle-out and currents near the cliffs. It's not a beginner's break.

Un reef classique seulement surfable à pleine marée basse par houle de sud. Marche trés rarement mais c'est un must. Une longue rame avec des courants dans tous les sens. Pas un spot de débutants.

ALEX WILLIAMS

Sutherland

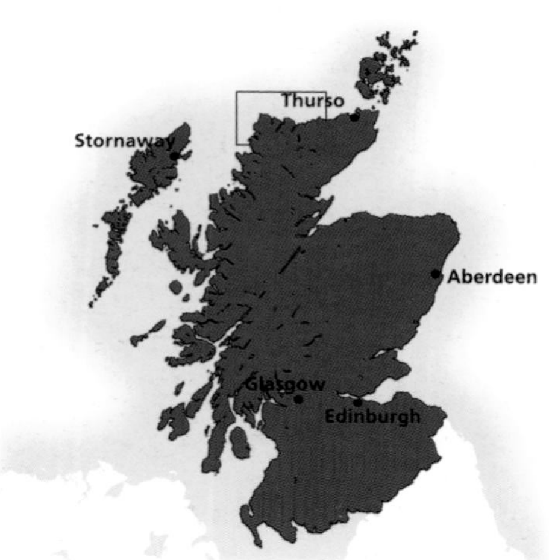

East Strathy

ALEX WILLIAMS

1. Oldshoremore

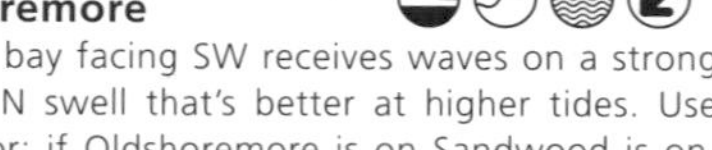

A sheltered bay facing SW receives waves on a strong W or even N swell that's better at higher tides. Use this indicator: if Oldshoremore is on Sandwood is on. It's just N of Kinlochbervie.

Une baie abritée exposée S-O, chope des vagues par grosse houle d'ouest et même de nord, mieux à marée haute. Un indicateur utile pour Sandwood: les deux marchent en même temps. Just au nord de Kinlochbervie.

2. Sandwood Bay

This kilometre-and-a-half long beach facing NW is one of Britain's finest with no fewer than nine different breaks. It has reefs at both ends and rock clusters marking its length. Save for birds and an occasional walker, it's deserted and the high cliffs offer protection from N and S winds. It receives as much swell as any other Scottish beach but the only access is a 7km (4mi) track located N of Blairmore. The first 3km (2mi) are navigable by car in summer, otherwise it's strictly a walk through the peat bog. The walk is as stunning as the beach.

Cette plage d'1,5 km, qui regarde le N-O, est une des plus belles de Grande-Bretagne avec pas moins de 9 vagues. Elle a des reefs de chaque côté, avec deux groupes de rochers qui définissent sa longueur et des hautes falaises qui empêchent les vents de nord et du sud de s'y engouffrer. Mise à part les oiseaux et les promeneurs éventuels, c'est désert. Reçoit la même houle que n'importe quelle autre plage d'Ecosse. Le seul accès se fait par un chemin de 6 kms juste au nord de Blairmore. Les 3 premiers kilomètres sont carrossables en été sinon il faut marcher tout le long dans les tourbières. La balade est aussi hallucinante que la plage.

3. Balnakiel Bay

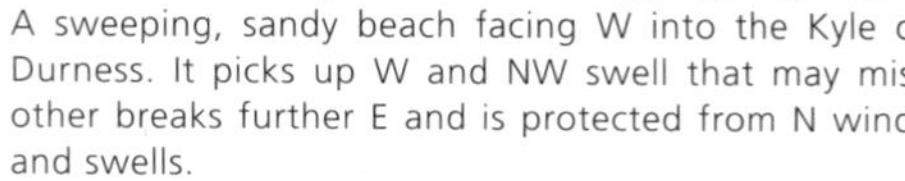

A sweeping, sandy beach facing W into the Kyle of Durness. It picks up W and NW swell that may miss other breaks further E and is protected from N winds and swells.

Une plage de sable instable exposée ouest dans le Kyle de Durness. Chope les houles d'ouest et nord-ouest qui peuvent manquer les autres spots à l'est. Abritée des vents et houles de nord.

4. Durness (Sango Bay)

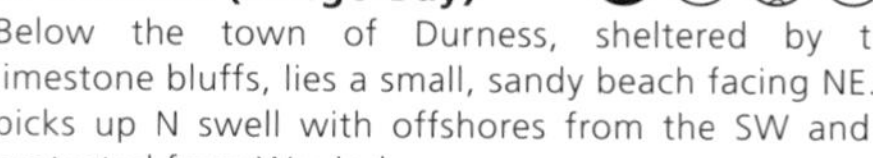

Below the town of Durness, sheltered by the limestone bluffs, lies a small, sandy beach facing NE. It picks up N swell with offshores from the SW and is protected from W wind.

Sous Durness, abritée par les a-pics de calcaire se trouve une petite plage de sable exposée N. Ca récupère les houles de nord avec de l'off-shore par vents de sud, à l'abri des vents d'ouest. Les autres spots s'appellent Ceannabeine beach (Rispond Bay) et Rabbit Island.

5. Kyle of Tongue

This is a sheltered glacial inlet that works in huge swells and offers protection from all but N winds. It's an area surfed very rarely, but waves are rideable for hundreds of metres up both sides in the right conditions.

Une baie protégée et glaciale qui marche quand ça rentre gras, abritée de tous les vents sauf ceux de nord. Une zone rarement surfée ou des vagues de plusieurs centaines de mètres sont surfables des deux côtés quand ça rentre bien.

6. Torrisdale

This is a beach break with a good right-hand rivermouth. The best sandbars are near the river; check for sinking sands along the bank. Low to mid tide is generally the best time to go.

Beach break avec une bonne droite à la rivière. Les meilleurs bancs sont prés de la rivière mais attention aux sables mouvants le long des berges. Off-shore par vents de sud, de préference de marée basse à mi-marée.

7. Farr Bay

Owing to its NW aspect, Farr picks up plenty of swell. Lefts are better at high tide and rights are better at low. Walk through the dunes after taking a turn-off at the Farr Bay Inn, but don't forget to close the gate as it is farmed land.

A cause de son orientation NW, Farr Bay chope des houles qui peuvent manquer Thurso. Les gauches sont meilleures à marée haute et inversement à marée basse. Traversez les dunes aprés avoir tourné à Farr Bay Inn. Ne laissez pas le portail ouvert car ce sont des champs cultivés.

8. Armadale Bay

Due N-facing beach break that's best at high tide. Access by following the rivermouth to or walking from town. Check it out from the main road.

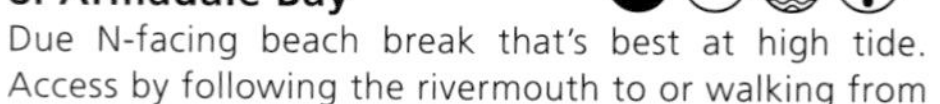

Exposé nord, visible depuis la route principale. Un beach break avec des pics meilleurs à marée haute. Suivez la rivière ou marchez depuis le village.

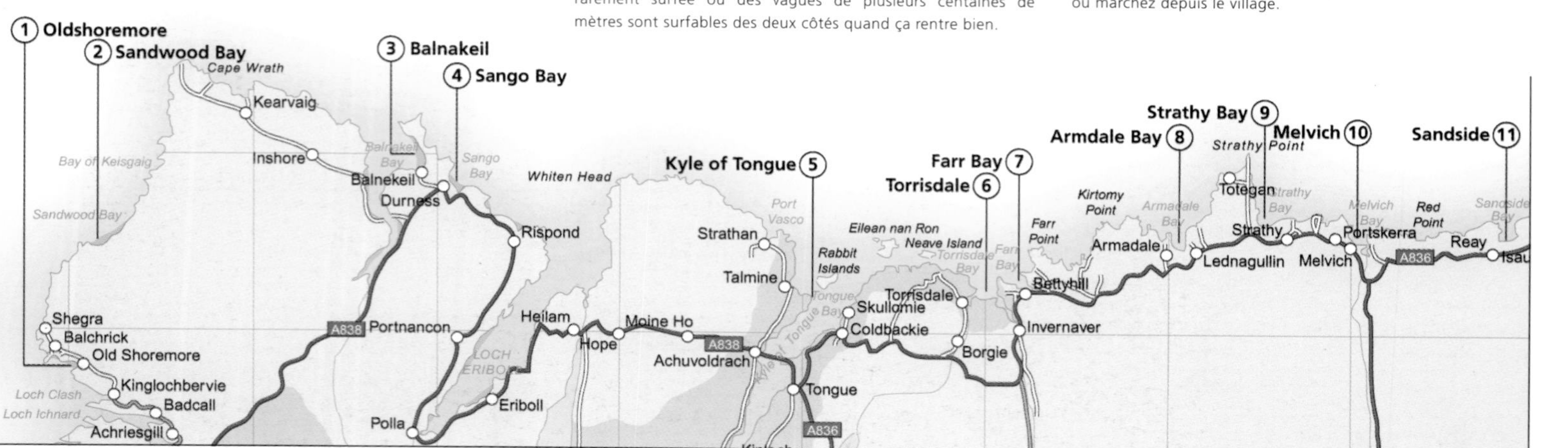

Jake Boex, Sandside

MIKE SEARLE

9. Strathy Bay

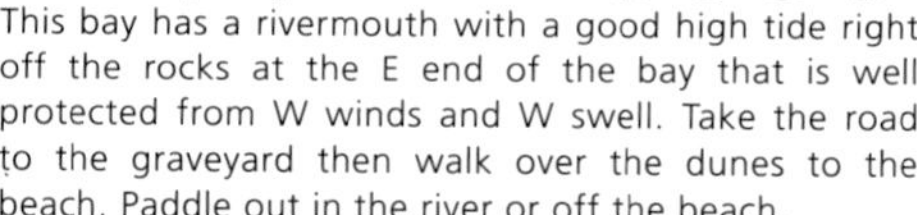

This bay has a rivermouth with a good high tide right off the rocks at the E end of the bay that is well protected from W winds and W swell. Take the road to the graveyard then walk over the dunes to the beach. Paddle out in the river or off the beach.

Une embouchure avec une bonne droite à marée haute sur les rochers à l'extrémité est de la baie. Bien protégé des vents d'ouest mais des swells d'Ouest aussi. Prenez la route jusqu'au cimetière et marchez sur les dunes. Ramez depuis la plage ou dans la rivière.

10. Melvich

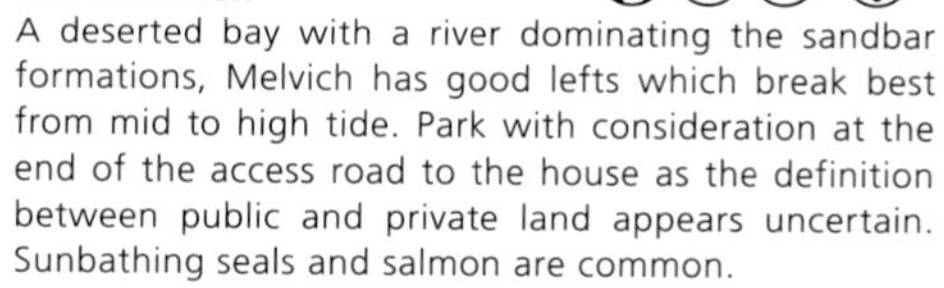

A deserted bay with a river dominating the sandbar formations, Melvich has good lefts which break best from mid to high tide. Park with consideration at the end of the access road to the house as the definition between public and private land appears uncertain. Sunbathing seals and salmon are common.

Une baie déserte avec une rivière qui influe sur la formation des bancs. De bonnes gauches cassent au mieux entre mi-marée et marée haute. Se garer avec précaution au bout de la route d'accés à la grosse maison. La définition entre le domaine public et privé n'a rien d'évident. On voit souvent des otaries qui se dorent la pillule.

11. Sandside Bay

A classic beach/reef setup: sandside faces N. Left-handers break into the bay from the harbour with occasional left and right bars on the beach. It works on an average N or big W swell and is best at mid to high tide (the left is rocky at low). It's within a stone's throw of the reactor at Dounreay – nice!

Une formation plage/Reef classique. Sandside est exposée au nord. Des gauches cassent dans la baie depuis le port avec des bancs pour droites et gauches de temps à autre. Ca marche par houle moyenne de nord ou un gros swell d'ouest, de préférence de mi-marée à marée haute (pas mal de cailloux sur la gauche à marée basse). Sandside Bay se situe à 18 Kms à l'ouest de Thurso, juste aprés le village de Reay, à portée de hallebarde du réacteur de Dounreay.

Torrisdale

MIKE SEARLE

Caithness

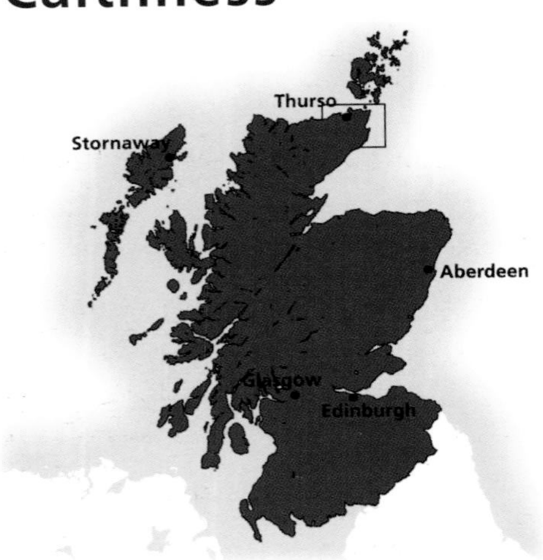

ALEX WILLIAMS

Thurso East

1. Brims Ness (Graveyards)

Brims Ness is Nordic for 'surf point' and that's what it is! While the long walk over the fields takes a bit of effort, especially in the cold, this point catches most of the swell in the area, and can be overhead when Thurso is flat. When seen from the road, the size can be misleading. Turn right just after you see the silos and the waves are on the point, 5km (3mi) W of Thurso. Go down to the farm and park respectfully among the machinery and sheds: it's private property!

Brims Ness signifie Nordic comme spot de surf et c'est rien de le dire ! Alors que la longue marche à travers les enclos demande un petit effort, surtout quand ça pèle, ces trois spots peuvent choper le plus de houle dans les environs .puisque ça peut faire un bon mètre cinquante quand il n'y a rien à Thurso.Depuis la route, on se rend pas bien compte de la taille . Tournez à droite aprés avoir vu les silos et les vagues sur le spot à 5 Kms par la route . Descendez jusqu'aux bâtiments de la ferme et garez-vous soigneusement entre les machines et les hangars, c'est une propriété privée.

The Bowl

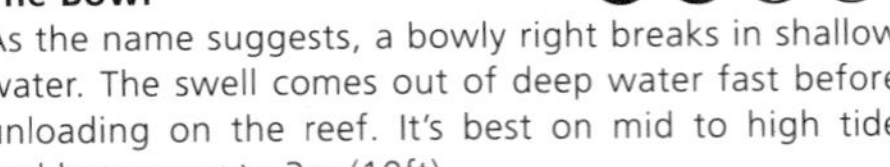

As the name suggests, a bowly right breaks in shallow water. The swell comes out of deep water fast before unloading on the reef. It's best on mid to high tide and heaves up to 3m (10ft).

Comme son nom l'indique, c'est une droite en bol qui casse dans peu d'eau. La houle arrive rapidement en eau profonde avant d'exploser sur le reef. Mieux de Mi-marée à marée haute, au montant, jusqu'à 2,5m.

The Cove

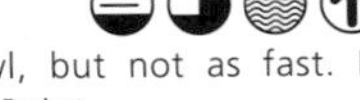

A similar set up to The Bowl, but not as fast. It's located 70m (60yd) down The Point.

Ressemble au Bowl mais en moins rapide. A 50m en bas du 'point'.

The Left/The Point

A classic left-hand point break, rideable for 100m (90yd) or more in the right conditions, but is easily blown out.

Une gauche qui s'enroule parfaitement, jusqu'à 100m ou plus avec les bonnes conditions. Ne supporte pas le vent.

2. The Shit Pipe

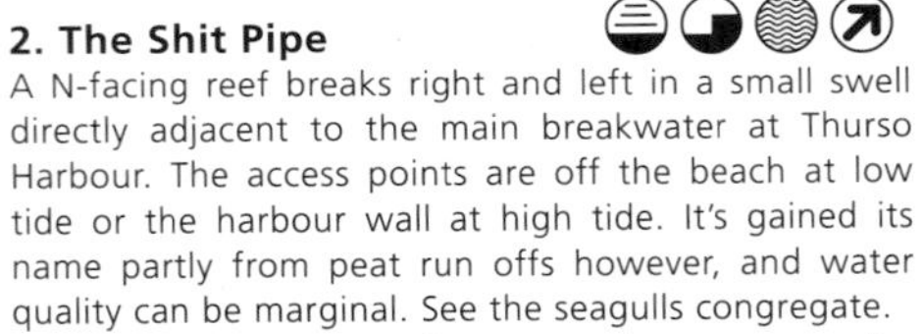

A N-facing reef breaks right and left in a small swell directly adjacent to the main breakwater at Thurso Harbour. The access points are off the beach at low tide or the harbour wall at high tide. It's gained its name partly from peat run offs however, and water quality can be marginal. See the seagulls congregate.

Par petite houle, ce reef exposé nord casse en gauche-droite. Directement relié à la jetée principale du port de Thurso. On y va depuis la plage à marée basse ou depuis le mur du port à marée haute. Ainsi nommé pour des raisons évidentes puisque l'eau y est détestable. On peut voir des hordes de mouettes à 400 mètres depuis le repère de marée basse.

3. Thurso East

Long tubes break here over a flat, kelp-covered reef. A slowish take-off and a long barrel subside into a fast, smaller inside section. It can work at all stages of the tide, but is considered best on an incoming to mid tide. An unsurfed bombora breaks in the middle of the bay, but when it's big enough to break, outside sets can close out from The Shit Pipe to the castle, so even a brave paddle out in the river could be a terminally bad move. The water always looks brown due to peat water flowing in from the river.

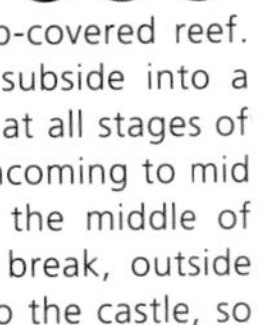

De longs tubes qui cassent sur un reef plat couvert de kelp. Un take-off mollasson suivi d'une longue section tubulaire s'affaissent pour reprendre à l'inside sur un mur rapide mais plus petit. Ca peut marcher à toutes les marées mais l'idéal semble être sur une marée montante à partir de mi-marée, avec un vent de SE. Un récif au large, que personne ne surfe, peut casser au milieu de la baie mais quand c'est assez gros pour casser, les séries au large peuvent fermer de Shit-Pipe jusqu'au château; ainsi même une rame courageuse depuis la rivière peut mal se terminer. L'eau y est toujours marron à cause de la tourbe charriée par la rivière.

4. Murkle Point

Several rock formations lie between Thurso and Dunnet Bay. A beautiful left breaks off the spur into the bay on a big swell.

Plusieurs groupes de rochers se trouvent entre Thurso et Dunnet Bay . Une superbe gauche casse à partir de "l'éperon" dans la baie avec une grande houle d'ouest ou de nord. Une petite route en sens unique y mène depuis le village de Murkle.

5. Nothing Left, Silos, The Pole

Three NE-facing reefs provide thick left peaks in a N or big W swell, but are rarely surfed as access is tricky... find and surf them if you can.

Trois reefs exposés Nord qui donnent des gauches épaisses avec un swell de nord ou un bon swell d'ouest . Rarement surfé parce que difficilement accessible. Trouvez les et surfez les si vous pouvez.

6. Dunnet Bay

Have fun at this 5km (3mi) long stretch of beach facing NW. There's sandbars along its length and excellent rights on the reef at the N end.

Une étendue de 5kms de plages exposées N-O. Bancs de sable moyens tout le long mais de super droites à l'extrémité nord.

R. GILLEY

The Bowl

ALEX WILLIAMS

7. Ham

Head to this left-hand reef breaking into deep water around the harbour. From Ham you'll see other reefs.

Gauche de reef cassant en eau profonde autour du port. Depuis Ham, on peut voir d'autres reefs aux alentours.

8. Kirk o' Tang, Scarfskerry, The Haven

This is a series of reefs visible at various points from the main road.

Une série de reefs visibles depuis la route principale.

9. Tang Head

This is a mid to high tide reef facing NW. Turn off the A836 at Mey village.

Un reef qui marche de mi-marée à marée haute, exposée N-O. Tournez sur l'A836 au village de Mey.

10. Gills Bay

The most E spot on the N coast, Gills has lefts at the W end of the bay and rights at the Ness of Quoys. Park near the graveyard and walk over the fields.

L'endroit le plus à l'est sur la côte nord. Gills a une gauche à l'extrémité ouest de la baie et des droites à Ness of Quoys. Garez- vous prés du cimetière et marcher à travers les champs.

11. Skirza Harbour

The most N break on the E coast faces into the North Sea, 5km (3mi) S of John O'Groats. Superb long lefts wind down the reef to a manmade harbour, which gets N to SE swells.

Le spot le plus au nord sur le continent exposé S-E en Mer du Nord, 5 kilomètres au sud de John o'Groats. Le port artificiel offre un abri contre les gauches dantesques qui balayent le reef.

12. Freswick Bay

A beautiful rivermouth with waves breaking on a sand-rock bottom.

Une rivière superbe avec des vagues sur fond de sable et rochers. Situé au S-O du port de Skirza.

13. Sinclair's Bay

Keiss is the name given to the N end of Sinclair's Bay. Lefts form off a N sandrock reef, and various sandbars form down the beach to Reiss, all visible from the A9. It can be huge.

Le nom donné à l'extrémité nord de la baie de Sinclair. Des gauches se forment à partir d'un reef de sable et de rochers au nord, et d'autres bancs de sable en bas de la plage, visible de l'A9.

14. Ackergill

Near the castle at Ackergill are two reefs that hold thick right-hand waves, working best at low tide when a SE swell wraps around the point. Travelling S from Ackergill are many interesting reefs and points that hold good swell during the winter.

A côté du château d'Ackergill, on trouve deux reefs qui tiennent des droites massives, de préférence à marée basse quand un swell de S-E s'enroule autour de la pointe.

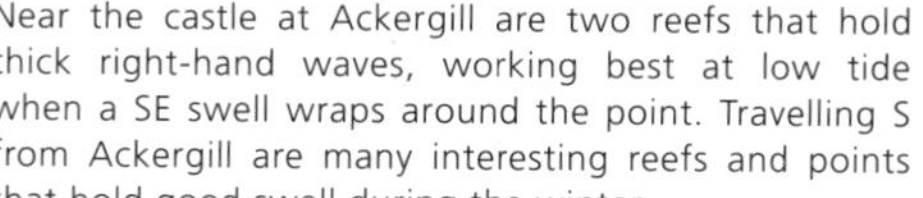

K. LUCAS

A Sutherland in Caithness, Skirza

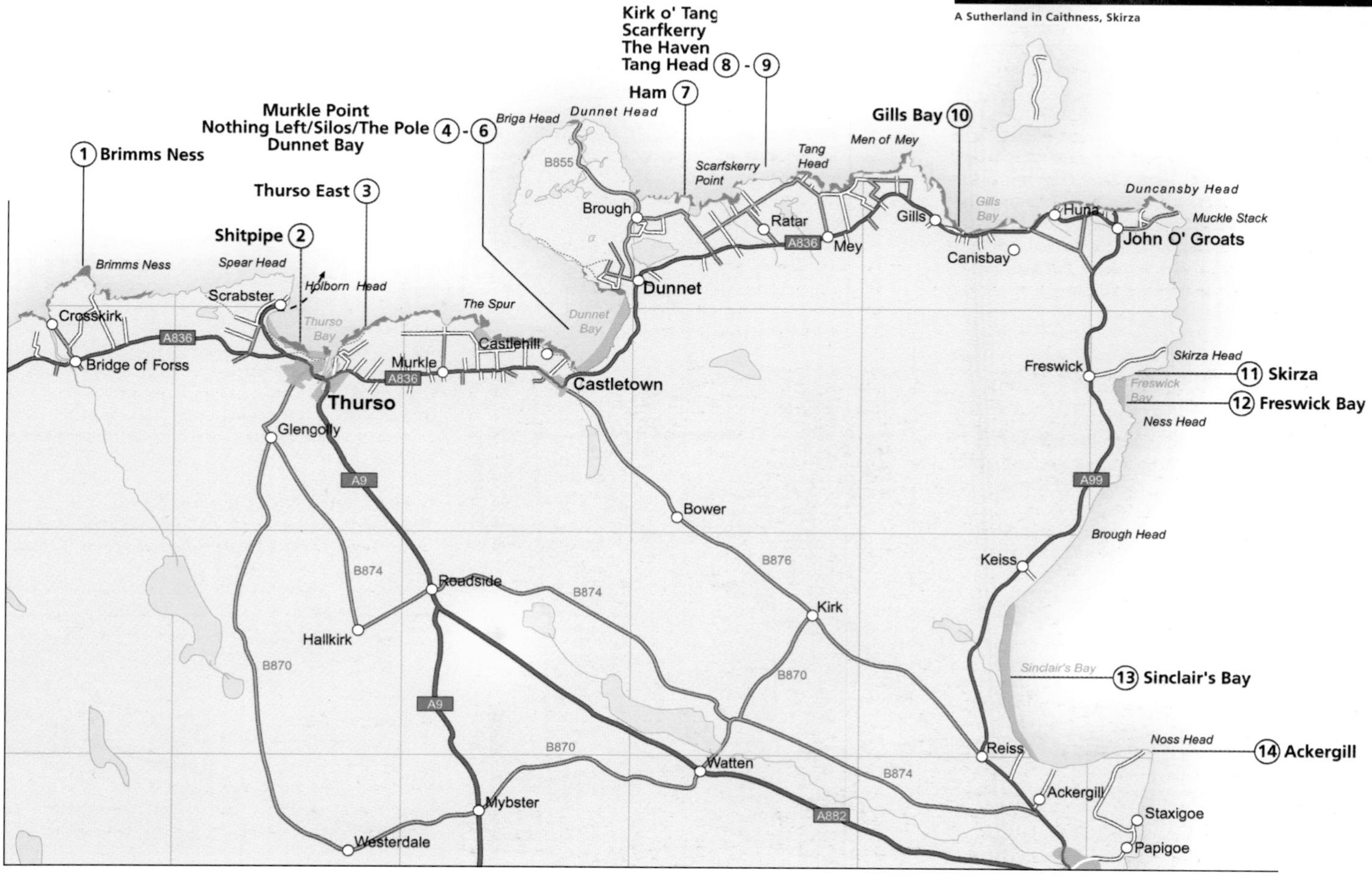

1 Brimms Ness
2 Shitpipe
3 Thurso East
4 - 6 Murkle Point, Nothing Left/Silos/The Pole, Dunnet Bay
7 Ham
8 - 9 Kirk o' Tang, Scarfkerry, The Haven, Tang Head
10 Gills Bay
11 Skirza
12 Freswick Bay
13 Sinclair's Bay
14 Ackergill

Moray Firth

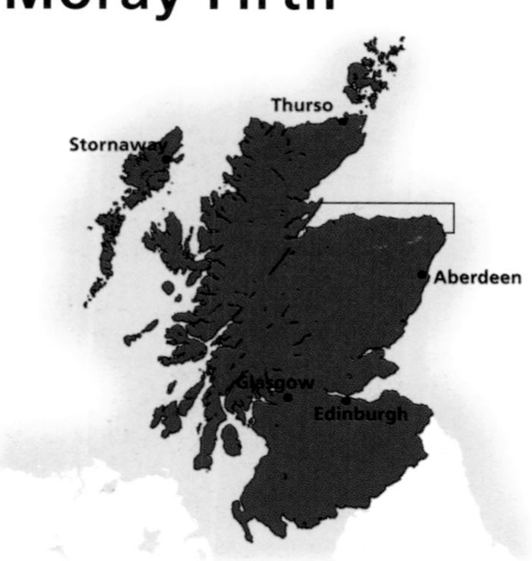

Lossiemouth

ROY MAJOR

1. Lossiemouth

The first real surf spot E of Inverness is an average but polluted beach that needs a big swell to work well. Beware the McWatt brothers.

Le premier vrai spot à l'est d' Inverness: une plage moyenne qui exige un gros swell pour bien marcher.

2. Spey Bay

Conditions here are similar to that of Lossiemouth. Distillerie-sville.

Mêmes conditions que Lossiemouth.

3. Cullen

Fast-breaking lefts and rights are visible from the A90.

Des droites et gauches rapides visibles depuis l'A90.

4. Sandend Bay

A quaint village with a harbour to the W of the bay harbours a beach, which has three main peaks: the most recognised is the left that breaks from the rocky point beside the harbour. Access by paddling off the sewer pipe. The middle peak and the right at the far side of the bay work on a similar swell but at a higher tide.

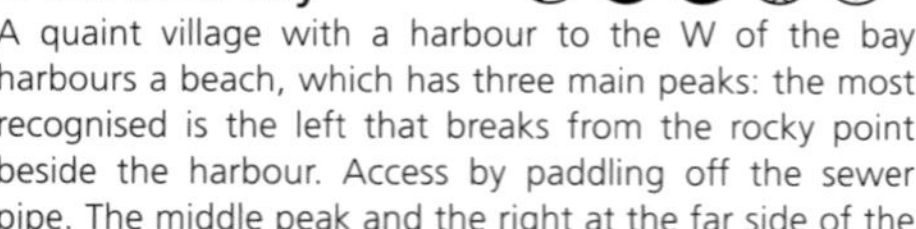

Village avec un port à l'ouest de la baie. Beach break avec trois pics principaux, le plus reconnaissable étant la gauche qui casse sur la pointe rocheuse à côté du port. L'accés se fait en marchant le long d'un tuyau d'égoûts et une petite rame jusqu'au pic. Le pic du milieu et celui de droite au bout de la baie marche avec la même houle mais avec une marée plus haute.

5. Boyndie Bay

This is a beach W of the point that has shifting peaks over a sand bottom. A small reef at the N end sucks like hell in a big swell.

Plage à l'ouest du point, avec des pics sur fond de sable. Une petite droite de reef au nord suce par gros swell.

6. Sunnyside Bay

This is a hard spot to find as it's signposted as a cliff walk, but if you get there you'll find a triangular reef in the middle of a sheltered bay. It's a bit of a mission, so say the few that have surfed this spot. Generally it has the same conditions as Sandend.

Petit village avec un port à l'ouest de la baie. Beach break avec trois pics principaux, le plus reconnaissable étant la gauche qui casse sur la pointe rocheuse à côté du port. L'accés se fait en marchant le long d'un tuyau d'égoûts et une petite rame jusqu'au pic. Le pic du milieu et celui de droite au bout de la baie marche avec la même houle mais avec une marée p.

7. Banff

Point

A good right point breaks here over a triangular reef at the E end of Banff Links beach. Fickle but worth checking, as it can handle solid, hollow barrels at mid to high tide.

Une bonne droite qui casse sur un reef triangulaire à l'extrémité est de la plage de Banff Links. Capricieux mais vaut le détour parce que ça peut envoyer des tubes solides à mi-marée.

Beach

You can find different peaks near Banff Harbour W of the river. At low tide these are hollow and powerful. Access by going down some metal stairs that also lead to the harbour. The water quality is bad.

Différents pics prés du port de Banff, à l'ouest de la rivière. Un spot particulièrement creux et puissant à marée basse. Il faut descendre des échelles en fer depuis le mur qui fait route aussi dans le port . La qualité de l'eau laisse à désirer.

8. Palmer Cove

A long, fast and occasionally hollow right breaks here into the mouth of the river Devoran. It's best at dead low tide.

Une droite longue et rapide et parfois creuse casse dans l'embouchure de la rivière Deveran, le meilleur étant à l'étale basse. Marche à toutes les marées quand c'est gros.

9. Pennan

A small village is perched here on top of steep cliffs. Below, a variety of reef waves in the small bay work on various tides and swells. It's easy to paddle out through the harbour, even in a big swell. Beware of rips, however.

Petit village et port avec la plupart des maisons perchées au sommet de falaises abruptes. Une palette de vagues de reef marchent dans la baie avec des marées et des houles différentes. Rame fastoche depuis le port, même quand ça rentre épais. Attention aux courants.

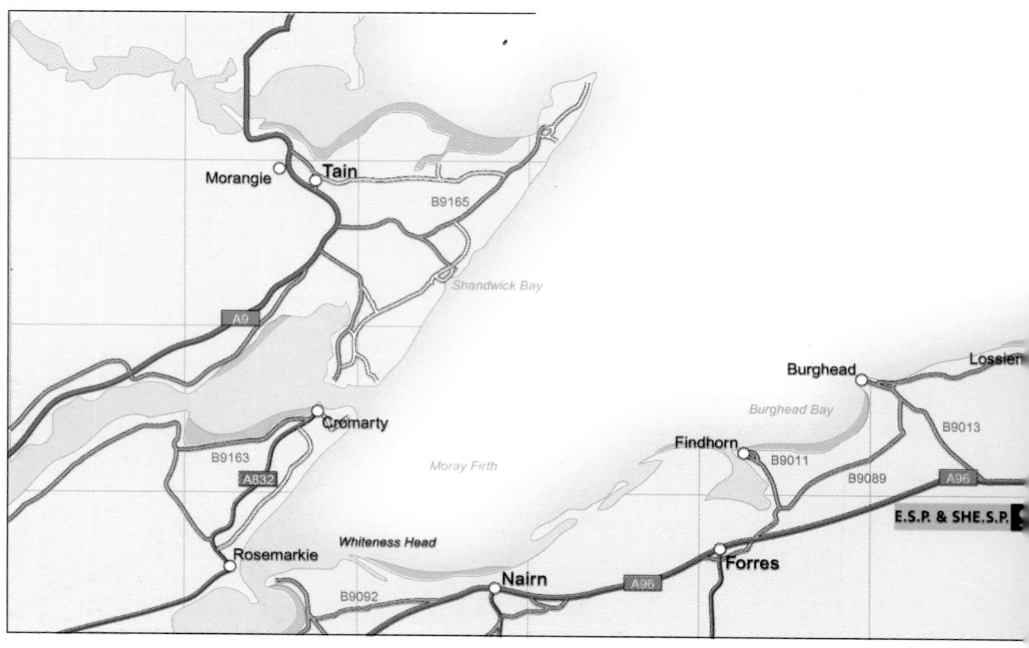

10. Wisemans

A short heavy left breaks beside Sandhaven Harbour. A hollow, chucking peak and barrel section before the wave peels onto the inside 'stone zone'. It breaks on a solid N swell and is no place for faint hearts. Water quality is poor.

Une droite courte et craignos qui à casse à côté du port de Sandhaven. Un pic creux qui jette au tube avant d'arriver à l'inside appelée la 'zone cailloux'. Par bon swell de nord, pour les téméraires seulement; L'eau est pas terrible.

11. Phingask

A long peeling left breaks between Fraserburgh and Sandhaven, in the same rocky bay as West Point.

Une longue droite entre Fraserburgh et Sandhaven, dans la même baie rocheuse que West Point.

12. West Point

Two right-hand point waves break on the outskirts of town, W of Fraserburgh. A local fish factory discharges waste nearby so water quality is rather fishy (doh!). A flock of seagulls marks the spot.

Deux droites qui cassent sur les abords de la ville, à l'ouest de Fraserburgh. Une usine de poissons locale rejete ses déchets dans l'eau à côté. Une horde de mouettes situe le spot.

13. Fraserburgh

Locally known as the 'Broch', Fraserburgh is home to many of Scotland's best surfers and has a long, hard-core history dating back to the 70s. The point beside the river produces good lefts in a N swell over a rock and sand bottom, while the beach E of town is home to various quality waves. The town end faces E, while the E end (known as Philorth) faces N and picks up any N swell. It also works in massive S winds, when the E coast is blown out.

Bien que Thurso soit connu pour avoir la vague la plus spectaculaire d' Ecosse, Fraserborough abrite nombre des meilleurs surfers écossais avec une équipe de durs des années soixante-dix. Localement, la ville s'appelle "Broch" et on voit aussi de bons spots sur la plage à l'est de la ville.

Pennan

NICK TAYLOR

Fraserburgh

GRANITE REEF

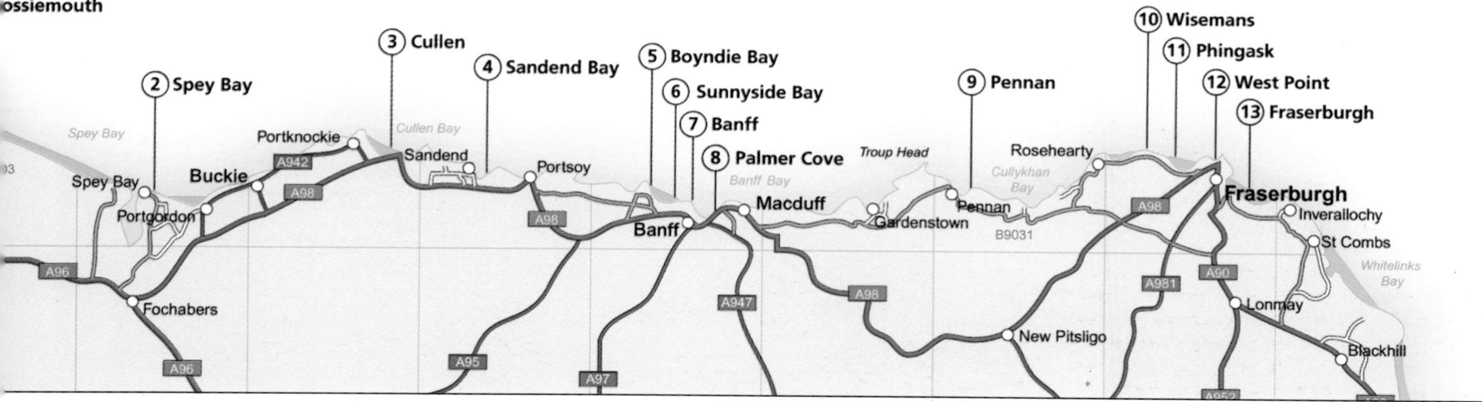

East Coast

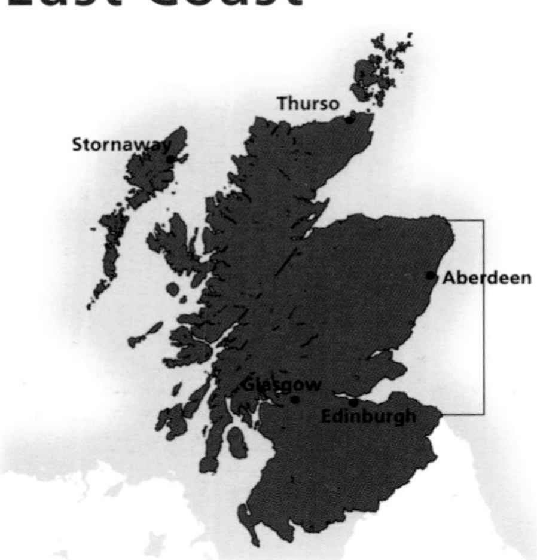

1. Inverallocchy to St Combs

Between Cairnbulg Point and Inzie Head, the coast is littered with reefs which break at different stages of the tide. The area is largely unsurfed but definitely worth exploring.

Entre Caimbulg Point et Inzie Head, la côte est gavée de reefs qui cassent à des marées différentes. La zone est peu surfée, mais mérite assurément l' exploration.

2. St Combs to Peterhead

Miles of empty beach are accessible only via a few roads and the St Fergus Gas Terminal. There's fickle peaks and strong currents, but also a few secret spots – bring your maps.

Des kilomètres de plages seulement interrompues par certaines pointes rocheuses et le terminal de gaz de St-Fergus. Des pics inconsistants et de forts courants, mais il y a des secret spots alors apportez vos cartes !

3. Sandford

Check out this deep, recessed bay with reef and beach peaks. The reef to the N pumps hollow, sucking lefts in a N or N/NE swell with good rights and lefts on the beach. The water is suspiciously warm due to outflow from the nearby Boddam power station, and consequently there is no need to wear boots and gloves even in winter. This spot is the home of quite a few seals: be respectful of their space in spring (mating season).

Baie profonde et encaissée avec des plages et des reefs . Le reef au nord soulève des gauches creuses qui sucent bien par houle de nord N-E. De bonnes droites et gauches aussi sur la plage. L'eau est bizarrement chaude puisque la centrale électrique de Boddam est à proximité: pas besoin de chaussons ni de gants même en hiver. Aussi squatté par les otaries qui sont trés curieuses à la saison des amours au printemps.

4. Cruden Bay

This is a crescent-shaped bay with a good peak near the harbour at the N end that's best in a clean S swell at lower tides. Paddle out from the harbour when it's big but watch out for salmon nets and shite hawks. The bay offers some protection from massive blown-out N swells.

Baie en forme de croissant avec un bon pic prés du port au nord, de préférence par une houle propre de sud à marée basse. Commencez à ramer depuis le port quand c'est gros tout en faisant gaffe aux filets à saumon et aux faucons excités. Quelque peu protégé des houles de nord complètement ventées.

5. Newburgh to Balmedie

Picking up the same swell as Aberdeen, this is an average stretch of beach which is not surfed often. Mind out for salmon nets along this stretch of coast.

Morceau de plage correct qui chope le même swell qu'Aberdeen, mais moins souvent surfé. Attention aux filets à saumon qui peuvent dériver, ça arrive!

6. Aberdeen

From Footdee, the beach runs N for 3km (1.8mi) to the mouth of the River Don. Groynes run the entire length, and hold good sandbars, which produce clean, hollow waves. Donmouth goes off with excellent rights. There's parking the length of the foreshore. Beware The Chief, the local longboarder. Water is OK.

Depuis Footdee, la plage s'étend au nord sur 3 bornes jusqu'à l'embouchure du Don. La construction d'épi s'étire sur toute la longueur et renferme de bons bancs sur lesquels cassent des vagues propres et creuses. Y'a une droite d'enfer à l'embouchure. Se garer directement sur la plage. Faites gaffe au chef, le longboarder local. L'eau n'est pas transcendante mais correcte.

7. The Harbour

Check this rarely surfed, perfect barreling right that can be sketchy due to oddball currents. In a huge swell, waves break inside the breakwater, but hazards include the Shetland ferry that sails through the line up and the harbour police. The water quality is pretty gnarly.

Rarement surfé alors que c'est une droite tubulaire et parfaite mais délicate aussi à cause de courants démentiels . Quand ça rentre énorme, les vagues cassent à l'intérieur de la jetée . Attention au ferry des Shetland qui navigue sur le pic et aux garde-côtes qui font chier .L'eau est complètement gerbique.

8. Nigg Bay

This is probably the best spot in the Grampian area with hollow rights and killer lefts. It is excellent at higher tides in big swells with long, deep barrels. The car park in the bay is often frequented by travellers (lock your car!); alternatively, park on the grass hill to the S of the bay. The water quality is unfortunately not good, especially after an E wind.

Probablement le meilleur spot dans la région de Grampian, avec des droites creuses et des gauches de folie. Peut bien fonctionner à des marées plus hautes mais avec de la taille. Des tuyaux profonds à choper quand les conditions sont optimales.

Aberdeen

GRANITE REEF

GRANITE REEF

Nigg Bay

9. Stonehaven

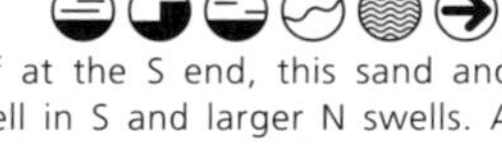

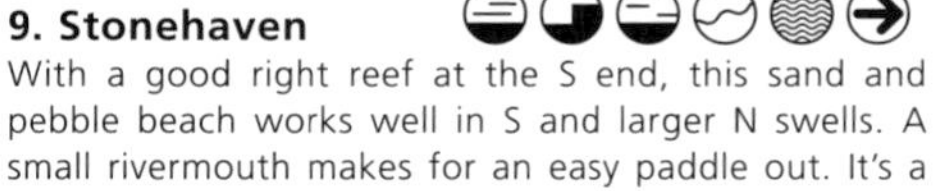

With a good right reef at the S end, this sand and pebble beach works well in S and larger N swells. A small rivermouth makes for an easy paddle out. It's a good spot to check when Aberdeen is blown out.

Plage de sable et de galets avec une bonne droite de reef au sud. Une petite rivière peut vous aider à passer la barre. Marche par houle de sud ou grosse houle de nord. A checker quand Aberden est trop venté.

10. Inverbervie

Normally breaking left off the point near the car park, this pebble beach is best on a clean S swell.

Plage de galet qui casse normalement en gauche sur la pointe à côté du parking, de préference par houle de sud sans vent.

11. Johnshaven

A fickle exposed reef break which needs a big, clean swell to work, but there's many other reef and point breaks in this area.

Vague de reef rare qui exige un swell gros et propre. Plein d'autres reefs et point breaks dans le coin.

12. Lunan Bay

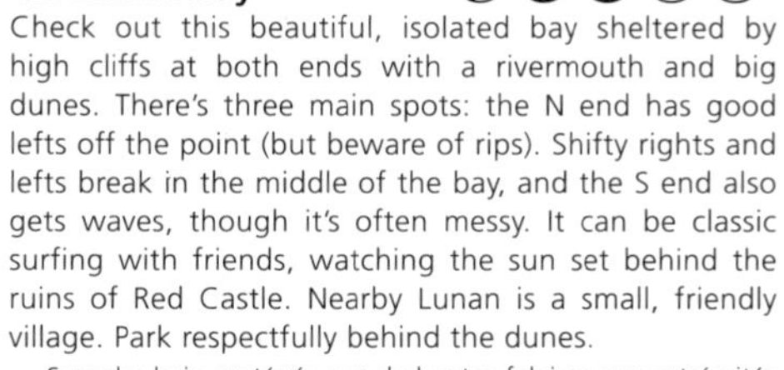

Check out this beautiful, isolated bay sheltered by high cliffs at both ends with a rivermouth and big dunes. There's three main spots: the N end has good lefts off the point (but beware of rips). Shifty rights and lefts break in the middle of the bay, and the S end also gets waves, though it's often messy. It can be classic surfing with friends, watching the sun set behind the ruins of Red Castle. Nearby Lunan is a small, friendly village. Park respectfully behind the dunes.

Superbe baie protégée par de hautes falaises aux extrémités avec une embouchure et des dunes massives au milieu où on se sent isolé. Trois spots principaux: la partie nord a des bonnes gauches sur le point mais attention au jus. Des gauches et droites sont au milieu de la baie; la partie sud reçoit aussi quelques vagues mais c'est souvent brouillon. On peut vraiment s'y éclater avec des potes, en regardant le coucher de soleil sur les ruines du Red Castle.

13. Arbroath

A 3km (1.8mi) beach break, known as Elliot, is located on the S outskirts of town. It's best on an incoming to high tide; the rock point N of the bay works well in N swells, but shallow rocks mean experienced surfers only. Elliot is located directly in front of the Elliot caravan park.

3kms de beachbreak qu'on appelle Elliot, situé dans la banlieue sud de la ville, mieux à marée montante jusqu'à marée haute. La pointe rocheuse au nord de la baie marche bien par houle de nord, mais vu le peu de fond, vous avez intérêt à assurer!

14. Saint Andrews

West Sands

There's shifty beach peaks here, better at low-mid tide – the central peak is usually the best. Water quality is OK.

Des pics changeants, mieux de marée basse à mi-marée. Le pic du milieu est souvent le meilleur où la qualité de l'eau est satisfaisante .

East Sands

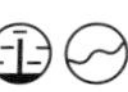

Take the rip out to good peaks breaking off the harbour wall. It usually closes out on outgoing tide. Unfortunately the town sewage affects the water quality, especially when the Gulf is on.

De bonnes droites et de bonnes gauches prés de la jetée du port. Sortir avec le courant, en général ça ferme à marée descendante. Les égoûts de la ville sont visibles.

15. Kingsbarns

This break hasn't been surfed much, but is worth checking out as there's reef and beach breaks, working only in a big swell.

Du reef et du beach break qui marche uniquement par gros swell. Pas beaucoup surfé mais mérite le coup d'oeil.

16. Pease Bay

Nestled at the foot of high cliffs, this classic beach faces due N. It's the most consistent and accessible bay for miles, although it can get blown out easily. Under these conditions the S end cleans up faster and is generally better. Facilities include holiday caravans, parking, loos and a shop. There are other spots nearby.

Plage renommée faisant face au nord et située au pied de hautes falaises. La baie la plus consistente et la plus accessible sur des kilomètres. 'S'il y a une vague quelque part, c'est sûrement à Pease Bay' bien que ça ne supporte pas bien le vent. Dans ce cas, la partie sud redevient lisse plus rapidement tout en étant meilleure. Il reste d'autres spots à découvrir dans les alentours.

GRANITE REEF

Pease Bay

17. Coldingham Bay

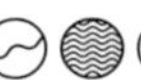

This bay faces E, and is an alternative to Pease, having the advantage of two small hotel/pubs but no campsite.

Exposé à l'est, c'est une alternative à Pease, avec l'avantage d'avoir deux petits hôtels/Pubs mais pas de camping .

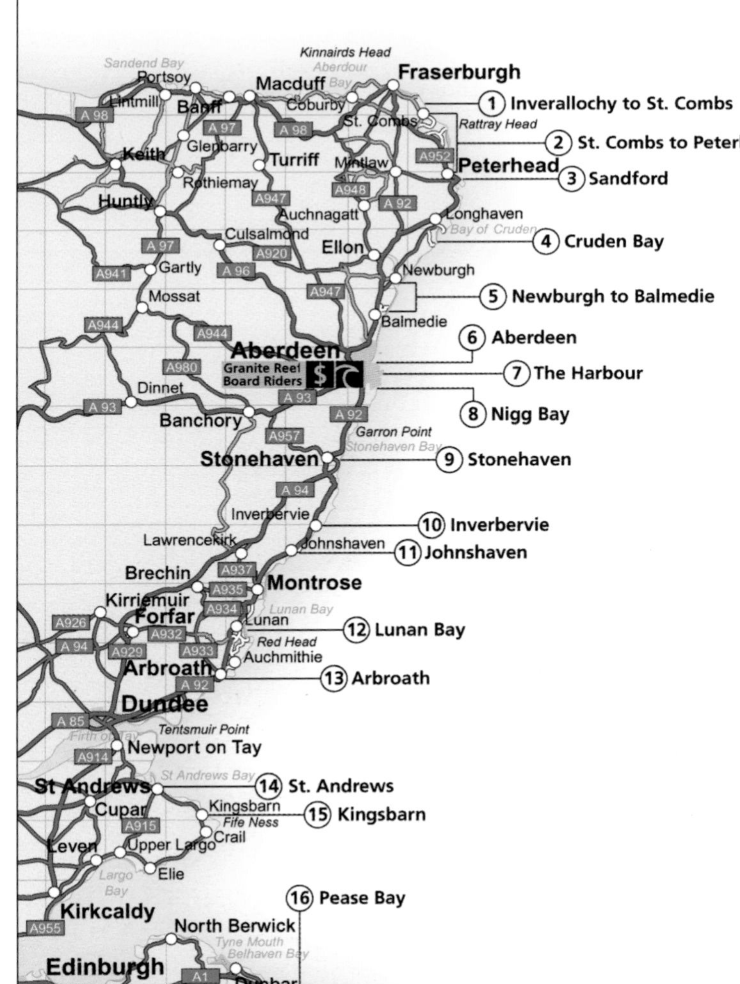

England

Make no mistake, the English know all about surfing with quality waves spinning onto their shores from three separate bodies of water. The English have been intrinsically linked to surf culture since Captain Cook delivered it to the West, after one of the most epic surfaris of all time. When Nelson and Drake's fleets sailed from Plymouth, they too cruised past a brace of gaping barrels before heading into the Bay of Biscay. Owing to a surprisingly moderate climate, regular swell and a massive variation in coastal aspect, old Blighty is home to Europe's largest, most hard-core surf population.

Angleterre

Ne vous y trompez pas, les Anglais savent tout du surf, puisqu'ils bénéficient de vagues de qualité venant de toutes les directions et de 3 mers différentes. Les Anglais ont été depuis longtemps liés à la culture surf depuis que la Capitaine Cook l'a ramené en Occident, après un des surfaris le plus incroyable de tous les temps. Quand les flottes de Nelson et de Drake mettaient les voiles depuis Plymouth, ils passaient le long de vagues vierges avant de s'aventurer dans le Golfe de Gascogne. Avec un climat étonnamment modéré, une houle régulière et une variation incessante du littoral, "Old Blighty" renferme une des plus importantes populations de surfers hardcore en Europe.

All the coasts get good waves which ever way they face. South coast perfection at Porthleven

SIMON McCOMB

The East Coast

The Peak – Yorkshire

Where to go

Surf Areas

The East Coast is enjoying growing recognition as a surfing area with consistent, quality waves around the Tynemouth and Scarborough areas. Colder air and water temperatures, coupled with pollution problems have limited the sport's growth rate, but with powerful surf and offshore winds, more people are taking to the water.

The north-east coast is a truly wild destination. Surfing started here in the mid 60s and by the 80s surfing was thriving. Pockets of local surfers exist in each coastal town, with surf shops in all the key locations (Seahouses, Tynemouth, South Shields, Hartlepool, Saltburn, Whitby and Scarborough). The rural coastline, dotted with small fishing villages and castles, is beautiful, but at the same time the throbbing night life of cities like Newcastle is never far away.

The best waves come from the north, but the coast also gets south-east swells up the channel and the surf can be great, with prevailing south-west winds offshore. Blessed with many reefs and quality beaches, there are still miles of unexplored coastline. Unfortunately the best time to catch surf is in autumn, winter and spring, so bring a warm wetsuit. Nigel Veitch, an East Coast legend, was the UK's first professional surfer and he paved the way for many others. He charged everything he did and inspired the next generation. H'way the lads. **Gabriel Davies**

The South Coast Infrequent and short duration swells, accompanied by onshore winds, typify the South Coast surf experience. The best sessions are with the presence of Biscay lows or Atlantic lows below or around Landsend. Despite this grim appraisal, there are classic days and the thriving surf population, centred around the main areas of Brighton, The Witterings, The Isle of Wight and Bournemouth, is often augmented by weekend trippers from London. The area from Paington to Weymouth is reputed to have some good spots working on occasion.

South Cornwall and Devon
Southerly storms in the Bay of Biscay or in the sea off Finistere produce powerful waves on the south coast of Devon and Cornwall. An east, north or north-west wind will provide the best conditions. Unfortunately, south coast swells are often accompanied by south or south-west winds, which drastically reduce the number of clean surfing days available. Ironically, England's premier reef break, Porthleven, is on the south coast, making the rideable tubes rare jewels indeed. Quite often a strong south-west wind will turn north-west for a time – so if a beach faces true south, such as Portwrinkle, the conditions will often clean up very quickly. The south coast is at its best between January and April when the winter storms take a southerly track across Europe.

South Cornwall and Devon

ALEX WILLIAMS

Porthleven

Ou Aller

Les zones de surf

La Côte Est est reconnue comme une région ayant des vagues de qualité et consistentes dont l'épicentre se situe autour de Tynemouth et Scarborough. Un temps frisquet et une eau froide ont limité le développement du sport à cet endroit bien qu'avec du surf costaud et des vents réguliérement offshore, la population surf augmente rapidement.

La côte nord-est est une destination "sauvage". Le surf a débuté ici au milieu des années 60 et depuis les années 80 la population surfeur se multiplie. On voit apparaître des bandes de surfeurs locaux dans chaque ville de la côte, avec des surf-shops dans tous les endroits stratégiques (Seahouses, Tynemouth, South Shields, Hartlepool, Saltburn, Whitby et Scarborough). La ligne côtière et rurale constituée de petits villages et de châteaux est charmante; et, en plus de posséder une industrie du surf florissante, certaines villes comme Newcastle sont victimes d'une certaine fièvre nocturne!

Les meilleures vagues proviennent des dépressions au large de la Scandinavie, mais la région reçoit également les houles de sud-est du"Channel" et le surf peut être super bon,lors de vents offshores de sud-ouest. Gâtée par de nombreux reefs et par des plages de qualité, il y a encore des kilomètres de côte inexlplorés, mais, puisque les meilleures périodes sont l'automne, l'hiver et le printemps, une épaisse combinaison est de rigueur.

Veitch, la légende de la côte est, était parmi l'un des premiers surfeurs professionnels du Royaume-Uni et il balisa le chemin pour les autres. Il faisait à fond ce qu'il entreprenait et il servit de modèle à une génération talentueuse de jeunes surfeurs. Ces surfeurs volent,maintenant, de leurs propres ailes. Bonne chance les gars.

La Côte Sud Houles éphémères et rares, accompagnées de vents onshores, caractérisent le surf sur la South Coast. Les meilleures sessions correspondent au passage des dépressions de la Baie de Biscay ou de l'Atlantique aux alentours de Landsend. Malgré cette appréciation quelque peu sinistre, quelques jolis surfs sont possibles, attirant les surfeurs de Brighton, des Witterings, de l'île de Wight et de Bournemouth tout en n'oubliant pas les Londoniens qui ne sont vraiment pas loin. La région de Paington à Weymouth est également reconnue pour avoir quelques bons spots qui marchent bien quelques fois par an.

Cornwall sud et Devon Les tempêtes du sud dans la baie de Biscay ou près du Finistère produisent des vagues pendant une courte période mais puissantes, elles déroulent sur la côte sud du Devon et du Cornwall. Un vent d'est,du nord ou nord-ouest fournissent les meilleures conditions.Malheureusement, les swells qui touchent la côte sud sont souvent accompagnés de vents du sud ou sud-ouest qui réduisent très fortement le nombre de jours réellement intéressants.

The West Country

West Cornwall The weather is often milder here than the rest of the UK and swells are as consistent as any other locations. Some of the most spectacular coast in Britain is left exclusively for the Cornish and a few travellers who have worked out that wintertime is the best surf season: the coast sees rideable 2-3m (6-8ft) waves for days on end. A big variety of spots present themselves and it is possible to find offshore waves on the north-facing beaches (like Harlyn, St Ives and St Agnes) in the prevailing south-west winds. Flat spells are common in summer, but easy to predict. Many of the spots also get very crowded in summer and sewage problems are obvious at most of them.

North Cornwall The coastline of North Cornwall is backed almost entirely by National Trust land, with very little development marring its windswept beauty. A maintained, world-renowned coastal path runs almost its entire length, offering extensive and unspoilt coastal views of its reefs, beaches and points, some of which are known to hold large swells.

North Devon The bulk of the best surf arrives on the west-facing beaches. The tidal flow up and down the Bristol Channel is similar to the current in a huge river; moving eastwards during the flood and westwards during the ebb. The 'push' effect of the incoming tide can be significant, by helping a weak swell on its way. Because of the vast range, there is also a difference in water level between low spring and low neap-tide. This effects the quality of some of the low tide breaks. A local tide table is a crucial investment.

The worst winds for most of North Devon's beaches are westerlies and north-westerlies, although in the summer when it's often flat, even these may give rideable waves for desperadoes. With surfers arriving at weekends from London and the big cities in the midlands, some spots like Croyde and Putsborough have been struggling to handle the crowds.

When to go

Although England has a poor record for producing surf when the summer competitions are held, it still receives year-round swell. Any coast may pump at any time of year, but generally speaking, September to April is prime time for both the Atlantic and North Sea. The West Country water gets up to 20°C/68°F in late summer, while the North Sea languishes around 15°C/62°F. Always pack a raincoat and umbrella.

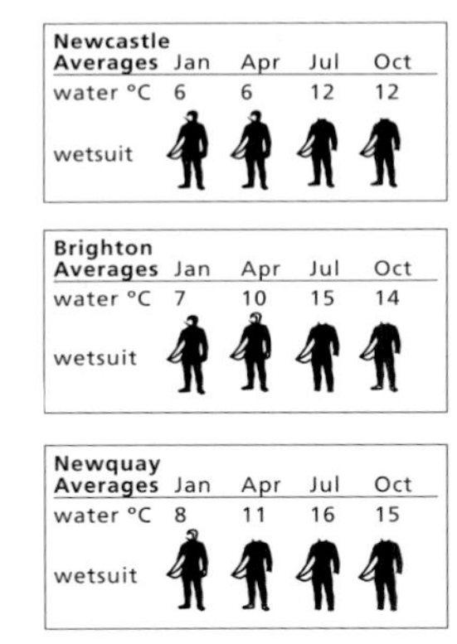

Newcastle Averages	Jan	Apr	Jul	Oct
water °C	6	6	12	12
wetsuit				

Brighton Averages	Jan	Apr	Jul	Oct
water °C	7	10	15	14
wetsuit				

Newquay Averages	Jan	Apr	Jul	Oct
water °C	8	11	16	15
wetsuit				

Porthtowan

Mike Raven – Black Rock, Widemouth

Lynmouth at high tide

La première vague de reef d'Angleterre, Porthleven, est sur la côte sud, produisant des petits bijous de tubes. Assez souvent, un fort vent de sud-ouest fini par passer nord-ouest - ainsi si une plage est exposée plein sud,telle que Portwrinkle, les conditions s'améliorent très rapidement. La côte sud est au sommet de sa forme entre janvier et avril quant les tempêtes d'hiver prennent un chemin plus au sud à travers l'Europe.

Cornwall Ouest Le temps est habituellement plus doux que dans le reste de l'Angleterre et les swells sont aussi consistants que n'importe où en Angleterre. Particulièrement en hiver, l'un des bords de mer les plus spectaculaires est le Cornish, de plus certains surfeurs ont pris conscience que l'hiver est la meilleure saison pour le surf avec des vagues surfables de 2-3 m durant des jours. Une grande variété de spots existe; il est très possible de trouver des vagues offshore sur les plages orientées au nord (par exemple Harlyn, St Ives et St Agnes), avec les vents de sud-ouest dominants.

Cornwall Nord fait partie presque entièrement du National Trustland, petite beauté sauvage balayée par les vents. La région s'étend du Hartland Point à Newquay et est un des endroits qui regorgent le plus de vagues en Angleterre. De célèbres sentiers côtiers, bien entretenus, s'étirent sur presque l'ensemble de la côte, offrant des points de vue magistraux et imprenables de ses reefs, plages et avancées, dont certains ont la réputation de tenir de grosses houles.

Devon Nord La majeure partie des bons jours ont lieu sur les plages exposées à l'ouest entre Sennen Cove et Lynmouth. Un swell correct assorti d'un léger vent d'est offriront d'excellentes conditions sur toute la côte, cependant le vent reste rarement un doux vent d'est très longtemps! C'est pour les jours de vent de travers, et les jours de très petit ou très gros swells , que ce guide a été conçu. La qualité du surf ne dépend pas seulement de la taille du swell et de la direction du vent, elle dépend aussi des fonds marins et des marées qui ont des amplitudes extrêmes dans ces régions. Le courant qui descend et remonte le Bristol Channel est comparable à celui d'une grosse rivière - se déplaçant vers l'est lors de la marée montante et vers l'ouest lors du reflux. L'effet de poussée du flux, en aidant au passage une houle faiblarde, est loin d'être négligeable.En raison d'un marnage important, il existe aussi une différence colossale entre lee mortes et les vives eaux. Cela nuit à la qualité de certains spots à marée basse. Une table locale des marées est un investissement vital.

Les pires vents sont les vents d'ouest et nord-ouest, bien qu'en été cela soit souvent plat, il se peut qu'il y ait des vagues surfables. North Devon est très couru au printemps, été, automne par les surfeurs des grandes villes du Midlands, et quelques spots tels que Croyde et Putsborough doivent admettre une imposante foule.

The Ocean Environment

Water Quality

England is one of the most densely populated nations on the planet, and the same is true of her coast. The south east is the population nucleus and water quality in this region is fairly dire. The combination of human excrement and commercial wastes which have plagued the British coast for too long begin to dissipate as you reach the west country, though in summer and near the few large towns, problems still exist. The east coast and the north west are England's most shameful areas, with heavy industry and nuclear power stations leading the list of primary culprits. SAS have obviously been leading the fight to clean the seas, with some success.

Chris Hines reports: 'Wessex and Yorkshire Water have adopted full treatment policies in line with the 1998 House of Commons Select Committee Inquiry into Sewage Treatment and Disposal which concluded that: 'All sewage should be treated to a tertiary level at all times and in all places.' Now other water companies have started to follow their example.

On Localism

Incidences of aggressive localism are extremely rare in Great Britain, which is explained to some degree by the lack of crowds at many spots and the large coastline, but also by the naturally mellow instincts of many of Britain's coastal inhabitants. A spirit of camaraderie is a naturally occurring phenomena when dealing with harsh elements: British champion Gabe Davies writes about growing up on the east coast which strike a familiar chord all over the British Isles.

'Hardened by cold weather, polluted and freezing seas and inconsistent swells, the locals are some of the keenest, most competitive and yet friendliest surfers anywhere, who give meaning to the term hard-core. There's an independent spirit and a strong local pride built on close friendships and a close-knit surfing network that exists along the coast, which becomes enriched by further discoveries of new breaks. Surfers who wait all winter for classic swells will not stand for visitors who arrive with a disrespectful attitude.'

Burning Issue – Surfers Against Sewage

It is ironic that a nation so fiercely proud of its maritime heritage has actually been guilty of crapping in the very thing that it claims makes it special. Traditionally the UK has used its coastline as a convenient sewer, dumping 400 million gallons a day into its waters. In May 1990, a bunch of surfers formed a group called Surfers Against Sewage (SAS). They were sick (sometimes literally) with surfing and swimming in a soup of human excrement with kilos of panty liners and condoms thrown in for good measure. SAS have campaigned hard and fast for clean seas – and they're winning!

Since forming, SAS have hugely raised the profile of beach and sea pollution. In so doing they encouraged Dwr Cymru/Welsh Water to adopt a full treatment policy (1993), which has subsequently been followed by Wessex Water in 1996 and Yorkshire Water in 1997. South West Water have recently decided to commit to a full treatment works including ultra violet light disinfection for Newquay by close of play 1999 as well as UV plants for Porthleven, Saint Agnes, Perranporth, the Camel Estuary and others.

The group has even been called in as independent advisor to the Environment Minister. In 1996 SAS were instrumental in a High Court Judicial Review of a council who claimed that 1.5kg (6lb) of panty liners and condoms per day, did not represent a threat to health or a nuisance. The action at the Royal Courts of Justice was successful and the council were told to think again.

Driven by two main pieces of European legislation, the privatised water industry has some clear heroes and some murky villains. Depending on where you surf, you can either get some of the best or the worst water quality available.

House of Commons Parliamentary Report

Year-round treatment of domestic waste and subsequent costs are two crucial issues in Britain. Some water companies have appealed against the requirement for annual treatment, only wanting to treat from May to September.

In late 1997, SAS were called to give oral evidence to a House of Commons Select Committee inquiry into sewage treatment and disposal. This is a bunch of MPs from all parties who investigate certain issues in depth. They have the power to call anyone in front of them and SAS were one of only 20 organisations, which included the Minister for the Environment. Luckily the politicians involved have recognised the use of the wetsuit and are endorsing year-round treatment.

BOB BOWEN

Chris opens Porlock Sewage Treatment works for Wessex Water featuring revolutionary tertiary treatment membrane microfiltration

The conclusions of the report make excellent reading for anyone who gives a shit about the state of our oceans: 'By the year 2002, all sewage should be treated to tertiary level at all times in all places.' This will undoubtedly cost someone. The issue now is whether the public are willing to pay for an improved environment. Surveys show that the younger generations are. SAS continue to fight those who say that surfers should pay for the water to be cleaned up. The coastline is a natural asset that millions of people enjoy and one that generates considerable revenue.

TIM RAINGER

SAS Regional Reps

Brighton
Andrew Coleman
(44) 01273 570261

Scotland
Alisdair Steel
44 0131 228 5416
Andrew Spragg
44 0131 228 5416

North East
Nick Noble
Saltburn Surf Shop
44 01287 625321
Simon Palmer
44 01287 638243
Roger Povey
Secret Surf Spot Shop
Scarborough

Wales
Huw John
Black Rock Surf Shop
Porthcrawl
01656 782220
Scott Tippings
01395 514920
Torbay Rob White
01803 525 677

Specificités du littoral

Qualité de l'eau

L'Angleterre est un des pays les plus peuplés de la planète et ceci est aussi vrai pour la côte. Le Sud-est est le coeur du pays et la qualité de l'eau est plutôt désastreuse. La combinaison de la pollution dû à l'homme et des rejets industriels qui a infecté la côte britannique depuis trop longtemps commence à se dissiper quand on atteint l'ouest du pays, bien qu'en été et à proximité des grandes villes des problèmes existent encore. La côte est et le nord-ouest sont les régions où le probléme semble le plus aigu, avec comme principaux responsables une industrie lourde et des centrales nucléaires. La SAS a bien évidemment mené le combat pour que l'océan soit propre, avec quelques succés il faut le reconnaître. Chris Hines rapporte "Le Wessex et le Yorkshire ont adopté des politiques de traitement des eaux et des ordures suite à la proposition de la commission d'enquête de la maison des Communes qui a conclu que".....tous les rejets doivent être traités à un troisième niveau n'importe quand et n'importe où...."La SAS était la seule organisation citée par la commission à traiter avec le ministère de l'environnement. Les négociations sont au point mort avec les autres assocations. Beaucoup d'endroits dans le Sud-ouest ont vu leur eau connaître des politiques de desinfection, en particulier l'estuaire de Camel, Porthleven, St Agnes, Perranporth et la région de Westward Ho! Newquay bénéficiera des mesures UV d'içi la fin 1999 et la SAS pense remporter encore d'autres victoires.

TIM RAINGER

Newquay waste

Localisme

Les cas de localisme agressif sont très rares en Grande-Bretagne. On peut l'expliquer d'une certaine façon par l'absence de foule sur pas mal de spots mais aussi par le tempérament flegmatique des Britanniques de la Côte. Un esprit de camaraderie se développe assez naturellement sur les spots, surtout quand les conditions sont austères.. Gabe Davies a rédigé un petit texte sur son enfance sur la côte est, qui a trouvé un écho dans toute la Grande-Bretagne.

Endurcis par le temps rude, une mer glaciale et polluée et enfin par l'iirégularité du swell, les locaux sont parmi les plus enthousiastes et les plus compétitifs tout en étant les plus sympathiques; ils sont l'illustration même de la notion d'"hard-core" (pur et dur). Il y régne un esprit d'indépendance et une forte fierté, ce qui est particulièrement vrai sur des spots spéciaux, qui se sont construits autour de fortes amitiés et un réseau de surf qui est présent le long de la côte, nourri par la découverte de nouvelles perles. Les surfeurs qui attendent tout l'hiver les super jours, ne supportent pas les touristes qui s'aménent avec une attitude irréspectueuse.

The North East

ALEX WILLIAMS

Gabe Davies at home

1. Scottish Border to Blyth

With its reefs and beaches this ancient, beautiful stretch of coastline offers great potential but is rarely surfed. There's no crowds and the further N you go the cleaner the water. Some spots are known at Newbiggin, Alnmouth, Beadnell and Sea Houses and Bamburgh (take the turn in the village to the beach) – it's great fun surfing here with the seals. Holy Island also has a fabled left that few have ridden.

Bien que rarement surfé, ce joli morceau de côte pleine d'histoire avec ses rochers et ses plages offre un bon potentiel. Quand les conditions sont bonnes, y'a pas vraiment de raisons de fuir les spots connus comme Newbiggin, Alnmouth, Beadnell ou Sea Houses. Pas grand monde à l'eau et plus on va au nord, plus l'eau est claire. Bonus: surfer avec les phoques de Bamburgh, aprés le virage de la plage. On raconte qu'Holy Island a une gauche, que peu ont surfé.

2. Blyth to Seaton Sluice

At the N end of the bay, Blyth is quite popular, but the S beaches are rarely surfed. The peaks of Blyth are of varying quality but the beach does offer shelter from larger swells.

Les plages du sud sont rarement surfées. On leur préfère Blyth au nord de la baie. Les pics sont de qualité variable mais c'est un endroit de repli en cas de grosse houle.

3. Hartley Reef

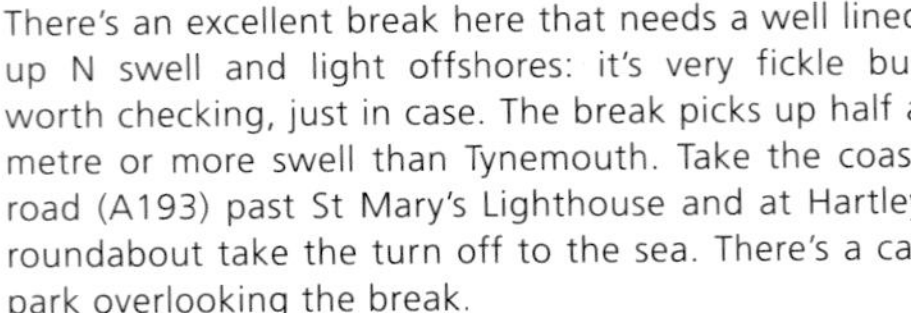

There's an excellent break here that needs a well lined up N swell and light offshores: it's very fickle but worth checking, just in case. The break picks up half a metre or more swell than Tynemouth. Take the coast road (A193) past St Mary's Lighthouse and at Hartley roundabout take the turn off to the sea. There's a car park overlooking the break.

Un super spot par houle propre de nord et léger off-shore. ne marche pas souvent mais vaut le détour, dès fois que. Prend 50 cms voire plus que Tynemouth. Prendre la côtière (A193) aprés le phare de St Mary et au rond-point d'Hartley, tourner vers la mer: 200m plus tard, c'est le parking juste au-dessus du spot.

4. Whitley Bay

This break is only surfed in storm conditions when it's more sheltered than Long Sands. Park towards the café at the N end of the beach.

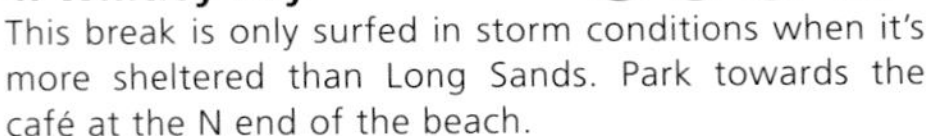

Uniquement surfé quand c'est tempête parce que mieux protégé que Long Sands. Se garer vers le café au nord de la plage.

5. Tynemouth

Long Sands

This spot is the centre of surfing on Tyneside. Long Sands is the main beach with the most reliable waves. The best peaks usually break near the outdoor pool on the S side of the bay, but the point is occasionally a better option.

Le noyau du surf de Tyneside, dont les vagues marchent le mieux sauf fin de printemps et été. Le plus régulier est Longsands, la plage principale dont les meilleurs pics sont souvent prés de la piscine extérieure au sud de la baie. La pointe devient parfois le meilleur spot.

Eddies

Depending on the swell direction and sandbanks, Eddies can be better than adjacent Long Sands.

Selon la direction de la houle et les bancs de sable, ça peut être meilleur que la plage d'à côté, Long Sands.

6. The Black Middens

The good news is that this is one of the best waves on the E Coast. The bad news is that it's polluted and seldom works. It is sited at the mouth of the Tyne River on the N bank. Two piers built to protect shipping from winter storms clean up the waves so it needs a large swell to get between them. Check it out from the coastguard's cottages or Lord Collingwood's monument.

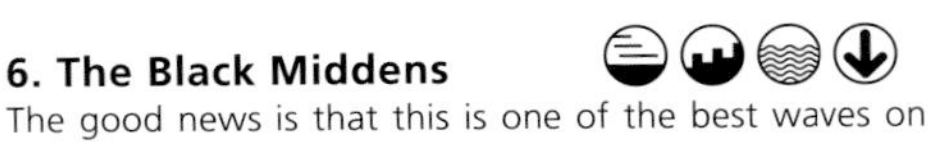

La bonne nouvelle, c'est que c'est une des meilleures vagues de la côte est. La mauvaise: ça marche rarement et c'est pollué. Situé sur la rive nord de la rivière Tyne. Les deux jetées prévues pour protéger le transit des bateaux des tempêtes ont aussi l 'avantage de lisser les vagues à l'intérieur, ce qui n'est le cas qu'avec une houle bien grasse. Visible depuis les cottages des garde-côtes et du monument de Lord Collingwood.

7. South Shields

A beach break of varying quality. Local surfers tend to surf in the middle of the beach in front of the lifeguard station, but better waves may be found at the S end.

Vagues de beach break sans qualité particulière. Les surfers locaux ont tendance à surfer au milieu de la plage en face du poste des MNS. Peut-être de meilleures vagues au sud et aprés les falaises.

THE GILL

Huntcliff and Penny Hale

8. Whitburn (Razor Blades)  

Three left-hand reefs produce good but fickle waves. Access is restricted, particularly at weekends as you walk across a firing range to the cliff path.

Trois gauches de reef: bien mais rare. L'accés se fait par un pare-feu sur le chemin longeant la falaise parfois interdit surtout le week-end.

9. Sunderland to South Shields

There are some sheltered breaks around here that work in heavy winter storms including Cats and Dogs by Roker Pier, Sunderland and the beach at Whitburn.

Voilà des spots abrités pour les bonnes vieilles tempêtes d'hiver: Cats and Dogs vers la jetée de Roker, Sunderland et la plage de Whitburn.

10. The Gare   

Located inside the mouth of the River Tees on the S bank about half a kilometre upstream from the lighthouse, this break – a world class wave at its best – only works on an E swell of a moderate size or above. The swell wraps around the headland producing a very fast wave that breaks over a man-made boulder dump, which makes it dangerous – and it's polluted. Access the break from Redcar along the Warrenby Road and on past British Steel out to the headland. Park by the lighthouse compound gates and walk over the grass bank to check it out.

A l'intérieur de la rivière Tees sur la rive sud à peu prés 300m en amont du phare. Marche seulement par houle d'Est de taille moyenne et au-dessus, qui s'enroule autour du petit cap pour donner des vagues ultra-rapides qui cassent sur fond de rejet de graviers: chaud dessous! Une vague épique quand tout est parfait, malgré la pollution. L'accés se fait depuis Redcar le long de Warrenby Rd, passé l'usine British Steel vers le cap. Se garer vers le portail du phare et marcher sur la rive herbeuse pour jeter un oei.

11. Coatham Sands to Saltburn

A large 8km (5mi) beach, broken at its mid-point by Redcar scars. Waves can be found at most points with swell from SE to NW and are accessible by walking over the 'stray' (dunes).

8km de plage, séparée au milieu par les dalles de reef de Redcar, où il y a généralement des vagues prés de tous les accés avec un swell de NO à SE. Accessible partout en marchant sur le 'Stray', à savoir les dunes.

12. Redcar Scars  

Good waves can be found off the scars at Redcar. People occasionally surf off the inside scars outside Denny's Garage and Lovett's Amusements but as yet no one has surfed the outer scars. There's a car park above the beach.

De bonnes vagues à côté des dalles de Redcar. Ca surfe parfois à l'intérieur de ces dalles en face du garage de Denny ou de la salle de jeux Lovetts. Pour l'instant, personne n'a surfé au large. Parking au-dessus de la plage.

13. Saltburn-by-Sea

Beach n5ho9

The most popular surfing beach in the NE but still not that good a break. It's a flat beach: waves tend to lose power a long way from shore.

Le spot le plus célèbre du nord-est bien que pas terrible. Comme le fond est plat, les vagues perdent de leur puissance au large.

Huntcliff    

A point break at the S end of the beach breaks off the huge scar lying beneath Huntcliff. When it's working, it's a fast powerful right.

Un point break au sud de la plage qui casse sur la méga-dalle situé sous Huntcliff: une droite puissante et rapide quand ça marche.

Saltburn Point

THE GILL

14. Skinningrove   

There are two beaches: one to the N of the jetty and one to the S. The S beach is sheltered to some extent from a W wind by a large stone jetty. To the S of Skinningrove Beck lies the long Hummersea Scar and a right which breaks off the Skinningrove end of the scar. The water quality here is disgusting. Go here if you're totally desperate and have had all the jabs.

Deux plages ici de part et d'autre de la jetée. Celle du sud est quelque peu protégée des vents d'ouest par un gros épi rocheux. Au sud de Skinningrove Beck s'étend la longue dalle de Hummersea avec une droite qui casse au bout de cette dalle.

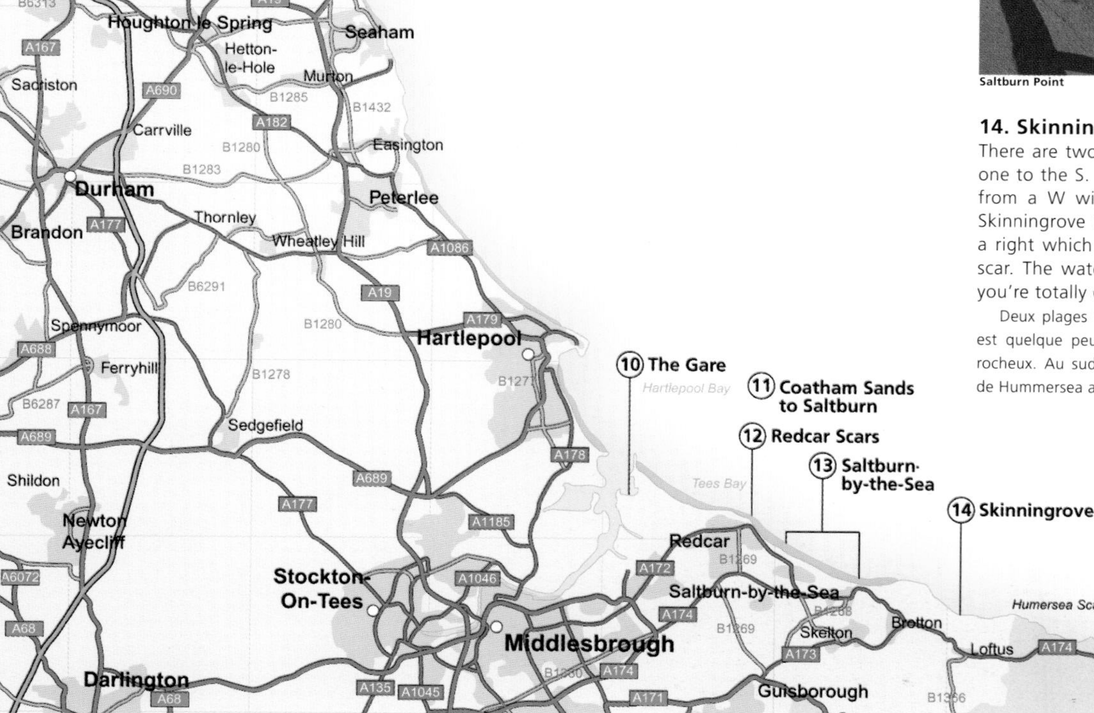

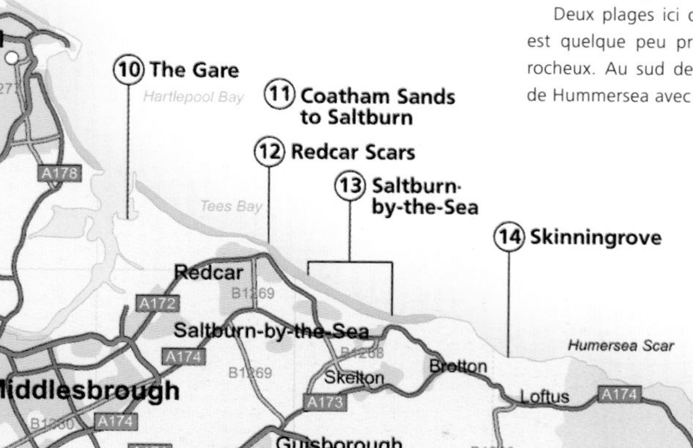

North Yorks and Humberside

Harbour reef

1. Runswick Bay

This is the place to head in a huge N swell when other places along the coast are too big. There are several breaks: the Cobble Dump is an impressive left breaking over rocks at most stages of the tide and is rarely surfed; Inner Reef is a well-protected right (1.2-2m/4-6ft when Saltburn is 2.5-3.5m/8-11ft) with easy rides and paddle out in front of the yacht house; while Middle Reef is often even bigger – it's a right that holds a good swell. Outer Reef bares the brunt of the swell working from low to mid tide with rideable rights up to 5m (15ft), unsurfed except by hell men.

L'endroit à checker par méga-houle de nord quand ça ferme partout sur la côte. Plusieurs spots: Le 'Cobble Dump' est une gauche impressionante qui casse sur des rochers à tous moments de la marée mais elle est rarement surfée. Inner Reef est une droite bien protégée (1,5-2m quand ça fait 2,5-3m à Saltburn) avec des vagues faciles et un endroit idéal pour ramer depuis le Yacht Club. Middle Reef fait toujours 50cms à 1m de plus, c'est une droite qui tient le gros. Outer Reef reçoit la houle de plein fouet de marée basse à mi-marée. Des droites surfables jusqu'à 4-5m, sans personne.

2. Sandsend Bay – Caves

Found underneath the cliffs in the left-hand corner of the bay, there's easy access to this break from the car park at the bottom of Lythe Bank. You'll get a long ride with an easy paddle out, which works up to 2m (6ft), but the break will start to bounce off the cliffs at high tide. The bay provides good shelter from strong W winds.

Située sous les falaises dans le coin gauche de la baie, son accés est facile depuis le parking en bas de Lythe Bank. La vague, plutôt longue et facile à atteindre à la rame, fonctionne jusqu'à un bon mètre cinquante. A marée haute, la vague rebondit sur la falaise: sortez avant. Bien abrité en cas de forts vents d'Ouest.

Beach

A classic beach with waves about quarter of a metre bigger than North Bay. It's a good indicator for the rest of the coast, but the beach itself can become crowded.

Un bon beach-break souvent un peu plus gros que North Bay qui est un bon indicateur de l'état des vagues sur la côte. Pas mal de monde donc, marche par swell de Nord et d'Est.

3. Whitby

 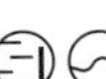  

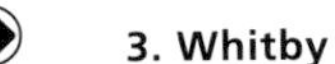

A good wave works on similar conditions as Sandsend and has a consistent left. There can be a hollow right breaking down the W side of the pier on an E swell.

Cette gauche consistente marche dans les mêmes conditions que Sandsend. Une droite bien creuse peut casser sur le côté Ouest de la jetée avec un swell d'est.

Scarborough Point

East coast secret spot

4. Robin Hood's Bay

This can often be the only place working on the E coast, but it's rarely surfed due to a long walk across the reef.

A essayer si rien ne marche ailleurs. Un marche pénible sur le reef limite le nombre de candidats.

5. Scarborough North Bay

All three waves are along a half kilometre stretch of sand and work on any swells.

Ces trés vagues marchent par n'importe quelle houle sur une étendue de sable de moins d'un km, contrairement à

Supersucks

Supersucks is a short, fickle wave at the N end of the bay and is best on a large SE swell.

Supersucks, une vague courte et aléatoire à l'extrémité nord de la baie, à checker par grosse houle de SE.

Middle Peak

A fun wave for beginner to intermediate surfers.

La vague préférée des débutants car sympa et facile.

Rights

On large, lined-up N swells, a wave breaks off the kelp-covered point. Access is through the tunnel S of the bay.

En général recouvert d'algues, ce pic fonctionne jusqu'à deux mètres avec un gros swell de nord bien rangé.

6. Scarborough South

When it's onshore at North Bay, South Bay tends to clean up N swells as they wrap around the harbour. On a SE swell, peaky high tide lefts and rights are popular with bodyboarders, and are crowded at weekends. Unsurfed reefs can be found at the far end of the bay. Park on the Foreshore, Spa, and Valley roads.

Quand le vent est onshore sur North Bay, South Bay a tendance à s'arranger avec les houles de nord qui s'enroulent autour du port du bout de la baie. Si ça vient du SE, on trouve des pics de gauches et droites à marée haute. Appréciée des jeunes en biscotte et donc pas mal fréquenté le week-end. Des spots plus tranquilles au bout de la baie. Laissez la caisse sur la Foreshore Rd, le Spa et Valley Rue.

7. Cayton Bay

The Point

Even on the messiest of days, swell wraps around the point into a calm bay, producing a fast, hollow ride. It works up to 3m (10ft) on huge N swells and can be world class, but strong rips, long paddles, wide sets, sewage, access and parking difficulties often put off all but a staunch local crew.

Même les jours les plus pourris, cette vague s'enroule dans une baie calme pour donner des sections creuses et rapides. Fonctionne jusqu'à 3 mètres sur une houle énorme de Nord. Ce peut être un must mais queqlues inconvéninets du style: forts courants, rame démente, des séries qui décalent et un accés et un parking pas évidents. En décourage beaucoup sauf une poignée d'irréductibles locaux.

Pumphouse

A fickle wave breaks with a huge clean N swell over a shallow suck rock in front of the old pumphouse. This can produce a wave at low-tide, but only on a SE swell. Park at the surf shop.

Une vague capricieuse qui marche plutôt par une houle propre et énorme de nord. Casse dans peu d'eau et suce pas mal en face d'une ancienne station de pompage. Peut aussi marcher à marée basse mais avec swell de SE.

Bunkers

A horseshoe-shaped sandbar produces hollow lefts and rights on a clean N swell. It's often packed at weekends and holidays.

Un banc de sable en forme de fer à cheval produit des vagues creuses par une houle de nord bien nette. Gavé aux heures de pointe.

8. Skeleton Reef

A recently discovered secret spot 8km (5mi) S of Scarborough. An intense, heaving wave, popular with transvestites and cross dressers. Watch out for the odd submerged motorbike. A local named Dennis rules the spot: don't cross him, you have been warned. Respect expected.

Récemment découvert, ce secret spot se trouve à 8km au sud de Scarborough. Une vague intense. Faites gaffe d'abord à une vieille moto submergée mais surtout à Dennis, un local pas fin qui sévit souvent; ne le droppez pas sinon... Secret spots parmi les secret spots, profil bas!

9. Filey Bay

Only surfed by locals under heavy wind and storm swell conditions, this break is not a quality wave but fun peaks hold up due to the protection of Filey Brigg.

Encore une vagues de locaux qui a quand même l'avantage d'être protégée des tempêtesgrâce à Filey Brigg. Pas une super vague mais de quoi s'amuser.

10. Primrose Valley

This sleeping beauty is rarely surfed as it only works under perfect conditions: a clean, large N swell. Beware of strong rips and the 'old guys' who rule it.

Un peu au Sud de Filey BAY, ce spot à moitié secret est rarement surfé car ne fonctionnant qu'avec des conditions optima, à savoir un bon swell nickel de nord. Attention aux courants et aux vieux locaux qui font la loi.

11. Withernsea

Only surfed when a huge swell is running and the rest of the East Coast is blown out, this break tends to produce mainly lefts.

Le dernier recours et seulement en cas d'énorme houle quand toute la côte sature. Plutôt des gauches. Parking directement sur la plage.

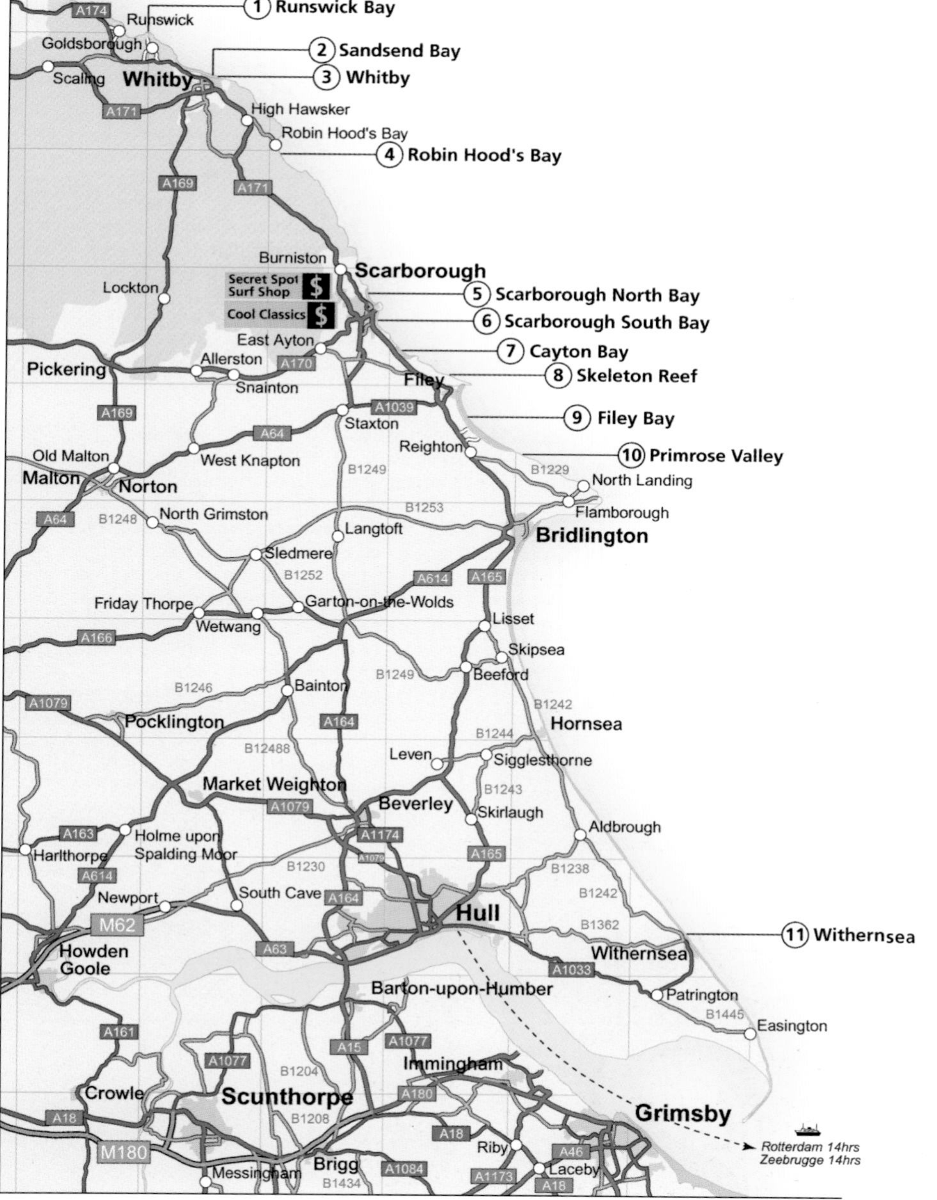

East Anglia

1. East Runton

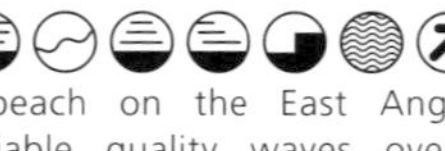

The premier surfing beach on the East Anglian coastline produces reliable quality waves over a shingle-sand bottom. The break has three peaks: the W most is a long right while the second is a left and slow right split by a sewage pipe. The third breaks over a reef made up of flint and rock and is mainly a left with a slower right, but all need a N swell to work. At high tide the shore break falls onto sharp flintstones: care should be taken as cuts can easily become infected due to untreated sewage from the short outfall pipe which has been polluting this break for 30 years. Anglian water has promised to remove it and build the region's first ever treatment plant. Many local surfers will obviously be happy to see water quality improve, but are sceptical as to how the pipe's removal will affect the break – only time will tell. Park above break.

Le berceau du surf de la région d'East Anglia offre des vagues plutôt régulières sur un fond de sable et de galets. Trois pics: le plus à l'ouest est une longue droite, celui du milieu une gauche et une droite molle séparée par une canalisation d'égoût. Le dernier casse sur un reef constitué de pierre et de silex, plutôt en gauche avec une droite plus lente. A marée haute, le shore break explose sur de silex tranchants, attention aux coupures qui peuvent facilement s'infecter à cause des risques élevés de pollution. Marche par swell de Nord, avec des courants quand c'est gros. Parking au-dessus du spot. Les rejets d'égoûts polluent ce break depuis 30 ans. On promet d'enlever tout ça bientôt et de construire une station de retraitement, ce que les locaux apprécieront sûrement sauf si l'enlèvement des tuyaux modifie le break, qui vivra verra.

Traditional Norfolk crab boats, East Runton

2. Cromer

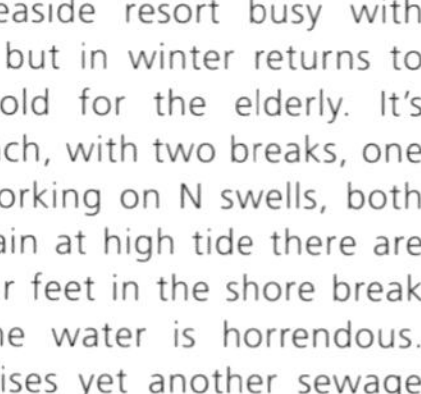

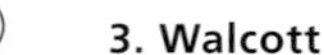

This is a popular family seaside resort busy with tourists during the summer, but in winter returns to being a retirement stronghold for the elderly. It's another sand and shingle beach, with two breaks, one on either side of the pier, working on N swells, both best at mid to high tide. Again at high tide there are sharp stones to mash up your feet in the shore break and again be careful as the water is horrendous. Cromer Pier cunningly disguises yet another sewage outfall pipe which turdinates at the end of the pier. Solids, sanitary towels and contraceptives are frequently seen in the water. Many local surfers have vowed never to surf this break again after experiencing the repulse first-hand. With onshore conditions the evidence is there for all to see, scattered a few hundred metres down the beach.

Petite station familiale agitée en été par le tourisme, elle retourne à son état de citadelle pour les vieux en hiver. Une autre plage de galets et de sable avec deux spots de part et d'autre de la jetée. Marche par swell de nord, préférablement de mi-marée à marée haute, même si le shore-break de marée haute peut vous lacérer les pieds sur les quelques tas de cailloux tranchants. La jetée de Cromer sournoisement dissimule une sortie d'égoûts, dont les rejets donnent la gerbe dans l'eau: tampons, capotes et autres délices font souvent partie du décor. Certains locaux se sont jurés de ne plus se remettre à l'eau après une expérience malheureuse. Avec des vents de mer, les délices s'éparpillent sur quelques centaines de mètres sur la plage.

3. Walcott

Short beach with a succession of wooden groynes. It's inconsistent and, as with other East Anglian waves, heavily affected by wind conditions. The best surf breaks on the outer sandbars at low tide.

Petite plage avec une succession d'épis de bois. Le spot manque de consistance et dépend terriblement des conditions de vent. Le meilleur spot est sur les bancs du fond à marée basse.

4. Happisburgh

Another N-facing sand and shingle beach which has a fickle peak with a longer right, but is heavily affected by wind conditions. It's at its best at mid tide. The water quality is bad.

Une autre plage de sable et de galets avec un pic capricieux et des droites plus longues, qui marchent mieux à mi-marée. Ne supporte pas le vent, l'eau est criticable.

5. Scratby

From the small cliff-top car park, two peaks become apparent: the first produces quality rights on strong S swells while the other, a decent left on N swells, is a short walking distance away. The take-off is critical followed by a short hollow wall with plenty of push. The shore break can be heavy and also works on E winds at low to mid tide after which wave quality deteriorates rapidly.

Depuis le parking en haut de la falaise, deux pics se détachent. Le premier offre de bonnes droites avec un forte houle de Sud. L'autre qu'on rejoint rapidement en marchant, est une gauche correcte par houle de nord. Take-off raide et petite épaule creuse et puissant. Le shore-break peut être carton. Marche aussi par vents d'Est et de marée basse à mi-marée après quoi la vague se pourrit rapidement.

East Anglian groyne

Mike Guymer, East Runton

NEIL WATSON

Paul Wicker, East Anglian secret spot

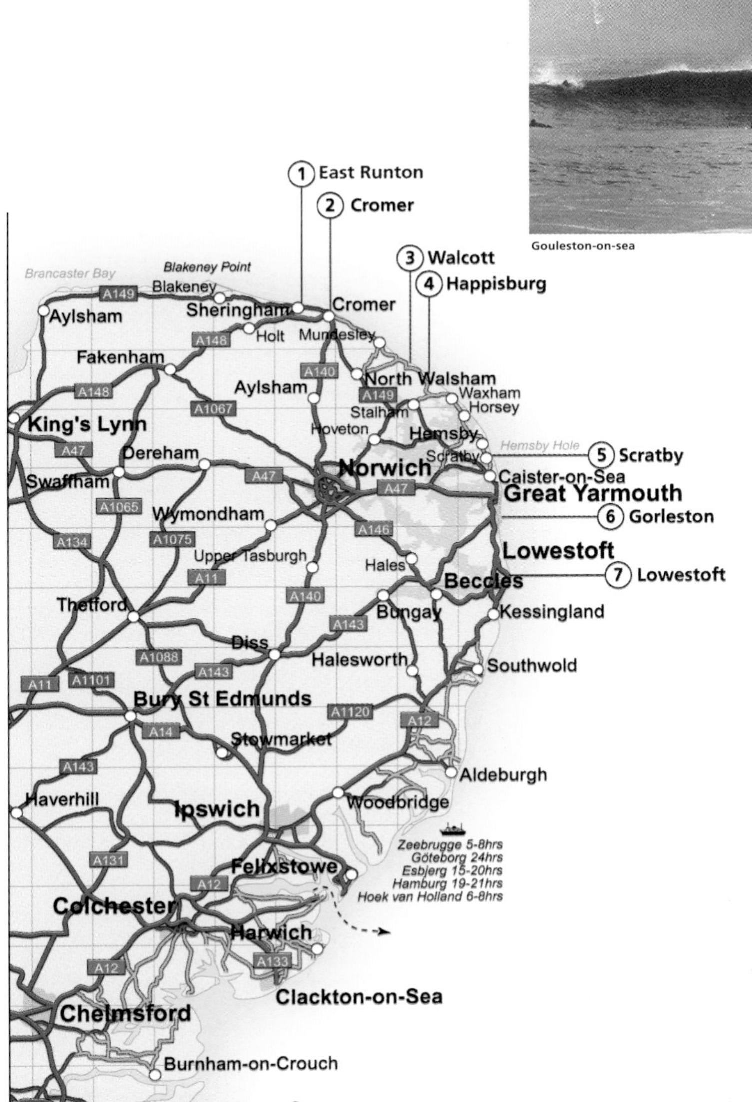

NEIL WATSON

Gouleston-on-sea

6. Gorleston

A popular but inconsistent beach that produces slow peaks. From the clifftop you can see 'Scroby Sands', a vast offshore sandbar that blocks much of the swell. To work, however, it needs a strong swell; a N swell is the most reliable, from mid to high tide. The promenade with its clusters of cafés, bars and amusement arcades has ample parking space. The water quality is bad as the port services the oil and gas industry and the accumulated pollution from this and sewage outfalls in the River Yare combine to make a foul situation.

En haut des falaises, on peut voir 'Scroby Sands', un méga-banc de sable au large qui bloque la houle. Il faut donc un méga-swell, nord de préférence, de mi-marée à marée haute. Le transit de déchets des industries pétrolières et autres ajouté aux rejets d'égoûts dans la rivière Yare rend l'eau vraiment gerbique.

7. Lowestoft

Popular with tourists, surfers and bodyboarders, Lowestoft has numerous peaks producing waves of varying quality, depending on swell direction and strength. Peaks on either side of the Claremont are favoured. Rides are often cut short by wooden groynes. A vast offshore sandbar which extends to Kessingland takes much of the power out of the waves. Rips become a problem on bigger swells.

Lowestoft a pas mal de pics, de qualité variable en fonction de la direction et de la puissance de la houle, mieux de part et d'autre de Claremont. Les vagues sont souvent interrompues par des jetées de bois. Encore une fois, un vaste banc de sable au large qui s'étend jusqu'à Kessingland absorbe l'essentiel de la houle.

NEIL WATSON

Lowestoft – Claremont Pier

South Coast

1. Paignton

E or NE winds blow wind swell in from the Channel. When winds turn offshore, Paignton will work for a few hours. Towards Lyme Regis there are a number of other spots that work in the similar conditions.

Les vents d'est ou nord-est soulèvent une houle de vent en Manche. Lorsque les vents tournent offshore, le spot marchera pendant quelques heures.

2. Kimmeridge Bay

The Ledges

Check these classic well-covered reefs that hold waves up to to 2.5m (8ft) with a ground swell in the Channel. There's a mellow wave that breaks a kilometre out to sea on a big day and though prone to blowing out easily, this is better as a left, although rights are also good. Crowded, especially with longboarders.

Des reefs 'classiques' avec pas mal d'eau qui tiennent jusqu'à 2.5m avec un swell en Manche. C'est une vague douce qui peut péter à 1.5 km du bord les jours de gros. Elle ne dure cependant pas très longtemps. Même si la gauche est meilleure, les droites sont pas mal. Bondé tous les jours; les longboarders y sont particulièrement nombreux.

The Bay

Located in the middle of the bay, this wave breaks a long way out. Similar to The Ledges (above) but has more power and is never as crowded. Occasionally, if it's onshore and big, it's great – an underrated wave!

Située au milieu de la baie, elle casse loin du bord. Ressemble à 'The Ledges' mais a plus de puissance et n'est jamais aussi peuplée. Parfois bon lorsque c'est onshore et gros. Une vague sous-estimée!

Broad Bench

A long powerful right with a short, hollow, shallow left, but there's a long walk to the break and restricted access. Go Monday to Friday as it's situated in an army firing range. Do not attempt to surf if it's off limits.

Une droite puissante et longue avec une courte gauche ultra creuse avec très peu de fond. L'accès est limité du lundi au vendredi étant donné que la vague se situe sur un champ de tir. Ne surtout pas tenter de surfer hors des limites! Les locaux 'purs et durs' ont en marre des artistes de la taxe.

3. Chapman's Pool

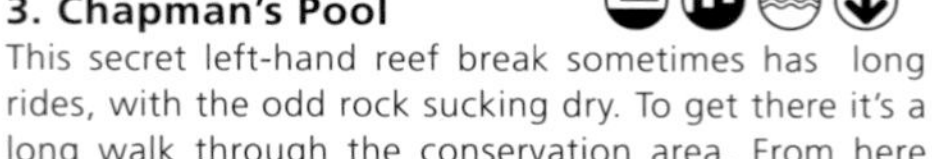

This secret left-hand reef break sometimes has long rides, with the odd rock sucking dry. To get there it's a long walk through the conservation area. From here two other breaks are visible: one, a right, is as yet unsurfed, while the other, Cloudbreak, breaks a quarter of a kilometre out to sea.

Une gauche de récif prétendue secrète qui peut dérouler sur une longue distance, avec un étrange rocher 'aspirant' à fond. Pour s'y rendre une longue marche à travers la zone protégée est nécessaire. De cet endroit, deux autres spots sont visibles, notamment une droite, pas encore surfée à ce jour. L'autre Cloudbreak, déferle à 400m du bord.

4. Bournemouth Pier

A crowded spot with the most popular peak on the E side of the pier. Don't use the pier to get out back – if you can't paddle out, you shouldn't be out. Drop-ins here are inevitable. Park in front of the peak.

Un spot bondé avec le pic le plus connu sur le côté est de la jetée. Ne pas emprunter la jetée pour sortir – si vous n'êtes pas capable de ramer, c'est que votre place n'est pas au large. C'est la guerre au pic. Il y a un parking en face du pic.

CHRIS POWER

Bournemouth Pier

5. Boscombe Pier

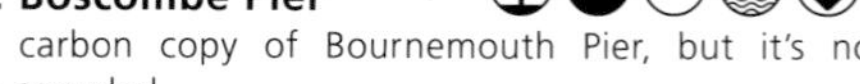

A carbon copy of Bournemouth Pier, but it's not as crowded.

La copie conforme de Bournemouth Pier, mais moins de monde.

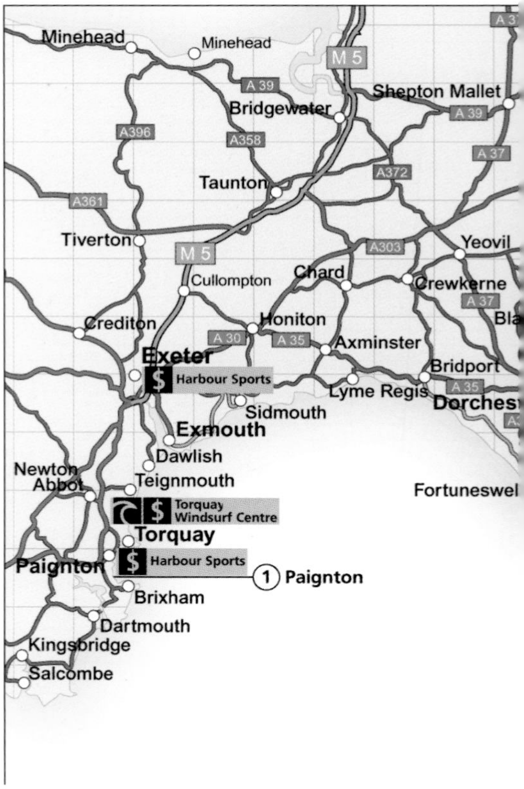

6. Southbourne

A succession of groynes between Boscombe and Hergistbury Head produce hard-breaking waves, picking up more swell than both piers, however, it's badly affected by the wind. If there's groundswell here K Bay will be going ballistic. Loads of young local bodyboarders.

Une succession d'épis de cailloux entre Boscombe et Hergistbury Head, peuvent donner des vagues très franches, recueillant plus de swell que les deux jetées mais elles sont plus gâchées par le vent. S'il y a un bon swell ici, K-bay sera parfait. Beaucoup de jeunes locaux qui font du bodyboard.

7. Highcliffe Area

This picks up more swell than the piers, but breaks a long way out and rolls on for a long way. A slow right can be amping if it's small at the piers. There's no protection from the wind.

Accepte plus la houle que les jetées mais casse au large et déroule sur une longue distance. Une droite un peu lente qui peut s'avérer bonne lorsque c'est petit près des jetées. La vague n'est pas abritée du vent.

8. Isle of Wight

From Freshwater and Compton Bay down to St Catherine's Point are various SW-facing breaks, which can get pretty good.

De Freshwater et Compton Bay jusqu'à St Catherine's Point, on peut trouver toutes sortes de spots exposés sud-ouest qui peuvent se révéler plutôt bons.

9. Hayling Island

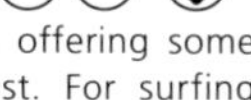

This is more popular with windsurfers offering some of the best conditions on the S coast. For surfing there are two spots at either end of the island.

Plus connue des windsurfeurs, elle offre parmi les meilleures conditions de la côte sud. On recense deux spots de surf, chacun à une extrémité de l'île.

ALEX WILLIAMS

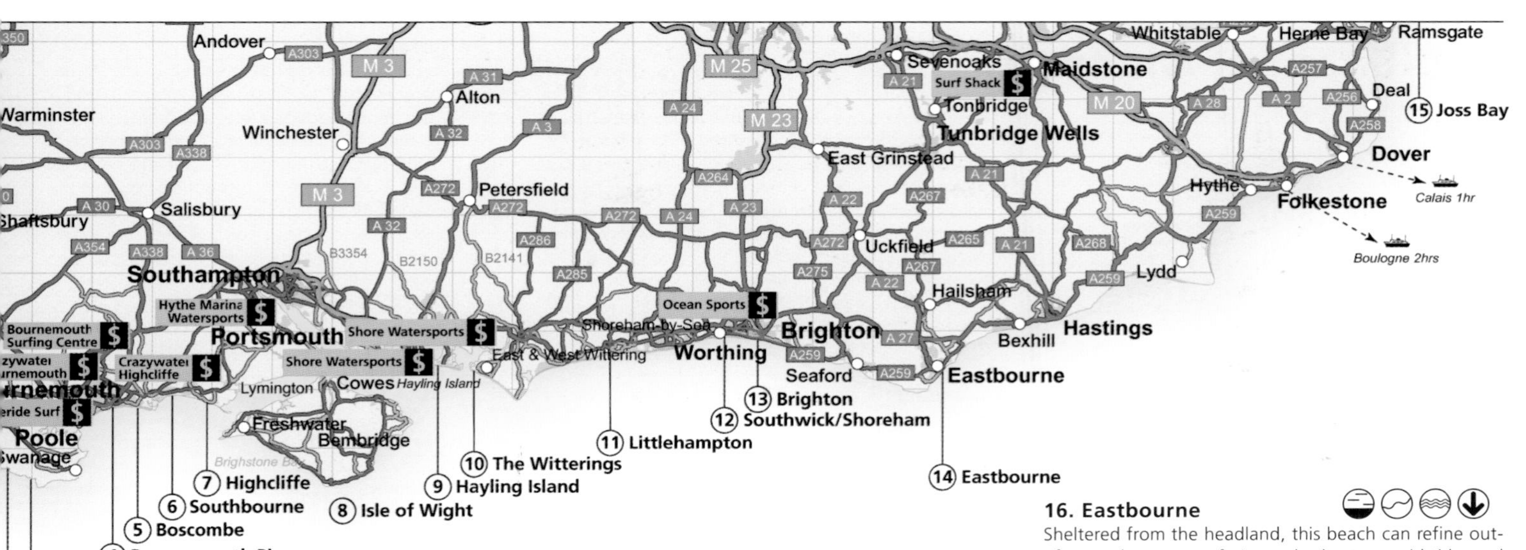

10. The Witterings

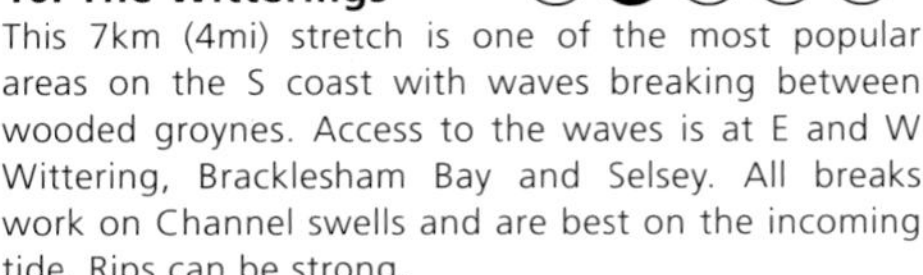

This 7km (4mi) stretch is one of the most popular areas on the S coast with waves breaking between wooded groynes. Access to the waves is at E and W Wittering, Bracklesham Bay and Selsey. All breaks work on Channel swells and are best on the incoming tide. Rips can be strong.

Cette zone qui s'étend sur 6kms est une des plus réputée de la côte sud avec des vagues cassant entre des pontons de bois. L'accès aux vagues se fait par Wittering Est ou Ouest, Bracklesham Bay et Selsey. Tous les spots marchent avec des swells provenant de la Manche et sont meilleurs avec la marée montante.

11. Littlehampton

A fickle rivermouth beach break that works only on large tides. It can be a classic but is always crowded with a keen bunch of locals. Still, worth a check if you're passing but don't hold your breath as it's very exposed and gets blown out quickly.

Un beachbreak à l'embouchure d'une rivière qui ne marche que par grosse marée. Ca peut être excellent mais y'a toujours du monde avec un groupe de locaux bien motivés. A checker si vous passez par là mais ne vous angoissez pas pour rien, le spot est très exposé et se dégrade très rapidement avec le vent.

12. Southwick/Shoreham

The main breaks (The Hot Pipe, Arms and New Beach) all offer good shelter from the wind with each break having its day during an average wind swell. All breaks work best at mid-tide with moderate SW winds. Friendly locals, a break for all types of surfer.

Les spots réguliers (The Hot Pipe, Arms et New Beach) sont bien protégés du vent avec chacun de ces spots marchant à un moment donné sur un swell correct. Ca marche mieux à mi-marée avec des vents modérés de sud-ouest. Convient à tous niveaux. Les locaux sont cools.

13. Brighton

The West Pier

Shallow sand bars provide fun, slow peeling lefts and rights and on a low tide ground swell. The Pier can be one of the area's best breaks, a Mecca for Brighton's large longboard community. Beware, this break is very exposed to the wind.

Dans peu d'eau, les bancs de sable donnent des gauches et des droites bien fun avec des gauches lentes. A marée basse, par bon swell, le Pier peut devenir un break top, la Mecque de la communauté des longboarders de Brighton. Avis, le spot est très exposé au vent.

14. The Wedge

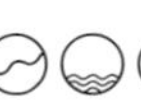

A fast, peeling right-hander breaks just off the beach, with a large groyne providing shelter from the wind. It's the area's best bodyboard wave but watch out for the heavy shore break and a competitive crew who surf there religiously.

Une droite rapide qui casse juste au large de la plage, avec une grosse jetée qui offre un bel abri par rapport au vent. C'est la meilleure vague de bodyboard du coin. On y trouve des mecs qui fracassent frénétiquement jusque dans le shorebreak le plus carton.

15. The Marina

Brighton's most sheltered break works best at mid-tide on a strong SW when ast peeling waves break over a shallow flint and chalk reef. The paddle out is easy but the crowd isn't. Don't venture out unless you're confident in the water.

Le spot le plus abrité de Brighton. Ca marche mieux à mi-marée avec de forts vents de sud-ouest. Les vagues cassent un peu en barre sur un fond de silex et de craie. La rame est cool contrairement aux locaux. N'y allez pas si vous n'êtes pas sûr de votre take-off.

16. Eastbourne

Sheltered from the headland, this beach can refine out-of-control storm surf. It works best at mid-tide and when it's big. Strong SE wind swells can offer relief from the summer heat but are often weak and fickle.

Niché dans un coin du cap, le spot peut filtrer certaines des plus grosses tempêtes. Ca marche mieux à mi-marée quand c'est gros. De bonnes houles de sud-ouest peuvent offrir une belle alternative à la pression des autres spots mais c'est mou et rarement bon.

17. Joss Bay

The most popular beach in the area gives beach break peaks mainly in big N winter swells. Tides from incoming mid to high are preferable.

La plage le plus populaire avec un beach break surtout avec les grosses houles de nord en hiver.

Brighton

OCEANSPORTS

Littlehampton

PETER CADE

The Channel Islands

Guernsey

1. Perelle Bay

Dom Hue

This is the jewel in the crown of Guernsey surf: it includes a variety of waves at mid to high tide and a big wave spot off the island. Far out to sea, and very rocky surfing, Perelle is generally left to the 'experts' and can be a daunting prospect.

La petite merveille du surf de l'île, comprenant une grande variété de vagues de la mi-marée à marée haute; c'est également le spot de gros de l'île. Vague au large et de rocher, Perelle est le plus souvent une gauche (d'après les habitués) et peut devenir une aventure intrépide.

The Peak

This big right breaks a long way out in the centre of Perelle Bay and is reached from the Islet of Dom Hue. The peak is very shifty and on a big day it's hard to suss the take-off point. To get there you have to pass two excellent breaks behind the island.

Cette grosse droite casse un long moment au centre de la baie de Perelle; on l'atteint par l'ilôt de Dom Hue. Le pic est traître et, un jour de gros, il est dur de repérer le take-off. Pour s'y rendre il faut passer deux excellentes vagues derriére l'ilot, relativement peu surfées.

The Left

This is the wave that's ridden most at Perelle. It generally picks up more swell than other breaks on the island. Because it's 300m (260yd) out to sea, it can suffer if the wind is blowing, but it provides the best shaped and longest rideable left on the islands. Breaking off or around a rocky outcrop, you can catch long, walling waves well into the shallows. Best on a smaller tide, it also can hold a swell up. Owing to the rocks and its positioning, this is only for the experienced surfers. Get caught on a big day and the rip can wash you to the other side of the island. On a small day you can lose a fin on the rocks below the surface as the tide recedes.

C'est la vague la plus surfée à Perelle. Elle reccueile plus de houles que les autres vagues de l'île. Parce qu'elle est située à 300m du bord, elle peut pâtir du vent, mais c'est la plus belle et la plus longue gauche des îles. Déferlant le long de rochers à fleur d'eau, on peut y surfer de longs murs sur des hauts-fonds. Meilleur lors de petites marées, la vague tient une houle de 3m. En raison des rochers et de son emplacement, la vague est réservée aux surfeurs confirmés. Un jour de petit, on risque de perdre une dérive lorsque la marée descend.

The Right

This is probably the best wave on Guernsey – it breaks on a big swell with a large tide. A sucking take-off, right next to a group of rocks, propels you onto a powerful, peeling wave and over a couple of large rocks that emerge as the tide drops. Don't get caught on the inside.

Certainement la meilleure vague de Guernsey, qui ne casse que par gros swell, lors d'une grosse marée. Un take-off aérien, tout près d'une barre de rochers, vous propulse dans une vague plutôt décoiffante, au dessus de deux gros rochers qui affleurent lorsque la marée descend. Ne vous faites pas avoir dans l'inside! Bonne chance!

2. Vazon Bay

Main Peak

The centre of Guernsey's surfing is predominantly a right-hander breaking from the centre of the bay diagonally towards the land drainage pipe. It's usually at its best from half tide up to the start of the backwash (caused by waves hitting the wall), and occasionally it's superb just before the high tide.

Le pôle du surf à Guernsey; une droite déferle en travers du centre de la baie vers la conduite d'égoût. Normalement, la vague est au meilleur de sa forme de la mi-marée jusqu'au début du backwash (dû au fait que les vagues rebondissent sur un mur), qui rend le spot impossible à surfer. De temps en tempsc'est parfait uste avant que la marée ne devienne trop haute.

Left

When the tide is too high for the beach, the left on the reef starts to break. It can offer an exhilarating drop with a fast, occasionally spitting, section. Increase your adrenaline by a confrontation with Nipple Rock smack in the middle of the reef.

Quand la marée devient trop haute pour la plage, la gauche du récif commence à fonctionner. Cela peut donner un super drop avec, de temps à autre, une section rapide qui en jette. Le 'Nipple Rock', en plein milieu du récif, vous permettra d'avoir des montées d'adrénaline tout à fait honorables!

Right

This wave needs a spring tide to cover the bigger rocks sufficiently. It's better than the left, providing a sucking take-off followed by a longish ride into the shallows. The right only works up to about 2m (6ft).

Cette vague a besoin d'une marée d'équinoxe pour recouvrir suffisamment les rochers les plus gros. Elle est meilleure que la gauche et commence par un take-off dans le vide suivi par un long surf sur les hauts-fonds. Cette droite marche jusqu'à environ 2m.

T' Other Side

The other side of the reef comes into its own on a big swell when the beach and the reef are closing out. It can provide long rights from the reef diagonally across the beach. There is no doubt that when everything gels this break can be classic.

L'autre côté du reef prend la relève lors des gros swells quand la plage et le récif ferment. La vague peut se transformer en de longues droites puis à travers la plage. Cela peut devenir un must quand les conditions sont réunies. L'absence de courants puissants la transforme en un surf pépère.

Pooh Poohs

This wave breaks over sand, with a peak that can be ridden left or right. The rides are usually short, very fast and break predominantly right. Rarer, equally fast, hollow lefts also wind across the beach into one of the ubiquitous land drainage pipes.

Une vague déferle sur du sable, avec un pic qui part en droite et en gauche. La vague est habituellement courte, très rapide et la droite marche plus souvent. Plus rare, également rapide et creuse, la gauche s'enroule le long d'une conduite de drainage; encore une!

3. Portinfer

A popular bay picks up more swell than Vazon, offering a consistent half tide break. At half tide a peak in the centre provides lefts and rights. As the tide drops the waves break more powerfully on the N headland to provide a right across the narrow part of the bay. On a small tide, a respectable left can be found breaking off the rocks just below the port.

Une baie réputée qui chope plus de swell que Vazon, offrant un break consistant à mi-marée. A mi-marée aussi, un pic au centre fournit des gauches et des droites. Quand la marée baisse, les vagues déferlent avec plus de puissance au nord du promontoire et balacent une droite à travers la partie étroite de la baie. Lors d'une petite marée, une gauche correcte peut casser sur de la caillasse juste en dessous du port.

4. Fort le Marchant

A difficult rock reef break wrapping around a headland (almost to 90 degrees) and throwing just off the rocks with a shoulder walling up into deep water. When everywhere else is totally huge, and blown out, head here and watch probably the best wave on the island break.

Un spot de récif difficile qui s'enroule autour d'un promontoire, et se jette sur des rochers avec une épaule venant mourir en eau profonde. Cette vague tourne à 90 degrés.Quand toutest énorme et impraticable, c'est certainement la meilleure vague de l'île.

Jersey

1. Greve De Lacq

A few times in winter, normally when the swells are huge, a visit to this little beach can be a good move. It only works on a 11m (33ft) tide.

Parfois en hiver, normalement quand le swell est énorme, cette petite plage vaut le déplacement. Marche seulement lors des marées à forts coefficients.

GERRY GEORGE

Sam George, Greve de Lacq

2. Plemont Beach

Only on big swells will you find worthwhile waves here. When these conditions are present surfing can be extremely rewarding: good waves, beautiful surroundings.

On trouvera des vagues valables seulement lors des gros swells. Quand les conditions sont réunies, on peut être récompensé par de bonnes vagues dans un joli cadre.

3. Stinky Bay

Located at the N end of St Ouen's Bay, this works like a point and will always be crowded. The name Stinky Bay comes from rotting seaweed in the gulley where you paddle out.

Située à l'extrême nord de la baie de St-Ouen. Marche comme un 'point' et sera toujours bondée. Le nom Stinky Bay ('baie puante') est due à la présence d'algues pourissantes dans lesquelles on rame.

4. Secrets

Long tubey, reef quality rides are surfable up to 3m (10ft). A left starts to work when the swell is over 1.2m (4ft).

Vagues de reef avec un long tube, surfable au dessus de 3m. Une gauche commence à marcher à partir d'1m.

5. Watersplash

If there's no swell at Watersplash then there's no swell anywhere. This makes this spot the most popular on the island. Watch out for rocks at low tide but beware of rips when it's really big.

S'il n'y a pas de swell à Watersplash alors il n'y a rien nulle part. C'est pourquoi c'est le spot le plus populaire de l'île. Faites gaffe aux rochers à marée basse et des chutes lorsque c'est gros.

6. Les Brayes

The waves here can pack a punch in this medium to big wave spot. The dropping tide is best and there's a rip running from S to N. There's an easy paddle out around the tower.

Un spot de vagues moyennes à grosses où les vagues percutent à max. La marée descendante est la meilleure et il y a une courant du sud au nord. Facile de sortir au niveau de la tour.

GERRY GEORGE

Sam George, Petit Port

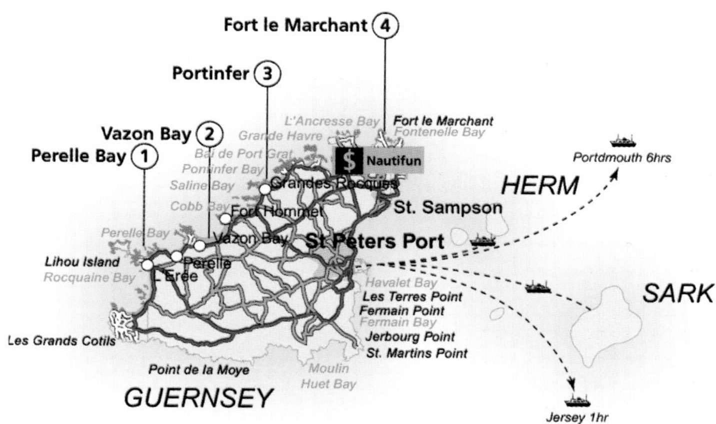

7. Corbière Reef

This break only starts to work when the swell reaches 5m (15ft). It has only ever been surfed by a handful of experienced locals and it's unlikely as a travelling surfer that you will have the right equipment. If you do decide to tackle it, ask the locals for advice, which they are more than happy to provide. Access is the same as Petit Port.

Ne daigne marcher que lorsque le swell atteint 4 à 5 m.N'a été surfé que par une poignée de locaux expérimentés et il est rare qu'un surfeur de passage ait l'équipement adéquat. Si vous décidez d'aller la taquiner, faites-vous conseiller par les locaux qui seront plus que ravis de vous renseigner. Même accés que pour Petit Port.

GERRY GEORGE

St Ouens Bay

8. Petit Port

Jersey's big wave spot: the right-hander here provides quality barrels up to 5m (15ft). The lower the tide, the more dangerous it becomes. To get out jump off the slipway and a rip will take you to the line up, but your timing is crucial. There is a car park next to the slipway.

Le spot de grosses vagues de Jersey. La droite envoie des tubes jusqu'à 4 à 5 mètres. Plus la marée est basse et plus cela devient dangereux. Le timing est crucial pour se jeter du chantier de construction, un courant vous poussera jusqu'au lineup. Il y a un parking près du chantier.

9. Saint Brelade's Bay

This is a popular tourist beach with windsurfing throughout the year. It receives waves only on the biggest swells when the W-facing breaks are closing out. The best peaks are found by the pier and it will be crowded when it's working.

Un lieu touristique branché où l'on pratique le windsurf tout au long de l'année. Il y a des vagues seulement lors des gros swells quand les spots exposés à l'ouest ferment. Les meilleures pics se trouvent près de la jetée et ils seront bondés lorsque ça marche.

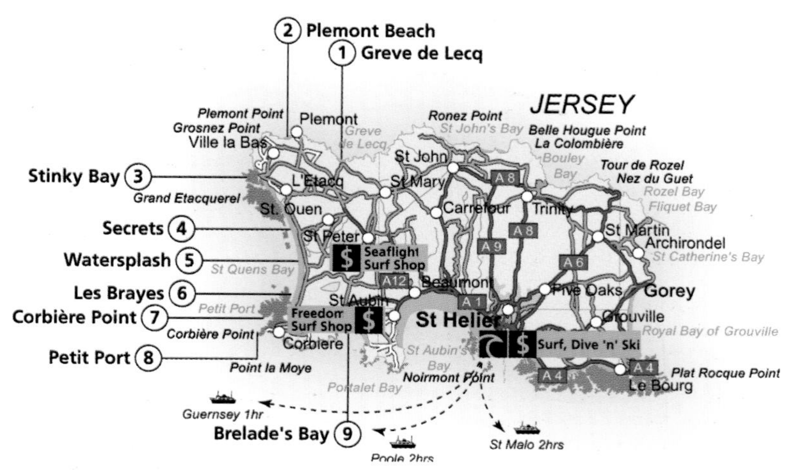

South Devon and Cornwall

1. Porthcurno 

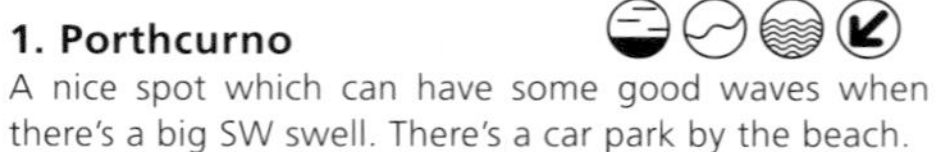

A nice spot which can have some good waves when there's a big SW swell. There's a car park by the beach.

Un bon spot qui peut bien marcher avec un gros swell de Sud-ouest. Méga-parking à côté de la plage.

2. Perranuthanoe  

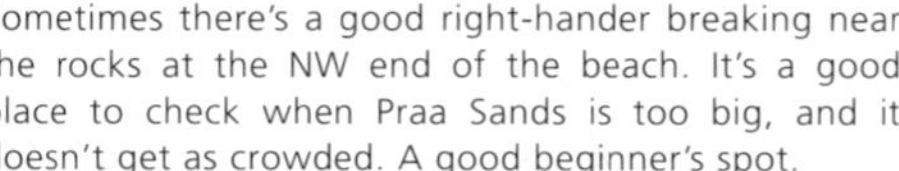

Sometimes there's a good right-hander breaking near the rocks at the NW end of the beach. It's a good place to check when Praa Sands is too big, and it doesn't get as crowded. A good beginner's spot.

Parfois une bonne droite à côté des rochers au nord-ouest de la plage. A checker quand Praa Sands est trop gros ou qu'il y a trop de monde. Bien pour les débutants.

3. Praa Sands 

One of the most popular beaches in the area, with surfers and holidaymakers. Picks up more swell than Perranuthanoe. The N end receives some protection from W winds by the point, off which a fast right sometimes breaks. The E end can have dangerous rips in a big swell. Park by the beach.

Une des plages les plus populaires du coin pour les surfers et les touristes. Prend mieux la houle que Perranuthanoe. L'extrémité nord est abritée des vents d'ouest par le cap, au bout duquel une droite rapide casse de tempe en temps. De l'autre côté, attention aux courants violents quand c'est gros. Parking sur la plage.

4. Porthleven     

Located on the W side of the harbour channel in Porthleven village is England's most talked about and respected reef break. It needs a big SW swell to get it pumping. Low tide is hollow and dangerous and at high tide the wave can be affected by the backwash. More injuries are caused here by flying surfboards than the reef due to the nature of the crowds. Watch out for strong rips when it's big. Park where possible in Porthleven.

Situé à l'ouest de l'entrée du port du village de Porthleven, le reef le plus respecté d'Angleterre, dont on parle souvent dans les chaumières. Exige un gros swell de sud-ouest pour marcher: ses tubes caverneux sont taquinés par les meilleurs surfers anglais qui gardent toujours un oeil attentif sur les conditions locales. A marée basse, c'est creux et dangereux tandis qu'il y a du backwash à marée haute. Les accidents sont plus souvent dûs aux planches perdues qu'au reef à cause de la foule. Méfiance quand c'est gros, il y du jus. Garez-vous dans Porthleven. On parle d'un projet de développement du port: encore un spot menacé!

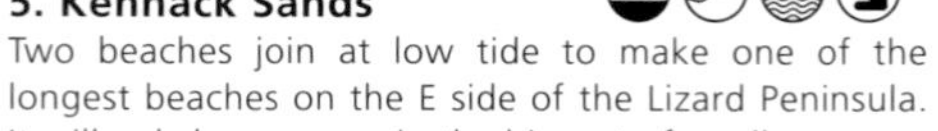

5. Kennack Sands

Two beaches join at low tide to make one of the longest beaches on the E side of the Lizard Peninsula. It will only have waves in the biggest of swells.

Deux plages qui se joignent à marée basse pour faire une des plus longues plages du côté oriental de la Péninsule de Lizard. Des vagues seulement avec des conditions énormes.

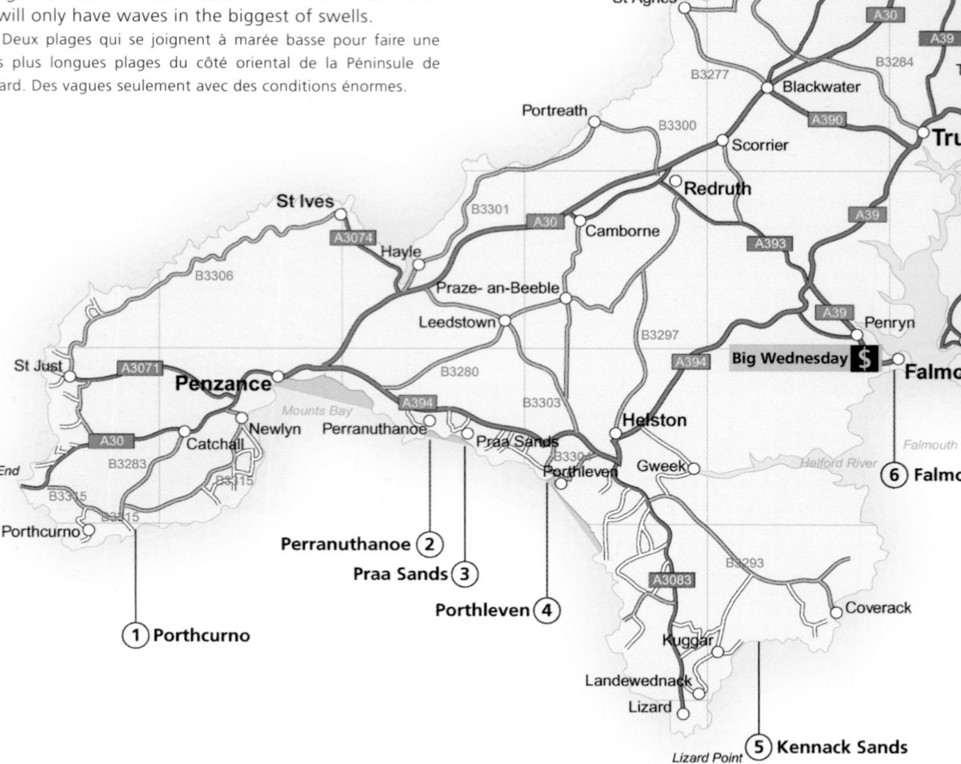

6. Falmouth Bay 

A number of waves working best on storm or SW swells. Maenporth, Swanpool and Gyllyngvase beaches all have waves on their day but word gets out quickly and they are always crowded. Gyllyngvase reef lies between Swanpool and Gyllyngvase beaches and about twice a year offers a good left with a fast take-off and short walling section as the tide covers the reef.

Un certain nombre de vagues qui marchent mieux quand c'est la tempête ou des houles de S-O. Les plages de Maenporth, Swanpool et Gyllyngvase ont toutes des vagues certains jours mais ça se sait vite et il y a pratiquement toujours du monde. Le reef de Gyllyngvase se trouve entre Swanpol et la plage de Gyllyngvase et donne deux fois par an une bonne gauche avec un take-off raide et des petits murs quand la marée recouvre le récif.

SIMON McCOMB

Falmouth Reef

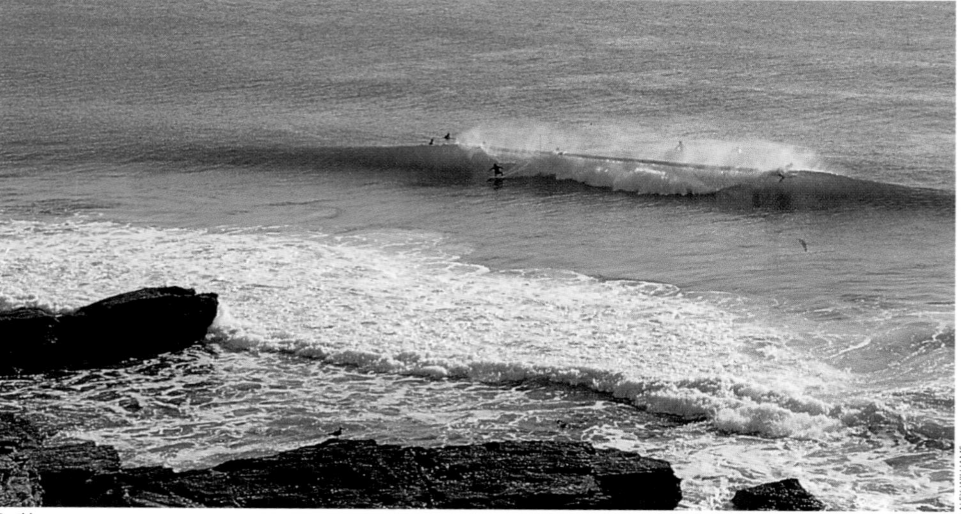
ALEX WILLIAMS

Porthleven

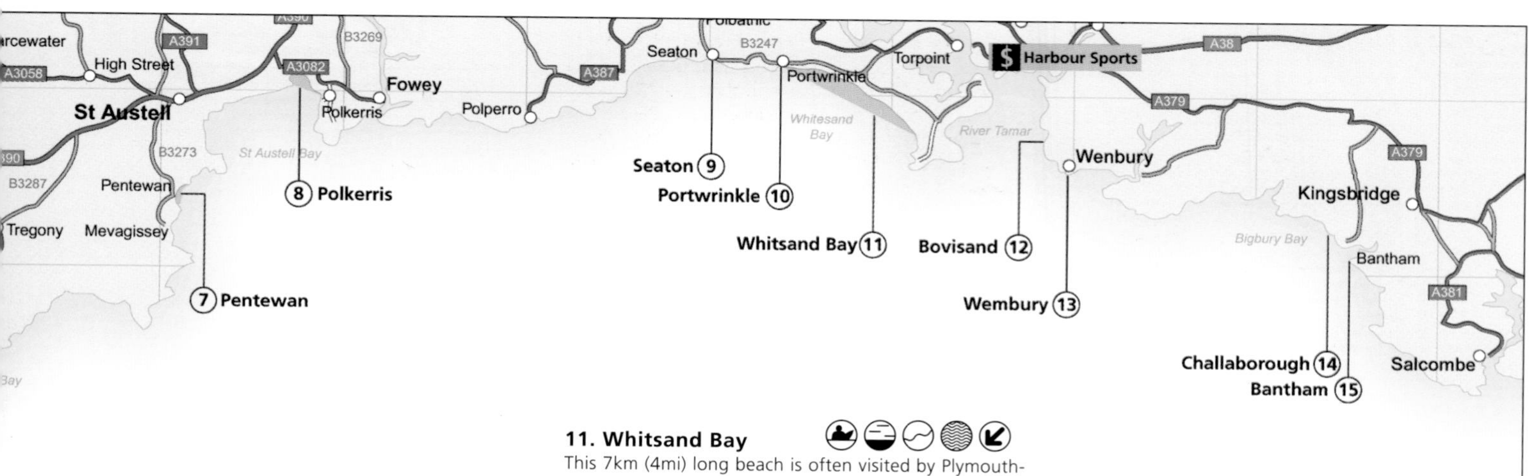

7. Pentewan

A sheltered beach about 6km (4mi) S of St Austell. It only works on a huge S swell and consequently is unlikely to work in the summer. The waves can get quite hollow at high tide when a fast beach break develops.

Par énorme swelde sud, cherchez pas en euvent y être assez creuses à marée haute quand un beach-break rapide se forme.

8. Polkerris

A popular beach which needs a big swell to work.

Encore une plage connue de tous, qui ne marche que pas gros swell.

9. Seaton

This beach, 5km (3mi) to the E of Looe, is quite sheltered. If Whitsands is 1.6m (5ft) expect half-a-metre (2ft-ish) waves at Seaton.

Cinq kms à l'Est de Looe, cette plage est abritée. Si Whitsands fait 1.5 m, ça ne fera que moins de la moitié à Seaton.

10. Portwrinkle

This is at the E end of Whitsand Bay and is usually smaller, but is favoured in big swells. A number of rocks get covered at high tide so watch your fins. Park above the beach and walk down the cliff path.

A l'extrémité Est de Whitsand Bat et normalement 50cms de moins, mieux quand c'est gros donc. Pas mal de rochers sont recouverts à marée haute, faites gaffe aux ailerons. Garez-vous au-dessus de la plage et cherchez le petit chemin qui descend.

11. Whitsand Bay

This 7km (4mi) long beach is often visited by Plymouth-based surfers. Tregantle, in the middle of the beach, works quite well at high tide, but access is restricted by the army who seem to know when the surf is good and always close the path for shooting. Rips are particularly strong here. There's no parking near the beach and it will take a 10-minute walk to get there.

Cette plage, longue de 6kms, est souvent visitée par les surfers de Plymouth. Tregantle au milieu de la plage marche plutôt bien à marée haute mais l'accès est restreint par l'Armée qui semble fermer pour les tirs seulement quand le surf est bon. Attention aux courants! Pas de parking prés de la plage, soyez prêts pour une bonne marche de 10 minutes.

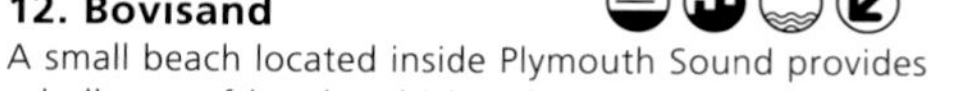

12. Bovisand

A small beach located inside Plymouth Sound provides a hollow reef break, which only works on huge S/SW swell. Very steep take-off, very rare event.

Petite plage situes dans Plymouth Sound, qui marche avec une grosse houle de S/SO. Un take-off bien raide. Ne marche que rarement.

ALEX WILLIAMS

John Copley

Looe

PETER CADE

13. Wembury

On smaller swells low to mid tide is best. The pick of the waves are often the lefts off Blackstone Rocks. Swell is normally half-a-metre smaller than Bantham. A popular place for Plymouth-based surfers.

Quand c'est tout petit, de marée basse à mi-marée. Les meilleurs vagues de la baie sont souvent les gauches de Blackstone Rocks. Ca fait en général 50cms de moins qu'à Bantham.

14. Challaborough

Check this surf with lefts off the cliffs when the sandbanks are happening. A low tide right-hand point works to the right of the beach and can be good. SW or W winds are OK.

Beach break qui donne des gauches vers les falaises quand les bancs sont favorables; Une droite à marée basse marche à droite de la plage, ça peut même être bon. Tient les vents de sud-ouest et ouest.

15. Bantham

Catching the most swell in the area with good beach peaks and tubing rights breaking into the mouth of the River Avon, Bantham rules on a pushing tide.

Bantham chope la plupart des houles dans le coin avec de bons pics et des droites qui tubent en sortie de la riviere Avon.

PETER CADE

Portwrinkle

ALEX WILLIAMS

Bantham

Right: Team
rider Jo Brown.
Below: Nigel —
surfer, shaper,
and Big Sato.
Photo: Alex Williams.
RETAIL 01637 850071
FACTORY / FAX 01637 852042
1973 — 1998 celebrating
25 YEARS OF EXCELLENCE
WORLD CLASS SURFBOARDS
NEWQUAY CORNWALL ENGLAND

The West Country

The most consistent, quality surfing conditions in England are found in the south west. Many surfers from 'up the line' have left work and family to share in a year-round lifestyle that has changed little in the last 20 years. On the coldest mornings in February you'll find surfers paddling out all along the coastline for a quick 'blast' before work or a more leisurely session for those probably with no work to go to.

There are perhaps a hundred or so surfing beaches in Cornwall and during the long winter season most are virtually deserted. Some of the most dramatic coastline in the British Isles is left exclusively to the Cornish surfers and a few travellers who have discovered that winter in Cornwall is by far the better surfing season.

The huge influx of summer surfers to Cornwall has neatly divided the current atmosphere into two very distinct seasons. From May to September Cornwall is awash with money, discos, packed surfing breaks, all types of surfcraft, hippies, punks, travellers and poseurs. The surf is not at its best at this time, lacking the power of winter groundswells. The novelty of searching for a parking space to gain access to half-a-metre (two foot) waves soon wears a bit thin.

Winter waves can reach a rideable offshore two to three metres (six to eight foot) for days on end. The weather is usually milder than the rest of the British Isles and it is possible to find some offshore or sheltered waves as long as a reasonable swell is running. There are so many beaches to choose from that you may well end up surfing on your own, particularly if it is a weekday and you are away from the towns.

Flat spells are not uncommon in the summer but they are not difficult to predict. Anyone who is keen to surf in Cornwall needs to become a part-time meteorologist if they want to avoid a wasted journey. In very general terms, a low pressure system in the mid Atlantic will provide waves two or three days later on the the north coast of Cornwall. A prevailing high pressure that covers most of the north Atlantic will eventually flatten all surf. The deeper the low, the bigger the waves. There are hundreds of variables that combine to thwart wave predictions but it is essential to grasp the elements of wave generation.

The prevailing winds are from a south-west direction so clean conditions are often sought on the few sheltered north-facing beaches. Harlyn, Towan, Saint Agnes and Saint Ives all have beaches facing north.

When the winds blow from the south or east, a large number of beaches will provide good surfing conditions. Every beach will have a favourite stage of tide when the sandbanks are better placed for longer or hollower rides, but these are often impossible to predict as storms and currents constantly move the sand around. Better waves are generally found on low to mid tide, but many beaches may close out until the water is deeper at high tide.

ALEX WILLIAMS

Spencer Hargraves, Fistral

Les conditions les plus consistantes d'un surf de qualité en Angleterre se trouvent sur la côte ouest. De nombreux surfers ont quitté leur boulot et leur famille pour profiter d'un style de vie "roots" qui a peu évolué en 20 ans. Même les matins les plus froids de février, vous tomberez sur des surfers qui rament vers le lineup pour se taper une petite session avant le boulot ou une session plus longue pour ceux qui n'iront pas bosser. Il existe peut-être une centaine de spots de surf dans le Cornwall qui sont désertés pendant la longue saison hivernale. Un des littoraux les plus pittoresques se réserve aux surfers du Cornwall et aux quelques voyageurs qui savent que l'hiver est de loin la meilleure saison pour surfer.

L'arrivée massive des surfers estivants dans le Cornwall divise vraiment l'atmosphère ambiante en deux saisons distinctes. De mai à septembre, le Cornwall se métamorphose sous l'effet de l'argent, des boites de nuit, des pics gavés de tous types de planches à vagues, de hippies, de punks, de voyageurs et de frimeurs. Le surf n'est pas à son meilleur car privé de houles puissantes. Le fait d'avoir à batailler pour trouver une place de parking pour avoir accès à des rougnes de 50 cm prend vite une dimension ridicule.

Les vagues hivernales peuvent atteindre les 2m/2,5m avec offshore, sur des périodes allant jusqu'à plusieurs jours. Le temps est généralement plus doux que dans le reste du Royaume-Uni et on peut toujours trouver un endroit offshore avec des vagues abritées à partir du moment où ça rentre correctement. On a tellement le choix parmi les plages qu'on peut finir par surfer seul, surtout en semaine et quand cette plage est loin des grandes villes. Les périodes de flat ne sont pas rares en été mais sont faciles à prévoir. Quiconque compte surfer là doit devenir un météorologue à mi-temps afin d'éviter des voyages inutiles. Grosso merdo, un système dépressionnaire au milieu de l'Atlantique enverra des vagues deux à trois jours plus tard sur la côte nord du conté. Un anticyclone établi sur tout l'Atlantique nord aura tendance à aplatir la houle. Plus la dépression est creuse et plus elle se déplace vite, plus les vagues sont grosses. Il existe une multitude de variables qui se conjuguent pour établir des prévisions de houles mais il est essentiel d'en saisir ces fondamentaux.

Les vents dominants viennent du sud-ouest. Il faut donc chercher les endroits abrités exposés au nord pour trouver des conditions propres. Harlyn, Towan, St Agnes et St-Ives sont des plages exposées nord.

Quand les vents sont de sud ou d'est, bon nombre de plages jouissent de bonnes conditions. Chaque spot a son meilleur moment de marée quand les bancs de sable sont bien formés pour un déferlement long et creux mais c'est impossible à prévoir dans la mesure où les tempêtes et courants déplacent sans cesse les bancs de sable. On surfe les meilleures vagues en général de marée basse à mi-marée même si pas mal de plages barrent jusqu'à ce qu'il y ait assez d'eau avec la marée haute.

PETER CADE

Fistral

West Cornwall

1. Sennen Cove

Britain's most westerly beach is located just to the N of Land's End. It gets crowded in summer, but for the rest of the year the waves are mostly empty. Sennen is well signposted and there's a car park and campsite by the beach.

La plage anglaise la plus à l'ouest juste au nord du Lands End. Peut être bondée en été mais c'est tranquille le reste de l'année. Sennen est bien indiquée et possède un parking.

PETER CADE

Sennen Cove

2. Gwenvor

One of Cornwall's most consistent beaches faces W and is exposed to all swell – if there's no swell here there's no swell anywhere. This point/reef works best at 1-2m (3-6ft), with the peak shifting with tidal movement and strong rips. Either walk from Sennen Cove, or turn right down Escall's Lane off the A30 and walk for about 15 minutes down cliff paths.

Une des vagues les plus consistantes de Cornwall.Exposée à l'ouest, elle reçoit tous les swells-s'il n'y a pas de vagues là, il n'y en a nulle part.Ce spot marche entre 1 et 2m, le pic bouge en fonction de la marée. Les courants peuvent être forts. Soit vous marchez à partir de Sennen Cove ou vous tournez à droite de Escalls Lane jusqu'à l'A30 suivi d'une marche de 15 minutes par des chemins jusqu'en bas de falaises.

3. Porthmeor

A popular beach with St Ives' locals, Porthmeor is reasonably consistent with good peaks in a S-SW wind. If Porthmeor is 33cm (1ft) then Gwenvor to the S will be 75cm-1m (2-3ft) as will Gwithian to the N. Park by beach.

C'est la vague des locaux de St Ives. Vague relativement consistante, avec de bons peaks par vent de sud ou sud-ouest. Si Porthmeor fait 30cm alors Gwenvor, au nord, fera le double ou le triple comme Gwithian, plus au nord. Il y a un parking sur la plage.

4. Carbis Bay

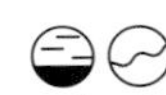  

This only works on the largest swells. At high tide entry is off the rocks at the end of a steep wooded path that crosses the railway tracks. There's rather limited parking.

Ne marche que lors des gros swells. A marée haute, l'accés se situe au niveau de rochers à la fin d'un sentier escarpé et boisé, qui traverse la voie de chemin de fer. Petit parking.

5. Hayle River

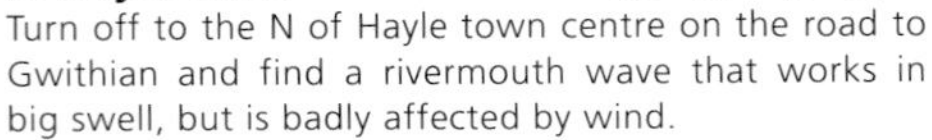

Turn off to the N of Hayle town centre on the road to Gwithian and find a rivermouth wave that works in big swell, but is badly affected by wind.

Prendre au nord du centre de Hayle town sur la route de Gwithian. La vague de l'embouchure peut être très défigurée par un vent trop fort.

6. Gwithian/Godrevy

This spot picks up the most swell in the area. In Gwithian the peaks below the car park are less powerful and thus more suited to beginners, but at high tide this area is cut off by rocks and then Godrevy to the N works. Access is via a turn off S of Gwithian, which leads to a car park.

A l'extrême nord-est dans la baie de St Ives, ces spots reçoivent la plupart des houles de la région. Gwithian, qui déferle en bas d'un parking, est moins puissant et par conséquent plus adapté aux débutants. A marée haute, la vague est interrompue dans son élan par les rochers, c'est alors que Godrevy plus au nord se met à marcher. L'accés se fait via un embranchement au sud de Gwithian Village jusqu'à un imposant parking.

PETER CADE

Godrevy

7. Portreath Harbour

On a decent-sized swell this is the best wave breaking at the N end of the beach.

Les débutants devront éviter la droite et surfer le beach break. Beaucoup de monde à l'eau pendant l'été.

Beach

Beginners should avoid the right and surf the beach break. This gets crowded in the summer months.

Les débutants devront éviter la droite et surfer le beach break. Beaucoup de monde à l'eau pendant l'été.

PETER CADE

Penhale

MIKE SEARLE

Portreath harbour wall

ALEX WILLIAMS

Chapel Porth

8. Porthtowan

A good quality beach break that can suffer crowds. The high tide is protected by the cliffs from SW winds. There's easy parking by the beach.

Un beach break de qualité mais que de monde à l'eau parfois. La vague à marée haute peut se retrouver abritée.

9. Chapel Porth

This is more powerful than many of Cornwall's other beaches. At high tide it is completely submerged, and at low it connects with Porthtowan to the S. It's signposted from St Agnes, and there is a National Trust car park by the beach.

Les vagues sont plus puissantes que la plupart des autres vagues du Cornwall. A marée haute il n'y a plus de plage, et à marée basse la connection est possible avec la plage au sud qui s'appelle Porthtowan. Indiqué à partir de St.Agnes, il y a un parking sûr près de la plage.

10. St Agnes

This can have some good, powerful surf especially at mid tide, although it needs a fair-sized swell to work. It's one of the few spots to get waves in the prevailing SW wind and hence tends to get crowded. There's a small parking area above the beach. Bad water quality, set to improve.

A mi-marée surtout, on peut avoir un bon surf bien puissant, bien que cela nécessite une houle honorable pour que cette vague donne sa pleine mesure. Un des rares spots qui marche par vent de sud-ouest dominant et a ainsi une fâcheuse tendance à être bondé. Il y a un petit parking au dessus de la plage.

11. Droskyn Beach

The lefts breaking off the headland in Perranporth can be especially good at mid tide when long rides are possible. The peaks shift with the tidal flow so it's good to keep assessing your position. There's a car park by the beach in Perranporth.

Les gauches cassent au niveau d'un promontoire. Cela peut être particulièrement bon à mi-marée avec de longues vagues. Les pics se déplacent en fonction de la marée, ainsi est il judicieux de bien observer ce qui se passe.

12. Penhale

Long walling rights peel off the rocks at the N end of Penhale with heaps of other peaks down the beach. Drive through Perran Sands Holiday Park and walk across the dunes.

Des droites formant de longs murs se levant devant des rochers à l'extrême nord du spot, également d'autres pics plus vers la plage. Traverser le Perran Sands Holiday Park, et marcher dans les dunes. Présence d'un parking à Perranporth près de la plage.

13. Holywell Bay

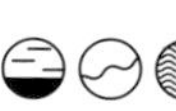 

There's an average beach break here reached from the car park by a 5-10 minute walk over the dunes. The S end receives some protection from SW winds.

Un beach break moyen. Il faut marcher 5 à10 mns à travers les dunes. La partie sud est protégée des vents sud-ouest.

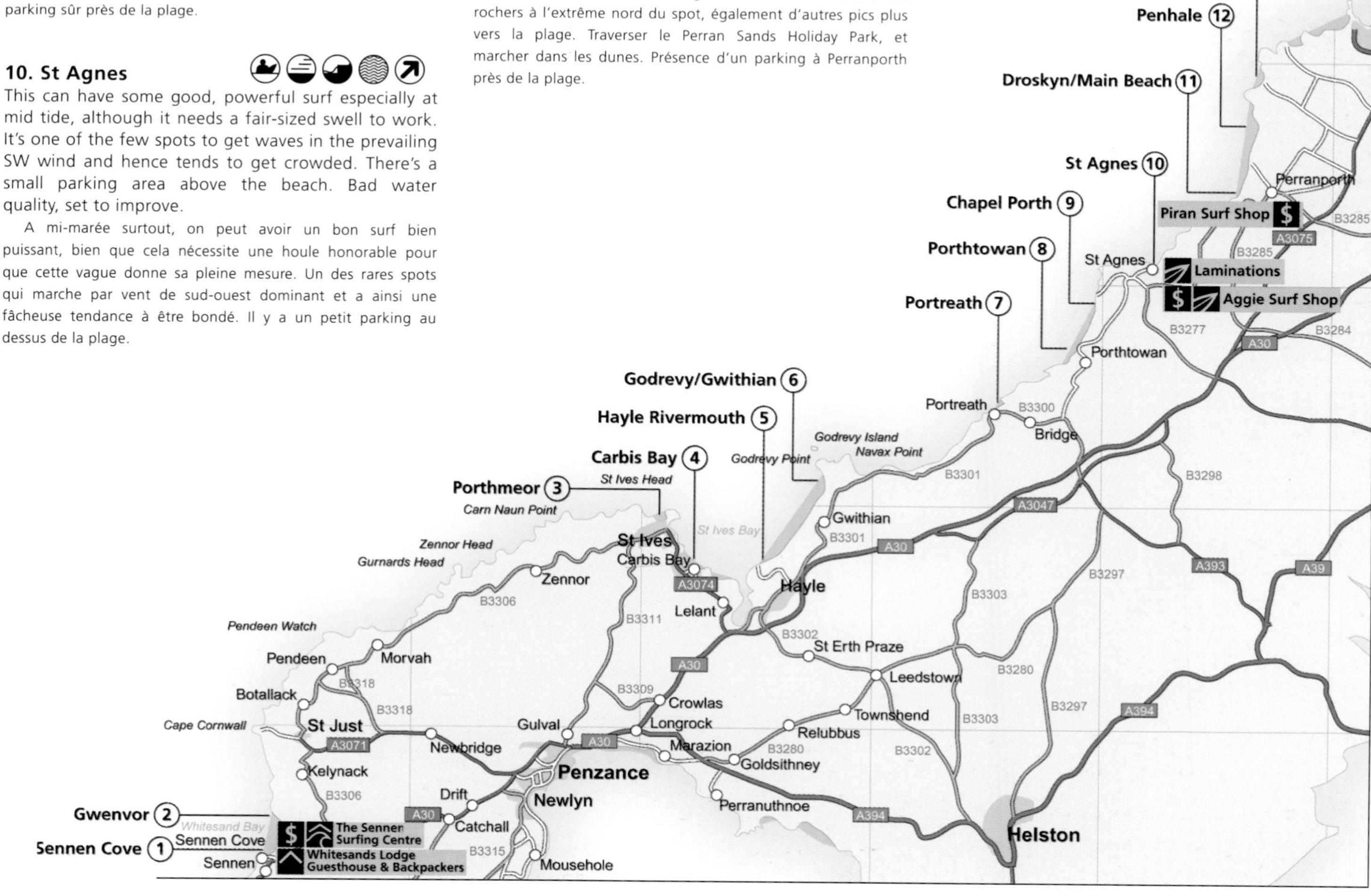

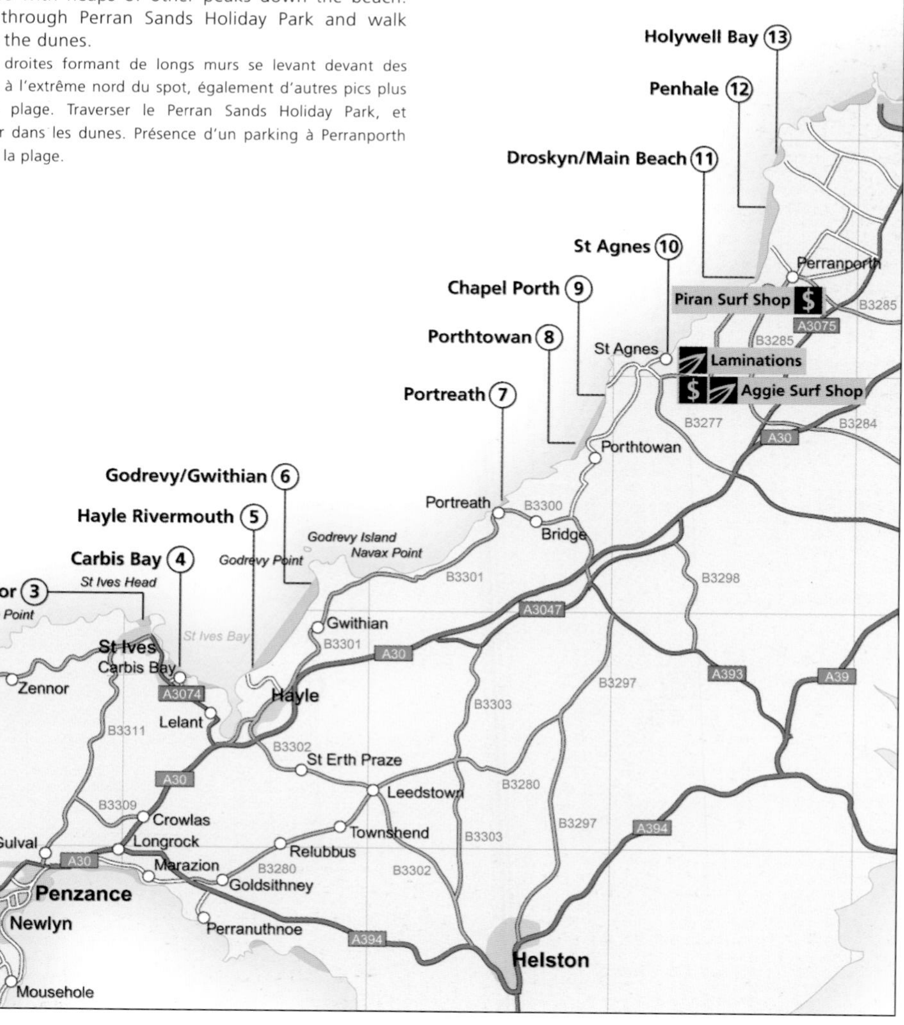

Newquay

Anthony Storer, Little Fistral

MIKE SEARLE

1. Crantock

The River Gannel runs out at the S end, giving more pronounced sand banks and it's here you'll find some long, hollow rights. There's some protection from N and NE winds, while the S end is sheltered from S and SW winds. When the S is huge, good lefts can be found at this point.

Le sud de la plage est prémuni des vents du sud et du sud-ouest, et par swell énorme, on peut trouver de bonnes gauches. Le River Gannel vient se jeter au nord de la plage, ce qui permet la formation de bancs de sable intéressants. De longues droites creuses se soulèvent, abritées des vents de nord et nord-est.

Crantock

ROD SUMPTER

2. Fistral

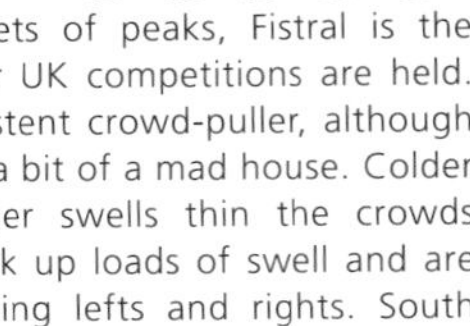

With three world-class sets of peaks, Fistral is the place where all the major UK competitions are held. Its fame makes it a consistent crowd-puller, although in summer this turns into a bit of a mad house. Colder winter months and bigger swells thin the crowds considerably. All spots pick up loads of swell and are renowned for peaky, tubing lefts and rights. South Fistral breaks left and is usually better at higher tides, while both North Fistral and Little Fistral break both ways. Though North Fistral breaks at high tide, it's undoubtedly the low tide barrels that have made the waves at the N end so famous.

La plage la plus célèbre d'Angleterre recèle trois spots de classe mondiale, qui ont vu les plus grandes compétition s'y dérouler. Sa réputation attire beaucoup de monde, et ça devient la Chine sur les vagues l'été. Au contraire, l'hiver avec ses mois plus froids et ses grosses vagues réduit considérablement la foule. Tous les spots prennent bien la houle et sont réputés pour avoir des pics droites-gauches tubulaires. Le sud de Fistral casse en gauche, en général meilleur à marée haute, tandis que Fistral-nord et petit Fistral n'ont pas vraiment de préférence. Alors que Fistral-nord casse à marée haute, c'est sans aucun doute les tubes à marée basse de l'extrême-nord qui lui ont donné ses lettres de noblesse.

Summer crowds

MIKE NEWMAN

3. The Cribber

One of England's big wave spots! Rarely ridden but much discussed: many locals have a board in the shed waiting for the right day. Rips and other obvious dangers associated with this kind of wave make it a venue for big wave surfers only.

Une des vagues de gros en Angleterre. Rarement surfée mais souvent un sujet de discussion: beaucoup de locaux ont un gun dans un coin attendant le bon jour. Les courants et autres dangers évidents associés à ce genre de spot en font un rendez-vous privilégié des surfers de gros.

North Fistral

ALEX WILLIAMS

4. Town Beaches 

At low tide the four beaches of Lusty Glaze, Tolcarne, Great Western and Towan link up to make a long, long stretch of sand. At high tide each beach, surrounded by high cliffs, becomes its own cove. At Towan, the most protected of them, lefts break off the Harbour Wall. On rare days this can be the only rideable wave in Newquay. The rest share the same sheltered characteristics and appeal especially to grommets and holidaymakers learning to surf. Local surfers head here only when there is no other choice.

A marée basse, les 4 plages de Lusty Glaze, Tolcarne, Great Western et Towan se rejoignent pour faire une seule plage d' 1,5Km. A marée haute, chaque plage devient une anse entourée par des hautes falaises. A Towan, la plus protégée des 4, des gauches déroulent depuis la jetée du port . Il arrive que ce soit la seule vague surfable de Newquay. Les autres plages sont également protégées et plaisent particulièrement aux vacanciers et aux débutants. Les locaux ne surfent qu'ici qu'en dernière limite.

5. Porth Beach   

Popular in the summer, this is an average beach break, which is good to head to when the town beaches become unbearably crowded. It receives protection from Porth Island. Park above the beach and walk down the steps to the water.

Beach-break moyen, fréquenté pendant les mois d'été quand les plages de la ville saturent de monde. Abrité de la houle par Porth Island. Garez-vous au-dessus de la plage et descendez les marches jusqu'à la mer.

Towan Beach

The annual 'Run to the Sun' VW event

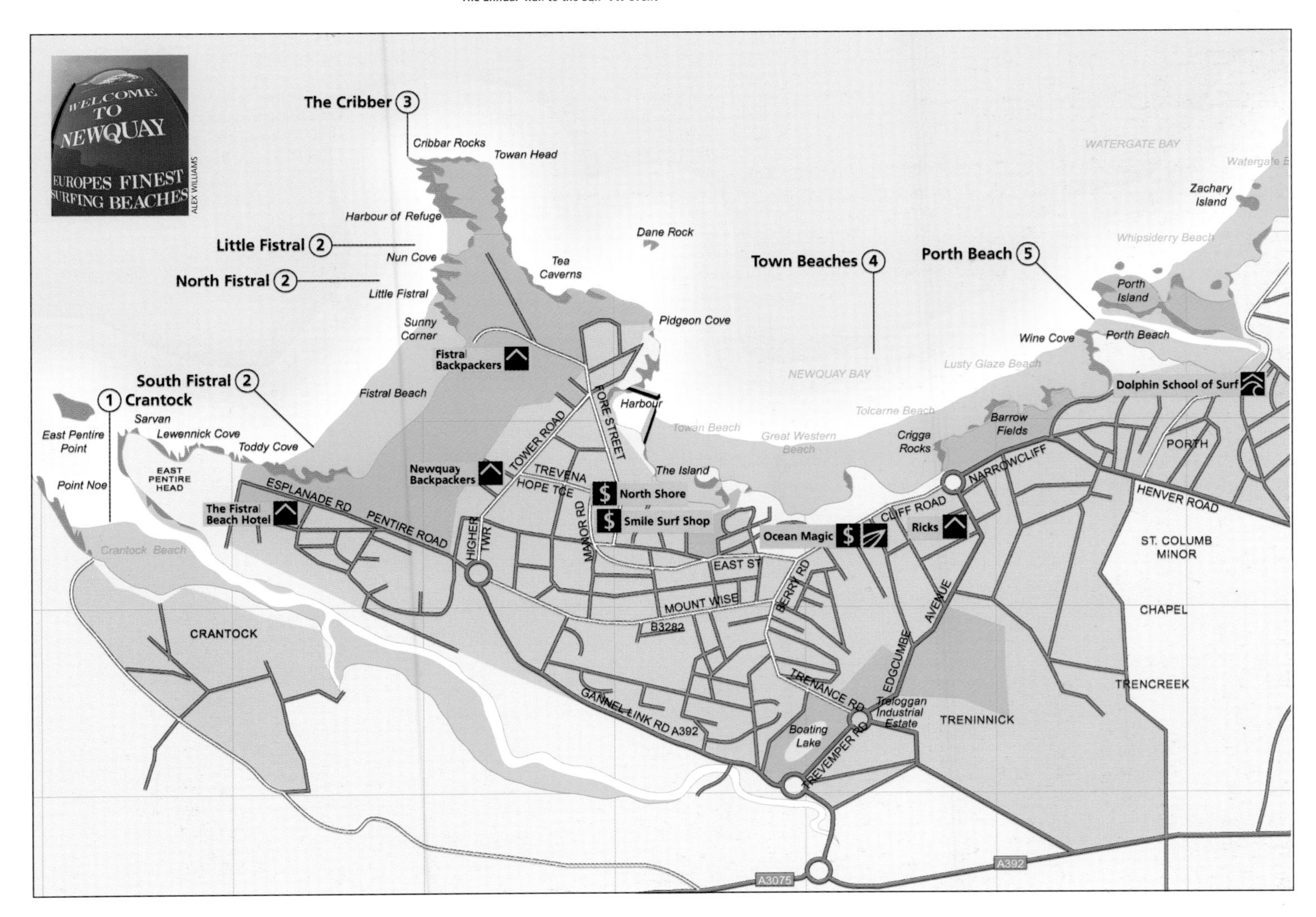

North Cornwall

1. Watergate Bay

You'll find a 3.2km (2mi) long stretch of sand with good beach break waves popular with Newquay locals.

Une étendue de 3kms de sable. Bon beach break bien connu des locaux de Newquay.

Watergate Bay

2. Mawgan Porth

This is a typical beach break that can favour lefts breaking into the river Menalhyl. Beacon Cove to the S also has waves but tends to be less crowded.

Beach break typique qui favorise les gauches entrant dans la rivière Manalhyl. Beacon Cove au sud a aussi des vagues et tend à être moins populeux.

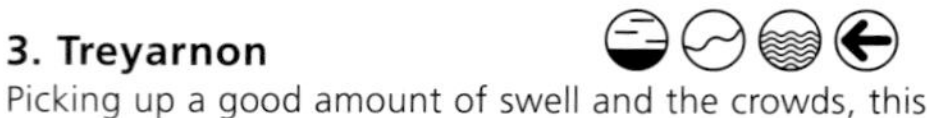

3. Treyarnon

Picking up a good amount of swell and the crowds, this is popular from mid to high tide with various peaks breaking at either end along the 1km (0.6mi) beach.

Récupère aussi pas mal de houle et plus fréquenté de mi-marée à marée haute. Plusieurs pics cassent des deux côtés et le long de cette plage d'un km.

4. Constantine

One of the best swell-pullers in North Cornwall, the waves found here in the middle of the bay are lefts and rights. At the S end a left will break off the reef. Booby's Bay to the N has a good but fickle right-hand reef break from low-mid tide. Beginners should be aware of strong rips.

Un des meilleurs 'aimants à houle' du nord-Cornwall. gauches et droites au mileiu de la baie. Au sud se trouve une gauche de reef. Booby's Bay au nord a une droite rare de marée basse à mi-marée. Débutants, méfiance, il y a du jus.

5. Harlyn Bay

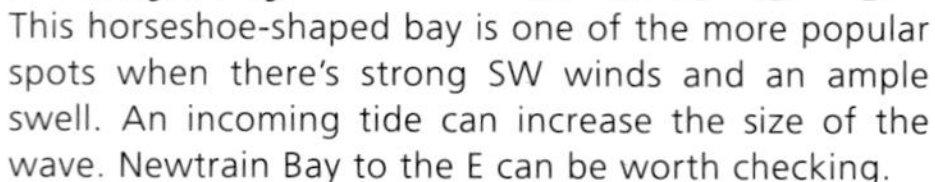

This horseshoe-shaped bay is one of the more popular spots when there's strong SW winds and an ample swell. An incoming tide can increase the size of the wave. Newtrain Bay to the E can be worth checking.

Une baie en forme de fer à cheval qui est un des spots les plus populaires quand c'est la tempête de SO. La marée montante peut augmenter la taille des vagues. Newtrain Bay à l'Est peut valoir le coup d'oeil.

6. Polzeath (Hayle)

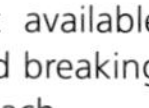

A very popular beach break picks up most available swell. There can be a right-hander at the N end breaking off Pentire Point on bigger days. Park by the beach.

Beach break super consistent et super fréquenté. Quand ça rentre, il peut y avoir une droite au nord qui casse à Pentire Point. Parking à proximité.

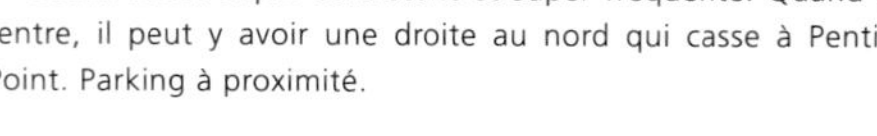

7. Lundy Bay

A good spot to check when big swells and strong SW winds blow out other breaks. The 10-minute walk from the car park keeps the beach crowd-free.

Un bon spot à checker quand ça rentre gros et que de violents vents de S-O bousillent les autres spots. Les 10 minutes de marche depuis le parking éloigne la foule.

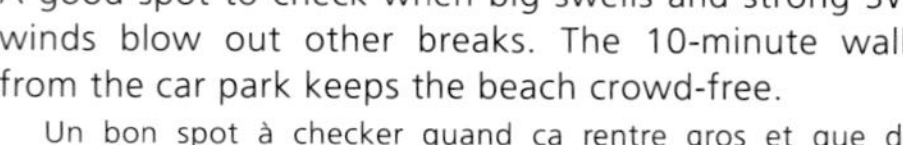

8. Trebarwith Strand

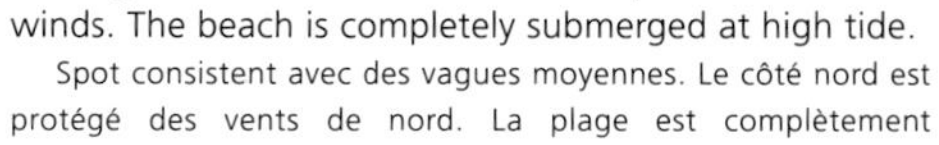

Average and consistant waves are found here: the S end has a good left which receives some protection from N winds. The beach is completely submerged at high tide.

Spot consistent avec des vagues moyennes. Le côté nord est protégé des vents de nord. La plage est complètement recouverte à marée haute.

9. Crackington Haven

Good waves tend to back off at high tide here, but it's sheltered from N winds and holds big swells. Imbibe good ales and feast at the Coombe Barton Inn. Close by is an excellent camping field.

Bonnes vagues qui ont tendance à s'affaiblir à marée haute. Protégées des vents de nord et tient le gros. L'auberge Coombe Barton sert des bonnes bières et de la bonne bouffe. Excellent camping.

10. Widemouth Bay

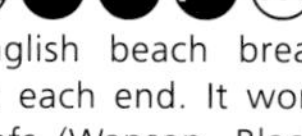

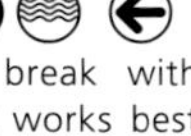

Welcome to a famous English beach break with various sand reef set-ups at each end. It works best up to 2m (6ft) and the reefs (Wanson, Black Rock) tend to get good with swell, though the banks shift continuously.

Un des meilleurs beach breaks anglais avec des reefs recouverts de sable à chaque extrémité. Marche mieux jusqu'à 2 mètres et les reefs de Wanson ou Black rock ont tendance à bien fonctionner bien que les bancs changent sans arrêt.

11. Upton

A semi-secret spot that's part reef part sand, Upton has good rights and lefts on the N and S side that are best on a 1.2-2m (4-6ft) swell. Access is by a dangerous descent down the cliff. No parking.

Un spot presque secret sur fond de sable et cailloux. De bonnes gauches et droites au nord comme au sud. Mieux par houle d'1 à 2 mètres. La descente par la falaise réserve parfois quelques frayeurs. Pas de parking à proximité.

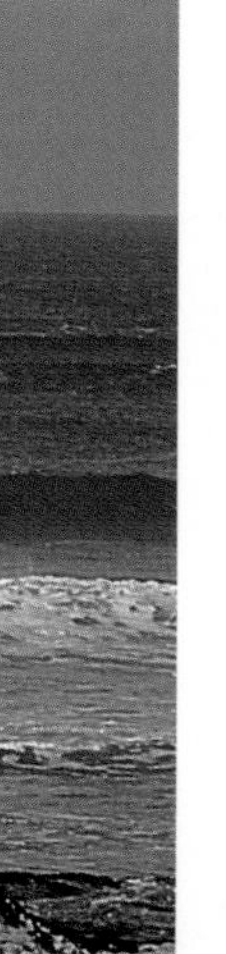

Constantine

Trebarwith

PETER CADE

14. Sandy Mouth

An excellent, small swell beach break with various banks can hold big swells but tends to have bad rips. Park in the National Trust car park and eat from the café in summer months. One of the cleanest beaches in the UK.

Super beach break avec plusieurs bancs de sable surtout par petit swell. Supporte aussi le gros mais avec des courants d'enfer. Pas de problème pour se garer et des cafés sympas en été. Une des plages les plus propres du Royaume-Uni.

15. Duckpool

A fickle low tide right breaks off the rocks up to 2m (6ft) and is sheltered from N winds. A clean, empty spot (usually).

Une droite à marée basse, capricieuse casse à côté des rochers jusqu'à 2 mètres. Abrité des vents de nord-ouest, c'est un spot souvent propre et vierge.

Bude - Summerleaze

A hollow left-hander works at low tide off The Barrel and holds most swell. From mid to high tide a right breaks into the harbour which can handle big swells and SW winds. The take-off can be steep and dangerous with strong rips.

Cette gauche creuse marche à marée basse en face du 'Barrel' et supporte la plupart des houles. De mi-marée à marée haute, une droite casse dans le port et peut tenir de gros swells ainsi que des vents de S-O. Le take-off peut être raide et dangereux à cause des courants.

Bude – Middle Beach

Between Crooklets and Summerleaze, there's excellent lefts and rights in swells up to 2m (6ft), but they're often crowded with locals.

Entre Crooklets et Summerleaze. Des gauches et des droites d' excellente qualité mais souvent peuplées de locaux.

Bude – Crooklet

Check hollow sandbank peaks and Wrangles Rocks to the N at low tide. At high tide Tower Rock produces a good, if shallow, wave. The infamous Crooklet's shore break also holds swell up to 2m (6ft).

Des pics creux sur fond de sable et Wrangles Rocks au nord qui marche à marée basse. A marée haute, Tower Rock offre une bonne vague, si elle est creuse. Le shorebreak infâme de Crooklets tient la houle aussi jusqu'à 2 mètres.

13. Northcott Mouth

The banks at low tide produce some heavy hollow waves, but they tend to back off at high tide, except on a big swell, which produces a good right-hander on the N side.

Les bancs à marée basse balancent de gros paquets. Tendance à mal casser à marée haute, sauf si la houle est massive auquel cas on trouve une bonne droite sur le côté nord.

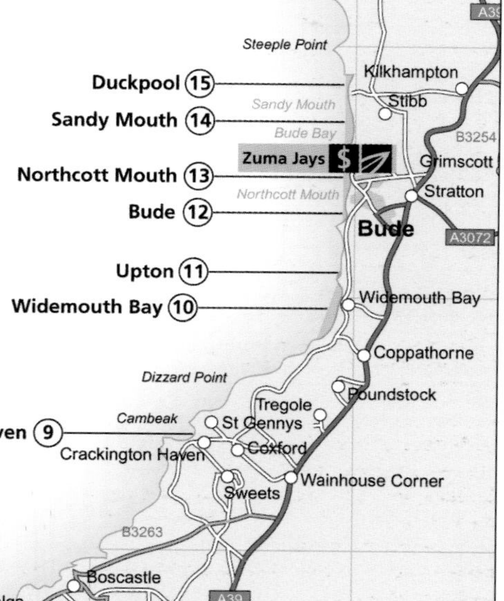

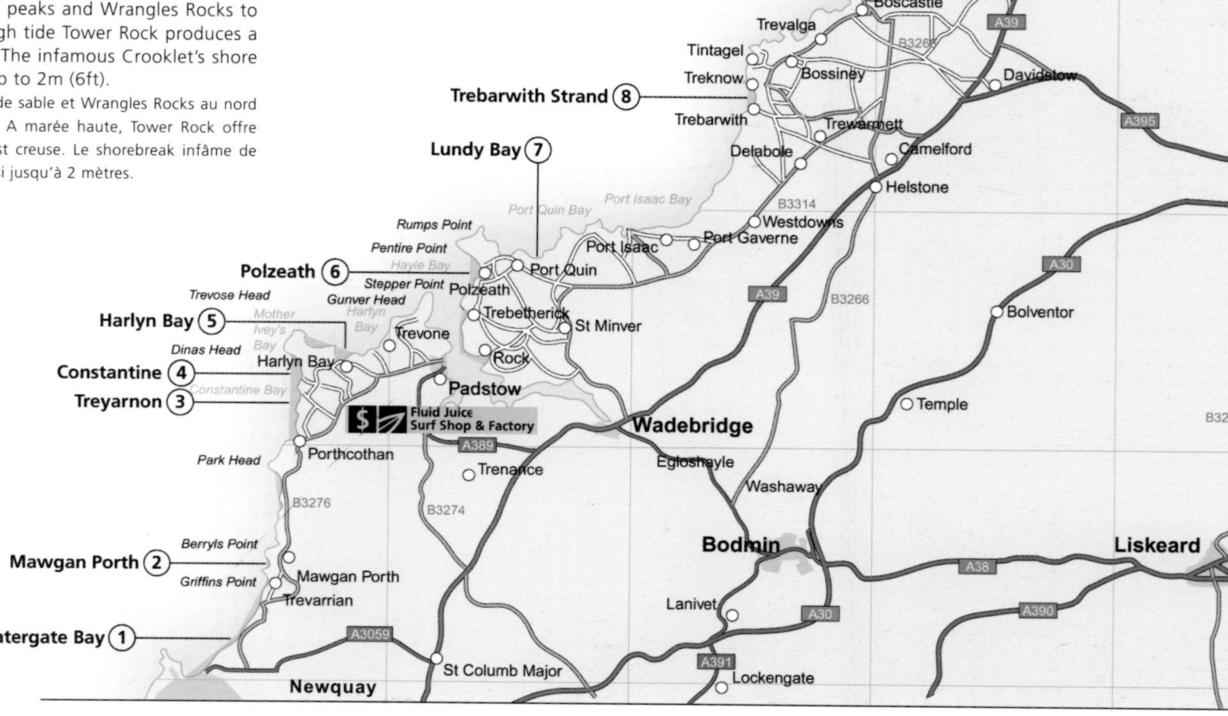

North Devon

1. Speke's Mill

This can have a rideable wave and lefts when everywhere else is flat, but it's not for beginners and has a difficult access. Respect the locals.

Peut avoir une vague surfable quand c'est le lac ailleurs. Des gauches par exemple. Par pour débutants. Accés difficile.

2. Buck's Mill

An attractive small village of thatched cottages overlooks a rock strewn shingle and sand beach. The wave here breaks along a rocky phalloid called The Gore and rates as one of North Devon's best spots in strong S or SW winds when huge swells are closing out in North Devon and Cornwall's W-facing breaks.

Un petit village attrayant de fermes de chaume qui surplombent cette plage graveleuse gavée de cailloux aussi. La vague casse sur un 'doigt' rocheux appelé 'The Gore'. Un des meilleurs spots du coin avec des forts vents de sud ou sud-ouest quand ça ferme à maximum sur les plages exposés ouest.

3. Westward Ho!

Only locals really surf the average quality waves in Westward Ho! and Bideford. Parking is easy.

Vagues moyennes seulement surfées par des locaux de Westward Ho! et Bideford. Parking facile.

Scott Rannochan, low tide Croyde

ESTPIX

4. Saunton

Extensive sands of over 5km (3mi) are backed by Braunton Burrows and are partly protected from N winds. It's the perfect place for grommets and windsurfers owing to its length and the slow breaking nature of the waves it receives. Park at the N end of the beach.

Cinq kms de sable avec Braunton Burrows en toile de fond. Protégé des vents de nord, c'est un endroit idéal pour les débutants et les windsurfers grâce à sa longueur et au déroulement lent des vagues. Parking facile au nord de la plage.

5. Croyde

Downend Point

In a large swell a good wave offers a fast take-off with long walls, but, you should exercise caution – the rocks are jagged and the peak has a habit of shifting around. Closely choose your entry and exit points. With good timing gulleys on either side of the point can save the pain of a damaged board or body.

Une bonne vague avec un take-off sportif et de longs murs, avec une bonne houle. Attention! Les rochers sont tranchants et le pic n'a rien de stable. Se mettre et sortir de l'eau n'ont rien d'évident, trouvez des channels entre les pierres, un bon timing devrez éviter des contacts éventuels avec la planche ou le corps.

Beach

This rates as one of England's best beach breaks due to the peaky, hollow waves it provides. The obvious drawback associated with this cred is crowding – and the break can become seriously dangerous. Low tide can be particularly powerful. If you're not experienced enough or if you don't like crowds then head somewhere else, especially in summer. The sandbars here are able to hold a bigger swell than Devon's other W-facing beaches. Water quality can be particularly bad.

Un des meilleurs beach breaks du Pays Grace aux vagues creuses en pic. L'in convenient est le monde qui peut etre dangereux. Si vous n'etes pas assez fort ou vous n'aimez pas la foule, auez ailleurs surtout en ete. Les bancs peuvent tener des plus grosses houles que les autres plages du Devon exposees ouest. A marée basse, c'est carrément puissant. Il faut que la houle soit bien grasse pour que ça marche. Si oui, le plus important est la premiere section en bol, rapide et creuse. Casse dans peu d'eau, ne convient qu'aux bons surfers.

Reef

The swell needs to be meaty for this to work and when it does the most important feature is the fast, hollow, initial bowl section. This wave breaks in shallow water and is best for experienced surfers.

Le swell ici doit tabasser pour ce reef fonctionne, mais il present un bowl section initial qui est rapid et creuse. Cette vague casse en mer peut profond et est seulement pour surfers avec experience.

6. Putsburough

 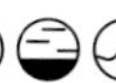 

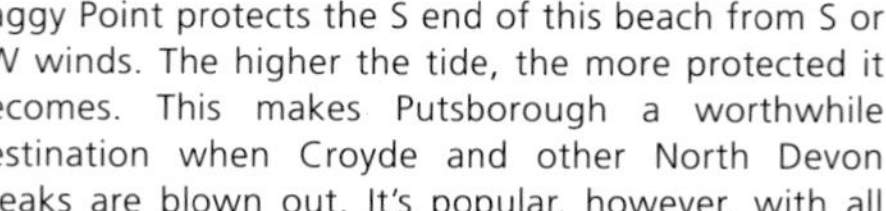

Baggy Point protects the S end of this beach from S or SW winds. The higher the tide, the more protected it becomes. This makes Putsborough a worthwhile destination when Croyde and other North Devon breaks are blown out. It's popular, however, with all forms of surf craft. Park and camp by the beach.

Baggy Point protège la partie sud de cette plage des vents de sud et sud-ouest. Plus la marée est haute, plus c'est protégé. Cela fait de Putborough une alternative à considérer quand ça ferme sur Croyde et les autres spots de la région. On y trouve tous les genres d'utilisateurs de vagues. Parking et camping prés de la plage.

Croyde Bay

CHRIS POWER

7. Woolacombe 

Woolacombe is left as a relatively unspoilt and mellow place to surf. In the longboard days, this was the hub of the surfing scene. Now that the emphasis has shifted to Croyde, The rocks at the N end of the main beach can produce some interesting rights above half tide. Barricane, known locally as Combesgate, can have some nice peaks at low tide, and receives protection from N winds. Park by the beach.

Dans les années longboard, c'était le centre du surf. Maintenant que l'attention s'est déplacée vers Croyde, Woolacombe est redevenu un endroit relativement peinard pour surfer. Les rochers au nord de la plage principale peuvent donner des droites intéressantes au dessus de la mi-marée. Barricane, aussi appelée localement Combesgate, peut avoir des pics sympas à marée basse, protégés des vents de nord. Parking prés de la plage.

8. Lynmouth 

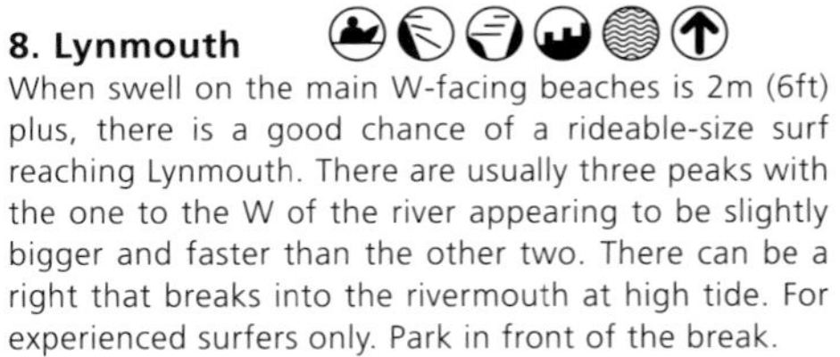

When swell on the main W-facing beaches is 2m (6ft) plus, there is a good chance of a rideable-size surf reaching Lynmouth. There are usually three peaks with the one to the W of the river appearing to be slightly bigger and faster than the other two. There can be a right that breaks into the rivermouth at high tide. For experienced surfers only. Park in front of the break.

Quand ça fait plus de 2m sur les plages exposées ouest, il est fort possible que des vagues tout à fait surfable atteignent Lynmouth. Trois pics en général: celui à l'ouest de la rivière semble souvent plus gros et plus rapide que les 2 autres. On peut trouver une droite dans l'embouchure à marée haute. Seulement pour surfers avertis. Se garer en face du spot.

9. Porlock Wier   

When huge swells are closing out in most of North Devon's and Cornwall's other breaks, Porlock Wier can provide some excellent fast waves. Park in the village.

Peut avoir de super vagues rapides quand une houle énorme fait fermer la plupart des spots du nord-Devon et du Cornwall. Se garer dans le village.

Lynmouth

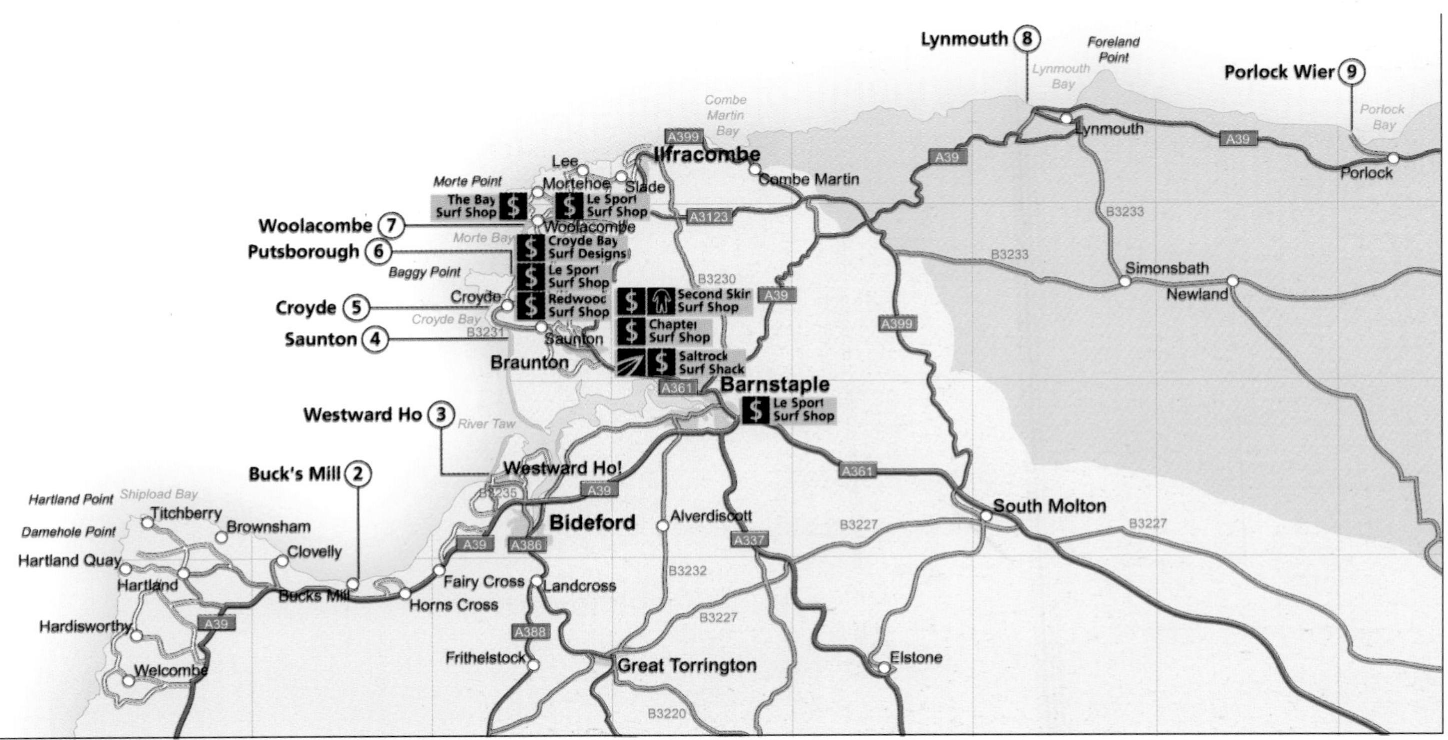

Wales

Wales is a land of striking contrasts. Despite being the British Isles' smallest nation, Wales is big on surf. It offers playful rolling beach breaks or square, shallow reefs, which break on pristine areas of coast interspersed with stark industrial landscapes. Surprising amounts of swell hit its convoluted coast and it's always offshore somewhere. The Welsh are a staunchly traditional people who are also friendly and humourous with their own rich culture and lyrical language. Put it all together and you've got a highly unusual but deceptively good place to go surfing.

Pays de Galles

Le Pays de Galles est une terre de contrastes étonnante. Bien que ce soit la plus petite des nations britanniques, le Pays de Galles possède un surf bien réel allant du beachbreak tranquille au reef craignos envoyant de gros barrels dans une eau cristalline, bien que le paysage soit souvent marqué par des traits de côtes salement industriels. De surprenantes tranches de swell viennent frapper sa côte découpée, dont l'exposition est toujours off-shore quelque part. Les Gallois ont toujours été des gens opiniâtres, amicaux, dotés d' un sens de l'humour développé. Leur culture s'exprime dans la musicalité de langue. Il en ressort de tout ça que c'est un endroit bizarre pour surfer, sous des apparences trompeuses qui cachent un bon potentiel de surf.

'You hear people say that it always rains in Wales, but we don't mind as long as there's surf' Carwyn Williams
A fine day at Crab Island

ALEX WILLIAMS

Where to go

Surf Areas

South Wales and The Gower Peninsula
As you cross the Bristol Channel past Newport, the M4 follows the coast. Set against one of the most industrial backdrops in the UK you'll find surf, especially in the biggest winter swells. Continuing west, you'll come to the Gower Peninsula. 'The Gower' is Wales' premier surfing area, ideally located to receive swells generated by mid and south Atlantic lows. The rugged, scenic coastline offers a wide variety of breaks, most within sheltered bays providing waves which smugglers rode in on centuries ago. These bays now offer secrets for the dedicated to find.

As Carwyn Williams, the area's best-known surfer says: 'The surf can sometimes be brilliant, but Welsh surfers must be one of the few bunches of people who get excited when the forecast is for gale force winds and rain. We don't mind that at all as long as there's surf. This breeds the hard-core element into Welsh surfing. When the surf is flat at Langland we normally go to Llangennith. This is the most consistent of all the breaks on the Gower and if there's no wind and you know the tides, there's some nice reef breaks to be found. It's touch and go whether you'll get perfect waves if you come to the Gower, but there are a few characters, the night life in Mumbles is classic and the sheep are friendly!'

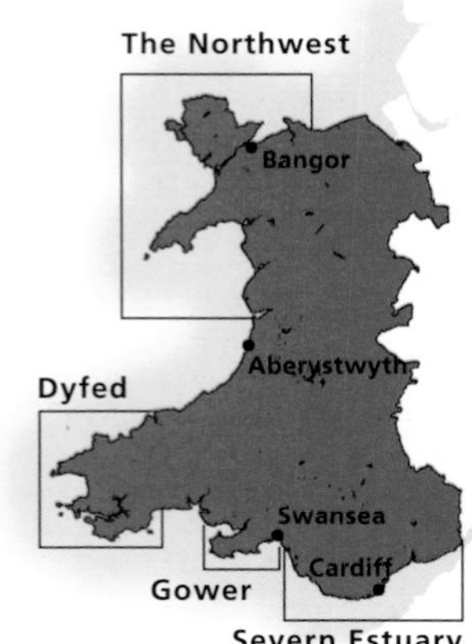
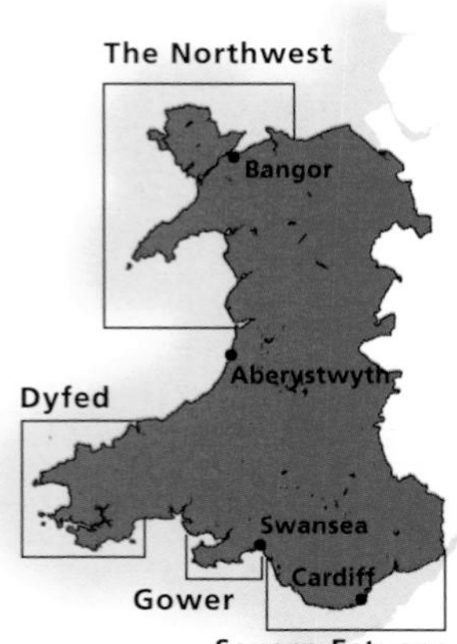

Severn Estuary

Aberavon

THE GILL

Pembrokeshire Little or no development has taken place to spoil the sand dunes and red sandstone cliffs that shelter the beaches and the surrounding National Parks. Whitesands is the focus for most surfing in North Dyfed. The wild, wide open Freshwater West extends in both directions and has become the focus of surfing in the south. Between Milford Haven and Abereiddy, there are numerous beaches and coves that require only a moderate swell to provide excellent surfing conditions. Many have remained unchanged for centuries. The occasional ice cream van can be the only source of sustenance.

North West Wales The coastline of mid and north Wales, including the Lleyn Peninsula and Anglesey, is not renowned for its surf. But, with patience, some decent waves are found, and as with all places, the right conditions can produce perfection. These areas definitely have their fair share of classic reefs points and beach breaks. You've just got to keep a very close eye on the weather maps.

When to go

It takes a lot for swell to get into the coastal areas of Wales: lows need to be south in the Atlantic to have an effect. This is least likely to happen in summer. The south-facing breaks need an accompanying northerly wind which tends to occur after the passage of a big low close to or over Britain. Again, a predominantly winter experience, as summer gets a lot of south-west (onshore) winds.

Swansea Bay Averages	Jan	Apr	Jul	Oct
water °C	8	11	16	15
wetsuit	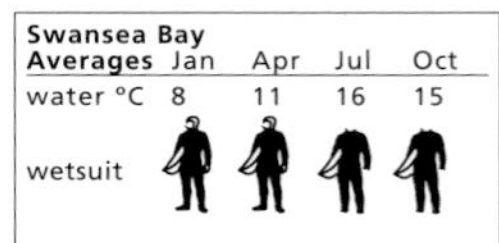			

Gower

Llangennith with Worms Head in the background

PHIL HOLDEN

Ou aller

Les zones de surf

La Gower Peninsula est la région de surf d'origine du Pays de Galles, idéalement placée pour recevoir les houles générées par les systèmes dépressionnaires du sud et du centre de l'Atlantique. La côte accidentée et panoramique offre une large variété de spots, la plupart à l'intérieur de baies protégées fournissant des vagues sur lesquelles "surfaient" les contrebandiers il y a des siècles. Ces baies offrent maintenant leurs secrets au surfeur prêt à les trouver.

Le surf peut parfois être excellent, mais nous devons être un des rares groupes de surfeurs qui se réjouissent lorsqu'il est annoncé de forts coups de vents et de la pluie. Cela nous était complétement égal du moment qu'il y a du surf. Cela rend compte de l'aspect "pur et dur" du surf gallois. Quand c'est calme à Langland, nous allons normalement à Llangennith. C'est le plus consistent de tous les spots sur le Gower et s'il n'y a pas de vent et si on connait les marées, il y a quelques jolis spots de récifs à trouver. On n'est pas certain d'avoir des vagues parfaites si on vient sur le Gower, mais il y a des personnages à découvrir, la nuit à Mumbles est un grand classique et les moutons sont sympathiques!

Pembrokeshire L'industrie peu développée de cette région n'a pas endommagé les dunes de sable et les falaises de grès rouge qui recouvrent les plages et les parcs nationaux alentours. Whitesands regroupe l'essentiel du surf dans le nord et la large ouverture sauvage de Freshwater West s'étend dans les deux directions et est devenu le spot principal pour le sud. Entre Milford Haven et Abereiddy, il y a de nombreuses plages et criques qui n'exigent qu'une houle modérée pour fourrnir des conditions de surf excellentes. Beaucoup sont restées les mêmes depuis des siècles. L'occasionnelle camionette de glaces est souvent la seule source de nourriture et les surfeurs locaux sont à la fois enthousiastes et sympathiques.

Le littoral nord et central du Pays de Galles, avec la péninsule Lleyn et Anglesy n'est pas renommé de par le monde pour ses vagues. Patience et vous trouverez !

Quand aller

Cela prend un bon bout de temps pour que les swells rentrent dans les régions côtières du Pays de Galles, pour cela il faut que les dépressions se situent plus au sud de l'Atlantique.

Evidemment il est peu probable que cela arrive en été. Pour que le côté exposé sud marche il faut un vent du nord qui se lève après le passage d'une grosse dépression sur ou près de l'île britannique. L'hiver semble la saison à privilégier, l'été recevant des vents de sud-ouest onshore.

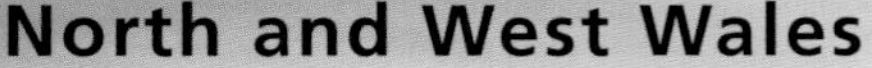

North and West Wales

PHIL HOLDEN

Top: classic secret spot – mid Wales Below: Freshwater West

Pembrokeshire

PHIL HOLDEN

Photo Brian Reid / TMRX
WISCONSIN
BACKSIDE NOSEGRIND SHUVIT OUT - TYRONE OLSON
Osiris
S K A T E B O A R D S H O E S
Dealer Enquiries: UK: Projects Distribution Tel: 0181 960 0555 Fax: 0181 960 0888 Web: www.osirisshoes.com
US: Alias Distribution 7130 Convoy Court San Diego CA 92111 Tel: 619.874.4970 Fax 619.278.3274
osiris
SHOES

ALEX WILLIAMS

Carwyn Williams in the bad old days

The Ocean Environment

Water Quality

Wales is one of the luckiest areas of the UK with regard to sewage pollution. Dwr Cymru/Welsh Water committed to a policy of full treatment to UV disinfection or microfiltration as far back as 1993. Many of these plants are already in place and deliver guideline water quality around the coastline. This will give Wales 50 EC blue flags by the year 2000 (in contrast, Cornwall only had one in 1998). Black spots such as Swansea Bay are now being cleaned up. The considerable risk of toxic discharges is also being dealt with by the Welsh regional Environment Agency who have a progressive policy of cessation of toxic discharges. However, there still remains the considerable risk from places such as British Steel at Port Talbot. Discharges from this huge industrial complex still hit the coastal waters and British Steel still seem unwilling to meet with SAS. There has even been a case of two sewer workers dying from toxic gases while working in the sewer. It seems that while many in Wales recognise the need for a safe environment, others allow greed to wipe away the guilt inherited by the blatant polluting of Wales' coastal waters.

On Localism

The Welsh are a totally friendly race who'll keep you drinking and laughing all night long if you let them, but their coastline isn't huge. Many of the best spots are regularly surfed, so like elsewhere, adhere to the rules. Carwyn Williams remembers his education: 'Surfing in Wales has a great heritage. I grew up in a spot called Langland Bay where I had to learn respect for the locals who were, by rights, the best surfers in the country. You would never paddle out onto the best breaks in the bay unless you did it early in the morning, or you were encouraged by the crew.' As a traveller, discretion is the better part of valour.

PHIL HOLDEN

SAS protest, Langland Bay 1994

Specificités du littoral

Qualité de l'eau

Le Pays de Galles est une région privilégiée en regard de sa pollution. Le Dwr Cymru/Welsh Water a engagé une politique de traitement complet des eaux par les techniques de désinfection UV et de filtrage dès 1993. Beaucoup de ces agences sont déjà en place et délivreront des directives en ce qui concerne la qualité de l'eau sur la côte. On attribuera au Pays de Galles 50 pavillons bleus de la communauté européenne d'içi l'an 2000 (par comparaison les Cornouailles n'ent ont qu'un en 1998). L'un des points noirs comme Swansea Bay est en train d'être nettoyé, toute la ville étant traitée. L'agence régionale galloise de l'environnement, s'occupe également de régler le problème des rejets toxiques. Cependant la menace perdure dans des endroits come British Steel à Port Talbot. Les déchets de ces énormes complexes industriels continuent à dégrader les eaux côtieres et British Steel ne veut toujours pas rencontrer la SAS. Il y'a même le cas de deux agents d'une usine de retraitement qui sont morts à cause des émanations toxiques alors qu'ils travaillaient sur un collecteur. Il semble alors que beaucoup reconnaissent la nécessité de protéger l'environnement d'autres continuent à se mentir à eux-mêmes quant à leur responsabilité sur la pollution de nos eaux côtières.

MARK GLEGHORN

Localisme

Les Gallois sont des gens très amicaux qui feront la fête avec vous si vous êtes cool, mais l'étendue de leur côte n'est pas infinie. Beaucoup des meilleurs spots sont régulièrement surfés, comme partout ailleurs les régles sont faites pour être respectées. Comme le souligne Carwyn Williams: Le surf sur le Gower est empreint d'un grand héritage. J'ai grandi sur un spot appelé Langland Bay où j'ai du apprendre à respecter les locaux qui étaient, sans problémes, les meilleurs surfeurs du pays. On n'allait jamais surfer les meilleurs spots de la baie si ce n'était tôt le matin ou si on n'y était pas encouragé par la "bande". En tant que voyageur, plus vous serez discret et mieux ça se passera.

Chris Hines, president of Surfers Against Sewage opened this tertiary treatment plant which is a tribute to the progressive policies of Welsh Water

Severn Estuary

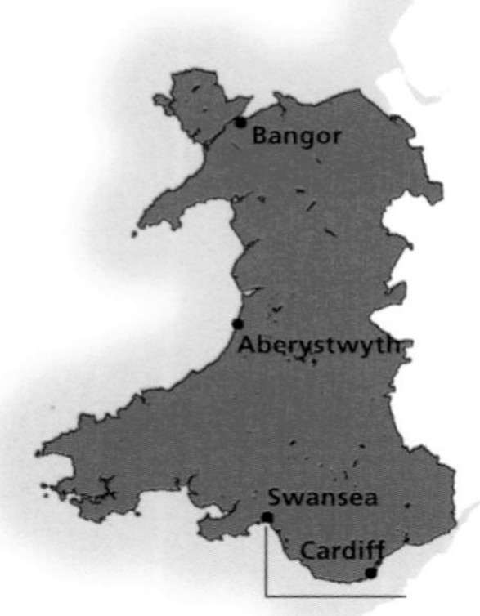

1. Aberavon

The last Stormrider said: 'One of S Wales' best (but most polluted waves) is under threat due to the planned construction of a massive breakwater. The local crew who've surfed this wave for over 20 years are fighting to save the wave in what is seen as the UK's test case.

Update from The City Surf Shop: 'Aberavon used to be an unreal wave before they built the poxy breakwater. It still works – but getting in and out is a bit of a death trap. Watch out for all the nasties floating in the water. If they don't get ya, the Scumpton crew will.'

Une des meilleures vagues du sud du Pays de Galles mais super polluée et menacée par la construction prévue d'une grosse jetée. Les locaux qui surfent cettevague depuis 20 ans luttent pour sauver cette vague, ce qui est considérée comme un exemple-test au Royaume-Uni. La gauche est une meilleure vague étant plus longue et plus creuse mais on peut taper quelques rollers sur la droite. Aberavon est un des seuls spots à marcher par vents de SE.

The Point

THE GILL

2. Rest Bay

  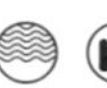

This can have good rights and lefts all the way to Margam Sands, but is often badly affected by common W winds. Pollution can be bad due to the heavy industrial site of Port Talbot to the N.

On peut trouver de bonnes droites et gauches tout le long jusqu'à Margam sands mais c'est souvent gavé de vents d'ouest. La pollution peut y être alarmante à cause de la proximité de Port Talbot.

3. The Point

Located between Sandy bay and Trecco Bay to the S of Porthcawl, this wave is always crowded. It can live up to the hype but only works in big swells.

Ca peut être fantastique mais seulement quand ça rentre balaise. Allez voir Sandy Bay ou Trecco Bay au sud de Porthcawl.

PHIL HOLDEN

PHIL HOLDEN

Aberavon

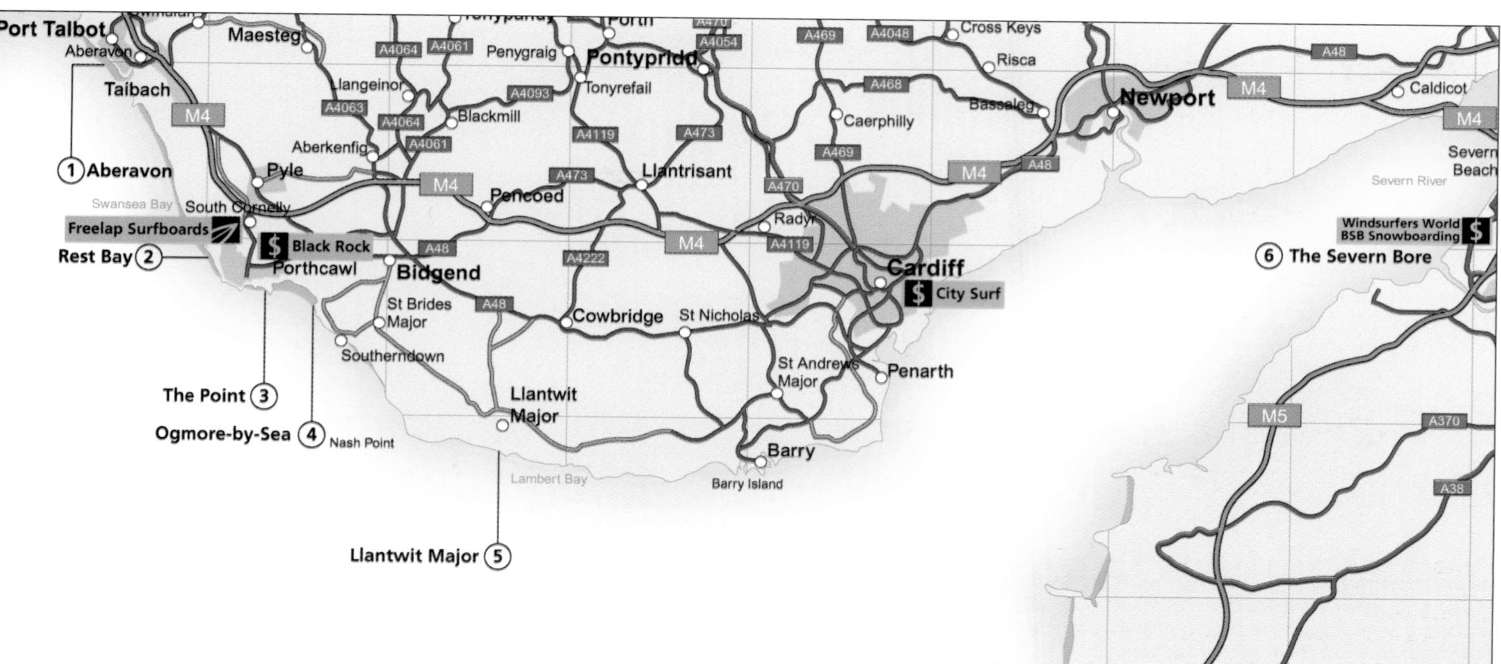

4. Ogmore-by-Sea

On the S side of the river there's a good left with rides of up to 100m (90yd): it needs a clean swell and works best from mid to high tide, but is polluted due to effluents outflowing from the river, which also causes strong rips. Beginners should definitely avoid the left at the rivermouth. The beach can have good peaks, depending on the state of the sandbanks.

Au sud de la rivière, une bonne gauche déroule sur prés de 100 mètres, avec une houle propre et de préférence de mi-marée à marée haute, débuitants s'abstenir. Pollué à cause de la rivière et attention aux courants. Ensuite, la plage peut avoir de bons pics, selon l'état des bancs de sable.

5. Llantwit Major

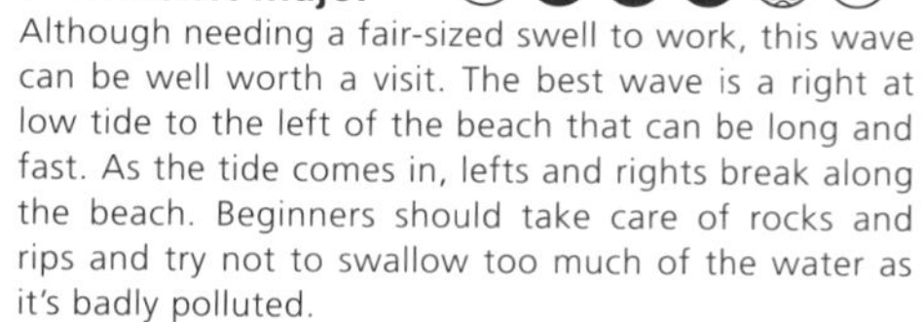

Although needing a fair-sized swell to work, this wave can be well worth a visit. The best wave is a right at low tide to the left of the beach that can be long and fast. As the tide comes in, lefts and rights break along the beach. Beginners should take care of rocks and rips and try not to swallow too much of the water as it's badly polluted.

Il faut une houle correcte pour que ça marche mais ça vaut le coup d'oeil quand même. La meilleure vague est une droite à marée basse sur la gauche de la plage, qui peut être longue et rapide. Quand la marée monte, des gauches et des droites cassent le long de la plage Les débutants doivent faire attention aux rochers et aux courants et attention aussi à ne pas trop avaler l'eau: ça craint !

6. The Severn Bore

At high spring tides a remarkable tidal bore pushes its way up the Bristol Channel and creates a waist-high surfable wave travelling at a speed of about 10km (6mi). It's best caught between Fretherne and Maisemore. It's in the record books for being the longest wave ever ridden, so the bigger the board the better time you'll have.

Aux grandes marées de printemps, un mascaret phénoménal remonte l'estuaire de Bristol pour créer une vague surfable à hauteur de la taille à une vitesse d'environ 10kms. Elle est meilleure entre Fretherne et Maisemore. Plus votre planche est grande, mieux c'est. C'est dans le livre des records comme la plus longue vague surfée au monde!

PHIL HOLDEN

Severn Bore

Gower

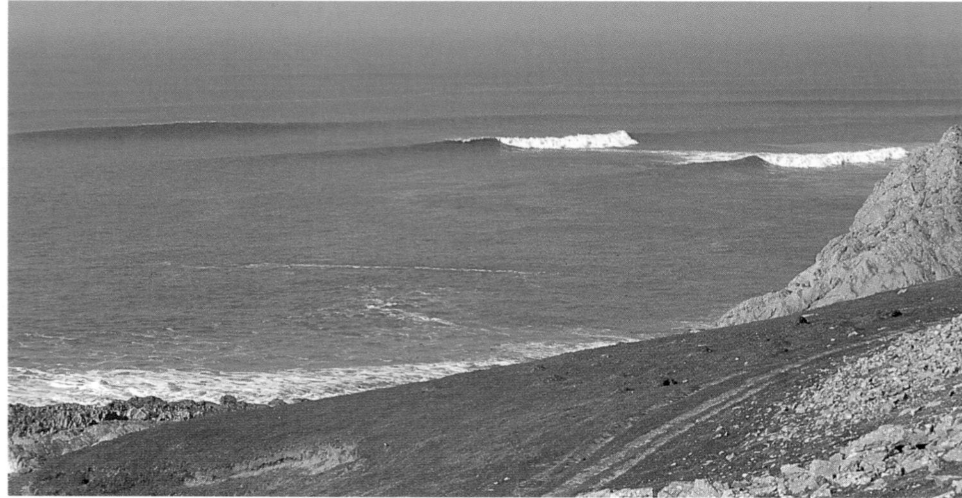
PHILL HOLDEN

Pete's Reef

1. Broughton Bay

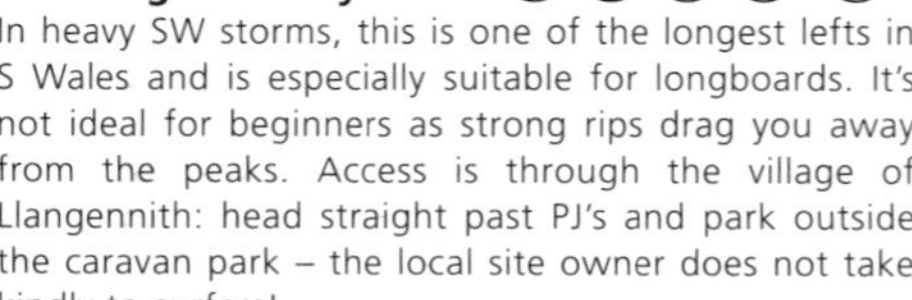

In heavy SW storms, this is one of the longest lefts in S Wales and is especially suitable for longboards. It's not ideal for beginners as strong rips drag you away from the peaks. Access is through the village of Llangennith: head straight past PJ's and park outside the caravan park – the local site owner does not take kindly to surfers!

Par grosse tempête de sud-ouest, c'est une des plus longues gauches du sud du Pays de Galles, idéal pour les longboards. De forts courants vous éloignent du pic, pas vraiment pour les débutants. Allez-y par Lalngennith, en passant PJ's et n'oubliez pas de vous garer à l'extérieur du caravaning parce que le proprio n'apprécie pas les surfers.

2. Llangennith Beach

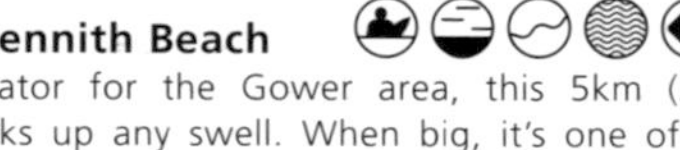

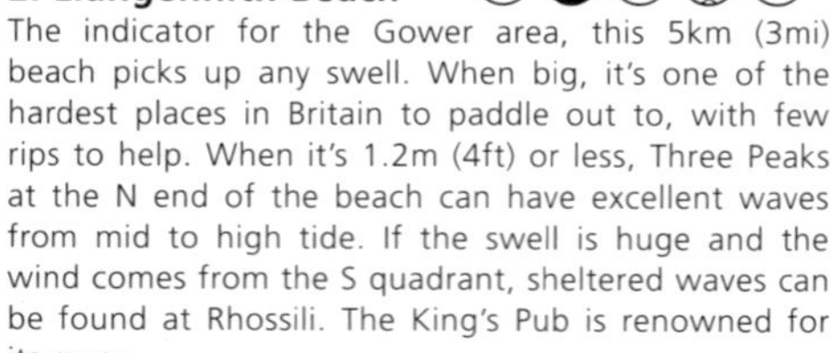

The indicator for the Gower area, this 5km (3mi) beach picks up any swell. When big, it's one of the hardest places in Britain to paddle out to, with few rips to help. When it's 1.2m (4ft) or less, Three Peaks at the N end of the beach can have excellent waves from mid to high tide. If the swell is huge and the wind comes from the S quadrant, sheltered waves can be found at Rhossili. The King's Pub is renowned for its raves.

Le spot indicateur de la zone de Gower: une plage de 5kms qui récupère toutes les houles. Quand c'est gros, c'est un des endroits les plus durs du pays pour passer la barre, avec peu de courants pour s'aider. Quand ça fait moins d'1,5m, le spot de Three Peaks au nord de la plage peut avoir d'excellentes vagues de mi-marée à marée haute. Quand c'est énorme et le vent de sud, on peut surfer abrité à Rhossili.

THE GILL

Llangennith

3. Fall Bay

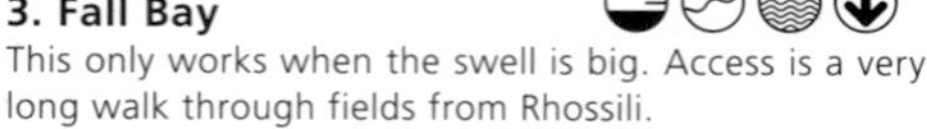

This only works when the swell is big. Access is a very long walk through fields from Rhossili.

Seulement quand ça rentre gros. Une trés longue marche à travers champs depuis Rhossili.

4. Pete's Reef

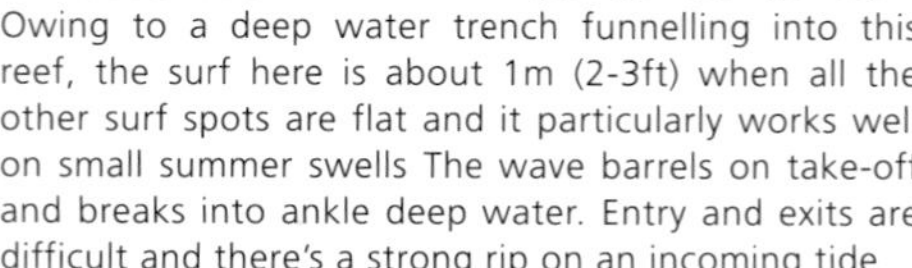

Owing to a deep water trench funnelling into this reef, the surf here is about 1m (2-3ft) when all the other surf spots are flat and it particularly works well on small summer swells The wave barrels on take-off and breaks into ankle deep water. Entry and exits are difficult and there's a strong rip on an incoming tide.

Due à une fosse profonde qui précède ce reef, les vagues peuvent faire un bon mètre quand les autres spots sont flat. Une vague qui tube au take-off avec de l'eau aux chevilles. Difficile d'y aller et d'en sortir. Marche bien avec les petits swells d'été. Fort courant à marée montante.

5. Boiler Reef

This wave breaks into a deep-water gully. Watch out for the take-off: any hesitation and you'll be picking barnacles out of your back! A strong rip constantly pulls you away from the impact zone. Don't be late leaving the water because as the bay fills, waves slam against the rocks. Difficult access.

Casse dans un goulet d'eau profonde. Attention au take-off car si vous hésitez une seconde, vous irez ramasser les bernacles avec votre dos! Un courant incessant vous tire hors de la zone d'impact. Ne sortez pas de l'eau trop tard car à marée haute, les vagues pètent sur les rochers. Accés difficile.

6. Sumpter's

This is the easiest of the Gower reefs to surf. A deep-water gully makes the paddle out easy, even when the swell is huge. Difficult access. Park respectfully.

Le plus facile des reefs de la Gower à surfer. Un chenal en eau rpofonde rend la rame facile même quand ça rentre énorme.Accès difficile et garez-vous correctement.

7. Port Eynon Point

Picking up more swell than the breaks to the E, this break is a sucky peak breaking in shallow water – the take-off and first section are best. As the wave peels into deeper ocean it flattens off.

Chope plus de houle que les spots à l'est. Un pic qui suce cassant sur trés peu d'eau, le take-off et la première section étant les meilleurs parce qu'aprés la vague va mourir en eau profonde.

PHIL HOLDEN

Gower Point Break

8. Horton

Llangennith needs to be about 2m (6ft) for Horton to get going but once it does it produces good shore-break barrels. It's excellent for beginners as it's usually uncrowded. Horton and Port Eynon Beach are two great Gower sailing spots.

Il faut que ça fasse 2m à Llangenith pour qu'Horton puisse envoyer des bonnes vagues de shore-break. Parfait pour les débutants car souvent tranquille. Horton et la plage de Port Eynon sont aussi deux super spots de funboard.

PHIL HOLDEN

PJ at Boilers

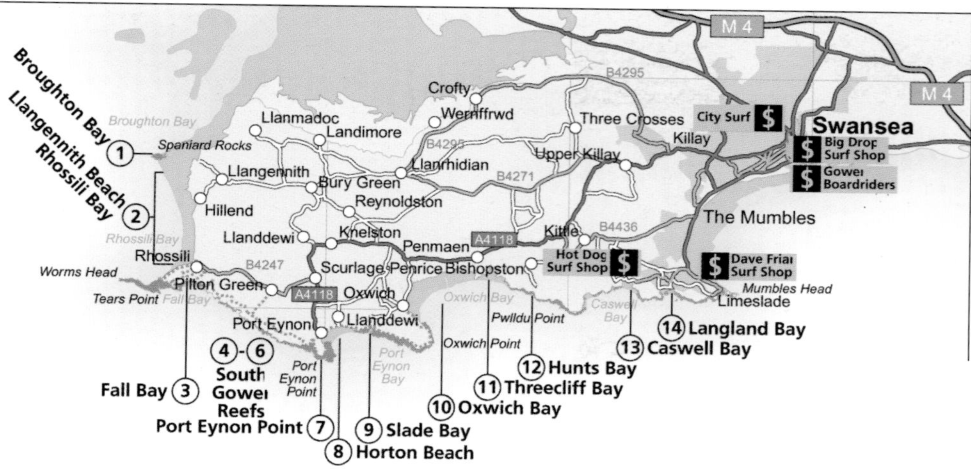

9. Slade Bay

This needs a solid swell to work. Access is via Horton followed by a pleasant walk around the coast path below the cliffs.

Encore par grosse houle. Allez à Horton et marchez le long de la côte en bas des falaises, c'est sympa.

10. Oxwich Bay

A beautiful, crescent-shaped bay, which is calm most of the year but comes alive during big winter storms, handling the howling W winds. It's always bigger as the tide turns back. When it's working, word spreads quickly and it's usually crowded. Access is via an expensive, privately-owned beach car park.

Une baie superbe en forme de croissant, calme le plus souvent sauf en hiver pendant les tempêtes; ça supporte les vents d'ouest déchaînés, toujours plus gros quand la marée descend. Attention, l'accés par la plage est payant car c'est privé.

11. Threecliff Bay

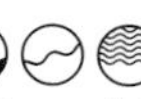
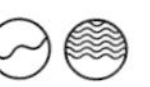

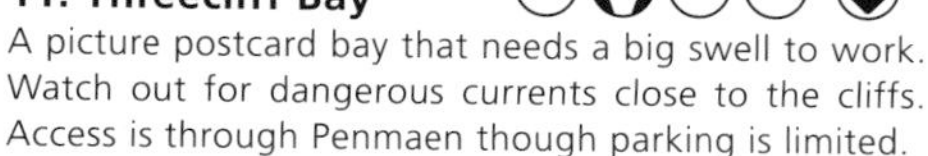

A picture postcard bay that needs a big swell to work. Watch out for dangerous currents close to the cliffs. Access is through Penmaen though parking is limited.

La baie style carte postale où il faut encore pas mal de houle pour espérer des vagues. Courants dangereux à côté de la falaise. Pour y aller, visez le petit parking de Penmaen.

12. Hunt's Bay

Head through Southgate village to find an uncrowded wave that needs a solid 2m (5-6ft) swell to work.

Exige au moins deux mètres de houle pou fonctionner correctement. Peu de monde en général. On y va par Southgate.

13. Caswell Bay

A stone's throw from Langland Bay, this break only works in a strong SW swell but is always smaller than Langland. The best wave is the left at the W end of the beach.

A une portée de fusil de Langland, la meilleure vague est une gauche à l'extrémité ouest de la plage. Ne marche que par bonne houle de sud-ouest, toujours plus petit que Langland.

14. Langland Bay

Langland produces a huge variety of waves. The high tide shore-break close outs are perfect for trying big manoeuvres in front of the crew on the promenade. As the tide drops, the (Rotherslade) lefts on the reef start to work: they're slow but near to perfect. This often turns into what is known as The Reef: a right and left that's normally crowded and pretty slow. As the tide goes out, the middle of the bay might start to work along with the lefts and Shit Pipe. At low tide Crab Island starts to become visible and a nice right-hander peels off the back of it. It's a great wave but has a heavy crew of older surfers on big boards along with some young whipper snappers. You should stay away unless you catch it with no one out (live in hope!). The other option is the point, a nice right with not too many people surfing it.

Une large variété de vagues. Le shore-break qui ferme à marée haute est idéal pour tenter des grosses manoeuvres devant la foule sur le remblai. Quand ça descend, les gauches de Rotherslade sur le reef se mettent à fonctionner: c'est lent mais c'est parfait. Ca se transforme souvent en ce qu'on appelle le 'Reef', un pic droite-gauche assez facile avec du monde d'habitude. Quand la marée descend vraiment, le milieu de la baie se met à marcher avec des gauches et 'Shit Pipe'. A marée basse, Crab island commence à être visible avec une belle droite qui déroule dessus. C'est une super vague mais attention aux vieux locaux avec des grosses planches et aux jeunes grommets qui fracassent, il ne faut démarrer que s'il n'y a personne au pic! Vous pouvez toujours essayer le Point, une droite sympa pas trop fréquentée.

ALEX WILLIAMS

Langland Bay

Pembrokeshire

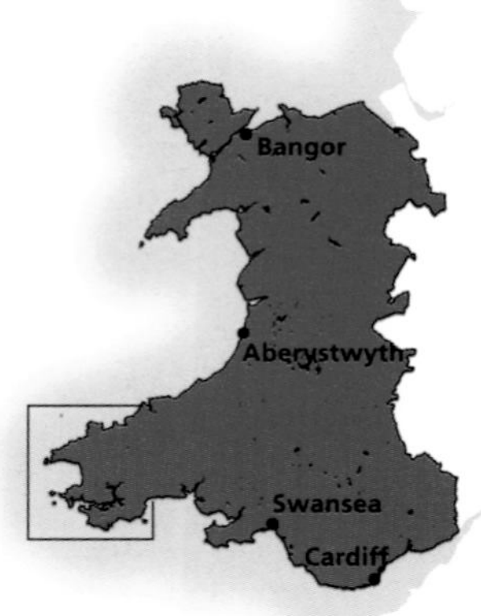

Tenby
THE GILL

1. Abereiddy

Enjoy great scenery; there's also none of the crowds found at Whitesand Bay. A bed of rock at the S end of the beach can produce a hollow left at mid tide. The break receives protection from all winds except a W, so check on a SW to SE wind. Park by the beach.

Un panorama splendide sans commune mesure avec la foule de Whitesand Bay. Une langue de rochers au sud de la plage qui envoie une gauche creuse à mi-marée. Offre une bonne protection des vents sauf ceux d'ouest. Checker par vents de sud-ouest ou de sud-est.

2. Whitesand Bay

Impressive setting, friendly locals, clean water and working up to 2-3m (6-8ft), it's small wonder this wave gets crowded (seals also wait in the line up). When it's working there are plenty of waves. To get out back when it's big there's a useful rip at the N end of the beach. A good beginner's spot.

Marche jusqu'à 2,5m. L'eau est propre, les locaux sont sympas et le paysage est à couper le souffle. Cela dit, y'a du peuple et des phoques aussi qui attendent au pic mais quand ça marche, y'a plein de vagues. Pour sortir quand c'est gros, il faut utiliser un courant au nord de la plage. Un bon spot pour débutants. Parking à proximité.

3. St Bride's Bay

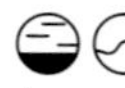   

With 8km (5mi) of consistent beach waves, Newgale has the most swell so is the most surfed. Broadhaven receives protection from SW wind but is usually half the size of Newgale. Druiston is not so accessible but is good for some solitude and suitable for beginners. Easy parking.

8 kms de vagues consistantes. Newgale chope le plus de houle et c'est l'endroit le plus surfé du coin. Broadhaven reçoit une bonne protection des vents de SO mais c'est souvent deux fois plus petit que Newgale. Druiston n'est pas aussi accessible mais parfait si l'on veut être seul. Parfait pour les débutants. Parking facile.

4. Marloes Sands

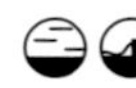  

A rarely ridden but consistent rocky beach break with good peaky waves. You should watch for the incoming tide, which can cover the whole beach. A 10-minute walk is signposted from the car park.

Rarement surfé mais consistant avec de bons petits pics. Il y des rochers éparpillés sur la plage et il faut faire gaffe à la marée montante, qui peut couvrir toute la plage. Une marche de 10 minutes est indiquée depuis le parking.

5. Freshwater West

Pembrokeshire's most consistent and popular break has a series of reefs linking two bays, with particularly good sandbars at the extremes of the tides. The best waves break on the ragged rocks at the S end, giving hollow rides up to 100m (90yd). The beach is MoD and firing times are indicated by red flags. Rips can be strong, so beware. Parking is easy.

Le spot le plus connu et le plus consistent de la Dyfed, où beaucoup de compétitions se sont déroulées. Une série de reefs joint les deux baies avec des bancs de sable particulièrement bons en été aux marées extrêmes. Les meilleures vagues cassent sur des rochers sauvages du côté sud, donnant des vagues creuses de prés de 100 mètres. Cependant, cette vague est une zone militaire dont les tirs sont indiqués avec des drapeaux rouges. Les courants peuvent être forts, méfiance. Parking fastoche.

Freshwater West
PHIL HOLDEN

6. Broadhaven

    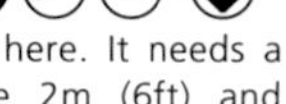

Good wedgy lefts are the speciality here. It needs a decent swell but closes out above 2m (6ft) and handles a strong W or SW wind. Park by the beach.

De bonnes gauches en coude qui sont la spécialité du coin mais il faut une houle de bonne taille et ça ferme au-dessus de 2m. Peut tenir de forts vents d'ouest ou de sud-ouest. Parking sur la plage.

PHIL HOLDEN
One good reason to spend £3.95 on a Land Survey map of Pembrokeshire

Broadhaven

7. Freshwater East

A winter break, best at the N end, picks up most of the swell and is favoured on the incoming tide. Park by the beach.

Un spot d'hiver dont l'extrémité nord chope le plus de swell. Meilleur à marée montante. Parking sur la plage.

8. Manorbier

A 12th-century Norman castle stands guard over a lovely sand and rock beach, which has impressive consistent, quality waves. Though it can be crowded, it works well, even in onshores. Park by beach.

Une charmante plage de sable et de rochers avec un impressionant château Normand du XII° siècle qui monte la garde sur des vagues souvent de qualité. Bien que ça puisse être bondé, sachez quand même que ça marche aussi avec de l'on-shore. Parking sur la plage.

9. Tenby (South Beach)

When all the other spots are blown out, this can be worth a visit in a storm swell. In the summer tourists crowd it out but for the rest of the year it's fine. It's popular with beginners and windsurfers.

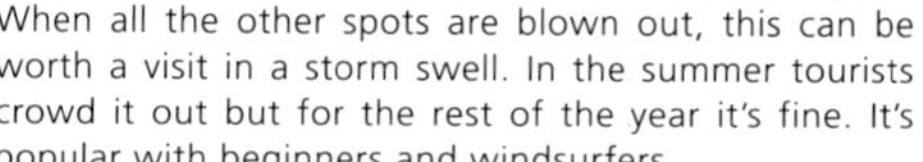

Peut valoir le détour si c'est la tempête quand tous les autres spots sont balayés par le vent. Est gavée de touristes en été, mais le reste de l'année, c'est cool.

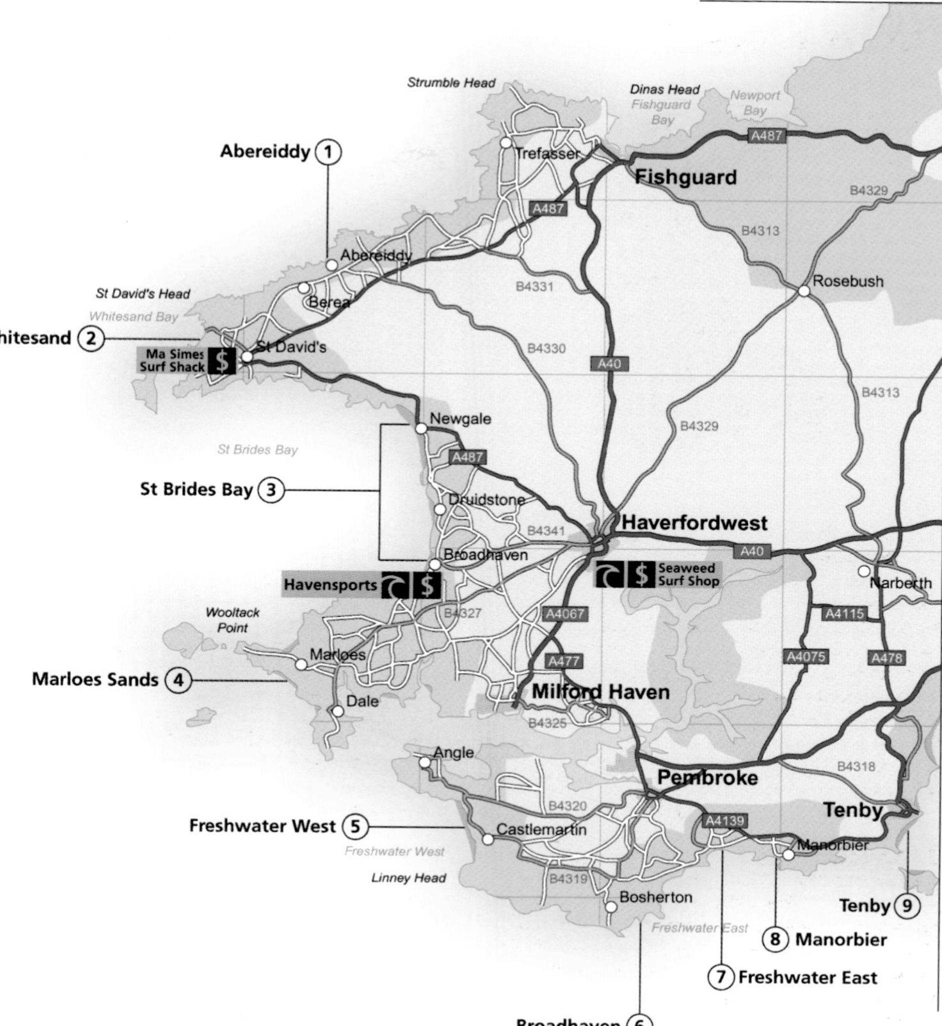

Manorbier

North West

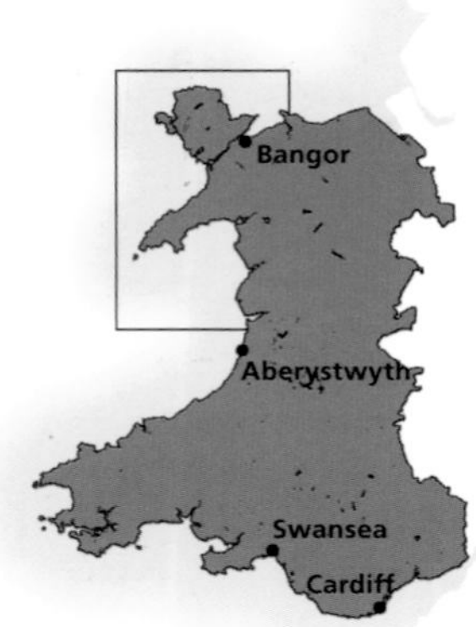

Mid Wales

1. Llandudno

A popular seaside resort with badly polluted water. It only works in a large W gale.

Marche seulement en présence d'un fort coup de vent d'ouest. Station balnéaire à la mode avec une eau très polluée.

2. Anglesey

The SW coast between Rhosneigr and Aberffraw has a number of different waves breaking when SW winds push swell up from the Irish Sea. A popular windsurfing venue with easy access to the beaches.

La côte Sud-Ouest enntre Rhosneigr et Aberffraw regorge de nombreuses vagues différentes déferlant quand les vents de Sud-Ouest soulèvent la mer d'Irelande. Un lieu connu pour le windsurf avec un accés facile aux plages.

3. Whistling Sands

Needing at least Force Eight gales to get going, this wraparound right is the pick and is also popular with bodyboarders. It's best at high tide from 1-1.5m (2-4ft).

A besoin d'un vent à décorner les boeufs pour marcher. Une droite qui s'enroule bien, fréquentée par les body boarders, c'est la meileure vague. Meilleure à marée haute à partir d'1m.

4. Aberdaron

Deserted for much of the year, this is a consistent and attractive beach break where waves come in right over the boulders. Survey the scene from a good pub overlooking the beach.

Vague consistante et intéressante, désertée depuis pas mal d'années. Des droites déroulent sur des rochers.

5. Fisherman's/Rhiw

Strong localism, difficult access and big boulders keep this spot relatively uncrowded.

Un 'localisme' affirmé, un accés difficile et de gros rochers permettent à ce spot d'être relativement peu fréquenté.

6.Hell's Mouth

Duckboards

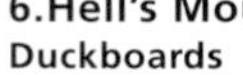

Probably the busiest spot in N Wales with 7km (4mi) of beach, this break has waves better from mid to high tide (30cm-1.2m/1-4ft). It's good for beginners.

Six kms de plages et certainement le spot du nord le plus surfé. Les vagues sont généralement meilleures de la mi-marée à marée haute pour de petites vagues. Bon pour les débutants.

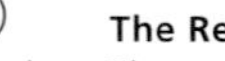

The Reef

The most consistent reef break on the Lleyn Peninsula is also probably the most crowded; works best either side of high tide.

Le récif le plus consistant se situe sur la Lleyn Peninsula mais c'est aussi le plus bondé. Meilleur avant et après la marée haute.

The Corner

Starting breaking on rock, finishing over sand and holding the biggest surf in the area, this is one fat wave. The break can link up with the reef and handles a S wind.

Commence à dérouler sur du rocher et finit sur du sable. Tient la grosse houle. Peut rejoindre le récif et marchera avec un vent du sud. A tendance à être une vague épaisse.

Hell's Mouth, middle and corner

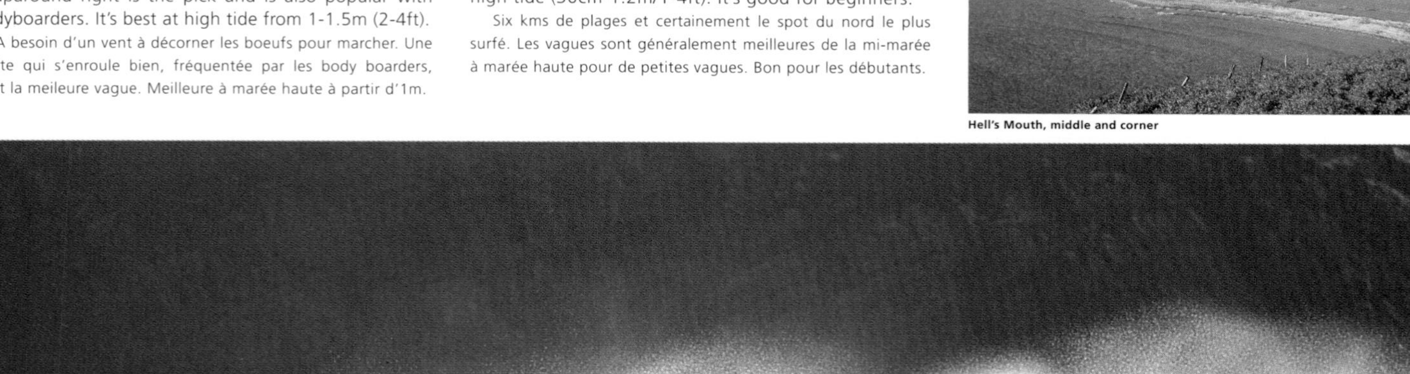

Hell's Mouth, corner

Chris Hookes, Porth Ceiriad

7. Porth Ceiriad

Swell bounces off the cliffs to form a series of hollow, powerful peaks and a worthwhile spot working to about 2m (6ft). Park and camp on the cliff edge overlooking the break.

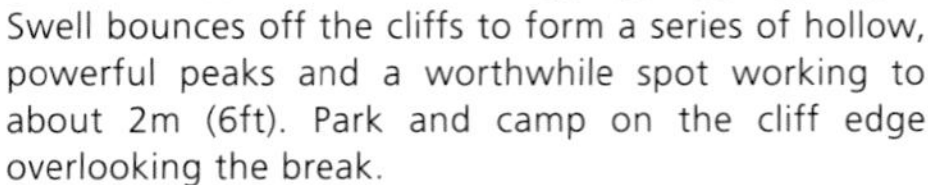

La houle rebondit sur les falaises pour former une succession de pics creux et puissants. Bon spot qui marche jusqu'aux alentours de 2 m. Il y a un parking et un camping sur le bord de la falaise surplombant le spot.

8. Harlech

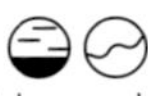  

The beach is 6km (3.5mi) long and has a classic castle worth a look on one of the many flat days.

Six kms de plages avec un château d'époque qui vaut une visite lors d'un des nombreux jours calmes.

9. Llandanwg to Barmouth

Explore an uncrowded 24km (15mi) stretch of exposed beach-break waves.

Des vagues de sable bien exposées qui s'étendent sur 24km.

10. Llwyngwril

This can be the best wave in mid-Wales when there's a big swell pushing up the Irish Channel. Only suitable for experienced surfers.

Peut-être la meilleure vague du centre du Pays de Galles quand une grosse houle remonte le Channel irlandais.Pour surfeurs confirmés seulement.

11. Borth

Small waves make this 3km (2mi) stretch of beach ideal for beginners – it's uncrowded and best on the pushing tide.

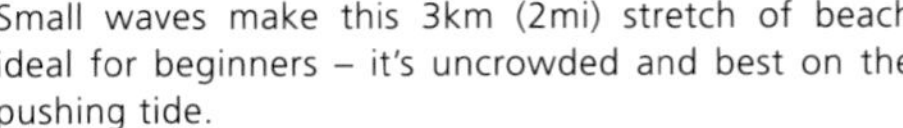

Station balnéaire renommée possédant 3kms de plage, meilleure à la marée montante. Peu de monde à l'eau et idéal pour les surfeurs de petites vagues et les débutants.

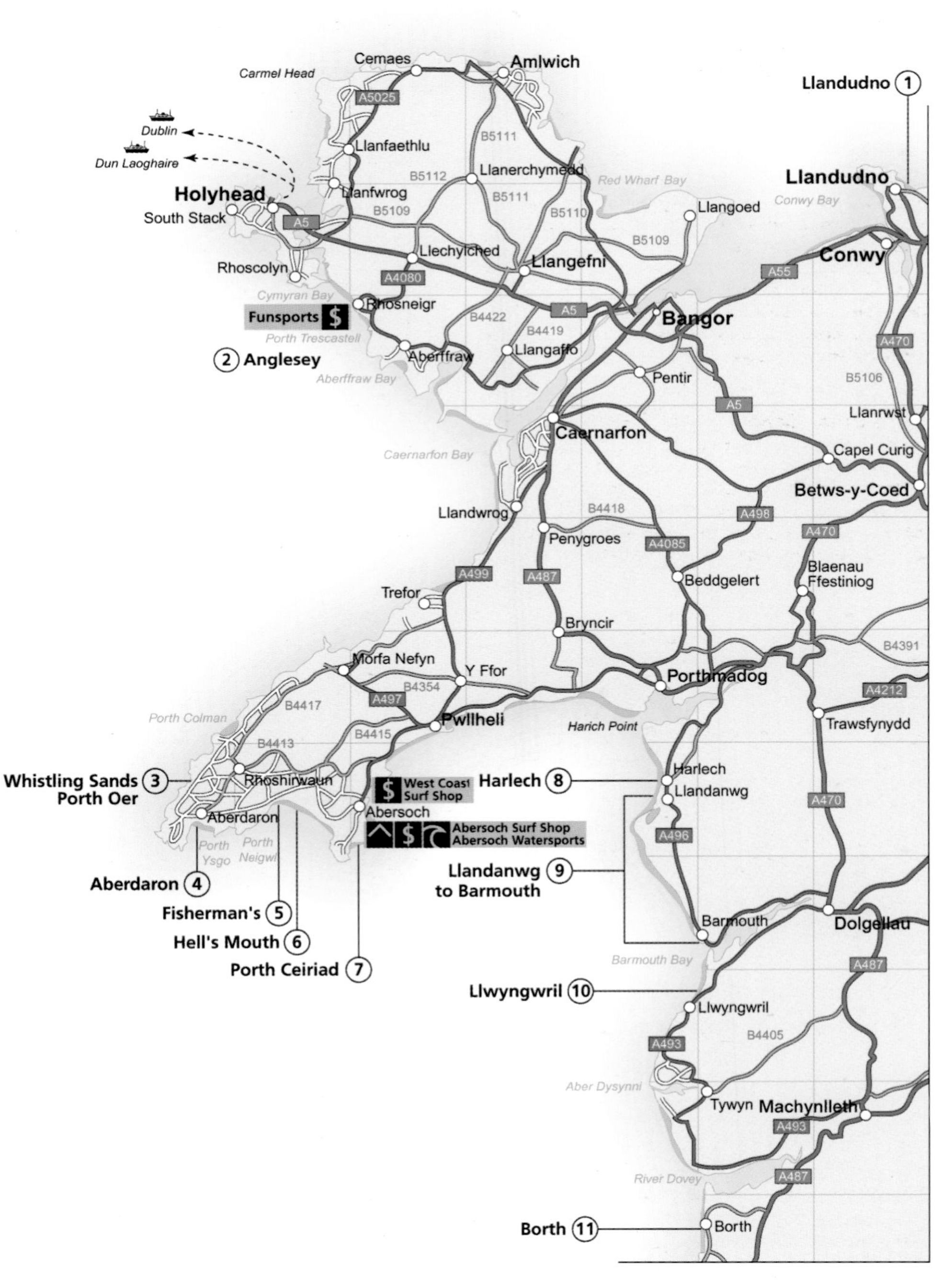

Llandudno (1)
Anglesey (2)
Whistling Sands (3) Porth Oer
Aberdaron (4)
Fisherman's (5)
Hell's Mouth (6)
Porth Ceiriad (7)
Harlech (8)
Llandanwg (9) to Barmouth
Llwyngwril (10)
Borth (11)
Funsports
West Coast Surf Shop
Abersoch Surf Shop
Abersoch Watersports
Dublin
Dun Laoghaire

This is one of many line ups that rarely get checked, let alone surfed. Walking through fields is an integral part of surfing in Norway

North Sea Nations

The coastlines of the North Sea are seeing a remarkable growth in surf culture: the seafaring Dutch are going back to their roots, Norway is unmasking its potential, while Germany, despite its tiny coast, is producing the biggest volume of afficionados. The Swedes and Danes are joining in, enthusiastically braving the frigid waters of the Baltic and Kattegat. In testimony to the sport's pull, where there are waves someone will end up riding them. Not surprisingly, travel is high on a North Sea surfer's agenda in winter, although this time is also when the dedicated are rewarded with some real North Sea juice.

la Mer du Nord

Les côtes qui se partagent la Mer du Nord connaissent une expansion rapide de la culture surf. On trouve même des surfers sur la Baltique en Suède et partout où il y a des vagues, on finira par trouver quelqu'un qui les surfe, ce qui prouve l'essor phénoménal de ce sport. Les Pays-Bas et la Norvège sont probablement les pays les plus développés, bien que l'Allemagne malgré sa portion de côte réduite, ait le plus grand nombre d'adeptes, qui surfent plus souvent en France ou aux Canaries que chez eux.

JAN ERIC JENSEN

JØRGEN MICHAELSEN - SURFSENTRUM

Ten centimetres of powder after a double overhead session at Kvassheim

Norway
Capital: Oslo
Population: 4.3 million
Area:323,900sqkm/83,657sqmi
Language: Norwegian, Lappish
Currency: kroner (Nok)

Telephone info:
Country code: 47
Dial out code: 095
Police: 112
Ambulance: 113

Sweden
Capital: Stockholm
Population: 8.6 million
Area:449,960sqkm/90,500sqmi
Language: Swedish, Finnish, Lappish
Currency: krona (Sek)

Telephone info:
Country code: 46
Dial out code: 009
Emergency: 112

RIMER S. HANSEN

A Danish crowd

Denmark
Capital: Copenhagen
Population: 5.2 million
Area: 43,094km/11,161sqmi
Language: Danish
Currency: kroner (Dkk)

Telephone info:
Country code: 45
Dial out code: 00
Emergency: 112
Directory Enquiries: 118
International Directory: 113

Germany
Capital: Berlin
Population: 80.3 million
Area:356,910sqkm/92,439sqmi
Language: German, Bavarian
Currency: Deutsche Mark (DM)

Telephone info:
Country code: 49
Dial out code: 00
Emergency: 112

The Netherlands
Capital: Amsterdam, The Hague
Population: 15.2 million
Area: 37,330sqkm/9,700sqmi
Currency: Guilder (fl)
Language: Dutch

Telephone info:
Country code: 31
Dial out code: 00
Emergency: 06 11

Belgium
Capital: Brussels
Population: 10 million
Area: 33,100sqkm/8,572sqmi
Currency: Belgian franc (BF)
Language: Dutch, French, German, Flemish

Telephone info:
Country code: 32
Dial out code: 00
Emergency: 112

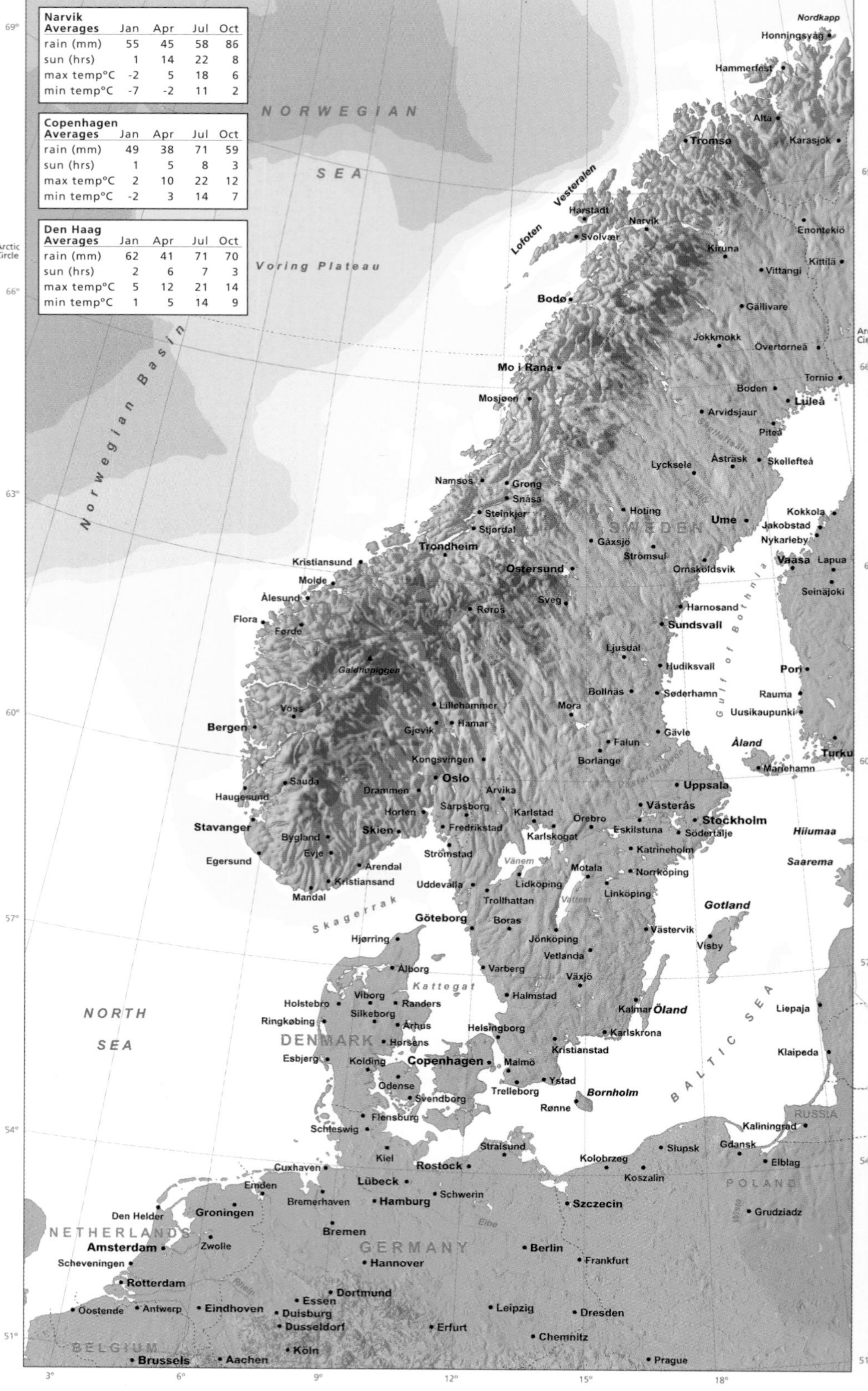

Narvik Averages	Jan	Apr	Jul	Oct
rain (mm)	55	45	58	86
sun (hrs)	1	14	22	8
max temp°C	-2	5	18	6
min temp°C	-7	-2	11	2

Copenhagen Averages	Jan	Apr	Jul	Oct
rain (mm)	49	38	71	59
sun (hrs)	1	5	8	3
max temp°C	2	10	22	12
min temp°C	-2	3	14	7

Den Haag Averages	Jan	Apr	Jul	Oct
rain (mm)	62	41	71	70
sun (hrs)	2	6	7	3
max temp°C	5	12	21	14
min temp°C	1	5	14	9

North Sea Nations Physical Map

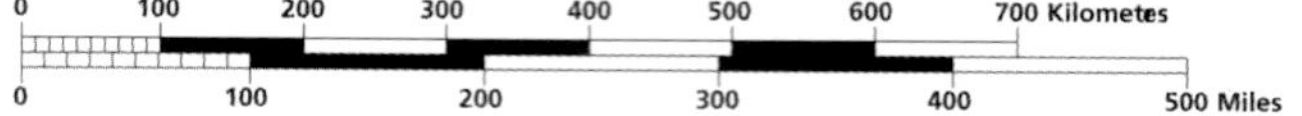

Surfsentrum shop owner Jørgen Michaelsen getting a few quiet ones, Fyret, Norway

Introduction

The North Sea is a relatively shallow body of water, but throughout the year, winds blow from south-westerly to north-westerly directions creating swell. These winds are associated with low pressure systems travelling from Iceland to Scandinavia and form in the Channel and North Sea; they provide the North Sea surfer with waves ranging from half to two metres (one to six foot) and bigger. The best waves occur from late August to April when the water temperature drops dramatically (in Norway it plummets to a mighty crisp 2°C (34°F). A typical winter scenario is overhead swell and offshore caused by a continental high pressure which also keeps the lows some distance from the coast. This can mean sub-zero temperatures and powder snow on the beach, so you'll understand why thick wetties, booties, gloves and hood are a must. Although water quality at spots near rural areas is OK, the general water quality of the North Sea is poor due to its history of abuse by industry.

Summertime (May until August) can be very flat, with only the occasional classic day. However, if there is a blocking anti-cyclone in the Atlantic, more low pressures are forced into the Norwegian Sea, creating some decent summer surf. A passage of weather fronts can also give good conditions when the prevailing onshore winds turn offshore and there are still the remains of swell. This gives rise to short sessions – head for the beach as soon as the wind changes. Water temperatures in Holland can rise to 18°C (66°F) in summer so surfing in a springy is possible in southern areas.

Introduction

La Mer du Nord est une étendue d'eau peu profonde mais tout au long de l'année, les vents soufflent du sud-ouest au nord-ouest en créant de la houle. Ces vents sont générés par les systèmes dépressionnaires voyageant depuis L'Islande en Scandinavie ou qui se forment en Manche et dans la Mer du Nord. Ils produisent des vagues de 30 cms à 2m, parfois plus. Les meilleures vagues arrivent de fin août à avril où la température de l'eau peut descendre à un 2 degrés polaire en Norvège. Une houle typique hivernale fait un bon mètre cinquante et ça peut être bon si le vent est off-shore. Malheureusement, ces houles correspondent aussi avec le temps glacial quand les autres pressions continentales gardent les dépressions à distance de la côte. Cela signifie des températures négatives avec de la poudreuse sur la plage! Vous comprendrez alors pourquoi une combinaison épaisse, des botillons, des gants et une cagoule sont indispensables.

L'été de mai à Août peut être désespéramment flat avec très peu de bons jours. Un passage de fronts dépressionnaires peut apporter de bonnes conditions quand les vents on-shore dominants tournent à 180° et qu'il reste encore de la houle. Ca donne lieu à de courtes sessions mais ça veut dire qu'il faut aller checker la plage dès que le vent tourne. La température de l'eau peut monter jusqu'à 18°C en été en Hollande, on peut donc sortir le springsuit dans cette partie méridionale.

En général pitoyable en sortie de rivière, des ports et à proximité des zones industrielles. Des preuves affolantes de pollution furent récemment découvertes par des surfers belges qui firent une ponction en Mer du Nord dans une bouteille de bière qu'ils mirent sur une télévision. Après 2 jours, elle explosa. Bien que les spots en zones rurales semblent satisfaisants, la moyenne générale en Mer du Nord n'est pas éniale vu les abus commis par l'industrie.

Further information

Norwegian Association
Jørgen Michaelsen,
Madlaveien 10
4008 Norway (51) 53 65 93

Swedish Association
Binge Eliasson, S Stundiun,
St Erics, Gotan 121
Stockholm 11343
(46) 833 4555

German Surfing Contact
DWV, UDO Tweckelmeier,
Herrenstr, 22, 48167
Münster (49) 02506 6816

Danish Surfing Association
Ruskør 53, 10 2610, Rødorre
(45) 36 47 4090

Holland Surfing Association
PO Box 84007, 2508 AA
The Hague, The Netherlands

Belgian Surfing Association
Contact Guy Fierens at
'Wave-Warriors'
(32) 059 809 897

Norway

Surf Culture Roar Berge is considered Norwegian surfing's 'grand old man'. Along with Per Grude and a crew of Americans residing in Norway with oil companies, they paddled out in the Jaeren area in 1982. The late 80s saw the next wave of Norsemen charging into the waves, although it wasn't until 1993 that surfboards and bare essentials were at last available from windsurf shops. The scene is concentrated around Stavanger: the locals are a friendly bunch, still stoked to have someone new to surf with.

Where to go Norway is one of the last surfing frontiers in Europe and there are still vast tracks of undiscovered waves along a significant proportion of its coastline. Only a few spots are surfed regularly. The coast is generally rocky and fringed with islets and skerries; getting around is time consuming, particularly when deep fjords and high mountains have to be crossed. The Jaeren area, extending from Stavanger to Eigersund, has the highest density of spots. The coastline here is unusually open and flat, providing almost 30 spots within an hour's drive of Stavanger. South of Egersund (around Lista), granite reefs hold many unridden possibilities. Areas further north around Molde and on Stat-landet are frequently visited by surfers from Oslo. This area picks up north swells far better than Jaeren, and focuses them onto some particularly heavy reefs. The tidal range is small in the south, but further north it reaches several metres. Way up north around Lofoten, killer waves lurk amongst stunning scenery, granite reefs and cobblestone-fringed beach breaks.

When to go The best month for quality waves is December, but this also coincides with the fewest winter daylight hours. October to May is the pick of the months, but summer can be good if the lows are pushed into the Norwegian Basin. An amping winter season will give two or three days of relatively good surf a week, while summer is more of a gamble.

Environment Although most of Norway's coast seems pristine and clean, a number of water quality issues exist. Apart from the odd fish factory 'chumming' at some spots, and the decision to extend outfall pipes rather than upgrade treatment plants, the main problem is phosphates and algae blooms. The North Sea Convention requires that all member states treat for phosphorous and nitrogen in order to help prevent the large red blooms of algae that devastate the marine eco-system. Offshore from Jaeren's main breaks, oil tankers wash out their storage tanks, which means lots of oily spots and dirty wax deposits. Large kelp beds are also commercially farmed (one of the extracts is used to make beer foam), a factor which has been blamed for increasing beach erosion and leg rope tangles.

The grand old man of Norwegian surfing: Roar Berge at Ervika, Stat-landet

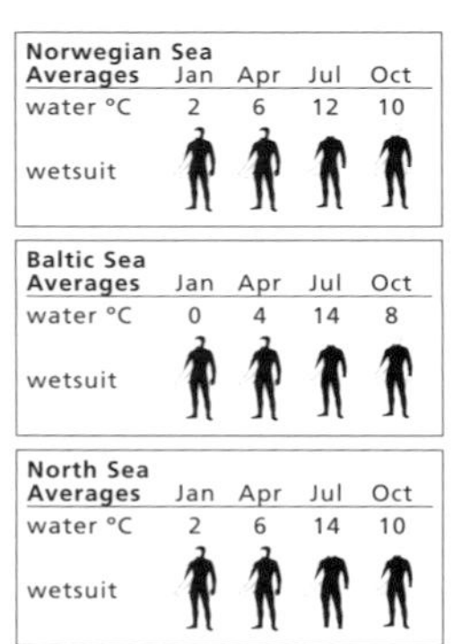

Norwegian Sea Averages	Jan	Apr	Jul	Oct
water °C	2	6	12	10
wetsuit				

Baltic Sea Averages	Jan	Apr	Jul	Oct
water °C	0	4	14	8
wetsuit				

North Sea Averages	Jan	Apr	Jul	Oct
water °C	2	6	14	10
wetsuit				

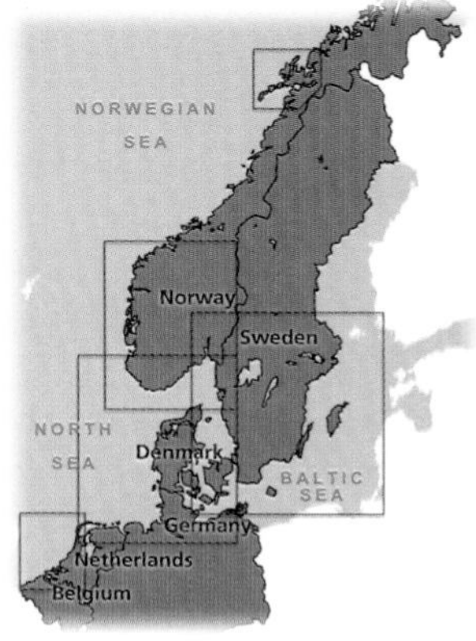

BINGE

Torö back in the days

Sweden

Surf Culture Sweden is not well known for its surf, but following the formation of the Swedish Surfing Association in 1985 by Janne Ekstedt, Swedish surfers have participated in the European Championships and come to the world's attention. Each year more and more people are taking to the waves, especially after Sweden's recent snowboarding boom. Some think it's impossible to ride waves up here, but there are a few legendary spots, so bring your board when you come to Sweden.

Where to go Sweden's east coast actually has more breaks than those on the west coast. Localised wind swells in the Baltic mean the islands of Gotland and Faro are a good call. The Kattegat area north of Goteborg receives winter groundswells from the North Sea and may be worth a check.

When to go The swell is best during autumn and winter when the storms are blowing, though there can be some decent waves during the summer. All you have to do is wait for a low pressure.

Environment The water quality is generally good in Swedish waters, though there were problems in the 80s with regard to a lack of oxygen in the water on the west coast. Sweden's coasts have also been affected by oil discharges.

Norvege

La Norvège est une des dernières frontières du surf en Europe avec des vagues sur une partie non négligeable de la côte. Malgré tout, seulement quelques spots peuvent être surfés régulièrement parce que cette côte est généralement rocheuse et entourée d'îlots et de cailloux. Rouler prend pas mal de temps quand il faut contourner les fjords profonds ou certaines montagnes assez élevées.

La zone de Jaeren qui possède la plus grande concentration de spots va de Stavanger à Eigersund. Le littoral y est anormalement ouvert avec presque 30 spots surfables à moins d'une heure de Stavanger. Pendant une bonne saison d'hiver, on peut surfer deux à trois jours par semaine. Les houles d'été sont rares et la qualité des vagues plutôt décevante. Les zones au nord aux environs de Molde jusqu'à Stat-Landet sont souvent fréquentées par les surfers d'Oslo. Le marnage des marées est minîme dans le sud alors qu'il atteint plusieurs mètres dans le nord. La qualité de l'eau est bonne sur tous les spots mentionnés.

Suède

La Suède n'est pas franchement réputée pour ses vagues mais la fédé suédoise fut constituée en 1985 par Janne Ekstedt, ce qui a permis, entre autre, aux suédois de participer à tous les championnats depuis. La houle est la meilleure en automne et en hiver quand les tempêtes soufflent, bien qu'il puisse y avoir quelques coups de surf en été où la seule chose à faire est d'attendre les dépressions. Chaque année, de plus en plus de gens se mettent au surf, surtout depuis le boom du snowboard ces dernières années. Certains pensent qu'il est impossible de surfer des vagues ici bien qu'il y ait quelques bons spots. Alors, si vous passez par la Suède, n'oubliez pas votre planche.

Qualité de l'eau: Elle est généralement bonne par ici, bien qu'il y eut quelques problèmes dans les années 80 à cause du manque d'oxygène dans les eux occidentales. Les côtes ont été aussi affectées par les vidanges d'huile. Le problème de la qualité de l'eau est crucial et demande plus d'attention que ces quelques lignes.

Allemagne

Le surf en Allemagne débuta dans le milieu des années 60 quand les maître-nageurs de Sylt entendirent parler de surf à Biarritz. Après avoir essayé en France, ils trouvèrent ça tellement génial qu'ils fabriquèrent des planches et chercher les spots sur l'île. C'était le début. Pendant les années 70, un étudiant nommé Uli Richter donnait des leçons de surf à Hendaye. I l écrivit un livre et son école devint célèbre. La communauté des surfers de Sylt se développa avec des voyageurs d'autres régions qui attrapèrent le virus. Ensuite, dans les années 80, quand le windsurf devint à la mode, certains adeptes essayèrent de surfer sans la voile. Les pères apprirent à leurs enfants et on en est maintenant à la deuxième génération.

En 1988, un groupe d'une douzaine de gars formèrent une équipe pour participer aux championnats du Monde amateurs et en 1991, la fédé allemande (DWV) fut constituée. Depuis, le nombre de surfers allemands aux compétitions européennes et

Denmark

Surf Culture Surfing in Denmark started in the mid to late 80s; Dane Rolf Eriksen was the first native to take to the waves. About a year later, another compatriot Reimer Hansen returned from Australia and started surfing with Eriksen. For a couple of years the pair surfed the North Shore of Sjølland in complete solitude, until another Dane Henrik Villadsen came along and, well, three's a crowd so word spread. The west coast of Denmark may have been first surfed by Germans. You'll still find more Germans surfing around Klitmøller than Danes, although most of them come to windsurf.

Although windsurfing was and still is the most popular watersport, a small hardcore surf tribe is beginning to grow. Some 'sailors' have even dropped their sails for real boards. More recently, 1995 saw the formation of the the Danish Surfing Association and 1996 witnessed the first Danish Championship, held in Klitmøller; later that year a team of five Danes went to the World Surfing Games. There are probably only around 100 surfers in Denmark and only half would be classified as 'core'.

Where to go The surf spots along the west coast of Denmark receive groundswell from the North Sea, but are usually of short duration. Wind swell is the most common source of rideable waves. For all the spots on Sjølland (Zealand) to work, it has be blowing hard. The piers can provide protection, giving side to offshore wind conditions.

When to go The season runs from April to November and will produce wind swells and bearable conditions. Only well-prepared hard-core types need apply for winter waves.

Environment The water quality around Denmark's shores isn't great, though with public lobbying for polluting industries to be shut down, including some nuclear processing plants on the east coast, it's improving (slowly).

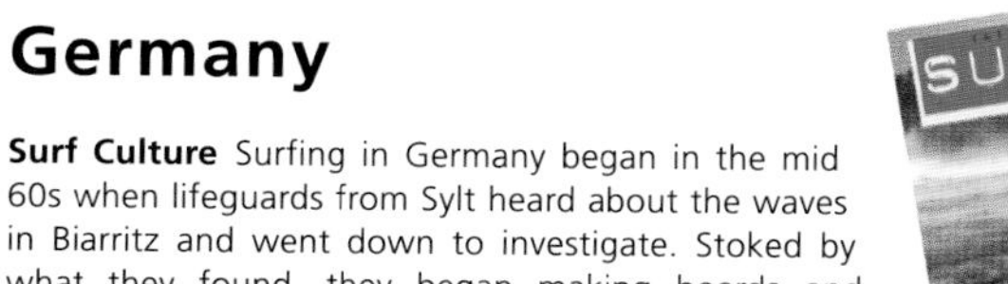

Germany

Surf Culture Surfing in Germany began in the mid 60s when lifeguards from Sylt heard about the waves in Biarritz and went down to investigate. Stoked by what they found, they began making boards and searching out spots in Germany. During the 70s, a student Uli Richter began giving lessons in Hendaye. He went on to author a book about surfing and word about his school spread. The Sylt community blossomed and travellers from other areas caught the bug. In 1988 a dozen enthusiasts formed a team to participate in the World Amateurs in Costa Rica; three years later the German Surfing Federation (DWV) was formed. There are now three surf magazines and more than 10,000 surfers, including a good percentage of women. Many travel the world avoiding the European winter but from time to time we hear about new spots on the north and eastern coasts.

Where to go Germany receives the same swells as Denmark, although Borkum and Nordeney are more open to northerly swell. Sylt is the seat of German surfing as it boasts the finest waves. The east coast is for desperadoes only.

When to go September to April receives the most swell, while summer will see crowds in the water with whatever swell – a longboard is a good idea.

Environment The problem of algae blooms off Sweden and Norway is caused by agricultural pollution (such as nutrients and fertilisers) flowing into mainland rivers, as they head to sea. Industrial and city run off – this can include heavy metals – add to the problems. However, most local surfers seem to think it's fairly clean.

GUIDO BREBACH

A foamy day in the North Sea

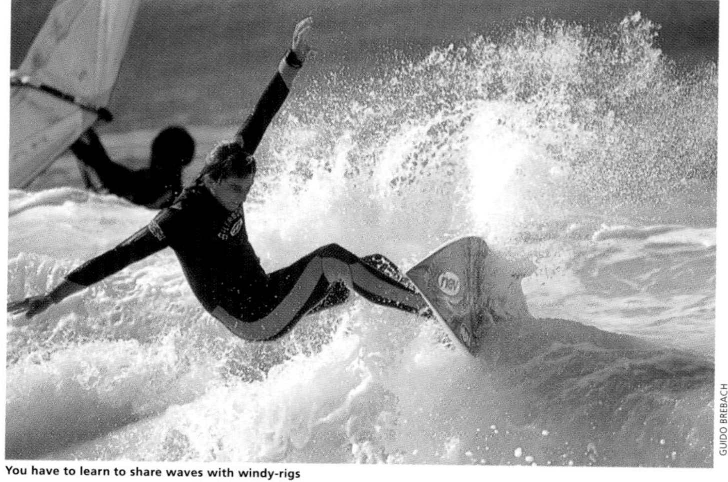

GUIDO BREBACH

You have to learn to share waves with windy-rigs

Netherlands and Belgium

Surf culture Pioneer Jan Nederveen surfed for the first time in the Netherlands in the 30s and was mostly on his own until the late 50s. The second generation of the 60s included names like Go Klap, Albert van Garderen, Arie Verbaan and Jaap van der Toorn. A friend who had visited the US lent Klap a Harbour longboard at a time when most of the other surfers were riding homemade planks. After riding his imported board, Klap immediately saw potential in the surf market and opened a shop in 1973.

The surfing story started in Belgium when a dude called Kobbe returned from an eight-month trip to Morocco in 1983. Once back home, he started riding the North Sea swells. To be able to surf the best spots, Dutch and Belgian surfers had to organise legally registered clubs. The Holland Surfing Association (HSA) was formed in 1973 and the Belgian Surf Association (BSA) in the early 90s. Both clubs organise surf events and publish magazines. The combined number of Dutch and Belgian surfers is estimated at around the 500 mark.

Where to go The Wadden Islands picks up north swell and warrants further investigation. Den Haag has the Scheveningen area which handles the bigger swells, while Maasvlakte has a concentration of quality waves and some cobblestone reef. If there's gonna be any waves in Belgium 'Surfer's Paradise' is the best place to look.

When to go It's undoubtedly a winter destination for decent-sized waves. Low pressures sitting south in the North Sea will whip up swell then head NE, leaving a strong chance of an offshore breeze. Summer will be flat other than occasional short fetch swells, which come and go very quickly, and are usually lumpy and inconsistent.

Environment Pollution is at its worst at river outlets, harbours and nearby industrial sites. Some Belgian surfers recently collected a scary sample of North Sea water in a beer bottle and placed it on their TV set. Two days later it exploded. In cities like Den Haag in the Netherlands, and in most Belgian seaside towns, surfing is only allowed in specially assigned areas during summer. Negotiations with Den Haag's local government has resulted in designated summer surf areas and in most Belgian seaside towns there are specially assigned 'surf zones'. In the Dutch wintertime (when the waves are best), the coast is unrestricted, but in Belgium you can be called out of the water anywhere, at any time. Respect the restricted areas. If you are called out by the police or the coast guard, leave the water. If not, you jeopardise HSA or BSA licences for the assigned areas and you'll also have hassles.

modiales a cru et en 1993, la première compète locale fut organisée sur Sylt. Y'avait 50 cms de vagues mais c'était top. La plupart des vagues sont générées par les vents bien que parfois de vraies houles passent par la Manche. Il y a maintenant 3 magazines de surf et plus de 10,000 surfers incluant une large proportion de filles. Beaucoup voyagent à travers le monde pour éviter l'hiver, de temps en temps on entend parler de nouveaux spots sur la mer du Nord ou de l'est. L'eau est froide mais la motivation est profonde.

Danemark

Le surf au Danemark est encore un peu mystérieux bien que la côte soit bien exposée aux fetchs de la Mer du Nord en recevant sans aucun doute les mêmes swells que la meilleure région allemande. En fait, Sylt est sur la frontière. On trouve une association de surfers danois et quelques centaines d'accros qui , comme leurs voisins allemands, voyagent beaucoup.

Pays-Bas et Belgique

Jan Willem Coenraads Nederveen surfa pour la première fois aux Pays-Bas dans les années 30, généralement tout seul jusqu'à la fin des années 50. La seconde génération des années 60 comptait dans ses rangs: Go Klap, Albert Van Garderen, Arie Verbaan et Jaap Van Der Toorn. Un ami qui séjourna aux E-U prêta un longboard "Harbour" alors qu'à l'époque la plupart des autres surfeurs se fabriquaient leur propre planche. Go ouvrit une boutique en 1973, et le surf se développa rapidement. En Belgique, le coup d'envoi fut donné lorsque qu'un gars s'appelant Kobbe passa 8 mois au Maroc en 1983. De retour chez lui, il commença à surfer les swells de la Mer Du Nord.

Le surf n'avait rien de facile. Les conditions en hiver sont très dures et pour des villes comme La Haye (avec son port Schevenigen) aux Pays-Bas, ou la plupart des villes du bord de mer en Belgique, le surf n'est autorisé que dans des zones bien déterminées pendant l'été. Afin de pouvoir surfer les meilleurs spots, les surfeurs hollandais et belges durent s'organiser en clubs officiels. La Holland Surfing Association (HSA) fut crée en 1973 et la Belgian Surfing Association (BSA) au début des années 90. Chacun des deux clubs organisent des compétitions et publie des magazines. Des pourparlers avec les autorités de La Haye, ont abouti à des zones réservées de surf pour l'été; sur la plupart des stations balnéaires belges, elles portent même le titre de "zones de surf".

En hiver (quand les vagues sont les meilleures) il n'y a pas de limites, mais en Belgique vous pouvez être rappelé au bord n'importe où, n'importe quand. Ne pas plaisanter avec ces zones réservées. SI vous êtes rappelé au bord par la police ou un MNS, quittez l'eau. Sinon, vous compromettez les autorisations HSA ou BSA pour les zones réservées et vous pouvez vous-mêmes avoir des problèmes.Le nombre de surfeurs hollandais et belges est estimé à environ 500. La HSA a plus de 100 membres.

Norway

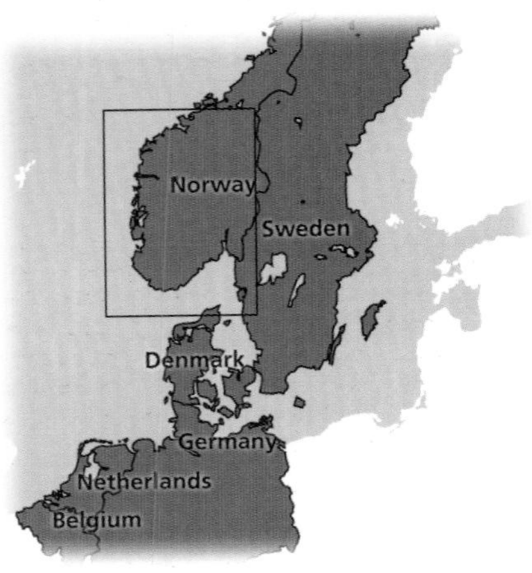

JAN GAARE

A Reve Havn rarity

1. The Lofoten Islands

One of the most scenic places in Norway, where steep mountains rising from sea level with a coastline of boulder and sand beaches facing into large fetches of Atlantic and Arctic ocean. You'll find a largely undiscovered surf zone, though this region has a huge swell catchment area. The easiest access point is at Undstad, a NW-facing bay receiving N to SW swells. There's solo surfing on cobblestone points at each end of many quality beachies.

Une zone de surf encore mal connue alors qu'elle reçoit un paquet de houles. Un des endroits de Norvège les plus spectaculaires avec des montagnes à pic qui surgissent tout droit de l'océan entrecoupées de plages de sable et de galets exposées aux méga-fetchs de l'Atlantique et de l'Artique.

2. Molde gj7

Powerful waves break here on a rock reef S of Hustadevika. Locals claim it is too hollow to be considered a hot-dog wave. A deep trench points at the reef, contributing to its power and consistency.

Un certain nombre de vagues puissantes sur du reef aux sud de Hustadevika. Les locaux les considèrent comme trop creuses pour être des vagues de hot-dog.

3. Godøy

An island off Aalesund, Godøy is known to produce a good right.

Une île au large de Aalesund, on sait que Godøy peut donner une droite.

4. Stad-landet Peninsula

There's three bays (two sandy) that are regularly visited by surfers from Oslo. Fossarevet is a reef N of Ervika that receives N swell when other spots are sheltered. It's the most hollow wave in the region and is sometimes known to produce A-frame barrels. Hoddevika picks up SW to W swell and is known for good beach peaks, especially at its N end. If the swell is from the NW, Ervika will be better but beware, there's a shipwreck in the bay, most of which is hidden at high tide, but clearly visible at low.

Fossarevet est un reef au nord d'Ervika qui chope les houles de nord tandis que les autres spots sont protégés. La vague la plus creuse de la région peut devenir des pics parfaits et tubulaires. Hoddevika prend mieux les swells de sud-ouest à ouest, avec de bons beach-breaks surtout au nord. Si la houle vient du nord-ouest, le mieux sera à Ervika mais attention, y'a une épave dans la baie pratiquement immergée à marée haute ,qui se découvre bien à marée basse.

5. Refsnes (North)

Named Norway's 'most scenic beach' in the early 90s, the coast here is characterised by high hills, fjords and islands. A little surfable territory is known S, before you hit Stavanger.

Cette côte se caractérise par de hautes collines, des fjords et des îles. Peu de surf répertorié au sud avant Stavanger.

6. Hellestø

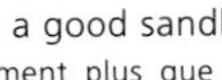

Hellestø has shifting peaks that close out more than Bore. Still, at the N end there's often a good sandbar.

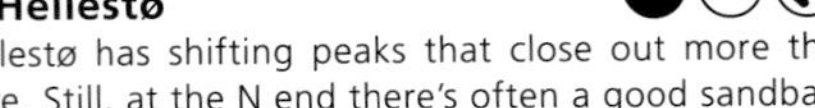

Hellestø a des pics irréguliers qui ferment plus que Bore. Cependant, y'a souvent un bon banc au nord.

7. Sele

A small point break and probably Norway's most crowded surf spot. Up to 20 surfers have been recorded here on a 1m-ish (2-3ft) day!

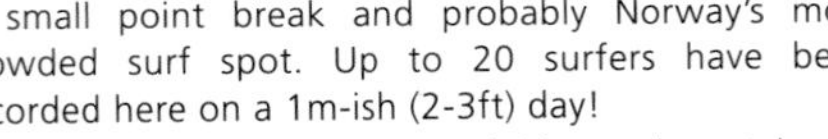

Un petit point-break qui est probablement le spot le plus couru. On y déjà vu jusqu'à 20 surfers sur des vagues de 50 cms.

8. Bore

This is the most consistent spot in the region, surfed frequently in summer. Sometimes the sandbars are good. It's signposted, with campsites at the S end. The dunes are susceptible to erosion, so use the paths.

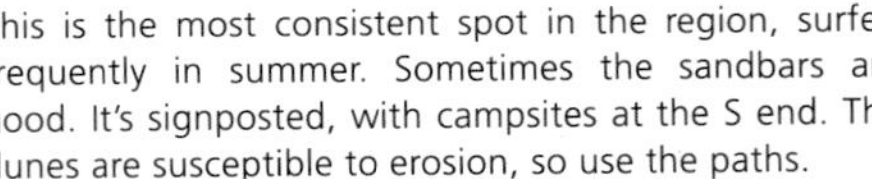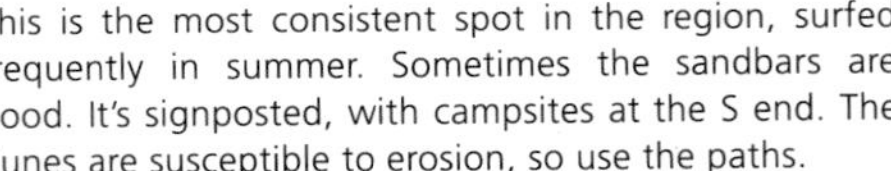

Le spot le plus consistant de la région souvent surfé en été. Souvent les bancs y font de bonnes vagues. Bien signalisé avec des campings au sud. Les dunes sont fragiles, merci pour elles de marcher sur les sentiers battus.

9. Steinen

There are several spots from along this stretch to Reve Havn: the most regularly surfed is Steinen. There are two spots between Steinen and Foglingane (the name given to two rocks outside the S end of Bore beach). Racetrack is a short, fast ride against some boulders sticking well above the water surface – kick out in time! Left-handers consist of large close out sections unless there's a classic swell when it can be ridden through its length. This may happen once or twice through winter.

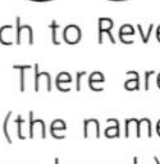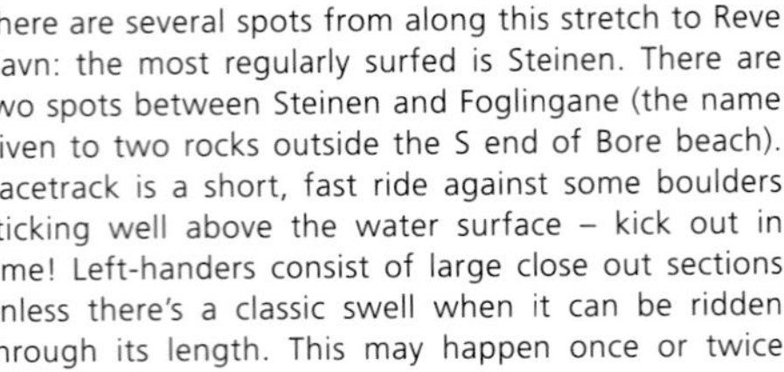

Plusieurs pics depuis Steinen au sud à Revehavn, le spot le plus surfé étant Steinen. On trouve deux spots entre Steinen et Foglingane. Racetrack est une vague courte et rapide sur des galets qui émergent de la surface. Faites votre kick-out au bon moment. Lefthanders consiste en une méga-section qui ferme à moins qu'une houle parfaite ne vienne arranger les choses, à savoir une ou deux fois dans l'hiver.

10. Reve Havn

Reve Havn is a bit of a sleeping beauty. It produces tubes but is unfortunately very inconsistent.

Reve Havn peut être tubulaire mais ça ne marche pas souvent.

11. Ghosthouse

Usually a close out close to the shore, this break can produce one of the hollowest waves in the area. Lined-up sandbars or messy swell can also make it surfable. It's located just N of Pigsty.

Souvent un close-out immonde sur le bord bien que ca puisse être une des vagues les plus creuses de la zone. Des bancs de sable bien formés ou un swell désordonné peuvent le rendre surfable.Juste au nord de Pigsty.

12. Pigsty

Pigsty is a one-man wave 500m (450yd) S of Reve Havn, but even the few locals create crowds here. Though inconsistent, Pigsty is a quality wave, even by international standards and picks up N swell better than other spots nearby.

Pigsty est une vague pour un seul surfer à 500m au sud de Revehavn tant et si bien que les locaux arrivent à saturer le pic. Bien qu'inconsistant, Pigsty est une bonne vague, même avec des critères internationaux.

13. Jaerens Rev

Jaerens Rev is a long, shallow water zone extending 1.6km (1mi) offshore producing a swell shadow S of it. The coast N of Jaerens Rev is referred to as the North Shore: the locals renamed Jaerens Rev 'Phantoms' because it breaks bigger than any other spots nearby. It's a risky call due to its distance from shore and strong currents. No locals have surfed it yet.

Jaerens Rev est une zone avec peu d'eau qui s'étend un mile au large, qui coupe le swell au sud. La côte au nord de Jaerens Rev est connu comme le North Shore ou Phantoms parce que ça casse toujours plus gros que les autres spots. Assez risqué parce que loin du bord et parce que les courants y sont forts. Aucun local n'a surfé ici encore.

14. Orre Beach

At the S end are two good boulder reefs which require a solid swell before they work. During an average season they are surfed a handful of times. There are camping facilities in the nearby vicinity.

Au sud, on trouve deux reefs sur des gros galets qui exigent une bonne houle pour fonctionner. Ca se surfe environ 4-5 fois dans la saison. Des possiblités de camping dans le coin.

15. Point Perfect

Point Perfect needs clean SW swells to live up to its name. If you are travelling by car, turn off along a dust road after the sign indicating Refsnes as a swimming beach. Park at Vik airfield.

Il faut une houle décente et propre pour que Point Perfect mérite son nom. Si vous conduisez, il faut tourner sur un chemin de terre après le panneau indiquant Refsnes comme une plage.

16. Refsnes Beach

An important windsurfing spot, this is also a good surf spot on the peninsula S of the beach. Raunen holds large swells but is susceptible to winds.

Un super spot de windsurf d'abord mais y'a aussi un bon spot de surf sur la péninsule de Raunen, au sud de la plage. Raunen tient le gros.

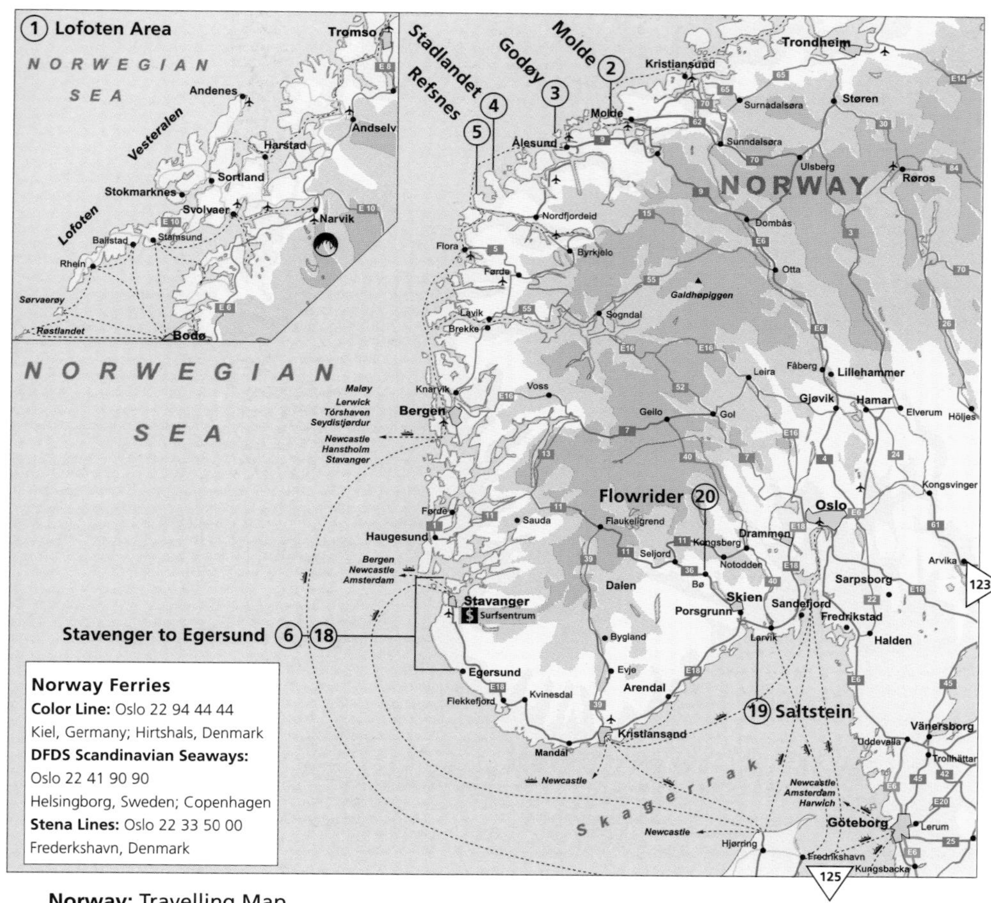

Norway: Travelling Map

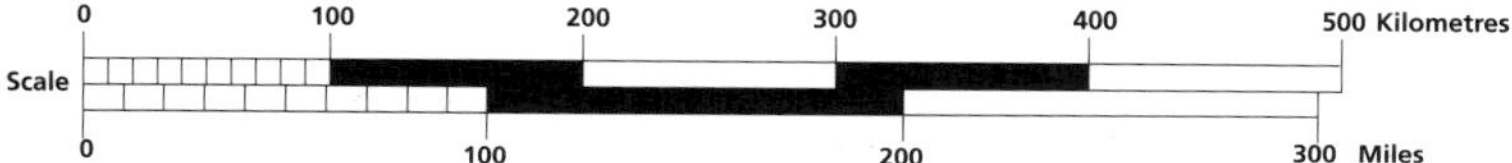

17.Kvassheim  

This is a classic point break that holds its shape, even during large swells and gives rides up to 150m (120yd). It's the best spot in the region in SW swell, located on the other side of the bay from the Kvassheim lighthouse.

Un point-break typique qui ne se déforme pas même avec les méga-houles de sud-ouest. Situé de l'autre côté de la baie avec le phare de Kvassheim.

18. Brusand 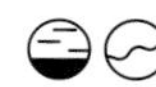 

The most S beach in Norway picks up S swell. The sandbars change, but the E end usually produces the best surf. Local campsites and cottages are for rent.

La plage la plus au sud de Norvège prend les houles de sud. Les bancs y changent mais le bout à l'est produit souvent les meilleures vagues. Des campings et des cottages à louer.

19. Saltstein  

Facing SE, this small bay is home to a few local surfers, as well as being the closest spot to Oslo. During summer, chop produced by afternoon sea-breezes can create rideable surf.

Une petite baie qui regarde le sud-est avec quelques surfers locaux, le spot le plus proche de d'Oslo. En été, les ondulations poussées par les thermiques de l'aprés-midi peuvent être surfables.

20. Flowrider – Bø

The Flowrider is a static or standing wave that is created by a fast flow of water over a sculpted obstacle. Unfortunately the Waterpark Telemark Sommarland at Bø can only be ridden on bodyboards. At occasional specialist events, surfers and snowboarders ride small, strap in, stand up boards, designed in San Diego by Carl Ekstrom. The wave itself is usually an open face, with a crumbling lip, because few surfers can handle the top to bottom barrel that's created when they crank it up to full speed. The water depth is only 10 to 15 cm (4–5 in) deep, but the whole face is coated in 2cm (1in) of shock absorbing foam. Exits at either shoulder deposit riders in a slow moving river which flows around the wave. When it's sunny, it's crowded out with 15-minute queues for a 30 second ride. Cost is 160 NOK for a day.
Open from 10am-8pm. (47) 35 95 16 99.

Le Flowrider est une vague statique seulment pour les bodyboards. Parfois il y a des événements pour les bodyboards et les surfers. Quant il fait beau il devient encombré. Parfois il faut faire la queue pour quinze minutes. Il coût 160 nok par jour.

JAYMIN ROWLANDS

This peak is somewhere between spot 17 and 18

JØRGEN MICHAELSEN - SURFSENTRUM

Terje Haakonsen, one of the lucky few allowed to strap in at the Flowrider

Sweden

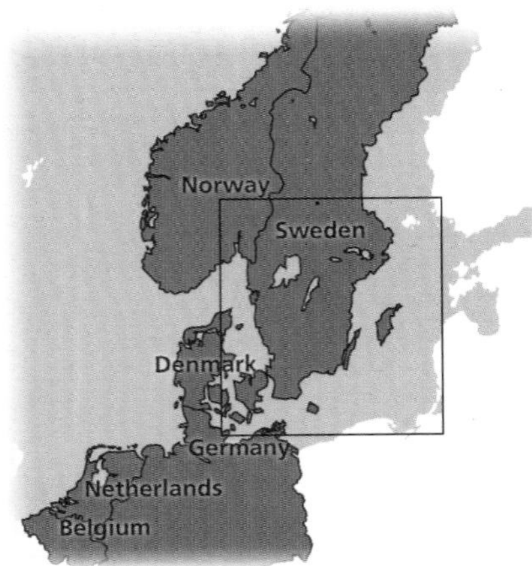

1. Åsa – Stenudden

A right point between Gothenburg and Varberg needs a strong SE wind to work.

Un pointbreak qui casse en droite entre Gothenburg et Varberg. Il faut un fort vent de sud-est.

2. Träslövsläge

Left point break, which is best in a S wind.

Un pointbreak de gauche. Le meilleur vent vient du sud.

3. Apelviken

The most famous windsurf location in Sweden was 'found' as a surf spot at the beginning of the 80s, and now people live here just for the surf. The best wind direction here is NE. The waves are OK in the S part of the bay when the wind is blowing from the SE. Talk to the guys working in the surf shop 'Surfer's Paradise' in Varberg. They have information about other places that are worth a visit on the W coast.

Le spot de windsurf le plus célèbre en Suède a été trouvé comme un surfspot au début des années 80 et maintenant certains y habitent uniquement pour surfer. Le meilleur vent vient du nord-est. Allez discuter le bout de gras avec les gars du surf shop "Surfers Paradise" à Varberg. Ils ont des infos sur des autres spots de la côte ouest qui valent le coup. Les vagues y sont correctes au sud de la baie quand le vent vient du sud-est.

4. Glommen

A point break, best when the wind direction is NE.

Point Break. Le meilleur vent vient du nord-est.

5. Mellbystrand

All wind directions can be good, but NW, W and S are the best. To get top waves, come when it's blowing from the NW, common during the summer. It's located about 20km (12mi) S of Halmstad, in Laholmsbukten.

Toutes les directions de vent sont propices mais ceux de nord-ouest, ouest et sud sont les meilleurs. Pour aller sur les meilleures vagues, venez-ici quand ça souffle au nord-ouest, ce qui est fréquent en été. Situé à environ 20 kms au sud d'Halmstad, à Laholmsbukten.

6. Vik

A great surf spot located just N of Simrishamn in Skåne. This point break is recommended when the wind is blowing from the SE or E.

Un super spot situé juste au nord de Simrishamn à Skåne. On recommande vraiment le détour sur ce point break quand le vent souffle au sud-est ou à l'est.

Sweden's most famous surf-spot: the peak at Torö

7. Grönhögen

Oland is an island on the E coast. To get here you go to Kalmar then take the bridge across Kalmarsund. The island is a small one and is easy to travel around. Gronhogen is a great spot on the SW side and has good surf between the campsite and the harbour. The best wind directions are SW and SE. Waves can range up to 3-4m (9-12ft).

Oland est une île sur la côte est. Pour y aller, il faut aller à Kalmar et prendre le pont jusqu'à Kalmarsund. L'île est petite et il y est facile de bouger. Gronhogen est un super spot au sud-ouest avec de bonnes vagues entre le camping et le port. La meilleure direction de vent est au sud-ouest ou sud-est. On peut y surfer des vagues de 3 à 4 mètres.

8. Haga Park

You'll find this fine spot W of the island. Go towards Färjestaden and then drive S for about 7km (4mi) towards Mörbylånga. The best wind directions are S and SW, when the waves break over a sandstone reef. You can park close to the spot.

A l'ouest de l'île, vous trouverez ce spot sympa. Il faut aller jusqu'à Färjestaden et rouler environ 7 kms vers Mörbylånga. Idéal par vent de sud et sud-ouest, quand les vagues cassent sur du sable et du rocher. On peut se garer à environ 25m du spot.

9. Ängjärnsudden

A sand beach on the N part of the island holds waves up to 2m (6ft), with easy parking.

Une plage de sable au nord de l'île qui tient des vagues jusqu'à deux mètres. Parking facile.

10. Tofta

Tofta is a spot on the E coast of Gotland and is the bigger of the two islands on the E coast. Since it's an island, you can find good surf with almost every wind direction. Gotland is a popular place during summer, so be prepared for a party if you come here. The best winds range from S to NW.

La plus grande des deux îles sur la côte est. Comme c'est une île, on peut trouver des vagues avec n'importe quelles conditions de vents. Gotland est une destination connue en été, soyez donc prêts à vous faire la fête si vous passez par là. Tofta est un spot sur la côte ouest de Gotland. Les meilleurs vents viennent du sud ou du nord-ouest.

11. Ireviken

On the NW part of Gotland you'll find a wave paradise. When the wind is blowing from N to W, it gets big.

Au nord-ouest de Gotland, on trouve cette vague paradisiaque. Ca peut être gros quand ça souffle du nord à l'ouest.

Strong onshores are the go for a lot of Sweden's waves

12. Fåro

When the wind is strong, you'll find some really good surf on this little island located just N of Gotland. Drive around and look for spots like Aursviken: when the wind is blowing from W to N, you'll find a quick left here. Ekeviken is best when it's blowing from the NW. Go here after a storm: you'll find that the waves stay around for a while.

Quand le vent est fort, on peut choper du bon surf ici sur cette petite île située juste au nord de Gotland. Roulez et cherchez des spots comme Aursviken avec des vents d'ouest à nord, ce sera une gauche rapide ici, ou Ekeviken, idéal par vents de N-O. Venez ici après une tempête, vous verrez que les vagues peuvent durer quelques temps.

13. Torö

Sweden's best known surf spot found 20km (12mi) S of Stockholm. You take Torövägen to Herrhamra gård and then turn to the right on a gravel road taking you down to the beach where you'll find a beach break with lefts and rights. The best wind direction is strong SE-SW. The Swedish Surf Association has held a couple of competitions here.

Un des spots suédois les plus célèbres du pays, à 20kms au sud de Stockholm. Il faut prendre direction Torövägen Gård en prenez à droite sur un chemin de gravier qui vous amène jusqu'à la plage. C'est un beach-break avec des gauches et des droites. Le meilleur vent est un fort vent de SE-SO. La Fédé suédoise a organisé quelques compétitions ici.

14. Sikhjälma

When the wind is blowing from NW to NE, you'll find this reasonably good spot S of Gävle.

De bonnes vagues avec des vents de NO à NE. On trouve ce spot au sud de Gävle.

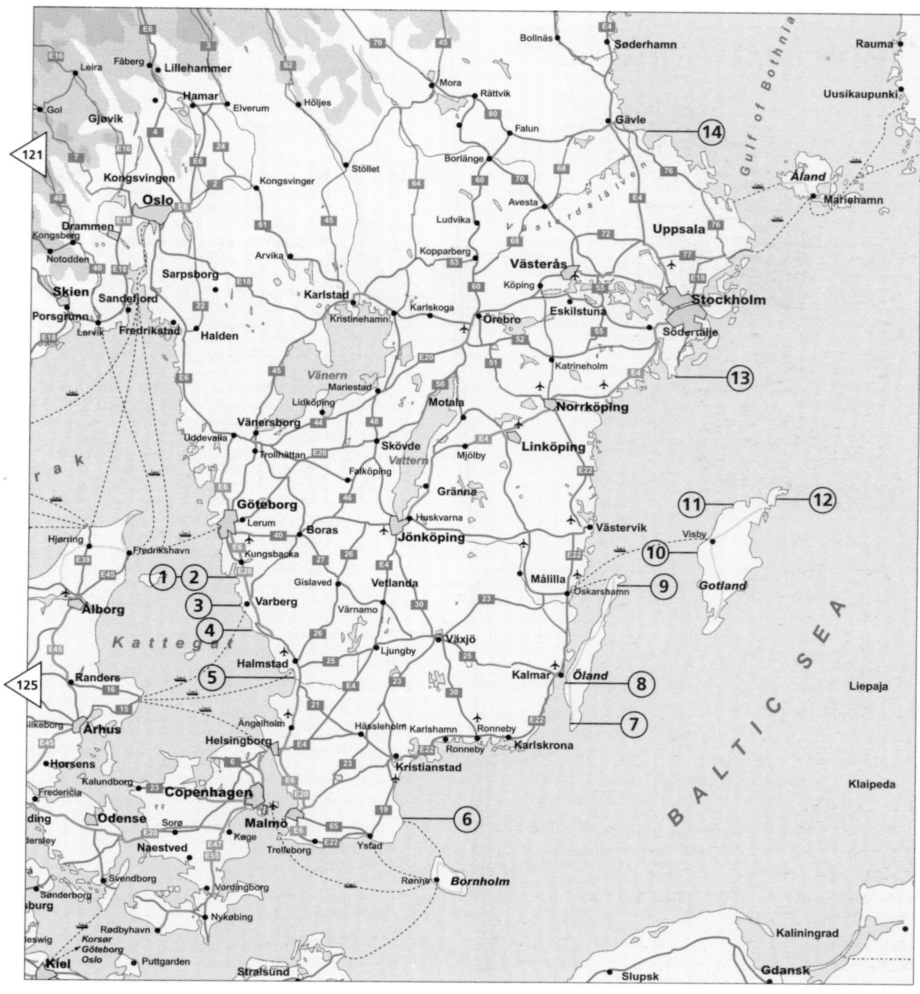

Sweden: Travelling Map

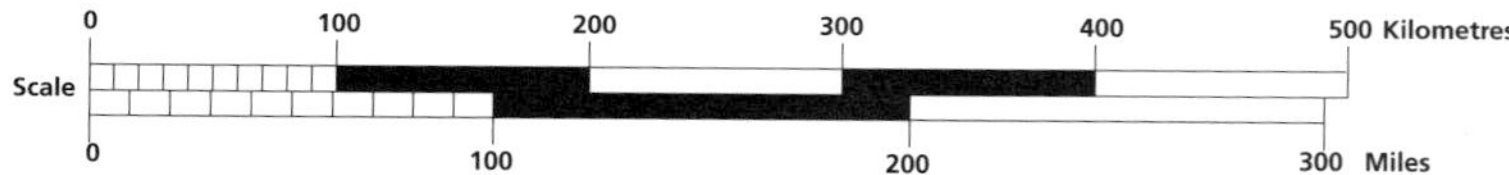

> **Sweden's Ferries**
> **Stena Line:** Gothenburg (031) 704 00 00
> Frederikshavn, Denmark; Kiel, Germany
> **Scandinavian Seaways:** Gothenburg (031) 65 06 66
> Newcastle, England; Copenhagen, Denmark

Going left at Torö

Denmark and Germany

Denmark

1. Aløgårde
A long left-hander that works on strong W/NW wind. The best way out is to walk to the end of the jetty and jump off.

Une gauche longe qui march sur un vent fort du ouest et du nord-ouest. Il faut sauter de l'extremité de la jetée.

2. Hornhole
Previously known for steep take-offs, this spot is now more mellow as a lot of sand has built up around the pier. A good place for beginners as the pier protects from the wind and current. It needs onshore NW/N winds.

Bien pour les débutants, protegé du vent et du courant par la jetée-promenade. Il faut des vents de terre (onshore) nord-ouests et du nords.

3. Gilleleje
Another pier spot that offers protection from the wind. In strong W/NW winds, you can almost find offshore conditions as the swell bends around the pier.

Autre spot de jetée-promenade protegé par le vent.

4. Smidstrop
When everywhere is flat and the wind is SW, Smidstrop usually has decent waves. It can produce a good left-hander, which breaks over a stone/mussel reef and then onto sand. If the wind is more W, right-handers begin to appear. It's popular with the windsurfing crew.

Quand c'est plat partout et il y a un vent du sud-ouest les vagues à Smidstrop sont d'habitudes bonnes. Elle casse sur un récif de moules et de roches et après sur le sable. Populaire pour les windsurfers.

5. Klitmøller
One of the most well-known windsurf spots in Europe. Coming out on the mussel reef, the waves can have huge 3m (10ft) faces and even bigger when it's really blowing. Wind from SW/W is best, and after a big storm when the wind dies down, the waves can be unreal. Strong winds can push waves around the point and down into the bay, which is an option when the outside is packed with German windsurfers. Respect the local people that live in Klitmøller and don't park in their driveways.

Une des 'spots' pour le windsurf en Europe. Les vent du sud-ouest et du ouest sont idéals. Les vagues sont formidables après une grande tempête. Il faut respecter les locaux!

6. Bunkers
The next beach S of Klitmøller has a large swell window from the S around to the N, but will be a mess if there is too much wind. A mussel reef to the N can produce a good right-hander.

Grande houle venante du sud. Un récif de moules vais le nord donne une bonne droite.

7. Nr Vorupør
A good place to find waves when the W coast is blown out. Look for the long left, N of the pier in a W wind.

Quand les vagues sont défigurées (gâchées) sur la côte oeste, il marche ici. Bonne gauche au nord de le jetée-promenade au vent de l'ouest.

8. Huide Sande
There used to be a really good right-hander S of the pier but since the pier was rebuilt the wave hasn't been the same. There are still good waves when the N/NW wind is blowing.

Depuis la jetée-promenade a été changée la droite n'est plus la même. Toujours des bonnes vagues quand il y a un vent du nord et du nord-ouest.

Germany

Eastern Sea
9. Pelzerhaken 10. Fehmarn
11. Hohwachter Bucht 12. Damp

Not quite Hawaii, but small wind swells during the winter months provide waves for a hardy, select group of surfers.

Pas vraiment Hawaii mais les petits swells de vents pendant l'hiver produisent quelques vagues pour un petit groupe de surfers élitistes.

Sylt: Spots 13-19
The best surfing area in Germany: various spots have waves along its 35km (24mi) length.

La meilleure zone de surf en Allemagne avec une brochette de spots le long des 35 kms de côtes. En aprtant du nord:

13. Buhne Kampen
Pretty fat beach break that has waves when there have been strong W winds for a few days. Owing to the walk through the dunes, it's not too crowded.

Un beach-break plutôt épais avec des vagues quand ça a soufflé d'ouest pendant quelques jours. Pas trop de monde parce qu'il faut marcher à travers les dunes.

GUIDO BREBACH

Westerland on Sylt

14. Sturmhaube Kampen
A sand and rock bottom spot with good rights between the stone jetties. Easy access.

Un spot de rochers et de sable avec de bonnes droites entre les jetées de pierre. Accès facile.

15. Nordseeklinik Westerland
A popular spot with waves when everywhere else is flat. In a S wind, it's a favourite spot for windsurfers.

Spot fréquenté avec des vagues alors que tout le reste est flat. Beaucoup de windsurfers par vent de sud.

16. Brandenburg Westerland
This rates as the most popular area in Germany and has powerful waves. The shoreline has a kink so waves break both ways. It's best at mid tide.

Le spot le plus branché d'Allemagne avec des vagues relativement puissantes. La côte fait un coude aussi les vagues cassent-elles en droite et en gauche. Meilleur à mi-marée.

17. Oase zur Sonne Westerland
A shore break with killer waves up 2m (6ft). Broken boards are a common sight. It works on all tides and like Nordseeklinik, it gets crowded.

Gros shore-break avec des vagues d'enfer jusqu'à deux mètres. On y voit souvent des planches cassées. Marche à toutes les marées et devient encombré comme Nordseeklinik.

18. Kilometerstein Vier Hörnum
Located at the very S end of Sylt, this is a good place for those wanting to avoid the crowds at Westerland.

Situé complètement au sud de l'île. Un bon endroit pour ceux qui veulent éviter la foule de Westerland.

19. Sansibar Rantum
Just five minutes' drive down from Westerland, it's not as crowded but can have little tubes in an offshore wind. Access is easy.

Quelques kms au sud de Westerland. Pas aussi encombré et des petits tubes avec off-shore. Accès facile.

GUIDO BREBACH

Thomas Lange, Sylt

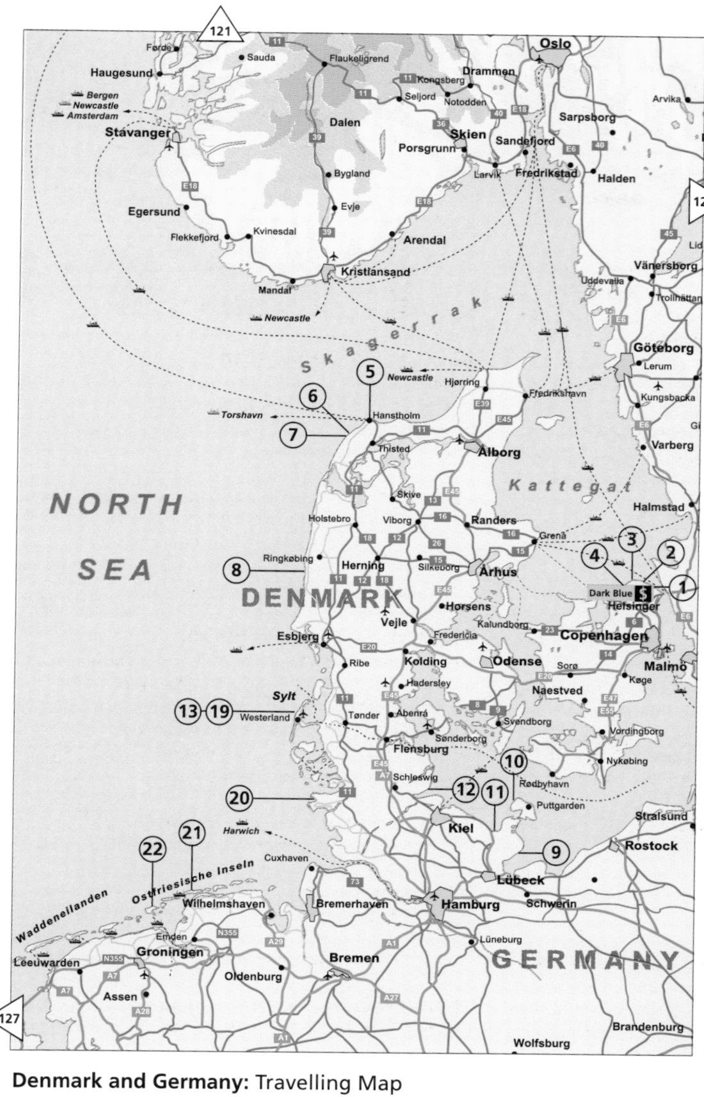

Denmark and Germany: Travelling Map

Scale 0 100 200 300 400 500 Km
0 100 200 300 Miles

Denmark Ferries
DFDS Scandinavian Seaways:
Copenhagen 33 42 33 42 - to Norway
Scandlines:
Copenhagen 35 29 02 00
Stena Line:
Copenhagen 96 20 02 00
to Sweden, Norway

Germany Ferries
TT-Linie: Rostock (0381) 67 07 90
to Trelleborg, Sweden
Scandlines Europa GT Links:
Rostock (0381) 670 06 67
to Gedser, Denmark
Scandinavian Seaways: Hamburg (040) 38 90 30
to England, Ireland, Copenhagen, Olso, Amsterdam

Quirin Rohleder, talented local at Munich's river wave, Eisbach

STEFFEN DITTRICH

20. St Peter Ording

Various sandbar peaks, popular with surfers and windsurfers. The area is busy with holidaymakers with heaps of campsites near the coast. Water quality is OK.

Un paquet de pics, bien connu des surfers et des windsurfers. Pas mal de touristes en saison avec des campings partout.

21. Norderney

A long thin island that works under the same conditions as Borkum but is more popular due to the shorter and cheaper ferry from Norddeich. It's mainly a tourist spot but increasingly you'll find surfers in the water at Januskopf (which has a surfer's café), Café Cornelius, Weiße Dune (close to the Happy Windsurfing School) and Strandsauna. The water around the island is generally OK.

Une île longue et étroite qui marche dans les mêmes conditions que Borkum avec plus de monde à l'eau parce que le ferry est plus court et moins cher depuis Norddeich. Principalement un endroit touristique mais on trouve de plus en plus de surfers à Januskopf (avec un café branché surf), Café Cornelius, Weiße Dune, et Strandsauna. L'eau est souvent de bonne qualité.

22. Borkum

The most W island in Germany has good wind waves and North Sea groundswells. Two spots are worthwhile: Jugendbad and FKK Strand (nudist beach), both of which are uncrowded and have good water. For more info, drop into 'Windsurfing Borkum' on the W side. Catch the ferry from Emden.

L'île la plus à l'ouest d'Allemagne qui fonctionne avec de bonnes vagues de vents et les houles de la Mer du Nord quand y'a eu des vents d'ouest pendant 3-4 jours. 2 spots: Jugendbad et FKK Strand (plage nudiste) où pas grand monde surfe. L'eau est impeccable. Pour plus d'infos, arrêtez-vous à Windsurfing Borkum du côté ouest. Prendre le ferry depuis Emden.

Eisbach – Munich's river wave

This so called 'wave', in the middle of metropolitan Munich, is like a natural Flowrider, occurring on a tributary of the River Isar (Eisbach). A waist-to-chest high, stationary wave is created by a fierce current flowing over three rows of box-shaped rocks. The result is a small, open face that's perfect for new school moves like shuvits and aerials performed on short, fat-tailed boards. The speed of the river flow increases any impact with the rocks, which lurk a mere 40cm (1ft) below the surface so care must be taken. Falls can also result in a long hold-down in 'the washing machine', a pool of deep turbulence just downstream. Boards can receive a good hammering on the rocks, with or without a leash. The most consistent time is March to November, but if the water level gets too high, the wave will close out. It's located just where the Isar flows out of a tunnel under the city, on Prinzregenterstr, which is next to the famous museum Haus der Kunst.

Vague de la rivière de Munich. Cette vague, se prèsentante sur un affluent de la rivière Isar est crée d'un courante fort. La face de la vague est ouverte; parfait pour les manoeuvres avec les planches courtes et larges. C'est preferable entre mars et novembre. Elle se trouve à côte du célèbre musée Haus der Kunst

Netherlands and Belgium

Netherlands

1. Waddeneilanden

Not much is known about surf on the Wadden Islands. The currents can be strong due to big tidal differences. The 'Slufter' on the island of Texel is a decent break.

On ne sait pas grand chose des iles Wadden, sauf que les courants y sont forts á cause des marnages importants. Cependant, Slufter'sur l'île de Texel est un bon break.

2. Camperduin & Hargen

   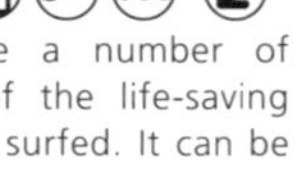

N and S of the dike there are a number of breakwaters. The breakwater, N of the life-saving club Hargen, is the most frequently surfed. It can be fast and hollow.

On peut trouver quelques jetées au nord et au sud de la digue, mais sachez que celles au nord du poste de secours d'Hargen ont les vagues les plus fréquentées, les plus creuses et les plus rapides.

3. Bergen/Egmond aan Zee

 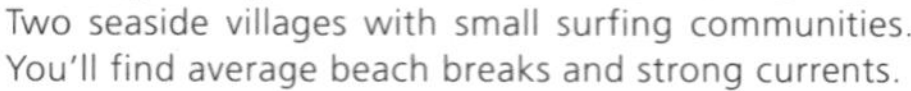

Two seaside villages with small surfing communities. You'll find average beach breaks and strong currents.

Villages côtiers pourvus d'une petite communauté de surfers et de beach-breaks moyens balayés par de puissants courants.

4. Wijk aan Zee Noordpier

One of the best beach breaks in the province of north Holland in front the massive Hoogoven's steel mill. In strong S or SW wind it becomes kind of slow, and is often invaded by windsurfers. Do not use the rip by the harbour wall or you'll get slammed. For a local surf check, call Egbert Visser (02517) 5826.

Un des meilleurs beach-breaks au nord de la province de Hollande en face de l'imposante acierie Hoogovens. Par fort vent de sud, sud-Ouest surtout, ça devient un peu mou et ça grouille de windsurfers. N'utilisez pas le courant de la jetée pour remonter ou vous risquez de vous ramasser. Infos surf: Egbert Visser (02517) 5826

5. Zandvoort to Katwijk

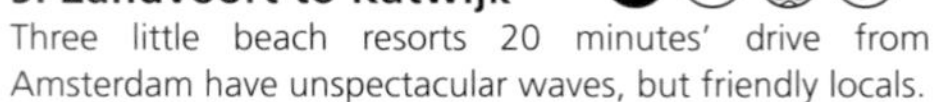

Three little beach resorts 20 minutes' drive from Amsterdam have unspectacular waves, but friendly locals.

Trois petites stations balnéaires á 20 minutes d'Amsterdam avec des vagues pas terribles mais des locaux plutôt accueillants.

6. Scheveningen

Pier

A pier with a restaurant about a mile to the N of the harbour has breaks that work well in a W swell. Watch out for strong currents.

Une jetée avec un restaurant environ 1.5km au nord du port Attention aux courants qui sont forts .Marche par houle d' ouest

Noord

Surf shifting sandbar waves: the lefts are usually longer and are best on a N to W swell with SW winds. Respect the locals.

Les bancs de sable bougent. Les gauches sont souvent plus longues, idéalement avec une houle de nord à ouest. Ca matche aussi avec des vents de sud-ouest. Respectez les locaux.

Zuid

  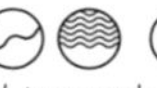 

This break needs more swell than Noord to work well, but rates as one of the better spots in Holland and it can handle sizable waves. The harbour wall protects against strong N winds. Usually it's not as crowded as the Noord. Inside a nice right is produced by a sandbar formed over a submerged jetty.

Exige plus de houle que le nord mais ça peut être un des meilleurs spots du pays et ça tient le gros. La jetée du port protège des vents de nord et dans le port casse une droite sur un banc formé sur un épi submergé Souvent moins de monde qu'au nord.

7. Kijkduin

   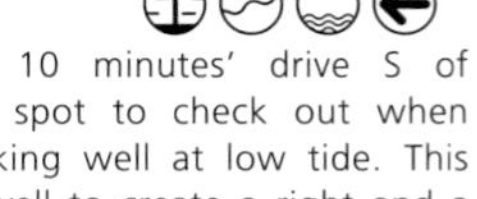

This small beach town 10 minutes' drive S of Scheveningen is a good spot to check out when Scheveningen is not working well at low tide. This beach break needs a N swell to create a right and a strong SW wind for long left-handers breaking off rock jetties. The waves can be very hollow and currents strong.

Petite station à 10 minutes au sud de Scheveningen. A checker quand Scheveningen ne marche pas à marée basse. Ce beach break a besoin d'une houle de nord pour créer une droite ou de forts vents de sud-ouest pour des gauches qui cassent prés d'epis de cailloux. Les vagues peuvent y être trés creuses mais encore une fois, les courants sont violents.

8. Ter Heyde

A nice beach town with a relaxed atmosphere. The sandbars are formed between small rock jetties.

Une petite station bien cool avec des bancs de sable entre des mini-jetées de cailloux.

9. Maasvlakte Area

Maasexpress

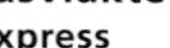    

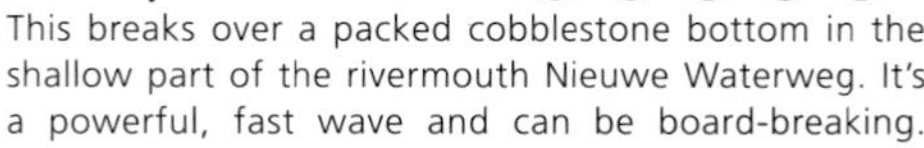

This breaks over a packed cobblestone bottom in the shallow part of the rivermouth Nieuwe Waterweg. It's a powerful, fast wave and can be board-breaking. There are three jetties: the main peak starts from the W jetty. The take-off is in front of or beside the second jetty. 'Impossibles' is a short section breaking off the third jetty. It peels straight in front of the rocks (bring short leashes). Pipeline construction has decreased the quality of the wave and it now needs a strong N swell to work. Rips can be severe.

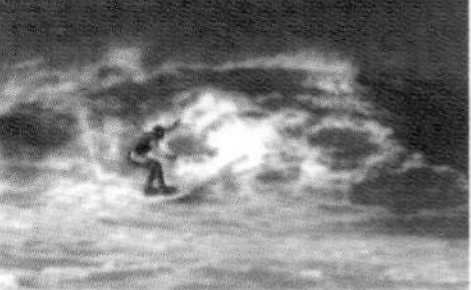

ROBBY BUTTNER

Casse sur des gros galets dans la partie peu profonde de l'embouchure de la Nieuwe Waterweg. On a vu des planches cassées sur ces vagues puissantes et rapides. Trois jetées: le pic principal casse sur celle à l'ouest; la zone de take-off est en face ou à côté de la jetée du milieu Impossible est une section courte de ce pic qui commence depuis la troisième jetée, juste en face des rochers, un petit leash est conseillé. La construction d'un oléoduc a amélioré la qualité de cette vague.

Blokken

Drive for seven minutes from the Maasexpress and you'll find a sheltered spot with a sandy bottom. Cooling water from a power plant causes the water to be warmer then elsewhere, which is nice in winter. In strong N swells there are various peaks and several paddle-out zones. The right from the main peak is the best break. To the SW there is a small left and here you find the easiest paddle out when it is big. The Blokken can hold all swells.

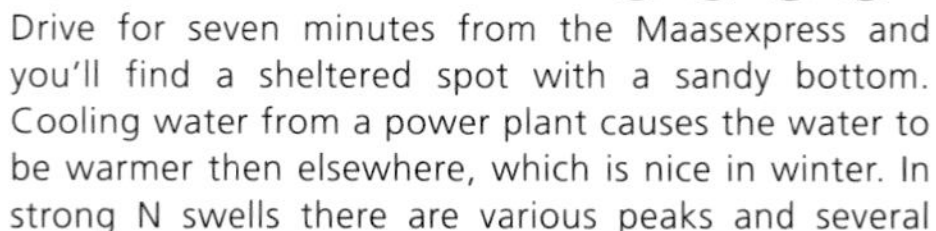

A 7 minutes de route du Maasepress, on trouve ce spot abrité avec un banc de sable. Une centrale thermique peut réchauffer l'eau jusqu'à 5°C en hiver. Avec un gros swell de N, on peut trouver quelques pics et des channels pour aller au fond. La droite est souvent la meilleure. Au SO, il y a une petite gauche et le meilleur channel quand ça rentre gros. Ca devrait tenir toutes les tailles.

Slufter

Further down, and visible from Blokken, you'll find a a stretch of beach called the Slufter. From the Blokken drive all the way around the point to access. The sandbars can become ultra shallow and hollow in bigger swells. Rips are strong in side-shore winds.

Plus au sud des Blokken, on peut voir une partie de la plage qu'on appelle le Slufter Pour y aller, il faut faire tout le tour. Ca peut casser sur trés peu d'eau quand c'est gros , c'est creux donc. Du courant par forts vents de côté.

ROBBY BUTTNER

Slufter

ROBBY BUTTNER

Maasvlakte – Maasxpress

10. Domburg

Domburg is a small village in the province of Zeeland, near the city of Middelburg. This beach break is at its best during low tide. Wind from the N is offshore which brings swell.

Petit village de la province de Zeeland, près de Middleburg, Dombourg est un beach-break qui marche mieux à marée basse. Ici, les vents de nord sont off-shores et amènent la houle.

Belgium

11. Surfer's Paradise

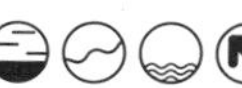

A popular spot and hang out with locals and visiting surfers since 1988. Depending on the tide, the waves can remain for days even after the wind dies down. Two sandbanks and a breakwall give peaky rights and lefts. SW and W winds are best at low tide and N and NW are better at high tide.

Le Premier spot en Belgique. Pour ceux qui se sentent une âme d'explorateur, c'est ce qu'il vous faut. Roulez jusqu'au dernier parking près d'une piscine et marche 15 min à travers la réserve naturelle. Meilleur par houle de N.

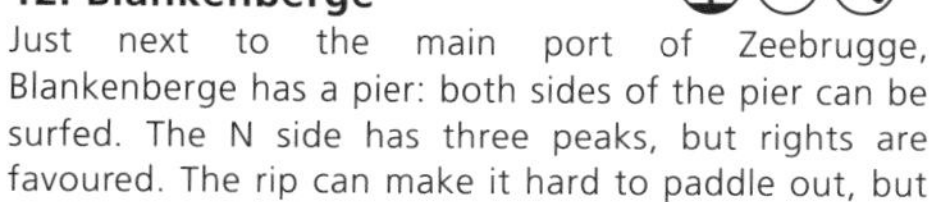

12. Blankenberge

Just next to the main port of Zeebrugge, Blankenberge has a pier: both sides of the pier can be surfed. The N side has three peaks, but rights are favoured. The rip can make it hard to paddle out, but you can jump from the pier.

Juste à côté du port de Zeebruge, allez à Blackenberge dont la jeté se surfe des deux côtés. Au nord, trois pics qui favorisent les droites. Si le courant rend la rame difficile, sautez de la jetée.

13. Oostende

Oostende is the biggest seaside town along the Belgian coast and features, among other things, a lively nightlife. You'll find several beach breaks, which work best in NW swell, in the middle of windsurf zones. There's restrictions on surfing during summer.

La plus grande station balnéaire de la côte belge qu'on appelle la Reine de stations grâce à une vie nocturne intense. On y trouve pas mal de beach-breaks, au milieu de la zone de windsurf, quand la houle vent de nord-ouest. Restrictions de surf en été.

14. Oostduinkerke to Mariakerke

Some good sandbars, formed between the numerous jetties along this part of the coast. At places like Oostduinkerke, Nieuwpoort Bad, Middelkerke Bad and Mariakerke you find designated 'surf zones'. In general surfing is only allowed in these zones during summer, but better surf can also be found outside these areas.

Bons bancs qui se forment entre les nombreuses jetées le long de cette partie de la côte. Aux endroits comme Oostduikerke, Nieuwpoort Bad, Middelkerke Bad et Mariakerke, on trouve des spots. En général, le surf n'est permis que dans les zones de surf en été, bien que de meilleures vagues puissent êtr1e trouvées en dehors.

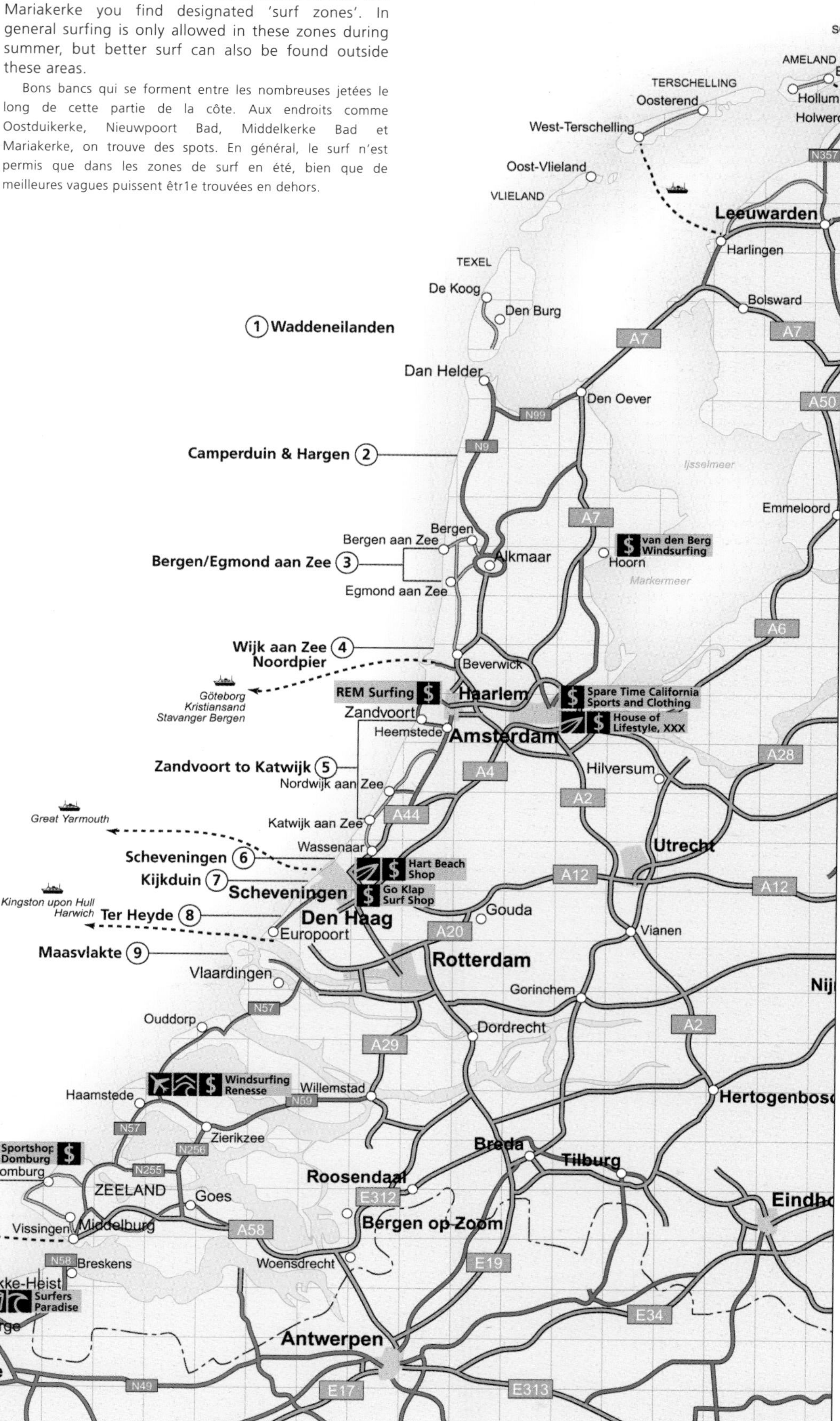

(1) Waddeneilanden
Camperduin & Hargen (2)
Bergen/Egmond aan Zee (3)
Wijk aan Zee (4) Noordpier
Zandvoort to Katwijk (5)
Scheveningen (6)
Kijkduin (7)
Ter Heyde (8)
Maasvlakte (9)
Domburg (10)
Surfers Paradise (11)
Blankenberge (12)
Oostende (13)
Oostduinkerke (14) to Mariakerke
REM Surfing
Spare Time California Sports and Clothing
House of Lifestyle, XXX
van den Berg Windsurfing
Hart Beach Shop
Go Klap Surf Shop
Windsurfing Renesse
Sportshop Domburg
Surfers Paradise
Ostend Surfing
Blue Marine
Göteborg Kristiansand Stavanger Bergen
Great Yarmouth
Kingston upon Hull Harwich
Sheerness
Kingston upon Hull Felixstowe Cover
Dover
TERSCHELLING
AMELAND
VLIELAND
TEXEL
ZEELAND
Ijsselmeer
Markermeer
Leeuwarden
Amsterdam
Haarlem
Den Haag
Rotterdam
Utrecht
Antwerpen
Brugge
Breda
Tilburg

France

Like France's fine wines which sit at the heart of European cuisine, the waves on her swell-drenched west coast occupy an equally romantic place in European surf lore. From the Celtic north to the Basque south, her 'grand-crux' beaches, points and reefs exhibit the variety and style one would expect from France's vineyards. The sweltering, semi-nude beaches of the south west offer the champagne of European summer surf. Moving from the Bordeaux region north wave quality stays high, though the essential characteristics include a dense bouquet of reefs and points. Surfing in Brittany is a curiously strong and very palatable experience. As for the Channel – well, it's a slab of Kronenberg.

France

De même que les grands vins français se situent au coeur de la cuisine européenne, les vagues concentrent le coeur du swell sur la côte ouest en exerçant un attrait d'un romantisme puissant. Depuis le nord celtique jusqu'au sud du Pays Basque, les plages, les reefs et les pointbreaks français offrent des grands crûs de la variété et de la classe des vignobles du pays. Les plages torrides constellées de seins nus offrent le champagne du surf d'été. En allant au nord de Bordeaux, la qualité ne se dégrade pas pour autant en présentant une belle brochette de reefs et de points. Le surf en Bretagne réserve aussi de bonnes surprises quand les dépressions passent et que certains reefs avec un vent offshore s'activent. Quant à la Manche...c'est rare mais mieux loti que la Mediterranée quand même!

This is France, pull in!

ERIC CHAUCHE

Introduction

The People

As with all of Europe, the history of France is an immense topic. The first inhabitants were hunters, cave dwellers and painters. As the Northern ice-cap receded around 1500BC, an agricultural and pastoral society developed. The Gauls were their iron age descendants and there were roughly 15 million of them when the Romans invaded in 52BC. The social and political contortions since then have been many and varied, and with them a succession of outrageous characters have asserted their place in history, notably Louis 14, Joan of Arc and Napoleon, whose military achievements are legendary. France has been invaded by a long succession of expansionist societies, starting with the Francs themselves, yet it remains one of Europe's strongest cultures, even through it's situated centrally between some tough neighbours. France's influence extends through the Mediterranean, Africa, Indo-China and the Pacific (currently a source of great debate). Their idiosyncratic way of life, reflected in the arts, culture and cuisine, is legendary.

Capital: Paris
Population: 57.2 million
Area: 551,500sqkm/212,930sqm
Time: GMT + 1
Language: French
Currency: Franc (FF)

FREDERIC LE LEANNEC

STEF CANDE

Marseille

The Land

France is western Europe's largest country and the landscape within its borders is incredibly diverse: it's home to western Europe's highest mountains, some of its largest rivers, longest beaches and most luscious hills. The flat north coast faces La Manche and the wild west confronts the Atlantic. The south is separated from Spain and Africa by the Pyrenees and the Mediterranean and eastern borders are shared with Italy, Switzerland, Germany, Luxembourg and Belgium. A high inland Plateau (the Massif Central) steps up to the Alps.

The Climate

France's climate is as varied as the landscape. While the north experiences similar rainfall and temperatures to south England, as you head south the climate becomes warmer and drier. During summer the North Atlantic feeds remarkably warm water along the west coast and regular morning winds blow offshore, a result of consistent high pressure over the south west. In winter the same east winds become freezing, coming off the snow-covered Alps. Snow sometimes falls on the beaches, but these cold months are tempered by long, warm summers.

PAUL DEEGAN

The Bosses Ridge, Mont Blanc 4,808m (15,770ft)

Introduction

La population

Comme ses voisins en Europe, la France posséde une histoire richissime. Les premier habitants étaient les hommes descavrenes, peintres et chasseurs. Alors que les galciers au nord se rétractèrent environ 1500 ans avant J-C, une société agricole se développa. Les gaulois en étaient leurs descendants de l'âge du fer et ils étaient environ 11 millions quand les romains arrivèrent en 52 avant J-C. Les contestations politiques et sociales depuis lors ont été variées avec une succession de personnalités qui ont marqué l'histoire, comme Jeanne d'Arc, Louis XIV et Napoléon, dont les conquêtes militaires restent légendaires. La France a été envahie plusieurs fois par une succession de peuplades, commençant avec les Francs. Le pays conserve

PETER CADE

une des cultures européennes les plus importantes, au milieu de ses voisin les plus redoutables. Les principaux agents qui ont formaté la culture française durant les derniers siècles furent la révolution de 1789, les deux guerres mondiales et la naissance de la CEE. L'influence française s'étend sur la Méditerrannée, l'Afrique, l'Indochine et le Pacifique (ce qui n'est pas sans poser problème) avec un"art de vivre" omniprésent dans les arts, l'artisanat, la cuisine... Il en résulte une toile de fonds culturelle partout où l'on va.

Le pays

La France est le plus grand pays d'Europe et contient une incroyable diversité à l'intérieur de ses frontières, allant des plus hautes montagnes d'Europe de l'ouest à certaines des plus grandes rivières en passant par de trés longues plages et des collines verdoyantes. La côte plane au nord fait face à la Manche tandis que l'ouest sauvage fait front à l'Atlantique. Le sud est séparé de l'Espagne et l'Afrique par les Pyrénées; la Méditérannée et les frontières orientales

France: Physical Geography

Scale: 0 50 100 150 200 250 300 Kilometres
0 50 100 150 200 Miles

PETER CADE

sont partagées par l'Italie, la Suisse, l'Allamagne, le Luxembourg et la Belgique. Un haut-plateau au centre (le massif Central) annonce les Alpes.

Le climat

La position dans ces latitudes tempérées rend les statistiques trés aléatoires dans la mesure ou les variations de températures sont considérables. En moyenne, les hivers oscillent de 5 à 10°C du nord au sud. On estime que les pluies sont plus fréquentes de Novembre à Mars aussi mieux vaut éviter cette période si l'on campe. Cependant, avec 170 à 180 jours de pluie par an, on ne peut que difficilement l'éviter. Aux demi-saisons, il fait environ 15°C avec des printemps plus secs au nord et des automnes plus souriants au sud. En été, il n'est pas rare d'avoir des jours de canicule à plus 25°C surtout en juillet-Août. Quant à la température de l'eau, on compte 3 à 5 degrés de différence du nord au sud. Pour le sud, comptez 12°C en hiver, 14°C jusqu'en Mai, 20°C voire plus jusqu'à mi-Septembre et 16°C jusqu'en Novembre. Les vents dominants sont de sud-ouest en hiver et de nord-ouest en été, ceci n'exclue pas une bonne fréquence de matinées off-shore et de quelques jours avec des vents de terre réguliers.

Cherbourg Averages	Jan	Apr	Jul	Oct
rain (mm)	109	49	55	99
sun (hr-day)	2	5	8	2
max temp°C	8	12	19	15
min temp°C	4	7	14	10

Bordeaux Averages	Jan	Apr	Jul	Oct
rain (mm)	90	48	56	83
sun (hr-day)	3	7	9	5
max temp°C	9	17	25	18
min temp°C	2	6	14	8

Marseille Averages	Jan	Apr	Jul	Oct
rain (mm)	43	42	11	76
sun (hr-day)	4	8	11	6
max temp°C	10	18	29	20
min temp°C	2	8	17	10

RENE BEGUE

Alain Bégué's imported Cadillac

Sainte – Ignace downhill team: François Lartigau, Jean Pierre 'La Fleur' Renault; Rene Bégué and his brother Alain with Claude Marcel squatting in front

Surf Culture

History

In 1956, Hollywood scriptwriter Peter Viertel was on the Basque coast shooting an adaptation of Hemingway's novel *The Sun Also Rises.* Amazed by the waves, he sent for a surfboard from California, but he was a strict beginner and shared his apprenticeship with a couple of Biarritz locals, George Hennebutte and Joel de Rosnay. His wife, the actress Deborah Kerr, became the patroness of France's first surf club, 'The Waikiki'. Within a year the sport had grown and Hennebutte, together with Michel Barland and Jacky Rott began to make longboards under Barland's name. Barland himself became a great innovator and has been credited, among other things, with designing the first pre-shape machine in 1981.

Culture Surf

Histoire

En 1956, le scénariste hollywoodien Peter Viertel passe un été sur la côte Basque pour tourner une adaptation d'un roman d' Hemingway, "Le Soleil se lève aussi". Conquis par la beauté des vagues, il se fait envoyer une planche de Californie bien qu'il fut un parfait débutant. Il partagea donc ses premières gamelles avec des locaux de Biarritz : George Hennebutte et Joël de Rosnay. Son épouse, Deborah Kerr, devint la marraine du premier surfclub du pays : le Waikiki. En l'espace d'une année, le sport avais pris racine et Hennebutte, en même temps que Michel Barland et Jacky Rott, se mirent à shaper des longboards. Barland lui-même devint un grand inventeur et a été crédité, entre autres, de la première machine à shaper. Quant à Hennebutte, son "fil à la patte" fut l'ancêtre du leash avant que des américains ne pompent l'idée et ne déposent le brevet.

Les années 60 furent témoins des premiers films de surf en Europe. Le premier fut "Waves of Change" de Greg Mac Gillivray et Jim Freeman à l'automne 1968, montrant les prouesses de Billy Hamilton, Keith Paul et Mark Martinson. Le second fut "Evolution", de Paul Witzig, un succès international où on voyait les sessions fabuleuses de Nat Young et Wayne Lynch à La Barre. Malgré cet attention de la part des média, le surf en France resta marginal jusqu'à la fin des années 70. Le changement se fit avec la création du Lacanau Pro en 1979 et le déroulement des championnats du monde amateurs à Hossegor en 1980. Le surf gagna rapidement l'attention de nouveaux adeptes. Les surfers des années 60 qui se déplaçaient toujours en bande furent remplacés peu à peu par des surfers au tempérament plus individualiste.

RENE BEGUE

The belza Castle, Biarritz

RENE BEGUE

REX

Today

France still has comparatively few surfers (40,000), though with two ASP competitions at Lacanau and Hossegor, a WCT event at Anglet and the Biarritz surf festival, and an ASP longboard competition, it's a crucial and always relaxing stop on the world tour. The current crew of young Frenchmen currently charging the EPSA circuit, including Didier Pitier, Boris Le Texier, Frederic Robin, Mickael Picon, are living examples of the upsurge in surfing's popularity, while Laurent Pujol has gained considerable respect for his abilities on the North Shore. At the Andre Malraux college in Biarritz, surfing has been introduced as a sporting option. The French Surf Federation now has a technical director and surfers are accepted as top level athletes. Boards are easy to find, and quality is generally high, but prices are possibly the most expensive in Europe.

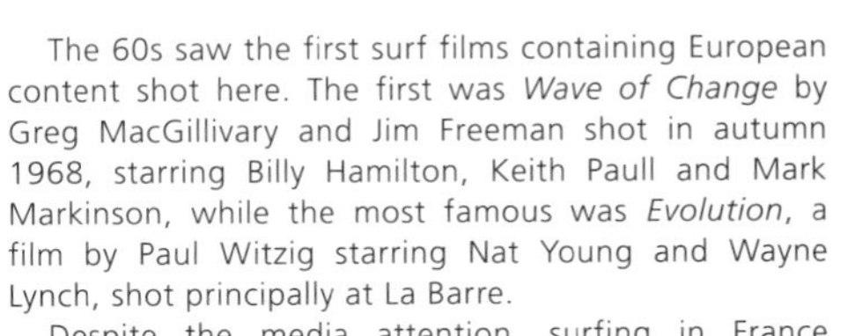

The 60s saw the first surf films containing European content shot here. The first was *Wave of Change* by Greg MacGillivary and Jim Freeman shot in autumn 1968, starring Billy Hamilton, Keith Paull and Mark Markinson, while the most famous was *Evolution*, a film by Paul Witzig starring Nat Young and Wayne Lynch, shot principally at La Barre.

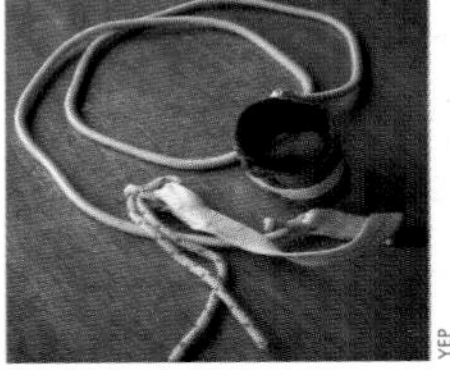

The first leash

YEP

Despite the media attention, surfing in France remained a marginal sport till the end of the 70s. This changed with the Lacanau Pro, created in 1979 and the World Amateurs in 1980. In those years surfing gained considerable recognition. The surfers of the 60s, who never went anywhere without a handful of guys in the car, were replaced by a generation of individualists.

FREDERIC LE LEANNEC

Aujourd'hui

Le nombre de surfers y est encore relativement faible (40.000) malgré le déroulement de nombreuses manifestations : 2 épreuves ASP à Lacanua et Hossegor, 2 épreuves WQS à Seignosse et Anglet et le Biarritz Surf Festival, incluant une épreuve ASP de longboard. Bien qu'absents du circuit mondial, une génération de français domine le surf européen EPSA avec des noms comme Didier Piter, Boris Le Texier, Frédéric Robin et l'espoir le plus réel : Mickael Picon. Signalons aussi Lauent Pujol dont la présence régulière sur le North Shore hawaiien force le respect. Au lycée André Malraux à Biarritz, une section "sports-étude surf" existe depuis plus de 5 ans. La FFS a recruté un Directeur Technique National ainsi qu'un personnel d'encadrants qui permet d'assister les surfers comme les autres sportifs de haut niveau. Les planches, fabriquées par certains des meilleurs shapers, sont faciles à trouver mais les prix sont les plus élevés en Europe.

YEP

Where to go

Surf Areas

The Channel is not the ideal location to catch waves, lacking both power and consistency, but it's worth mentioning firstly because it's the closest surf to Paris and secondly for its scenery. The most consistent area is the northern part of the Cotentin Peninsula, which catches all west swell, while the coast of Normandy works mostly in south-west storms. Some of those spots also work on north westerlies. Winter is the best time to come here, but the tides (creating heavy rips) and freezing water temperatures challenge most hardy surfers.

JEAN-MARC HEBERT
Etretat

Brittany occupies a special place in the heart of visitors here disproportionate to the quality of the surf. Its 1,300 kilometres (800 miles) of rugged coastline is home to a courageous Celtic people who love their hearty local bars (*fest-noz*). Tides of up to 14 metres (40 feet) have been measured on the north coast and its rugged cliffs, islands, rocks and winds give an imposing feel to the surroundings, reflected in many place names, like Baie des Trepasses (Bay of the Dead), Fromveur (Channel of Great Fear). The real bonus is being able to take advantage of the varying orientation of the coastline, and (like Cornwall) you can find waves every day. Virgin spots await.

The *departments* of **Vendée** and **Charentes** make up the 700 kilometre (400 mile) Côte de Lumière. *Lumière* means 'light' and it's a fact that this region receives the highest sunshine hours on the French Atlantic coast. It's an interesting mix of

P. CHIGLIA
Bud Bud

Aquitaine's dunes and Brittany's creeks, with a great array of underrated waves. Despite a less convenient swell exposure than south-west France and a somewhat extended continental shelf, there are many quality reefs which work well in big swells as well as good beaches for summer swells.

The River Gironde marks a psychological line dividing north France from the south and below it, **Aquitaine** stretches in an almost uninterrupted line from Pointe de Grave to Boucau, sharing the honours with the Basque coast of being France's most popular surf region. Encompassing the *departments* of **Gironde** and **Landes** the sheer immensity of the beaches combine a plethora of peaks which remain relatively uncrowded (except in July and August). The Aquitaine Coast is made up of the departments Gironde and Landes, and wave quality is high in both. Since the earliest days **Hossegor**, at the far south end of the region has stunned visitors and locals with the punishing power of its legendary peaks, in the process gaining a reputation as one of the most hollow, consistent beach breaks on the globe. The predominant swell angle favours rights, however the lefts get sculpted by the fairly consistent north-to-south undertow, and tend to become hollow. Channels to get to the line-up are rarely deep (except for a few spots), so it tends to close out over three metres (eight feet). Offshore winds can quickly change and tidal ranges can be large, which means waves can evolve or devolve with incredible speed. Perfect spitting peaks can turn into mush within minutes. Nonetheless, it's one of the best summer trips in Europe with boardies wearable for four months of the year in consistent, hollow surf.

The Basque Coast, its more refined southern neighbour, has a selection of epic points and reefs, and offers a perfect alternative when the beachies further north are maxing out.

FREDERIC LE LEANNEC
Cap de le Chevre

ERIC CHAUCHE
Avalanche

Ou aller

Les zones de surf

La Manche n'est pas l'endroit idéal pour prendre de bonnes vagues car ça manque de régularité et de puissance. Cependant, il faut en parler parce que c'est ce qu'il y a de plus proche de Paris et aussi parce que le panorama des spots y est parfois grandiose. La zone de surf la plus consistante est la partie nord du Cotentin qui chope toutes les houles d'ouest, tandis que la côte normande marche surtout avec les tempêtes de sud-ouest. Certains de ces spots s'activent aussi avec les vents de nord-ouest, voire nord-est dans le Nord. L'hiver est la période la plus régulière bien que l'eau descende souvent au-dessous du supportable (7-8°c). Attention aux variations de marée qui créent de violents courants.

La **Bretagne** exerce une fascination chez le surfer en décalage avec la fréquence du bon surf. Ses 1300 km de côtes découpées dessinent le territoire d'un peuple Celte courageux

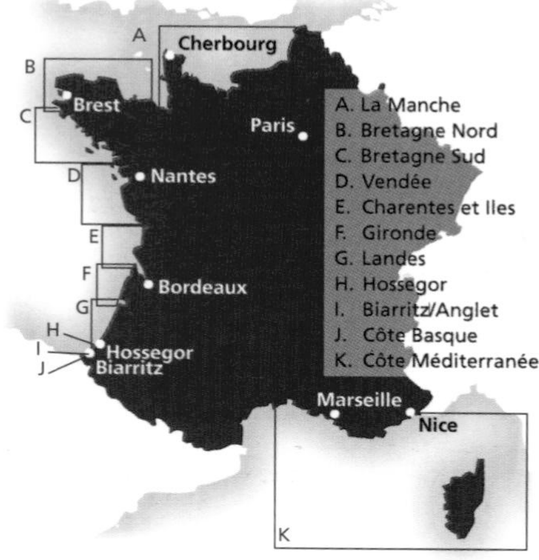

qui adore traîner dans les bars lors des traditionnelles fest-noze. Des marnages de près de 13-14 mètres sont atteints en Bretagne nord lors des grands coeffs d'equinoxe. Falaises, îles, rochers et vents hurlants confèrent aux alentours un décor intimidant, dont certains noms témoignent d'un passé terrible : La Baie des Trépassés, Fromveur (Le chenal de la Grande Peur en breton)... L'avantage géographique est sans doute le découpage extrême de la côte qui permet de trouver systématiquement des spots offshore avec une houle filtrée avec cette condition : il faut que ça rentre ! C'est le réservoir de reefs vierges le plus important en France, surtout en Bretagne nord!

La **Vendée** et les **Charentes** constituent sur 700 km la Côte de Lumière, dû à son ensoleillement exceptionnel, le plus élevé de toute la côte atlantique. C'est un mélange intéressant entre les dunes landaises et la côte rocheuse bretonne, avec des platiers rocheux sous-estimés. Malgré une exposition aux houles de nord moins bonne et un plateau continental plus étendu, il existe nombre de reefs de qualité qui ne saturent pas ainsi que

Aquitaine

Hossegor pit

T. GIBAUD

Cassis

S. CANDE

Formerly considered a bit of a joke, surfing in the French Med has become a reality in the last couple of years. Swell can produce short period waves up to two metres (six feet), depending on the wind strength and fetch. If the wind drops, conditions can be clean, but an offshore will flatten it very quickly. Easterly winds, regular in winter, especially on the Côte d'Azur also provide good sessions. Winds are deeply linked to North Atlantic lows so it's advisable to avoid the summer months. Even during winter swell is inconsistent.

When to go

The south west's beaches can produce some of Europe's best summer waves, though autumn, winter and spring are the most consistent and powerful surf seasons, also the least crowded. The legendary summer beach scene down south is a lot of fun, but can be hazardous for your health due to the huge sewage problems twinned with the high likelihood of contracting alcoholic poisoning or sexually transmitted diseases during flat spells.

Brest Averages	Jan	Apr	Jul	Oct
water °C	8	9	15	14
wetsuit				

Biarritz Averages	Jan	Apr	Jul	Oct
water °C	13	15	20	18
wetsuit				

nombre de beachbreaks qui offrent un surf d'été correct.

La **Gironde** marque une ligne psychologique entre le nord de la France et le 'Sud-ouest' marquée par la région Aquitaine. C'est d'abord une ligne droite à peine entamée par le Bassin d'Arcachon qui rejoint le Boucau à la Pointe de Grave sur 230 km. Puis, c'est la Côte Basque, la région de surf la plus fréquentée. L'immensité des plages concentre une pléthore de pics qui restent pour beaucoup sans prétendant à l'exception de juillet-août. Elle combine deux départements: la Gironde au nord, les **Landes** au sud. La direction dominante de la houle a tendance à favoriser les longues droites, bien que le courant nord-sud forme aussi des bancs parfaits dans les 'baïnes' pour des gauches courtes mais tubulaires. Les passages pour aller au lineup sont rarement profonds et les vagues ont tendance à fermer au-dessus de 2,5m-3m. Mieux vaut choisir marée basse quand c'est petit et marée haute quand c'est gros. Les vents de terre améliorent sensiblement la surfabilité de ces vagues plutôt rapides. Inversement, ces vagues sont fragiles aux vents de mer. Les différences de marées font évoluer les spots à toute allure. Les pics parfaits peuvent dégénérer en d' immondes rougnes en moins d'une heure. C'est une des zones estivales les plus consistantes d'été où on surfe en short 3 mois de bonnes vagues creuses entre les quelques 'flats'.

Depuis les débuts du surf, **Hossegor** a toujours impressionné les visiteurs et les locaux par la puissance dévastatrice de ses pics considérés aujourd'hui par les pros comme un des meilleurs beachbreaks au monde. La Côte Basque est la version plus nuancée du paradis du surf français avec une gamme composée de quelques pointbreaks de qualité et de beachbreaks protégés, offrant de belles alternatives surtout quand ça rentre et que ça souffle

Autrefois considéré comme une boutade, le surf en **Méditerranée** est devenu une réalité depuis quelques années. Les houles de vent provoquées par les coups de Mistral en Provence, peuvent envoyer des vagues rarement puissantes mais parfois creuses jusqu'à 2 mètres, selon la force du vent et le fetch. Les jours de swell sont rares mais intenses. Si le vent tombe ou se renverse, ça devient épique même si ça ne dure pas longtemps Les vents d'est, assez fréquents en hiver, produisent de bonnes sessions sur la Côte d'Azur. L'activité de ces vents est étroitement liée aux dépressions de l'Atlantique nord. Evitez l'été absolument. Attention, les vrais spots sont rares et déjà saturés. Pour ceux qui cherchent des spots vierges, il faut aller en Corse où seule la Baie d'Ajaccio est déjà bien jalonnée...

Quand aller

Les plages de sud-ouest possèdent probablement les vagues idéales d'été dont la plupart des surfers rêvent. Les autres saisons ne peuvent être négligées car les houles sont puissantes, régulières sans la pression de la foule estivale. Attention aux dangers de l'été : rejets d'eaux usées non traitées, excès alcooliques et parties de jambes en l'air non sécurisées.

Kelly Slater, Australie, 1998.
Photo Joli.

SURF session

D'année en année,
le surf ne cesse d'évoluer.
Les champions changent.
De nouvelles manoeuvres apparaissent.
De nouveaux spots sont découverts.
De nouveaux défis sont lancés.

Tom Curren, Pipeline, 1988.
Photo W.Bolster

Indonésie.
Photo T.Grambeau

D'année en année, depuis plus de 12 ans,
Surf Session ne cesse de coller, tous les mois,
à l'actualité du surf, sans jamais oublier de faire parler
les vagues... et de vous faire rêver.

The Ocean Environment

Water Quality

Summer's here! Where are you going on holiday? Will you choose the petrochemicals of Pas de Calais, the radioactivity of Normandy, the nitrates of Brittany, the bacteria of the Côte Basque or the timber mills and human waste of the Aquitane? The Surfrider Foundation would like to help you choose your destination.

For the second year, Surfrider Foundation Europe have published their Black Flag system of water quality rankings, aimed at informing you exactly what you're getting into before plunging innocently into the water. Regional information is all based on info provided by surfers and Surfrider Foundation members. They are the reflection of one of surfing's sad realities.

Surfrider Foundation Europe
79 bis, rue d'Espagne 64200 Biarritz
tel 05 59 23 54 99 fax 05 59 41 11 04
email surfrider.europe@hol.fr

The difference between the Black Flags and the Blue Flags awarded by government agencies is that Surfrider's observations are not based solely on the period from July to September, which establishes a 'right' to pollute during the rest of the year. Swimmers, surfers, fishers, and windsurfers are more and more plunging into the waves twelve months of the year. The other difference between the water quality reports administered by the Ministry of Health is that Surfrider refuses to limit their evaluation of water cleanliness to just three bacterium. Chemical pollution, hydrocarbons, floating rubbish, odours – are all included in the analysis.

In 1997, 25 Black Flags were attributed to beaches with pollution problems effecting surfers. In 1998, 118 Black Flags were awarded to beaches with real pollution problems. We have one hope for Black Flag 1999; the number diminishes. High human bacterial levels and chemical pollution are the main determining factors for the attribution of a Black Flag. Studies enable us to measure the effect of these pollutants on each beach. It is, however, much more difficult to measure the tonnes of floating rubbish and oil that soil our beaches all year round. Surfers and swimmers are the main victims, so we put the question to the official guardians of our coast.

Of France's coastguards, 304 have given their verdict. They responded to a a questionaire circulated by the Surfrider Foundation, covering 175 french surf spots which were put under the magnifying glass. This is a summary of their findings.

- 30% judged their beach 'always or often polluted'.
- 97% were finding rubbish on their surf spot.
- 77% thought their beach was insufficiently cleaned.
- 47% claimed to have fallen ill after a session in the water.

On Localism

As with everywhere in the world, locals want foreigners to respect their spots and the atmosphere in the water, but generally it is quite cool. Summer and early fall are the most crowded seasons, and when there are crowds there are sometimes struggles for waves. But they can be avoided. For wild and truly solitary surfing, the Landes Coast is still full of secret spots as soon as you walk a bit. In summer there are more and more longboarders, while in the water, you will find all generations of surfers from kids to 50 year old guys.

J.M.HERBERT

Specificités du littoral

Qualité de l'eau

L'été est là ! Où allez-vous en vacances ? Allez-vous choisir les dérivés pétrochimiques du Pas-de-Calais, la radioactivité de la Normandie, les nitrates de Bretagne, les bactéries de la Côte Basque où les rejets des usines papetières ou des eaux usées de l'Aquitaine? La Surfrider Foundation va vous aider à choisir votre destination.

Pour la deuxième année, Surfrider Foundation a publié sa carte des pavillons Noirs, qui décèle les poinst noirs du littoral en matière de pollution de l'eau et de la plage. Cette information se base sur les témoignages de surfers comme sur les relevés hebdomdaires de la DDASS. La réalité est désastreuse.

La différence entre les Pavillons Noirs et les Pavillons Bleus, décernés par un organisme gouvernemental réside dans le fait que les observations de Surfrider ne sont pas seulement faites entre juillet et septembre, ce qui implique indirectement une "permission" de polluer le reste de l'année. Baigneurs, surfers, pêcheurs et windsurfers sont de plus en plus nombreux à être dans l'eau 12 mois sur 12. L'autre différence est que le Ministère de la Santé se restreint à l'évaluation de 3 bactéries alors que Surfrider inclut aussi les métaux lourds, les hydrocarbures, les déchets flottants et même les odeurs suspectes !

En 1997, les surfers plantaient 25 Pavillons Noirs sur les spots. En 1998, on est passé à 118 ! On espère qu'en 1999, ce chiffre va pouvoir baisser. Les pollutions organiques et chimiques sont les facteurs déterminants pour l'attribution de ces Pavillons. Des études nous permettent de connaître l'impact de ces polluants sur les plages. Il est en revanche plus difficile de mesurer l'importance des déchets flottants qui souillent les plages tous les mois où il n'y a pas de nettoyage. Surfers et baigneurs en sont les premières victimes : c'est donc à ces "gardiens de la côte " qu'il faut poser la question.

Ils sont plus de 300 à avoir donné leur verdict. Ils ont répondu à un questionnaire où 175 des principaux spots ont été passé au crible. Voci un résumé des résultats.

30% jugent leur spot " toujours ou souvent pollué"
97% ont déjà trouvé des déchets sur leur spot
77% pensent que le nettoayge de plage est insuffisant
47% sont tombés malades après une session.

Le localisme

Comme partout dans le monde, les locaux veulent que les étrangers respectent leur spots afin d'y conserver une bonne ambiance, ce qui souvent est le cas. La fin de l'été et le début de l'automne sont les périodes de friction au lineup. Rappelons qu'il y existe encore des zones de surf esseulées comme les Landes ou la Gironde où il suffit de marcher dans le sable pour être tranquille. En été, les longboarders sont de plus en plus nombreux. Le lineup est souvent composé d'une multitude d'âges allant du kid de 10 ans en bodyboard au Tonton quiquagénaire en malibu.

Travelling

Getting There

By air If you are arriving in France from international destinations, Paris is the main international point of arrival. From there you can take an internal flight to Bordeaux or Biarritz, of which Bordeaux is significantly cheaper at most times of the year, but leaves you at the north of Les Landes. If flying within Europe, Bordeaux is without doubt the best and cheapest way to get to the southwest. Either catch a bus from there to Lacanau (about one hour) or a train or bus south to Biarritz (about two and a half hours). Rental cars are available from both airports.

S. CANDE

By sea Car ferries are cheap and convenient: the overnight crossings from Plymouth to Roscoff, and Portsmouth to Saint Malo, can leave you rested and ready to hit the water within a few hours. Prices vary according to season: peak time is from mid July to September. Several companies ply the shortest and cheapest Dover-Calais route; ferries leave regularly throughout the day and night. It does however add a few more hours to your drive time and a few more francs to your petrol bill.

By train From Britain, the Eurostar is a quick and easy way to get to France. At the moment, trains connecting London's Waterloo or Ashford directly with Paris run twice an hour and fares range from £85 – £135. Boards cost £20 for a single journey and have to be checked in as registered baggage at the Euro Dispatch Counter. There's a 24-hour delivery time, so plan on a night in Paris before you and your board are reunited.

Getting Around

RIGHEZZA

By car French roads are some of the best in the world. You will nearly always have the choice between the high speed *péage* (which is more expensive) or good RN roads (RN stands for Routes Nationales). Petrol prices in France are among the highest in Europe: they're even more expensive on the *peage*. The cheapest place to buy fuel is from the supermarkets. French roads are often congested at the beginning of August and long drives should be avoided at these times. You must always carry vehicle registration documents, insurance, license and passport with you. Police checks are often just after péage booths. A clean appearance and van can save you hassles.

By train The French train network (SNCF) has a reputation for efficiency and speed. The TGV (France's hi-speed train) runs (amongst other destinations) from Paris to Bayonne and can be an excellent way to get to the coast from the north.

Infos voyage

Y aller

En avion Si vous arrivez de l'étranger, Paris est le point de chute incontournable. De là, il suffit de rejoindre Bordeaux ou Biarritz, sachant que Bordeaux est moins cher car ouvert à la concurrence. Depuis l'Europe, Bordeaux est sûrement le meilleur aéroport à viser. De là, vous pouvez prendre un bus pour Lacanau (environ une heure) ou un train pour Biarritz (2 heures). On trouve des locations de voiture aux deux aéroports.

En bateaux De loin la méthode la plus utilisée par les anglo-saxons est eclle du ferry. Les traversées nocturnes (en général moins chères) Plymouth-Roscoff et Porstmouth-St-Malo peuvent vous amener tout frais à quelques heures des vagues. Les prix varient en fonction de la saison qui va de la mi-juillet à début septembre. Les prix hors-saison peuvent être avantageux surtout si vous êtes en groupe dasn un van. Quelques compagnies assurent la liaison Douvres-Calais jour et nuit. C'est de loin le plus court et le moins cher pour traverser la Manche (surtout de minuit à l'aube) bien que ça rallonge le trajet par la route et surtout un bon pactole pour l' essence.

Se deplacer

En voiture Les routes françaises sont parmi les meilleures du monde en ayant souvent le choix entre une route natioanle (RN) et les autoroutes à péages (cher). Roulez à droite et n'oubliez pas non plus la priorité à droite, sauf indication contraire comme sur les rond-points qui ont tendance à se miltiplier. Les prix à la pompe sont les plus élevés d'Europe avec une différence notable (jusqu'à 80 centimes) entre les stations sur l'autoroute et celles des supermarchés où avoir une carte de crédit permet de faire le plein 24h/24. En été, pas mal de routes côtières sont encombrées, les parkings saturent et les flics sont partout, mieux vaut être en règle avec tous les papiers nécessaires.

En train La réseau de la SNCF est rapide et efficace surtout avec le TGV qui relie Paris à toutes les côtes dans des temps record. Pas toujours trés pratique avec les planches, il permet quand même à beaucoup de parisiens d'aller surfer en week-end. Renseignez-vous pour les abonnements parce que le tarif plein est assez lourd.

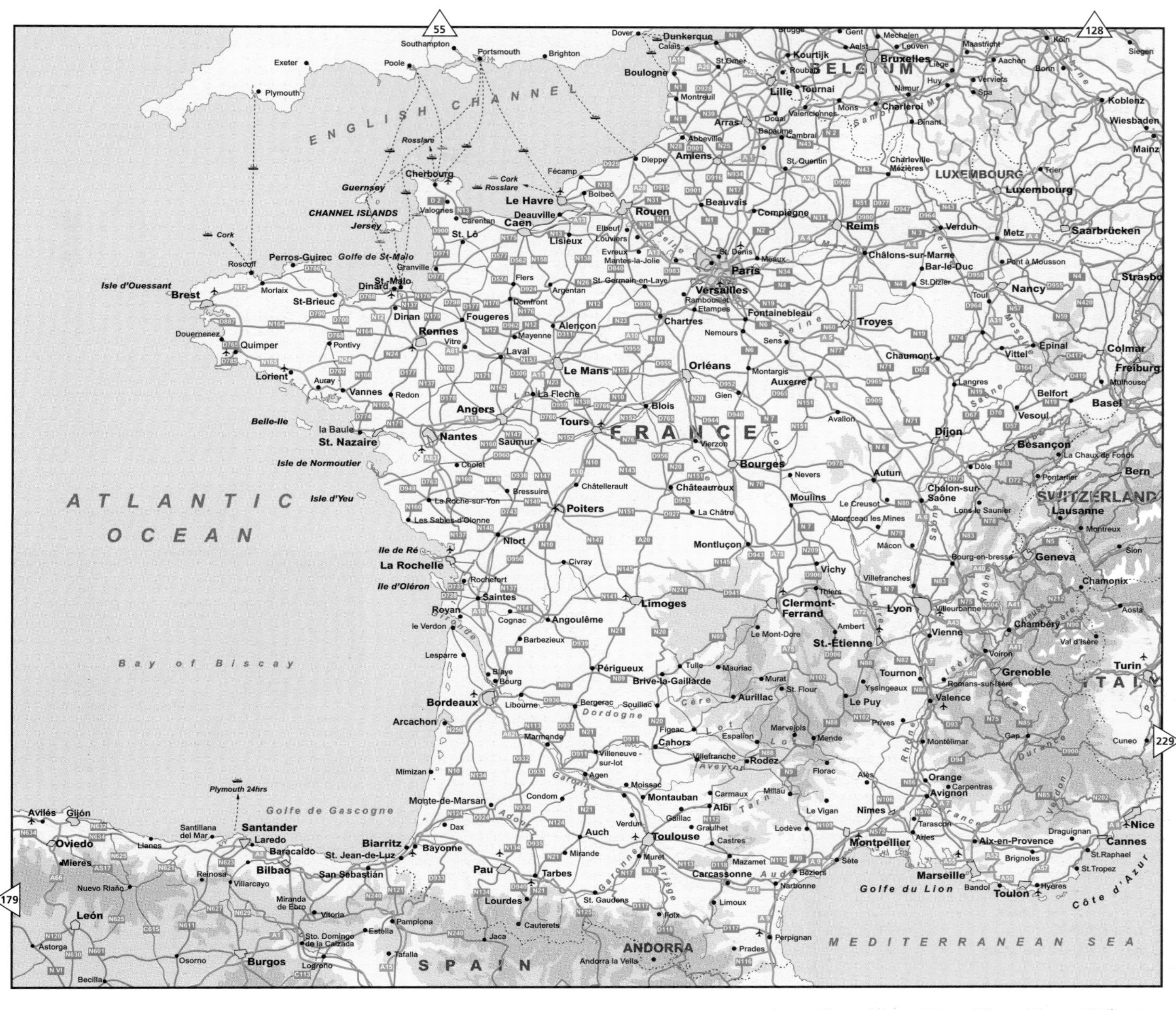

France: Travelling Map

Scale 0 50 100 150 200 250 300 Kilometres
0 50 100 150 200 Miles

Travel

Airports

Aeroport Roissy-Charles de Gaulle: (01) 48 62 12 12
Aeroport d'Orly: (01) 49 75 15 15
Bordeaux: (05) 56 34 50 50
Biarritz: (05) 59 43 83 83

Ferries

Brittany Ferries - Roscoff: (02) 98 29 28 00
Caen: (02) 31 36 36 36
General: 0800 382 861
P&O - Calais: (03) 21 46 04 40
Cherbourg: (08) 03 01 30 13
Hoverspeed Calais: (03) 21 46 14 14
SNCM Marseille – Corsica: (04) 91 56 38 63

Trains

Paris SNCF (Grandes lignes): (01) 45 82 50 50
Paris SNCF (Ile de France only): (01) 45 65 60 00
Bordeaux Gare St Jean: (08) 36 35 35 35 (info)
Bayonne SNCF: (08) 36 35 35 35
Eurostar: 0990 300 003

Buses

Eurolines Paris: (01) 49 72 51 51
Bayonne Sud-ouest: (05) 59 59 19 33

Driving

Le Shuttle is the car carrying tunnel from Folkestone to Calais - 35 minutes: 0990 353 535

Speed Limits

Autoroutes: 130 kph/80mph
Routes Nationales/Departmentales: 100kph

Tolls

Privatised toll paying motorways cover most of France. National motorways are usually toll free, mostly in the NW.

Petrol Prices

6,34FF/l
Diesel: 4,28 FF/l
Autoroutes informations: (08) 36 68 10 77 or (01) 47 05 90 01

Greencard/Bail Bonds

If you rent a car, you will need a green card or International Insurance Certificate to prove you have liability insurance. Carry a letter of authorisation from the owner if the car is not registered in your name.

Other Info

Visas

Citizens of most european countries, the US, Australians, Canada and New Zealand do not require visas. All others including and South Africans and those planning to stay more than three months, must obtain a visa from the French consulate in their home country.

Tourist Authority

Bureu d'Accueil (01) 49 52 53 54
Charles de Gaulle airport office: (01) 48 62 27 29

Telephone Info

International Country Code: 33
Dial Out Code: 00
Emergencies: 15
International Operator: 00 33 11
International Directory: 00 33 12 + country code
Directory Enquiries:12
Operator: 13

The Channel

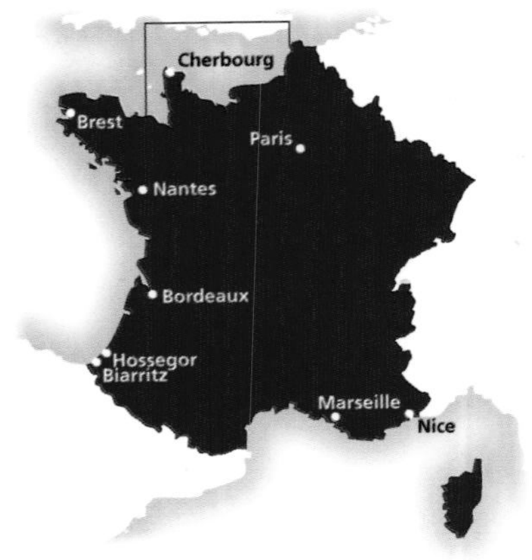

1. Wissant

A long stretch of NW-oriented,beach 20km (12mi) from Calais. The conditions are best on W/SW swells. Beware of the strong current that rips through this spot on strong W winds.

Longue plage de sable à 20 kms de Calais orientée nord-ouest. Les conditions sont bonnes par houle d'ouest sud-ouest. Attention au fort courant qui balaye le spot quand le vent d'ouest dépote à max.

2. Cap Gris-Nez

Probably the best spot on the entire nothern France coastline, this is a rocky bottomed spot working on big west W-SW swells, which can deliver beautiful waves up to 2m (6ft). There's also spots at Cap Blanc Nez on the D940. Mid tide only.

Fonds rocheux pour ce spot qui fonctionne par grosse houle d'ouest/sud-ouest et offre parfois de superbes vagues pouvant aller jusqu'à 2 mètres. C'est certainement le meilleur spot de l'extrême nord de la France. Il existe aussi un cap Blanc-Nez sur la D940.

3. Wimereux

The break of Pointe des Oies is only a few kilometres from Boulogne. The full W orientation of this beach makes it a wave magnet on any SW swell. But the strong W winds can often spoil the party.

Le spot de la Pointe aux Oies se trouve à quelques kilomètres de Boulogne. L'orientation plein ouest de cette plage de sable lui permet de recevoir parfaitement la moindre houle de sud-ouest mais le spot est très sensible au vent qui souffle souvent exagérément de secteur ouest.

4. Mers

Right next to the town of Le Tréport, and on the border of Normandy, this beach is famous for its lack of crowds. The reason is that it only works on big W-SW swells. Worth checking out in autumn when the sandbars are still settled.

Pile à la limite de la Normandie, collée au Tréport, cette plage de galets a le mérite d'être encore peu fréquentée. Et pour cause, le spot ne fonctionne correctement qu'avec une grosee houlasse d'ouest/sud-ouest. Un pari à faire de préférence en automne.

5. Pourville

Just ask any guy from the local Surf Club Espace Fun how good it gets on big swells. It can be perfect when its glassy, but then again, it's rare. Have patience.

Demandez au Pourville Espace Fun, le club local, ils vous raconteront comment ça rentre par gros swell! Ce spot peut marcher terrible sans vent mais là encore, c'est rare. Patience !

J.M.HERBERT

Yann Le Her, Pourville-Dieppe

6. Petites Dalles

À very famous sailboarding spot, this shingle beach can also produce more-than-decent waves. This reef-like break is best at mid-tide, on SW but also on NE swells. A bad option when the winds are up because this place is immediately squatted by... windsurfers.

Spot très réputé pour le funboard, cette plage de galets peut aussi devenir un spot de surf plus que correct. Un haut-fond rocheux lève de belles séries à mi-marée. Favorable par houle de sud-ouest mais aussi par nord-est. A éviter quand le zef souffle à donf à cause d'une surpopulation de ...windsurfers !

7. Fécamp

Some ridable curls on the S part of the beach, mostly lefts that peel nicely on flat rocks when there's swell is up (but not the wind!). It's packed with sailboarders when a storm is in full swing.

On trouve des vagues au sud de la plage sur une longue dalle rocheuse, plutôt des gauches, qui déferlent joliment les jours de houle sans trop de vent d'ouest. Gavé de funboarders en cas de tempête.

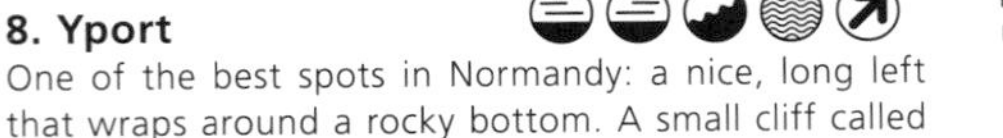

8. Yport

One of the best spots in Normandy: a nice, long left that wraps around a rocky bottom. A small cliff called Pointe de Chicard keeps the line up glassy when the SW blow. On big days, a smaller right starts rolling on inside the bay. Just beware of the rip pulling you towards Fécamp.

Un des meilleurs spots de Normandie. Une belle et longue gauche déroule régulièrement sur des fonds rocheux . Une petite falaise appelée Pointe de Chicard protège ce spot des éventuels vents de sud-ouest. Par gros gros swell, une droite pète au milieu de la baie mais attention au jus qui vous tire vers Fécamp.

9. Vaucottes

Hidden between the legendary cliffs of Normandy, a small shingle beach that ends up with a stretch of rocks. This set up delivers rather mushy waves, making it a beginner's favourite.

Petite plage de galets, encastrée dans les falaises, se terminant par une dalle rocheuse sur laquelle la houle vient se fracasser. La vague manque parfois de punch, ce qui n'est pas pour déplaire aux débutants.

10. Etretat

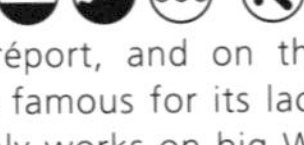

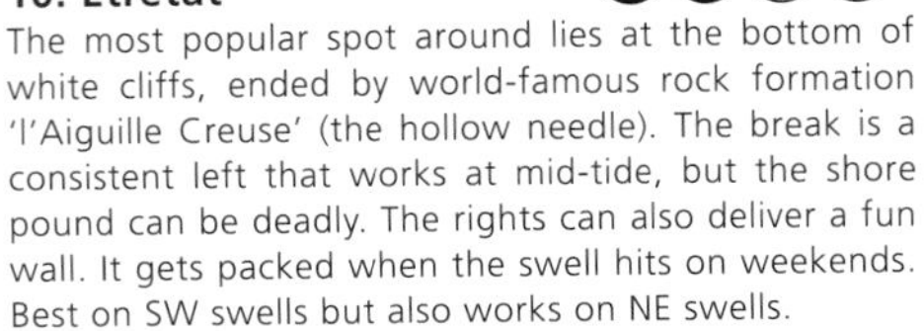

The most popular spot around lies at the bottom of white cliffs, ended by world-famous rock formation 'l'Aiguille Creuse' (the hollow needle). The break is a consistent left that works at mid-tide, but the shore pound can be deadly. The rights can also deliver a fun wall. It gets packed when the swell hits on weekends. Best on SW swells but also works on NE swells.

Le spot le plus célèbre de la région est au pied d'une haute falaise blanche de calcaire se terminant par une aiguille rocheuse : bienvenu sur l'Aiguille creuse ! La gauche marche régulèrement à la mi-marée et se termine parfois sur un shorebreak de galets explosif. on peut aussi partir en droite sur un bon petit creux. Surpeuplé quand la houle tombe le week-end. Houle de sud-ouest bien sûr mais aussi nord-est.

J.M.HERBERT

Etretat

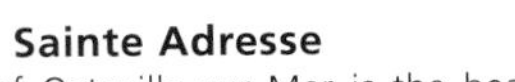

11. Sainte Adresse

W of Octeville sur Mer is the beach break of Sainte-Adresse. It features mostly lefts, but the water is often of very poor quality.

Juste à l'ouest d'Octeville/mer, on trouve le beachbreak de Ste-Adresse qui lève plutôt des gauches dans une eau parfois dégueu...

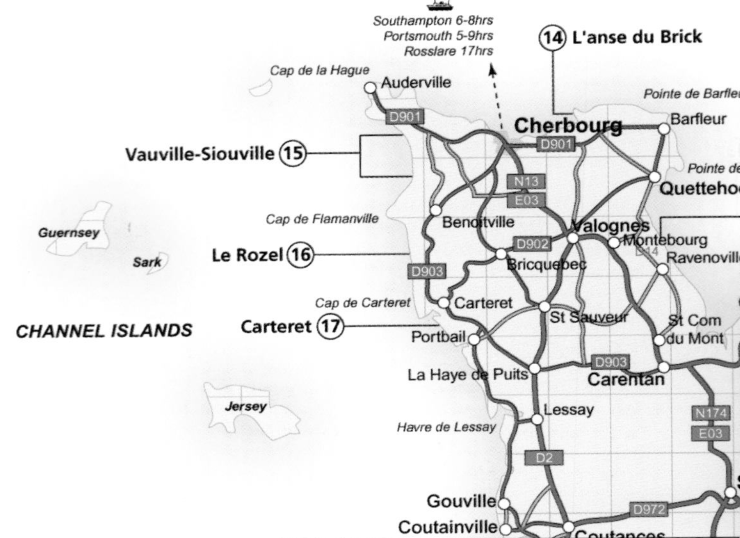

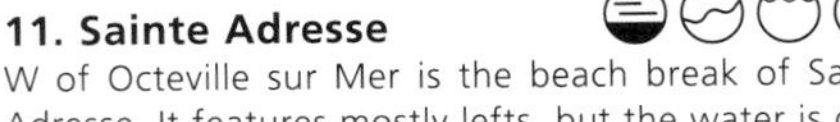

J.M.HERBERT

Le Havre

12. Trouville

On the main beach, the best break is located close to the jetty at low tide. It's only worth checking on big NW swells and SE winds.

Sur la plage principale, on trouve une vague près de la jetée à marée basse. A checker seulement par vent de sud-est et gros swell de nord-ouest.

13. Les Plages Du Débarquement

Hard to call it a surf spot, but this succession of sandy beaches (apart from a few mushy breakers on big swells) recalls June 6, 1944, when it got blasted by the meatiest swell: hoards of allied troops, determined to put an end to nazi domination.

Pas vraiment un spot de surf mais une guirlande de plages qui réveille non seulement quelques vagues mollassonnes par grosse houle mais surtout le souvenir qu'un 6 Juin 1944, c'est rentré gras de soldats alliés pour endiguer l'impérialisme nazi.

14. L'anse du Brick

When the W coast of the Channel is either blown out from the SW or closing out, all it takes is a 12km (7mi) drive from Cherbourg to score waves. The take-off spot isn't very large so expect competition for positioning.

Quand la côte ouest de la Manche sature de houle ou de vent de sud-ouest, il suffit d'aller à 10 kms à1'est de Cherbourg et trouver cette petite baie qui produit de belles vagues. Le lineup est restreint, ça bataille vite pour la priorité.

15. Vauville

If you're looking for solitude, head to Vauville where there's no less than 16km (10mi) of beaches that work any swell coming from the W. The best bet along this stretch of coast is Siouville, where the locals have sights of Les Landes when it's grinding. Word is spreading around about a reef break at Diélette that goes Indonesian every once in a while.

Pas moins de 15km de beachbreaks qui reçoivent la moindre houle d'ouest. L'embarras du choix pour surfer un pic seul mais le meilleur reste souvent Siouville où les locaux se croiraient dans les Landes quand c'est bien creux.On parle d'un reef à Diélette qui devient indonésien une fois l'an.

16. Le Rozel

This is the best spot of the Cotentin coastline and if you're lucky you'll score good waves (surfable up to 3m/10ft), though often it's blown out.

Loue plage rectiligne, orientée plein ouest, offrant de belles vagues lorsque le vent on-shore ne souffle pas fort. Ca peut rentrer à 2,5m/3m avec une puissance rare par ici. Le meilleur spot du Cotentin.

17. Carteret

Although this is not as consisant as the other breaks in this area, there are some waves at this sandy-bottomed location on good days. To the S, the boardwalk of Barneville gives a panorama of the excellent beginner's beach.

Fond sableux pour ce spot qui est tout de même moins régulier que les précédents. Quelques belles séries les meilleurs jours. Idéal pour débuter. Au sud, le front de mer de Barneville permet de checker pas mal de pics.

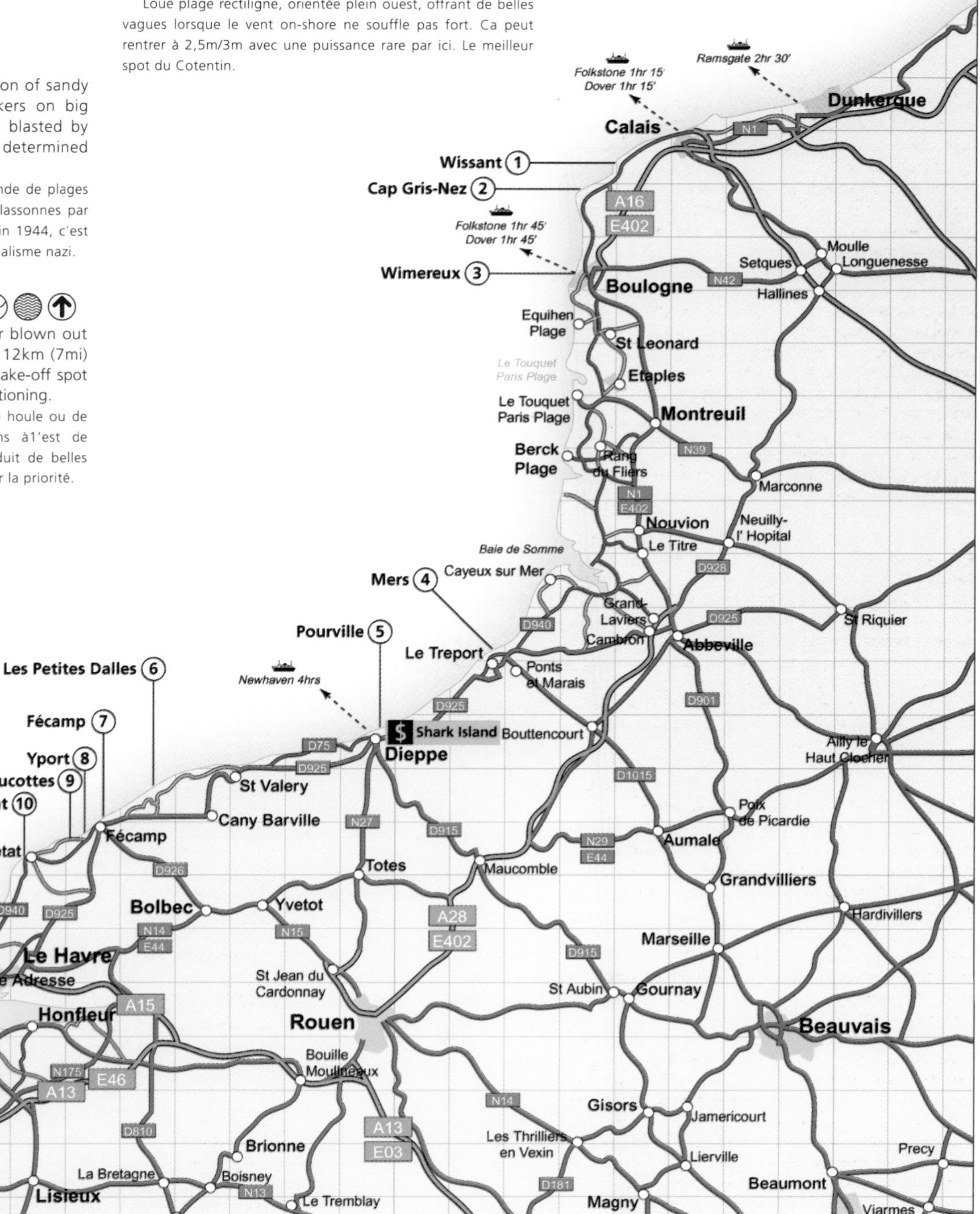

North Brittany

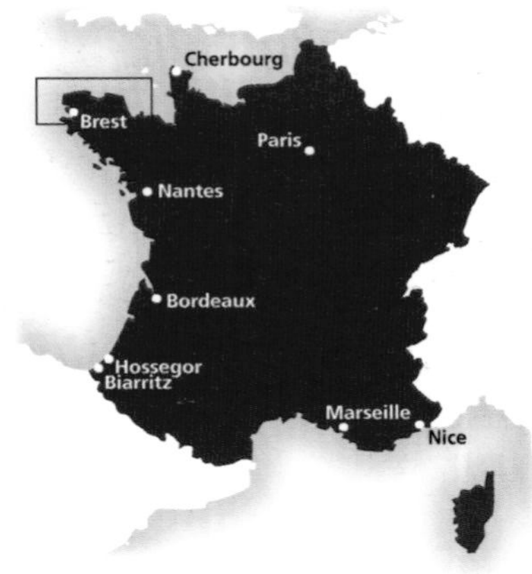

1. La Plage du Sillon

Between Paramé and St Malo mushy waves break close to the promenade, often with a SW storm.

Entre Paramé et St-Malo, on trouve quelques vagues le long du remblai, le plus souvent par tempête de Sud-Ouest.

2 La Garde-Guerin

Heading towards St-Lunaire and Longchamps beach, you'll find one of the only real surf spots around with hollow waves.

Direction St-Lunaire et la plage de Longchamps, on trouve le spot de surf du coin: des vagues assez creuses pour glisseurs en tous genres.

3. Pleherel

Head 3km (2mi) W of the Vieux-Port beach and drive up to Cap Fréhel to take a look at its postcard-coloured cliffs. This is a perfect viewpoint to check the surf at Plevenon and surrounds.

Trés kms à l'ouest de la plage du Vieux-Port. Poussez jusqu'au Cap Fréhel et ses falaises colorées. Point de vue pour mater Plevenon et le reste aussi.

Pleherel Plage

4. Tregastel Plage

Between the coast and Tomé Island there's a few waves occasionally.

Entre la côte et l'île deTomé, vagues de temps en temps.

5. Beg Leguer

One of the most consistent rivermouth spots.

Littéralement 'embouchure de la Leguer'. Consistent région.

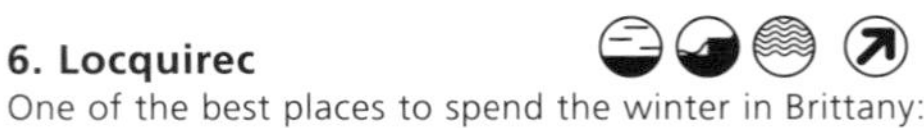

Le Petit Minou

6. Locquirec

One of the best places to spend the winter in Brittany: the locals are cool and there's a couple of good spots protected from SW storms including Pors Ar Ville (the most consistent), Poul Rodou and Moulin La Rive. Take the road for Morlaix and follow the signs for Locquirec.

Une des meilleures places en Bretagne pour passer l'hiver. Les locaux y sont encore sympas. Un paquet de spots protégé des tempêtes de sud-ouest, Pors Ar Villec le plus consistent Poul Rodou, Moulin La Rive. Prendre morlaix puis Locquirec .

7. Primel-Tregastel

Not much happens in this part of Brittany, but if you are lucky, take look around the area of St-Jean du Doigt at low tide and there might be a surprise.

Comme dans toute cette partie nord de la Bretagne, ça rentre rarement mais dès fois que vous soyez là au bon moment. Si la marée est basse, allez zoner du côté de St-Jean du Doigt.

8. Le Dossen

As it's pretty sloppy and exposed, windsurfers are in heaven. It's better to surf at La Mauvaise Greve (a popular reef), or, if you like hardcore waves, go to L'Ile de Sieck, where you'll find a hollow, powerful right breaking on a shallow reef. Between Le Dossen and Penfoul you'll find one of richest areas of reef breaks in Brittany. Surfers who know about these don't let on too much.

Un paradis de Windsurfer; très mou et venté pour les surfers, aller plutôt a la Mauvaise Grève (reef populaire) ou si vous aimez le surf hard core, allez a L'Ile de Sieck, droite puissante et creuse sur un reef craignos. Entre Le Dossen et Penfoul, une des régions les plus riches en reefs, les surfers qui connaissent sont avares d'indications.

9. Penfoul

A pretty messy spot. It's better to find the secret reefs of La Chapelle and Le Triangle. Go to Ploudalmézeau and follow signs for Penfoul.

Trés mou, aller plutôt chercher les reefs secrets La Chapelle, Le Triangle. Prendre Ploudalmézeau puis Penfoul.

10. Le Gouerou

A short, hollow wave breaks close to the shore. Follow the signs for Lampaul-Plouarzel.

Vague trés creuse et courte près du bord. Prendre Lampaul-Plouarzel.

11. Blancs-Sablons

This is a sloppy beach break that closes out easily, but is good for beginners. Take the road for Le Conquet.

Beach break mou qui ferme, idéal pour débutants. Prendre le Conquet.

12. Le Petit Minou

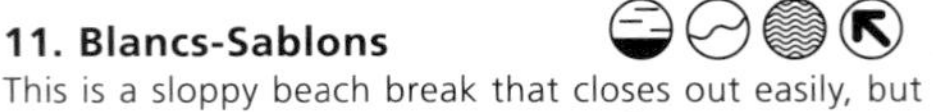

This is a hollow beach break that works only at low tide. Often it's crowded out with bodyboarders and grommets and when it is, head for Deolen, Talbosse or Le Trez-Hir. These three spots are also protected from N winds.

Beach break creux, ne marche qu'à marée basse. Bodyboards et grommets vous feront regretter de vous y être attardé. Allez plutôt voir Deolen, Talbosse ou le Trez-Hir, tous ces spots sont protégés des vents de N et NO.

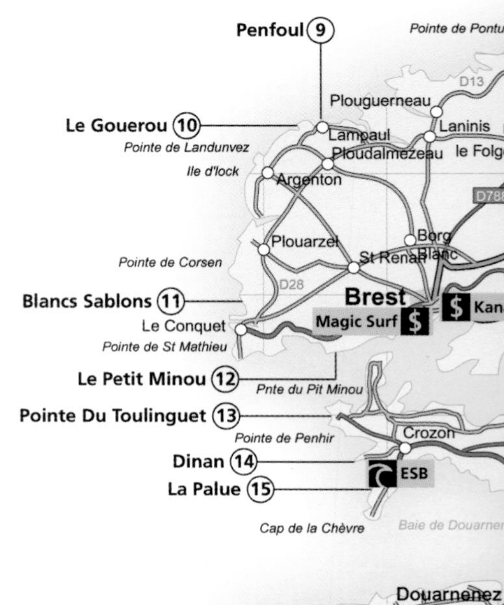

13. Pointe Du Toulinguet  

Not as crowded but with less swell than La Palue, there's a nice hollow beach break here that's exposed to the W. Be careful of the rip.

Beach break creux exposé plein ouest, la houle et la foule y sont toujours plus petites qu'à la Palue, attention aux courants. Prendre Camaret puis la pointe du Toulinguet.

14. Pointe De Dinan 

There's a good right on the reef here protected from N winds: in good conditions you can ride for 200m (180yd), but when it's small you'll end up slaloming between the rocks. If you like beach breaks check out Goulien or Kerloch – you'll be in for a pleasant surprise.

Très panoramique, belle droite sur du reef, par bonnes conditions, surfable sur 200m quand c'est petit on fait du slalom entre les rochers. La gauche plus facile, casse sur du sable à marée haute; spot protégé des vents de nord. Si vous aimez le sable allez voir Goulien ou Kerloch, peut réserver des surprises.

15. La Palue   

The most consistent and popular of the spots on the Crozon peninsular, this break works better on a high tide. At low tide check Lostmarc'h, which is rideable up to 3m (10ft). If it's big and you want more, check out Cap de la Chevre; guns and a long leg rope are necessary here while dolphins are frequent visitors. to this spot. At night go to Morgat where there's a couple of decent crêperies.

Spot le plus consistent et le plus populaire de la presqu'ile de Crozon. Marche mieux à marée haute et Lostmarc'h à marée basse tient la houle jusqu'a 3m. Par tempêtes les vagues par dessus le Guéneron. Si c'est trop gros et que vous en vouliez plus, allez voir du coté du cap de la Chèvre, guns et grand leash obligatoire. Les orques sont fréquents, attention. Le soir rendez-vous à Morgat.

La Palue, Lostmarch

F. LE LEANNEC

La Palue, Cap de la Chevre

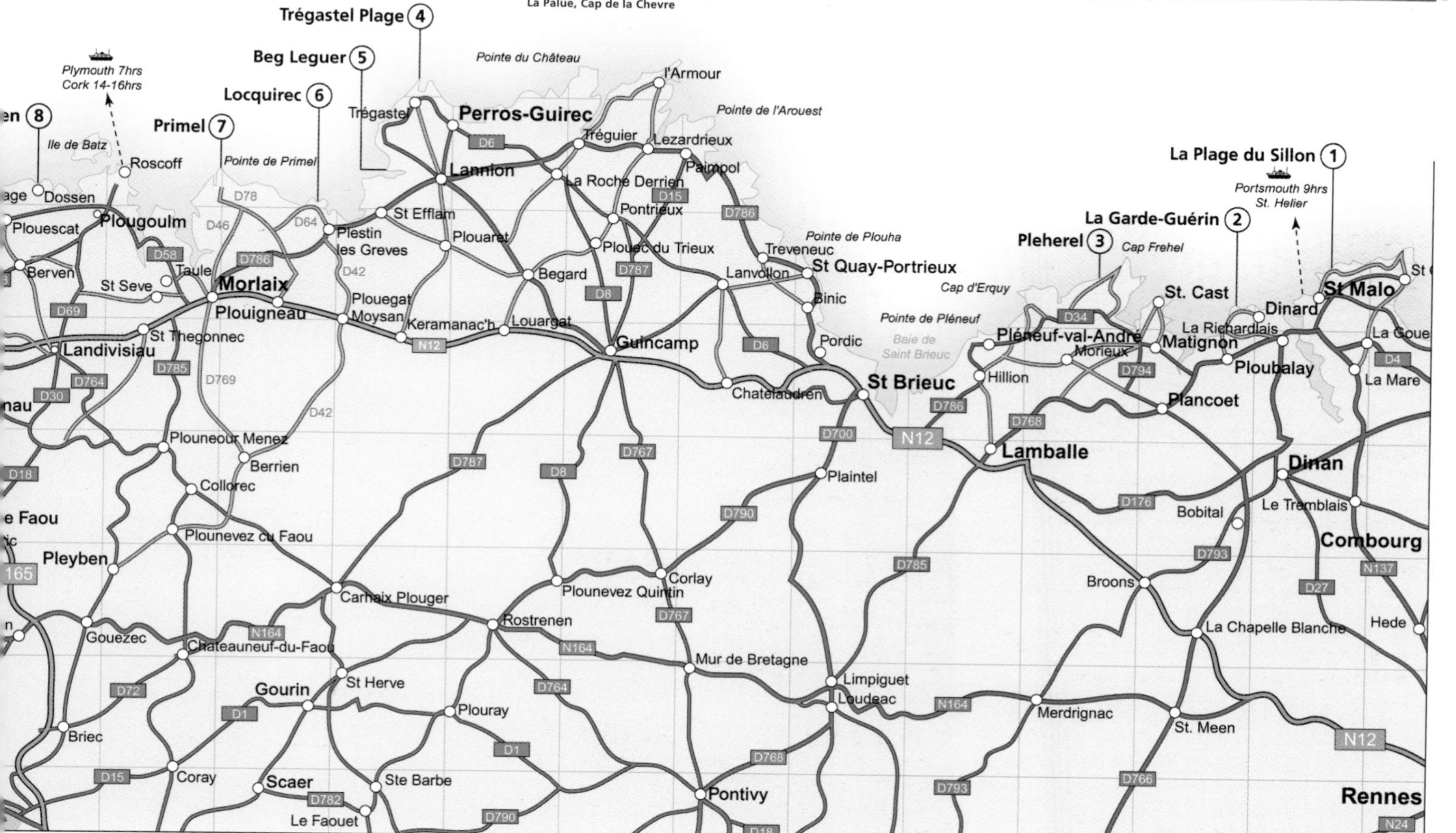

F. LE LEANNEC

Trégastel Plage 4
Beg Leguer 5
Locquirec 6
Primel 7
8
La Plage du Sillon 1
La Garde-Guérin 2
Pleherel 3
Plymouth 7hrs
Cork 14-16hrs
Portsmouth 9hrs
St. Helier
Ile de Batz
Roscoff
Dossen
Plouescat
Plougoulm
Berven
St Seve
Taule
Morlaix
Plouigneau
St Thegonnec
Landivisiau
Pointe de Primel
Plestin les Greves
St Efflam
Plouegat Moysan
Keramanac'h
Trégastel
Perros-Guirec
Pointe du Château
l'Armour
Pointe de l'Arouest
Tréguier
Lezardrieux
Paimpol
Lannion
La Roche Derrien
Pontrieux
Plouaret
Plouec du Trieux
Begard
Louargat
Guincamp
Lanvollon
Treveneuc
Pointe de Plouha
St Quay-Portrieux
Binic
Cap d'Erquy
Pointe de Pléneuf
Baie de Saint Brieuc
Pordic
Chatelaudren
St Brieuc
Hillion
Pléneuf-val-André
Morieux
Lamballe
Cap Frehel
St. Cast
Matignon
Plancoet
Dinard
La Richardlais
St Malo
Ploubalay
La Goue
La Mare
Dinan
Le Tremblais
Bobital
Combourg
Broons
La Chapelle Blanche
Hede
Plouneour Menez
Berrien
Collorec
Plounevez du Faou
Pleyben
Carhaix Plouger
Gouezec
Chateauneuf-du-Faou
Gourin
St Herve
Plouray
Rostrenen
Plounevez Quintin
Corlay
Plaintel
Mur de Bretagne
Limpiguet
Loudeac
Merdrignac
St. Meen
Briec
Coray
Scaer
Ste Barbe
Le Faouet
Pontivy
Rennes
D6 D15 D786 D787 D8 D6 D34 D794 D786 D768 D700 N12 D176 D793 N137 D27 D4 D78 D46 D64 D58 D786 D42 D69 D785 D769 D764 D30 D42 D18 D787 D8 D767 D790 D785 N164 D767 N164 D764 D72 D1 D1 D15 D782 D790 D768 D18 D793 D766 N164 N12 N24 N12

South Brittany

1. Baie de Douarnenez

Pors ar Vag is a good beach break for beginners – follow the signs for Plomodier, while Le Riz is more mellow and is protected from stormy SW winds by high cliffs. Pointe de Leydé or Roches Blanches has a very good left, but if you miss the take off, your board will kiss a big rock. It needs a big swell and is perfect in a SW storm. In Douarnenez take the road for Les Sables Blancs and follow the coast for 500m to find some other choice waves.

Pors ar Vag bon beach break pour les débutants et par vents d'ouest. Le Riz encore plus mou que le premier, mais des falaises la protègent des vents de sud ouest. Avant d'arriver à Douarnenez.Pointe de Leydé ou Roches Blanches dues à la couleur des rochers qui embrasseront votre planche au take off raté. Très belle gauche qui pète à raz la callaisse. Nécessite une très grosse houle d'ouest, idéal par tempêtes de sud-ouest. Dans Douarnenez prendre les Sables-Blancs et suivre la côte sur 500m. Attention aux locaux.

2. Baie des Trépasses   

(Translates as 'Bay of Death') and the name says it all. It might well be called this as it's the coldest spot on the Finistere. This is a good beach break working in a W or N swell: it's better at low tide with a small SW swell when can produce long rides. If you've time, check out Ile de Sein where there's some good reefs (take the boat at Audierne).

Bon beach break, le vent de sud y tourne offshore dans la baie. Ne reçoit que les houles d'ouest et de nord ouest. Marche mieux à marée basse et avec de petites houles qui peuvent vous offrir de trés longs rides, c'est le spot le plus froid du Finistère. Si vous avez le temps, allez sur l'Ile de Sein, de bons reefs vous y attendent (prendre le bateau à Audierne)

3. Saint Tugen   

The pearl of Cap Sizun is a good S-facing beach break, working only at low tide. If the swell is above 2m (6ft), there's stand-up barrels. Follow signs for La Pointe du Raz and turn off near Primelin à la Chapelle St Tugen.

(Ou Anse de Cabestan.) La perle du Cap Sizun, trés bon beach break, ne marche qu'à marée basse, à plus de 2m vous rentrez debout dans le tube. La plage est orientée plein sud. Prendre 'la Pointe du Raz' et tourner au niveau de Primelin à 'la Chapelle St Tugen'.

4. Pointe de Lervily 

A long right breaks over a shallow reef here. There's a peak close to the Island of Cows and another peak in the bay.

Une longue droite sur un reef craignos. Un pic près de l'Ile des Vaches et un pic dans la baie.

F. LE LEANNEC

La Torche

5. La Torche    

This is a popular beach break that gets crowded at weekends. Check out the good right on the point, but in a SW wind go to Pors Carn (to the left). If you like soul surfing, go up the beach to Tronoën and Penhorsou Guendrez, where you'll find quality waves.

Beach-break trés populaire, éviter les week-ends. Trés belle droite à la Pointe, beaucoup de monde aussi. Si vous aimez le soul surfing remontez la plage jusqu'a Tronoën, Penhors ou Guendrez des vagues de qualité vous y attendent.

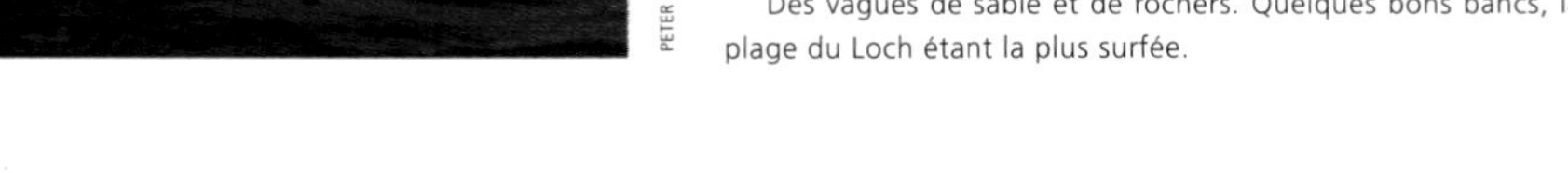

PETER CADE

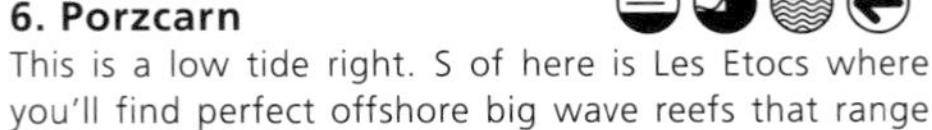

La Torche

6. Porzcarn    

This is a low tide right. S of here is Les Etocs where you'll find perfect offshore big wave reefs that range from 3-6m (8-18ft) – only for daredevils.

Une droite à marée basse, une érosion rapide sur la dune. Au sud, on trouve les Etocs, des reefs parfaits au large pour les couillus du gros surf, jusqu'à 6m.

7. Lesconil   

Windsurfers go crazy over this spot where there's excellent conditions between Benodet and Beg Meil; occasionally the surfing fraternity enjoys waves as well on big SW, W swells. The reef favours lefts on an incoming low to mid-tide close to the harbour.

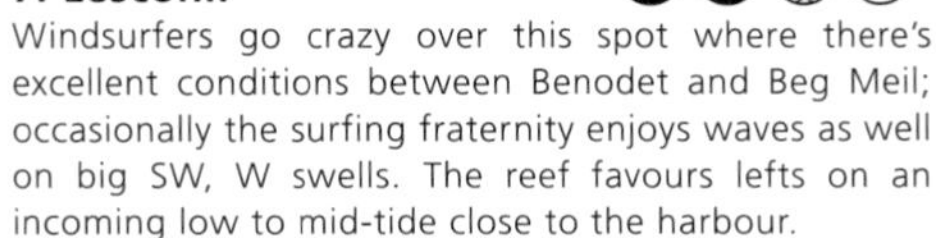

Les windsurfeurs l'aime ce spot, avec conditions excellent entre Benodet et Beg Meil. Le surfer gagnez des vagues avec houle de sud ouest. Les gauches marchant plus bonne sur le récife.

8. Guidel

Plages 

Reef, beach and a few good sandbank breaks are located here. The Plage du Loch is the most popular wave.

Des vagues de sable et de rochers. Quelques bons bancs, la plage du Loch étant la plus surfée.

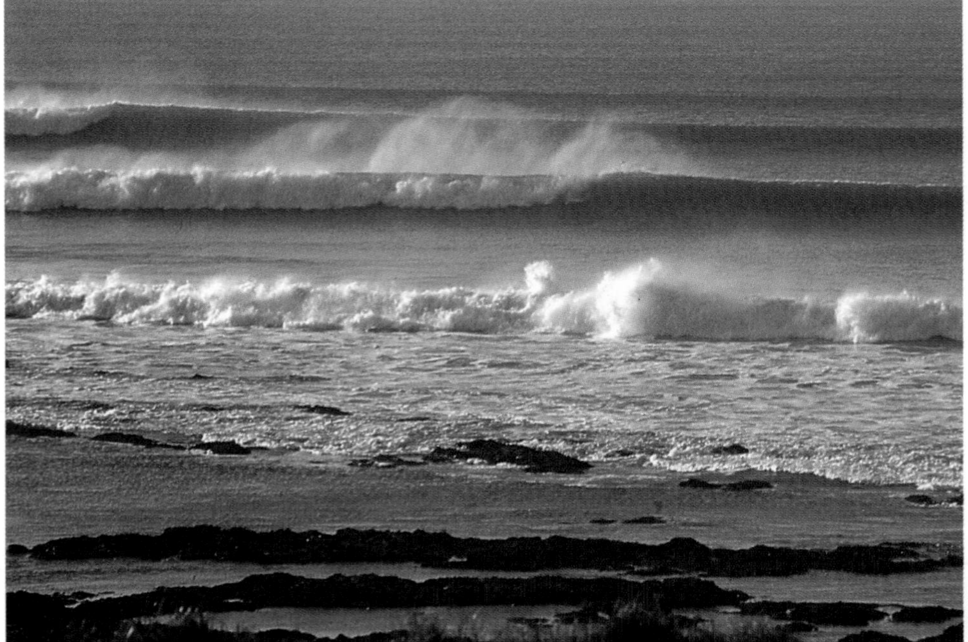

F. LE LEANNEC

Plage du Loch, Guidel

Baie des Douarnenez (1)
Baie des Treppasses (2)
St-Tugen (3)
Pointe de Lervily (4)
La Torche (5)
Porzcarn (6)
Lesconil (7)
Guidel (8)
Etel (9)
Penthièvre (10)
Quiberon (11)
Les Donnants (12)

ESB
Desert Point $
$ Atlantic
Action Line $
ESB $
$ Authentic

Kaolin

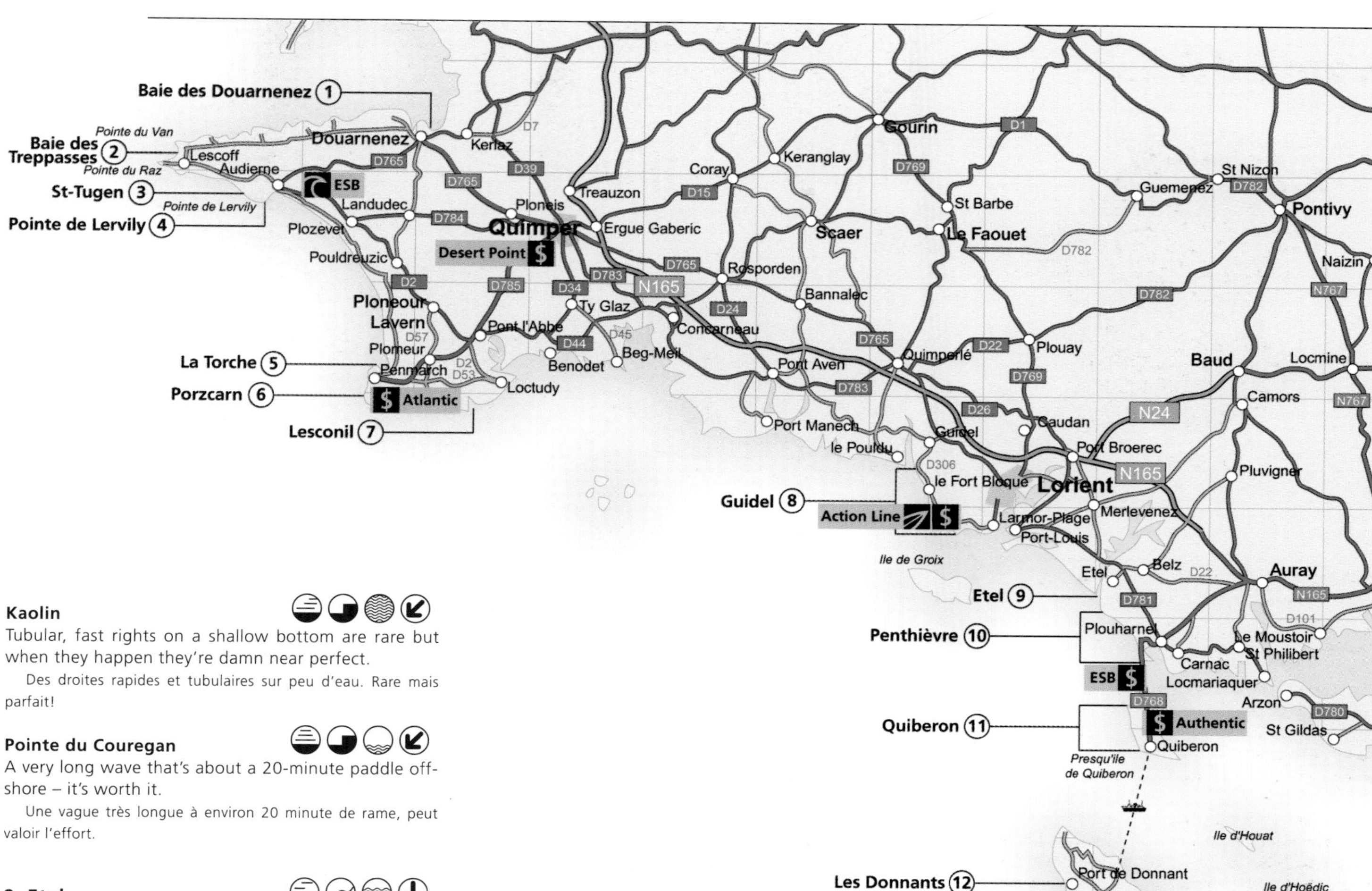

Tubular, fast rights on a shallow bottom are rare but when they happen they're damn near perfect.

Des droites rapides et tubulaires sur peu d'eau. Rare mais parfait!

Pointe du Couregan

A very long wave that's about a 20-minute paddle off-shore – it's worth it.

Une vague très longue à environ 20 minute de rame, peut valoir l'effort.

9. Etel

This break often looks like a close out but sometimes, when offshore winds and vicious currents hollow, some tubular sections are makeable – be quick.

Ressemble souvent à une immonde barre qui ferme mais parfois quand le vent de terre et les courants infernaux permettent de creuser la vague, les sections tubulaires sont exploitables: le turbo est de rigueur!

10. Penthièvre

When the tide is high in Quiberon, this area might work along with other spots like Kirminhy, Sainte-Barbe or Le Fozo.

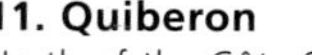

Quand la marée est haute à Quiberon, cette zone peut marcher tout comme Kirminhy, Sainte-Barbe ou Le Fozo.

11. Quiberon

North of the Côte Sauvage, this spot rates among the best in Brittany. Port-Blanc and Port-Rhu are two creeks with powerful rights, while the easier break is Port-Bara, a large beach that can become packed out. When the tide goes in, head N of Penthièvre.

La péninsule concentre au nord de la Côte Sauvage certains des meilleurs spots de Bretagne avec une consistence appréciable. Port-Blanc et Port-Rhu sont deux cales avec 2 gauches assez puissantes. Plus facile, la longue plage de Port-Bara sature parfois de monde ou ferme. D'autres spots plus au sud comme le Château.

F. LE LEANNEC

Kaolin

F. LE LEANNEC

Quiberon, Port-Rhu

12. Les Donnants

Les Donnants is the most consistent break of the lot.

Belle-ile mérite le détour car recèle certainement d'autres vagues que celle du port des Donnants, qu'on soupçonne de marcher souvent.

Vendée

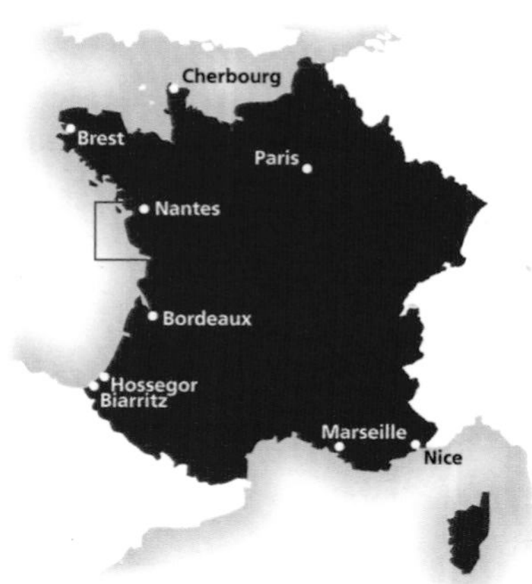

La Sauzaie

M. FENIES

1. Batz/Mer

When there is a swell, La Govelle is the most famous crossroads for La Baule surfers. It's nothing stupendous but there can be good rides, particularly to the right.

La Govelle est le rendez-vous privilégié des surfers de la Baule quand ça veut bien rentrer. Rien d'extraordinaire mais y'a de quoi faire surtout sur la droite.

2. Saint-Marc

The little beach of La Courance receives a few average waves when there's a lot of swell. At higher tides, head for St Marguerite and the Grand Trait as there's sometimes a right. Watch out for rocks underneath.

La petite plage de la Courance, parfois, avec beaucoup de houle s'agite et crache quelques vagues moyennes. A marée haute, de l'autre côté du cap à Ste-Marguerite, la droite du Grand Trait peut se réveiller. Ouvrez les yeux, y'a du rocher.

3. Préfaille

Between the Pointe St-Gildas and Préfaille, surfers from Nantes have discovered a few breaks, however get a pair of binoculars and sniff them out yourself. Your last wave options S of La Loire are Rochelets and Ermitage.

Entre la Pointe St-Gildas et Préfaille, les surfers nantais écument les reefs et trouvent. A vos jumelles! Dernière option au sud de la Loire: les beach-breaks des Rochelets ou de l'Ermitage.

La Sauzaie

T. ORGANOFF

Sauveterre

F. LE LEANNEC

Pointe du Croisic
Le Croisic
Batz
La Baule
Batz/Mer 1
Pornichet
Saint-Marc 2
St Nazaire
L'Immaculee
Loire
St Brevin les Pins
St Brevin l'Ocean
Plaimboeuf
Campbon
Nantes
St Pere
La Sicaudais
Vue
Launay
Theron Plage
St Michel Chef Chef
Bouguenais
Pointe de St Gildas
Préfailles
Préfailles 3
Pornic
La Birochere
Le Pont Beranger
Arthon en Retz
Port St Piere
Viais
la Bernerie-en-Retz
Ste Pazanne
Tournebride
les Moutiers
Bourgneuf
Pointe de l'Herbaudière
Noirmoutier
Machecoul
l'Epine
Le Vrignais
Bouin
Barbatre
Beavoir de Mer
Touvois
Fromentine
Lege
Challans
Notre-Dame-de-Monts
la Tonnelle
Plage de la Tonnelle
Plage St Jean
St Jean de Monts
Plage des Demoiselles
les Vases
la Pége
Port Joinville
Ile d'Yeu
Aizenay
Pointbreak
St-Gilles-Croix-de-Vie
St-Gilles Croix-de-Vie 4
le Pont-Jaunay
le Sauzaie
La Sauzaie 5
Brétignolles/Mer
La Mothe Achard
Les Dunes 6
Sauveterre 7
la Chaume
Les Sables-d'Olonne
Bahia
Les Sables d'Olonne 8
Seatime
Talmont-St-Hilaire

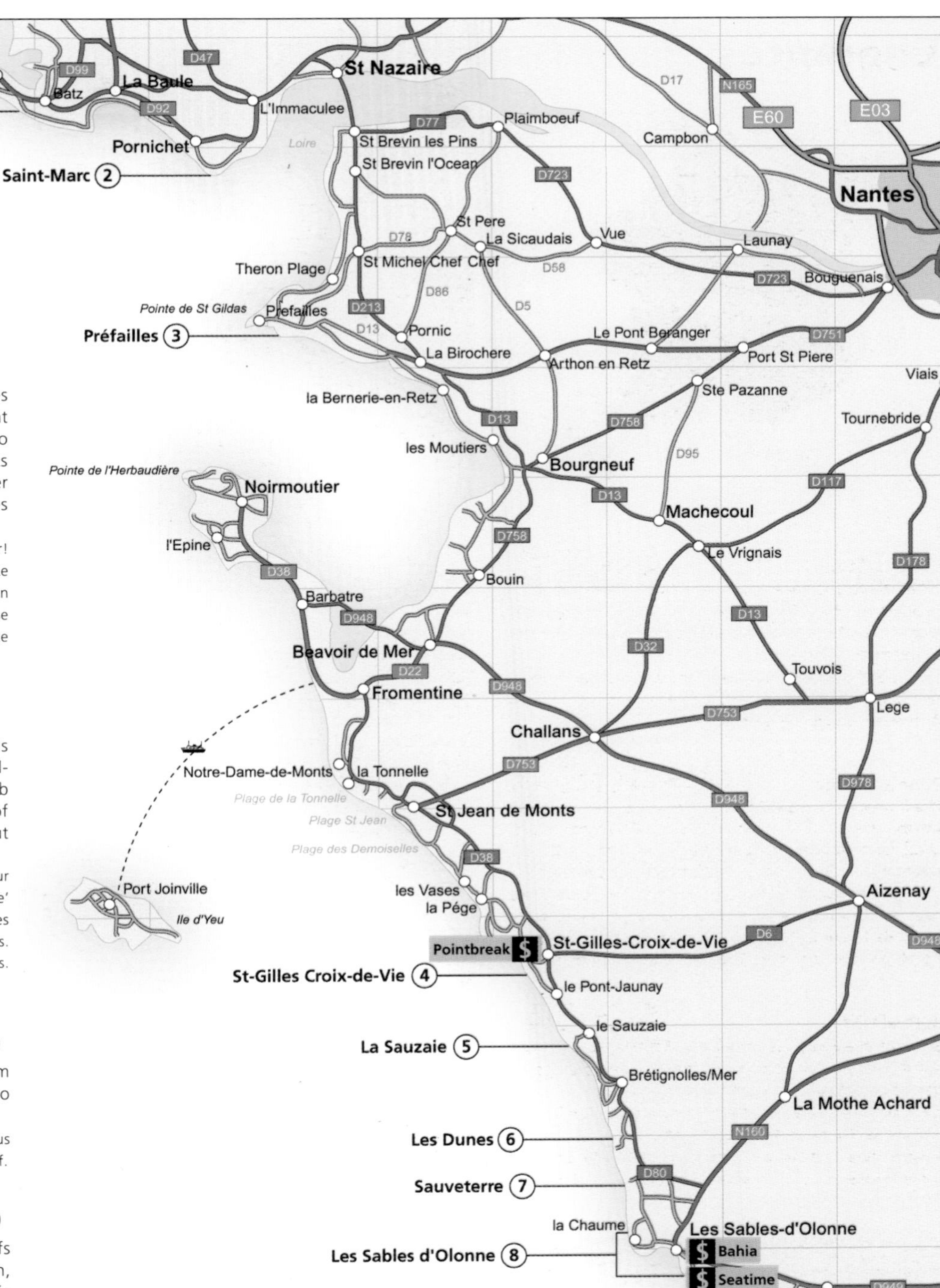

4. Saint-Gilles Croix-de-Vie

This is a rather mushy beach break that rarely closes out. The concrete promenade creates backwash at high tide and from here onlookers are guaranteed to see poseurs in need of admiration. When it gets bigger, the break is more protected from winds closer to the jetty. To the N, the continental shelf becomes shallower and filters even the most powerful swells.

Croix de Bois, Croix de fer, si c'est puissant, je vais en enfer! Plutôt mou donc mais ne sature pratiquement jamais. Le remblai fait du backwash à marée haute mais peut garantir un public attentif pour les frimeurs. Plus c'est gros, plus il faut se rapprocher de la jetée. Au nord, le plateau continental remonte et filtre mêmes les houles les plus puissantes.

5. La Sauzaie

Curling around the coastline, the high point of this seaside road has an awesome view of seaweed-covered reef, an exceptional break. 'Sauze' has superb tubular sections and brilliant waves that hold a bit of wind – and more than 30 surfers. Keep your eye out for a right, nicknamed 'killer', immediately to the N.

La corniche offre une vue imprenable à marée basse sur cette dalle rocheuse recouverte d'algues. Choper la 'Sauze' quand ça marche (assez souvent d'ailleurs), ça veut dire des sections tubulaires et d'excellentes vagues en tous cas. Supporte mal le vent et plus de trente surfers ou assimilés. N'oubliez pas la droite de Killer juste à côté.

6. Les Dunes

A mellow beach break that tends to close out over 2m (6ft) that has good walls for longboarders and it's also a popular wave-jumping spot.

Beach-break plutôt mou, qui a tendance à fermer au-dessus de 2m. De bons murs pour le longboard. Bon spot de windsurf.

7. Sauveterre

In the heart of the Olonne Woods are two good reefs and a well-exposed beach break. With a clean, average swell, choose between Pic du Large and Pic du Phoque – both have long rides.

Au beau milieu de la forêt d'Olonne, se trouvent pas moins de deux bons reefs et un beach break bien exposé. Avec une houle moyenne et bien rangée, vous n'avez plus qu'à choisir entre le Pic du large et ou le Pic du Phoque: c'est long et c'est bon! Mais attention, c'est du reef en dessous. Sinon, le beach-break marche bien jusqu'au blockhaus.

8. Les Sables d'Olonne

The Bay of Les Sables often closes out. The best formed waves are at Tanchet to the S and at L'Aubraie, which is well hidden in La Chaume to the N, sited between a cemetary and a large transmitter. There's a bit of a walk, but it's worthwhile.

La Baie des Sables peut se surfer un peut partout mais ça ferme souvent. Meilleures ouvertures à Tanchet (pointe sud) et surtout à L'Aubraie, bien caché à la Chaume au Nord, entre cimetière et antenne télécom. Il faut marcher quelques minutes mais on ne le regrette pas souvent.

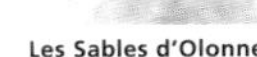

T. ORGANOFF

Les Sables d'Olonne

Charentes

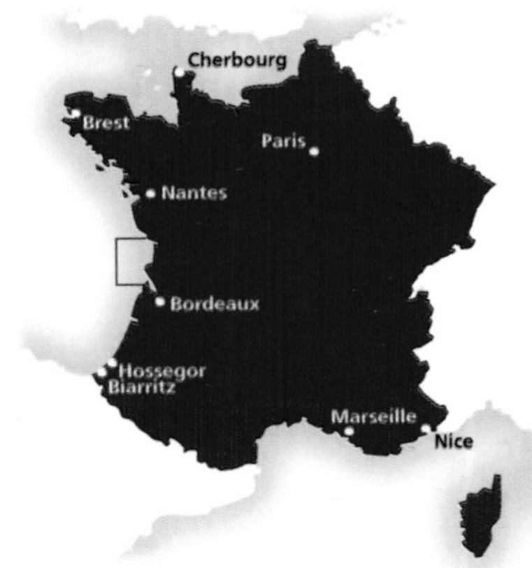

M. FENIES

Les Alassins

1. Saint-Nicolas

In a big storm, see if you can find a few secret spots scattered on the way up to Les Sables. The one we can tell you about is the left-handers of Plage de la Mine close to Park de la Grange – you have to find the other ones!

Quelques secret spots en cas de grosse houle jalonnent la côte jusqu'aux Sables. La seule référence connue: les gauches de la plage de la Mine prés du Parc de la Grange. A vous de trouver les autres !

2. Longeville

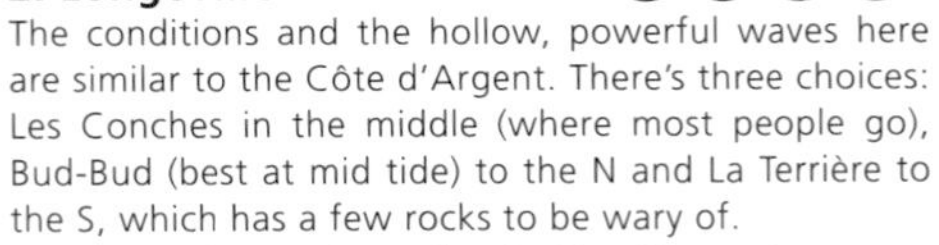

The conditions and the hollow, powerful waves here are similar to the Côte d'Argent. There's three choices: Les Conches in the middle (where most people go), Bud-Bud (best at mid tide) to the N and La Terrière to the S, which has a few rocks to be wary of.

Plusieurs plages qui rappellent la Côte d'Argent. Les vagues aussi d'ailleurs puisque creuses et puissantes. Trois choix: Les Conches au centre qui est le lieu de ralliement, Bud-Bud (mi-marée) au Nord ou La Terrière au Sud avec quelques cailloux.

3. La Tranche sur Mer

This is the pick in a storm swell. The jetty of La Tranche, 'Embarcadère', has mushy rights that are best ridden with longboards. A more consistent option is the Groin lighthouse.

Lieu de repli pour les tempêtes, la jetée ou l'Embarcadère de la Tranche donne des droites molles idéales pour les malibus.Une option plus consistente: Le phare du Groin.

F. BOURDIER

La Côte Sauvage

Ile de Ré

4. Le Lizay  

When it's on, this break is powerful, but be careful not to bounce off the rocks.

Puissant quand ça marche. Ca peut même bastonner sévère sur les rochers.

Ile de Ré

Y. LE TOQUIN

5. La Couarde/Mer 

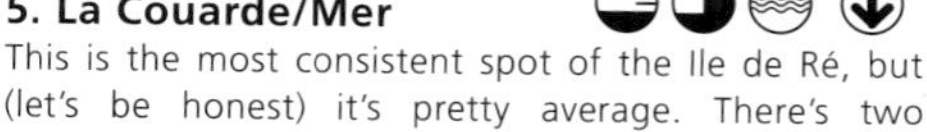

This is the most consistent spot of the Ile de Ré, but (let's be honest) it's pretty average. There's two rideable peaks on either side of a wooden jetty in front of the Pergola parking lot.

La vague qui marche le plus souvent sur Ré mais n'exagérons rien, l'exposition est loin d'être idéale. Deux pics moyens de part et d'autre d'une jetée en bois devant le parking de La Pergola.Ne marche pas à marée basse.

Ile d'Oleron

6. Chassiron 

The Pointe de Chassiron has various reef breaks and is probably the best spot on the island when there's enough swell and SE winds. Beware of the rocks and rips. In case of a big storm, head towards St-Denis and the Pointe des Boulassiers where other lefts await you.

Probalement le meilleur spot de l'île avec suffisamment de houle et de vents d'est à Sud-Est, la Pointe de Chassiron compte plusieurs reefs. Attention aux cailloux donc et aux violents courants. En cas de grosse tempête, farfouillez vers St-Denis et la Pointe des Boulassiers, d'autres gauches peuvent vous attendre.

Chassiròn

ERIC CHAUCHE

7. Les Huttes   

Often associated with Trois Pierres, Les Huttes is a pounding shore break that can be sometimes tubey.

Souvent associé aux Trois Pierres, les Huttes est un shore-break assez massif, parfois tubulaire. Vous ne serez certainement pas seul à venir voir. Le spot se trouve en fait de l'autre côté des Huttes .

8. Les Alassins 

Vert-Bois is the most consistent and the most surfed spot of the island providing heaps of peaks.

Vert-Bois est le spot le plus consistant de l'île, le plus fréquenté aussi. Droites et gauches.

9. St-Trojan   

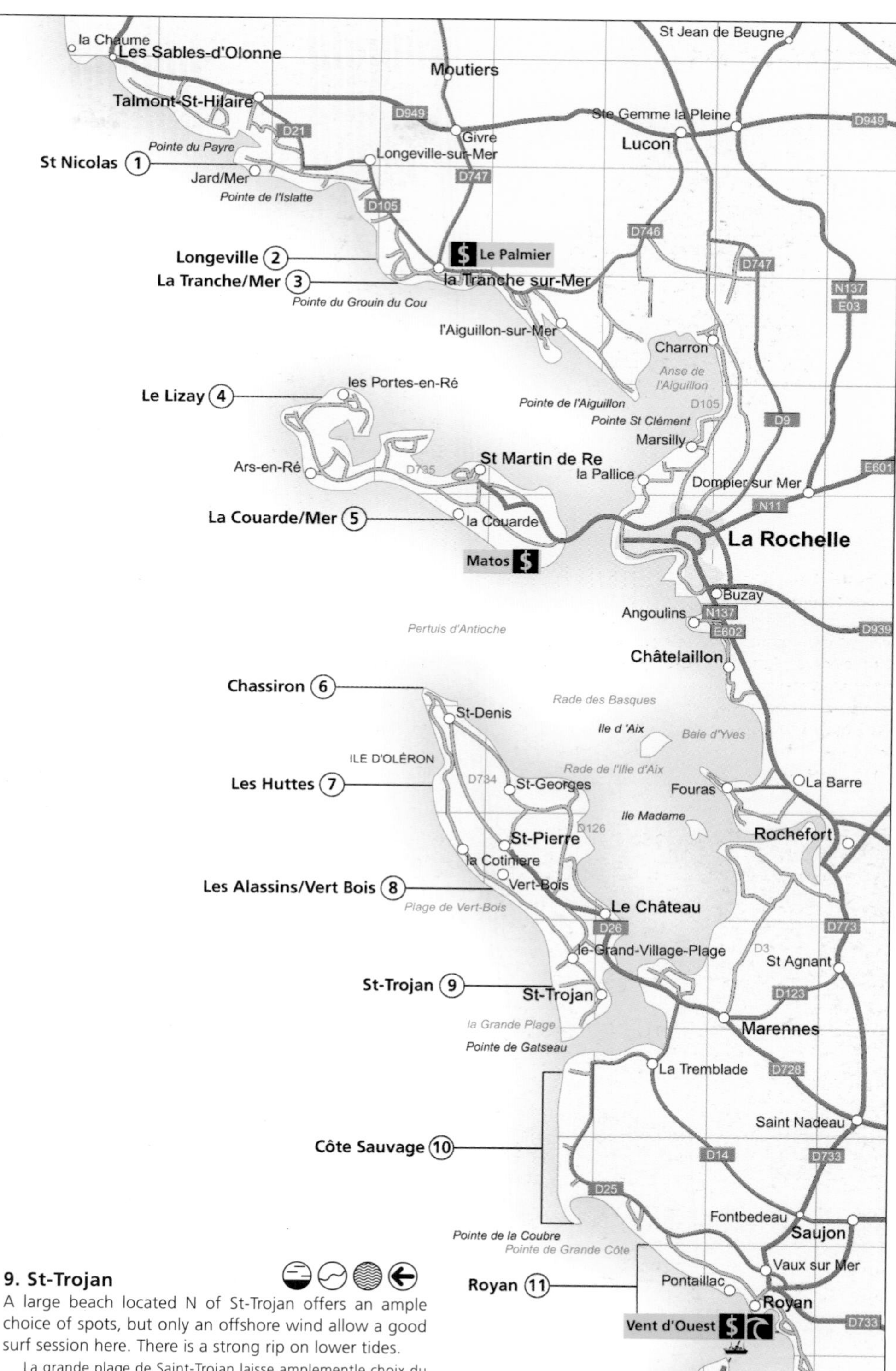

A large beach located N of St-Trojan offers an ample choice of spots, but only an offshore wind allow a good surf session here. There is a strong rip on lower tides.

La grande plage de Saint-Trojan laisse amplementle choix du spot. Seul un vent de terre peut vous faire espérer un bon surf. En tous cas, il y a du jus à marée basse.

10. La Côte Sauvage

You'll find 16km (10mi) of consistent and mushy beach breaks here resembling Côte d'Argent. The N part, towards the Pointe Espagnole, offers better conditions than further S towards the Coubre lighthouse. Water quality is bad and there are strong undercurrents.

15 kms de beach-break consistant plutôt mou dans un décor qui rappelle étrangement celui de la côte d'Argent. La partie Nord vers la Pointe Espagnole semble offrir de meilleures conditions que l'accès Sud au phare de la Coubre. Courants et pollution au programme.

11. Royan  

If it closes out on the Côte Sauvage, go inside the estuary towards Royan. Check Nauzan, Pontaillac or Suzac, which all favour rights.

Si ça ferme sur la Côte Sauvage, allez voir dans l'estuaire vers Royan. Checker des criques comme Nauzan, Pontaillac ou Suzac. Plutôt des droites.

KANABEACH tm

ERIC CHAUCHE

Aquitaine

If there's a surf area in Europe that needs no introduction, its the Acquitaine. Few of you will know its proper name, but this 160km long ruler-straight beach constitutes the largest potential stretch of unridden summer barrels in the entire continent. Call it 'grand crux', call it what you want, but if you're sitting in your dark home on any old summer day, you can take it for granted that there's barrels unloading on this exquisitely sandy, hollow coast at most times of both day and night.

Hossegor is the best known spot on the beach. Why? A finger of extremely deep water points directly at Hossegor. The 'Fosse de Capbreton', as it is known, is the signature of the River Ardour on the ocean bottom, a deep scar formed over millions of years of powerful water flow. It used to come out at Capbreton but Napoleon re-directed it to Bayonne in the 18th century in an attempt to create a safer harbour, away from the tempestuous waves along this 10km (6mi) stretch of coast. An incredibly grand vision has had spectacular results for the French surfing communities.

Not surprisingly on such a long, deep beach, dominant north to south rips are a huge factor, especially in a big swell. Unfortunately, so is pollution, which unfortunately is pretty horrific at all beach towns during summer, with few signs of positive change.

R. GILLEY

M. FENIES

It used to be a pretty quiet affair but with extreme recent mainstream exposure this is changing rapidly and there's a lot of flotsam and stink eye in the line ups. Travellers invariably make this their first point of contact with Europe. Summertime sees good waves, no doubt, but unfortunately lots of pretenders. The social atmosphere is relaxed on the surface, the night life good and in summer the beaches become a writhing mass of sun-tanned bodies playing and surfing in the sun. Go see for yourself.

Aquitaine

Compte tenu de marnages importants, la physionomie des vagues évolue à une vitesse parfois déroutante: un close-out immonde à midi peut devenir un pic parfait deux heures plus tard. Leur orientation favorise les droites bien que les gauches déferlant à contre-courant sont peut-être plus puissantes. Le chenal d'évacuation de l'eau n'est jamais très profond aussi les vagues au-dessus de 2m-2,5m auront tendance à fermer. Les baïnes sont rapidement défigurées par les tempêtes, il faut donc réexaminer les bancs après chaque hiver. Peu de spots de repli donc quand la mer est agitée: le nord de la Gironde, l'entrée du Bassin, Capbreton ou le Boucau sans garanties. Une population réduite à de petites villes côtières et une forêt de pins quasi-omniprésente rendent l'endroit merveilleusement sauvage sauf en été où les plages font le plein .Une destination d'été

ERIC CHAUCHE

donc dont Lacanau et Hossegor sont les têtes d'affiches. Pour ceux que marcher dans le sable n'effraie pas...

Une fosse trés profonde au large en forme de doigt pointe sur Hossegor . Le "Gouf" de Capbreton, ainsi nommé donc, est la cicatrice laissée par l' Adour pendant des millions d'années sur le fond, à l'époque où le puissant flot s'écoulait à Capbreton . C'est au XVIII siècle que Napoleon l'a déviée sur Bayonne pour créer un port sûr, à l'abri de ces côtes battues par les tempêtes . Cette initiative devait donner un résultat spectaculaire pour la communauté du surf dans le monde.

Gironde

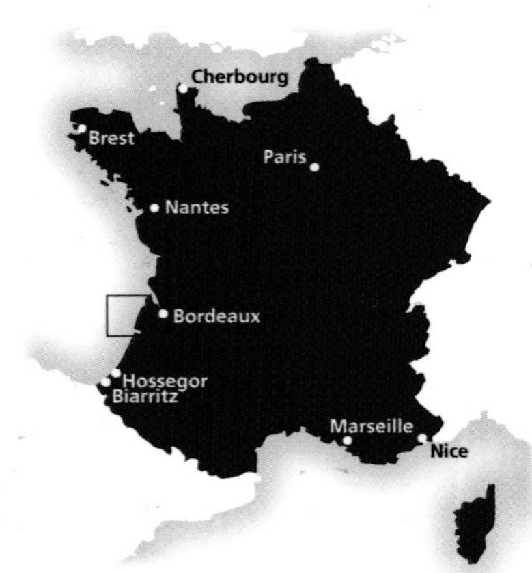

Y. LE TOQUIN

1. Le Mascaret de la Dordogne

On the biggest spring tides, you'll find a very slow tidal bore. Enjoy rides of 200-300m (180-280yd) on your longest board.

Aux équinoxes, une vague d'environ 200-300m au Bec d'Ambes à St-Pardon. Longboard ou Bodyboard. Le record est de 15 minutes en Kayak surf.

Pictogrammes   

Due to their similarity, these pictograms apply to all the breaks that follow.

De par leur ressemblance, les vagues correspondent toutes à ces pictogrammes.

2. Verdon-sur-Mer

Owing to the proximity of the Gironde Estuary, this spot only works with big swells. On the Pointe de Grave, even bigger swells are needed to get good waves. Watch out for gnarly rips and water pollution.

Compte tenu de la proximité de l'estuaire de la Gironde, ce spot ne marche que par grosse houle voire très grosse en amont de la pointe de Grave. Courants et pollution au menu.

3. Soulac-sur-Mer

When everywhere else is closed out, this is still rideable as the rivermouth creates offshore sandbanks.

Vagues de repli en cas de tempête compte tenu de l'ensablement des fonds par la Gironde.

4. L'Amelie

Heading off D101, there's a tiny access to a non-developed, uncrowded spot.

Depuis la D101, cet accès discret sans aucun aménagement ouvre une nouvelle option.

5. Le Gurp

When it's out-of-control down S, this is the best spot to head for – look for the beaches of Négade or Dépé (with a german bunker). The break is made up of filthy tubing lefts. Naturalists should head to the nudist camp at Euronat.

On y a souvent vu des surfers bordelais ou canaulais venir ici choper des gauches tubulaires alors que ça sature complètement au Sud. Cherchez la plage de la Négade et Dépé prés d'un blockhaus. Camp naturiste d'Euronat.

ALEX WILLIAMS

Lacanau

6. Montalivet-les-Bains

This is another choice spot for naked tourists. From the central car park, there's views of the wave peaks.

Encore un haut-lieu du Naturisme au sud de la ville. Bonnes vagues et parking facile.

7. Le Pin Sec

If there's a crowd here, you're unlucky. The zone between spots 7-9 has rapid erosion and low tide uncovers clay and a soft reef named Alios.

Si vous trouvez du monde ici, vous avez vraiment pas de bol. La zone 7-9 subit une érosion rapide qui découvre l'argile et l'alios à marée basse.

8. Hourtin-Plage

During the summer this popular British hang out can become packed out. When it does, explore the mountainbiking tracks between the lakes and woods which offer leads for new spots.

Rendez-vous habituel des Britanniques l'été, on commence donc à trouver quelques pics saturés l'été. Plein de pistes cyclables entre lacs et forêts peuvent donner des idées pour les activités annexes.

9. Carcans-Plage

This is an escape from the crowds at Lacanau and often has good – if not better – waves.

Alternative à Lacanau pour éviter les encombrements au pic.

10. Lacanau-Ocean

Close to Bordeaux, with a beachfront that allows anyone to check the surf from the car, this ASP contest venue is surf central and has been so since the contests started in 1979. But, there's a reason for that – the surf's consistently good. The best camping is at Les Grands Pins.

Avec un front de mer qui permet de mater les vagues depuis la voiture, avec une compétition ASP depuis 1979 et avec un accés direct depuis Bordeaux, Lacanau est le noyau du surf girondin. Camping des Grands Pins.

11. Le Porge

This is the closest spot to Bordeaux. The beach is a two-minute walk from the parking lot.

Peut-être la route la plus courte depuis Bordeaux mais deux minutes de marche pour traverser la dune.

12. La Jenny

Turn off the D3 at Lauros, N of the nudist camp entrance. There's a long walk to the beach which few can be bothered with.

Sur la D3, tournez à Lauros au Nord de l'entrée du camp naturiste. Longue marche donc... pas de monde.

13. Le Grand Crohot

This is a spot for surfers from Bordeaux or Andernos for a reason... check it out.

Un des spots privilégiés des surfers bordelais ou d'Andernos.

14. Le Truc Vert and Le Petit Train

Tucked away from the tourist hub, this place is a rootsie soul surfer destination. If you need of more social life, camp at Sables d'Or. The wooden pole jetty on the beach helps to build decent sandbars.

Primo, un camping branché surfer un peu a l'écart des trépidations estivales. Autre option pour camper aux Sables d'Or. Ca s'agite pas mal l'été et la jetée stabilise parfois des fonds corrects.

15. Cap Ferret

Sited at the entrance to the Bassin d'Arcachon, currents are powerful here, especially on the outgoing tide. There can be excellent surf when there's a big swell N.

Au bout de l'isthme à l'entrée du Bassin d'Arcachon, les courants sont violents surtout à la descendante mais ça peut rester surfable alors que ça sature au nord.

Y. LE TOQUIN

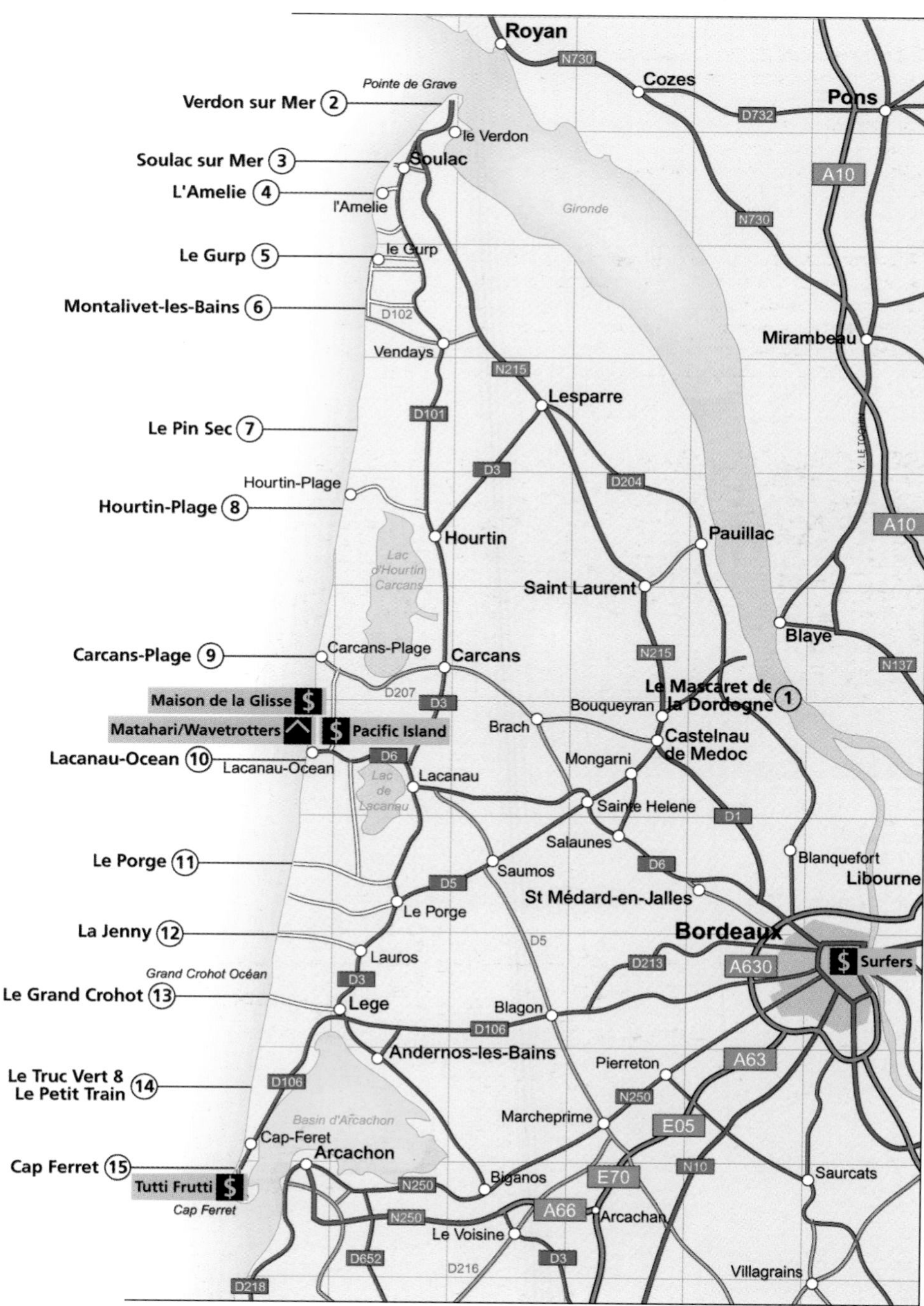

Landes

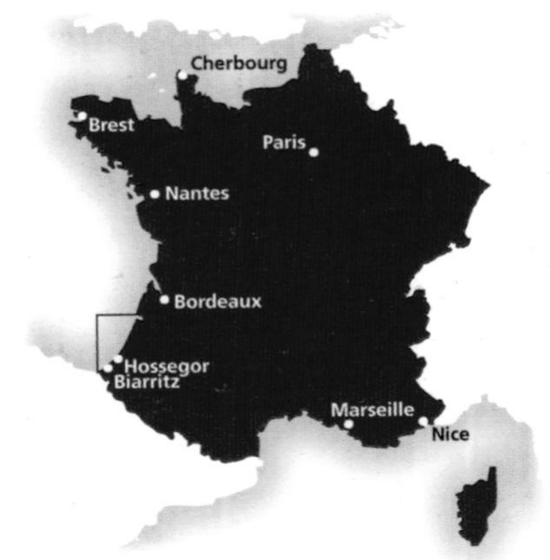

Pictogrammes

 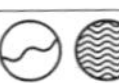 

Due to their similarity, these pictograms apply to all the breaks.

De par leur ressemblance, les vagues correspondent toutes à ces pictogrammes.

1. La Salie

These sandbars shift incredibly fast: the best and the worst are located at the two access points. The most reliable banks are beside the first wharf, but around here is also a stinky, suspicious foam. If it's flat, surf the highest dunes in Europe (110m/95yd).

La Salie dépend terriblement des bancs de sable qui se détachent du bassin. Deux accès dont celui du Wharf mène aux spots les plus réguliers. Malheureusement, la jetée de fer crache des eaux pas trés rassurantes qui puent. Si c'est flat, on peut faire une reconstitution d'Endless Summer sur les hautes dunes (100m) du Pyla.

M. FENIES

La Salie

2. Biscarrosse-Plage

There's two obvious access points to the beach with the usual crowds. To the S, as far as Mimizan, it's a military zone: access is strictly forbidden. Camp at Les Viviers towards the N.

Deux accès directs sur la plage et du monde à l'eau. Camping Le Vivier au Nord. Au sud commence une zone militaire dont l'accès est interdit jusqu'à Mimizan.

Y. LE TOQUIN

Biscarrosse

3. Mimizan-Plage

With a pole jetty and a rivermouth that shape good sandbars on some years, this beach has good waves. If there's a foul smell from nearby paper factories, rejoice... it's blowing offshore! There are no crowds.

Mimizan-Plage a un front de mer de quelques centaines de mètres, un courant (rivière) qui donne certaines années de bons bancs avec finalement peu de surfers. Des jetées de bois sur la plage. Si vous sentez des bouffées d' activités papetières, le vent est à l'est.

4. Lespecier

From here to Spot 3 is a remote area with difficult access. This resort is no exception.

Jusqu'au spot 3 commence une zone d'ombre d'accés relativement long depuis les villes. Exemple flagrant ici.

5. Contis-Plage

Try to visit the lighthouse with binoculars during clear weather and a clean swell to check out what's going on with the sandbanks, especially those N, close to the rivermouth. Assess and surf.

Débrouillez-vous pour visiter le phare de 183 marches par temps calme et bonne houle et mater avec des jumelles les environs, surtout vers la rivière au nord. Vous verrez facilement les bons bancs.

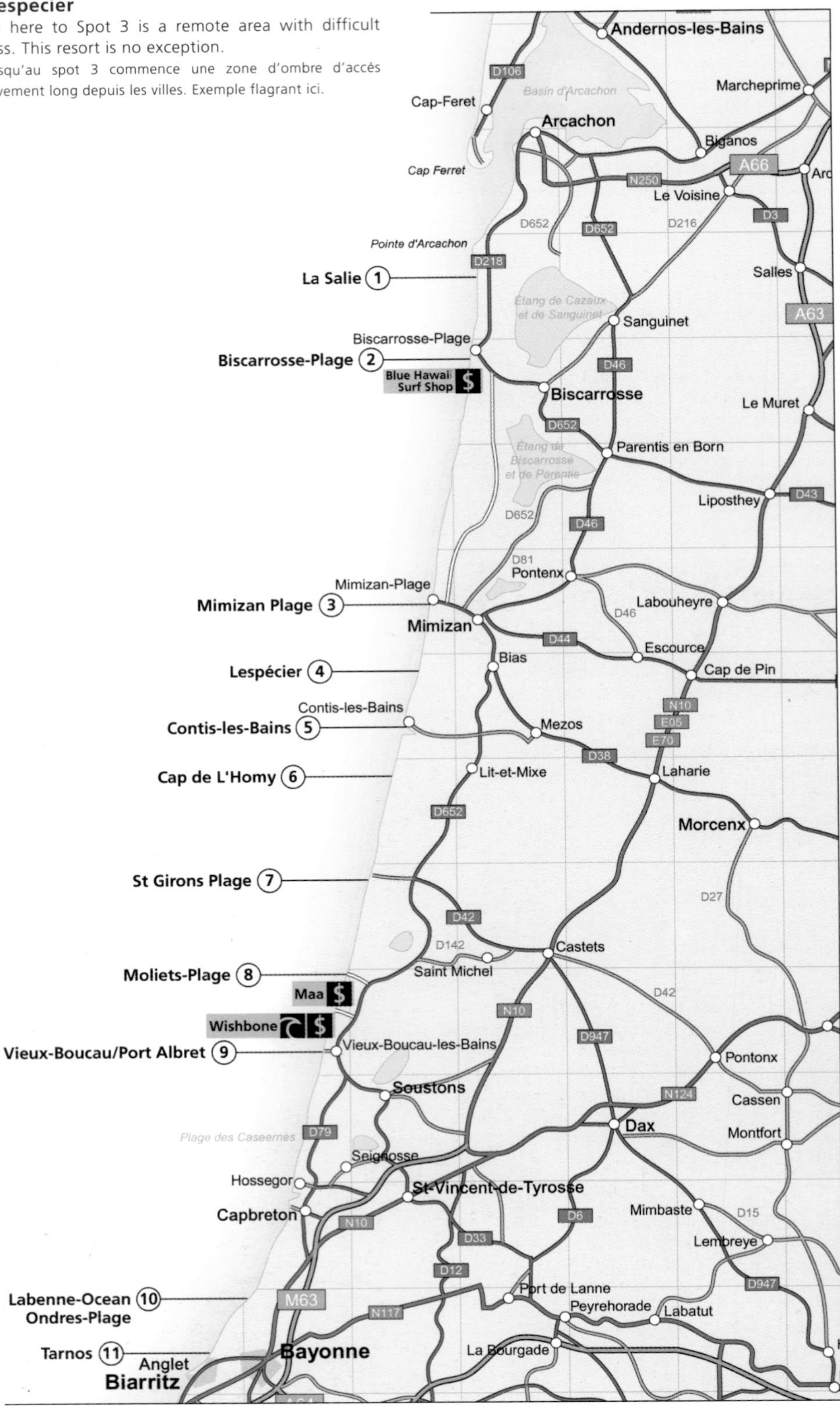

La Salie 1
Biscarrosse-Plage 2
Mimizan Plage 3
Lespécier 4
Contis-les-Bains 5
Cap de L'Homy 6
St Girons Plage 7
Moliets-Plage 8
Vieux-Boucau/Port Albret 9
Labenne-Ocean Ondres-Plage 10
Tarnos 11

6. Cap de L'Homy

This isn't really a cape but has year-round peace, solitude and a few good waves.

Pas vraiment de cap mais une petite station balnéaire.

7. St-Girons Plage

Although you can find nude people all over the Silver Coast, this beach is teaming with both nude bodies and barrels.

Encore un camp naturiste bien qu'il y ait des nudistes partout sur la Côte d'argent.

8. Moliets Plage

Have fun: paddle down the Huchet River from Leon Lake and you'll end up at the best break around.

Une idée fun: descendez le courant d'Huchet avec votre planche depuis le lac de Léon. Vous arrivez peut-être sur le meilleur break à l'embouchure.

9. Vieux Boucau – Port d'Albret

The D652 gets closer to the coast here. There's waves on both entrances to the lake, Port d'Albret is the name given to the S side.

A partir d'ici, la D652 se rapproche du littoral, ce qui permet donc de checker plus de vagues. Avant d'arriver sur les vagues de Vieux-Boucau, vous traverserez Port-d'Albret, un bassin artificiel plutôt sympathique mais légérement pollué par Soustons. Des bancs de sable intéressants qui méritent le détour.

10. Labenne-Ocean / Ondres Plage

Discover pounding shore breaks at high tide. Even though it's close to the N10, it's never very crowded.

Pas bien loin de la N10 et peu de surfers viennent traîner leurs slaps ici. Tendance à former des shore-breaks épais à marée haute.

Y. LE TOQUIN

Blockhaus

11. Tarnos Plage

The Metro beach is nothing special, unlike Boucau. It has a long jetty, crane, and submerged shipwreck that shapes perfect sandbanks giving tubing lefts. It's protected from S winds. An industrial area of dirty factories, unfriendly chimneys and like-minded locals.

La plage du métro n'a rien de transcendant contrairement au Boucau avec sa digue, sa grue et son bateau échoué qu'on ne voit plus mais qu'on devine. Ici, protégées des vent de sud, les gauches peuvent être tubulaires et rappeler l'époque d'avant la digue. Attention, les locaux sont chauds et le paysage industriel peu romantique.

M. FENIES

The line-up at Boucau

M. FENIES

Boucau

Hossegor

Tom Curren, La Gravière

T. GIBAUD

1. Le Penon

A small wooden jetty to the S sometimes creates worthwhile sandbars.

Le village le plus tranquille de la zone. Plus au nord, un parking largement squatté par les vans. Au sud, une petite jetée de bois favorise parfois de bons bancs.

2. Les Bourdaines

The uncrowded break here starts S of the long steel jetty.

Commence au sud d'une longue jetée en acier. Peut-être un peu moins de monde parce qu'on ne se gare pas aussi facilement qu'ailleurs et que les camps de vacances sont des propriétés privées.

3. Les Estagnots

Until the town's mayor moved in, the car park by the beach was a popular surfers' hang out and former site of Rip Curl Pro contests. It's still a popular stretch of beach breaks which have well-formed, consistent peaks.

Un nom célèbre parce que médiatisé par le Rip Curl Pro et souvent squatté par les voyageurs. Il est maintenant interdit d'y dormir. Souvent, on y trouve une bonne vague.

4. Les Culs Nuls

This is Hossegor's naturalist beach: the name literally means 'bare-bums'. It was also the site of the 1995 Rip Curl Pro contest as it always receives consistent, hollow banks. Park and head over the dunes.

Le maillot de bains n'y est donc pas indispensable. Garez-vous sur les côtés et traversez la dune. A partir d'ici, le shore-break devient carton.

5. La Gravière

This is Hossegor's 'tube station': it has monsterous barrels rideable in clean conditions. When it's on there's always a crowd – be prepared to wait and get slammed.

La machine à tubes d'Hossegor avec des droites monstrueuses surfables quand les conditions sont propres. Toujours la Chine quand c'est bon: soyez prêts à attendre et à vous faire touiller.

Hossegor shore break

T. GIBAUD

les Estagnots

ERIC CHAUCHE

Poupinel, L'Epi Nord

T. GIBAUD

6. L'Epi Nord

When sandbanks are in good shape and with a big swell, the outside has huge rideable rights. There's a suicide shore break on the beach, facing the 'Front de Mer'. Towards the pier are some low tide shore breaks with good peaks in big swell.

Spot de grosses vagues au large avec des droites surfables quand les bancs sont là. Le shore-break du Front de Mer est suicidaire. Plus au sud, y'a de bons shore-breaks à marée basse avec assez de houle.

7. Capbreton/le Prevent

Access the beaches between the jetties, which are the only places to surf when it's big and blown-out elsewhere. However, this catches less swell than the N and it's packed-out when on.

Les plages les plus accessibles entre des jetées. Le spot de repli quand c'est tempête ou que ça sature mais ça prend moins la houle et la foule est loin d'etre sentimentale quand ça marche.

La Piste/VVF (very, very fast)

R. GILLEY

8. La Piste/VVF

S of scattered WW11 German bunkers start remote beaches with breaks that are often fast and tubular at lower tides. It favours rights and there's a 'don't drop-in' attitude among the tube-seekers around you.

Au sud des blockhaus se trouvent des plages un peu à l'écart qui balancent des vagues rapides et tubulaires aux marées basses. Plutôt des droites où il vaut mieux ne pas griller les priorités de ceux qui cherchent le tube, comme vous.

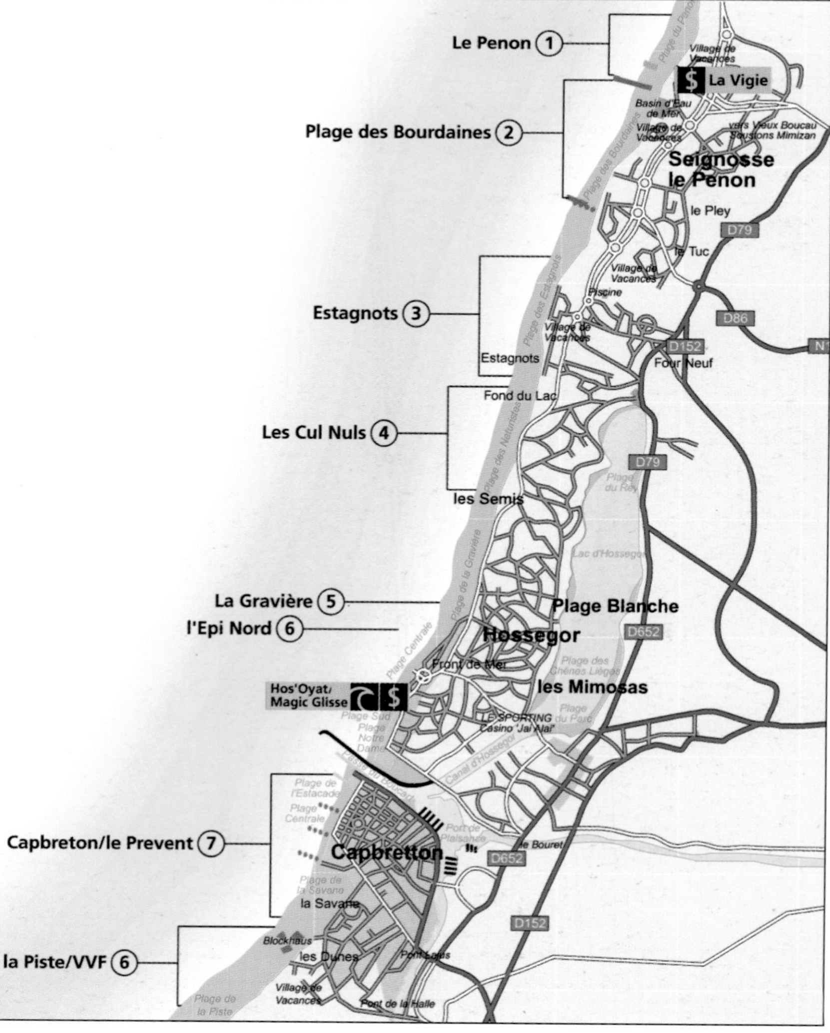

billabong
Luke Egan

Photo: Sean Davey

MARC FENIES

The Pyrenees

The Basque Coast

The Basque coast is the cradle of surfing in Europe, a region rich in surf and surf culture. Unlike Aquitaine further north, SW France is home to some excellent and hollow reefs, jetties and points (which hold huge swells), as well as her celebrated and variously orientated beaches. Although many spots are close to well populated towns, crowds for most of the year remain minimal. Unfortunately you can't say the same thing regarding the pollution problems. Summer can get a bit crazy, and localism can also be potent at some spots. However, with such a variety of surf, snowfields or a trip to Spain only hours away, this coast has been a lure for travellers from all over the world for many years. Not surprisingly, the French Basque are proud of their unique culture, as are their Spanish cousins.

TIM RAINGER

La Côte Basque

Premier cailloux en arrivant du Nord, Biarritz sonne le glas des plages à perte de vue pour donner une côte rocheuse avec quelques excellents reefs (Guethary, Lafitenia) entrecoupées de quelques plages (Grande plage, Côte des Basques, St-Jean de luz, Hendaye) relativement protégées, sans oublier Anglet et ses digues. Territoire de vagues puissantes et rondes, la Côte Basque offre une variété de vagues se pliant à presque toutes les conditions. Seules ombres au tableau, les spots saturent de monde en été peut-être plus qu'ailleurs et la pollution peut y être alarmante. Tant que possible, evitez les jours de pointe et n'oubliez pas les activités environnantes: stations de ski entre une et deux heures, les paysages hallucinants de l'intérieur, les escapades en Espagne et la formidable culture basque qui force le respect.

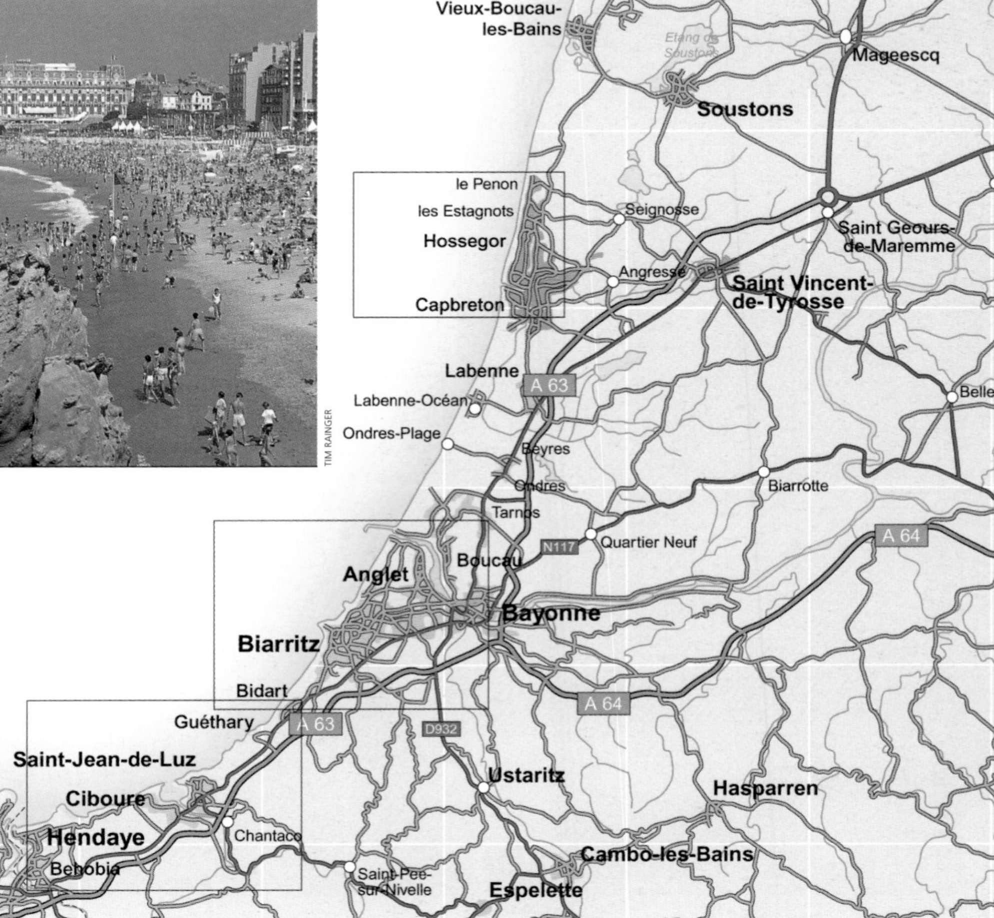

Biarritz

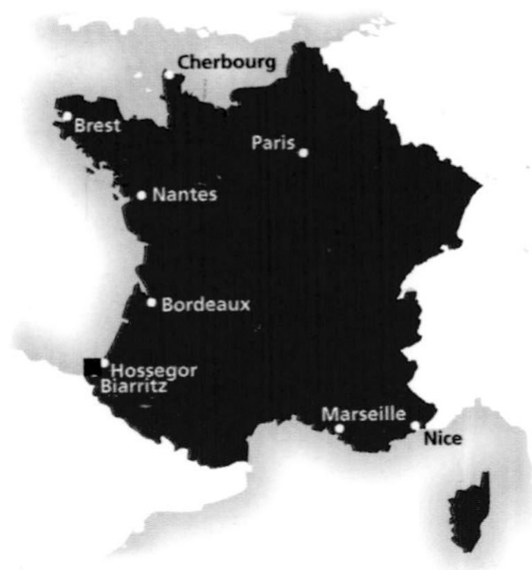

Anglet

1. La Barre

This is a once famous wave sited at the Adour rivermouth. With the construction of a jetty in the 60s, its quality has been sharply reduced, but a few peaks still break here in a big swell. It's protected from cross-shore winds, but often there's too much backwash at high tide. The water quality is negligible due to effluents snaking down the Adour.

Vague célèbre dans les années 60 à l'embouchure de l'Adour dont la qualité s'est dégradée avec la construction de la jetée. Il reste encore de bonnes gauches avec suffisamment de houle, protégées des vents de Sud et Nord. Trop de backwash à marée haute. Aprés de forte pluies, l'eau n'est pas franchement appétissante.

2. Les Cavaliers

Often bigger than other Anglet beaches, the tubes here are known to rival those of Hossegor. They're located on the side of the La Barre jetty. Watch out for heavy backwash at high tide. Hundreds of surfers come here in the summer, but maybe not for too much longer as this break is threatened by harbour development.

De l'autre côté de la Barre se trouve ce super spot dont les tubes à marée basse n'ont rien à envier à ceux d'Hossegor. Souvent, plus de taille que les autres plages d'Anglet. Trop de backwash à marée haute. Menacée par la construction d'une marina. Plusieurs pics mais il n'est malheureusement pas rare de voir une centaine de surfers à l'eau en été, voire plus.

Côte des Basques

Les Cavaliers

3. Les Plages d'Anglet

There are several access points to Anglet's beach breaks, but, if they're crowded, head to L'Ocean and La Madrague, a long, but worthwhile walk from the car park. Good peaks break at all points between the jetties.

Bons beachbreaks. Plusieurs accès à ces plages d'Anglet, les deux premières proches de Chiberta sont moins fréquentées en raison de la marche depuis le parking. La Marinela est la plage du camping de Fontaine Laborde.

4. Sables D'or VVF

These two spots are directly visible from the road and car parks of Chambre d'Amour and hence have a crowd factor to consider; but then again, there's always a wave working somewhere and plenty of room for everyone. A wedging left breaks near the lighthouse cliffs giving nice, long rides.

Ce sont les spots de la Chambre d'Amour directement visibles depuis la route et des parkings: du monde à l'eau donc. Marche aussi à marée haute. Toujours un spot qui marche. Du côté de la falaise du phare casse une gauche correcte à marée basse.

S. MIRA

Sables D'or/VVF

ERIC CHAUCHE

Biarritz Sunset

5. Grande Plage 

The Basque Coast's most mythical beach is protected from S winds but has a narrower swell window than Anglet. Only the S half receives surf. On the downside there's bathing zone restrictions in the summer and difficult, expensive car parking. It's often crowded and the water is not particularly clean – to avoid the crowds, surf at night.

La plage frime de la Cote Basque. protégée des vents de Sud qui prend moins la houle qu'Anglet. Seule la moitié sud est surfable. En été, cette moitié est reduite par la zone de baignade. En plus, il est difficile, en tous cas payant de se garer. Souvent peuplé mais éclairé la nuit.

6. Côte des Basques 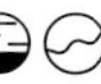   

One of the birthplaces of Europe's surfing scene, this is today popular with longboarders on account of the mushy waves that generally lack form. To the S are some reefs worth checking out: one in particular is called La Mouscariette.

Le berceau de surf en France et des Tontons surfers. Une atmosphère décontractée, trés prisée des longboarders avec des vagues plutôt molles sans vraiment de bancs de sable. Vers le Sud, quelques reefs corrects dont la Mouscariette.

7. Ilbarritz   

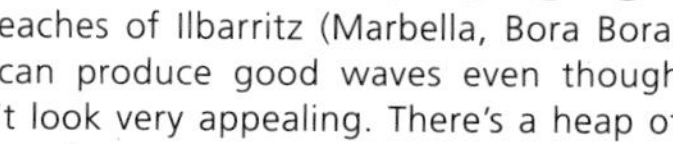

The various beaches of Ilbarritz (Marbella, Bora Bora, Edouard VII) can produce good waves even though the reefs don't look very appealing. There's a heap of rocks to look out for.

Les plages d'Ilbarritz (Marbella, Bora Bora, Edouard VII) peuvent mériter le coup d'oeil même si les reefs ne produisent pas de fonds particulièrement bons. Beaucoup de rochers donc.

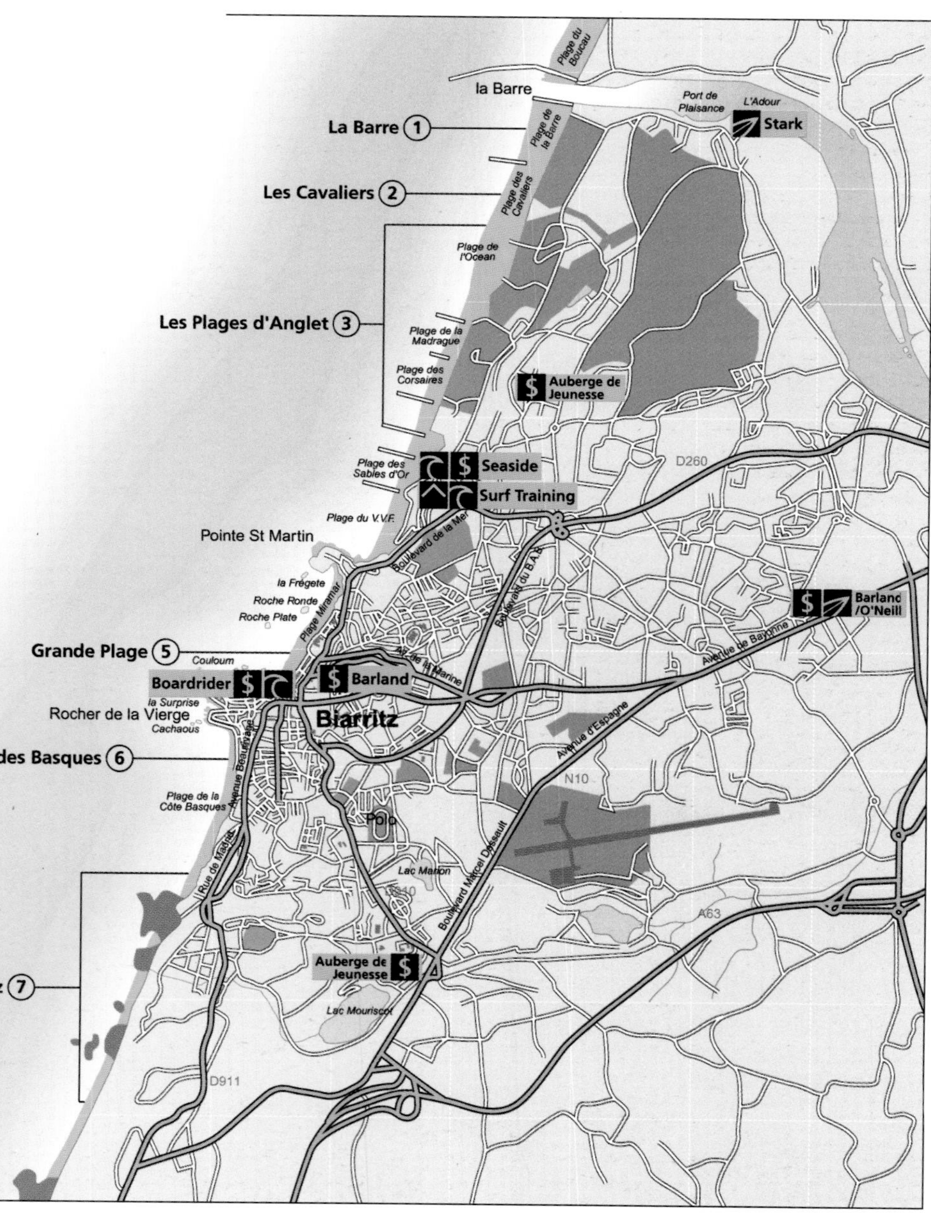

The Basque Coast

Bidart

M. FENIES

1. Bidart

The central beach doesn't have a clear access point and also has a disadvantage of gnarly rocks – but it does have some heavenly days. However, Ouhabia, visible from the N10, can be badly polluted by the river.

La plage centrale n'est pas facilement accessible. Malgré quelques rochers, elle peut réserver de bonnes surprises, contrairement à Ouhabia, visible depuis la N10, qui peut en réserver de très mauvaises à cause des rejets de la rivière.

2. Guéthary

At Guéthary, you'll find a sunset-like right with a shifting peak and short shoulder that holds up to 5m (15ft) on a clean, NW swell. The inside wave has good walls at higher tides and the left can be ridden, but you'll end up in the impact zone. Crowds and longboarders are a downer. Guéthary Harbour and village are worth a detour at any rate.

Bonne droite puissante et ronde qui tient jusqu' à 4-5 mètres. La gauche peut être surfable mais on risque de bouffer la série au retour. L'inside peut être creux avec de bons murs à marée haute. Beaucoup de monde, beaucoup de longboards. Le port et le village de Guéthary valent le détour.

Guethary

ERIC CHAUCHE

Guéthary

ERIC CHAUCHE

3. Les Alcyons/Avalanche

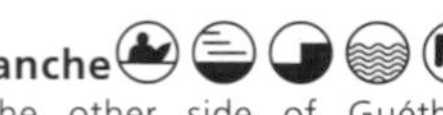

Down the road, on the other side of Guéthary Harbour, you'll find Alcyons, a short but powerful left that holds swell up to 4m (12ft). A heavy current dominates at mid tide and a shallow bottom means these are best left to big wave surfers. With the right board, the outside lefts can be ridden up to 7m (20ft).

Descendez la route de l'autre côté du port de Guéthary. D'abord les Alcyons, une gauche courte et intense qui tient jusqu'à 4m. Pas mal de courant en milieu de marée. Peu de fonds et un drop vraiment impressionnant. Pour les plus courageux, la vague du fond, Avalanche, se surfe jusqu'à 6m, sortez le gun.

Les Alcyons/Avalanche

ERIC CHAUCHE

4. Lafitenia

A beautiful, consistent right with tubes on the inside. Park in Acotz and Lafitenia Bay.

Belle droite consistente qui peut être longue quand la section du milieu de la baie connecte avec le premier pic au niveau des remous. Marche d'escalier au take-off. Tubes à l'inside. Suivre Acotz pour trouver le parking et la baie de Lafitenia.

Inside Lafitenia

5. Erromardie

Good waves are rare but there are a few nice lefts which face the lifeguard house or head towards the cliffs.

Les bonnes vagues y sont rares mais quelques gauches cassent en face du poste de secours ou vers la falaise.

6. Sainte-Barbe

A long right with a rad take off wraps around the jetty N of the bay. At the end of the wave is 'Le Flots Bleus', a peaky point break. Concrete blocks used for beach protection may destroy the wave.

Cette longue droite déroule depuis la jetée nord de la baie. Le take-off y est radical. En bout de vague se trouve une deuxième section, 'les Flots Bleus' dans la baie qui devient un spot de funboard quand ça souffle. Ce spot est menacé par des blocs de béton qu'on dépose pour ramener le sable sur la plage.

7. Ciboure/Socoa

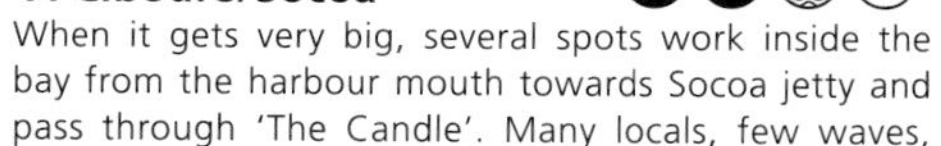

When it gets very big, several spots work inside the bay from the harbour mouth towards Socoa jetty and pass through 'The Candle'. Many locals, few waves, respect due.

Quand ça rentre trés gros, plusiers spots marchent du port à la digue de Socoa en passant par la Bougie. Beaucoup de locaux et des vagues au compte-goutte: chaud devant!

Sainte-Barbe, St Jean de Luz

8. Hendaye Plage

This is the answer when everything else is closing out. A long stretch of average beach breaks offers a wide choice of peaks; the best is not far from the casino. The two rocks to the N hold a right that requires patience, but is perfect for beginners.

L'ultime solution quand tout sature. Longue plage qui offre le choix pour trouver un pic correct selon les marées, plutôt vers le casino. Idéal pour débutants. Vagues moyennes sauf vers les 'Deux Jumeaux' au nòrd de la baie: une droite qui demande patience et détermination.

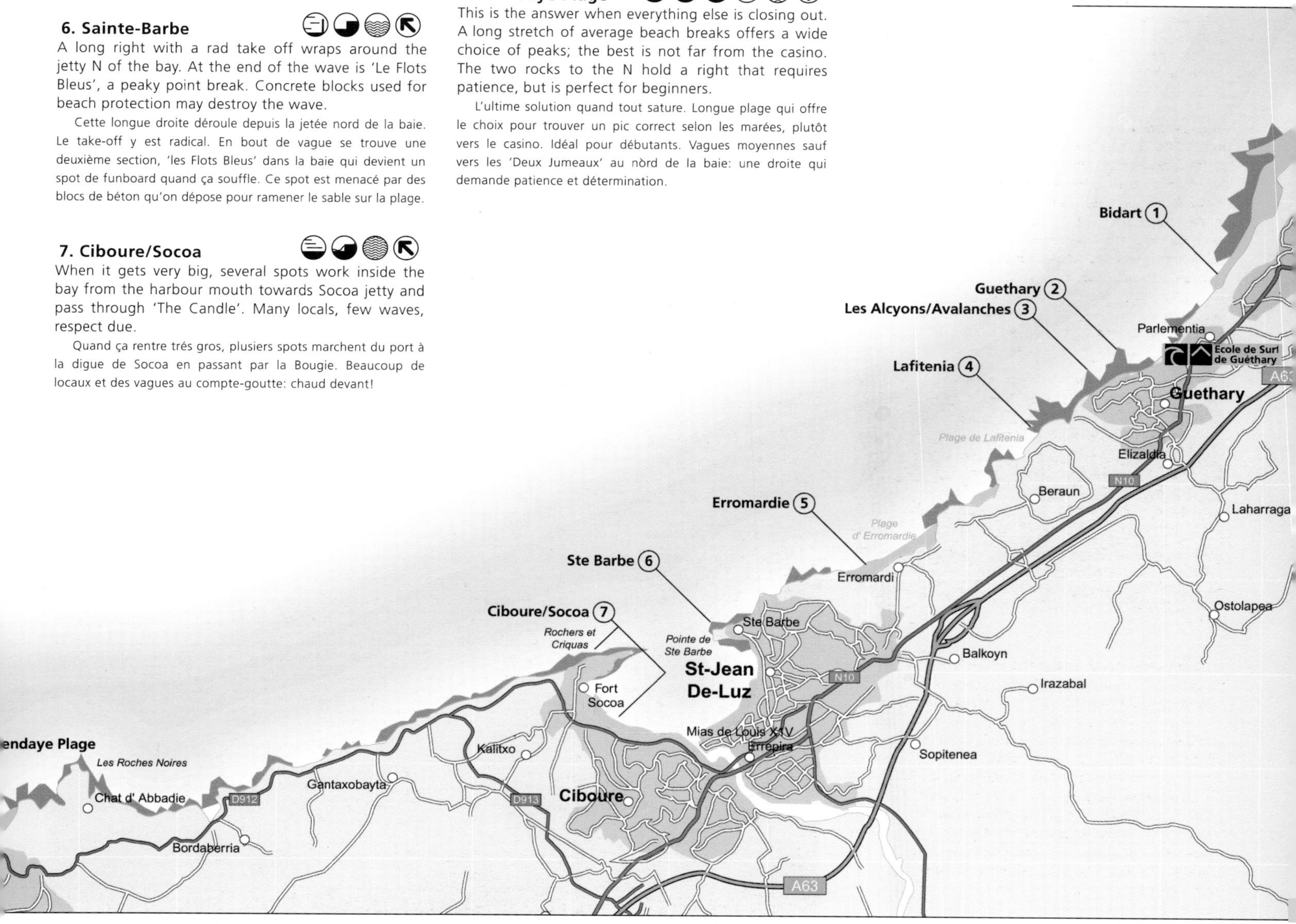

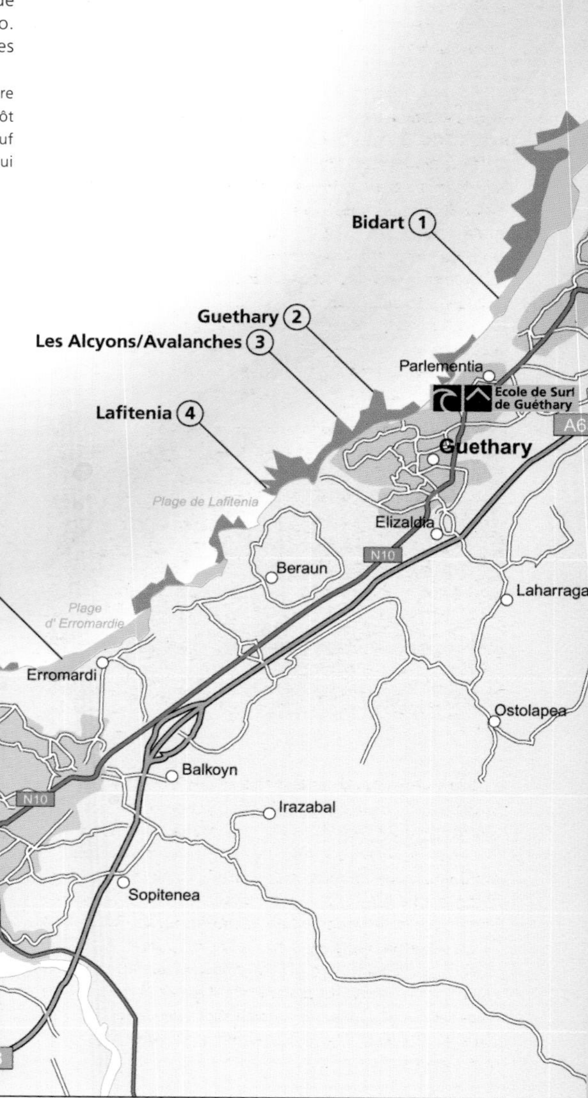

The Mediterranean

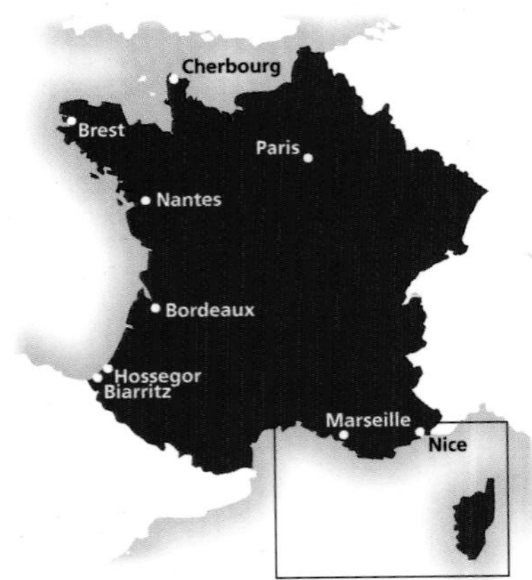

1. Palavas-les-Flots

There's a set of four spots between Palavas Harbour and Maguelonne. The best spot for camping is Maguelonne.

Une série de 4 spots depuis celui du port de Palavas jusqu'à Maguelonne. Prés des jetées, vous trouverez le pic du pêcheur ou le Canal du Prévost, à moins que vous ne poussiez jusqu'au camping de Maguelonne.

2. Saintes-Maries

In the very heart of Camargue, this long stretch of beach receives most swells but lacks power. On the right-hand side of the harbour, facing the bull arena or at Petit Rhône rivermouth (on an unusually big swell), there is occasional surf

En pleine Camargue, cette longue étendue de sable chope tous les swells (ou presque) mais manque cruellement de puissance. A droite du port devant les arènes, ça surfe de temps à autre ou au petit Rhône à Beauduc si ça rentre vraiment.

S. CANDÉ

Ponteau, Côte Bleue

3. Sausset-La Couronne

In the right conditions, a group of relatively, consistent reef breaks are nice to session, and are particularly good when there's any winds from SW to SE or the mistral wind. Carro, Couronne-vieille, L'Arquet et Ponteau are the names to etch on your memory. Rocks and crowds, however.

Un groupe de reefs relativement consistants qui s'activent avec du Mistral. Carro, Couronne-vieille, l'Arquet et Ponteau font partie des noms à retenir. Des sessions épiques quand les conditions veulent bien être là. Du monde et des rochers.

4. Le Prado

Have a laugh at this hip Marseille beach with tons of wave-sailors, sponges and trash. There's a bodyboard spot at Pointe Rouge.

La plage fun de Marseille avec son lot de windsurfers, de bodyboarders et de détritus. Un spot de bodyboard à la Pointe-Rouge. Rien d'extraordinaire mais c'est la frime!

5. Cassis

A fickle wave that can produce a surprisingly hollow left and much mellower right in the premium conditions: look for Arène beach and you'll find it. When the mistral blows, it's sheltered. Parking can be difficult.

Rien de régulier ici mais ça peut bien rentrer en gauche avec une droite mollassonne à la plage de l'Arène. Bien abrité par Mistral, un décor dantesque. Parking difficile.

S. CANDE

Cassis

6. La Ciotat

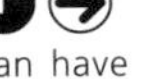

It's rare – but with heaps of E winds – this can have some good lefts.

Rare aussi mais si ça souffle ou ça a soufflé d'Est, les gauches valent le déplacement.

7. Cap Saint-Louis

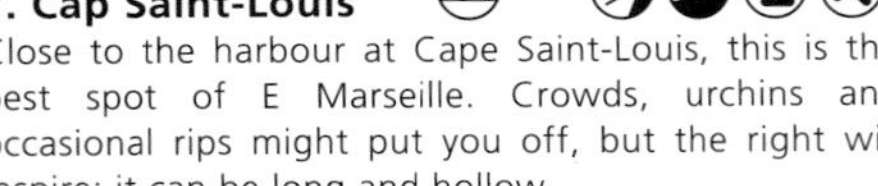

Close to the harbour at Cape Saint-Louis, this is the best spot of E Marseille. Crowds, urchins and occasional rips might put you off, but the right will inspire: it can be long and hollow.

Certainement le meilleur spot à l'est de Marseille au près du port des Lecques. Du monde, des oursins et parfois du courant mais la droite peut être longue et creuse.

8. Bandol

To the W of the central beach is a short left that is hard to locate. Try Bendor Island right in front of you – it has a decent reef break but the paddle out is long.

A l'ouest de la plage centrale, une gauche courte, difficile à trouver. L'ile de Bendor à un reef aussi. Bonne rame!

9. Six-Fours les Plages

This peninsula offers the widest swell window and has the best wind exposure. You can't miss La Coudoulière, a right-hander that fires when the wind is nil. On the E side, drive to Les Sablettes to check Verne beach, Pin-Rolland or La Seyne.

La péninsule offre certainement la meilleure palette de swell et de vent de toute la région. Difficile de louper Brutal Beach, souvent gavée de windsurfers. Tout prés se trouve la Coudoulière, une droite qui n'est bonne que sans vent. De l'autre côté, à la Seyne, aux Sablettes, il faut checker la plage de la Verne ou de Saint-Asile à Pin-Rolland.

10. Gigaro

If you don't find any surf, enjoy the unique scenery.

S'il n' y a pas de surf, vous pourrez au moins profiter d'un panaroma unique.

11. Beauvallon

Sheltered from nasty winds, you'll find fast and hollow waves here. It's not as crowded as the hip resort of St-Tropez but, if it works, there will be a plenty of people surfing around you.

Des vagues creuses et rapides abritées de quelques mauvais vents. Moins de monde qu'à St Tropez en face mais pas la solitude non plus.

RHIGHEZZA

Cap St. Louis

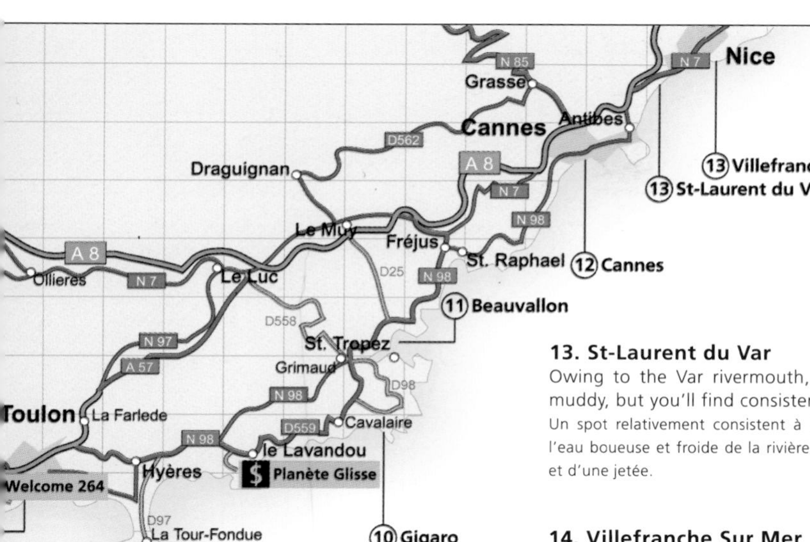

12. Cannes

This central beach can have small tubes with W winds. If the wind is blowing from the E, head to the other side of the Croisette Cape in front of the Palm Beach Casino. You may want to explore Sainte-Marguerite Island: go there by ferry and check Batéguier and Dragon Points.

La plage peut donner des petits tubes avec du vent d'Ouest. Si ça vient de l'Est, passez de l'autre côté du cap de la Croisette en face du Palm Beach Casino. Peut-être un trip en bateau pour l'île de Sainte-Marguerite et les pointes du Batéguier et du Dragon.

13. St-Laurent du Var

Owing to the Var rivermouth, the water is cold and muddy, but you'll find consistent, small waves.

Un spot relativement consistent à l'embouchure du Var, avec l'eau boueuse et froide de la rivière. Près d'un centre nautique et d'une jetée.

14. Villefranche Sur Mer

Even though the odds of finding it flat are high, this place is worth checking out. Deep in the bay, the peaks can be powerful.

Même si c'est flat, il faut y aller. Au fond de la baie, le pic droite-gauche peut être puissant .

Corsica

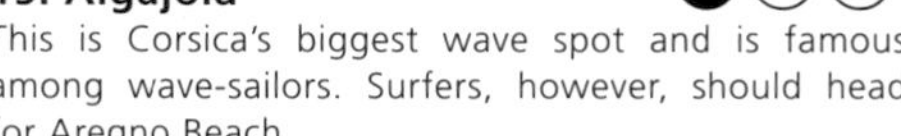

15. Algajola

This is Corsica's biggest wave spot and is famous among wave-sailors. Surfers, however, should head for Aregno Beach.

Probablement le spot le plus gros de Corse, bien connu des windsurfers: direction la plage d'Aregno!

16. Capo di Feno

It's difficult to access this break, but when you get there it's quite consistent. Drive past Tino Rossi's house or CRS on the road towards the Sanguinaires Islands.

Accés difficile mais ça rentre souvent. Roulez sur la route des Iles Sanguinaires et jetez un oeil aux CRS ou devant la maison de Tino Rossi.

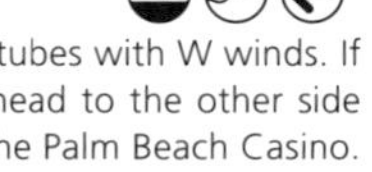

17. Le Ruppione

Past Punta di Sette Nave, this spot is a fat shore break. Close by is La Castagne, a much better wave on a reef.

Passé Punta di Sette Nave, ce spot est un shorebreak assez gras. La Castagne à quelques encablures est un reef digne de ce nom.

18. Figari

North of Ste-Lucie de Porto-Vecchio you'll find waves on the E side of the bay. De l'autre côté de la baie, on peut surfer de temps en temps. Surtout fréquenté par les windsurfers.

19. Pinarellu

N of Sainte-Lucie de Porto-Vecchio, this experiences the most consistent waves on the E coast.

Au nord de Ste-Lucie de Porto-Vecchio, les vagues plus consistentes de la côte Est. Rare quand même.

S. CANDE

Porticcio, Ajacio

S. CANDE

Balagne, Algajola

The lefts powering their way into the mouth of the river Gernika are some of the most famous in the world

Spain

Spain is an incredibly varied and satisfying surf destination with some of the biggest, longest and most perfect waves on the planet. Surfing is a highly sociable experience in line with other aspects of Spanish cultural life. Naturally animated, colourful and hospitable, the Spanish have retained a friendly curiousity towards the international surf tribes who wander through their rich land. If you're prepared to fit it in, Spain offers an exotic and quintessential European travel experience.

Espagne

A la fois intense et varié, ce pays haut en couleurs à tout d'une destination surf à ne pas manquer. Un peu à l'écart de son voisin à la culture surf très developpée, l'Espagne bénéficie de nombreuses vagues parmi les plus longues et les plus parfaites d'Europe. Le surf est un merveilleux vecteur de découvertes sociales, et qui pense à un trip en Espagne imagine les éfluves du poisson grillé, du bon vin, et des cigares corsées qui enfument les nuits blanches, sans oublier les berets et les corridas! Les Espagnols sont un peuple chaleureux et vivant, qui ne manquent pas d'une accueillante curiosité envers les tribus de surfers qui viennent découvrir leur riche héritage. Si vous êtes partant pour le dépaysement, l'Espagne est une destination d'un exotisme unique.

JAKUE ANDIKOETXEA

Introduction

The People

The Spanish are a *mestizo*, an eclectic cultural mélange resulting from a history that spans many centuries, religions and rulers. With the fall of the Romans, the country was, from 705 AD, nearly all Islamic after the Moors invaded and occupied the southern peninsula. Moors and Christians largely resided in peace until 1469, when the marriage of Isabel de Castilla and Ferdinando de Aragón cemented two prominently Christian regions, and filled a power vacuum left by the loss of the Muslim leader Sultan Almanazor. When Christopher Columbus discovered America in 1492, a whole new era of wealth and power began for Spain, and luckily for the coffers of the Spanish treasury, the Aztec and Inca civilisations lay in the way. Isabel's daughter Juana married into the powerful Hapsburg dynasty, which lead Spain of the 16th and 17th centuries to continue to dominate European events. Stridently Catholic, Spain became both the victim and propagator of countless wars and conspiracies over the next couple of centuries, including Napoleon's invasion in the early 19th century.

Capital: Madrid
Population: 40 million
Area: 32,714 sq km/202,382 sqmi
Time: GMT +1
Language: Spanish, Catalan, Basque (Euskera)
Currency: Peseta (pta)

All was fairly quiet until 1936 when Civil War broke out. With the throne abandoned ignominiously by King Alfonso X111, liberals from around the globe arrived to fight the Fascists, led by General Franco, who triumphed, thanks to some timely help by Hitler. Since the death of Franco in 1975, the monarchy was restored and Spain has managed a rapid and relatively peaceful transition to democracy under the supervision of King Juan Carlos I. In recent years, it has been governed by a succession of socialist administrations led by Felipe González. Since joining the EC in 1986, there has been an increasing devolution of power to the regions. The Ballearic islands in the Mediterranean and the Canary Islands off the north west coast of Africa are also administered by Spain.

The old and the new in Bilbao

J. AMEZAGA

TIM RAINGER

Bullfighting is still popular in Spain

The Land

Spain occupies the majority of the Iberian peninsula, an ancient landmass surrounded by the ocean. Her mountainous north border rises from the Med to 3,404m (1,1168ft) in the Pyrenees and stretches along the Cordillera Cantabrica and Picos de Europa, ending on Galicia's rocky fingers.

The desert-like interior is dominated by a broad, flat central plateau that only centuries ago was heavily forested. It is punctuated by the Cordillera Central and drained by the Duero, Tagus and Guadiana Menor rivers. The Sierra Estrella and Sierra de Gata mark the western border with Portugal while the southern fringes of the landmass face the Strait of Gibraltar and eastwards into the Mediterranean. The Sierra Nevadas are possibly Spain's best-known range, featured in countless spaghetti westerns.

The Climate

Spain's climate is primarily influenced by the oceans that surround it. When talking about such a large country, it's difficult to generalise about weather conditions due to the existence of several distinct micro-climates.

Most of the low pressure weather systems come from the north and west and consequently there's a wet north and west Atlantic coast and a drier, warmer Mediterranean influence to the south and east. North Spain is the coldest, wettest and windiest part of the country and the coast here is also exposed to swells, which come in from the same systems. Luckily, because of its chequered weather patterns, it has escaped the fate of tourist traps like the Costa del Sol and the Costa Brava.

Galicia occupies a peculiar and exposed geographical situation and lies at the same latitude as Marseilles but is much wetter, with a climate more similar to Cornwall or Brittany than southern France. Air temperatures around both north and west coasts are moderate, though in winter, snow does fall in the Cordillera Cantabrica at altitude. The interior suffers extreme and rapid temperature variations ranging from below zero to baking hot. Most of the precipitation falls in the winter months taking the form of mountain snow, but the summers are hot, long and very dry, plagued by searing, dusty winds. What rain there is comes in spring and early summer in short, intense bursts.

The eastern and southern coasts are home to the Mediterranean resorts that are renown for their long hours of sunshine, tempered by warm gentle sea breezes which often come up from the deserts of Africa.

Introduction

La population

Les Espagnols sont un peuple trés latin, issu de la tradition catholique, convaincu par l'Europe, avec un fort penchant pour les fêtes et les discussions animées, Julio Iglésias, le Pape, le football, le Flamenco, les courses de taureaux et autres corridas. Mais 700 ans après la chute de l'Empire Romain, la quasi totalité du pays était islamique, avant d'être reconquit par les habitants de la Cantabrie. Outre ces conquérants nationaux, l'emblème catholique fut l'inspiration des "conquistadores" qui bâtirent l'empire du Nouveau Monde. A l'époque des grandes découvertes, la couronne espagnole fut la seule a adopter le projet fou de naviguer non-stop vers l'ouest, soutenu par un certain Christophe Colomb. Heureusement, les trésors des civilisations Incas et Azteques vinrent à point pour remplir les coffres du royaume. Les Espagnols ont toujours été tournés vers la côte, attendant le retour des galions chargés d'or, qui auraient échappé aux pirates portugais et anglais. La cour d'Espagne a mené la danse en Europe au 16e et 17e siècle. Extrêmement catholique, elle fut la victime et la provocatrice de nombreuses guerres et conspirations. Tombée dans l'oubli durant plusieurs siècles, l'Espagne souleva un regain d'attention à l'occasion de la guerre civile, lorsque les libéraux du monde entier se sont mobilisés pour barrer la route aux fascistes du Général Franco. Il trompha avec l'aide d'Hitler, sans toutefois avoir son destin, car il ne fut pas son allié en 1939. Depuis la mort de Franco en 1975, la monarchie a été rétablie, et l'Espagne a opéré une rapide et plutôt pacifique transition à la démocratie, sous l'égide du roi Juan Carlos 1er. Depuis, le gouvernement a été longtemps à tendance socialiste, mené par notamment par Felipe Gonzales. Depuis son entrée dans la CEE en 1986, la décentralisation du pouvoir a été une priorité. Les îles Baléares en Méditerrannée, et les îles Canaries à l'ouest de l'Afrique sont toujours sous administration espagnole.

F. MUNOZ

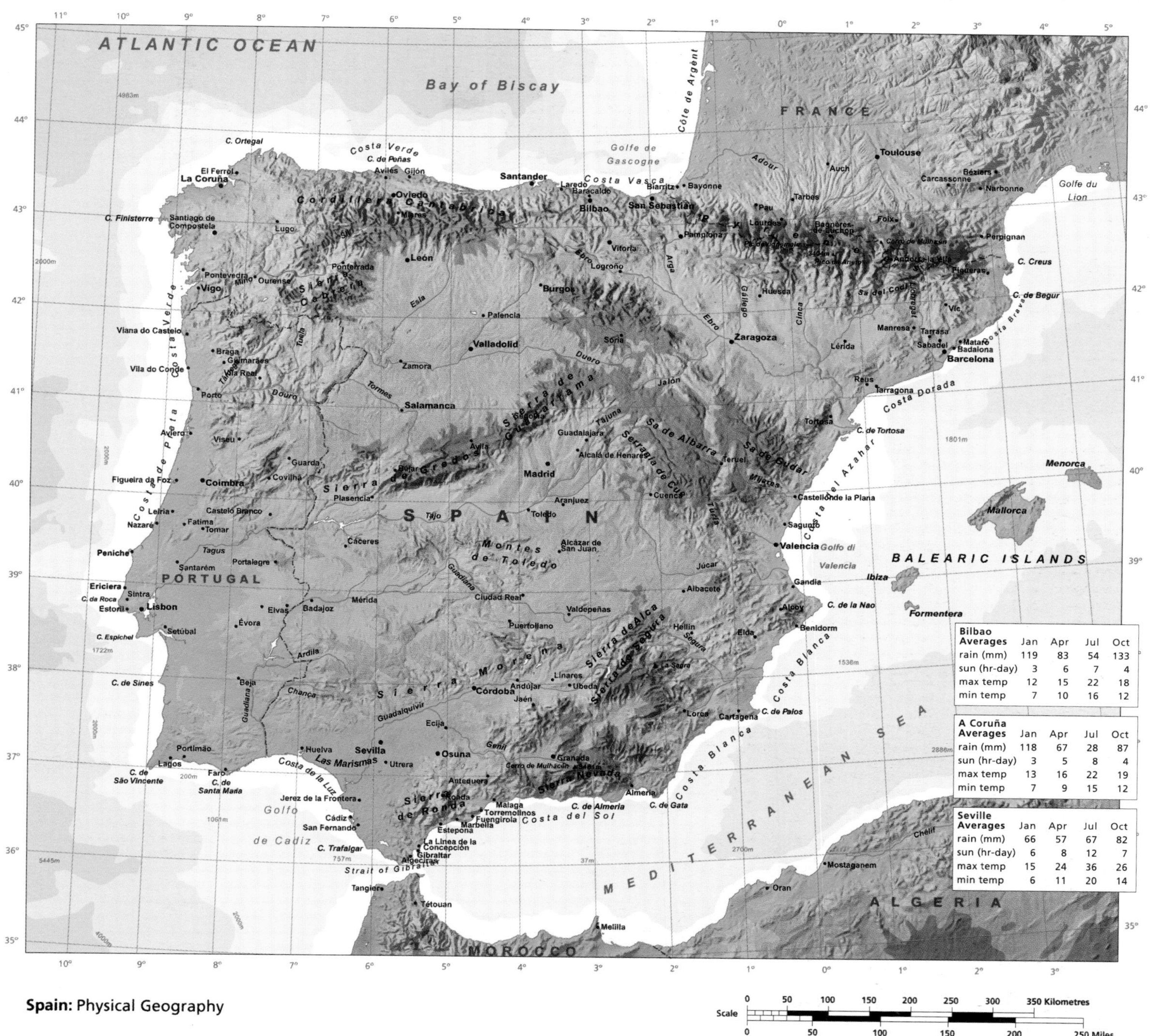

Bilbao Averages	Jan	Apr	Jul	Oct
rain (mm)	119	83	54	133
sun (hr-day)	3	6	7	4
max temp	12	15	22	18
min temp	7	10	16	12

A Coruña Averages	Jan	Apr	Jul	Oct
rain (mm)	118	67	28	87
sun (hr-day)	3	5	8	4
max temp	13	16	22	19
min temp	7	9	15	12

Seville Averages	Jan	Apr	Jul	Oct
rain (mm)	66	57	67	82
sun (hr-day)	6	8	12	7
max temp	15	24	36	26
min temp	6	11	20	14

Spain: Physical Geography

Scale 0 50 100 150 200 250 300 350 Kilometres; 0 50 100 150 200 250 Miles

Le pays

L'Espagne occupe la quasi totalité de la péninsule ibérique, grande avancée de terre dans l'océan. Le Nord est trés montagneux, avec les Pyrénnées qui culminent à 3404m, puis la cordillière Cantabrique, et Picos de Europa, jusqu'aux pointes rocheuses de Galice. La côte nord est une terre de légendes, lorsque les brumes descendent les vallées, poussées par les vents, les locaux racontent encore les histoires de "Santa Campana" (la procession des fantômes). C'est une terre de vertes collines recouvertes de fougères, parsemées de forêts, qui viennent sa marier avec la beauté de l'océan.

L'interieur du pays se résume à un grand plateau désertique, qui fut abondamment boisé il y a quelques siècles. La monotonie est toutefois rompue par la cordillière centrale où les rivières de Douro, le Tage et la Guadiana prennent leur source.

A l'ouest, les chaines montagneuses Sierra Estella et Sierra de Gata marquent la frontière avec le Portugal, et se terminent au sud par le rocher de Gilbraltar. La Sierra Nevada a été rendue célèbre par d'innombrables westerns spaghettis.

Le climat

Le climat de la péninsule ibérique est sous l'influence des océans qui l'entourent. Il est difficile d'émettre des généralités tant les micro-climats sont nombreux. Le nord et l'ouest sont plutôt humides à cause des dépressions qui balaient ces régions. Le Sud et l'Est sont sous l'influence plus sèche du climat méditerrannéen. Le Nord n'est pas seulement la région la plus humide, mais également la plus froide et la plus ventée.

La côte nord est également la mieux exposée aux swells et a échappé au destin bétonné des Costa del Sol et autres Costa Brava. La Galice est tant exposée que sa latitude, indentique à celle de Marseille, ne lui épargne pas un climat plus proche de celui de la Bretagne que de celui de la Côte d'Azur! Les températures sont tempérées sur les deux côtes, mais des chutes de neige sont possibles en altitude du coté de Picos de Europa.

Le Centre subit de grandes amplitudes, de glacial à torride, en peu de temps. L'essentiel des précipitations est hivernal, voire sous forme de neige. Les étés sont longs, chauds et secs, balayées par des vents brûlants. On peut toutefois s'attendre à de la pluie au printemps et en début d'été sous la forme d'averses violentes. Plus on se déplace vers le sud, plus les étés sont longs.

Les côtes Sud et Est sont connues pour leurs stations balnéaires, qui doivent leur succès à un ensoleillement généreux, mais tempéré par des brises côtières. Ceux qui visitent le Nord en éspérant le soleil mediterranéen seront trés surpris de ne trouver bien souvent que pluie et nuages venus de l'Atlantique.

Surf Culture

History

In May 1962 Jesús Fiochi ordered a surfboard from the Barland workshop in Bayonne, France, entering the ocean at the Primera Playa of Playa del Sardinero, Cantabria. From the beginning, a group of swimmers and divers accompanied Jesús armed with their own homemade plywood boards with rounded tips. They soon realised that proper boards were available in Bayonne (Jesús had rubbed out the trademark and said that he'd ordered his from Australia!) and promptly bought a Barland each, forming two core groups consisting of some 12 surfers in total.

Jesús Fiochi still charging at 55 years old

By 1969 José Merodio began crafting boards for himself and later for his friends under the name MB Surfboards. In the early 70s, he moved to the Euskadi where his compadres included Iñigo and Carlos Beraza. They were affectionately known as the 'Tanganazo Boys' and lived the surfing lifestyle with long hair, good music and surf, surf, surf. With suits and ties banished, they sought to find a way to lead the life they loved and yet still earn a living. In a familiar response to an age-old dilemma, making boards seemed to be the only answer. The legendary Santa Marina Surfboards, the first board factory in Spain, was born and single-handedly hot housed much of Spain's early surf culture.

In Asturias, Diego Mendez has experienced surfing's gradual evolution since the 60s and remembers: 'It was in Tapia de Casariego, Gijón and later in El Espartal that the first surfers began to appear. I wish I could describe the atmosphere that surrounded those championships. I will never forget those days – they were the best! I don't mean they're bad now, but times change.'

In Galicia, the sport's beginnings were predictable: the first glimpse of a big Malibu was love at first sight. Says surfer Carlos Bremon: 'The first waves were ridden in Vigo (1969) and La Coruña (1970). I remember the first contest at Nemiña (100km/60miles from La Coruña) that ended up as a beach party because the surf was too small. We were continually looking for new places to surf: we'd open a map and see lots of beaches but nobody knew exactly where to go, so with map in hand we discovered many spots. In Ferrol, where we first made our surf boards, we spotted Doniños as a white line in the distance. One afternoon we decided to try it. What we found was the quintessential surf dream – an infinity of empty, perfect peaks. I remember the crazy race we had down the hill to get there. The water was crystal clear and cold, but the sun shone. It was an unforgettable moment. Despite the years, nothing has really changed and the same waves still break in the same places. I guess 20 years in the multi-coloured history of one man is only a tiny second in the long history of a beach. I feel small when I contemplate the quiet cliffs that have presided over so many geological eras. In this land without haste, surfing has slept quietly for these last 25 years.'

English travellers, Zarautz

PETER CADE

JAKUE ANDIKOETXEA

By the mid 70s the national surfing population had grown to a tight-knit community of several hundred people, focused around País Vasco. Iñigo Letamendia started up Geronimo Surfboards with an American called Jay and an artist named Txema Elexpuru, who gave the boards their 70s style spray jobs. Around this time the brand Pukas appeared. Surfers like Raúl Dordil, Estanis Escauriaza, Jon Susaeta and Gonzalo Gandarias stood out. By the early 80s, surfing had expanded across the peninsula to the coasts around Cádiz and Tarifa and surf shops, clothing brands, wetsuits, boards and accessories were readily available. In 1987 the first Spanish surf mag *Tres 60* was published and from this time the market rocketed.

Culture Surf

Histoire

C'est en Mai 1962 que Jésus Fiochi a commandé sa première planche à l'usine Barland de Bayonne, pour attaquer les vagues de "Primera Playa" de Playa del Sardinero (Cantabrie). Au départ, un groupe de nageurs et de plongeurs a suivi Jésus, armés de planches de contre-plaqué à l'avant arrondi. Ils ont bien fini par apprendre que de vraies planches étaient disponibles à Bayonne (en effet, Jésus avait effacé le logo de sa planche, et prétendait l'avoir commandée en Australie !). Chacun des douze surfers s'était rapidement procuré une "Barland", pour former deux groupes distincts.

En 1969, José Merodio a shapé ses premières planches, pour lui-même puis pour ses amis, sous le logo "MB Surfboards". Ce doit être en 1972 qu'il déménagea au Pays Basque, pour retrouver ses amis Inigo Letamendia et Carlos Beraza. Connu sous le nom des "Tanganazo Boys", ils vivèrent à fond le style de vie surf: cheveux longs, musique, jolies filles et bien sûr du surf et encore du surf. Une fois leurs costumes et leurs cravates aux oubliettes, leur objectif était de poursuivre ce style de vie, mais aussi d'arriver à en vivre. La fabrication de planches était la réponse naturelle à ce vieux dilemme. La légendaire marque Santa Marina Surfboards fut non seulement la première marque espagnole, mais représentait à cette époque toute sa culture surf.

Dans les Asturies, Diego Mendes a connu toute l'évolution depuis les sixties, et se souvient:"C'est à Tapia de Casariego, à Gijon puis à El Espartal que sont apparus les premiers surfers. J'aimerais pouvoir décrire l'ambiance qui règnait lors de nos premiers championnats. Jamais je n'oublierai cette époque fabuleuse. Je ne veux pas dire que c'était mieux qu'aujourd'hui, mais les temps changent!"

En Galice, les débuts étaient prévisibles. Et ce fut le coup de foudre, avec les premières vagues surfées à Vigo en 1969, puis à La Corogne en 1970. Carlos se souvient: "la première compétition à Nemina (100 km de La Corogne) a fini en beach party par manque de vagues. Nous étions toujours à l'affût de nouvelles vagues à surfer. On dépliait une carte, et à la vue de toutes ces plages, on était pas plus renseignés! Nous avons tout de même découvert pas

JAKUE ANDIKOETXEA

JAKUE ANDIKOETXEA

Jamie Fernandez, Meñakoz

Today

All Spain's coasts are popular and local communities are still gaining numbers rapidly. Surfing is even practiced in the Mediterranean, in the provinces of Málaga, Valencia and Cataluña and on the Ballearics in the occasional swells. Bodyboarding is especially popular and is increasing at an alarming rate. In some regions where surfing is relatively new, bodyboarders greatly outnumber surfers. Two excellent surf mags *Tres 60* and *Surfer Rule* service an ever-growing market of more than 15,000 regular watergoers (60% surfers, 40% bodyboarders). Local board making, especially in the Basque region is of the highest international standards. Pukas is still the most advanced board company in Spain, producing boards with the likes of Pat Rawson, Maurice Cole and Wayne Lynch as well as domestic shapers for the local market. Board prices are equivalent to the rest of Europe (depending on current exchange rates).

JAKUE ANDIKOETXEA

The main competitive focus is the European Pro-Am calendar which includes events like the 'Pantin Classic' and the 'Tapia Pro Am', both held annually. Zarautz has held ASP events and on a smaller scale, most regions also have internal comp circuits. The standard of surfing at any given beach is solid and standards are improving rapidly. On the big days the locals charge most spots and guys like Jamie Fernandez, Ibon Amatriain, Pelo Etxebarria and others command respect from any travelling pro on a big day at Mundaka, Menakoz or Roca Puta.

mal de spots de cette manière. Nous pouvions voir Doniños depuis l'abri où nous fabriquions nos premières planches, à Ferrol. C e n'était qu'une ligne blanche au loin, mais un jour, on s'est lançé. Nous avons pu vivre le rêve de tout surfer: découvrir une réserve infinie de vagues parfaites. Je nous vois encore courir au pied de la colline. L'eau était cristalline mais froide, et le soleil brillait. Un moment inoubliable. Depuis les années ont passées, mais rien n'a vraiment changé, et les mêmes vagues déroulent toujours au même endroit. Je suppose que la durée de vie d'une personne est insignifiante dans la vie d'une plage. Je me sens tout petit quand je contemple ces falaises immobiles qui ont vu défiler tant d'ères géologiques. Dans cette région que rien ne presse, les vagues déroulent tranquillement depuis 25 ans.

Au milieu des années 70, la population atteignait 100 à 200 surfers se connaissant tous. Inigo Letamendia, a créé Géronimo Surfboards, épaulé par un américain nommé Jay et l'artiste Txema Elexpuru. C'est à la même époque que les premières Pukas firent leur apparition. Les surfers Raùl Dordil, Estanis Escauriaza, Jon Susaeta et Gonzalo Gandarias faisaient parler d'eux. La Fédération Espagnole de Surf fut créée en 1982. Au début des années 80, le surf s'était développé à travers la péninsule, jusqu'à Tarifa et Cadix, où l'on pouvait déjà trouver des surf-shops, ainsi que des vêtements, des planches, des combinaisons et des accessoires. Depuis la parution du magazine "Tres 60", le marché n'a cessé de se developper.

Aujourd'hui

Toutes les côtes sont surfées, et chaque communauté se développe rapidement. On surfe en Méditerrannée, dans les provinces de Màlaga et de Valence, en Catalogne, et même aux Baléares quand le swell le permet. Le Bodyboard séduit tous ces nouveaux surfers, et en Andalousie où le surf est une neuf, le nombre de bodyboarders dépasse largement les surfers. Deux excellents magazines "Tres 60" et "Surfer Rule" sont lus par d'innombrables pratiquants. La manufacture de planche, notamment au Pays Basque, répond aux meilleurs standards internationaux et les prix sont équivalent aux autres marques européennes (suivant les taux de change).

Au niveau compétition, les temps forts sont les étapes annuelles du cicuit pro-am européen EPSA, dont la Pantin Classic et le Tapia Pro-Am. Zarautz a accueilli à deux reprises le circuit ASP et, à moindre échelle, la plupart des régions reçoivent des compétitions internationales. Pukas est la plus grosse et la plus célebre marque espagnole, qui utilise les talents de Pat Rawson, Maurice Cole et Wayne Lynch, à la plus grande joie des locaux. Le niveau de surf que l'on peut rencontrer sur les spots, s' il n'est pas le meilleur du monde, est souvent solide. Les jours de gros swell, les locaux sont de plus en plus présents, et des gars tels que Jaime Fernandez, Ibon Amatriain et Pelo Etxebarria forcent le respect des pros de passage à Mundaka ou Meñakoz.

País Vasco

Roca Puta

Where to Go

Surf Areas

Owing to the good quality of some of the waves in the north, the **País Vasco** coast is the most frequently visited by travelling surfers. The majority head for the legendary Mundaka, then move along the north coast towards Portugal. Mundaka, a world famous left rivermouth with super fast, heavy barrels, is the main spot, although Menakoz and Roca Puta are also intense wave areas that hold anything the Atlantic can throw at them. The cities of Bilbao and San Sebastian hold the major surf crowds as these have good but populated beach breaks.

Now there are surfers at the majority of beaches in **Cantabria**. El Brusco and Los Locos are excellent peaky beach breaks, while Somo, Sardinaro and the waves at Liencres keep the surfers of Santander smiling. Other spots tend to be fairly empty except during weekends and holidays.

Asturias has a coastline of approximately 500km (300mi) with many good quality beaches, reefs, points and rivermouths. It's a region is full of contrasts with ocean, forests, mountains, flora and fauna combining to create breathtaking vistas. One of the best spots, Rodiles, is an excellent left-hand rivermouth, similar to

Los Locos, Luis Malibu

Ou Aller

Les Espace de Surf

Pays Basque La qualité des vagues dans le nord du pays explique que cette région soit la plus visitée par les surfers. La plupart s'arrêtent d'abord à la vague légendaire de Mundaka, puis continuent le long de la côte vers le Portugal. Pour ne parler que des spots les plus connus, on trouve Mundaka, gauche tubulaire de classe mondiale à l'embouchure d'une rivière, puis Meñakoz et Roca Punta, spots de gros qui ne saturent pratiquement jamais. La grande majorité des surfers locaux vivent à Bilbao et San Sebastian. On trouvera donc beaucoup de monde à l'eau sur les beach breaks avoisinants.

Cantabrie Chaque plage a désormais sa population de surfers. Somo, à coté de El Sardinero, et Los Locos sont considérés comme étant les meilleurs spots. El Brusco et Los locos sont d'excellents beachbreaks. Somo, Sardinero et Liencres font le bonheur des surfers de Santander. On trouvera peu de monde à l'eau sur les autres spots, à part peut-être durant les vacances et les week-ends.

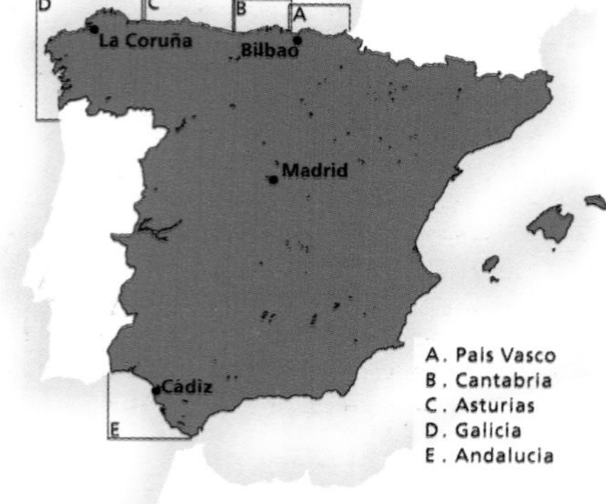

Asturies La côte des Asturies s'étend sur 500km de plages, récifs, pointbreaks et embouchures, tous de bonnes qualité. Les montagnes, les forêts, la flore et la faune locale, créent des paysages grandioses et contrastés. Rodiles est une gauche d'embouchure type Mundaka, sans être aussi radicale. Tapia, joli village de pêcheurs avec son ambiance relaxe. La densité de population étant supérieur de Gijon à Salinas, il y a du monde de ce coté là toute l'année.

Galice La côte de La Galice est très découpée, et, sur une portion du littoral, vous pouvez trouver tous les types de vagues. Quelle que soit la direction du vent ou du swell, il ya toujours un spot qui marche. Il y a fort à parier que vous serez seul avec le grondement de l'océan. Vos pas ne croiseront que des pêcheurs,

F. MUNOZ

Shaun Bevan, Pantin

F. MUNOZ

El Palmar, Cadiz

Mundaka but not as heavy or as crowded. Tapia is a cool fishing village with good waves and a mellow local scene. The area from Gijón to Salinas is the most frequented and it has waves perennially.

The coast of **Galicia** has a tortuous outline and on its sandy beaches you can find a-thousand-and-one different waves. Regardless of wind and swell direction, somewhere is going off all the time. It's more than likely you'll be alone with the ocean's roar, your footsteps alongside those of a fisherman who impassively observes your manoeuvres without losing sight of his rod. All of Galicia's coasts get waves in various conditions, generally speaking, the breaks in the north are the most consistent. In summer the area around Ferrol can be exceptional. Within easy reach of the towns of Ferrol and La Coruña are the beaches of Pantin and Doniños, which have the best-known quality beach-breaks. Patos, near the Portuguese border, also has fine waves

Andalucia has a consistently warm, dry and windy climate along its west-facing coast. The swell shadow cast by Cabo St Vincent means that the southern stretches pick up more swell, especially in winter when it can be a good uncrowded area to search for surf. The Cadiz area is the nucleus of the scene, while El Palmar is the best beach break in the area. Other notable spots include Canos de Meca (a long, hollow left reef) and Barbate (a rivermouth left).

F. MUNOZ

Rodiles

When to go

The ideal time for waves is September to November since the water and air temperatures are still bearable and swells coming from the north west are powerful and consistent. The fiestas continue and core surfers go into underground overdrive. A good time to be between jobs. The most pleasant time to surf is in the summer but swells are inconsistent, not normally reaching above 1.5m (4ft). In winter the waves are as good as in autumn but the water temperature is 9-13°C (43-52°F) and with similar air temperatures many people think twice, even on good days. The southern coasts are the warmest in winter and can be a worthwhile effort. With spring comes warmer weather although the surf becomes erratic and unpredictable. There could be back-to-back swells or you may wait for months with mushy seas coming from the north.

qui vous observeront sans quitter leurs lignes des yeux. Toute la Galice est toujours surfable, mais le nord semble être plus consistant, donc plus prisé par les surfers. En été, la région de Ferrol peut être exceptionnelle. L'avantage de cette région est l'accès facile et la variété de vagues surfables en toutes conditions.

A deux pas du Ferrol et de La Corogne, se trouvent quelques excellentes plages. Pantin et Doniños sont les plus connues par leurs bons bancs de sable. Patos, près de la frontière portugaise réserve différentes vagues de qualité.

Andalousie La côte fait face à l'ouest, et le climat y est plus chaud et sec. La partie la plus au sud reçoit moins de swell, car située derrière le cap St Vincent. C'est un bon repli en hiver, lorsque les dépressions descendent très au sud, le climat y reste agréable. La région de Cadix est la plus prisée et El Palmar est le meilleur beach break du coin. Caños de la Mecca est une longue et creuse gauche de reef. Barbate est une gauche d'estuaire,comme Mundaka mais en miniature.

Quand Aller

La période idéale pour les vagues court d'octobre à novembre quand les températures de l'eau et de l'air sont encore supportables et que les swells du nord-ouest commencent à envoyer la patate. Le plus agréable pour surfer est bien sûr l'été mais on chope rarement de bonnes vagues de plus d1,50m. En hiver les vagues sont aussi bonnes qu'en automne mais la température de l'eau descend vers les 13°C avec une température terrestre qui peut tomber à 5°C. Quand tel est le cas, y'en beaucoup de surfers qui hésitent. C'est donc l'occasion de surfer sans la foule. Au printemps, il commence à faire chaud à nouveau, par petites périodes, mais l'eau tarde à suivre. En plus, de nombreuses perturbations s'enroulent sur la péninsule ibérique et ramènent du mauvais temps. Soyez patients !

Bilbao Averages	Jan	Apr	Jul	Oct
water °C	11	12	19	18
wetsuit				

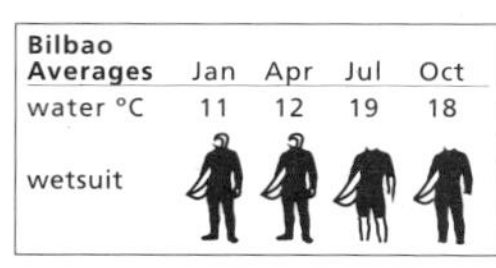

A Coruña Averages	Jan	Apr	Jul	Oct
water °C	12	13	18	17
wetsuit				

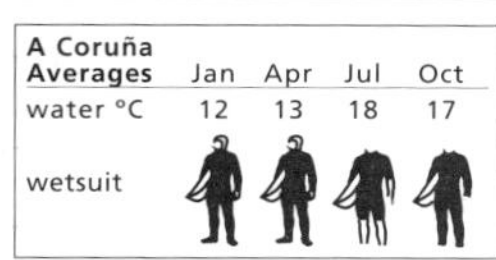

Cadiz Averages	Jan	Apr	Jul	Oct
water °C	14	15	20	20
wetsuit				

The Ocean Environment

Water Quality

Talking about the ocean environment in Spain means talking money and politics. The Spanish government is supposed to have a system to control and sanction the industries that send waste into the ocean, but European legislation is far from dilligently applied. If you look along the north coast, you'll see some obviously dirty areas where effluent is dumped directly into the sea, in some cases due to the proximity of big cities, such as San Sebastian, Bilbao, Gijón, La Coruña and others because of their proximity to industrial areas, like Bilbao, Suances, Avilés and Vigo.

There are, at least, no nukes on the Spanish Atlantic coast. One was built in Lemonia in the Basque Country, next to a good reef break, but it never operated and luckily never will because of opposition from the entire Basque population. Unfortunately, knowing politicians and businessmen, the biggest fear is that of the unknown. Alarm bells started ringing in Andalucia last spring when a storage reservoir being used by a Swedish mining company, cracked, releasing a tide of corrosive black 'spoil' along the Guardiamar river, up to the border of the Parque de Doñana. The chemicals contained in the toxic 'mud' (zinc, cadmium, lead, mercury and thalium) flowed into the wetlands surrounding the park, and into the ocean in the surf zone between Huelva and Cadiz. The crisis was so severe it warranted immense attention Europe-wide, which caused a shameful blame laying war between those responsible. Nobody knows how many other dangerous enterprises are currently threatening Spain's waters, and other than Greenpeace, there are no environmental organisations in Spain. Despite this dire appraisal, the latest clean up efforts in the Basque country (see Basque intro p179), are some grounds for optimism.

On Localism

As with everywhere in the world, localism is present in Spain but it's not as radical as some. There are no spots where the black shorts are going to hassle you off the beach, but there are some where you must be careful. The most representative of these is Mundaka, the Queen of Europe. Between September and December there are so many international travellers in the line-up that maybe you'll feel comfortable. However you'll soon realise that it's difficult to get a wave and that the locals claim the first section exclusively for themselves. Normal stuff. In Cantabria, you'd better park discreetly at beaches like El Brusco, Liencres or Los Locos. And in Asturias, be careful at Rodiles. Along the rest of the coast, take the regular precautions, but in general the people are warm and mellow. **Javier Amezaga**

Punta Galea: clean lines, dirty water

Specificités du littoral

La qualité de l'eau

Parler de l'environnement aquatique en Espagne revient à parler d'argent et de politique. Le gouvernement espagnol est supposé avoir un système pour contrôler et sanctionner les industries qui déversent des déchets dans l'océan, mais la législation européenne est loin d'y être appliquée assidûment. Si vous regardez le long de la Côte Nord, vous y verrez quelques zones franchement polluées là où les eaux se déversent dans l'Océan, dans certains cas causées par la proximité de grandes villes comme San Sebastian, Bilbao, Gijon, La Corogne, dans d'autres cas dues à la proximité des zones industrielles comme par exemple Bilbao, Suances, Aviles, Vigo entre autres.

Au moins il n'y a pas de centrales nucléaires sur la Côte altlantique espagnole. Une a été construite à Lemonia dans le Pays Basque, près d'un bon reefbreak, mais elle n'a jamais été opérationnelle et en le sera jamais grâce à l'opposition de toute la population basque. Mais connaissant les politiciens et les hommes d'affaires, on ne peut jamais présager de rien. Une sonnette d'alarme a commencé à sonner le printemps dernier en Andalousie quand un bassin de retenue utilisé par une compagnie minière suédoise fut fendu, déversant une marée noire corrosive le long de la rivière Guardiamar jusqu'en bordure du parc de Donana. Les produits chimiques que contenait la boue toxique (zinc, calinium, plomb, mercure et thalium) s'écoulait dans les marais entourant le parc et dans l'océan dans la zone de surf entre Huelva et Cadiz. La crise fut tellement sévère qu'elle justifia l'indignation de l'Europe entière, ce qui provoqua une vague de reproches honteux à l'égard des politiciens responsables. Personne ne sait combien d'autres entreprises dangereuses sont en train de menacer nos eaux et à part Greenpeace, il n'y a pas d'organisation surf de protection de l'environnement en Espagne. En dépit de cela, les derniers efforts d'assainissement du Pays basque (voir intro Pays Basque P†.179) nous laissent espérer pour l'avenir.

Le localisme

Tout comme partout dans le monde, le localisme est présent en Espagne: mais pas radicalement. Il n' y a pas de spots où les black shorts viennent vous virer de la plage, mais il y a tout de même quelques endroits où vous devez rester prudent. Le cas le plus représentatif est celui de Mundaka, la vague reine de l' Europe. Entre septembre et décembre, il y tellement de voyageurs internationaux que peut-être vous vous sentirez bien au line up, mais bientôt vous réaliserez qu' il est difficile de prendre une vague et que les locaux réclament l' exclusivité de la première section. Autre chose, en Cantabrie, il vaut mieux se garer discrètement sur des plages comme El Brusco, Liencres ou Los Locos et en Asturies, attention à Rodiles. Sinon le long du reste de la Côte, prenez vos habituelles précautions, mais en général les gens sont chaleureux et accueillants.

Tapia, Asturias

Travelling

Getting There

By air In the summer months, Bilbao airport, only 30 minutes' drive from Mundaka, is the best place to fly to. Within Europe, prices can be very cheap and car hire, if booked with your flight, is as reasonable as you'll find. If you want to get away from it all, Galicia's airport at Santiago de Compostela is not as cheap, but gives easy access to some of Spain's more beautiful surf spots. In winter Málaga is often a ridiculously cheap place to fly and can also be an economical way of starting a Moroccan surfari. Most long haul flights will arrive in Madrid, about 400km (240 mi) from the nearest surf. Be warned: Iberian Airways has a strict charge for surfboards – at nearly 15,000 pts its not cheap.

By sea One of the most relaxing ways of getting to Spain from Britain is by ferry. Brittany Ferries operates a service from Plymouth to Santander and P&O from Portsmouth to Bilbao, both twice weekly. It can be quite expensive and takes 24 hours, but drops you and your car at surf central. South Spain can be your springboard to Morocco or the Canaries, and although it's a long drive from the north, it's advantageous to have your own transport in either destination.

By foot The Christian pilgrimages to Santiago de Campostello were the subject of the first ever travel guide book, a Baedecker, which described the walking trails and routes that many suppliants performed on their knees, coming from as far afield as Ireland, Scotland and central Europe.

Getting Around

By car Spanish roads have improved over the last few years, but northern Spain is mountainous with windy, single lane roads that make journey times often a lot longer than expected, especially in summer. Most driving licenses are recognised, but you must have a green card from your insurers and a bail bond or extra legal cover on your travel policy. Car security is a nightmare in Spain: never leave posessions visible in a locked car where possible. Around the País Vasco (Euskadi), many road signs are in both Euskadi and Spanish, with the Spanish sprayed out on many – keep your map open!

By public transport If you choose this mode of travel, remember that half the fun of the journey is the journey itself, not the destination! Buses are the choice for short trips: there's a plethora of bus companies albeit no centralised service. For long trips trains are the best option: Spain's national railway RENFE is normally clean, punctual and reasonable. If you're there for a short while, buy the Tarjeta Turista which permits unmitigated travel for three to 10 days.

Accommodation Camping facilities, mainly open from May to October, are excellent everywhere, providing showers, sinks and toilets. At off-peak times, *pensiones* and *hostales* offer a basic room at a reasonable price, which you can haggle over. It's advisable to go and view the room and secure the price. Another alternative are the 165 Youth Hostels throughout the country. Their prices are cheap and often include breakfast.

Infos Voyage

Comment s'y Rendre

En avion Bilbao, à 1/2h de Mundaka, est la meilleure destination. Le prix des billets depuis une autre ville d'Europe peut être trés bon marché, et les locations de voiture, lorsque réservées avec le billet, sont raisonnables. Si vous souhaitez plus d'évasion, l'aéroport de St-Jacques de Compostelle en Galice est une destination plus onéreuse, mais à deux pas de certaines de plus belles vagues d'Espagne. Pourquoi ne pas en faire le point de départ d'un surfari au Maroc? La plupart des vols longs courriers arrivent à Madrid, à 400km de la première plage. Attention, emporter sa planche en Espagne coûte cher, environ 600 francs (et impossible de négocier). Bilbao est célèbre pour cela, mais apparement cela s'applique à tous les vols sur l'Espagne. Renseignez-vous auprès de votre agence de voyage.

En bateau C'est là une des façons les plus relaxantes de voyager. La traversée peut être un peu chère et durer 24h, mais avec une location de voiture à l'arrivée, vous êtes pile sur les spots! Du sud de l'Espagne, vous pouver embarquer pour le Maroc ou les Canaries et, même si la route est longue jusque là, avoir sa voiture ou son minibus là-bas est trés appréciable.

A pied Les pélérinages chrétiens à St Jacques de Compostelle furent le sujet des premiers guides de voyage, décrivant les sentiers et chemins que certains pelerins parcouraient à genoux depuis l'Irlande, l'Ecosse ou l'Europe Centrale!

Une fois sur Place

En voiture Si les routes espagnoles se sont beaucoup améliorées, les routes restent étroites et sinueuses, dans les montagnes du nord, rendent souvent les trajets plus longs que prévu, sourtout en été. Profitez du paysage, et soyez patients derrière les convois de camions qui parcourent ces routes jour et nuit. Sinon, vous pouvez toujours prendre l'autoroute mais c'est cher. L'Espagne n'est pas plus épargnée que les autres pays d'Europe en ce qui concerne les vols et effractions. Ne laissez rien de visible à l'interieur. Au Pays Basque, où les signalisations sont bilingues, les indications en Espagnol sont souvent taggées. Attention aux erreurs et... gardez votre Stormrider à portée de main.

Se loger Ouverts généralement de mai à octobre, les campings sont npmbreux et d'excellente qualité. Hors saison et lorsqu'il pleut trop, les "pensiones" offrent des chambres à des prix raisonnables. A part quelques hotels plutôt chers, Mundaka propose un camping ouvert toute l'année.

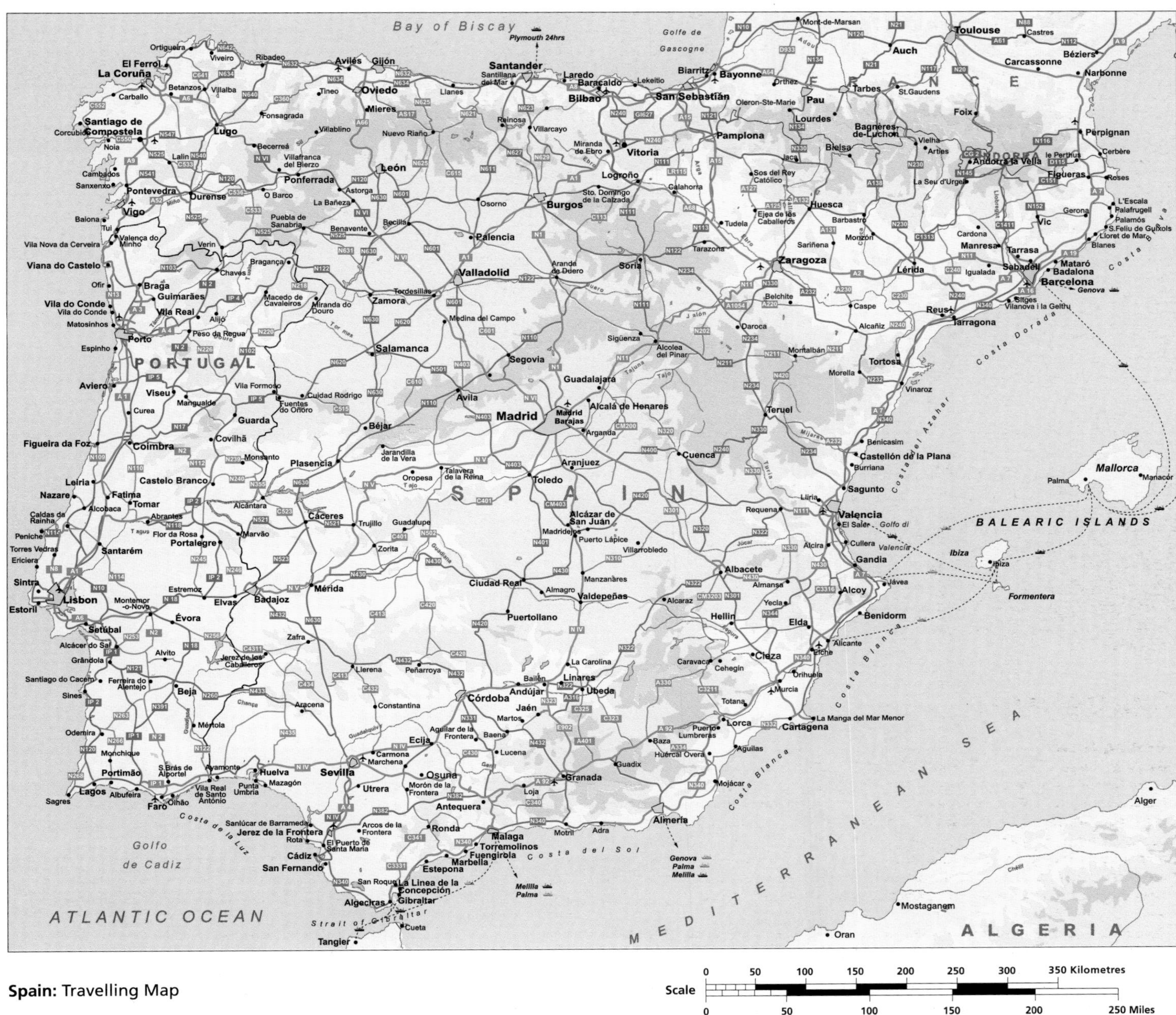

Spain: Travelling Map

Other Info

Visas

Passports required by US, Canadian, British, Australian and New Zealand citizens to remain for 90 days. South African citizens need a visa to enter Spanish territory.

Tourist Authority

Iniciativo de turismo or Informacio
Madrid: Tel: (1) 541 23 25

Telephone info

Country Code: 349
Dial Out Code: 07+ cc (on December 31, 1998 = 00+ cc)
Emergencies: 091 or 092
Operator
9198 – Europe
9191 – intercontinental
Directory Enquiries: 003

Travel

Ferries

Brittany Ferries, HQ: 0990 360 360 (Plymouth)
Santander: (4) 222 00 00
Transmediterrania Ferries, Barcelona: (3) 443 25 32
Run between Tangier, Morocco and Málaga, Gibraltar or Algeciras. Also service the Ballearic and Canary Islands.

Trains RENFE (National Rail System)

Barcelona: (3) 490 1122
Bilbao: (4) 423 86 23
Santander: (42) 28 02 02
Vigo: (86) 43 11 14
La Coruña: (81) 15 02 02

Buses

Only way to get to isolated areas. There's a multitude of private companies rather than a central national company. Viajes TIVE or bus windows will give you information. The one in Madrid at the Estación Sur de Autobuses is very useful.
ALSA: (1) 528 28 03 – Madrid, Galicia, Asturias.
Continental-Auto: (1) 356 23 07 – Madrid, País Vasco
PESA: (902) 10 12 10 – San Sebastian, Bilbao
Empresa Portillo: (56) 65 10 55 – Algeciras, Marbella, Málaga

Driving

Speed Limits

Built-up area: 50km/h (31m/h)
B roads: 90km/h (55 m/h)
Category: 100km/h (62m/h)
Motorways: 120km/h (74m/h)

Tolls

Motorway tolls: Between 100-2810 ptas
Very few motorways are toll free, mainly in the Barcelona and Madrid areas.

Petrol Prices

Unleaded 116.90 ptas/litre

Greencard/Bail Bonds

You'll need a greencard from your insurer and a bail bond is also worth having, as if you do have an accident, it'll be your fault, as a foreigner, regardless of the circumstances. Without a bail bond, you and your car will probably be locked up pending investigation. It's compulsory to carry replacement bulbs for headlights.

sunny garcia

A Change in Bilbao

Introduction

The decline of the steel mills and shipyards in the Basque Country during the 70s and 80s produced a deep economic recession and as a result the main source of income in Bizkaia disappeared, with resulting high unemployment. The Basque government realised that supporting big industry was simply throwing money away and that the local economy needed a radical change. Big factories located along the Bilbao river became redundant and the biggest steel factory in Spain, Altos Hornos de Vizcaya was reduced to a tenth of its former size, becoming a small, electric, competitive steel producer. The positive effect, however, of this reduction in industry has been that water tributaries have arrived at the coast a little bit cleaner.

To transform an economy based on steel into a service economy, the Basque Government centred its efforts on Bilbao. As the city of San Sebastian is already recognised by tourists worldwide for its beauty, the Government decided they needed to spread the wealth further west. Money was made available to build a bigger harbours and improve improve infrastructures like roads and railroads. Then came the Guggenheim Museum, one of the biggest and most ambitious projects that has transformed Bilbao's status into one of the capitals of Modern Art. The museum stands alongside other impressive new buildings like the Palace of Music and Congress, the bridge by Calatrava and the subway designed by Norman Foster.

Unfortunately there have already been casualties to the surf community. The enlarged Bilbao Harbour wall has already destroyed one surf spot (Freaga Beach). On a positive note one of the biggest parts of this process of development and beautification involves cleaning the water in Basque Country. The Government has already begun an ambitious campaign to build residual water collectors and purifying plants all along the coast. The first are working already making the water notably cleaner than they were 10 years ago. The project will be fully functioning by 2002 and finally Basque surfers can look forward to a future that includes improving rather than deteriorating water quality.

JAKUE ANDIKOETXEA

Petro No Protestors

AMEZAGA

Guggenheim museum

Burning Issue

Environmental efforts don't get an easy ride in Spain. Take, for example, a group of Basque surfers from Playa La Arena who organised a surf contest in protest against the oil spills from the petrol refinery located next to the beach. The local politicians went ballistic and began campaigning against the contest, turning local people against the organisers. It got so crazed that even some of the surfers from the local surf club decided not to support the contest because the petrol company that was polluting their waters sponsored another local surfing contest. Despite all the controversy, 'Petro-No' was a big success and the Basque Government eventually decided to remove the oil tanks for good. In 1998, surfers from Playa Sabon with the same problem tried to organise a second Petro-No contest, but finally gave up because of the opposition from the local population and institutions.

JAKUE ANDIKOETXEA

La Arena

Pays Basque

Le déclin des mines d'acier et des chantiers navals dans le pays basque durant les années 70 et 80 produisirent une récession économique, la principale source de revenus dans la province de Bizkaia a largement disparu à ce moment, ce qui provoqua un fort taux de chômage. Le gouvernement basque réalisa que de supporter cette lourde industrie équivalait tout simplement à jeter de l'argent par les fenêtres, et que l'économie locale nécessitait un changement radical. Les grosses usines qui étaient situées tout le long de la rivière de Bilbao disparurent et la plus grosse usine d'acier d'Espagne, Altos Hornos de Vizcaya fur réduit à un dixième de sa taille initiale, devenant une petite production d'acier moderne, électrique et compétitive.

Le premier effet positif de cette réduction industrielle fut que désormais les eaux de la rivière arrivèrent alors un peu plus propres sur les côtes.

Le concept économique était et reste encore: la volonté de transformer une économie basée sur l'acier en une économie de services. Le gouvernement basque concentra ses efforts sur Bilbao qui était à la fois bien situé et peu développé. De même que la ville de St-Sébastien est toujours reconnue par les touristes du monde entier pour sa beauté, il était nécessaire de faire de même plus loin à l'ouest. De l'argent a alors été débloqué pour construire un plus grand port et améliorer les infrastructures ferroviaires et routières. Vint alors le musée de Guggenheim, un des plus grands et ambitieux projets qui a transformé le statut de la ville de Bilbao en l'une des capitales de l'art moderne. Le musée se tient le long d'autres nouveaux immeubles impressionnants comme le palais des musiques et congrès, le pont de Calavetra et le métro de Norman Foster.

Malheureusement, ceux-ci ont déjà causé des dégradations. Les agrandissements des murs du port de Bilbao ont déjà détruit un spot de surf (la plage de Freaga). La note positive est que l'une des plus grosses parties de ce processus de développement et de réaménagement inclut l'assainissement de l'eau dans le Pays basque. Le gouvernement a déjà commencé cette ambitieuse campagne : de construire des collecteurs d'eaux usées et des points de purification tout au long de la côte. Le premier fonctionne déjà, ce qui rend l'eau sur certains spots beaucoup plus propre qu'il y a dix ans. Le projet sera pleinement achevé et fonctionnera à partir de 2002, et finalement les surfers basques peuvent envisager l'avenir tourné vers des améliorations plutôt que des détériorations de la qualité de l'eau.

Point chaud

Les efforts consacrés à l'environnement ne furent pas facilités en Espagne, comme en témoigne l'organisation d'une compétition par les surfers basques de la plage La Arena, en protestation contre les nappes de pétrole de la raffinerie située à proximité de la plage. Les politiciens locaux prirent position contre cette compétition en retournant la population locale contre les organisateurs. Cela devenait tellement confus que même quelques surfers locaux décidèrent de ne pas supporter cette compétition car la compagnie de pétrole qui polluait leurs eaux sponsorisaient d'autres événements locaux de surf qu'ils voulaient alors préserver. En dépit de toute cette polémique, Petro-No fut un vif succès et le gouvernement basque décida finalement d'enlever les réservoirs de pétrole pour de bon. En 1998, les surfers de la plage de Sabon qui connaissaient le même problème tentèrent d'organiser une deuxième Petro-No. Mais finalement, ils furent contraints d'abandonner à cause de l'opposition de la population locale et des institutions.

Pais Vasco

1. La Arena

Various peaks, best at high tide. Close by there is a petrol refinery, consequently the water is very polluted. There's parking at the beach, camping facilities and quite a few local surfers. Good atmosphere.

Des pics pas terribles meilleurs à marée haute. A proximité, une raffinerie de pétrole, imaginez donc la qualité de l'eau. Parking sur la plage, camping et quelques locaux. Endroit sympa malgré tout.

2. Playa de Ereaga

The jetty extension of the Superpuerto of Bilbao has definitely ruined this spot. It's only a shadow of the past. Water quality is very bad, but improving.

Cette plage plus fréquentée est situer au centre d'Algorta. Assez protégé, donc il faut un bon swell, genre tempête en hiver. On trouve une gauche sévère prés de la jetée alors que du côté est, c'est Jeffries, une droite qui peut casser à marée basse.

3. Punta Galea

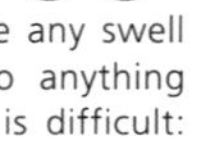

A long, perfect right point that can handle any swell size. It breaks very close to the cliffs so anything above 3m (9ft) is virtually suicide. Access is difficult: you have to walk down a dodgy dirt road or take a boat out.

Une droite longue et parfaite qui tient toutes les houles. Ca casse tout prés des cailloux et aprés 3 mètres, il faut être kamikaze. Trés difficile de sortir de l'eau et d'accéder au spot: sentier casse-gueule ou bateau...

4. Sopelana

4km (2.4mi) of coastline with dozens of peaks that pick up all swells. From W to E, there is Playa Salvaja (Batidora and La Triangular). The latter is consistent and can hold a 4m (12ft) swell. The Playa de Sopelana has two distinctive areas: Larrabasterra and Peña Txuri, which both offer good quality peaks up to 2m (6ft). Further on, there's a rocky cove called El Sitio where a good low tide left breaks up to 2.5m (8ft). This is a popular area to surf in summer, expect crowds and pollution.

4 kms de côtes avec une douzaine de pics qui chopent tous le swell. D'est en ouest, on trouve Playa Salvaje (Batidora et la Triangular, celui -ci pouvant tenir jusqu'à 4 m). La plage de Sopelana a 2 zones distinctes: Larrabastera et Peña Txuri qui donnent de bons pics jusqu'à 2 mètres. C'est la concentration de surfers la plus élevée en Espagne. Ensuite, on trouve El Sitio dans une crique qui peut casser à maére basse jusqu'à 2,5 m.

5. Meñakoz

One of the biggest, most powerful rights in Europe, holds waves up to 6m (18ft), which can break with exceptional violence. Access is by a dirt road with the last kilometre on foot.

Une des plus grosses et puissantes droites d'Europe, pas trés long mais qui casse avec une violence rare jusqu'à 6 mètres! Un gros rochers au milieu, qui en a fait flipper plus d'un. L'accés est délicat par un chemin de terre puis un sentier d'1 km.

JAKUE ANDIKOETXEA

Meñakoz

6. Bakio/Baquio

Good quality consistent peaks which can become crowded with local crew. Park next to the beach. The water quality has improved over the last few years.

Plage avec de bons pics et plein de locaux à respecter; On se gare prés de la plage. Quand tout va bien, l'eau est correcte.

7. Mundaka/Mundaca

Some of the longest, hollowest lefts in Europe. break over sandbanks at the mouth of the river Gernike. It's best at low tide, when the rivers current (a useful conveyor belt) is less intense, and holds swell up to 4m (12ft). On the other side of the rivermouth are the beaches of Laida and Laga where you can find waves in small swells. The river and its estuary are a Worldwide Fund for Nature reserve, but even so, the water is not as clean as could be expected.

Plus tellement de secrets à dévoiler. La gauche la plus longue et la plus creuse en Europe qui casse sur un banc de sable formé par la Gernika. Marche mieux à marée basse montante jusqu'à 4 mètres. De l'autre côté, on trouve les plages de Laïda et Laga où ça surfe quand Mundaka est flat (souvent). La rivière et son estuaire est au patrimoine écologique de l'UNESCO, c'est donc un monument de propreté et de limpidité. Evitez les jours de pointes, c'est chaud.

8. Ogeia/Oguella

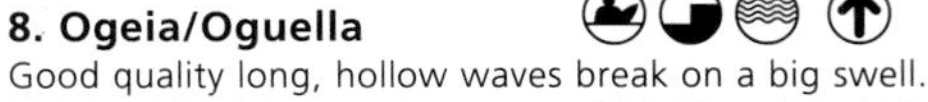

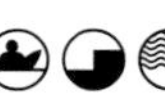

Good quality long, hollow waves break on a big swell. Fortunately plans to create an artificial beach, which would have made the waves disappear, have been put on hold.

De bonnes gauches longues qui cassent par gros swell. Malheureusement, on y veut y construire une plage artificielle qui feraient disparaître les vagues.

9. Zumaia/Zumaya

In front of the new jetty that forms the entrance to the port, there's a right which can hold a substantial swell.

En face de la nouvelle jetée qui ferme le port, y'a une droite qui tient le gros.

10. Orrua

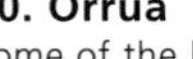

Some of the biggest, gnarliest rights in the País Vasco. Locally known as Roca Puta (Whore Rock), it breaks over rocks and can hold a solid 6m (18ft) swell. As with Ogeia, a project to build another breakwater has been put on hold.

Orrua, alias Roca Puta, une des meilleures droites du Pays Basque, qui casse dangeureusement sur des cailloux qui se surfe jusqu'à 6m. Une construction de jetée en projet à laquelle les surfers s'opposent.

JAKUE ANDIKOETXEA

Mundaka

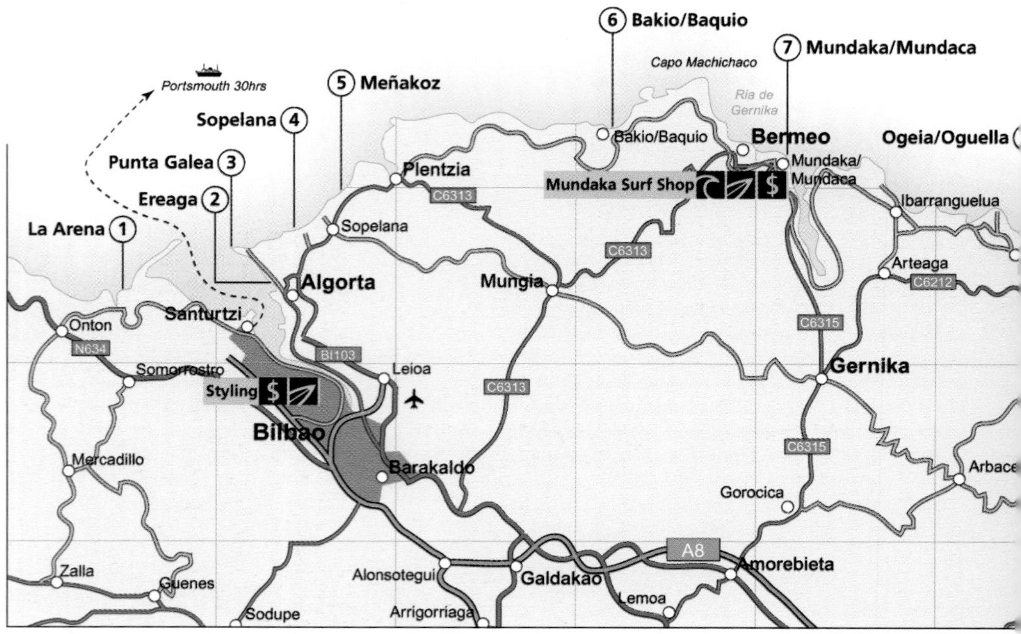

11. Zarautz

The most popular beach town in Gipuzkoa (and occasional ASP venue) has a variety of peaks, which are all the better at high tide. The lights of the streets and bars illuminate the beach at night allowing you to surf. A polluted spot.

La plage la plus célèbre du Gipuzkoa site de compétitions internationales avec des pics meilleurs à marée haute; Les loupiotes des rues et des bars permettent de surfer la nuit. L'eau est gerbique.

12. Orio

There's a little beach situated next to the River Orio. When the swell is up, a peak may break into the rivermouth at low tide. The wave is visible from the motorway.

Une petite plage située à côté de l'Orio. Marche parfois à marée basse quand c'est gros. Visible depuis l'autoroute.

13. Concha/Ondarreta

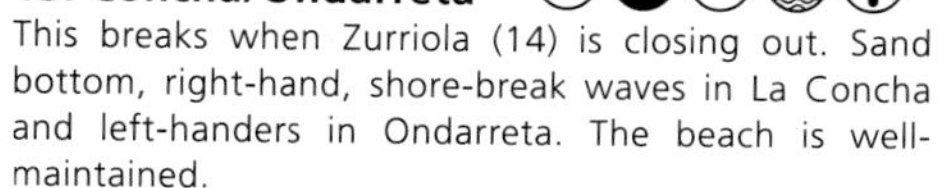

This breaks when Zurriola (14) is closing out. Sand bottom, right-hand, shore-break waves in La Concha and left-handers in Ondarreta. The beach is well-maintained.

Quand ça ferme à Gros, venez checker ici pour y trouver peut-être des droites de sable à la Concha et des gauches à Ondaretta. La plage est bien tenue.

14. Zurriola

This beach used to be called Playa de Gros. It has suffered several changes and the sandbars are different but it still has good quality shore-break waves. The water is polluted due to its proximity to the river.

La plage la plus surfée de San Sebastian avec des vagues de shore-break sur fond de sable. Sur la gauche, il n'y a plus de vagues à cause de la jetée construite en 94. L'eau est carrément polluée par la rivière toute proche.

F. MUÑOZ

Zurriola (Playa de Gros)

JAKUE ANDIKOETXEA

Orrua (Roca Puta)

F. MUNOZ

Un-named big wave right

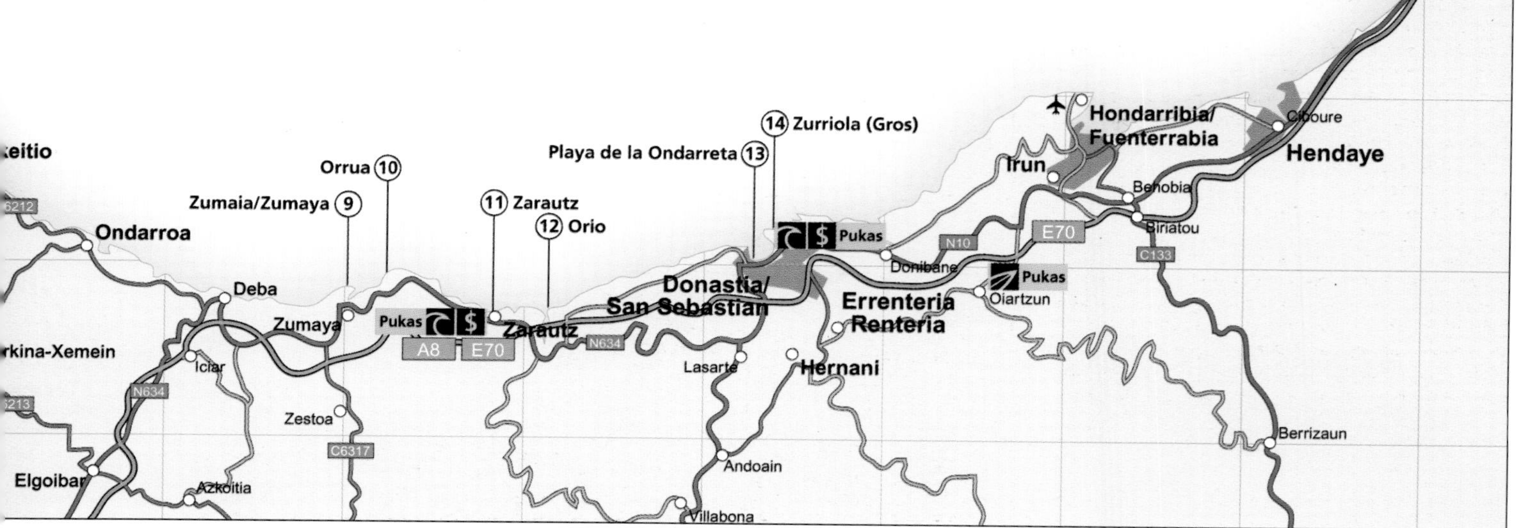

Cantabria

JAKUE ANDIKOETXEA

Pablo Solar

1. Playa de Meron

On the E side of the river is a very good sandbank. The left is generally better, being a longer faster ride which can tube, especially at low tide, with an energy-saving channel to the left of the peak. Playa de Meron gets quite busy with a lot of surfers staying for the weekend in the campsite right next to the beach. There's also a rivermouth wave but it only breaks in a heavy swell.

Du côté est de la rivière se trouve un bon banc de sable. La gauche est en général meilleure étant plus rapide avec de sections à tubes surtout à marée basse avec un channel remonte-vagues à gauche du pic. Meron s'agite pas mal le week-end sur un camping directement sur la plage. Aussi une vague de rivière qui ne casse qua quand c'est gros.

2. Playa de Oyambre

Facing E, this beach holds W and NW winds and big winter swells at its W end (near Cabo de Oyambre). This area is a nature reserve and it's usually uncrowded.

Le gros avantage, c'est que ç'est exposé SE et que ça chope quand même de la houle: bonne alternative à San Vicente sauf que peu de surfers viennent ici. A Oyambre, vers la rivière, y'a un petit peu plus de houle. L'eau est impeccable.

3. Los Locos

One of Spain's best beach breaks! Catch it on a clean 2m (6ft) swell and you'll see why. When the swell reaches 1.5m (4.5ft), sometimes a right-hand sand point E of the beach breaks off the rocks giving hollow, fast waves. Naturally it's popular and is the only beach in summer that's well situated for the dominating winds that come from the NE. At high tide the beach is covered and waves will only break in a large swell. Pretty good water quality.

Un des meilleurs beach-breaks d'Espagne: chopez 2 mètres propres et vous verrez pourquoi. A 1,5m, une droite creuse et rapide à l'est de la baie. A l'évidence, y'a foule surtout si c'est la seule plage qui marche, la seule bien située par vents de NE. Ne marche à marée haute que par gros swell. Plutôt propre.

JAKUE ANDIKOETXEA

Oscar Ruíz, Los Locos

4. Playa de Concha

A large headland offers decent protection from the winds without blocking out all the swell and is best at mid tide. At low tide a sandbar is formed in the rivermouth of San Martín, but surfers need to go in with anti-contamination equipment as the water gets badly polluted with all sorts of industrial residues.

Une tête rocheuse protège des vents sans trop filtrer la houle. Mieux à mi-marée. Du monde et une eau agrémentée de déchets industriels. A marée basse, un banc s'expose à la sortie de la San Martin: pour ceux que la reconstitution d'une marée noire intéresse...

5. Liencres Area

The coast around Liencres offers a number of good rights and lefts, sand and rock reef breaks. The area faces W to NW and consequently picks up a lot of swell, with different peaks breaking throughout the tides. Along with Los Locos, this is the most consistent spot in Cantabria. The long beach is separated in the E area into various sections by rocks. The E coves usually have the best peaks, but the W beach is worth a look, especially the rivermouth at low tide.

La côte offre ici une belle palette de droites et de gauches, sur fond de sable et rochers. La zone regarde de l'ouest au nord-ouest et chope un max de houle à toutes les marées. Avec Los Locos, c'est le plus consistent de toute la Cantabrie. Cette longue plage est scindée dans sa partie ouest par des rochers. A marée haute, vous y trouverez les meilleurs pics avec du monde dessus. Y'a plus de taille sur l'ouest, idéal aux marées plus basses avec des vents de sud. L'eau est propre.

6. Playa del Sardinero

In a big swell, with strong SW or W winds, Sardinero can be a worthwhile spot to check out. Otherwise it's very miss-able. A far better idea is to make the short trip to the breaks E or W of Santander. In summer it's forbidden to surf and it is difficult to even find a place to lay down a towel.

Par grosse houle, avec forts vents de S/S-O, Sardinero peut soulever un petit quelque chose mais attention aux déceptions. Allez plutôt voir ailleurs, surf interdit l'été où les grande serviettes ne trouvent pas toujours de la place sur le sable. C'est là que le surf a commencé en Espagne.

7. Playa de Somo

Because of its proximity to Santander and with a ferry over the river every 20 minutes, this beach draws the most surfers in all of Cantabria. Nevertheless, the waves are good and incidents in the water are rare.

Des vagues régulières et des paquets de surfers de Santander qui débarquent aussi par le ferry (toutes les 20 mn). Ca se passe bien à en croire les locaux, surtout en hiver.

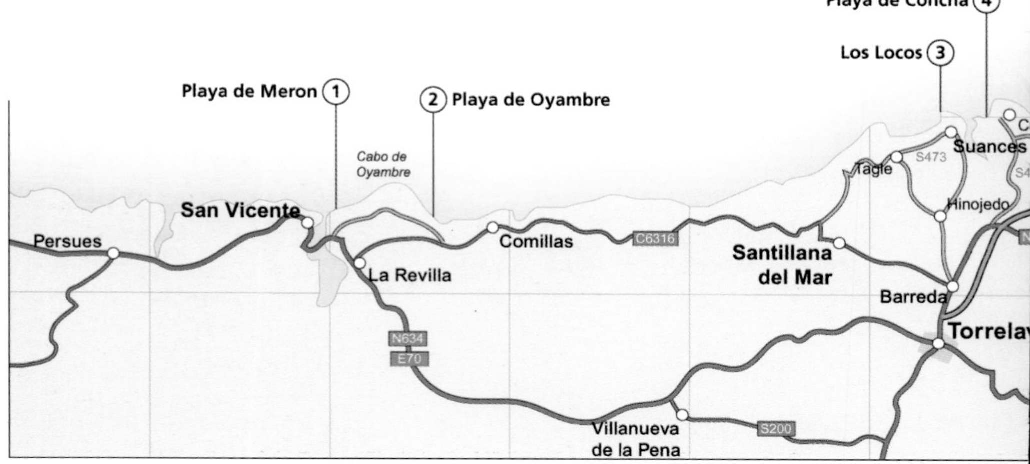

JAKUE ANDIKOETXEA

Gontzal Mendiola, Laredo

8. Playa de Langre

A path leads to the centre of the beach down cliffs which protect the surf from W and NW winds. The setting for surfing here is impressive. A good left breaks at the centre of the beach and it's best from low to mid tide up to 2m (6ft). Good water quality.

Des falaises escarpées protègent des vents de O/N-O, avec un sentier qui descend vers le milieu de la plage. Cadre imposant avec une bonne gauche au centre jusqu'à 2 mètres de marée basse à mi-marée. Eau limpide.

9. Galizano

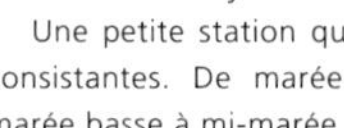

In the tiny village of Galizano you can find three different breaks in two small coves with a point between them. There are always waves but quality days are few. It holds NE winds. Usually uncrowded.

On peut trouver trois spots près du petit village de Galizano: deux criques et un 'point'. Les vagues y sont consistantes et sans monde mais ça ne casse pas souvent bien. Tient les vents de NO.

10. Playa de Ajo

Ajo beach and the nearby cove of Antuerta provide good, powerful peaks. The sandbanks shift a lot, but there are always waves.

Une petite station qui bouge en été avec des vagues assez consistantes. De marée basse à mi-marée consistentes. De marée basse à mi-marée. Checker la crique d'Antverta à côté.

11. Playa del Ris

The best wave is a peak that breaks left and right at high tide. It's a fun wave that tends to get crowded as it's located in the touristy village of Noja.

La meilleure vague est un pic droite-gauche qui se forme à marée haute. C'est une vague amusante et assez fréquentée. Situé à Noja.

12. El Brusco

Excellent beach break with tubey peaks and perfect walls. From the parking area nearby the waves always look much smaller than they are. It works up to 3m (9ft), but is perfect at 1-2m (3-6ft).

Un excellent beachbreak avec des pics tubulaires et de bons murs. Depuis le parking, on a l'impression que les vagues sont petites mais vous êtes à 400m du pic. Peut atteindre 3m.

JAKUE ANDIKOETXEA

John Mills, El Brusco

13. Playa de Berria

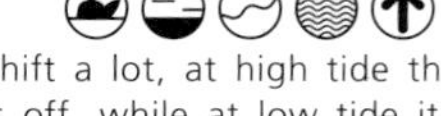

Although the sandbanks shift a lot, at high tide the central area normally goes off, while at low tide it's the ends of the beach that work.

Bien que les bancs bougent beaucoup, normalement la partie centrale envoie le pâté à marée haute tandis qu'à marée basse, ça marche mieux aus extrémités.

14. Playa de Laredo

A good place to check out in a big N swell. It's mainly a winter spot with the best peaks usually around the centre of the beach. Howling winds from the W and NW are no problem here. Other breaks in the bay are worth a look.

Un endroit à checker quand la houle rentre épaisse de nord, surtout en hiver avec les meilleurs pics souvent au milieu de la plage. Pas de problèmes pour les grands vents de N-O/O. Il y a aussi d' autres spots dans la baie.

15. Playa de Oriñon

This is more protected against strong winds than Arenillas and has an excellent left that needs a big swell to work properly.

Plus protégé des vents qu'Arenillas mais nécessite un plus gros swell. Une super gauche dans un cadre dantesque.

16. Playa de Arenillas

A weak but fun wave that can handle a light NW wind. Close to the rocks there's a current (useful for experienced surfers, dangerous for beginners) that helps you get out the back.

Une vague molle qui supporte de légers vents de NO. Prés des rochers, il y a un courant quipeut vous aider à passer au fond, si tenté que vous sachiez vous en sortir.

Asturias

Salinas y Espartal

1. Playa de Peñarronda

Choose between here and Tapia because when the conditions are right for one, they're not for the other.

Comparez avec Tapia, normalement y'a toujours un spot qui marche sur les deux.

2. Tapia de Casariego

This lovely fishing village has an excellent small beach with fun waves. It's here that some of the first surfing took place in Asturias and there's still a small but dedicated surfing population. There are two spots: a beach giving rights and lefts and a rock reef on the W side of the bay. The reef breaks as a left and is best from 1.5-2.5m (4-8ft) at mid tide. The water is clean.

Ce charmant village de pêcheurs possède une super plage avec de bonnes vagues qui accueille parfois une épreuve EPSA. Un des berceaux du surf en Asturies et il reste une petite population de surfers cool. 2 spots: le beach-break correct et une gauche de reef à l'ouest de la baie de 1,5m à 2,5m à mi-marée. Pas de problème avec l'eau.

3. Navia

A sandbar gives excellent rights and lefts in the middle of the beach and holds a good swell. To the E a point named El Moro produces a good right that works on all tides. It's badly polluted.

Au milieu de la plage, un bon banc de sable avec de super gauches et droites qui ne saturent pas toujours quand c'est gros. Sur la droite, y'a un Point 'El Moro' qui est une droite respectable qui marche à toutes les marées. Méga-pollué.

4. Playa de Frejulfe

A little village set amongst wild surroundings with a beach that has powerful, hollow waves and no crowds. Unfortunately it's badly affected by pollution from Navia. There are plans to make it a nature reserve so it could improve.

Un petit village dans un environnement sauvage avec des vagues creuses et puissantes, sans monde. Le hic vient de Navia qui pollue à fond. Un projet est dans l'air pour en faire une réserve naturelle, à suivre...

5. Playa de Otur

A sheltered beach break best in spring and autumn.

Un beach-break peinard, abrité plutôt en mi-saison.

6. Playa de Cueva

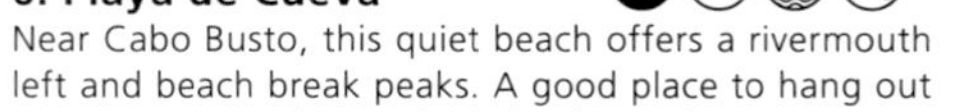

Near Cabo Busto, this quiet beach offers a rivermouth left and beach break peaks. A good place to hang out in a campervan due to the lack of crowds.

Pas loins de Cabo Busto, cette plage tranquille offre une gauche a la bouche de la riviere et des beach break pics. Bonne place pour squatter en break pour raison de manque de foule.

7. Playon de Bayas

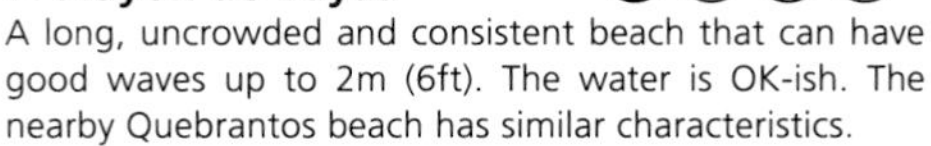

A long, uncrowded and consistent beach that can have good waves up to 2m (6ft). The water is OK-ish. The nearby Quebrantos beach has similar characteristics.

Une longue plage consistante sans monde qui marche bien jusqu'à 2m. L'eau y est propre.

8. Salinas y Espartal

A popular beach. To the right, in Espartal, there's a breakwater that forms a decent sandbank. Powerful rights with hollow sections break at low tide, while at high tide left peaks form. The best winds are from the SE. Towards Salinas, there's an abundance of peaks with good quality waves. Owing to its length, the beach picks up all types of wind and swell, so depending on the conditions, there is always something to choose from, and because of this it draws the crowds. Polluted water.

Plage très courue avec une bonne ambiance. Du côté droit, à Espartal, y'a une jetée qui favorise la formation de droites puissantes avec des sections creuses à marée basse, alors qu'à marée haute c'est plutôt une gauche. Mieux par vents de NE. En poussant vers Salinas, une bonne moisson de pics est à attendre. La forme et la taille de la plage permettent presque toutes les conditions de vent et de houle. Ca tient bien la taille mais vu la proximité des zones urbaines, ça se bouscule parfois et l'eau est pas terrible.

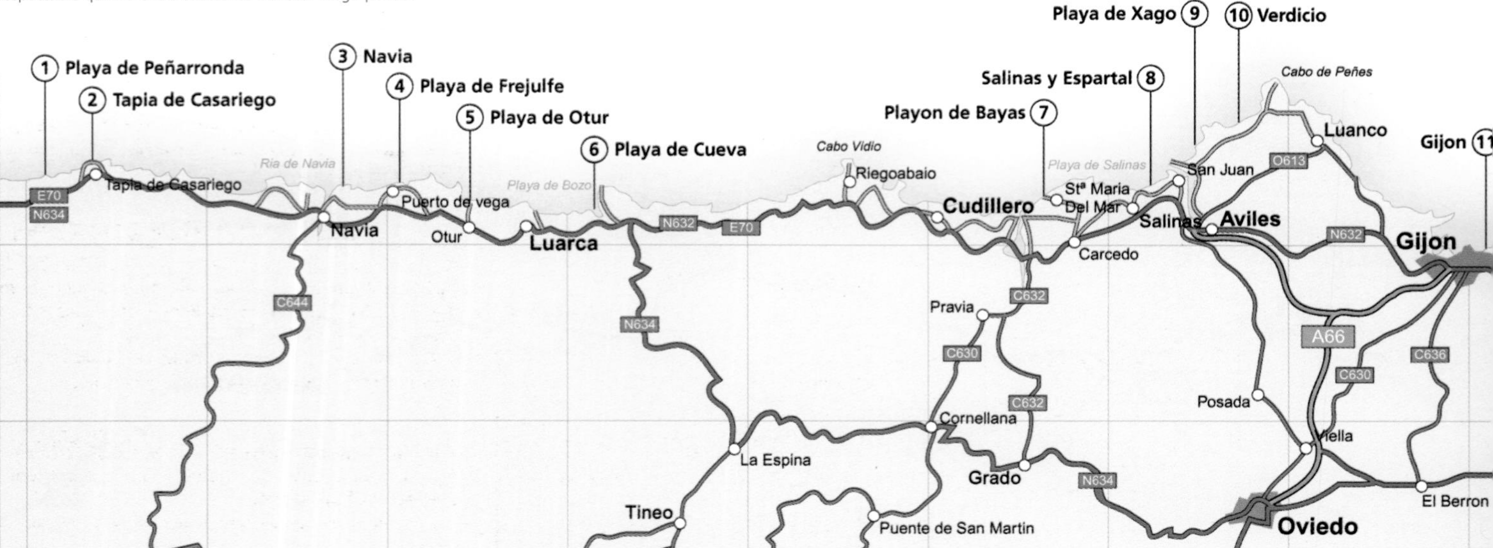

9. Playa de Xagó

As it's exposed and works well with very small swells, this is a sure choice for the summer season. It gets crowded because of its proximity to the nucleus of surfers in Aviles and Salinas.

Une plage destinée aux sessions d'été parce que très exposée. Marche avec très peu de houle, pas mal de monde car proche des noyaux de surfers d'Aviles et Salinas.

F. MUÑOZ

Cocó Carril, Xagó

10. Verdicio

An attractive spot with hollow waves in the right conditions. The small beach town is quiet and mellow.

Spot attrayant avec de bonnes vagues creuses dans les bonnes conditions. Le petit village est tranquille.

11. Gijón
Playa de San Lorenzo

Since it's a city beach, there's always a load of people here. At low tide there can be good rights over a sand and rock bottom.

La plage la plus peuplée puisqu'en plein centre ville. A marée basse, sur la droite, on peut trouver de bonnes droites sur fond de sable et rochers.

F. MUÑOZ

Dani García, Salinas

F. MUÑOZ

Rodiles

P. CADE

Rodiles' take-off

El Mongol

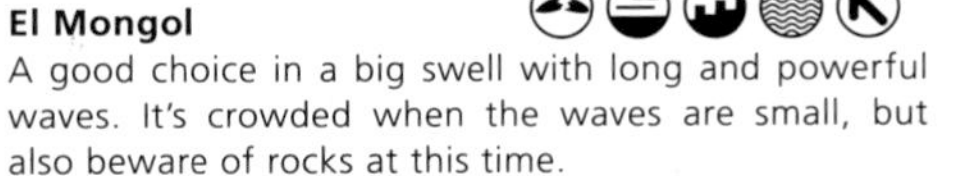

A good choice in a big swell with long and powerful waves. It's crowded when the waves are small, but also beware of rocks at this time.

L'option gros swell: vague longue et puissante. Moins de monde quand c'est gros. Attention aux cailloux!

Peñarrubia

On the E outskirts of Gijón you'll find a boulder and sand beach that holds a big swell. There's easy parking by all three beaches.

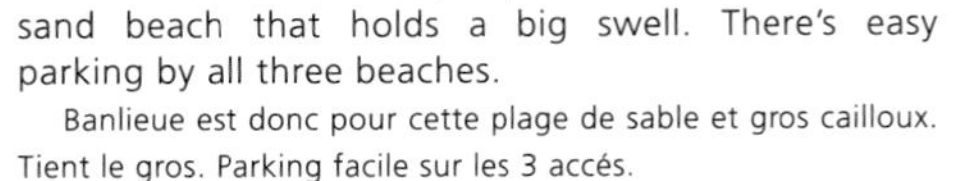

Banlieue est donc pour cette plage de sable et gros cailloux. Tient le gros. Parking facile sur les 3 accès.

12. Playa de España

AsO it's close by to Gijón, this beach draws in the surfers, but it's a pretty setting and has some lively waves that are best around mid tide.

Comme c'est prés de Gijon, y'a foule sur cette plage sympa avec des bonnes vagues vers la mi-marée.

13. Rodiles

There's a wave at the rivermouth of Villaviciosa. To the W of the beach a sandbank gives some perfect lefts, and at high tide on the E side of the beach, there are lovely peaks, but the rights are usually better. It's the most famed spot in Asturias and because of this, there is a 'localism' factor to contend with. The place is a paradise and, when conditions are perfect, it can even be hallucinogenic. Fun camping, bars and the like. Rodiles is a nature reserve and the water is kept clean.

Par bonne houle, une super gauche tubulaire d'abord à la sortie de la Villaviciosa, à l'ouest de la plage: plus la marée est basse, mieux c'est. A marée haute de l'autre côté, on trouve un beach break correct avec plutôt des droites. C'est LE SPOT des asturies donc vous ne serez pas seul, les locaux sont chauds. Trois campings, des bars, une réserve naturelle, une eau limpide: un petit paradis, quoi!

14. Playa de Vega

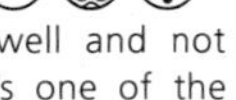

There are sizeable waves in a small swell and not many surfers here. On the bad side it's one of the most polluted beaches on the Asturian coast due to the little creek that flows into it which is used to wash out fluorite from the mines upstream. Bad news.

Bonnes vagues par petit swell avec de rares surfers. Une des plages les plus polluées des Asturies, à cause de la petite crique qui s'y jette. L'eau est en contact avec du fluor qui descend des mines en amont. Gargl!

15. Ribadesella

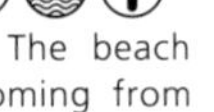

A fishing village, popular with tourists. The beach sheltered from all winds except those coming from the N. With a local surfing tradition, you'll always find people in the water.

Petit village de pêcheurs bien touristique. A l'abri de tous les vents sauf ceux de nord, toujours quelques surfers ici.

16. Playa de San Antolin

An uncrowded spot that holds a big swell. There's easy views of the waves.

Spot peu fréquenté qui tient le gros. Vues rapides sur les vagues.

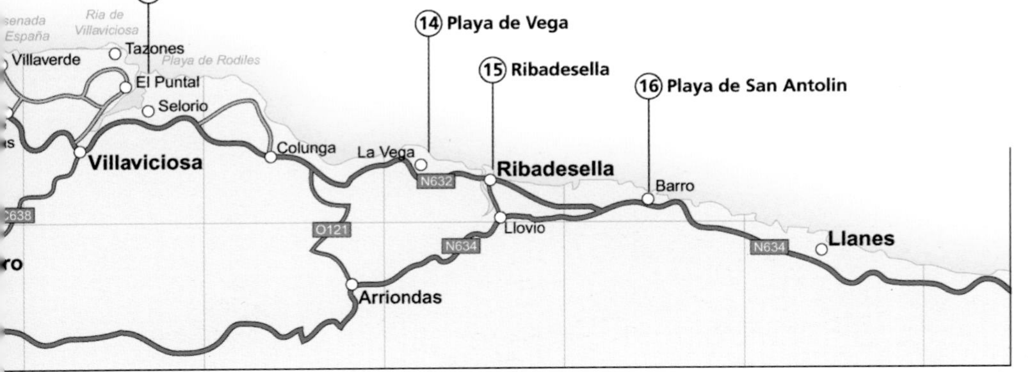

Galicia

1. Patos

Patos has some awesome reefs. At the S end, a point breaks both rights and left. In the centre of the beach a reasonable right breaks over rock. To the N another right breaks over a rocky ledge. The first two spots are only safely surfed at high tide and the third is best at mid tide. All break in a big NW swell and need S to W winds. The water is often polluted to the S of the bay.

Une kyrielle de super reefs. A gauche, une pointe rocheuse envoie d'excellentes droites et gauches. Au centre de la plage, une bonne droite sur fond rocheux. Complètement à droite, une 3° droite casse correctement sur une corniche caillouteuse. Les deux premiers spots ne sont inoffensifs qu'à marée haute, le troisième est idéal à mi-marée. Toutes ces vagues ne marchent que par gros NO avec des vents de sud ou d'ouest. A gauche, ça peut être pollué.

2. Playa de Lanzada

A beautiful bay more popular with windsurfers, but it only produces waves on large swells.

Superbe baie, très populaire parmi les windsurfers, qui ne marche quand ça cartonne au large.

3. Playa de Ladeira

Head here when NW swells are closing out of the beaches on the N shore of this peninsula. Otherwise, this beach needs a W or SW swell.

Venez ici quand un bon swell de NO fait fermer les plages sur la partie nord de la péninsule. Sinon, il faut un swell normal d'ouest ou de sud-ouest.

4. Playa de Rio Sieira

A fairly consistent break situated in some of Galica's more remote countryside. Crowds here are non-existent and the water quality is as clean as you'll find anywhere on Europe's Atlantic coast.

ment consistant situé dans la campagne, une des plus reculées de Galice. Envoyez-nous une carte si vous surfez à plus de 20.

5. Playas de Louro/Lariño

Both these beaches work best on a W or SW swell and are only surfable up to 1.5m (4.5ft). Louro is the most surfed of the two. Both can be seen from the road.

Ces plages marchent idéalement par houle d'ouest ou de sud-ouest et sont seulement surfables jusqu' à 1,5m. Louro est le plus surfé des deux, tous les deux sont visibles depuis la route.

F. MUNOZ

Dave Malherbe, Doniños

6. Nemiña

This is a beautiful, uncrowded remote area. There is a left rivermouth and a bèach break. When it's on, it's all for you. All the area near Cabo Finisterre has a multitude of spots.

Ceci est une location belle, tranquille, et lointaine. Il y a une bouche de riviere gauchiere et un beach break. Quand cest allume ...cest tout pour toit. toute la region pres de Cabo Finistre a une multitudes de spots.

7. Playa de Traba

With a good clean NW swell you can find tubey surf here. There are a number of dirt tracks leading to the beach. Water quality is excellent.

Avec une houle décente et propre de NO, on peut trouver des tubes ici. On trouve bon nombre de chemins de terre qui vont jusqu'à la plage.

8. Malpica

This is best at mid tide up to 2m (6ft). Few crowds appear here, although in summer you may find a handful of travellers due to the good waves and the pleasant surroundings. Good water quality.

Mieux à mi-marée jusqu'à deux mètres. C'est rare de voir la foule ici bien qu'on trouve des voyageurs en été attirés par les vagues sympas et le décor grandiose.

9. Playa de Razo

Consistent beach waves, no crowds, but this beach is exposed to N and NW winds that are common and often strong.

Vagues de beach break consistantes sans monde. Exposée aux vents de N/N-O qui sont réguliers et souvent forts.

10. Caión (Cayon)

A small beach, relentlessly pounded by Atlantic swells, is best from mid to high tide. Good water quality.

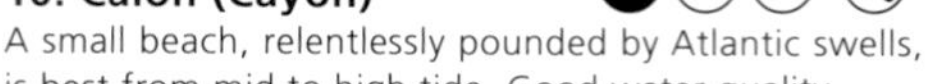

Une petite plage qui est sans cesse battue par le houles de l'Atlantique, mieux de mi-amrée à marée haute. La qualité de l'eau est bonne.

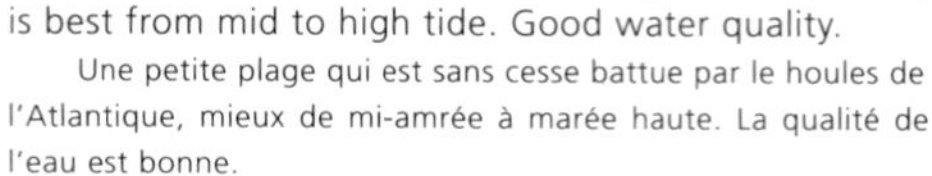

11. Barrañan

A long beach which picks up most swells. Watch out for rocks inconveniently placed along the beach.

Une longue plage qui chope la plupart des houles. Attention aux rochers au large de la plage.

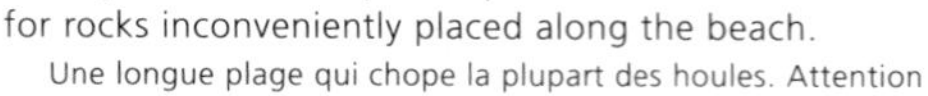

12. Sabón

A highly-regarded beach with rideable waves when everywhere else is flat. However, the water quality is generally poor, so only surf here if it's going off.

Hautement considérée par les surfers Galiciens mais à cause de la pollution du polygone industriel, on ne vous conseille de venir surfer ici que si il n'y a rien de mieux ailleurs. Malheureusement, c'est souvent le cas parce que cette plage reçoit trés bien la houle.

13. Riazor/Orzan

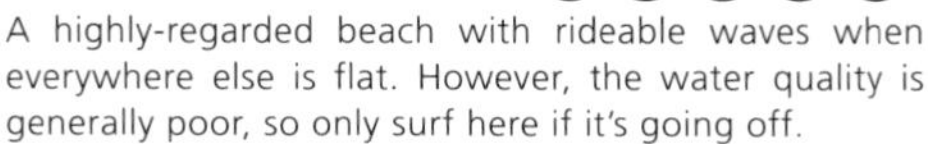

A couple of mediocre breaks: a left in the middle of the beach works best from 1-2m (2-6ft) at low tide, and a rock reef gives a right at mid tide. Being town breaks, both get crowded and the water quality is usually very poor.

Deux breaks médiocres: une gauche au milieu de la plage qui marche mieux de 50 cms à 2ms à marée basse et un reef qui envoie une droite à mi-marée. Comme c'est en ville, attendez vous à trouver sur ces 2 spots du monde et une eau dégueu.

F. MUNOZ

Orzan, A Coruña

14. Doniños

Consistent tubey waves here are best surfed from low to mid tide. Two access points: N and S, with the N end nearly always the best. One of Galicia's most popular spots.

Vagues consistentes et tubulaires meilleures de marée basse à mi-marée . Deux accès, dont celui du nord est presque toujours le meilleur. Un des spots les plus connus en Galice.

15. Playa de San Jorge

The S end of this sweeping bay is the place to head for when Doniños is blown out by S winds. From low to mid tide there can be an excellent left breaking over a sand bottom with a useful channel near the rocks. The rest of the bay can also have decent waves (especially the N end) on big swells when Doniños and the left are closing out.

L'extrémité sud de cette baie profonde est l'endoit où il faut aller quand Doninõs est gavée de vents de sud. De marée basse à mi-marée, il peut y avoir une super gauche qui casse sur du sable avec un chenal prés des rochers. Le reste de la baie peut aussi avoir de bonnes vagues (surtout au nord) par grosse houle, quand Doniños sature et que la gauche ferme.

16. Campelo

One of Galicia's best spots and undoubtedly one of its most beautiful with excellent surf that can be crowded in summer. Excellent water quality.

Un des meilleurs spot de Galice et sans doute un des plus beaux, avec des vagues remarquables qui peuvent saturer en été.

17. Valdoviño (Frouxeira)

Check when the surrounding beaches are flat. Frouxeira is a 2km (1.2mi) curving beach with three access points, and is easiest to approach from the N.

Un bon spot à checker quand tout le reste est plat. Frouxeira est une plage en croissant de 2 kms. 3 accés principaux, plus facile au nord.

18. Pantín

Pantín picks up a lot of swell and has some of the best beach waves in Galicia. A channel to the right of the beach through the rocks will take you out to the best peaks. Decent waves make it a popular competition venue and also a hit with local and visiting surfers. Water quality is excellent.

Pantin reçoit très bien la houle avec certaines des meilleures vagues de sable de Galice. Un chenal à droite de la plage vous amènera à travers les rochers vers les meilleurs pics. La qualité des vagues en fait un carrefour pour les compétiteurs et les voyageurs.

JAKUE ANDIKOETXEA

Pantin

19. Foz Area

A number of good beaches: Playa de Barreiros, Playa de Rapadoira and Playa de Peizas are all within easy access and happen on small swells. A lively area in summer with lively bars, restaurants and good campgrounds (therefore crowded peaks). Water quality is variable.

Toute une série de beach-breaks. Les plages de Barreiros, de Rapadoira sont d'accés facile et marchent aussi par petite houle; si ça grossit allez vers l'ouest à la plage de Peizas. Un endroit animé en été avec des bars, des restaurants et des campings (où les vagues récupèrent la foule). L'eau est variable.

20. Playa Reinante

Playa Reinante and the beaches to the W produce many empty peaks. A coast road provides ocean vantage points.

Playa Reinante et les plages à l'ouest ont plein de pics vierges. De bonnes vues sur l'océan depuis la route côtière.

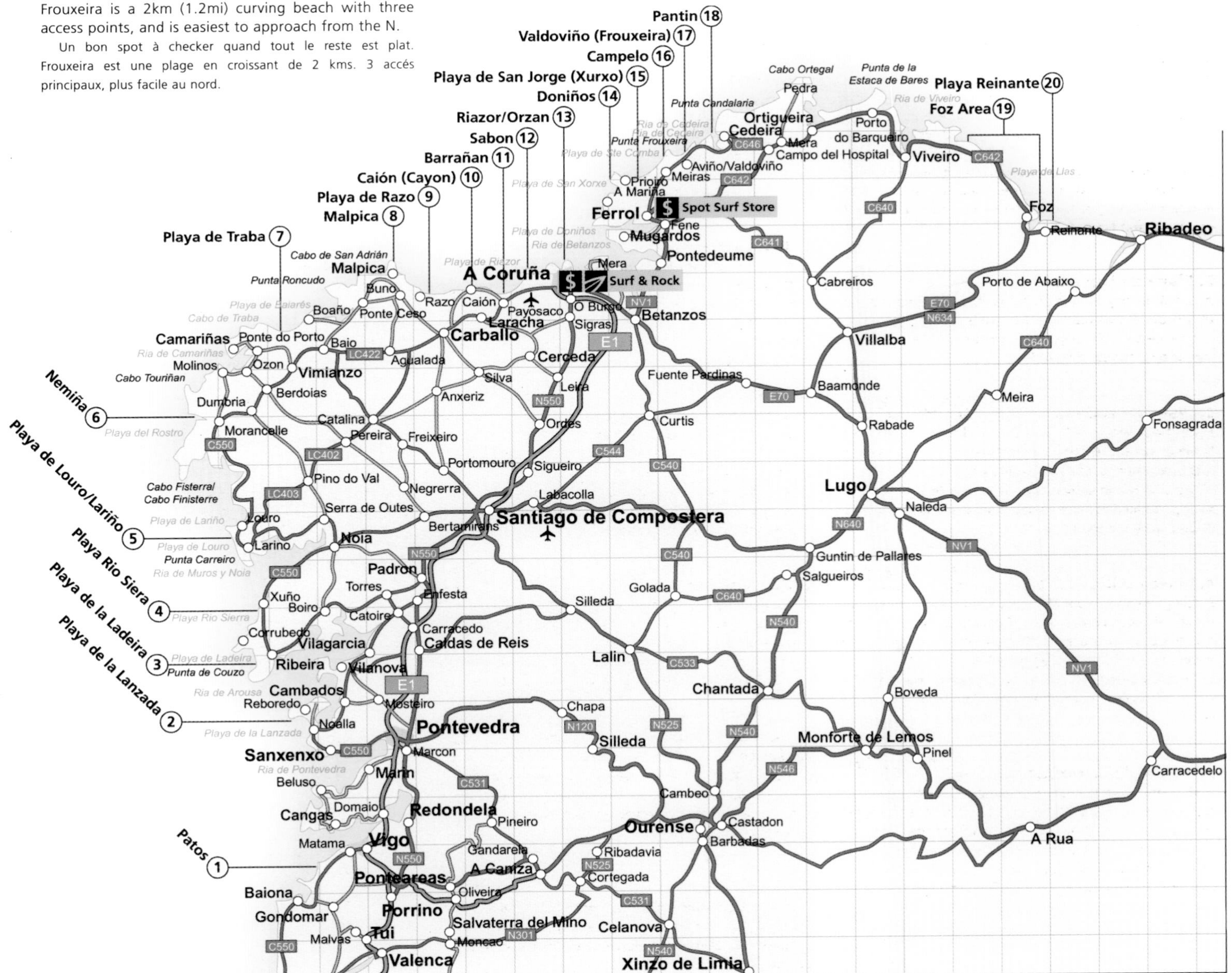

Pantin (18)
Valdoviño (Frouxeira) (17)
Campelo (16)
Playa de San Jorge (Xurxo) (15)
Doniños (14)
Riazor/Orzan (13)
Sabon (12)
Barrañan (11)
Caión (Cayon) (10)
Playa de Razo (9)
Malpica (8)
Playa de Traba (7)
Nemiña (6)
Playa de Louro/Lariño (5)
Playa Rio Siera (4)
Playa de la Ladeira (3)
Playa de la Lanzada (2)
Patos (1)
Playa Reinante (20)
Foz Area (19)
Spot Surf Store
Surf & Rock

Andalucia

1. Cádiz

The city of Cádiz is built along an extensive peninsula. On one side is the Bay of Cádiz (with no waves) and on the other a long beach facing the Atlantic (which does have waves). About halfway down the main avenue is Santa María del Mar, between two dikes. It is the most surfed beach in Cádiz, though it's rarely bigger than 1.5 m (4ft). It's best at low to mid tide, at high tide the backwash makes it unsurfable. The part of the beach at the entrance of the city is called La Cortadura. It's totally open here and at high tide the waves break with more strength. The beach of Cádiz extends to the city of San Fernando, where the beach of Camposoto has the same characteristics of La Cortadura.

La ville de Cadiz s'étend au large d'une méga-péninsule, à côté duquel on trouve la baie de Cadiz (pas de vagues) et de l'autre, une plage étendue qui donne sur l'Atlantique, des vagues donc. Vers le milieu de l'avenue principale, on trouve la plage de Santa Maria del Mar, entre deux digues. C'est la plage la plus surfée de Cadix, elle peut être bonne avec n'importe quelle taille (difficile si plus d'un mètre et demi) par marée basse ou moyenne. A marée haute, y'a du back-wash. La plage à l'entrée de la ville s'appelle la Cortadura. Complètement exposées, les vagues y cassent avec plus de puissance à marée haute. La plage s'étend jusque à San Fernando, où la plage de Camposoto présente les mêmes caractéristiques.

2. Chiclana

This is the next location after San Fernando in the direction of Tarifa. It has waves on the beach of La Barrosa and can get tubey, but it needs a very strong swell. Generally it's smaller than elsewhere.

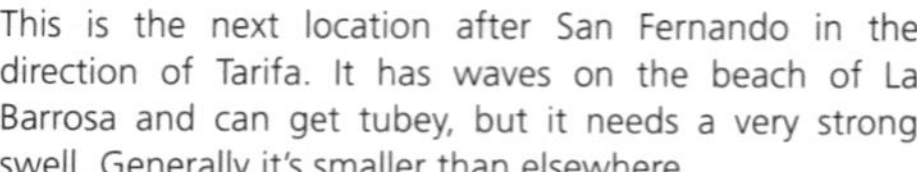

C'est le prochain village aprés San Fernando. Vagues sur la plage de Barrosa, plage de sable et idem à a précédente. Y'a une vague qui casse parfois avec un tube mais il faut que ça rentre vraiment. Engénéral, c'est petit.

3. Cabo Roche

A few kilometres before reaching Conil, on the road, there is an entrance that says 'Urbanización Roche'. Cabo Roche, 1.5km (a mile-ish) from here, has a long beach which stretches to Chiclana. Cabo Roche is the point on the coast of Cádiz that receives the most swell and there are almost always waves there. A strong, hollow shore break.

Quelques kilomètres avant Conil, sur la route, y'a une entrée marquée "Urbanizacion Roche". A un kilomètre et demi de cette pointe, on trouve le Cabo Roche, avec une grande plage qui va jusqu'a Chiclana. Cabo Roche est le point de la côte le plus agité. On trouve presque tout le temps une vague. On peut surfer à toutes les marées ce shore-break puissant.

F. MUNOZ

El Palmar

4. Conil

The village of Conil is the surfing epicentre on this coast. The beach is immense, beautiful, and extends from Cabo Roche to Cabo Trafalgar. If swell is bigger than 1m (3ft), you can surf in Conil itself, but the best spot is El Palmar.

Conil est l'épicentre du surf sur cette côte. La plage est immense, d'une beauté extrême, en s'étendant du Cabo Roche au Cap Trafalgar. Si les vagues font plus d'un mètre, on peut surfer Conil même mais le meilleur spot c'est Palmar.

5. El Palmar

The best surfing beach of the Cádiz area is 2km (1.2mi) from Conil. From even half-a-metre high the waves already are stong and it can hold a swell up to 2.5m (7.5ft). It has fast shore-break waves that are powerful and can be long.

La meilleure plage de Cadix est à 2kms de Conil. A partir de presqu'un mètre, les vagues ont toujours de la puissance et tiennent jusqu'à 2,5m. Des vagues de shore-break rapides, puissantes et longues. Spot à noter dans les carnets.

6. Caños De Meca

A bed of flat rock forms a stable peak next to Cabo de Trafalgar. It breaks at low tide, protected from W winds. This is a left, although it also has poor quality rights. At low tide the wave breaks in shallow water andwhen it does, it walls up, hollow and long. A classic reef spot. It breaks when El Palmar is at least 1m (3ft).

A côté du cap de Trafalgar. Une langue de rocher plat soulève un pic stable. Marche à marée basse et c'est plutôt bien protégé du Ponant. C'est une gauche bien que ça puisse être une droite moyenne. A marée basse, y'a pas d'eau et c'est là que c'est bon avec du surf sur des murs creux et longs. Spot de reef typique. Casse à partir de 50 cms, quand y'a au moins un mètre à El Palmar.

7. Yerbabuena

The most well-known wave in Andalucia and a classic right point. It needs a decent swell to work and it's not that easy to find. Don't leave things unattended.

La plus fameuse vague de l'Andalucia un pic droit classique. Il a besoin d'une bonne houle pour fonctioner et cest pas facille a trouver. Ne laisse jamais tont matosse non-surveillait.

STEFFAN DITTRICH

Yerbabuena

8. Barbate

Like Mundaka, but in miniature, the rivermouth forms a tongue of sand. It gives a long, playful left-hander that you can surf at all tides. It doesn't need a lot of swell (half a metre is sufficient) but it's a little dangerous: fishermen put hooks in the bottom of the seabed.

A la sortie de Barbate, vers Zahara, y'a une sortie de rivère qui forme une langue de sable comme Mundaka mais miniature. Ca donne une trés longue gauche amusante à toutes les marées. Pas besoin de beaucoup de mer, 50 cms à peine. Danger à cause des pêcheurs qui mettent des hameçons au fond de l'eau.

9. Zahara de Los Atunes

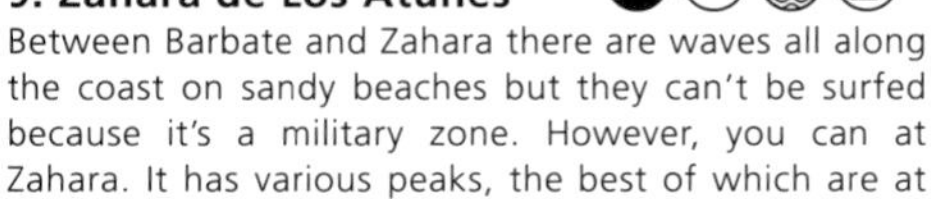

Between Barbate and Zahara there are waves all along the coast on sandy beaches but they can't be surfed because it's a military zone. However, you can at Zahara. It has various peaks, the best of which are at the exit of the village going S. Sandy bottoms and shore breaks.

Entre Barbate et Zahara, des vagues cassent le long de la côte sur du sable, mais on ne peut pas surfer parce que c'est une zone militaire. Pourtant, en entrant par Zahara, ça marche. Plusieurs pics dont les meilleurs sont à la sortie du village vers le sud. Shore-break.

10. Bolonia

There's a 4km (2.4mi) beach that's a blast when Tarifa is blowing strong E. The small bay, surrounded by bits of driftwood and sandy dunes, is very beautiful. Check the ruins of an ancient Roman village.

4kms de plages qui marche quand Tarifa est surventée d'est. La petite baie entourée de bois et de dunes est superbe. A voir: es ruines d'un ancient village romain.

11. Los Lances

An extensive beach that stretches to Tarifa. As you get closer to Tarifa the waves are better, but it doesn't receive much swell and is generally battered by the wind (good for windsurfers). Along the road there are campsites and about 20 hotels.

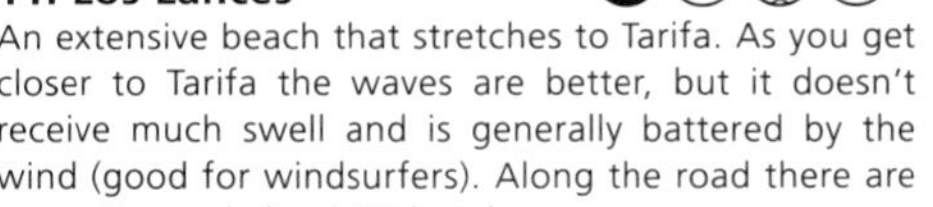

Plage immense qui s'étend jusqu'à Tarifa. Plus on s'approche de Tarifa, plus y'a des vagues. Shore-break qui ne reçoit que peu la houle et généralement trop venté. Surtout pour les windsurfers, mais les jours sans vents peuvent offrir des supers vagues. Le long de la route, on trouve quelques campings et au moins une vingtaine d'hôtels.

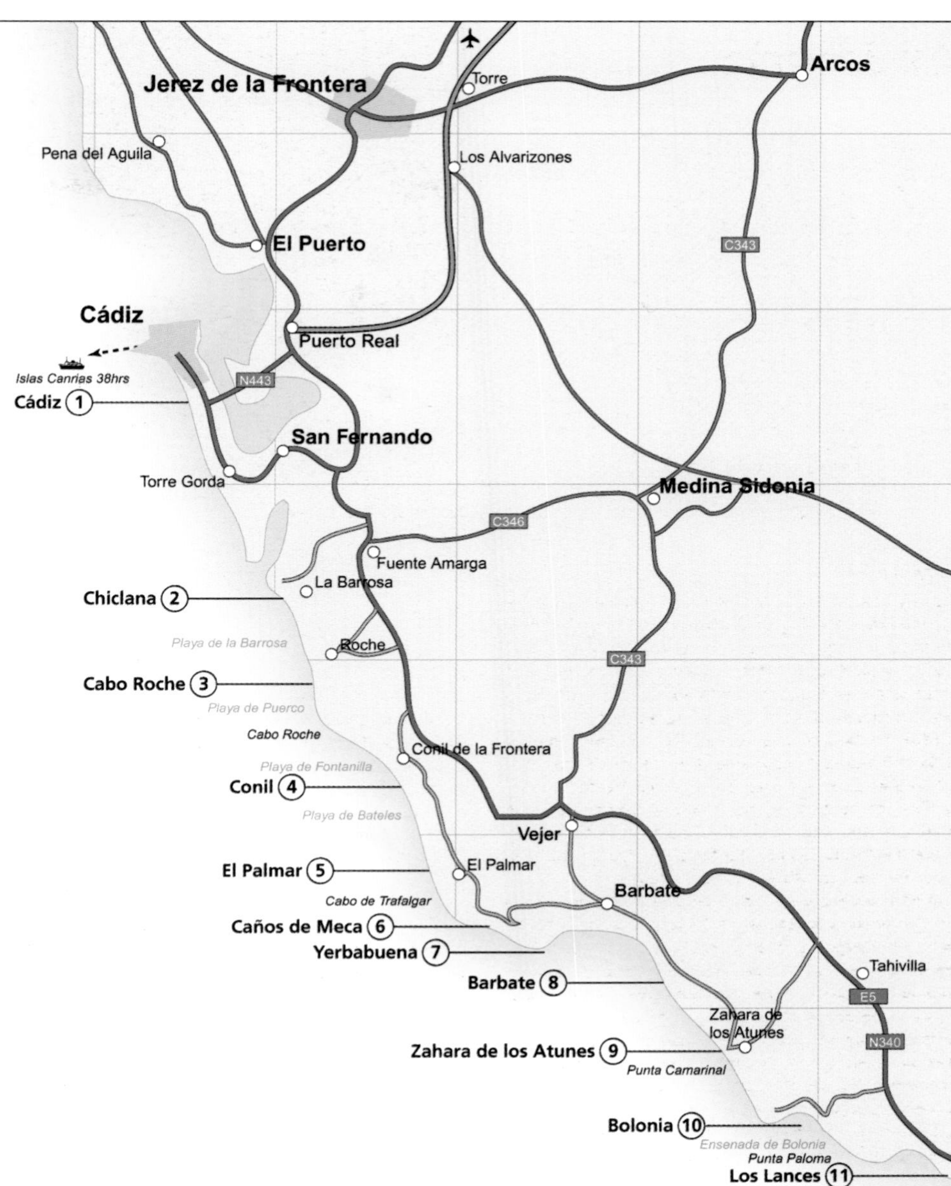

Barbate

Carcavelos' sparkling tubes have been an integral and inspirational element of Portugal's surfing scene since day one

Portugal

A strange and beautiful nation of the most obscure European flavour forms the mainland's western seaboard. That Portugal is saturated with epic spots should go without saying, yet the wider world still has a thing or two to learn about its true surf potential. This country's cool waters are home to a legendary year-round menu of tasty waves ranging from the squarest reefs to the most mellow beaches. Combine this with one of Europe's most enchanting coastal cultures and you'll see why it vies heavily for 'main course' status on Europe's overladen banquet table.

Portugal

Le Portugal se présente comme une nation étrange et colorée qui reflète la souche européenne la plus exotique ; les découvertes maritimes du pays en ont fait un pionnier dans son ouverture sur l'océan atlantique. Ses eaux fraîches hébergent une palette désormais bien connue de spots qui marchent toute l'année, qui vont des reefs les plus sauvages aux beachbreaks les plus cools. Le fait que le littoral portugais soit gavé de bons spots ne peut plus être un secret pour personne. Ajoutez à ce super potentiel une des cultures martimes les plus riches et vous comprendrez pourquoi le pays concentre tous les regards des surfers européens en mal d'une destination de bon surf, pas chère et dépaysante.

JOÃO VALENTE

Introduction

The People

Little is known of Portugal's earliest inhabitants, the Iberians, but the successive visits and conquests by the Celts, Moors, Visigoths, Romans, French and Spanish have all left their idiosyncratic genetic, architectural and social impressions on its personality. Portugal's fortunes have been firmly linked to the ebb and flow of the Atlantic since Prince Henry 'the Navigator' focused the Church's attention and finances seaward, founding a school of navigation at Sagres (then considered world's end). Madeira and the Azores were discovered in 1419 and 1427 respectively, and by Henry's death in 1460, the Cap Verde Islands and the west coast of Africa had been explored. In 1487, Bartolemeu Dias navigated the southern tip of Africa and named it Cabo da Boa Esperanca (Cape of Good Hope) in the hope of good things to come. Within a decade, explorer Vasco de Gamma had opened up trade routes with India. The cargo of pepper he bought back on his first trip was enough to pay its expenses 60 times over and Portugal very quickly became the richest monarchy in Europe.

Capital: Lisbon
Population: 10,524,000
Land area: 92,389sqkm/35,672sqmi
Currency: Escudo (Esc)
Official language: Portuguese

ALEX WILLIAMS

MARK STEVENSON

The Portuguese version of beach sports

In 1494, Spain and Portugal divided the world between themselves along an imaginary line 370 leagues west of the Cap Verde Islands. For the next 30 years, Portuguese wealth and power were at their zenith until a combination of social and political factors brought a rapid end to the dynasty of the House of Avis. The sadness of its demise reputably contributed to the term *saudade*, which gives a name to the deeply melancholic inclination of many Portuguese people. Political life since then has been tumultuous. On April 25, 1974, a bloodless coup ended half a century of near fascist rule, giving independence to all Portugal's former colonies. Since 1975 there has been a period of growth and consolidation, which has included the country's full membership of the EC in1992.

The Land

Portugal occupies mainland Europe's most westerly seaboard and falls into two broad geo-climatic regions, separated by the River Tagus. The northern interior is mountainous, lush and green, punctuated by peaks and plateaus drained by the rivers Minho, Douro and Montega. South of the River Tagus, you encounter the undulating hills and dry, dusty plains that stretch to the Algarve and the Spanish border.

The Climate

Portugal has a mild Mediterranean climate which is heavily moderated by the Atlantic ocean. There's an adaption of the old adage that circulates amongst winter visitors: 'The rain in Spain falls mainly on Portugal'. It might be a bit unfair, but is borne out in the rainfall figures, especially in the north. The mountains act as a cloud barrier for the weather systems coming in off the Atlantic from both the north and west. While some areas above Lisbon receive in excess of 1,000mm (40 inches) of rain each year, just south of the Tagus the climate rapidly turns Mediterranean. Droughts are common in the south, however groves of carob, olives, almonds and figs still flourish. Prevailing winds flow over the entire Iberian Peninsula but are unfortunately from the north and west; land breezes are a common occurrence in the early mornings. *Diario de Noticias* is the daily newspaper with the best satellite pictures and weather charts. On television, Channel One has the best evening predictions, including maps and satellite pictures.

MARK STEVENSON

Summer fun

Introduction

La population

Le Portugal conserve la trace d'influences successives par les conquêtes des Moors, des Visigoths, des Romans, des Français et des Espagnols, qui ont donc laissé une partie de leurs gènes, de leur architecture ou de leur société.

La destinée du pays a toujours été liée aux allées et venues par l'Atlantique depuis qu'Henry le Navigateur a concentré l'attention et les finances de l'Eglise, en fondant une école de navigation à Sagres, alors considérée comme le bout du monde. Madère et les Açores furent respectivement découvertes en 1419 et en 1427; à la mort d'Henry les îles du Cap Vert avaient été explorées en 1460 jusqu'aux fins fond de l'Afrique de l'ouest (Sierra Leone). En 1487, Barolomeu Dias navigua jusqu'au sud de l'Afrique et le nomma le Cap de Bonne Esperance, en espoir de ce qui allait se passer. En 10 ans, Vasco de Gama avait ouvert les routes commerciales vers l'Inde. Le cargo de Poivre qu'il avait ramené de son premier voyage fut suffisant pour rembourser 60 fois ses frais. Le Portugal devient rapidement la monarchie la plus riche d'Europe.

En 1494, L'Espagne et le Portugal se partagaient le monde le long d'une ligne imaginaire 370 miles à l'ouest des îles du Cap Vert et pour les 30 années à venir, la richesse et la puissance furent au sommet, jusqu'à ce qu'une combinaison de facteurs sociaux et politiques amenèrent une fin rapide à la dynastie de la Maison d'Avis. La tristesse de cette déroute contribua à forger l'esprit du Saudade; qui évoque le tempérament souvent mélancolique de nombreux portugais.

La vie politique depuis lors a été tumultueuse. Le 25 Avril 1974, un coup d'Etat sans effusion de sang mis fin à un demi-siècle de quasi-fascisme, donnant son indépendance aux anciennes colonies. Depuis 1975, on a observé une période de croissance dont l'intégration dans la CEE en 1992 en est la preuve.

Le pays

Le Portugal, comme l'Irlande, occupe la place la plus orientale de l'Europe et l'Atlantique y exerce une influence majeure sur ces terres d'une diversité hallucinante. Alors que le nord intérieur est montagneux, exubérant et vert, ça devient plus aride au fur et à mesure que l(on avance vers le sud. La côte est longue, entrecoupées de plages de sable fin, de reefs de classe mondiale, de "points" et de jetées.

Le climat

Le Portugal jouit d'un climat méditerranéen puissamment modéré par les entrées océaniques. Il existe un vieux proverbe qui cicrcule entre les premiers visiteurs du Pays qui dit : "La

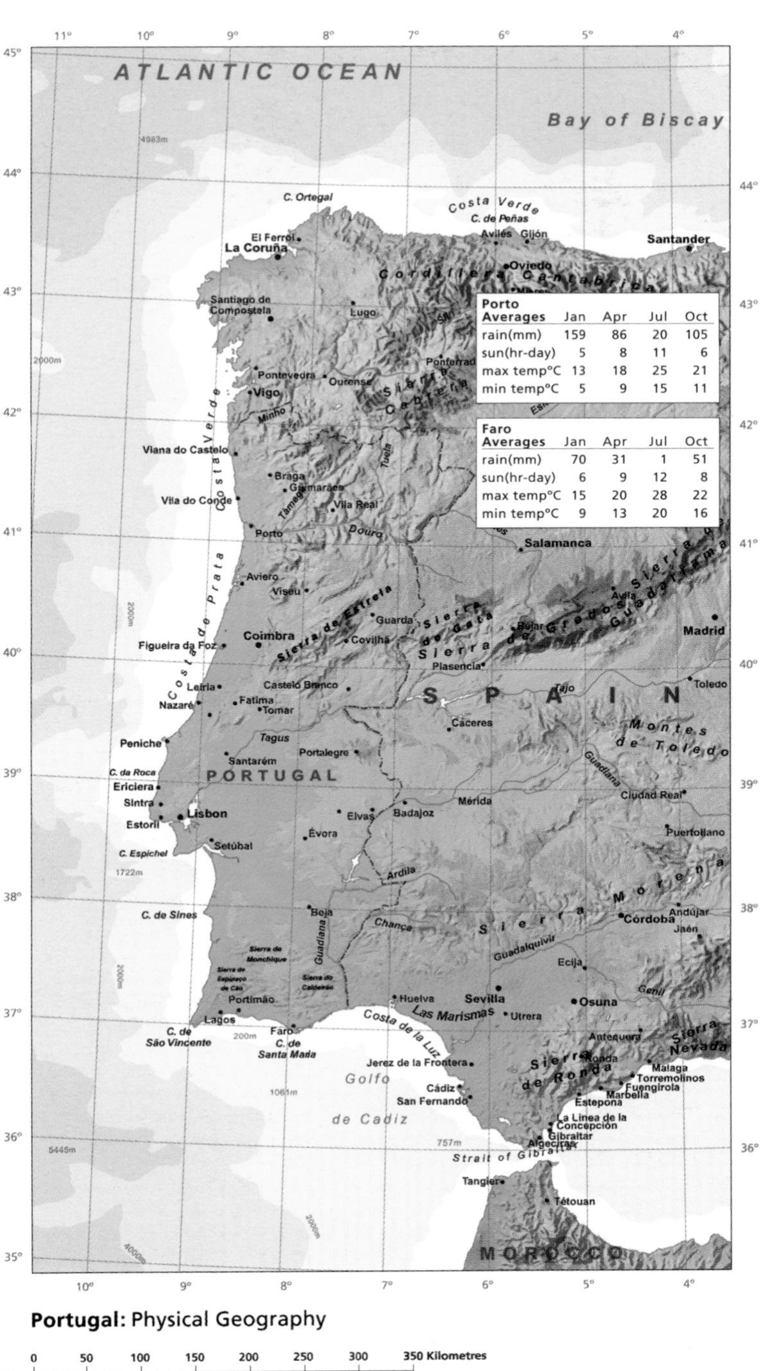

Porto Averages	Jan	Apr	Jul	Oct
rain(mm)	159	86	20	105
sun(hr-day)	5	8	11	6
max temp°C	13	18	25	21
min temp°C	5	9	15	11

Faro Averages	Jan	Apr	Jul	Oct
rain(mm)	70	31	1	51
sun(hr-day)	6	9	12	8
max temp°C	15	20	28	22
min temp°C	9	13	20	16

Portugal: Physical Geography

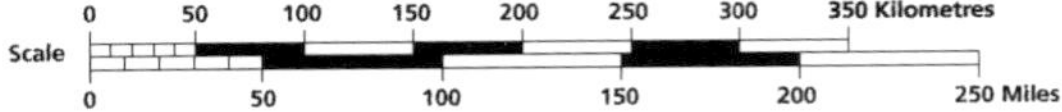

PHIL HOLDEN

Old skool rules

PETER CADE

Ericeira view

pluie en Espagne tombe surtout au Portugal." Cela peut sembler sévère mais les statistiques de précipitations sont là pour le prouver, surtout dans le nord. Les montagnes agissent comme un aimant à perturbations arrivant depuis un cadran nord jusqu'à l'ouest. Certaines régions au nord de Lisbonne reçoivent jusqu'à 1 mètre d'eau par an. Ensuite, passé la Tage, les pluies se font de plus en rares. La sécheresse sévit régulièrement dans le sud ; olives, amandes et figues y poussent très bien. Les vents dominants d'ouest au nord balayent toute la péninsule ibérique, ce qui donnent parfois des conditions on-shore défavorables. Quand le temps est calme, les brises côtières off-shore du matin garantissent de belles conditions. Le quotiden "Diario de Noticias" donne une superbe page météo avec une carte isobarique. A la télé, c'est Channel One qui offre le soir les meilleures prévisions marines avec des cartes et des images de satellites.

TIM RAINGER

Surf Culture

History – 'The Early Days' by Nuno Jonet

'The identity of the first person to ride waves on the Portugal coast is debatable, let's call him/her surfer incognito. What is known is that the first Portuguese surfer was Pedro Martins de Lima, an accomplished sailor, who still surfs Malibus. His son, Pedro Lima II also surfs, so does his grandson, Pedro Lima III. Another pioneer was António Jonet, a Navy officer and Olympic pentathlete. During a trip to Hawaii in 1953 he brought a Koa board and tried it in Costa de Caparica. On his second attempt, the heavy board broke loose and shattered some lady's leg on the shore break. Jonet quit and hung the board on his garage wall. Photos of huge surf at Uncho, published in *Surfer Mag* in 1976, first made the world aware of Portugal's surf potential and the first semblance of a local surf culture began to develop in the early 70s.

'I returned from Angola in 1975 and found a vanguard of six or seven Portuguese surfers who were surfing with a handful of foreigners who either lived here or visited frequently. There were no boards available and precious little of anything else. Everything had to be sent away for or purchased off the travellers. An Aussie shaper, Bruce Palmer, who'd been working in Wales, was a notable visitor who contributed a lot in those early days.

'The first surf competition was held in April 1977 at Ribeira D'Ilhas: João Rocha, Alberto Pais and myself were the organisers. Out of 60 competitors (we had Junior, Men's and Open events), João scored first place, I came second, while Alberto forked out the 60,000Esc the event cost us. We got our money back from sponsors like Coca Cola. The surf was a decent metre high, the creek that fed the break was still clean then and the whole bottom of the valley was taken by the tents of the different 'tribes' from Aveiro, Porto, Figueira da Foz and Lisbon – what a glorious weekend it was. The final party, thrown by the city of Ericeira at the Santa Clara Park, was a total gas, at least for us. Great seafood, lots of wine and spirits and then, chocolate mousse... can you imagine the explosive mix in the making here, considering what a fired-up bunch we were? Anyway, nothing got seriously vandalised; the concept of 'food-fight' had to be introduced in the area sooner or later, and the only annoyed person in the end was the bus driver who drove us back to Lisbon... (two-thirds of the passengers ended up talking to 'Rolf').

'Later the same year, we had the first international comp, held in Peniche, at Molhe Leste (East Jetty), won by Bruce Palmer. Pedro Lima II came second and a very slim (then) Al Hunt, who later became ASP Tour Rep and a hundred kilos heavier, came third. With the help of the 'old man' Narciso, who owned the hotel and restaurant on the beach, we hosted the Four Nations Tournaments in 1978 and 1979, with teams from the UK, France, Spain and Portugal. Both years there were big waves in Carcavelos and once we had to move the event to Praia da Torre (around the fortress, at the south end of Carcavelos). Nigel Semmens and Gerard Dabadie were the big names then, and I remember the diplomatic efforts we had to make to keep things smooth both in and out of the water. Put it this way: there was no love lost between Pommies and Frogs even in those days.

'At that point the main surf areas were Carcavelos, São Pedro and Guincho before Costa de Caparica became popular. Ericeira was also always on our minds.

'A friend and surfer Nick Urrichio arrived in 1978 and stayed at my place for a while. We started doing BonaFide and later Sol Skateboards together. I used to go on trips to London's Alpine Sports Show and pick up wheels and trucks, assemble them on to our plywood/fibreglass decks and sell them from home.

'In 1979 a good friend I had taught to surf in Angola called António Pereira Caldas arrived from Brazil and began working with Nick. He had a beach house at Caparica and they decided to build boards together in the garage. Since there were no blanks around, they had to go to Espinho to the only polyurethane factory in the country where they literally dared their main engineer to come up with a formula. Boy, could those blanks soak up resin! But thirsty or not, Lipsticks, the first boards made in Portugal, were born from there. After António's untimely death, Nick carried on in Ericeira, teaming up with Miguel Katzenstein and Semente Surfboards evolved from there. I kept doing skimboards and skateboards then met and became good friends with Greg Curtis, an Aussie surfer and entrepreneur who invited me to go to Australia to learn how to make wetsuits at the Aleeda factory on the Gold Coast. I came back in 1980 armed with a licence and my newfound skills and opened the Aleeda Surfshop, the first in Portugal. These efforts signaled the beginnings of an indigenous industry which has kept on growing ever since.'

Today

PIC COURTESY OF NICK URRICHIO

António Perira Caldas and Nick Urrichio with the first Lipsticks,1979

Strangers in a Strange Land

'I first travelled to Portugal in 1978 with no intention of surfing. I was ignorant of the quality and quantity of waves in this strange and beautiful country. It took me roughly two days to change my game plan, having seen perfect barrels at Carcavelos. Surfboards and wetsuits were unavailable at that time so I was forced to head to France, where I bought a secondhand board and wetsuit. Upon my return, I spent two months' surfing perfect Carcavelos. It was fall of 1978 and there were maybe 200 surfers in Portugal. They'll all remember it was a classic year – there have been many more since. It was a magic time as I guess it must have been everywhere in surfing's early days. The general public were amazed by the madmen paddling out in 2-3m (6-9ft) waves. It was a crowd pleaser: people would watch us for hours on end.

Like the rest of the world, wherever surfing starts, it explodes with an almost cancerous growth. Portugal is no exception and in the 20 years I've been here, the population has grown into the tens of thousands, due to magazine exposure and a number of ASP and EPSA competitions. But that's all part of the evolution of surfing. Board builders have grown to meet the demand and with input from travelling shapers, professional surfers and killer waves, local surfers and surfboards have evolved on par with the rest of the world.'

by Nick Urrichio

Histoire –"Premiers takeoffs" par Nuno Jonet

L'identité de la première personne à surfer des vagues au Portugal donne lieu à débat, appelons-le "INCOGNITO". Ce qu'on sait est que le premier surfer portugais était Pedro Martins de Lima, un navigateur accompli, qui surfe encore en longboard. Son fils, Pedro Lima surfe aussi ainsi que son petit fils, Pedro Lima III. Antonio Jonet était officier dans la marine et champion olympique de pentathlon. Lors d'un trip à Hawaii en 1953, il ramena une planche Koa et l'essaya à Costa da Caparica. A son 2ème essai, la très lourde planche s'échappa et alla briser la jambe d'une jeune femme dans le shorebreak. Il cessa donc de surfer et rangeant la planche dans son garage. Le premier semblant de culture surf se fit sentir ensuite au début des années 70. Je revins d'Angola en 1975 où je tombais sur une avant-garde de 6 à 7 surfers qui se partageaient les vagues avec une poignée d'étrangers résidents ou de visiteurs réguliers. On ne trouvait pas de planches sur place et les accessoires étaient précieux. Tout devait être commandé à l'étranger ou acheté à des étrangers de passage. Un shaper australien, Bruce Palmer, qui venait juste de bosser au Pays de Galles, fut un visiteur privilégié qui apporta beaucoup lors de cette période balbutiante. La première compétition fut organisée en avril 1977 à Ribeira d'Ilhas. João Rocha, Alberto Pais et moi-même en furent les instigateurs.

João termina premier, moi second et Alberto dût payer les 60.000 escudos que coûta cet évènement. Il récupéra sa mise avec des sponsors comme Coca Cola. Il y eut presque 60 compétiteurs toutes divisions confondues. Les vagues faisaient un bon petit mètre, l'eau de la baie était encore limpide et tout le bas de la vallée était couvert de tentes occupées par les différents clans de chaque ville : Aveiro, Porto, Figueira da Foz et Lisbonne. Quel week-end épique ce fut ! La fête finale, goupillée par la mairie d'Ericeira dans le parc de Santa Clara, fut un délire inénarrable, du moins pour nous les surfers. Des fruits de mer à volonté, vins & alcools aussi et une mousse au chocolat bien crémeuse : imaginez un peu le mélange explosif pour les surfers complètement allumés que nous étions ! Il n'y eut pas de dégradations majeures et puis il fallait bien que le principe de la "lutte alimentaire" se fasse connaître tôt au tard ! La seule vraie victime fut le chauffeur qui nous ramena à Lisbonne : plus de la moitié d'entre nous déposa une gerbe en souvenir de cette célébration mémorable !zPlus tard la même année, eut lieu la première compétition internationale à Péniche sur le spot de Molho Leste, remportée par Bruce Palmer. Pedro Lima II fit deuxième (logique) et le troisième fut un petit rachitique nommé Al Hunt, qui devint plus tard représentant de l' ASP avec en prime un quintal autour des hanches. Avec l'aide du "Vieux " Narciso, qui tenait l'hôtel et le restaurant sur la plage se déroula le "tournoi des 4 Nations" en 1978 et 1979 avec les équipes de Grande-Bretagne, de France, d'Espagne et du Portugal. Les deux années, il y eut de grosses vagues à Carcavelos et il fallut déplacer le site de compet à Praia da Torre (de l'autre côté du fort, au sud). Nigel Semmens et Gérard Dabbadie étaient les vedettes et je me souviens de toute la diplomatie employée pour refroidir les esprits à l'eau comme sur la plage. Imaginez le tableau : ça n'était pas franchement amical entre les Rosbeefs et les Froggies déjà en ce temps-là.

A cette époque, on surfait le plus souvent à Carcavelos, São Pedro et Guincho avant que Costa da Caparica ne devienne connu. Ericeira était déjà sur toutes les lèvres. Nick Urrichio débarqua en 1978 et squatta chez moi pendant un moment. On lança ensemble la marque BonaFide et plus tard les skateboards Sol. J'avais pour habitude d'aller à l'Alpine Sports Show à Londres pour ramener des trucks et des roues. Ensuite, je les

Lisbon beach scene

João Valente, the editor of *Surf Portugal*, estimates the combined surf/bodyboard population to be about 20,000. 'However, due to the comparative youth of the sport here, we're only now seeing a generation of older surfers appear to help the younger ones into the water,' he says. Meanwhile surfboard companies such as Polen and Semente rank among the best in Europe.

Big wave contestants

Names such as Dapin, Jorge Leote, João Antunes, Bruno Charneca, Rodrigo Herédia and Nuno Matta are well-known to any core European surfer. There are some rippers that few people outside Portugal have heard about like Pires, Ruben Gonzalez, David Luis, Marcos Anastácio, Felipe Gatinho and Hugo Zagalo. There's also an active big-wave crew who almost never compete but who don't miss any serious days. Anyone who has spent some time at Ericeira will have met guys like Miguel Fortes, Miguel Ruivo, Faneca, Zé Menezes, João Pedro and Tó Gama, who besides being a great big wave surfer, is also one of the best *forcados* in Portugal bullfighting is done by groups of six bare-handed men. The *forcado* 'face' is the guy that cops it first.

Media coverage has been improving and today there is one main surfing mag *Surf Portugal*. Also, there's also an all bodyboard publication *Body Board Portugal* and a newspaper that covers the surf and bodyboard scene on a regular basis *Notícias do Mar*. There are about five regular radio programs and two TV series with surf content. The most established has been running successfully for five years now, originally featuring a daring new format that has become a classic. There's no repetitions and every show covers local and international events of the previous week. To cut a long story short, they now produce six 12-minute shows per week aired at 7am and repeated around 3am on SIC. *Portugal Radical* is an extreme sports show, made with assistance from Nuno Jonet; surfing takes the lead role. The show also produces a quarterly magazine, plus a website and daily radio show aired nationwide.

assemblais sur les plateaux de contreplaqué et fibre de verre puis les vendais à la maison. En 1979, Antonio Pereira Caldas, un pote à qui j'avais appris à surfer en Angola, arriva du Brésil et se mit à bosser avec Nick. Il avait une maison sur la plage de Caparica et ils décidèrent de shaper des planches. Comme on ne trouvait pas de pains de mousse, il leur fallait aller à Espinho, la seule usine de polyuréthane dans le pays où ils tarabustèrent l'ingénieur en chef jusqu'à ce qu'il trouve une formule magique. Horreur, pourquoi ces pains absorbaient-ils autant de résine ? Plus ou moins gavées de résine, les planches Liptsick furent les premières produites au Portugal grâce à cette usine. Après la mort d'Antonio, Nick continua sur Ericeira, s'associant avec Miguel Katzenstein. D'où naquirent les Semente Surfboards. Quant à moi, je continuai à faire des skimboards et des skateboards avant de rencontrer Greg Curtis, surfer et businessman australien qui me proposa d'aller en Australie pour apprendre à fabriquer des combinaisons à l'usine Aleeda sur la Gold Coast. J'en revins avec une solide expérience et une licence de fabrication. En 1980, j'ouvrai le premier surf shop au Portugal: Aleeda bien sûr. Ce furent donc les prémisses de l'industrie du surf qui ne cesse de se développer à toute allure jusqu'à maintenant.

Aujourd'hui

João Valente de Surf Portugal estime la population combinée de surfers et de bodyboarders à environ 20.000. Comme le sport est relativement jeune, il n'existe qu'une seule génération de surfers plus vieux qui montrent le chemin à la nouvelle garde. Des fabricants de planches comme Polen et Semente se placent parmi les plus compétitives en Europe. Des noms comme Dapin, Jorge Leote, João Antunes, Bruno Charneca, Rodrigo Heredia and Nuno Matta sont désormais bien connus des surfers européens dignes de ce nom. Il existe aussi des mecs qui fracassent dont les gens ont peu entendu parler hors du pays comme Pires, Ruben Gonzalez, David Luis, Marcos Anastacio, Felipe Gatinho et Hugo Zagalo. On trouve aussi un groupe actif de Big Wave Riders qui ne font presque jamais de compets mais qui ne ratent jamais les jours de gros swells. Quiconque a passé un peu de temps à Ericeira a forcément entendu parler de Miguel Fortes, Miguel Ruivo, Faneca, Zé Menezes, João Pedro and Té Gama, un type qui est aussi un des meilleurs "forcados" du pays. ("Forcado" est la corrida portugaise où il s'agit de faire tomber le taureau en le saisissant à mains nues)

La couverture médiatique du surf s'est nettement améliorée avec le magazine principal qu'est Surf Portugal, à quoi il faut ajouter un mag de bodyboard (Bodyboard Portugal) et un journal qui parle souvent de tous les sports de vagues (Noticias do Mar). Il existe 5 émissions radios et 2 émissions télé qui traitent de surf. La plus établie existe depuis 5 ans maintenant, proposant dès le début un format révolutionnaire dont personne ne peut plus se passer désormais. Pas de rediffusion, une couverture intégrale des compets internationales comme locales de la semaine précédente. Pour résumer, les producteurs montent 6 X 12 minutes par semaine, diffusée à 7 heures du matin et 15 heures sur SIC. "Portugal Radical" est un programme de sports extrêmes, réalisé avec l'aide de Nuno Jonet, où le surf prend une part prépondérante. Portugal Radical produit aussi un mag trimestriel, un site internet et une émission radio quotidienne diffusée nationalement.

Where to go

Surf Areas

Minho and Douro Surfing is strong in this area. A combination of beaches, rivermouths and points all hold good waves in most swell directions, however with predominant winds coming from the north west ideal conditions can be frustratingly rare. Porto is the industrial capital of Portugal and the most crowded region in the north – it's also the home of nationally renowned surfing figures like the Ribas brothers. The main spots, like Viana do Castelo and Espinho are surfed regularly, though the whole region holds potential for further discovery. Numbers in the water are generally much fewer than further south.

PANCHO VILLA

Cabadelo

The **Beira Litoral** is best described as semi-explored. Jetties, rivermouths and the odd well-placed rock break the kilometres of almost empty beaches which stretch northwards. João Valente has described Nazaré as the most underrated spot in the country: it certainly has a reputation for big waves that funnel down a finger of extremely deep water pointing straight at the town. Figueira da Foz has also gained a good reputation among keen European travellers and Buarcos, which is relatively unknown, has to be one of the longest rights in Europe. Tomaz da Figueira is the most noted surfer in the area.

Peniche is one of Portugal's busiest fishing ports and was an island until the 12th century. It's now joined to the mainland by a narrow causeway. The town has been a magnet for surfers for at least a decade due to the large variety of spots working in different conditions within a five kilometre (three mile) radius. Small north swells which hardly register around Ericeira can be found breaking on the beaches north of town, while in south swells or north winds 'supers', turn on with board-snapping power. The surrounding areas are small, rural and have a friendly vibe. Europe's surfers realised this quickly and the number of campervans bear colourful witness to nearly three decades of welcome.

JOAO VALENTE

Supertubes, aka Supertubos!

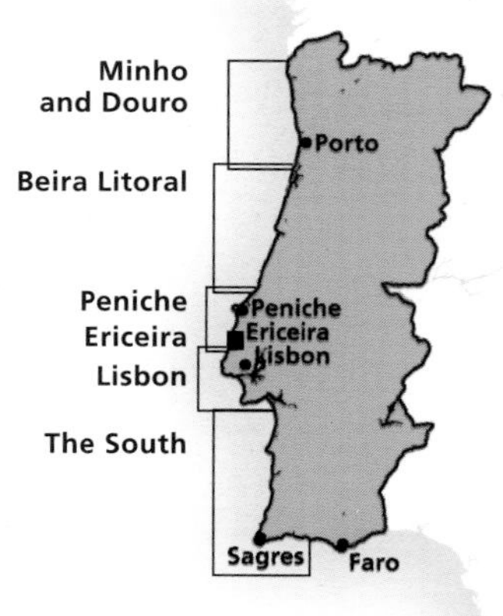

Ericeira was and is the Mecca of Portuguese surfing. In the early days it was a remote fishing village and trips here were rare and exciting. Food and lodging were dirt cheap, the surrounding beaches were unspoilt, car parks were non-existent and crowds never a problem. With a tourist explosion over the last 10 years, it has begun to change, but it's still a cool place to hang out. The spots cover 20km (12 miles) by road and about 11km (seven miles) by water. They include some of the best reefs, points and beach breaks in Europe. Offshore winds for all spots come from the east quadrant.

Lisbon lies on seven low hills at the mouth of the River Tagus. Its origins are shrouded in mystery, but the name is derived from the Phoenician 'Allis Ubbo' or 'delightful port'. Though the old town was raised in a massive earthquake in 1755, the city and the royal palaces at Sintra provide a breathtaking glimpse into history.

CHRIS POWER

Pedra Branca

All three coasts pump. North and west swells break consistently on the beaches at Guincho, Praia Grande and Costa da Caparica. In big west and south swells, the points and beaches along the Estoril line become the scene of frantic surf activity for Lisbon's bustling surf community. It was undoubtedly along this coast that wave sports had their birth and it is here that a good percentage of the surf industry can be found, close to international travel routes, markets and good waves.

South Portugal remains one of Europe's enigmas. Various decent-sized peaks have been found and many more are rumoured. Kilometres of empty beaches with unfound points and reefs keep the feeling of adventure strong. The west-facing Atlantic coast is undoubtedly the most consistent, but the Algarve's pretty coves and Mediterranean style beaches definitely receive amping waves. The climate is one of Europe's most favourable, making camping an enjoyable experience, and if you avoid the tourist traps, the water is remarkably clean. Faro is the cheapest place to fly to and car rentals are easy to arrange.

Ou Aller

Les zones de surf

Minho et Douro Le surf est bien développé bien qu'on y trouve moins de surfers que dans le sud. La côte est surtout adaptée au saut de vagues avec des vents dominants de NO. La région reste encore à explorer. Porto est la capitale industrielle du pays et la région du nord la plus peuplée. Certains des meilleurs surfers en viennent comme les frères Ribas, parmi les premier surfers au Portugal, et Zé Skate qui partagea pendant les honneurs des compétitions nationales avec Dapim, le surfer portugais le plus célèbre.

Beira Litoral Cette zone reste encore à moitié explorée. Jetées, sorties de rivières et des rochers bien placés de temps en temps interrompent des kilomètres de plages désertes qui s'étendent jusqu'au nord. Nazaré s'est fait connaître comme un spot de gros grâce à un doigt d'eau profonde qui se dirige vers la ville. João Valente le considère comme le spot le plus sous-estimé du pays. Figueira da Foz est bien connue aussi de surfers européens avec de Tomaz de Figueira, le plus local des locaux surtout dans les grosses vagues. On y trouve Buarcos, une des plus longues vagues du Portugal.

Peniche est un des ports les plus animés du Portugal. C'était une île jusqu'au XII° siècle, maintenant reliée au continent par une étroite bande de terres. Sa forteresse du XII° était l'une des prisons les plus célèbres, reconvertie aujourd'hui en un monument impressionnant contre le fascisme.
La ville agit comme un aimant à surfers depuis une dizaine d'années, grâce à la grande variété de spots qui marchent avec des conditions différentes dans un rayon de 15 kms. Les swells de nord qui ne donnent presque rien sur Ericeira peuvent bien casser sur les breaks du nord. Par houle de sud et vents de nord, 'Supers' devient une machine à casser des planches. Au Nord, la foule se réduit considérablement. Les villages environnant sont de petite taille et l'atmosphère y est relax.

Ericeira était et est encore la Mecque du surf Portugais. Au début, c'était un petit village de pêcheurs avec peu de voyageurs. Les piaules et la bouffe étaient ridiculement pas chers, les villages environnant étaient superbes avec des maisons en murs blanchis et on trouvait une ambiance campagnarde partout. Les plages étaient vierges, les parkings inexistants et il n'y avait jamais la foule. Bien que ça ait changé aujourd'hui, ces caractéristiques restent globalement valables.
Les spots couvrent environ 20 kms par la route et 11 par la mer. Ils incluent certains des meilleurs reefs, 'points' et beach-breaks d'Europe. Surfer motivé mais aussi plongeur

South Portugal

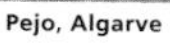

Pejo, Algarve

MARC FENIES

Rodriga Heredia, Carcavelos

JOÃO VALENTE

When to go

As with the rest of Atlantic Europe, summer is usually the least consistent and costliest season, though undoubtedly the warmest. Autumn, winter and spring are the primo surf seasons with constant swells accompanied by varied and often wet weather conditions, especially in the north. The Peniche/Ericeira region is a fairly consistent and climactically moderate year-round bet, which has traditionally been Portugal's biggest drawcard. Down south, the baking sun and consequent tourist frenzy subsides by autumn and while summer is a fun time to visit, the darker months that follow are a joyous time to surf there, featuring the possibility of good south, west and north-west swells.

Porto Averages	Jan	Apr	Jul	Oct
water °C	12	14	16	16
wetsuit				

Faro Averages	Jan	Apr	Jul	Oct
water °C	14	15	18	18
wetsuit				

passionné, j'ai fouillé srupuleusement les fonds marins. Les vents off-shore pour tous les spots sont dans le quart Est.

Lisbonne se trouve sur 7 collines à l'embouchure du Tage. Ses origines sont voilées de mystère mais son nom vient du Phénicien "Allis Ubbo" ou "Port Délicieux" et bien que la vieille ville ait été soulevée pendant le tremblement de terre de 1755, la ville et les palaces royaux de Sintra offrent des vues plongeantes dans l'histoire à en perdre haleine. Les trois côtes fonctionnent. Les houles de nord et d'ouest cassent de façon consistante sur les plages de Guincho, Praia Grande et Costa da Caparica. Par grosse houle de N-O ou de sud, les "points" et les reefs de la ligne d'Estoril deviennent le théâtre d'une activité surf débordante de la communauté trépidante des surfers locaux. C'est sans conteste le long de cette côte que les sports de vagues sont nés et c'est donc ici qu'on peut trouver la majorité de l'industrie du surf, proche des grands axes de communication, des marchés et des bonnes plages.

Le sud du Portugal reste encore une énigme pour beaucoup, certains pics ont été trouvés, d'autres sont uniquement soupçonnés. Des kilomètres de plages et de spots secrets y conservent ici un goût d'aventure. La côte Atlantique exposée ouest est certainement la plus consistente et l'Algarve, entre Sagres et Faro, reçoit aussi des vagues. Le climat est un des plus favorables d'Europe, ce qui rend le camping vraiment agréable et si vous évitez les pièges à touristes, l'eau est remarquablement propre. Faro est la destination aérienne la moins chère du Portugal avec des locations de voitures faciles à trouver.

Quand partir

Comme le reste de l'Europe de l'ouest, l'été est évidemment la période la moins consistante et la plus chère bien qu'indubitablement la plus chaude. L'automne, l'hiver et le printemps sont les saisons de surf privilégiées avec des houles régulières accompagnées par des conditions climatiques plutôt humides, surtout dans le nord. La région de Peniche/Ericeira offre une consistance appréciable tout au long de l'année. C'est depuis longtemps le premier choix de destination des surfers. Au sud, l' ensoleillement généreux provoque un tourisme massif en été qui se résorbe à l'automne. Même si l'été garantit une ambiance d'enfer, mieux vaut venir ensuite pour profiter de bien meilleures conditions de surf qui se traduisent par un mélange explosif de swells de sud, d'ouest et de nord-ouest, surtout à la fin de l'hiver.

The Ocean Environment

Introduction
The oceans surrounding Portugal are bypassed by the Gulf stream and in summer when air temps can soar, the Lisbon water temperatures often go no higher than a comparatively chilly 16°C (58°F). Booties are valuable year round especially as sharp rocks and urchins abound – be warned! Most waves come from north Atlantic lows, though west and south swells are common.

Water Quality
Portugal is one of Western Europe's poorer nations and as is often the case, when money is tight, the environment is usually the first to suffer. The seemingly unrestricted development of the tourist industry in areas like the Algarve, and massive investment of European finance in harbours, breakwaters and groynes are having a detrimental effect on the coast. Toxic waste is often disposed of in the oceans or on any available land as regulations are few and lightly policed. Tragic examples include the timber mills of the north coast and the hideous marina development proposed for the rivermouth of Douro, thankfully stalled due to the withdrawal of funds.

JOÃO VALENTE

Evidence of increased awareness is seen in the new water treatment plant being built at Ribira d'Ilhas in an attempt to solve the area's growing sewage problems.

Burning Issue
By the time you read this, the plight of Portugal's oceans will have been decided by referendum. Not surprisingly, the fight will take place in the political realm. It comes from a government-sponsored referendum to decide whether or not to decentralise a greater degree of executive power to local government, a possibility that João Valente feels will become an environmental nightmare. 'This concept may be fine in the wealthier nations like Switzerland or Germany where environmental issues are at the top of any list of considerations,' he says, 'but in Portugal where these matters can aren't a priority, this won't work. If control over these issues passes down to the regions, and local business interests have more opportunity to change the outcomes of difficult environmental decisions, disasters invariably follow.'

JOÃO VALENTE

Treatment plant – Ribeira d'ilhas

On Localism
João Valente comments: 'Portuguese surfers have a special feeling (like most others) about their homeland: they really enjoy their own waters. That's probably one of the reasons why they don't travel as much as other surfers – they know the surf-trip potential they have on their own doorsteps. Accordingly, Portuguese locals can sometimes seem a little difficult, but after the first verbal contact, and if the sport's laws are respected, they can be really friendly. The Portuguese level of performance is high on a European scale as the climatic conditions that allow you to surf round the calendar.'

PHIL HOLDEN

Harbour wall, Molho Leste

'When travelling, one must treat others as one would like to be treated. People here are very friendly and helpful: treat them and their property with respect so you and other surfers will be welcome in the future. Nobody likes a wave-hog or bad manners in the water. Remember at all times... you are here to surf and have a good time, not to make enemies!'

Nick Urrichio/Semente Surfboards

Spécificités du littoral

Introduction
Les eaux qui baignent le Portugal sont influencées par le Gulf Stream qui se refroidit par un phénomène d'upwelling (remontée d'eaux profondes). Alors que la température de l'air en été devient suffocante, l'eau devient comparativement glaciale en oscillant autour de 16°c. Il faut donc porter des chaussons toute l'année surtout que les reefs tranchants plantés d'oursins sont légion. La plupart des vagues proviennent des dépressions de l'Atlantique nord accompagnées de rares houles d'ouest et de sud.

Qualité de l'eau
Le Portugal est une des nations d'Europe de l'ouest les moins riches et comme souvent quand les budgets sont serrés, les mesures pour protéger l'environnement sont les premières à sauter. L'industrie touristique dont le développement semble galopant comme dans le sud, provoque l'émergence de ports, de jetées et de remblais qui dégradent le littoral. Les eaux usées sont souvent rejetées directement dans l'océan où sur tout terrain où la règlementation est faible ou exempte de sanctions adaptées au préjudice. Les exemples les plus terribles concernent les industries du bois de la côte nord ou le développement horrible d'une marina à l'embouchure du Douro, heureusement interrompu par le retrait des investisseurs.

Des preuves d'une prise de conscience croissante se révèlent comme à Ribeira d'Ilhas où une station d'épuration vient d'être construite pour résoudre les problèmes de retraitement des eaux usées de cette zone dont la croissance est rapide.
Organisations environnementales au Portugal
Quercus tél: 351 1 395 1630

Problème brûlant
Au moment où vosu lirez ces lignes, l' avenir de l' océan au Portugal aura été décidé par référendum. Evidemment, la lutte se joue sur un plan politique. Cela vient d'un référendum piloté par le gouvernement de décider si oui ou non il faut décentraliser le pouvoir exécutif à un niveau régional, une option que Joao Valente considère comme un cauchemar environnemental. "Ce concept peut être acceptable pour des nations plus riches comme la Suisse ou l'Allemagne où ces considérations sont prioritaires mais au Portugal où l'environnement passe en dernier, ceci ne marchera pas. Si le contrôle s'exerce au niveau des régions où les intérêts particuliers plus vifs d'entreprises auront plus d'impact sur des mesures environnementales difficiles, il est inévitable que des désastres se produiront au nom de la productivité ou de l'emploi."

Le localisme
Les surfers portugais éprouvent un sentiment territorial puissant (comme beaucoup d'autres) par rapport à leurs spots : ils adorent leur littoral. C'est probablement une des raisons pour lesquelles ils ne voyagent que peu, ils connaissent donc bien le potentiel de spots que recèle le pays. Ainsi, les locaux sont parfois agressifs même si après un contact verbal radical, si les priorités sont respectées, ils peuvent devenir plus amicaux. Le niveau de surf y est très élevé sur un plan européen, dû en partie au fait que les conditions climatiques sont favorables toute l'année.

PHOTO: Chauché

Travelling

Getting There

By air Most of the bargain flights within Europe to Portugal are charter flights to Faro, Lisbon and Porto; the Faro option is usually the cheapest.

By car The traditional route into Portugal from the north is via San Sebastian, Burgos, Valladolid and Salamanca to Coimbra. The road from Madrid to Lisbon is longer, packed with lorries and consequently slower.

By train If you're coming by an international train, you'll arrive at Lisbon's Estação Santa Apolónia.

By bus International buses travellers will disembark at Rodoviária da Estremadura.

Getting Around

By car Lisbon at rush hour is capable of fraying the nerves of the steeliest drivers. Remain calm but drive assertively at all times or be crushed. Once in Portugal, the roads are radical; it's no comfort to know road mortality rates are among the highest in Europe. If you're looking to rent, cars cost around £100 per week, and again are cheaper in the south.

By public transport Caminhos de Ferro Portugueses is Portugal's national railway, but unless you're travelling the Braga-Porto-Coimbra-Lisbon line, take the bus: it's cheaper and more frequent. Special tickets may be available on some train routes, though, especially on trips of over 100 kilometres (60 miles) or more.

Portugal's national bus company has recently been privatised and Rodoviária has been split into several smaller companies dealing with particular regions, such as Rodoviária Alentejo, or Minho e Douro. Generally though, it's known by its old name. There are also private regional companies dealing with the more obscure routes. With both buses and trains, beware the published timetable as they are often out of date. It's advisable to get the ticket vendor to write out the departure times for you.

Accommodation Basic rooms in private houses are an extremely good way of scoring cheap accommodation. If you're in the busy part of any town or village, especially in tourist season, you'll be hustled for one of these straight away as for many local residents, it pays the rent. Don't be afraid to shop around and haggle: prices range from 3600–6000Ecu depending on the season. *Pensaōs* are another option and are graded like hotels in stars, according to quality. Most of them lay on one or two meals a day: expect to pay between 4200–18,000Ecu depending on season and level of comfort. Camping is not officially allowed in National Parks or on beaches, but there are plenty of campsites; every town on the south coast has at least one. Ask at the local *turismo* for more information, or try your luck in the local cafés and bars where you might stumble upon a cheap, friendly room in a local's home.

ALEX WILLIAMS

The Surf Experience - driving to the office

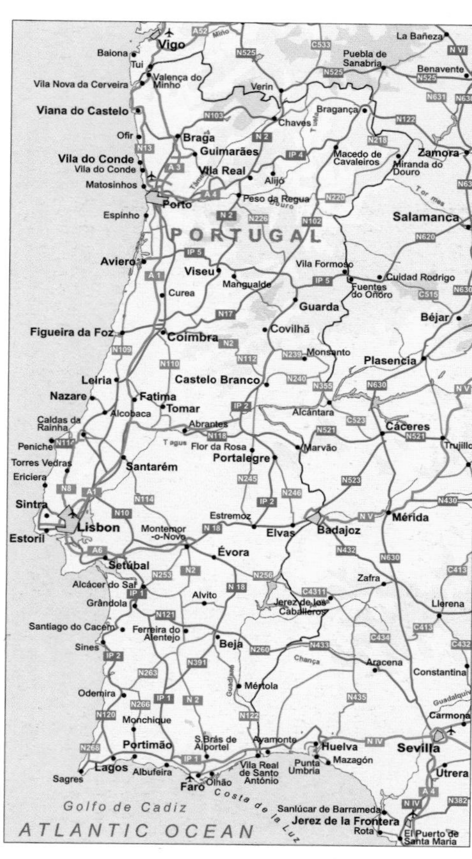

Portugal: Travelling Map

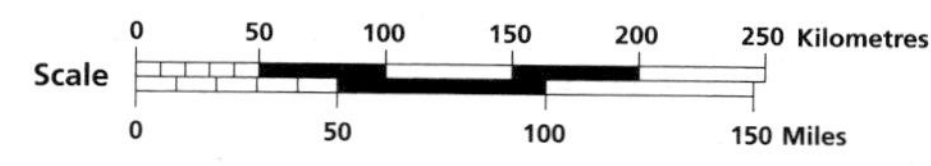

Travel

Airports

Lisbon:
Aeroporto de Lisboa (01) 840 20 60
Oporto: Aeroporto Francisco de Sá Carneiro (02) 941 32 70
Faro: (089) 800 800

Airlines

TAP Air Portugal (01) 386 40 80
Iberia (01) 355 81 19
Portugália Airlines (domestic destinations) (01) 848 66 93

Trains

Caminhos de Ferro Portugueses – CP
General: (01) 888 40 25
Porto: (02) 56 41 41
Faro: (089) 80 17 26
Lagos: (082) 76 29 87
http://www.cp.pt

Buses

Rodoviária Da Estremadura:
(01) 54 54 35
Caima (express service to Algarve):
(01) 888 63 69
EVA (Faro): (089) 89 97 00

Driving

Legal identification, valid national driving licence, both with photographs, car registration, insurance certificate and hire contract should be carried at all times.

Speed Limits

Cities – 50km/h, 30m/h
National Roads – 90/100km/h
Motorways – 120km/h

Car Rental

Hertz
Lisbon: (01) 941 55 41
Lagos: (082) 76 00 08
Rental cars start at 10,000 Ecu per day, but are less in winter.
Often it's cheapest to rent in a package with flights.

Tolls

In general tolls in Portugal are low.

Petrol Prices

Super: 168 Ecu
Unleaded: 95 Ecu
95 Octane: 163 Ecu
Diesel: 115 Ecu

Other Info

Visas

Citizens of the US, Canada, UK and New Zealand can visit Portugal visa free for up to 90 days. Australians need only a passport, but South African citizens need a visa.

Tourist Authority

Direcção Geral do Turismo (DGT)
Lisbon (01) 849 36 89

Local Tourist Offices

Ericeira (061) 63 122
Peniche (062) 78 95 71
Lagos (082) 76 30 31
Faro (089) 80 36 04

Telephone Info

International Country Code: 351
International Dial Out Code: 00
Emergencies: 112
International Operator:
099 - Europe
098 - Intercontinental
Local Directory Enquiries: 118
Emergencies:
(01) 942 91 03 (S of Coimbra)
(02) 205 67 32 (N of Coimbra)

Infos Voyage

Y aller

Par avion La plupart des vols pas chers depuis l'Europe sont des charters pour Lisbonne ou Porto ou Faro, ce dernier étant souvent le moins cher.

Par la route La route classique du Portugal depuis le nord passe par San Sebastien, Vitoria, Burgos, Valladolid, Salamanque et Coimbra. La route par Madrid est plus longue, plus chère et plus lente. Lisbonne aux heures de pointe est un enfer, capable même d'user les nerfs d'habitués du périf parisien. Attention aux routes à 3 voies où les dépassements intempestifs provoquent souvent des frayeurs. Sur les mêmes routes circulent les charettes et les chauffards, conduire la nuit sur une route secondaire peut être une épreuve dangereuse. Le taux de mortalité par conducteur est le plus élevé d'Europe. Les voitures de location coûtent à peu près 1000 ff par semaine dans le sud, un peu plus vers Lisbonne.

En train Les trains internationaux arrivent à Lisbonne à 'Estação Santa Apolónia'.

En bus Les bus internationaux arrivent au 'Rodoviária da Estremadura'.

Se déplacer

Avec les transports publics Caminhos de Ferro Portugueses est la compagnie nationale de chemin de fer, c'est bien sûr la ligne Braga-Porto-Coimbra-Lisbonne, sinon, le bus est moins cher avec une meilleure desserte. Des billets spéciaux existent sur certaines routes de plus de 100 km

La compagnie de bus portugaise a été récemment privatisée. Rodoviaria a donc été morcellée entre plusieurs petites compagnies de bus régionales. Exemple : Alentejo, Minho ou Douro. Attention, on se réfère encore souvent à Rodoviaria national. Il existe aussi d'autres compagnies privées pour les routes les moins fréquentées. Atttention aux horaires qui sont souvent dépassés. Demandez au guichetier de vous marquer les heures de départ et d'arrivée sur le billet à l'achat.

Logement De simples chambres dans la maison de particulier sont le moyen idéal de se loger pas cher. Si vous vous trouvez dans la partie commerciale de la ville, surtout en saison, vous n'aurez que l'embarras du choix par rapport aux panneaux "Quartos". Pour beaucoup de locaux, c'est le moyen pour eux de payer leur loyer. N'hésitez pas à tourner un peu pour batailler le prix d'attaque. Les prix varient entre 3500 et 6000 esc. selon la saison. Les pensions représentent une bonne option, elles sont classées avec des étoiles comme les hôtels. La plupart proposent un forfait avec petit dèj ou en demi-pension. Attendez vous à payer entre 4200 et 18000 esc. Le camping sauvage n'est pas franchement autorisé dans les parcs nationaux ou sur les plages, mais on trouve beaucoup de terrains aménagés, surtout dans le sud. Allez voir le "Turismo", l'office de tourisme ou essayez dans les cafés et les bars où vous pouvez tomber sur une chambre bon marché dans une famille.

Minho and Douro

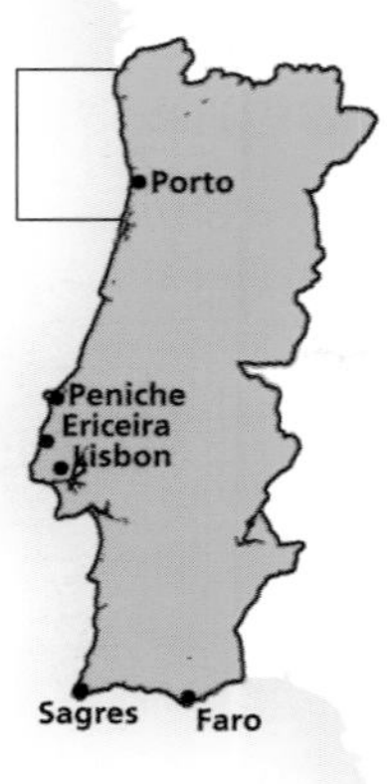

1. Moledo

 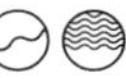  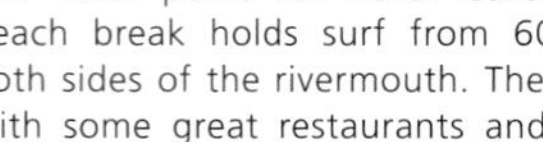

The river here constitutes the border between Portugal and Spain; a half-ruined fort guards the rivermouth from a long spit. A good beach break offers fun conditions for both surfing and wave sailing.

Un vieux fort à moitié en ruine protège la rivière d'une grande langue de sable. Cette rivière est la frontière entre le Portugal et l'Espagne. Un bon beach-break offre des conditions sympas pour le surf et le windsurf.

2. Vila Praia de Âncora

   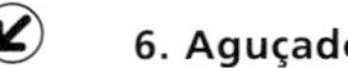

A long rivermouth break that can be one of the best spots in the area depending on the sandbar. The water is a little polluted and there's constant crowds.

Une vague longue à la sortie d'une rivière, qui peut être une des meilleures vagues du coin. L'eau est un peu polluée et du monde à l'eau en permanence.

3. Afife

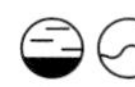 

The most consistent wave in Viana do Castelo is this multiple-peak beach break that can handle a big swell. In the summer it's almost never flat and the water is pretty clean.

La vague la plus consistante de Viana do Castelo, une plage avec plusieurs pics qui tient bien le gros. Même en été, il y a toujours quelque chose et l'eau est propre.

4. Viana do Castelo

The focal point for north coast wave sailors, this beach break holds surf from 60cm-3m (2-10ft) on both sides of the rivermouth. The town is really lively, with some great restaurants and bars. A ferry from here takes you to Cabedelo.

Beach break qui marche de 50cms à 3m des deux côtés de la rivière. Lieu principal pour la pratique du Fun-board en été. Une ville animée avec de bons restos, prenez le ferry pour aller à Cabadelo.

5. Esposende

Another stretch of W-facing beach, broken by a moderately sized river.

Encore une étendue de plage exposée ouest, partagée par une rivière plus ou moins grande.

6. Aguçadoura

A long, sandy beach with consistent peaks. On small days you'll find bigger waves here than elsewhere.

Une plage longue avec des pics consistants. Quand c'est petit ailleurs, c'est souvent plus gros ici.

7. Póvoa do Varzim

There's a left-hander off the rock and sandbars on the beach, but it needs a good-sized swell to work. The rocks are sharp, making surfing at mid to high tide a safer bet.

Une gauche sur fond de rochers mélangés avec du sable. Gaffe aux cailloux qui sont plutôt tranchants, mieux vaut éviter les marées basses. Il faut un bon swell pour que ça marche.

8. Vila do Conde

Located S of Póvoa do Varzim, this beach break is very consistent and is considered a good spot for windsurfing.

Plage de sable au sud de Povoa. Des breaks trés consistents, souvent favorables au windsurf aussi.

9. Azurára

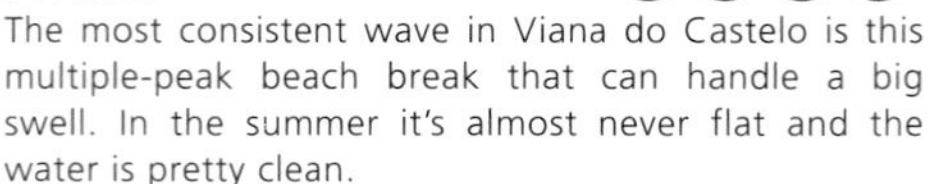

With similar conditions to Vila do Conde, this is a good beach for bodyboarding due to the heavy shore break. It's not usually crowded and the water quality is very good.

Mêmes conditions que Vila do Conde. Un shore-break carton parfait pour le bodyboard. Pas forcément du monde et une eau impeccable.

JOÃO VALENTE

Espinho

MIKE NEWMAN

Porto

Porto

10. Leça

The most consistent spot in the Porto area, this break rarely gets flat, even in the summer. The harbour helps form good sandbars in the winter. The water quality is, however, abysmal.

Le pic le plus régulier de Porto, où ça surfe toujours même en été. Le port aves ses digues de cailloux favorise de bons bancs de sable en hiver. L'eau est plutôt gerbique.

11. Matosinhos

This beach needs a big swell to get decent-sized waves, an option when all the other spots are closing out. It is also particularly good for beginners. The down sides are that it's usually crowded and the water is dirty due to the sewage pipes on the beach.

Ce spot exige une bonne houle pour que les vagues cassent. Spot de repli donc quand tout ferme ailleurs et parfait pour les débutants. Souvent peuplé avec une flotte qui sort directos des égoûts sur la plage.

12. Luz

There are usually good sandbar spot in front of Foz Avenue. The waves aren't usually great, though with big swells you can have a good time surfing here.

En face de L'Avenida da Foz, avec un bar branché prés de la plage. D'habitude, les vagues n'ont rien d'extraordinaire sauf en cas de gros swell où on peut choper une bonne session.

13. Barra do Douro

One of Portugal's sleeping beauties breaks on sandbars on the mouth of the Douro and can turn on superb waves in the right conditions.

14. Miramar

Depending on the direction of the swell, the waves here can be perfect, but it can't handle big swells. This beach has a rocky bottom: booties are recommended.

Selon la direction du swell, ça peut être correct mais pas si ça rentre gros. Des cailloux partout, mieux vaut donc des botillons pour vos petits petons.

15. Espinho

The N's big-surf spot handles waves from 1-3m (3-10ft). Take off beside the jetty where the wave then breaks through to the inside, before closing out over the rocks. At high tide there is a lot of backwash.

Le spot de grosses vagues du nord du Portugal. qui tient jusqu'à 3m. Ca démarre à côté de la jetée puis l'inside continue jusqu'à un close-out final, sur les rochers. Beaucoup de backwash à marée haute. Quand c'est gros, y'a pas foule!

16. Furadouro

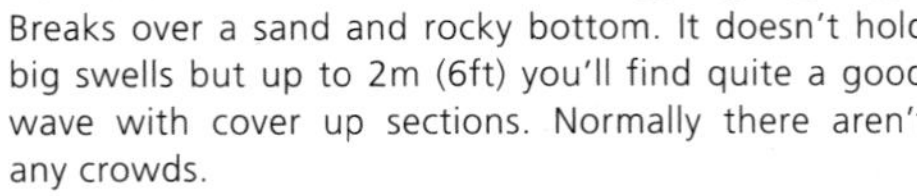

Breaks over a sand and rocky bottom. It doesn't hold big swells but up to 2m (6ft) you'll find quite a good wave with cover up sections. Normally there aren't any crowds.

Casse sur fond de sable et de cailloux. Ca tient pas le gros mais jusqu'à 2m, vous devriez avoir une vague agréable avec des sections à tubes. Normalement, y'a pas grand monde et un bon hôtel tout prés.

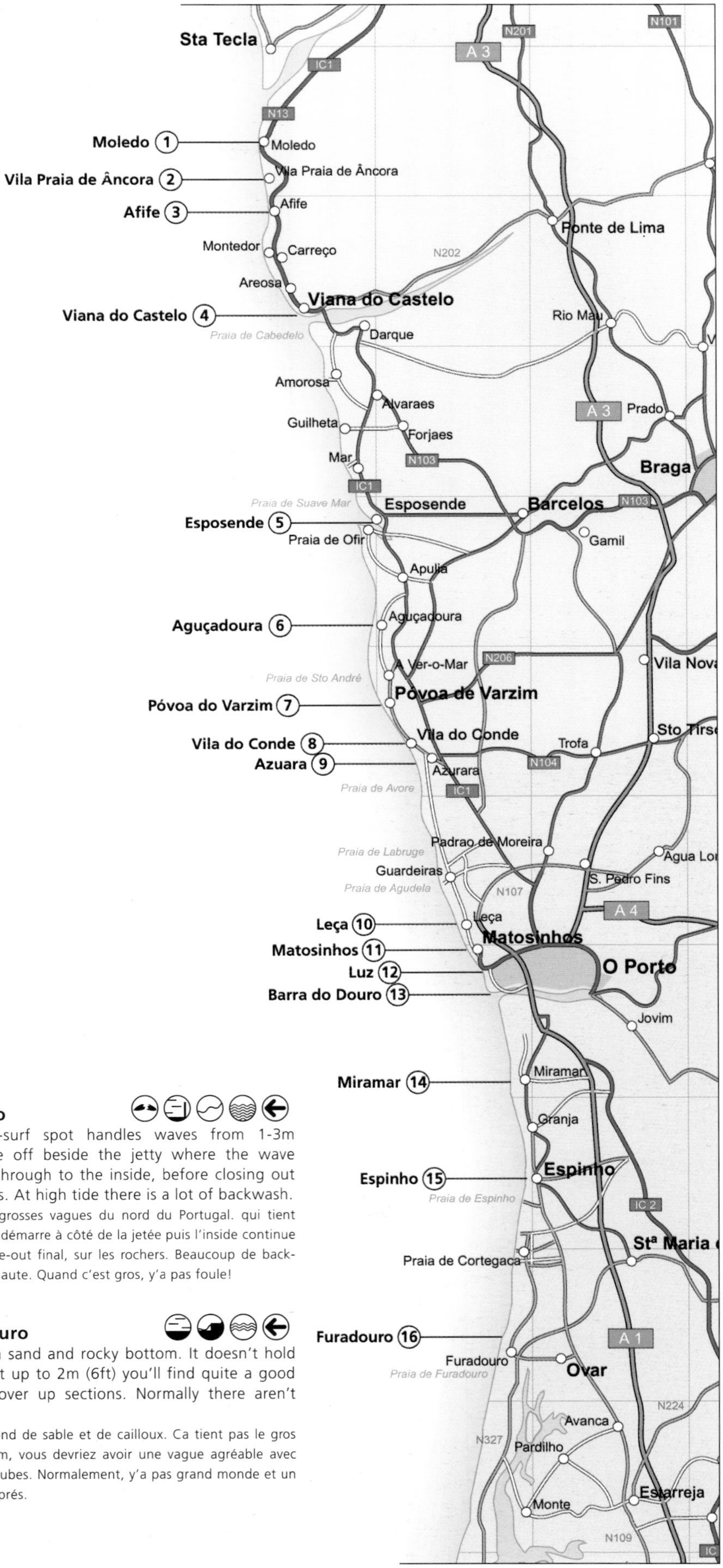

Beira Litoral

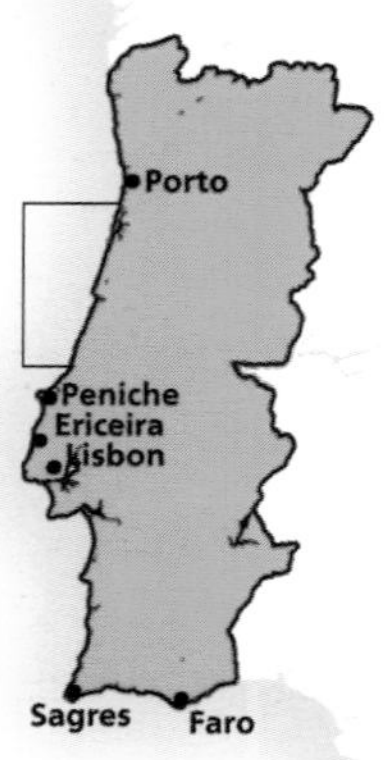

Nazaré

1. Praia da Barra

Beach developments killed this spot: it used to work all the time but now only breaks on big swells.

Ne marche plus aujourd'hui que par gros swell, de part et d'autre de la jetée. Les constructions ont défiguré cette vague.

2. Costa Nova

Good jetties S of the River Vouga produce some of the best waves along this stretch of coast. When it's big, the paddle out can be arduous, so finding a rip to go out on can be well worthwhile.

De bonnes jetées au sud de Vouga ont permis la formation de bons bancs de sable, parmi les meilleurs du coin. Quand c'est gros, passer la barre n'a rien d'évident alors essayez de repérer un chenal qui vous aidera à ramer.

3. Praia de Mira

A typical beach town. Set amongst extensive dunes, you'll surf consistent, uncrowded beach waves.

Plage de ville typique avec des vagues supra-consistentes derrière des dune qui n'en finissent plus. Rarement peuplé .

4. Buarcos

A very long right breaks over rocks and sand, situated in front of Hotel Tamagueira. It holds good-sized swells with no crowds outside summer.

Une trés longue droite sur fond de sable et rochers, en face de l'hôtel Tamagueira. Cette vague tient presque toute les tailles et n'est pas souvent prise d'assaut sauf en été. Courants.

5. Cabedelo

On the S side of the River Mondego, a tarmac pier runs out to sea for about a half a kilometre. A long classic right with thick lips and grinding barrels breaks on the sandbanks. Use the useful rip alongside the pier to get out. Usually it's crowded but there's more than enough waves for everyone.

Au sud de la Montego, une jetée goudronnée va en mer sur 500 mètres. Une droite classique et longue avec une lèvre épaisse et des tubes déments. Un courant utile le long de la jetée. Toujours un peu de monde mais souvent une vague pour chacun.

6. São Pedro de Muel

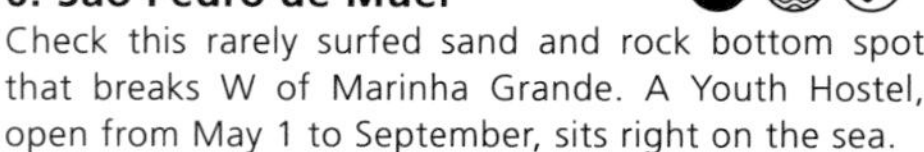

Check this rarely surfed sand and rock bottom spot that breaks W of Marinha Grande. A Youth Hostel, open from May 1 to September, sits right on the sea.

Rarement surfée, cette vague casse sur fond de sable et rochers, à l'ouest de Marinha Grande. Une auberge de jeunesse sur le sable de Mai à Septembre.

7. Nazaré

   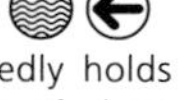

Another highly underated spot that reportedly holds waves from 1-5m (3-16ft). A long finger of deep ocean points to Nazaré and consequently swells hit the beaches with speed and ferocity – rideable.

Le Surf Report la décrit ainsi 'Le spot du gros du Portugal de 2m à 6-7m sur fond de sable'. Une plage qui tient les méga-houles donc avec une fosse au large faisant un doigt qui pointe Nazaré et qui concentre la puissance de la houle. Des conditions extrêmes et la vague la plus sous-estimée selon Joao Valente de Surf Portugal.

Buarcos

JOÃO BARBOSA

Secret spot north of Peniche

DAN HUTTON

Cabedelo

ZÉ SURF

Praia de Barra (1)
Costa Nova (2)
Praia de Mira (3)
Buarcos (4)
Cabedelo (5)
São Pedro de Muel (6)
Nazaré (7)

S Jacinto
Praia da Barra
Aviero
Costa Nova
Ilhavo
N235
Vagos
Palhaca
N235
N335
Barra de Mira
Mamarrosa
Praia de Mira
Cabeco
Covoes
Mira
N234
N335
Ermida
Cantanhede
Praia de Tocha
Tocha
N335
Arazede
N109
N335
Praia de Quiaios
Quiaios
Miradouro
Buarcos
N111
Figueira da Foz
Gala
Abrunheira
N342
N348
Soure
Carvalhais
Praia de Leirosa
Leirosa
Marinha das Ondas
Lourical
Carrico
Grau
N109
A 1
Pom
Pedrógão
Coimbrao
Monte Redondo
Praia da Vieira
Vieira de Leiria
Varzeas
Monte Real
Pedras Negras
Barracao
Gandara
Praia Velha
Sao Pedro de Moet
N242
Leira
Agua de Madeiros
Marinha Grande
Pedra do Ouro
Padrao
Polvoeira
Vale Furado
Martinganca
Légua
Falca
Batalha
Pataias
N356
N242
Santuario
Sao Jorge
Porto de Mos
Nazare
Cruz da Legua
A 1
Praia Nova
Fervenca
Praia do Salgado
A2242

L.M.FRAZAO
G. Bonneville, Sto. Amaro

JOÃO VALENTE
Ribeira D'ilhas

PHIL HOLDEN
Supertubos

Enter the Heartland

The coastline stretching from Lisbon to Peniche is a wave feast of epic proportions that'll bring out the glutton in the most moderate surfer of the tribe.

JOÃO VALENTE
Carcavelos, Lisbon

If you arrive in Lisbon, you could by rights go no more than 20 kilometres (12 miles) either way and have a killer surf trip. There are so many waves to choose from, and despite the regular crowds of local guys, they're lots of fun to surf. Lisbon, spectacularly built on one of the world's most famous harbours, is one of Europe's most interesting cities. The first town heading north from Lisbon is Sintra, an enlightening time warp that's a historian's answer to Disneyland, with a community of royal castles inviting a glimpse back in time. You drive a few more miles then the feast continues.

TIM RAINGER
Ericeira

Arriving at Ericeira is like walking into a Portuguese pastry shop: there's a thousand choices and they're all good. One of everything will probably kill you but you want to sample anyway so you pull up a chair and settle in for a long session. Many's the good person who arrived for a week and ended up staying longer than they imagined. This sleepy piece of coast has been a magnet for Portugal's locals since way back in the day as it's conveniently situated within an hour's drive of Lisbon and offers a complete selection of wave types that are packed in as densely as the rides at a funpark.

Driving north there are a few little-known spots that offer great waves, but after 20 kilometres (12 miles), you hit Peniche, with a 14th century fort built on the end of a small peninsula and a small town focused intensely on the sea. The busy fishing port and associated services dominate the environment, but for surfers it's the waves peeling deliciously into the bays on both sides of the peninsula that have made this such a special place.

PHIL HOLDEN
Peniche

No matter what the conditions, there's almost certainly going to be an offshore wave somewhere in these three conveniently accessible areas. In small swells, you'll find yourself plumbing the beaches and rivermouths north of Ericeira and Peniche, and when the Atlantic turns on the power, you can either take it on the head at Coxos and Supers, or skuttle down to Lisbon where the capital's classic south-facing beaches and points will be sheltered and firing. The surf community is strong all over the region and this is definitely not the place to play games with locals, who've been charging with the best for two decades. Accommodation, food and nightlife are as cheap and plentiful as anywhere on the Atlantic coast, and despite the growth in recent years, it's still a super chilled place to visit, remaining one of Europe's most venerated wave theatres and sumptuous travel destinations.

Entrez dans l'épicentre du surf portugais

La côte qui s'étend de Lisbonne à Péniche regorge de spots de tous types qui sauront rassasier n'importe quel surfer en mal de sessions interminables. Si vous arrivez à Lisbonne, il suffit juste de faire 20 km vers l'ouest ou vers le sud pour se taper une bonne session. Les spots sont si nombreux que malgré la foule, on peut toujours prendre des vagues. Lisbonne, bâti sur un des ports les plus célèbres dans le monde, est aussi une ville fascinante. La première ville au nord est Sintra, une ville d'histoire qui offre une version plus authentique que Disneyland, avec une tripotée de châteaux qui vous plongent dans le passé.

Arriver à Ericeira, c'est comme rentrer dans une pâtisserie : on a l'embarras du choix parce que tout est bon. Un peu de tout vous tuerai alors il faut donc choisir un spot pour se caler pour la journée. Nombreux sont ceux qui croyaient rester une semaine et sont restés beaucoup plus. Ce village tranquille a lontemps été un aimant pour les habitants de Lisbonne, à moins d'une heure de route. La palette de spots disponible est aussi variée qu'on peut l'imaginer.

En allant vers le nord, on rencontre d'autres bons spots avant de tomber sur Péniche, avec sa forteresse du XIVème siècle et une petite péninsule dédiée à 100% aux activités maritimes. Le port est actif : il suffit de regarder autour. Pour les surfers, ce sont les vagues qui déroulent des 2 côtés qui rendent l'endroit unique.

Quelles que soient les conditions, le vent sera toujours offshore quelque part. En cas de petit swell, il faudra sillonner les petits chemins au nord de Baleal. Quand ça rentre gros, il faudra redescendre vers Supertubos ou Coxos ou rentrer vers Lisbonne où les spots orientés au sud offrent un abri idéal. Les surfers locaux sont présents partout dans cette zone et il ne s'agit pas de jouer au plus fin avec eux. Le logement, la bouffe et les sorties sont bon marché. Malgré la croissance de ces dernières années, c'est encore un endroit bien cool, qui reste une zone de surf incontournable en Europe.

Peniche

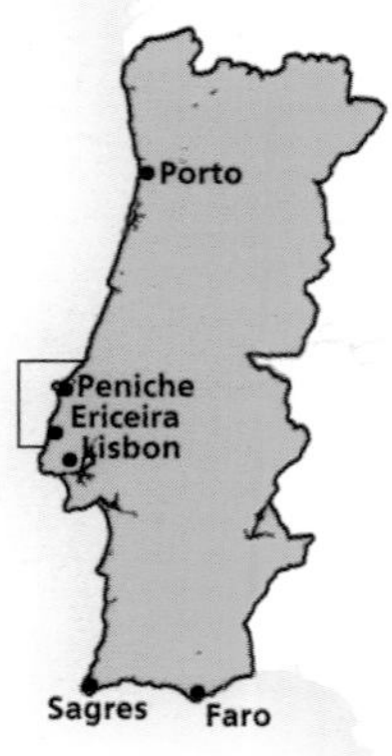

ERIC CHAUCHE

Supertubos

1. Praia da Foz do Arelho

Stretching from Foz to Peniche this beach is only interrupted by the occasional small rivermouth.

Cette plage qui va de Peniche à Foz est sans interruption. Bonnes vagues à l'embouchure.

2. Ferrel

You can see the beach from Baleal: in a small N swell when everywhere else is crap and the wind SW, Ferrel can be head high and pumping. A track runs along the length of the beach – finding it can be tricky but persevere.

Visible depuis Baleal; quand c'est petit pourri par vents de S-O à Baleal, Ferrel peut être mieux que surprenant. Des pistes sillonnent le long de la côte, pas faciles à s'orienter mais ça vaut la galère.

3. Lagide

A high quality left breaks over an urchin-infested reef, that's dangerously shallow at low tide. Loads of campervans hang out in the car park.

Une belle gauche sur un reef infesté d'oursins, d'où certains risques à marée basse. Pas mal de vans sur le parking en face en général.

4. Praia do Baleal

This protected scallop-shaped beach just N of Peniche works best in large swells or when the rest of the coast has a cross-shore wind.

Plage en croissant de lune juste au nord de Peniche qui marche bien par grosse houle quand les vents sur les autres plages sont cross-shore.

PHIL HOLDEN

Lagide

5. Molho Leste

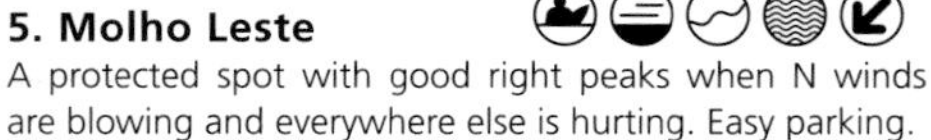

A protected spot with good right peaks when N winds are blowing and everywhere else is hurting. Easy parking.

Spot protégé par les digues avec, à l'abri des vents de nord, avec de bonnes droites rapides. Parking à proximité.

PHIL HOLDEN

Molho Leste, Peniche

CHRIS POWER

Consolação rights

JOÃO VALENTE

Consolação lefts

6. Supertubos

The name speaks for itself: Supertubos is one of the most legendary beaches in Europe. The nearby fish factory lends a pungent odour to the experience and although the lefts are wicked, crowds can mar the enjoyment. Supertubos is a S swell break and can handle N winds.

Tout est dans le nom. L'usine de poisson à côté balance une odeur pestilentielle. Par houle de sud, les gauches peuvent y être démentes mais attention au monde.

7. Consolação

A right-hander that's often fat breaks over a rocky bottom, with a hollower left on the N side of the point. Less swell gets in here than at Supertubos, but it's a very pretty spot with excellent water quality.

Une droite, souvent épaisse, sur fond de rochers. D'habitude plus petit qu'à Supertubos mais le décor est grandiose et l'eau impeccable. Décor est grandiose et l'eau impeccable.

8. Praia da Areia Branca

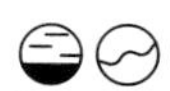  

A good beach break with rivermouth waves.

Bon beach break et une sortie de rivière.

9. Santa Cruz

A particularly good beach works in similar conditions to the Ericeira breaks and is also a popular summer wave-sailing venue.

Une plage vraiment bonne avec les mêmes conditions que les spots d'Ericeira. Très prise des windsurfers surtout en été.

10. Praia Azul

One of the most consistent waves in this area that's always 30-70cm (1-2ft) bigger than the other breaks. When the sandbars are good, it can have heavy barrels.

Une des vagues les plus consistantes de la zone, toujours environ 50cms plus gros que les autres breaks. Quand les bancs sont bons, on peut y trouver du tube.

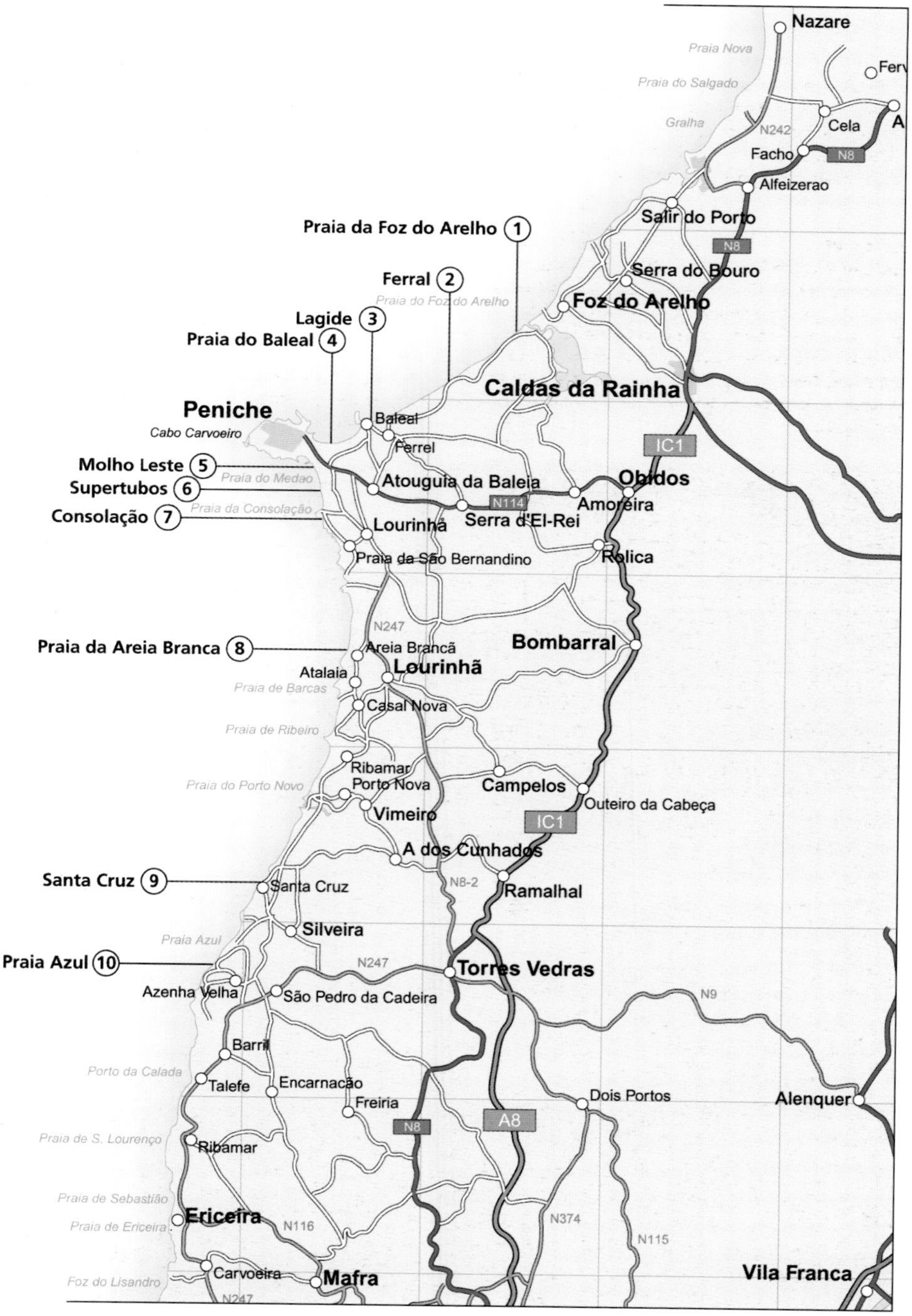

Praia da Foz do Arelho (1)
Ferral (2)
Lagide (3)
Praia do Baleal (4)
Molho Leste (5)
Supertubos (6)
Consolação (7)
Praia da Areia Branca (8)
Santa Cruz (9)
Praia Azul (10)
Nazare
Cela
Facho
Alfeizerao
Salir do Porto
Serra do Bouro
Foz do Arelho
Caldas da Rainha
Peniche
Cabo Carvoeiro
Baleal
Ferrel
Atouguia da Baleia
Obidos
Amoreira
Serra d'El-Rei
Lourinhã
Praia da São Bernandino
Rolica
Areia Brancã
Bombarral
Atalaia
Lourinhã
Casal Nova
Ribamar
Porto Nova
Campelos
Outeiro da Cabeça
Vimeiro
A dos Cunhados
Santa Cruz
Ramalhal
Silveira
Torres Vedras
Azenha Velha
São Pedro da Cadeira
Barril
Talefe
Encarnação
Freiria
Dois Portos
Alenquer
Ribamar
Ericeira
Carvoeira
Mafra
Vila Franca

Ericeira

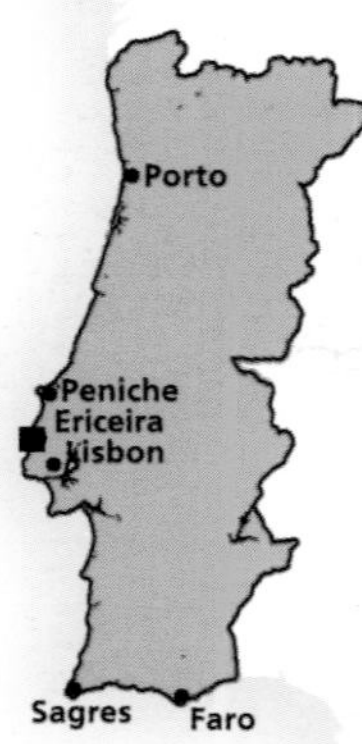

São Lourenco

JOÃO VALENTE

1. São Lourenço 

The Portuguese version of 'Sunset' can hold giant surf if the swell direction is correct. Keep an eye out for sneaker sets from the W when it's big. Expect elevator drops and fast hollow sections. N and NW swell is the best and it will hold a little S wind.

La version portugaise de Sunset qui peut tenir des méga-houles si la direction est adéquate, à savoir N/N-O. Quand c'est gros, faites gaffe aux séries surprise qui viennent de l'ouest. Un take-off dans le vide et des sections rapides et creuses. Tient un peu le vent de sud.

2. Coxos     

One of Europe's most legendary rights points breaks in a small bay. Swells come from deep water and unload on a sharp reef bottom. It's best in a N/NW swell from low to mid tide, but when it's big currents can be heavy. Waves change according to swell direction and size, but are unforgiving, powerful and humbling on big days – always fun.

Droite légendaire, par heule de N/N-O de marée ba sse à mi-marée, qui peut être surfée jusqu'à la marée haute mais attention à la sortie. C'est une petite baie c'est pourquoi ça brasse terrible quand ç'est gros: puissant.

Coxos

PEDRO JORGE

3. Crazy Left 

A tubey wave on the S side of Coxos Bay has – on S-SW days – hollow, fast and powerful waves breaking over a rocky bottom. The high tide is better.

Une vague tubulaire au sud de la baie de Coxos. Par houle de S/S-O, c'est creux, rapide et puissant avec un fond craignos. Meilleur à marée haute.

4. Pontinha   

You can either paddle or walk N from Ribeira D'Ilhas to this 1-4m (3-12 ft) break. On N-NW swells the wave can be perfect, but closes out when becomes too W. Watch out for the urchin-infested reef.

A distance de rame ou de marche depuis Ribeira. Par houle de N/N-O, ça peut être parfait mais ferme dès que c'est trop ouest. Fond plat et infesté d'oursins, de 1 à 4 mètres.

5. Ribeira D'ilhas    

A versatile bay with various peaks that work on most swells but are best on W-NW. When good, this boasts one of the longest waves in the area. It's one of the most consistent spots in the summer, holding a 1-4m (2-12ft) swell.

Une baie changeante avec divers pics. Trés consistant et meilleur par N/N-O. Quand c'est bon, une des droites les plus longues qui tient jusqu'à 4 mètres. Du monde à l'eau.

6. The Reef    

It's 7m (20ft) deep to the right side of the peak and 1m (3ft) where you drop in, getting shallower on the inside. Waves range from 1-2m (3-6ft) and when it's on it's pure magic but no one surfs it a lot without paying the fiddler.

Y'a 6 mètres de fond à droite du pic et 1 mètre au take-off, avec encore moins de fond à l'inside. Quand c'est clean, c'est magique mais quiconque surfe ici souvent paye un tribu un jour ou l'autre. De 1 à 2 mètres.

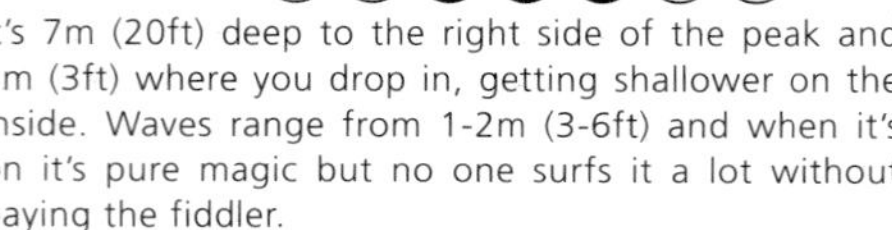

7. Backdoor     

Normally a summer break, this works best on N-NW swells. It holds some very hollow sections and is sketchy on low tide. Maxes out at double-overhead.

Généralement, un spot d'été qui marche par N/N-O avec des sections ultra-creuses. Casse-gueule à marée basse.

8. Pedra Branca    

An extremely hollow left reef located in front of the camping and caravan park N of Ericeira, which works best on S-SW swells, holding large surf if the swell direction is perfect. The bottom is a rock platform with big holes. The swell comes out of deep water, so peaks with speed and power. It's got a pipe-ish look on good days; goes from 1-3m (3-10ft). It's suicide at low tide.

Mieux par houle de S/S-O, qui tient le gros si la direction est optimale. Le fond est une plateforme avec des cavernes. La houle arrive en eau profonde donc vitesse et puissance au programme, suicidaire à marée basse avec un look pipelinesque quand c'est parfait, de 1 à 3 mètres.

Coxos overview

CHRIS POWER

Tadeu Pereira, Pedra Blanca

JOÃO VALENTE

Shane Herring, Reef

ZÉ PIRRAYT

9. Praia do Norte 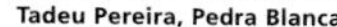  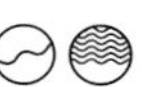 

This will work with all swell directions from 1-4m (3-12ft), but is best known for the the long rights from the N. The point is very dry on low tide.

Marche avec toutes les houles, mais plus réputé pour les droites par houle de nord. Peu d'eau sur la zone de take-off à marée basse. De 1 à 4 mètres.

10. Praia do Peixe    

In a solid swell waves break inside the harbour. The raw sewage outlet will soon be hopefully redirected.

Spot de repli par tempête. Pollué en été à cause des égoûts.

11. Furnas  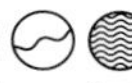 

This only works with a big N-NW swell. It's your last chance when everything thing else in Ericeira is huge and you don't feel like driving.

Marche uniquement par grosse houle de N/N-O, dernier recours quand tout ferme et que vous ne vous sentez pas prêt à tailler la route.

12. Foz do Lizandro  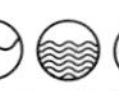  

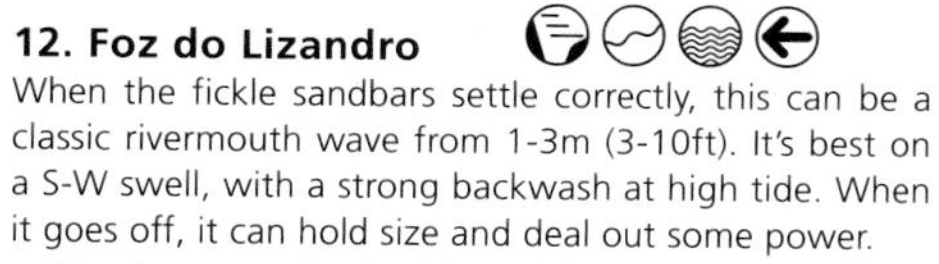

When the fickle sandbars settle correctly, this can be a classic rivermouth wave from 1-3m (3-10ft). It's best on a S-W swell, with a strong backwash at high tide. When it goes off, it can hold size and deal out some power.

Une bonne sortie de rivière si les bancs capricieux se forment correctement. Mieux par houle de S-O, avec un méchant back-wash à marée haute. Peut tenir la taille et envoyer le pâté. De 1 à 3 m.

13. São Julião   

This works on most swell directions and tides depending on the sand flow. This is a small spot that maxes out easily.

Marche par toutes les directions de houle et marées selon les courants. Beach break de 50cms à 2 mètres qui sature facilement.

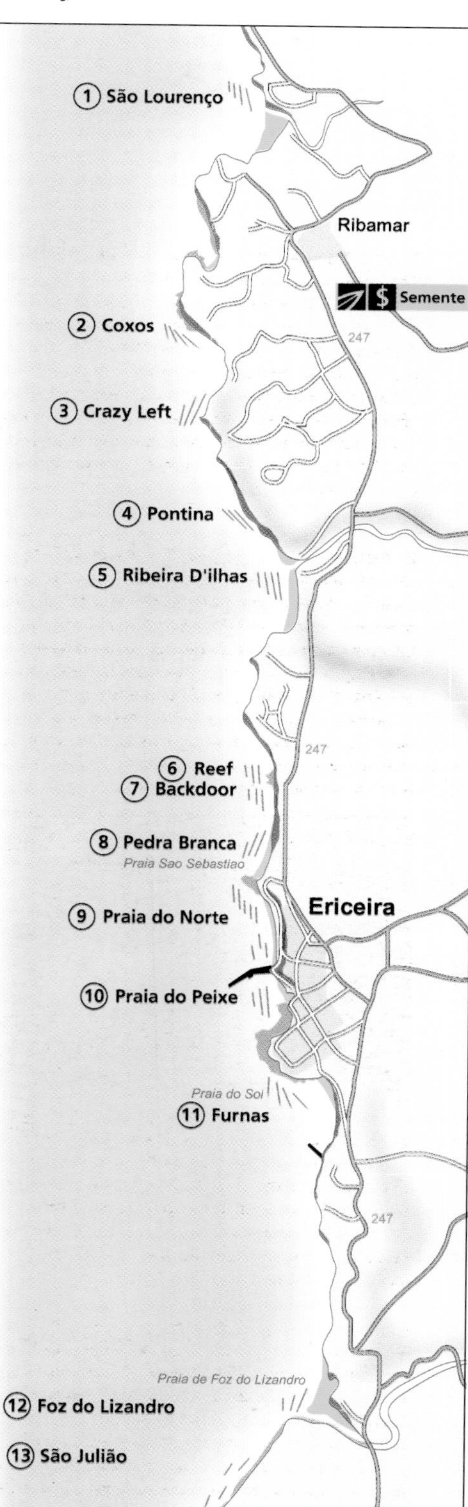

Foz do Lizandro

MIKE NEWMAN

Lisbon

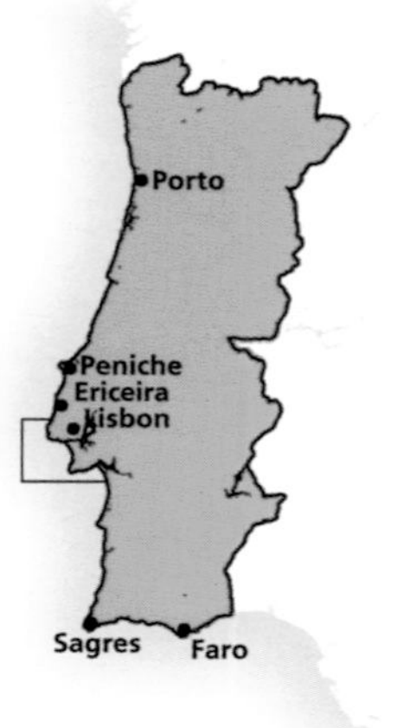

Punta Pequena

1. Praia Grande/Pequena

The most consistent spot in the Lisbon area, and one of few places protected from summer N winds, this has powerful waves and an infamous shore break. Praia Pequena is the N continuation of the same beach with similar characteristics but not so many crowds. The water is some of the cleanest on this part of the coast.

Le spot le plus consistent autour de Lisbonne, qui plus est, protégé des vents de nord en été. Vagues puissantes avec un shore-break carton. Praia Pequena est juste au nord avec quelques rochers en plus et du monde en moins. L'eau la plus clean du coin aussi.

2. Praia do Guincho

Photos of huge surf published in *Surfer Magazine* in September 1967 first made the world aware of Portugal's surf potential. Guincho is Portugal's most popular wave sailing location with strong summer NW winds providing classic sailing conditions. Strong swells do the same for the surf conditions.

Des photos publiées dans SURFER en Septembre 1967 d'énormes paquets à Guincho ont donné au monde l'image du potentiel de surf au Portugal. C'est d'abord un spot de windsurf en été avec de forts vents de NO. Souvent du bon surf aussi avec des gauches qui tiennent la taille.

3. Monte Estoril

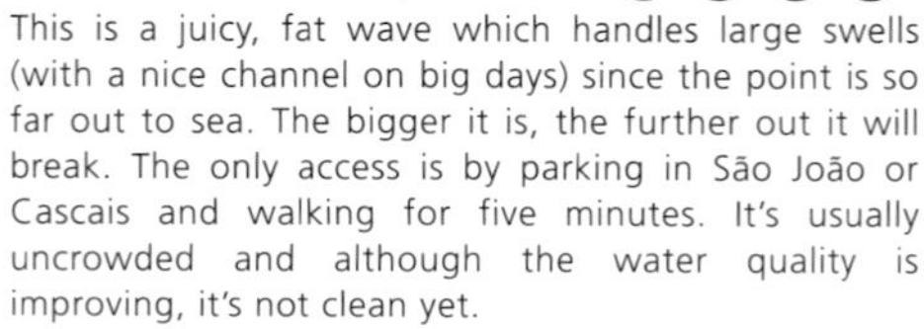

This is a juicy, fat wave which handles large swells (with a nice channel on big days) since the point is so far out to sea. The bigger it is, the further out it will break. The only access is by parking in São João or Cascais and walking for five minutes. It's usually uncrowded and although the water quality is improving, it's not clean yet.

Une vague épaisse qui tient le gros avec un chenal idéal quand c'est gros, assez loin du bord. Plus gros c'est, plus ça pète loin. L'accès se fait par le parking de São João ou Cascais, en marchant 5 minutes. Pas trop de monde en général.

4. São João
Bolina

One of the best spots on the Linha do Estoril is an intense, hollow wave that ends over the rocks, so it's not recommended for beginners. Usually it's crowded and respect for the locals is essential. Water quality is bad due to a sewage pipe in front of the point.

Un des meilleurs spots de la "ligne Estoril (train)", une vague creuse et intense qui termine sur la caillasse; par forcément pour débutants. Bien pris d'assaut par les locaux, méfiance! Une sortie d'égoût en face du spot.

Ricardo Santos, Costa da Caparica

Poça

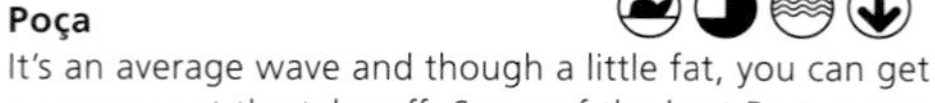

It's an average wave and though a little fat, you can get a cover up at the take-off. Some of the best Portuguese surfers began their careers here, including João Bonne Ville, Pirujinho, Paulo do Bairro and Gatinho. It's usually crowded but the water quality is improving.

Une vague moyenne, un peu épaisse malgré une section à tube au départ. Souvent peuplé et jardin de pas mal de champions.

Azarujinja

This is probably one of the best small waves on the Estoril line and is very protected from onshore winds. The take-off is over a rock bottom, but ends on sand. Water quality poor but improving.

Un des meilleurs paris quand c'est petit, trés protégé des vents on-shore. Le take-off se fait sur du rocher et termine sur du sable. L'eau n'est pas terrible.

5. São Pedro
Bica

   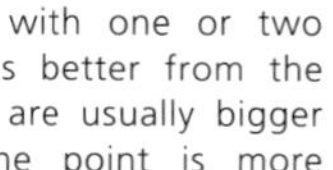

A very long generally fat wave with one or two hollower sections. Usually it looks better from the parking lot than it is, but waves are usually bigger here than elsewhere because the point is more exposed to swell. Normally it's crowded, but on good days there are plenty of waves for everyone. The water quality is not bad and improving.

Une droite trés longue, un peu épaisse avec une ou deux sections creuses. Parait depuis le parking mieux qu'elle n'est en réalité mais ça prend mieux la houle que partout ailleurs. Souvent du monde mais quand ça marche, ça débite!

Bafureira

Located right beside Bico and handling the same kind of swell, this wave is a little shorter, but usually less crowded than elsewhere. Average water quality.

Juste à côté de Bico avec la même exposition à la houle à quelque chose prés. Un petit peu plus court mais moins fréquenté: une bonne option donc quand c'est la Chine à côté.

6. Parede

Possibly the rarest wave in Portugal to break to its full potential: it's been compared to J-Bay when it does. Normally the locals just surf one or two sections of it. The water quality is not bad and a new development may improve it.

Rare, trés rare pour que ça casse à 100%: parfois comparé à la Jeffreys' Bay, droite trés rapide donc. Normalement, les locaux surfent une ou deux sections.

Praia Grande/Pequena (1)
Praia do Guincho (2)
Monte Estoril (3)
São João (4)
São Pedro (5)
Parede (6)
Carcavelos (7)
Sto Amaro (8)
Costa da Caparica (9)
Praia do Castello (10)
Bicas (11)

7. Carcavelos

History has this as one of the first Portuguese surf breaks to be ridden and as it's a central-city break, it's usually crowded these days. In strong NW swell, lefts predominate. Sewage problems, which have been terrible in the past, are in the process of improvement as a new sewage pipe will take waste further out to sea.

Un des premiers spots du Portugal. Par bon swell de NO, les gauches prédominent. Etant un spot urbain, y'a toujours foule. Les problèmes d'écoulement des eaux usées sont résolus, en jetant tout plus au large.

8. Santo Amaro 

This wave only works when the rest of the Linha do Estoril is closing out. It's very hollow with two cover-up sections and is not recommended for beginners. Water quality is extremely bad.

Ne marche que si tout le reste ferme. Trés creux avec deux sections à tubes. Pas de débutants et une pollution abominable.

Santo Amaro

PEDRO JORGE

9. Costa da Caparica

Rates as one of the most popular surf spots in Lisbon. Jetties have been placed along the beach creating good waves on every one of them. This is a choice spot for beginners, not only for the quantity of peaks, but because the waves are mellow. When it's good, Costa da Caparica can be a dream. The water quality is OK.

Le plus long beach-break de Lisbonne. Les jetées sur la plage créent de bons bancs de sable. Un endroit idéal pour débutants non seulement pour le nombre de pics mais pour la mollesse des vagues. Cela dit, ça peut être fantastique. L'eau y est propre.

10. Praia do Castello   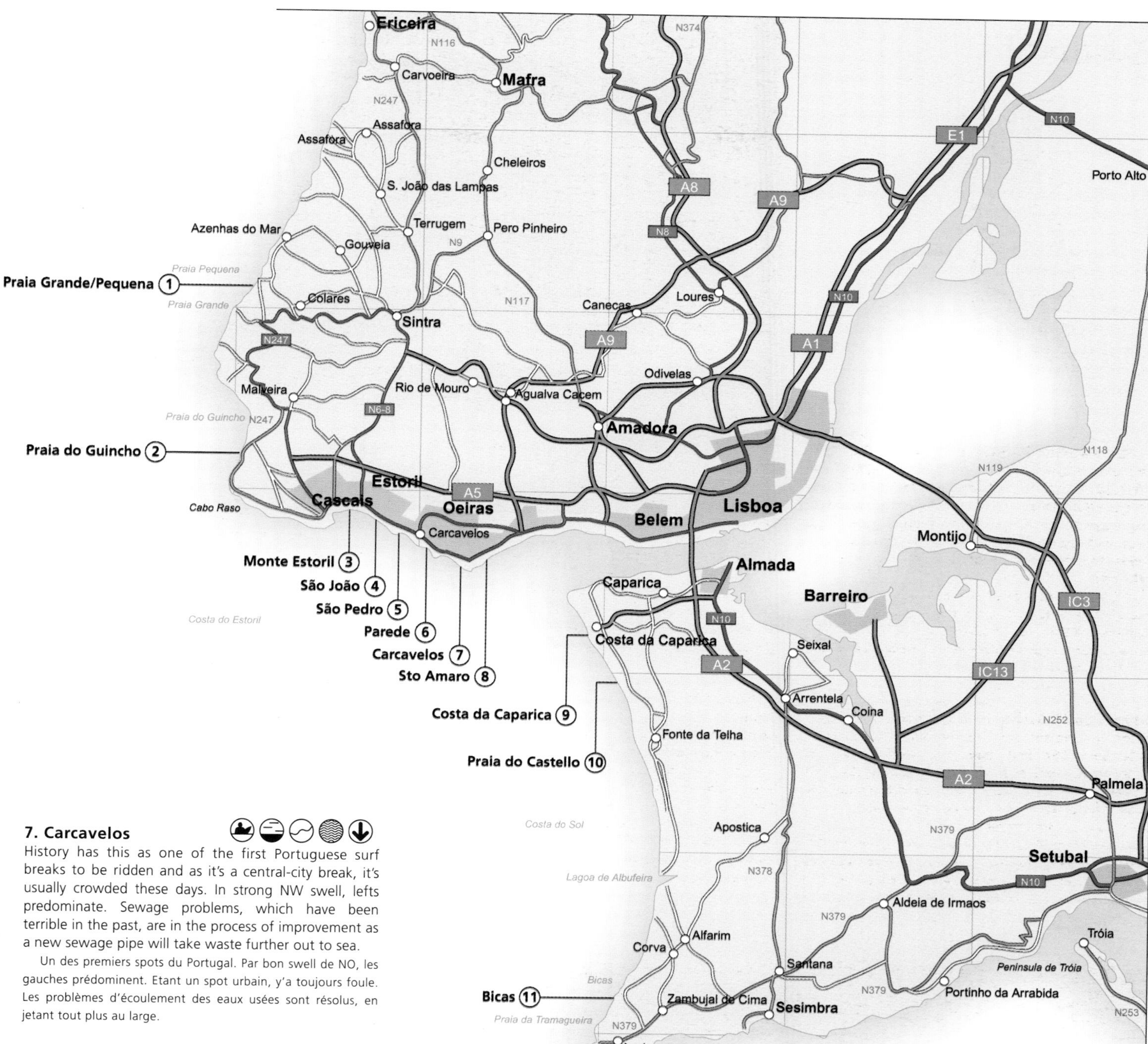 

Depending on the sandbar, the break can be a right or a left, but normally it has multiple peaks of a consistently high quality. The water is some of the cleanest in the Lisbon area and crowds are minimal.

Selon les bancs, c'est droite ou gauche mais y'a souvent pas mal de pics de trés bonne qualité. L'eau est parmi les plus pures de Lisbonne et la foule est minime.

11. Bicas  

This only breaks a couple of times a year and when it does it's a perfect left-hander which handles substantial amounts of swell. Water quality is excellent.

Quelques fois par an seulement pour cette gauche magique qui attend patiemment les gros swells pour s'activer. Tubes.

The South

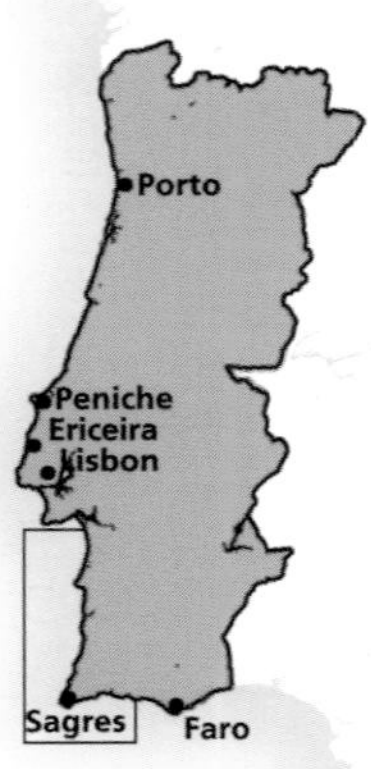

1. Cabo de Sines

This spot is located in front of the infamous Sines' industrial plant. The wave starts on a jetty and, depending on the sandbars, it can be quite good. It's usually uncrowded.

Ce spot se situe en face de l'infâme complexe industriel. La vague part d'une jetée et en fonction des bancs, peut être sympathique. Pas de monde normalement.

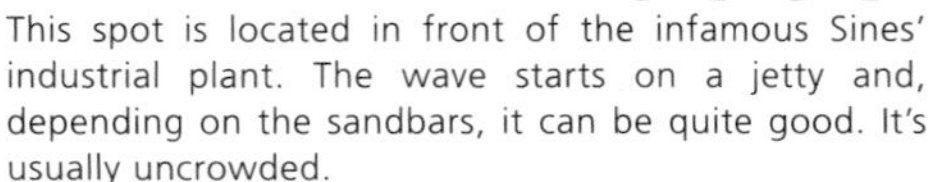

2. São Torpes

An average wave that works well here in the same conditions as Sines and is normally uncrowded. The water is pretty good.

Une vague correcte qui marche dans les mêmes conditions que Sines. L'eau y est de bonne qualité.

3. Porto Corvo

This wave breaks between Pesseguiro Island and the shore. It can hold big swell and, depending on the tide, it has cover up sections.

La vague casse entre l'île de Pessiguiro et le rivage. Peut tenir la houle et à la bonne marée, il y a des petites sections à tubes.

Arrifana rights and lefts

JOÃO VALENTE

4. Malhão

The most famous spot in the Nova area is rarely flat. The quality of the wave depends on the sandbar, but it's consistently good and the water is clear.

Le spot la plus couru de la zone de Vila Nova qui peut être ultra-consistant, étant rarement flat. La qualité de la vague est variable mais souvent bien formée et l'eau est cristalline.

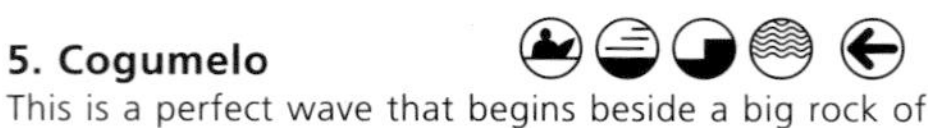

5. Cogumelo

This is a perfect wave that begins beside a big rock of the same name and rolls all the way to the inside over a rocky bottom. Normally it needs a bigger swell to work well. Good quality water.

Un pic parfait, qui démarre prés d'un rocher 'le Cogumelo' et déroulant jusqu'à l'inside sur un fond rocher. Par houle de bonne taille pour être classique. Rien à dire sur l'eau.

6. Praia de Odeceixe

Located a few kilometres down a windy, hazardous road, you'll find a good beach break. When everywhere nearby is suffering from strong winds, the protection offered by the cliffs here makes it a reliable choice.

Un bon beach break, protégé des vents par les falaises quand les spots alentours sont gavés de vents.

7. Carriagem

Working in the same conditions as Odeceixe, this break is not so protected from the winds.

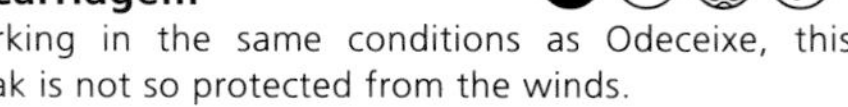

Mêmes conditions qu'Odeceixe, bien que moins abrité. La vague est correcte et l'eau est propre.

8. Monte Clérigo

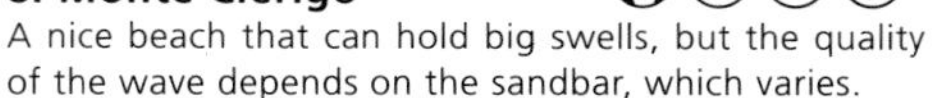

A nice beach that can hold big swells, but the quality of the wave depends on the sandbar, which varies.

Une superbe plage qui tient bien les grosses houles mais la qualité de la vague dépend des bancs de sable, qui bougent beaucoup.

9. Arrifana

The most versatile spot in the S of Portugal. On big days, there's a huge right breaking from the N of the bay that occasionally runs over two big rocks on the inside. On small days there's a peaky wave in the middle of the beach with nice little tubes.

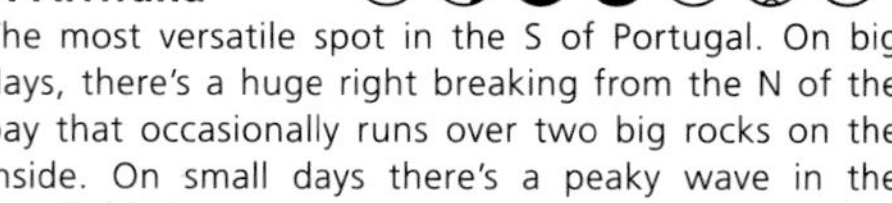

Le spot le plus versatile du sud du Portugal. Quand c'est gros, une méga-droite casse au nord de la baie, qui passe de temps en temps sur deux gros rochers qui émergent. Quand c'est plus petit, on trouve une gauche courte au milieu de la baie avec des tubes sympas.

10. Carrapateira

A nice spot, sheltered from heavy S winds and normally uncrowded. A left peak bowls off the headland at low tide. As the tide gets higher the beach turns on, the best peak breaking right into the rivermouth. Depending on the sandbars waves can either be hollow and fast or long and mellow. When its good, its very, very good. Check beaches S as well.

Un spot agréable, abrité des vents forts et souvent sans monde. Les bancs de sable déterminent la qualité de la vague et ça peut être fantastique.

One of the many spots on the south west coast

ALEX WILLIAMS

ALEX WILLIAMS

The guys at *Surfer's Path* named this new spot 'Pussy Galau'

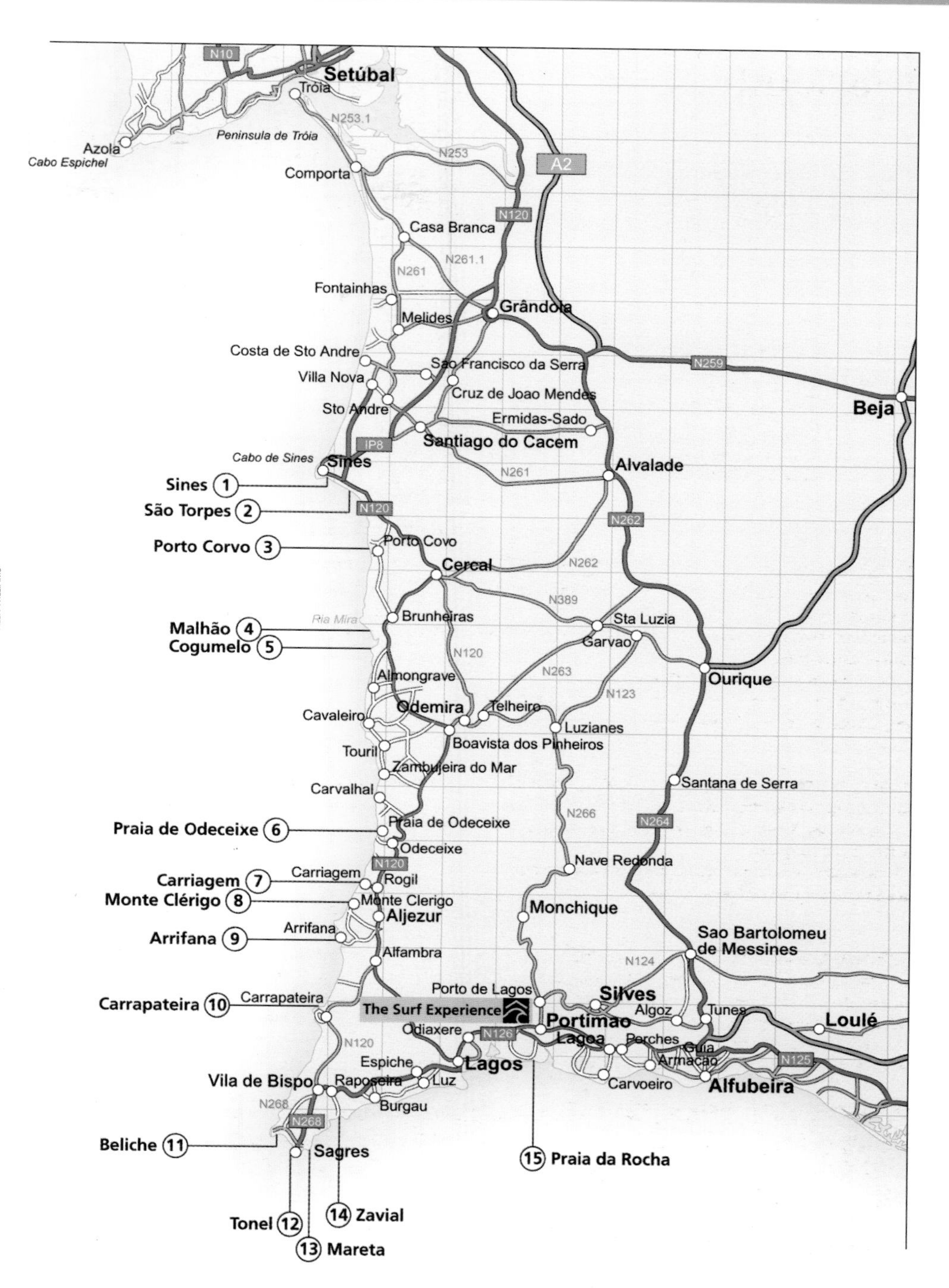

Setúbal
Tróia
N10
N253.1
Peninsula de Tróia
Azola
Cabo Espichel
Comporta
N253
A2
N120
Casa Branca
N261
N261.1
Fontainhas
Grândola
Melides
Costa de Sto Andre
São Francisco da Serra
N259
Villa Nova
Cruz de Joao Mendes
Sto Andre
Ermidas-Sado
Beja
IP8
Santiago do Cacem
Cabo de Sines
Sines
Alvalade
Sines (1)
N261
São Torpes (2)
N120
N262
Porto Corvo (3)
Porto Covo
Cercal
N262
N389
Ria Mira
Malhão (4)
Brunheiras
Sta Luzia
Cogumelo (5)
Garvao
N120
N263
Almongrave
Ourique
N123
Cavaleiro
Odemira
Telheiro
Luzianes
Touril
Boavista dos Pinheiros
Zambujeira do Mar
Santana de Serra
Carvalhal
N266
N264
Praia de Odeceixe (6)
Praia de Odeceixe
Odeceixe
Nave Redonda
Carriagem (7)
Carriagem
N120
Rogil
Monte Clérigo (8)
Monte Clerigo
Aljezur
Monchique
Arrifana (9)
Arrifana
Alfambra
Sao Bartolomeu de Messines
N124
Porto de Lagos
Carrapateira (10)
Carrapateira
Silves
The Surf Experience
Algoz
Tunes
Loulé
Portimao
Odiaxere
N125
Lagoa
Perches
N120
Guia
Espiche
Lagos
Armacao
N125
Vila de Bispo
Raposeira
Luz
Carvoeiro
Alfubeira
N268
Burgau
N268
Beliche (11)
Sagres
(15) Praia da Rocha
(14) Zavial
Tonel (12)
(13) Mareta

11. Beliche

This is a hollow wave that needs either a good size N swell, or an average S swell to make it work. It's usually very crowded as it's a perfect peak with tube sections on most waves.

Une vague creuse qui demande un bon swell de nord ou un swell de sud pour marcher. Souvent beaucoup de monde parce que les pics sont parfaits avec des sections à tubes sur la plupart des vagues.

12. Tonel

This works in the same conditions as Beliche. There is a Youth Hostel overlooking the point, so accommodation isn't a problem, especially in the winter.

Marche avec les mêmes conditions que Belixe, mais plus exposé et donc plus de houle. Il y a une auberge de jeunesse qui surplombe la baie, donc pas de problème de logement surtout en hiver.

13. Mareta

A perfect peak, but it takes a big swell to make it break. It's usually a good option when Tonel is closing out.

Un pic parfait mais il faut que ça rentre énorme pour activer les bancs, il faut que Tunel sature à max.

14. Zavial

Zavial breaks in the same conditions as Mareta. It's a long right-hander and has a cover up section. Good quality water.

Zavial casse dans les mêmes conditions que Mareta. Une longue droite avec des sections à tubes. L'eau y est super propre.

15. Praia da Rocha

Famous for its barrels, which normally break left, this was the first known Algarve break and is the closest spot to Faro. Owing to the location of the spot it can become crowded on good days.

C'était le premier break connu du Portugal car le plus proche de Faro. Célèbre pour ses tubes qui cassent normalement en gauche. Attention au peuple!

MARC FENIES

South coast lineup

The seas surrounding Italy can have good waves in the 1-2m (3-6ft) range

Italy

Few surfers would have guessed it, but Italy actually receives regular waves, sometimes as high as double overhead. With 8,000 kilometres (4,971 miles) of coast there is a remarkable variety of surf, explaining the growing number of Italian surfers that have appeared in the 90s. Regular winds can kick up short fetch swells, from several directions in this sea of no tides and while summer can have its flat periods, the Mediterranean climate, food, culture and water temperatures balance out the equation. Winter offers the best chance of quality waves in the Med, where swells may be short but they sure can be sweet.

Italia

Trés peu du monde le savent mais il y a des vagues régulieres en Italy. Parfois elles font trois metres. Avec 8000km de côte c'est normal qu'il y des belles vagues. Ce qui explique une croissance des surfeurs dans les années quatre vingts dix. Il y a un vent régulier qui crè de la houle qui va dans plusies directions cette, mer qui à des marrées de petits coefficients. Pendent l'été ca peut être calme mais la culture, la nourriture, le climat et la température de l'eau donnent une envie de tout laisser tomber pour y aller. Pendent l'hiver les vagues sont meilleures et même si les houles de la Méditerranée ne durent pas longtemps elles sont bonnes.

STEFFAN DITRICH

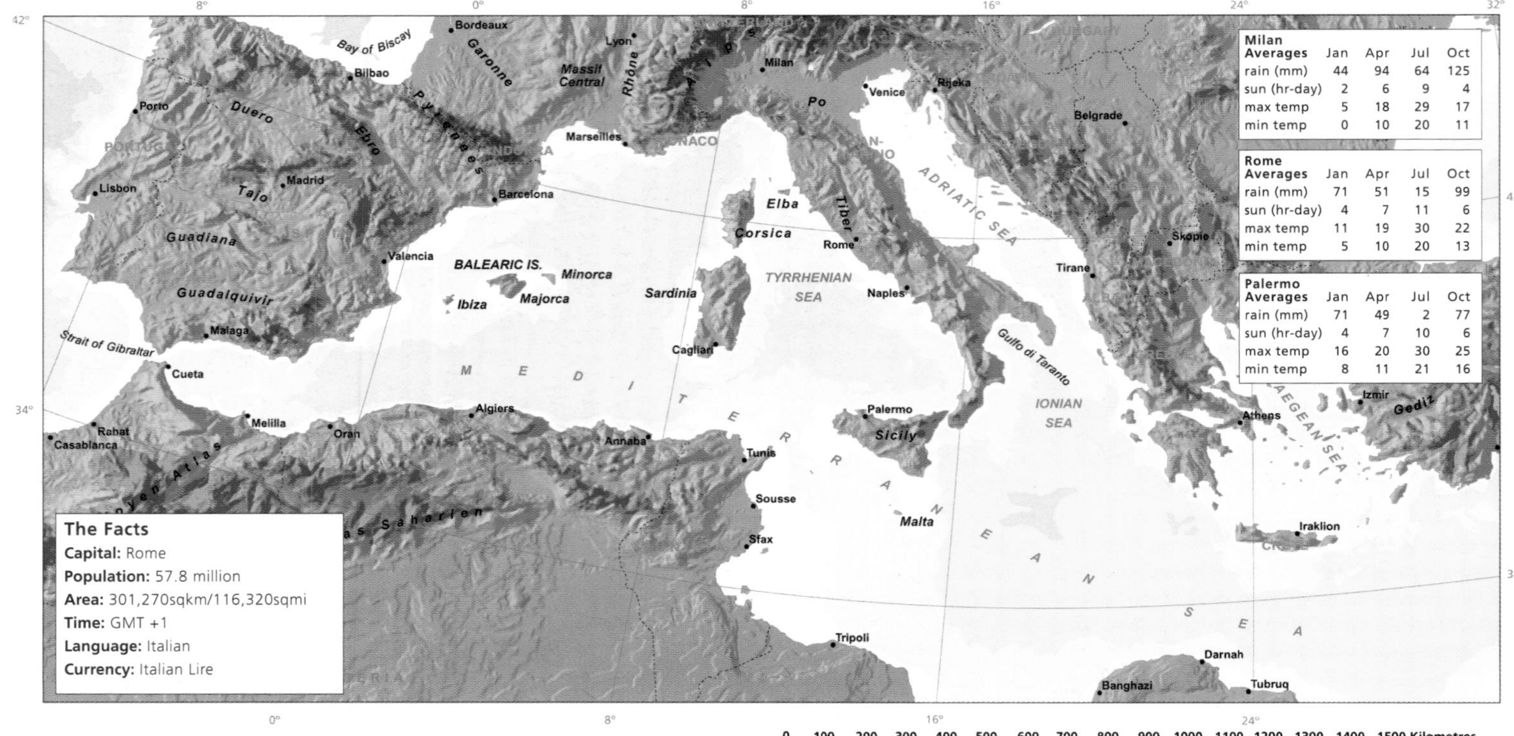

Milan Averages	Jan	Apr	Jul	Oct
rain (mm)	44	94	64	125
sun (hr-day)	2	6	9	4
max temp	5	18	29	17
min temp	0	10	20	11

Rome Averages	Jan	Apr	Jul	Oct
rain (mm)	71	51	15	99
sun (hr-day)	4	7	11	6
max temp	11	19	30	22
min temp	5	10	20	13

Palermo Averages	Jan	Apr	Jul	Oct
rain (mm)	71	49	2	77
sun (hr-day)	4	7	10	6
max temp	16	20	30	25
min temp	8	11	21	16

The Facts
Capital: Rome
Population: 57.8 million
Area: 301,270sqkm/116,320sqmi
Time: GMT +1
Language: Italian
Currency: Italian Lire

The Mediterranean: Physical geography

Scale 0 100 200 300 400 500 600 700 800 900 1000 1100 1200 1300 1400 1500 Kilometres
0 100 200 300 400 500 600 700 800 900 1000 Miles

Introduction

Surf Culture

In the late 70s to early 80s alongside the windsurf boom, and the release of the Hollywood cult classic, *Big Wednesday*, the first 'wave surfers' appeared in Italy. Viareggio was the centre of Italian surfing, where the first club (Italia Wave Surf Team), the first shop (Natural Surf), and the first contests started up. This area was pioneered by the Farina brothers and the Dini brothers, while up in Genova the instigators were the Fracas brothers. Carlo Piccini and Fabio Gini were the early starters around Rome, while Maurizio Spinas, Diddo Ciani and Giuseppe Meleddu were already enjoying Sardinia. The east coast push came from Andrea Tazzari and Angelo Manca at the Adriatic breaks around Ravenna. Initially numbers were small, but now there are 10,000 to 15,000 surfers and that figure is ever increasing. Since the early 90s the number of surf shops went from four to 50 and specialised magazines from zero to three. The surfing federation, FISURF, has 30 affiliated clubs, and organises all official competitions.

The Ocean Environment

The water quality in the Italian Basin is generally poor, and in industrialised areas and at rivermouths the quality deteriorates further. Many waves, such as Banzai and Lillatro are currently under threat from sea wall constructions. Coccia de Morto has heavily polluted water flowing down the river from Rome, carrying the possibility of ear infections and worse. Most major rivers and harbours are polluted with residential and commercial effluent, but things are improving with better sewerage treatment plants in some areas. Algae blooms in the Adriatic are a problem, suffocating everything in the water. Seven years ago tight controls were imposed, funded by government agencies. 'Green Schooner' certificates are supposed to bear testament to the quality of the water, but it's a bit of a lottery depending on location and season.

Forte dé Marmi
STEFFEN DITTRICH

Introduction

Culture Surf

Dans le début des années 80 avec le boom du windsurf, les premiers surfers "de vagues" apparurent. Au départ, les effectifs étaient minimes mais une fois que la difficulté d'expliquer que les eaux italiennes étaient parfaitement surfables fut surmontée, les adeptes se sont multipliés régulièrement. Actuellement, il y a à peu près 4000 surfers. Depuis le début des années 90, le nombre de surf-shops est passé de 4 à 20 et les magazines spécialisés de 0 à 3. Il y a aussi deux federacion de surf. Le SFI qui organise les competitions. Avec 8000 kms de côtes, l'Italie reste encore largement inexplorée, surtout dans l'extrême sud, où les surfers sont encore une curiosité. Pour l'instant, la FISO a répertorié une centaine de spots mais ce n'est qu'un début.

FISURF
FEDERAZIONE ITALIANA SURFING

L'Evirons Ocean

La qualité de l'eau est correcte bien que dans les zones industrialisées et aux sorties de rivières, elle soit inquiétante. En 1988, des contrôles sévères furent imposés par des institutions gouvernementales. Le "Green Schooner" (bannière verte) certifie la qualité de l'eau.

Ou Aller

Le nord et l'Adriatique La plus grande concentration des surfeurs est située aux environs de Rome. Cependant la région au nord de Livorno est considerée comme le lieu de naissance du surf Italien. C'est ici que vous trouverez les meilleures

Venice
TIM RAINGER

Varraze

Where to go

The North and Adriatic The area north of Livorno is the birthplace of Italian surfing. This is where you'll find some of the best waves, like the big wave spot, Levanto, and consistent spots around Forte dé Marmi and Viareggio, where most competitions are held. The Adriatic coast receives wind swells, but a lack of fetch means short swells, which mainly occur in the depth of winter.

Rome, Sardinia and the South The greatest concentration of surfers is around Rome. Its most consistent spot, Banzai, and all the surrounding area, is now suffering from crowded conditions and isolated localism, though this lessens towards the southern breaks of Santa Agostino. Sardinia is rapidly gaining popularity, with breaks like Capo Mannu earning a reputation for being one of the Med's most powerful tubes. The island is centrally positioned to pick up any local swell, and has

Pellegrini, Banzai

Buggerru, Sardinia

some good reefs to extract what power there is. Localism is on the increase as mainlanders are realising the potential just across the Tyrrhenian Sea. Be cool.

Southern Italy is largely unexplored, especially Sicily, and down on 'the boot' of Italy, where surfers are still a rare sight. Calabria hides some great waves on both sides of the coast. Swell windows on the west coast range from north to south west, while a trip over the mountains will see north to south swells on the east side. Sicily has equally impressive swell windows, with only a handful of locals pioneering many of the difficult access reefs.

When to go

Mediterranean Averages	Jan	Apr	Jul	Oct
water °C	13	15	26	22
wetsuit				

Adriatic Averages	Jan	Apr	Jul	Oct
water °C	13	15	28	24
wetsuit				

Waist-high surf is a common occurrence caused by trade winds, fronts, or with luck, an established low, west of Sardinia. The most frequent meteorological conditions are fronts associated with lows crossing north and west from the Atlantic towards the Med. The contrast of temperatures between the cooler air arriving from the ocean generates gusty sea breezes that affect the whole Italian coastline and islands. South winds from Africa can also produce swell for the south and west coasts. A favourable set of conditions for wave generation in the Adriatic is the descent of cold air currents from the former Soviet block triggering a strong east to north-east wind. Usually disturbances cross Italy swiftly, producing waves and favourable conditions for a couple of days. The best surf period is September to June, when disturbances passing across the Med are most frequent. The number of surfable days varies, depending on the position of the spots, from a minimum of 60 days to a maximum of 200 a year. During the colder periods on the west coast and on the islands, the air temps rarely fall below 10°C (50°F), while the water stays round 12°C-14°C (55-58°F), but rises to 26°C (81°F) in summer. The east coast is colder during winter, but summer temps rise to a bath-like 30°C (88°F).

vagues, comme à Levanto ainsi que les spots qui marchent toujours à côté de Forte dei Marmi et Viareggio où les competitions prenent lieu. Les meilleurs spots de Rome se trouvent dans la région de Banzai. Récemment ils ont été envahis ce qui enerve les locaux, mais plus qu'on va vers le sud plus ils sont calmes. La côte Adriatique récoit des petits houles dont la plupart arrivent en plein hiver.

Rome, Sardaigne et le Sud La Sardaigne devient très populaire grâce à des spots comme Capu Mannu connu pour le tube le plus puissant de la Méditerranée. D'ailleurs l'ile est située pour recevoir toutes les houles locales qui augmentent sa puissance par les récifs qui l'entourent. Pour les locaux c'est très populaire, donc ici fait gaffe et respect. L'Italie du sud-est est et peu explorée, surtout la Sicile et la côte qui longe la 'botte' d'Italie d'où les surfeurs sont rares. En Calabria il y a des spots cachés sur les deux côtes. Les houles sur la côte oeust varient du nord au sud-oeust alors que sur la côte est les houles viennent du nord-est et du sud. Les houles en Sicile sont égalements très variées avec seulement une poignée des surfeurs locaux sur les spot les plus inaccessibles .

Quand Aller

Grâce à de bonnes conditions climatiques, les mers qui entourent l'Italie ont souvent un bon potentiel pour des vagues de 1 à 2 mètres. On peut même parfois surfer jusqu'à 2,5m. Les conditions météo les plus fréquentes sont le passage de perturbations du nord-ouest au sud depuis l'Atlantique nord. Après que la dépression a traversé la France et l'Espagne, elle heurte le bassin Méditerranéen. Le contraste de températures entre les mers entourant l'Italie et l'air arrivant de l'océan génère des vents violents qui affectent tout le littoral italien et ses îles. Un situation favorable pouur la formation de vagues est la descente de courants d'air froid depuis l'ex-bloc soviétique qui provoquent de forts vents d'est/nord-est sur le littoral italien. Il y a aussi la situation d'un air océanique froid qui entre violemment en Afrique du Nord, ce qui amène dÜes vents de sud sur toutes les mers italiennes et donc des vagues. Souvent, les perturbations circulent sur le pays rapidement, donnant des vagues et des conditions favorables pour un ou deux jours. La meilleure période pour surfer s'étend de septembre à Juin, quand ces dépressions sont les plus fréquentes. La fréquence des jours surfables varient énormément en fonction de la position des spots: de 60 au minimum à 200 jours par an. Le climat italien est particulièrement clément. Pendant les périodes les plus froides sur la côte ouest et les îles, les températures descendent rarement au-dessous de 10°c avec une eau entre 12°c et 14°c. La côte orientale est plus froide pendant l'hiver mais l'été, ça peut monter jusqu'à 30°c.

The North

Levanto

1. Varazze

This Italian jewel breaks over an artificial reef. Heavy, hollow and crowded, it works on small swells. Wipe-outs can lead to a confrontation with the jagged rock. Water quality is good.

Un autre joyau des spots de la Mediterranée sur un reef artificiel. Carton, creux et peuplé. Prenez une gamelle et vous irez tâter les formations rocheuses déchiquetées. Marche par petit swell. L'eau est propre.

2. Levanto

Situated deep in the bay is one of Italy's biggest lefts. A SW swell will give the best waves.

Située dans la baie, cette gauche est une des plus grosses du pays. Une houle de S-O donnera les meilleures vagues.

3. Lerici

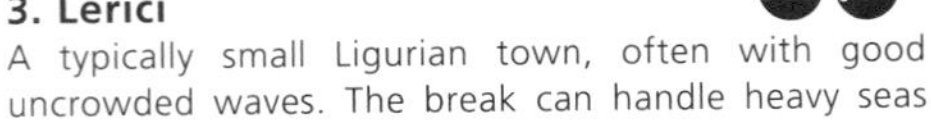

A typically small Ligurian town, often with good uncrowded waves. The break can handle heavy seas and SW winds. Good water quality.

Une petite ville typique de Ligurie avec de bonnes vagues régulières sans la foule. Peut tenir des mers démontées avec des vents de SO.

4. Forte dé Marmi (Pontile)

There are good sandbars but strong currents consistently alter wave characteristics. It's located about 15km (9mi) N of Viareggio. Mediocre water quality.

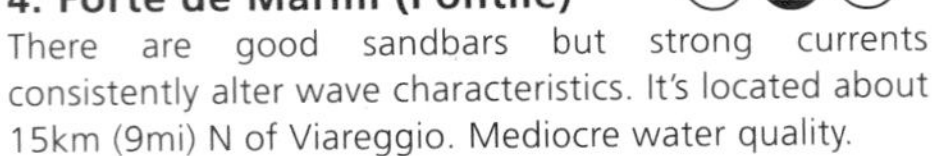

De bons bancs de sable mais des courants infernaux qui changent constamment les caractéristiques de la vague. Situé à 15 kms au nord de Viarregio avec une qualité de l'eau qui est médiocre.

Viareggio
5. Tito del Molo

The N side of the port has long and powerful waves with a strong SW swell. When it works, it's crowded.

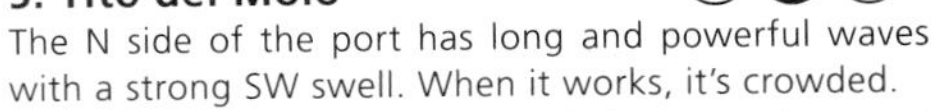

L'extrémité nord du port peut avoir des vagues longues et puissantes par forte houle de sud-ouest. La Chine quand ça marche.

6. Piazza Mazzini

A shallow sandbar created by the dredging of the port has provided Viareggio with one of Italy's best waves S of the port. It's consistent and very crowded.

Un haut-fond créé par le draguage du port est maintenant une des meilleures vagues d'Italie. Consistant et bondé.

A. DINI

Varazze rights, Liguria

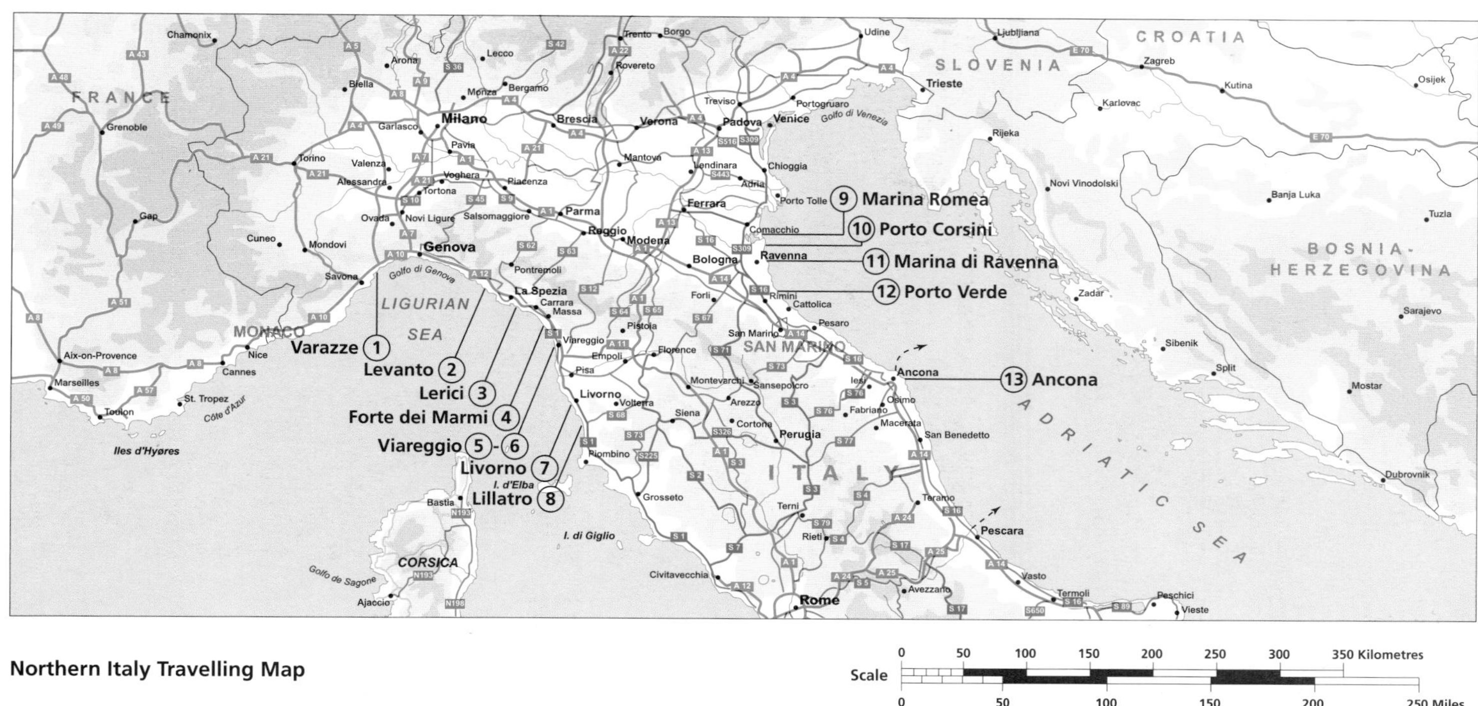

Northern Italy Travelling Map

A. DINI

Stefano Giuliani at Il Molo, Viareggio

7. Livorno (Il Sale)

One of the best spots in Italy, this has a powerful, tubey peak which breaks in shallow water. It needs a good swell to break and when it does it's dominated by a hot local crew.

Un pic puissant et tubulaire casse dans peu d'eau, dominé par une bande un peu survoltée. Marche avec un swell correct.

8. Lillatro

Four peaks give short but good waves. Water is bad due to a detergent factory which nonetheless gives a photogenic blue quality to the water.

Quatre pics qui donnent de bonnes vagues mais courtes. L'eau est détestable à cause d'une usine de détergents qui donne à l'eau néanmoins une belle couleur bleue très photogénique.

Adriatic Sea

9. Marina Romea

The rivermouth has created sandbanks which hold the most consistent waves in the N Adriatic. It's best in S swell up to 2m (6ft).

Les vagues les plus consistantes du nord de l'Adriatique. L'embouchure de la rivière a créé des bancs avec de bonnes vagues jusqu'à 2m. Meilleur par houle de sud.

10. Porto Corsini (Diga Nord)

A popular spot in the centre of town. At the port of Ravenna a sandbar forms a long right, which can be especially good on a longboard. Dirty water.

Un spot bien connu au centre de la ville. Dans le port de Ravenna, un banc de sable forme une droite qui peut être longue, surtout en longboard. L'eau est médiocre.

11. Marina di Ravenna

A good contemplation spot, which handles the bigger swells. It needs a NE or E swell to amp.

Bon spot pour le paysage. Par houle de nord-est à est.

12. Porto Verde

The only rock/reef in the area holding good rights on a NE or E swell; located 200m (180yd) S of the port. Average water quality.

Le seul reef dans le coin qui donne de bonnes droites par houle de nord-est et est. Situé à 200m au sud du port.

13. Ancona (La Trave)

Three km (2mi) S of Ancona, you'll find good water and quality waves in most swells.

Trois kilometre au sud d'Ancona. Eau et vague de ûqualité qui chope la plupart des houles.

ANDREA TAZZARI

Marina di Ravenna, Adriatic Sea

STEFFEN DITTRICH

Viareggio backdrop

Rome and Sardinia

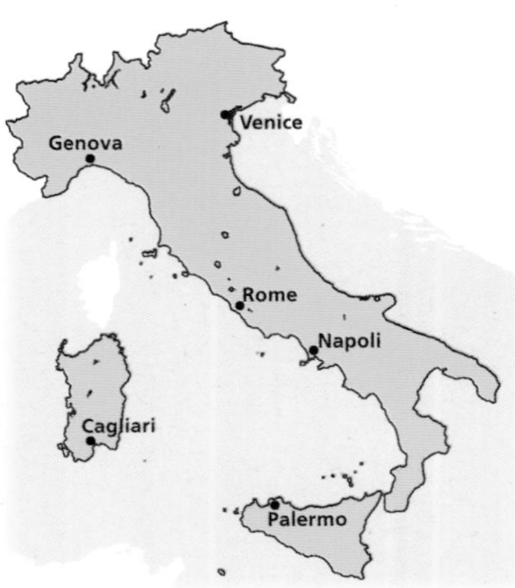

Santa Marinella

1. Porto

One of the best spots in the area that's good in a SW swell. It's a decent size but water quality is bad due to the port.

Un des meilleurs spots de la zone, idéal par houle de sud-ouest. Peut tenir une bonne taille de houle mais l'eau est polluée par le port..

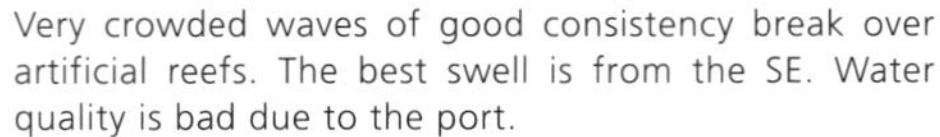

STEFFEN DITTRICH

2. Bunker

A good wave breaking in shallow water, which is best in a NW wind.

Une bonne vague qui casse dans peu d'eau meilleure par vents de nord-ouest

3. Ristorante

This picks up a bit less swell than Banzai but has good fast waves and is not always crowded.

Chope un peu moins de swell que Banzai mais les vagues y sont plus rapides. Pas forcément la foule.

4. Banzai

Called 'The Prince of the Lazio Coast', Banzai is a powerful break and consequently gets crowded with some of Italy's best surfers. Good water quality.

Appelé 'le Prince du Lazio', Banzai est puissant et est rippé par certains des meilleurs surfers italiens.

5. Off The Wall

A good peak with very short waves that can work well when Banzai is flat.

Peut bien marcher quand y'a rien à Banzai. Un bon pic mais les vagues sont ultra-courtes.

6. Focene

A crowded spot that works well in a small swell.

Le spot le plus peuplé par petite houle.

7. Coccia de Morto

Very crowded waves of good consistency break over artificial reefs. The best swell is from the SE. Water quality is bad due to the port.

Des vagues bondées bien consistantes qui cassent sur un reef artificiel. La meilleure houle vient du sud-est. Un port à côté donc l'eau est moins que moyenne.

8. Lido Garda

The most popular beach break in the area N of Anzio. Water quality can be bad.

Le beach break le plus fréquenté au nord d'Anzio. Pollution.

9. Porto de Anzio

A consistent spot that holds big surf and is best with a SW swell. Water quality can be bad.

Spot consistant qui tient le gros surf, meilleur par houle de sud-ouest. Pollution.

10. Carrubo

Protected from N winds by the Circeo headland, this is a good spot with clean water and no crowds.

Protégé des vents de nord par la péninsule de Circeo. Bon spot avec une eau limpide et pas de monde.

A. DINI

P. Perucci, Coccia di Morto, Rome

DINI

Mini Capo, Sardinia

11. Santa Agostino

A good spot especially with winds from the SE. Waves have power and speed.

Bon spot surtout par vents de sud-est. Les vagues sont puissantes et rapides.

Sardinia

North Coast

12. Isola Rossa

A narrow beach surrounded by rocks; this break can have powerful tubes.

Une plage étroite entourée par des rochers.

13. Badesi

A wide beach with various peaks best in a NW swell.

Une plage avec des pics variés meilleurs par houle de nord-ouest.

14. La Ciaccia (Valledoria)

This break can have good long lefts.

Peut avoir de longues vagues de qualité.

15. Sotto Il Castello

A short but powerful peak breaks right. It needs a big swell to work.

Un pic court mais puissant qui casse en droite. Demande un gros swell.

16. Lu Bagnu

This tubing left peak works up to 2m (6ft) with swell from the SW-NW.

Marche jusqu'à 2m avec une houle de SO à NO. Un pic en gauche qui donne un bon tube.

17. Alghero – Porto Ferro

A bay needing swell from SW-N and no wind. It's good from 1-4m (3-9ft), but blows out easily.

Une baie qui nécessite une houle de sud-ouest à nord mais sans trop de vents. Marche de 1 à 4 mètres!

Puzzu Idu

Some of the best waves in the Med break in an area 30km (20mi) NW of Oristano. It also works in mistral conditions.

Parmi les meilleures vagues de la Mediterranée dans un rayon de 30 kms au nord-ouest d'Oristano.

18. Capo Mannu

A powerful peak with a long tubey right and a shorter steeper left. Sharp rocks and urchins mean boots are a good idea.

Un pic puissant qui donne une droite puissante et tubulaire avec une gauche plus courte et plus raide encore. Des rochers coupants et des oursins, n'oubliez pas vos chaussons.

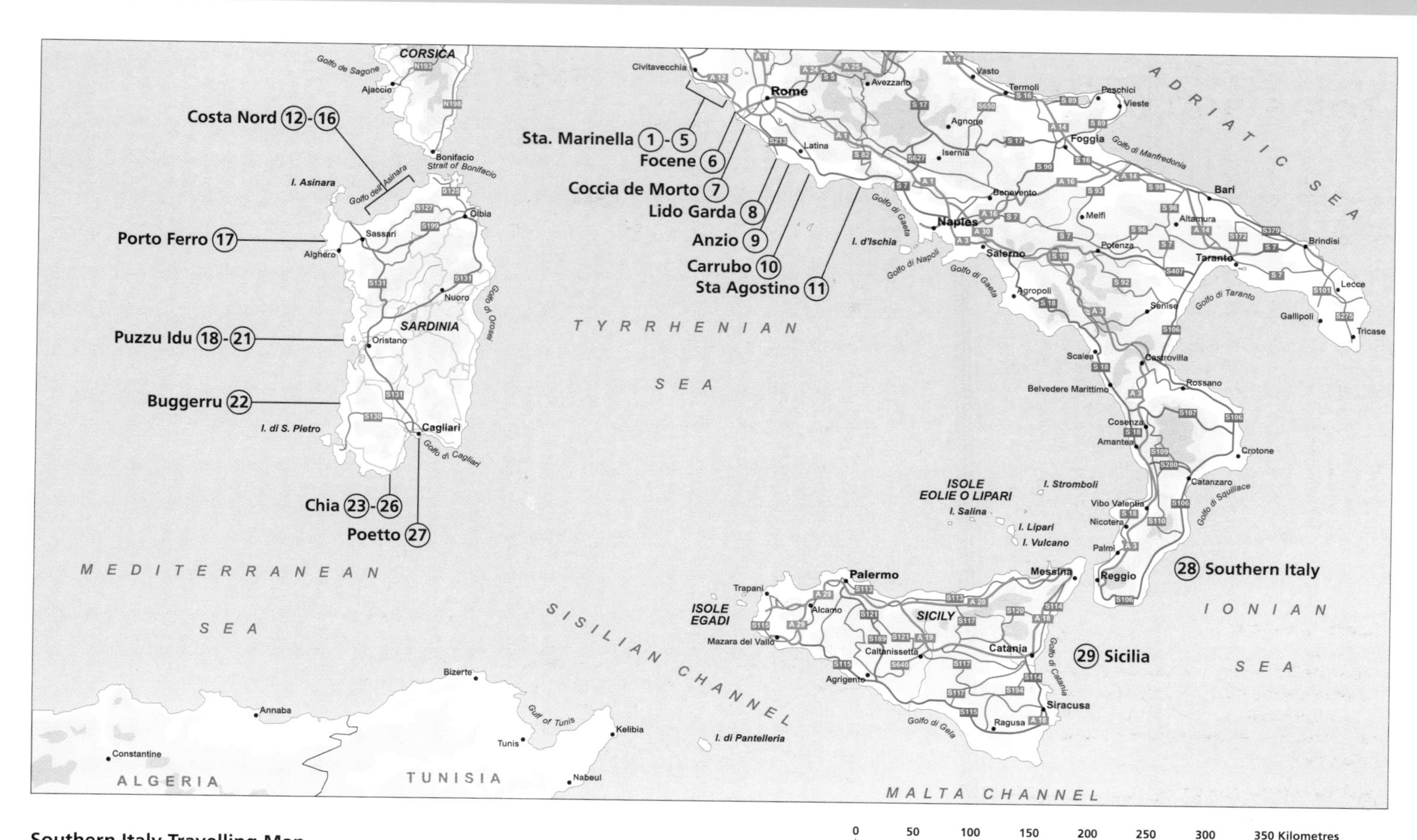

Southern Italy Travelling Map

19. Mini Cap

This wave starts to break when Capo Mannu is big and when it does it's a good steep peak.

Commence à casser quand Capo Mannu est gros. Un bon pic bien creux.

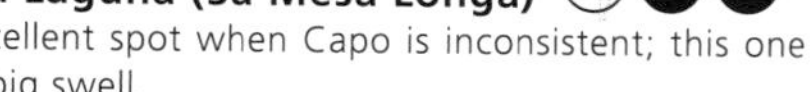

20. La Laguna (Sa Mesa Longa)

An excellent spot when Capo is inconsistent; this one holds big swell.

Excellent spot quand Capo est irrégulier. Tient bien le gros quand ça vient du nord au sud-ouest.

21. Su Paulo Su

A long, powerful wave that works in the same conditions as La Laguna.

Une vague très longue et puissante marchant dans les mêmes conditions que la Lagune.

22. Buggerru

A heavy left that tubes on take-off. There's an easy paddle out along the pier. Also waves at Porti Sceddu.

Une gauche carton qui tube au take-off. Il est facile de ramer le long de la jetée. Des vagues aussi à Porti Sceddu.

Chia

About 50km (36mi) from Cagliari is one of the best areas on Sardinia with various good quality waves.

A 50 kms dela Sardaigne se trouve une des meilleures zones de surf en Sardaigne avec quelques vagues de qualité variable.

23. Il Pontile

A tubey left wave that holds a good-sized swell. It needs a NE swell to work well.

Une gauche tubulaire.

24. Il Morto

With huge seas from the W, this spot harbours some very long, lined up rights.

De très longues droites avec une mer agitée vers l'ouest.

25. L'Isolotto

When Il Morto is small, this area can have waves.

Peut marcher quand c'est trop petit à Il Morto.

26. Pipeline

Long rights and also a good steep shore break.

Tres longues droites et aussi un bon gros shore-break.

27. Cagliari (Poetto)

One of the best spots on the island with long, mellow waves ideal for beginners.

Un des meilleurs spots de l'île. Des vagues longues et molles idéales pour débuter.

Other spots Southern Italy

Rodi Garganico, Peschici, Vieste, Barletta, Bari, Monopoli, Otranto, Gallipoli, Lido di Policoro, Capo, Spulico and Pizzo Colabrohave.

Sicilia

Mazzara Del Vallo (various spots), Tre Fontane, Triscina, Elora, Siracusa, Cefalu, Terrasini Capo D'Orlando and Pozzallo.

A. DINI

Maddaleni, Terrasini, Sicily

A. DINI

David Malherbe, Chia area

Morocco

For the past three decades, Morocco's myriad right-hand points and abundant, hollow beach breaks have attracted surf travellers the world over. This wave-rich kingdom, which sits at the frontier of European civilisation, has become a natural conclusion to the well-worn European surf trail and can be its most rewarding stop. An untapped stash of uncrowded rights in a warm climate with no sharks, no coral and few diseases create a perfect Northern Hemisphere winter escape. From the verdant, mountainous north to the harsh, arid deserts of the Saharan south, Morocco is a trip of vital intensity.

Maroc

Le Maroc, dernier arrêt d'une visite des spots européens, pourrait bien être le meilleur. Un climat idéal, une réserve illimitée de droites désertes, aucune des maladies typiques d'Afrique, font du Maroc le refuge hivernal rêvé pour les européens. La population est sympa, curieuse, et les paysages varient des collines verdoyantes du nord aux déserts arides du Sahara au Sud. Depuis plus de 30 ans, de nombreux européens, attirés par ses innombrables droites et autres beach breaks, ont poussé les locaux à se mettre au surf pour en profiter.

Many gems like thes await discovery

MARC FENIES

Introduction

The People

Morocco lies on the north-western tip of the African continent; consequently you might be wondering what it's doing in this book, and that has as much to do with historical as well as recent links to Europe. It's nonetheless the last refuge for descendants of the original north African people, the Berbers, who have borne an almost silent witness to the many foreign powers which have come and gone through their land. Back in the 7th century AD, the ubiquitous Romans were overrun by Muslim Arabs, who were then thwarted by the Berbers in the 11th century; the Berbers went on to even occupy parts of Spain. During 1896 Spain took over Morocco's Saharan territory, but in 1912 Morocco changed hands to become a protectorate of France. Nationalists gained momentum during WW11 and in 1956, under the rule of Sultan Mohammed V, Morocco gained independence. A third of the population are Berber; their language is mainly used in the mountains and villages, while the Arab majority inhabit the lowlands and cities. French is widely spoken along with a growing number of European languages that young Moroccans learn in order to service the burgeoning tourist industry. Tourism, agriculture and mining of 75% of the world's phosphate reserves are the backbone of the economy.

Capital: Rabat
Population: 28,558,635
Area: 458, 730 sqkm/177,117sqmi
Time: GMT +1
Language: Arabic, French, Spanish, Berber
Currency: Moroccan Dirham (DH)

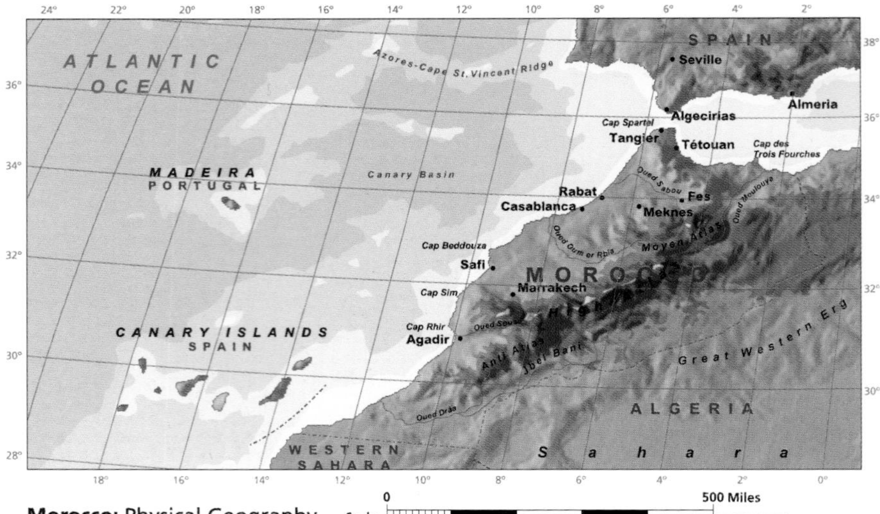

Morocco: Physical Geography

TIM RAINGER

More than 99% of the population are Sunni Muslims, leaving very few Christians and about 45,000 Jews. The tolerant national attitude reflects the moderate religious stance of King Hussan II (Commander of the Faithful), avoiding the fundamentalist Islamic militancy that engulfs Morocco's neighbours.

The Land

This corner of Africa contains a vast backbone of mountains, which run from the north-east Med to the south-west Atlantic. At 4,165m (10,576ft) Jebel Toubkal is the highest peak in north Africa and only marginally lower than Mount Blanc. The rest of the country sits on a plateau with very little land at sea level. The Rif Mountains in the north and the adjacent alluvial lowlands are verdant and agriculturally productive. Extensive forests of oak and cedar plus the illegal but tolerated forests of cannabis provide the north with some natural resources. The middle Atlas area begins to become more arid, while the High Atlas and Anti-Atlas border the Sahara desert with little vegetation. Date palm-fringed oases are dotted around the south, fed by water sources from the High Atlas.

BRUCE SUTHERLAND

Tizi-n-Test in the high atlas, only two hours' drive from Tarhazoute

The Climate

Morocco's weather is as diverse as the geography, which starts with a Mediterranean feel in the north and finishes in the deserts of the Saharan south. Throw in the alpine regions of the High Atlas and the balmy coastal areas near Agadir, and Morocco can truly be described as a four seasons' destination.

Hot summers and mild, wet winters are the rule for the north and coastal areas down to Agadir. A stable microclimate in Agadir gives 300 days of sunshine a year, which makes the winter months dry and warm before the scorching 'sirocco' and 'chergui' winds blow in from the desert during summer. It's a mere two hours' drive from Agadir to the snow-covered peaks of the High Atlas meaning that in winter a surf and snowboard session are both possible from the same low pressure on the same day.

Rabat Averages	Jan	Apr	Jul	Oct
rain (mm)	66	43	0	48
sun (hr-day)	5	9	11	8
max temp	17	22	28	25
min temp	8	11	17	14

Introduction

La Population

Le Maroc, à l'extrème nord-ouest du continent Africain, est entouré par la Mediterrannée et par l'Atlantique. Ce fut le refuge des plus anciennes tribus Berbère d'Afrique du nord. Elles ont depuis traversé l'histoire du pays, quels que soient les pouvoirs en place. Au 7e siècle avant J.C., les arabes ont défait les Romains, avant d'être écrasés par les berbères au 11e siècle. Les Sultans ont règnés jusqu'en 1912, date de la colonisation française. De nombreux pays ont tenté d'avoir leur part, et il n'y a que l'Espagne qui a pu annexer les ports mediterrannéens de Ceuta et Mellilla., ainsi que les vastes territoires du sud Sahara. L'indépendence fut signée avec la France en 1956.

Un tiers de la population parle berbère, notamment dans les montagnes et les villages, alors que la majorité arabe réside en plaine et dans les villes. Le français et d'autre langues européennes sont régulièrement enseignées, afin de répondre aux besoins du tourisme en pleine expansion. Le tourisme, l'agriculture, ainsi que l'exploitation de 75% des réserves mondiales de phosphates, sont le fer de lance de l'économie.

Si 99% de la population est musulmane sunnite, il y a étonnamment 45 000 juifs et peu de chrétiens, qui disposent de toutes leurs libertés et droits civiques. Ce panorama unique reflète la position modérée du roi Hassan II, qui a su éviter les dérives intègristes de ses proches voisins.

Le Pays

Ce coin d'Afrique est caracterisé par une grande dorsale montagneuse, qui s'étend du nord-est méditerranéen, au sud-ouest Atlantique. Le Mont Jébel Toubkal qui culmine à 4165 m, est le plus haut sommet d'Afrique du Nord, à peine plus modeste que le Mont-Blanc. La majorité restante du pays est située sur un plateau, les plaines cotières étant minimes.

Les Monts du Rif, au nord, et les vallées adjascentes sont les plus fertiles. De grandes forêts de cèdres et de chênes, et la culture, interdite mais tolérée, du cannabis, assurent les ressources naturelles du nord.

Dès le Moyen-Atlas, le climat devient plus arride, tandis que le Haut-Atlas et l'Anti-Atlas bordent le Sahara avec peu de végétation.Le sud-est est connu pour ses oasis abreuvés par les sources du Haut-Atlas, et bordées de palmiers datiers.

Le Climat

Aussi varié que sa géographie, le climat méditerranéen du nord contraste avec les amplitudes extrêmes du Sahara au sud. Au centre, le Haut-Atlas et son climat de montagne et, à l'ouest, la côte près d'Agadir bénéficie d'un régime tempéré. Le Maroc est destination pour toutes les saisons.

Surf Culture

History

US servicemen stationed in Morocco introduced surfing to the country during the early 60s. The next wave of foreign surfers arrived with the hippy trail in the late 60s and early 70s, which extended south to Agadir and the now famous waves of Tarhazoute. French ex-pats and a handful of Moroccans slowly began to surf, but their only source of experience and equipment was from the foreigners. As the country became better known for quality waves, a small surf industry has gradually evolved with its nucleus in Casablanca, providing the essentials for a growing number of locals and visitors alike. Today the association Cap Surf helps organise contests and Morocco now boasts its own national amateur team. King Hussan's family have provided support, as well as funds, to build a surf club at Rabat.

The Moroccan team in Brazil

Morocco 1974

The Ocean Environment

Water Quality

Morocco's more isolated coastal waters offer alluring, emerald waves, however, there are obvious problems associated with the large coastal cities of Tangier, Rabat and Casablanca. Agadir has a growing number of tourist developments and a large commercial harbour – it's safe to say these haven't done the environment any favours. After periods of rain, all rivermouths (nature's drains) can become fouled up, increasing the likelihood of picking up infections when surfing. While this is a rule of thumb around the globe, it's especially marked in densely populated or underdeveloped countries. The national attitude to household rubbish is dubious: it's often thrown into the ocean or roadside scrub and can be a dilemma for all.

On the whole Maroc is saved by its low coastal population density and comparative lack of industry, though in a developing nation with little environmental awareness this must pose a threat in years to come.

Most of Morocco's waves are crystal clear

On Localism

The Moroccan locals demand respect, but are extremely friendly towards relaxed visitors. At crowded locations such as Tarhazoute, where foreigners outnumber the locals, their understandable attempts to control the peak can cause problems. Yet in such a wave-rich country, with miles of empty waves, any confrontation can be easily avoided. Maroc is so laid back, that a bad attitude has no place in day-to-day life.

Speaking of which, the freakiest thing presently happening on the Moroccan coast is linked to the existence of a surf camp in El Oualidia, run by a French ex-pat. Despite being the instigator of countless pages of press in world surfing magazines showing and telling of a legendary right, he is allegedly the instigator of consistently violent, threatening behaviour in an attempt to limit access for non-clients. Unfortunately – as it's Morocco – these matters are difficult to take to the police, though the karmic wheel must keep spinning. Ownership of the world's waves is a preposterous idea and an individual's personal or business ideals should not prevent any travelling surfer from searching out and riding any swells anywhere, at any time. Humbly seek waves and you deserve to find them.

Getting to the point

Can anyone own this wave?

La culture surf

Les hommes des services américains introduirent le surf dans le pays au début des années 60'. La seconde vague de surfers étrangers correspond aux voyages hippies de la fin des années 60 et du début des années 70, qui découvrirent les vagues plus au Sud et notamment les dorénavant célèbres vagues de Taghazoute. Quelques expatriés français et une poignée de Marocains commencèrent à surfer, mais leurs sources d'expérience et leur équipement était de provenance étrangère. Au fur et à mesure que le pays devenait connu pour ses vagues, une petite industrie du surf s'est développée avec son cœur à Casablanca et Rabat, fournissant l'essentiel aux locaux de plus en plus nombreux et aux visiteurs. Le pays organise des compétitions, et le Maroc peut se vanter d'une équipe nationale amateur de talent. La famille du roi Hassan a apporté son support ainsi que des fonds pour développer le Surf Club des Oudayas à Rabat afin de proposer aux jeunes de la Medina une planche et les conseils avisés de moniteurs formés.

Qualité de l'eau

Les eaux les plus isolées des côtes marocaines offrent de séduisantes vagues vert-bleu, même si les grandes villes côtières de Tanger, Rabat et Casablanca posent problèmes. Agadir connaît une industrie touristique florissante et possède un grand port commercial, mais les conséquences sur l'environnement sont toujours inconnues, même si l'on se doute qu'elles ne sont pas bonnes. Après les périodes de pluie, les embouchures des rivières peuvent être très nauséabondes, augmentant les probabilités d'attraper des infections en surfant. Si c'est le cas partout dans le monde, ceci est particulièrement accentué dans les pays fortement peuplés ou pauvres. L'attitude nationale face aux déchets ménagers est extrêmement douteuse; le plus souvent jetées dans l'océan ou sur les bas-côtés. Ceci peut finir par poser des problèmes. Au final, le Maroc est préservé de par sa faible population et industrialisation, mais dans un pays en plein développement et se préoccupant aussi peu de l'environnement, la pollution peut devenir une menace ces prochaines années.

Le localisme

Les surfers marocains demandent qu' on les respecte, mais peuvent s' avérer extrêmement amicaux envers les étrangers qui se comportent bien. Sur des spots surpeuplés où les étrangers sont largement plus nombreux que les locaux, leur tentative légitime de rester maîtres du pic peuvent poser des problèmes. Malgré tout, dans un pays si riche en vagues avec des kilomètres de spots vierges, les confrontations peuvent être facilement évitées. Les mauvais comportements n' ont pas leur place au Maroc. Le pire exemple de ce qui s'est est passé sur les côtes marocaines est lié à l' existence d' un surf camp géré par un expatrié français basé à El Oualidia. Même s' il est l' instigateur de nombreux articles de presse dans les magazines de surf où il revendiquait son droit légendaire, il est connu pour avoir été l' instigateur de violences et de menaces pour limiter l' accès au spot aux non-clients. Malheureusement, s' agissant du Maroc, il est difficile de faire intervenir la police, bien que la roue Karmique continue de tourner.

Where to go

Surf Areas

The North Nearly all visitors to Morocco head south to the famous waves around Agadir and miss out on some of the most consistent surfing areas the northern hemisphere has to offer. With a thousand kilometres of coastline facing north-west into the Atlantic, it seems incredible that this unreal surf region has been ignored for so long. The area from Tangier to Rabat is predominantly beach. Between Rabat and Safi the coast becomes rugged and here a far greater variety of waves await discovery. Having a northerly aspect, the waves here can be head high when the south is flat, but in winter the northerly windflow can blow it out easily.

The port at Imessouane

TIM RAINGER

The North

Jelaba Man watches this northern point break

ALEX WILLIAMS

Ou Aller

Les Espace de Surf

Le Nord Le circuit classique consiste à partir d'Agadir et de remonter plus au nord. Cette solution peut vous faire rater les excellentes vagues au nord du pays. Avec des miliers de km de côte orientée face au nord-ouest Atlantique, une latitude assez sud pour echapper au vent et à la grisaille, et les mêmes swells que les canaries, c'est étonnant que le nord ait été ignoré depuis si longtemps. Une majorité de beach breaks de Tanger à Rabat. Depuis Rabat, passez Casablanca vers Safi, la côte devient plus découpée ce qui augmente la variété des vagues. L'orientation de cette côte la rend plus sensible au swells. Cela peut être surfable au nord, et flat au sud. Toutefois le vent vient plus fréquemment gâcher la partie, surtout en hiver.

Le Sud Les meilleurs spots du Maroc se trouvent à Taharazoute, à environ 30 minutes au nord-ouest d'Agadir. C'est l'épicentre du surf marocain car sur une petie étendue de côte se trouvent quatre point-breaks et récifs de qualité. Des vagues de 20 pieds qui déroulent sur 1,5 km autour d'Anchor Point, les locaux pourront vous en raconter. De plus, la quantité de vagues de la région limite la surpopulation de chaque spot. La géographie des montagnes avoisinantes canalisent le vent plein off-shore, de Agadir au cap Rhir. Au nord de ce cap, encore de nombreux récifs, pointes et beach breaks. C'est une région qui, bien que plus ventée, capte mieux le swell que la région d'Agadir. L'accès aux spots peut être difficile lorsque les pluies torrentielles balaient les chemins de terre. Essaouira est un haut lieu touristique, avec l'ancienne piste des hippies, et la ville que Jimmy Hendrix a tenté d'acheter. Quelques bons beach break dans ce coin là qui reste avant tout un spot de funboard.

Au sud d'Agadir, certains surfers bravent le désert pour surfer des spots tels que Sidi Ifni et Tarfaya. Du sable, des dunes, pas d'eau douce, et des falaises qui compliquent la mise à l'eau, voilà ce que réserve un surf trip au Sahara.

Quand s'y Rendre

L'hiver a toujours été la saison la plus courrue. La côte est bombardée par les swells des dépressions de l'Atlantique nord, mais la latitude sud épargne au Maroc les fronts pluvieux qui balaient l'Europe. La température est parfaite, et le surf est majoritairement solide et glassy. Moins de monde à l'eau au printemps et en automne, avec un surf similaire mais des températures en hausse. L'été est fréquement plat et très chaud comme partout ailleurs en Europe. A l'interieur des terres, les chaînes montagneuses subissent des températures torrides le jour et fraîches la nuit. Prévoyez en fonction.

The Desert South

MARK FENIES

Tifnit

ERIC CHAUCHE

Central Morocco (extending from El Jadida south to Agadir.) Essaouira is popular with tourists checking the old hippy trail and the town that Jimmy Hendrix tried to buy. There are some good breaks around Essaouira but it's generally regarded as a windsurfing area. The coastline between Essaouira and Cap Rhir hides many quality reefs, points and beach breaks, which receive more swell than further south, but also more wind. Imessouane is the most popular with hard-core campers and vans. A small shop, fish market and a couple of cafés are the only facilities, but there's a mellow vibe and great waves. Access can be difficult especially in rain. The desert south of Agadir is still frontiersville; some surfers make the arduous desert journey to places like Sidi Ifni and Tarfaya. Soft sand, no water and coastal cliffs are some of the problems associated with surfing in this area.

Many of the best winter spots in Morocco are found around **Tarhazoute** (or Taghazoute), which has gained world fame for its four quality point and reef breaks in one area. Tales of seven metre (21 foot) waves breaking for at least a kilometre down Anka Point can not be discounted. Even on smaller days a host of brilliant peaks break within a small area. Coastal mountain ranges tend to funnel the predominant northerly winds in a more offshore direction for the breaks from Agadir to Cap Rhir.

When to go

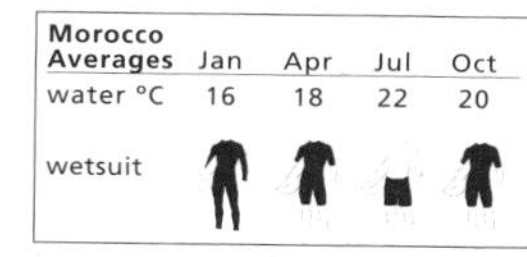

Morocco Averages	Jan	Apr	Jul	Oct
water °C	16	18	22	20
wetsuit				

Winter time has always been the most popular season. Consistent low pressure systems winding up in the North Atlantic provide all the swell, but, as it's so far south, Morocco usually misses out on the cold weather and frontal systems that blow over Europe. Clean, solid surf is a regular occurrence and the air and water temperatures are perfect. It's also possible to find good powder sessions in the Atlas Mountains at this time so bring a snowboard and you could score freshies as well as barrels. The surf in spring and autumn is similar but the air is hotter and it's less crowded. Summer, like elsewhere in Europe, sees long flat spells and soaring temperatures. The mountainous interior and southern desert bake during the day but cool significantly at night. Go prepared.

Mystery free camp

Tarhazoute

RIGHEZZA

Travelling

Getting There

By air Nearly all surfers will fly to either Tangier, Agadir or Casablanca. Prices from the UK are reasonable but from France, Spain or Portugal, driving or catching a train is cheaper.

By sea The most popular, frequent and cheapest route for vehicles is Algeciras to Ceuta (a Spanish enclave), but for pedestrians the ferry route to Tangier saves time and aggravation.

Bonded consumer items On arrival at Ceuta by ferry you will be faced with customs. Anything of value you take into the country will be recorded and declared on your passport (surfboards, cameras etc). You must leave with these items or you will be charged 100% duty. If your belongings are stolen, you will need a letter from the police, while broken boards must be brought back to the border.

Other Info

Visas

South Africans require a visa, most other countries do not. UK and Europeans (except Dutch, Belgium and Luxembourg), USA, Oz and NZ do not require a visa for stays of up to 90 days. If you have an Israeli stamp in your passport, you may be refused entry.

Telephone Info

Country Code: 212
Dial Out Code: 00 212
Emergencies: 177 – Gendarmerie Royale
International Operator: 16
International Directory: 16
Police: 19

Getting Around

Car hire is widely available: the cheapest and most widespread option is the trusty-rusty Renault 4. It's a good idea to organise car hire when booking a flight as deals can be cheaper. If you do it when you arrive you'll have to barter.

Driving Getting around Morocco is fairly easy. In the North you'll be greeted with a new coastal motorway which runs from Larache to Casablanca with a projected extension to Tangier. Further south beyond Safi the coast road deteriorates fast, especially in winter when rain washes out large sections. In the event of a breakdown Moroccan mechanics are cheap and efficient. Visitors intending to drive in Morocco must show proof of an international driving licence – police routinely pull cars over for safety checks particularly around major northern cities and the hash-producing Rif. Fines for traffic violations may have to be paid on the spot, but like all things, you can usually negotiate. Moroccan roads are extremely dangerous: reckless driving and excessive speeds are common.

By bus The bus network is also very cheap and often fun, though patience and a guaranteed sore butt make it an option for the more hardy or budget minded traveller. Boards on the bus are a bit of a hassle if they are over 2m (6ft, 8in).

Accommodation All options are available from free camping and basic rooms to package accommodation and high class hotels. A cheap room at the coast could cost 30dh per night. Choose depending on budget!

Infos Voyage

Y aller

En avion Presque tous les surfers passeront par Tanger, Agadir ou Casablanca, les prix en provenance de Grande Bretagne et du nord de l' Europe restent raisonnables, mais de la France, l' Espagne ou du Portugal, conduire ou partir en train reste la solution la moins cher. Les prix des vols ont considérablement augmenté du fait de la diminution du nombre de compagnies assurant la liaison.

En bateau Le plus fréquent, meilleur marché et par conséquent la plus populaire route pour les véhicule est: Algerciras-Ceuta (une enclave espagnole). Pour les piétons, la route de Tanger vous épargne du temps et de l' énervement.

Se deplacer

Par la route Si vous descendez d' Europe, vous serez accueilli par un bon réseau routier du Nord au Sud, le long de la côte, et de plus les mécaniciens sont bon marché et rapides en cas de panne éventuelle. Une autoroute côtière quasi -neuve va maintenant de Casablanca jusqu' à Larache avec le projet d' une extension jusqu' à Tanger. Soyez tout de même prudent car en cas de pluie, la route côtière entre Essaouira et Agadir peut fermer à tout instant. Des conducteurs dangereux, des vitesses excessives et des bas côtés en mauvais état font partie du quotidien. Les touristes qui ont l' intention de conduire au Maroc devront se fournir un permis de conduire international. La police effectue des contrôles de routine régulièrement, particulièrement autour des principales villes du nord, et du Rif. Les amendes pour infraction au code de la route sont à régler sur place et habituellement il est possible de ne payer que 10%.

En bus Le réseau des bus est aussi très bon marché et en plus amusant, même si une bonne dose de patience et un solide derrière sont de mise pour les budgets les plus serrés. Les planches peuvent être admises dans les bus locaux, mais elles ne doivent pas dépasser 6' 8' '.

Biens personnels Tous les objets de valeur que vous emportez au Maroc seront déclarés et enregistrés sur votre passeport. (planches de surf) Vous devez repartir avec ces objets ou vous serez taxé à 100% à la douane. Si ce qui vous appartient vous a été volé, vous aurez besoin d' un formulaire de la police, les surfs cassés doivent être également rapportés à la douane.

Location de voiture On peut facilement louer des voitures. La moins chère et la plus répandue, mais aussi la plus sûre et la plus rouillée est une Renault 4L. C' est souvent une bonne idée de réserver la location de voiture en même temps que les vols, et c' est aussi moins coûteux. Si vous arrivez par avion dans n' importe quel endroit cité plus haut, faites le tour et soyez prêt à négocier âprement pour obtenir le meilleur prix. Les taxis de l' aéroport sont relativement peu cher et facilement accessibles.

Travel

Airports

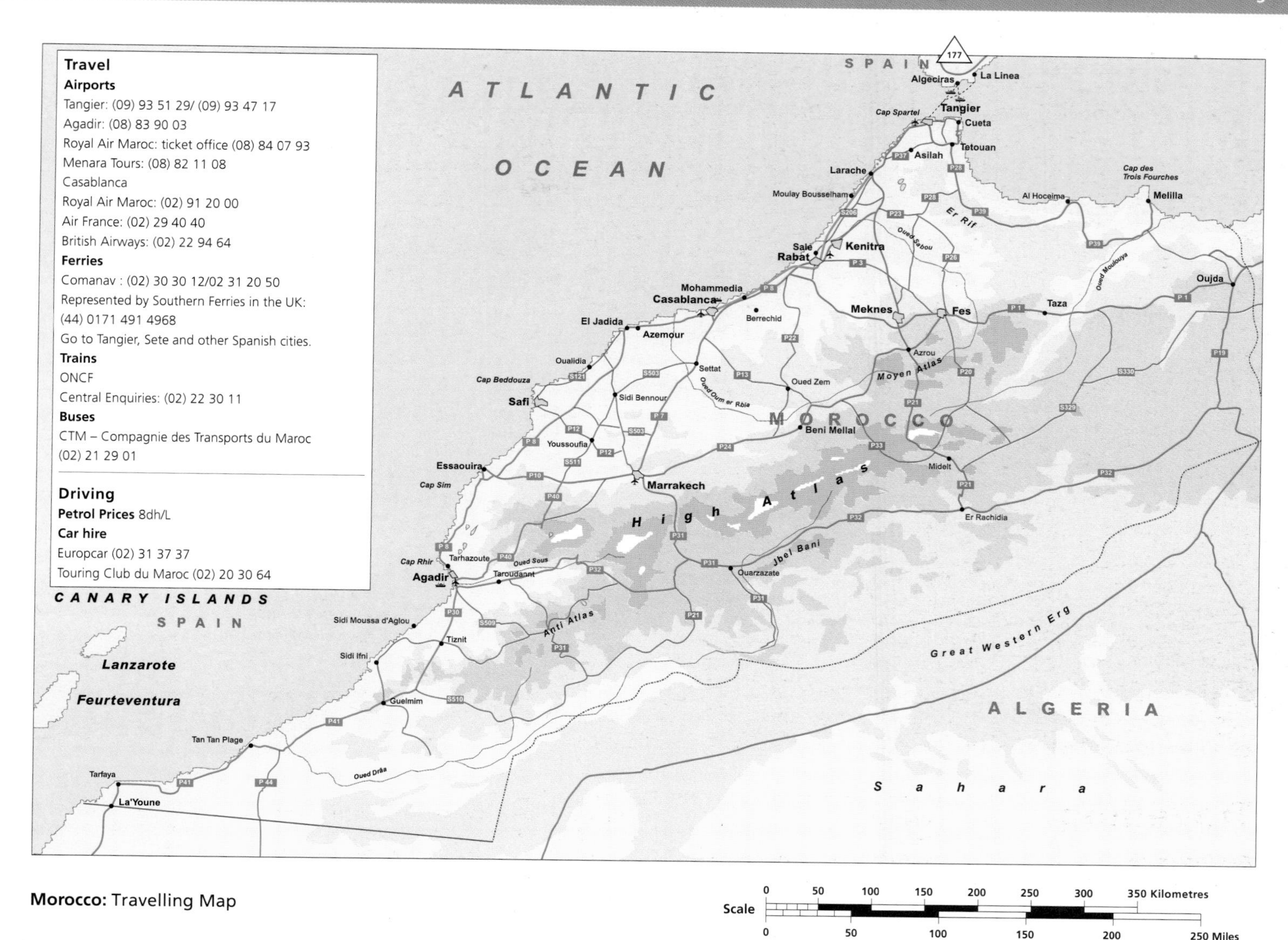

Tangier: (09) 93 51 29/ (09) 93 47 17
Agadir: (08) 83 90 03
Royal Air Maroc: ticket office (08) 84 07 93
Menara Tours: (08) 82 11 08
Casablanca
Royal Air Maroc: (02) 91 20 00
Air France: (02) 29 40 40
British Airways: (02) 22 94 64

Ferries

Comanav : (02) 30 30 12/02 31 20 50
Represented by Southern Ferries in the UK: (44) 0171 491 4968
Go to Tangier, Sete and other Spanish cities.

Trains

ONCF
Central Enquiries: (02) 22 30 11

Buses

CTM – Compagnie des Transports du Maroc
(02) 21 29 01

Driving

Petrol Prices 8dh/L
Car hire
Europcar (02) 31 37 37
Touring Club du Maroc (02) 20 30 64

Morocco: Travelling Map

Scale: 0 50 100 150 200 250 300 350 Kilometres / 0 50 100 150 200 250 Miles

Other

Barter Like in most poorer countries in the world, bartering is standard practice. A taxi driver might ask for 500dh when other people are paying 200-300dh. Always be friendly, always smile, don't get hassled and don't be in a hurry.

Food Eating in Morocco is usually an extremely pleasant experience. Local culinary delights include the traditional tahgine, a mini cone-shaped clay oven, stuffed full of vegetables and seafood or meat, which is then steamed over hot coals. Fresh organic produce of excellent quality is available in most towns, or at the wild weekly souk with absolutely everything. The seafood is superb and can be bought directly from the fishermen at the port or at the market. The meat is halal, rarely refrigerated and best avoided. Bottled water is the safest way to go, but is generally one of the most expensive items on the shopping list.

Drugs Contrary to popular belief, smoking hash or the seed and stalk mix, kif, is illegal. Though Morocco has a reputation for being a great place to smoke good, cheap hash, the police and informers are active, especially in the Rif Mountains (the hash producing area), where random roadblocks and search points have taken out many an otherwise careful traveller. Be warned.

TIM RAINGER

TIM RAINGER

Living the simple life

Hébergement Toutes les options sont disponibles du camping sauvage aux chambres simples jusqu' au package et hôtel de grande classe. Une chambre à petit prix sur la côte coûte environ 30dh (25 FF) par nuit. Choisissez donc en fonction de votre budget.

Marchandage Comme dans la plupart des pays les plus pauvres dans le monde, marchander est une pratique courante. Un conducteur de taxi pourra vous demander 500 dh, alors que d' autres ne paieront 200 ou 300 dh. Il faut toujours être sympahique, souriant, ne soyez pas stressé, ni pressé.

Nourriture Manger au Maroc est habituellement une expérience plaisante. Les nourritures traditionnelles telles que le Tajine cuit dans un plat conique au four plein de légumes, poissons ou viandes, est un vrai délice. Les produits frais sont d' excellente qualité et disponibles dans la plupart des villes et souks hebdomadaires o˘ ils vendent absolument de tout. On trouve des poissons à profusion, pas chers et d' excellente qualité que vous pouvez achetez n' importe o˘. La viande est halal, rarement réfrigérée, il vaut mieux éviter. L' eau en bouteille est la plus s˚re et reste l' un des produits courants les plus chers.

Drogue Contrairement à la rumeur, fumer du hasch ou toute autre dérivé est illégal, bien que largement disponible. Bien que le Maroc ait la réputation d' être un bon endroit pour fumer du shit de bonne qualité et pas cher, la police et les indics rôdent.

The North
Tangier to El Jadida

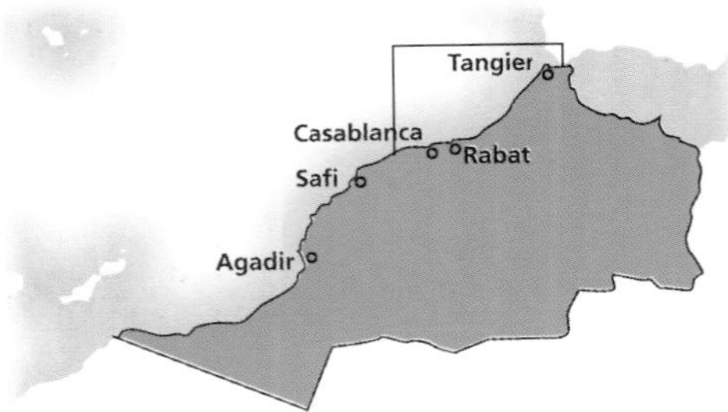

1. Tangier
Not the most primo surf zone, but worth a visit for its beauty and culture. The area lacks consistency, but there are brilliant reefs and beaches like Plage Sol that works in small swell. Check Aroussa Bahe 12km (7mi) W at Cape Spartel (facing the Ba Kacem Café), a right over reef and sand. Beware of the rock at the peak.

Pas forcément la première zone de surf mais vaut le coup d'oeil pour le pittoresque et la culture. Un carrefour depuis la nuit des temps de toutes sortes de contrebandiers, réinventé par les écrivains de la Beat generation. Manque cruellement de consistance mais on y trouve de super reefs et de belles plages comme la plage Sol, qui marche quand c'est petit ou Aroussa Bahe au Cap Spartel, une droite sur du reef et du sable. Attention aux rochers au pic.

2. Briech

A consistent beach that's best at mid to high tide. Check the famous music festival in summer.

Une plage consistente qui reçoit un festival de musique en été.

3. Plage Loukos

This beach is 7km (4mi) N of Larache and here you'll find a left alongside the jetty at mid tide. It's offshore nearly all the time.

7kms au nord de Larache. Une gauche le long de la jetée à mi-marée. Off-shore pratiquement tout le temps.

4. Mouslay Bousselham

A beach that works best from mid to high tide. There's a nice lagoon, but it's hard to reach without a 4WD.

Plage correcte qui marche mieux de mi-marée à marée haute. Un joli lagon difficile à atteindre sans un 4x4.

5. Mehdiya Plage

Find the rock groyne then wait for a big swell: there should be a right breaking off it, but it's usually better at mid to high tide. This is the cradle of surfing in Morocco due to the US military base nearby.

Le berceau du surf au Maroc puisque les soldats de la base américaine y ont commencé à surfer dans les années 50. Une droite qui casse à partir d'une jetée rocheuse par grosse houle .

Miles of empty beach breaks

Beach break north of Casablanca

6. Plage des Nations

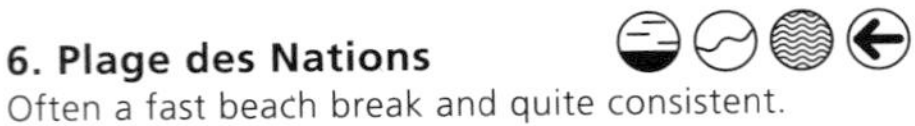

Often a fast beach break and quite consistent.

Souvent un beach break trop rapide. Plutôt consistant.

7. Rabat-Salé
Enjoy the scenery of the capital and its magic atmosphere, but don't miss the waves close to the jetty. There's no less than four lefts (Plongeoir, Cascade, Kbair and Bergama) and four rights (La Pointe, Doura, Brema, shore-break De Salé) that all need a big swell to work.

Profitez des curiosités de la capitale et de son ambiance magique. N'oubliez pas ses vagues non plus, proches de la jetée encore une fois. Pas moins de 4 gauches (plongeoir, Cascade, Kbair & Bergama) et 4 droites (La pointe, Doura, Brema,shore-break de Salé). Il faut que ca rentre gros.

8. Skhirat-Plage
 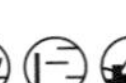   

This point is a left, breaking alongside the jetty and is best at incoming low to mid tide. In a small swell (up to 2m/6ft) it goes off. Try the beach break if the point becomes too crowded.

Un point-break de gauches le long d'une jetée, de préférence au montant de marée basse à mi-marée. Marche par petite houle. Allez sur la plage si le point-break est trop encombré.

9. Oued Cherrat

A reef and beach break here breaks all year round and is very popular – it also handles W winds. Beware of the reefs and bodyboarders when going out.

Spot de sable et de rochers qui résiste les vents d'ouest, fréquenté toute l'année surtout par les bodyboards. Attention aux rochers quand vous ramez.

10. Bouznika Plage

A good right point, which on a medium to big swell (best with N-NE winds at low tide) breaks into a cove sheltered from the trade winds. Avoid currents when it's big and urchins.

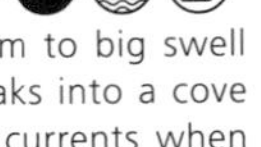

Une anse sympa abritée des alizés, avec de bonnes droites avec une houle moyenne à grosse. Attention aux courants et aux oursins. Meilleur par vents de N/N-E à marée basse.

11. Sablette-Plage

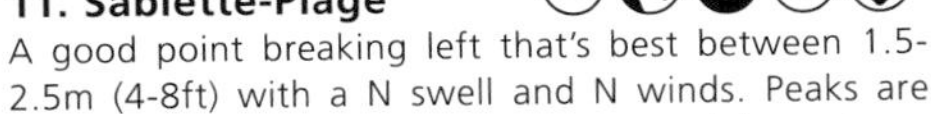

A good point breaking left that's best between 1.5-2.5m (4-8ft) with a N swell and N winds. Peaks are disputed over, even before you've entered the water.

Une bonne gauche, meilleure entre 1 et 2 mètres par houle et vent de nord.

12. Pont Blondin

Named after a soldier who fought here during the American debarkment, Blondin has some good days enjoyed with friendly locals.

Ainsi nommé aprés qu'un soldat combattit ici pendant le débarquement américain de la deuxième guerre mondiale. Quelques bons jours avec pas mal de locaux.

13. Casablanca
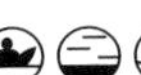 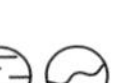  

Morocco's financial capital has consistent beaches, which include Monica Plage, Zeneta Plage, Mohammedia Plage y Paloma Plage. They work all year and have currents when big.

La capitale économique du Maroc a des plages consistantes comme Monica, Mohammedia, Zeneta ou Paloma qui marchent toute l'année. Toutes ces plages sont gavées de courants quand c'est gros.

14. Dar Bouazza

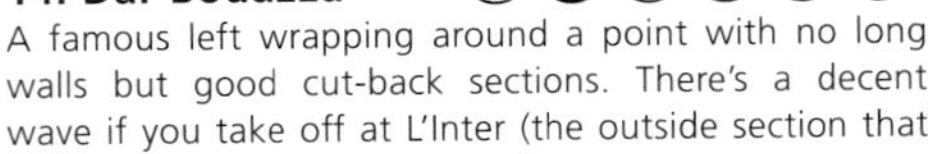

A famous left wrapping around a point with no long walls but good cut-back sections. There's a decent wave if you take off at L'Inter (the outside section that sometimes connects with the point), which is best at low tide. Beware of a ship boiler called La Bobine when surfing the final section. There's sharp rocks and urchins, so hard-sole booties are advisable. Crowds out.

Une gauche réputée qui s'enroule autour d'un cap, meilleur à marée basse. C'est une vague longue si vous démarrez à l'Inter, le pic au large qui connecte parfois avec le pointbreak. Attention à la Bobine, une chaudière d'un bateau qui a coulé, en fin de vague. Des rochers à éviter aussi et surtout une concentration d'oursins phénoménale qui vous feront certainement penser à avoir des chaussons à semelle dure ainsi qu'une pince à épiler. Beaucoup de monde à l'évidence.

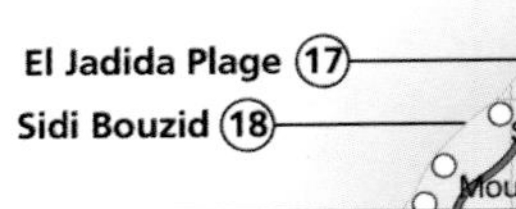

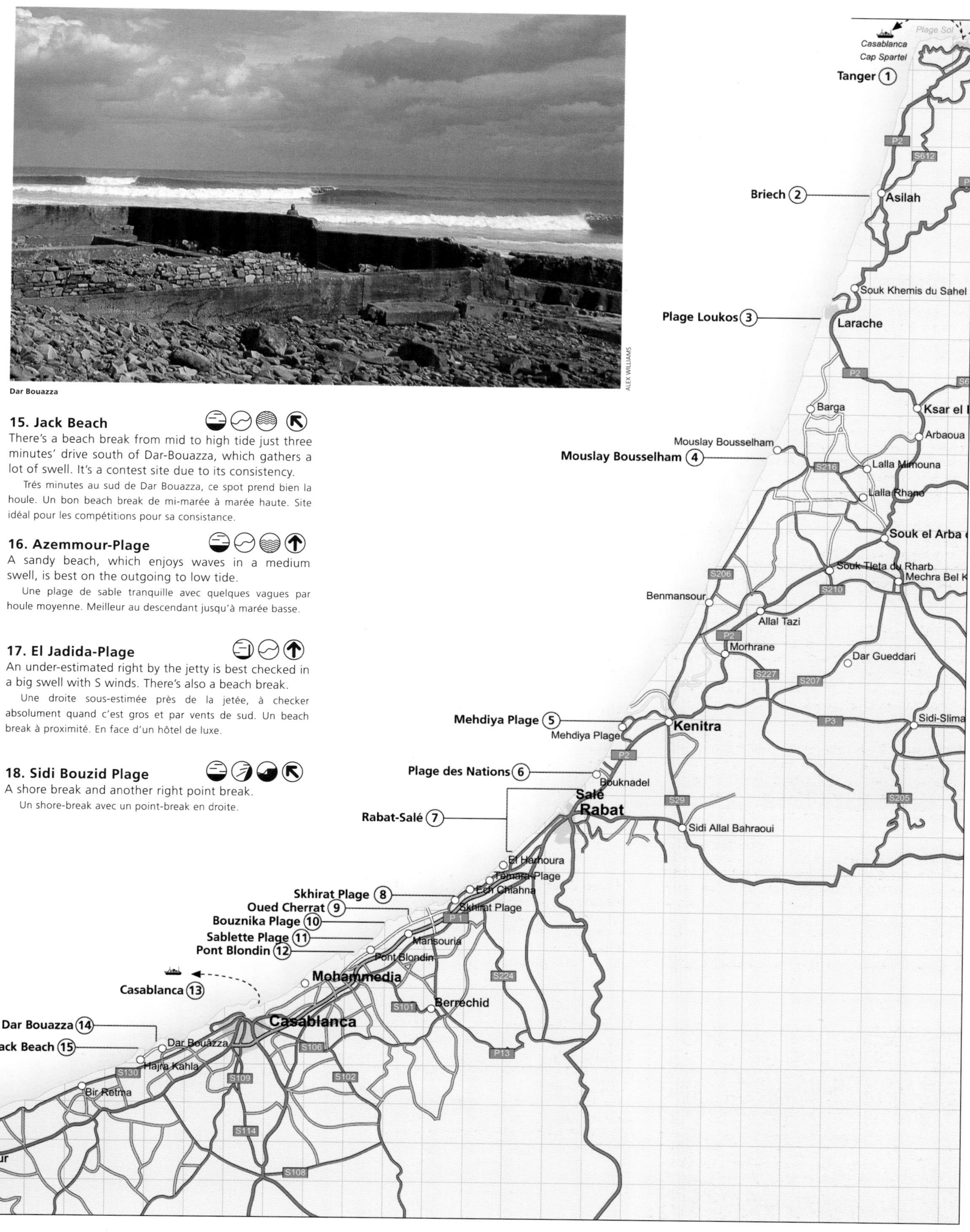

Dar Bouazza

15. Jack Beach

There's a beach break from mid to high tide just three minutes' drive south of Dar-Bouazza, which gathers a lot of swell. It's a contest site due to its consistency.

Trés minutes au sud de Dar Bouazza, ce spot prend bien la houle. Un bon beach break de mi-marée à marée haute. Site idéal pour les compétitions pour sa consistance.

16. Azemmour-Plage

A sandy beach, which enjoys waves in a medium swell, is best on the outgoing to low tide.

Une plage de sable tranquille avec quelques vagues par houle moyenne. Meilleur au descendant jusqu'à marée basse.

17. El Jadida-Plage

An under-estimated right by the jetty is best checked in a big swell with S winds. There's also a beach break.

Une droite sous-estimée près de la jetée, à checker absolument quand c'est gros et par vents de sud. Un beach break à proximité. En face d'un hôtel de luxe.

18. Sidi Bouzid Plage

A shore break and another right point break.

Un shore-break avec un point-break en droite.

Central Morocco
El Oualidia to Agadir

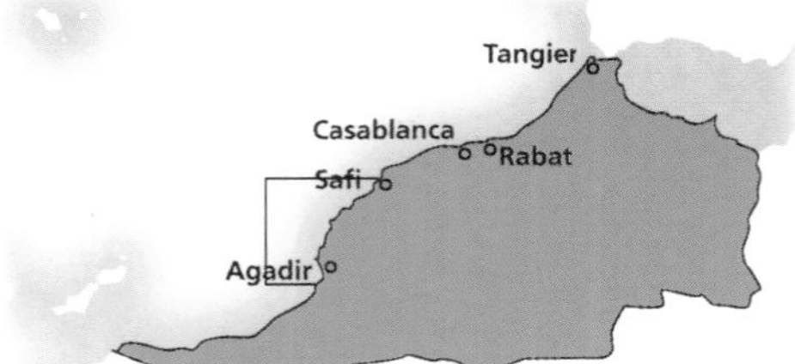

1. El Oualidia

This sheltered bay is something of a paradise for beginners and has a well-organised surf-camp with good but pricey facilities.

Une baie abritée idéale pour les débutants. La preuve, c'est un surf-camp organisé avec toutes les installations, surtout en tente. Un petit paradis pour apprendre à surfer.

ERIC CHAUCHE
El Oualidia

TIM RAINGER
Pointe d'Imessouane

2. Safi

There's another right reef 2km (1.2mi) north of Safi named Racelafaa. It needs a big swell to be one of the best waves in the country.

Une autre droite de reef au nord de Safi nommé Racelafaa. Par grosse houle, c'est une des meilleures vagues du pays.

3. Pointe d'Immesouane

Good waves that are rarely surfed.

Bonnes vagues rarement surfées.

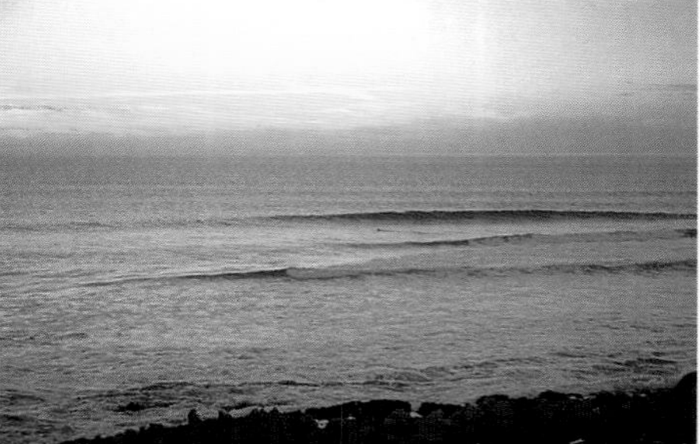
TIM RAINGER
Like many, this break is named after a kilometre marker post north of Boilers

4. Tamri-plage

A good beach break about 4km (2.4mi) from the village. Check it at low tide with a small swell and offshore winds.

Bon beach break à environ 4 kms du village. Passez à marée basse par petite houle et vents off-shore.

5. Boilers

This consistent and powerful wave can be found just south of the lighthouse of Cap Rhir. There's easy parking and a good overview. Take-off in front of the washed up ship boiler. When Boilers closes out on the reef, Draculas reels off at high speed 200m S. It's tricky getting in and out because of the urchins.

On peut trouver cette vague puissante et consistante juste au sud du phare de Cap Ghir. Parking fastoche et une vue panoramique pour la photo. La grosse bouilloire: démarrez en face des bouillons. Pas facile d'entrer et de sortir de l'eau, surtout à cause des oursins.

RIGHEZZA
Boilers

TIM RAINGER

The Desert South

The Moroccan coast still extends almost unexplored for nearly 1000km (600mi) to the border area with Occidental Sahara. You're going to hit the desert so be prepared for it! Check the spots below and others like Mirleft-Plage (a medium swell right), Sidi-Ifni (jetties and harbour breaks), Tarfaya (shipwrecks on beach), Laayoun (sheltered from N winds) and Ad Dakhla.

La côte marocaine s'étend encore, complètement vierge, sur presque 1,000kms jusqu'à la frontière avec l'ex-Sahara Occidental. Vous serez en plein désert alors équiipez-vous en conséquence. Passez sur des spots comme Mirleft-plage (une droite par houle moyenne), Sidi-Ifni (des breaks sur des jetées près du port), Tarfaya (une épave sur la plage), Laayoun (abrité des vents de nord), Ad Dakhla et Lagouira.

6. Tifnite

An undevelqped beach just S of Agadir.

Une portion de plage sans aménagements juste au sud d'Agadir.

MARC FENIES

Tifnite

Oued Massa

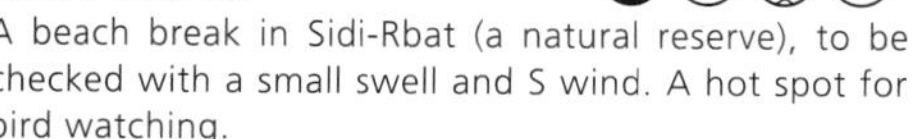

A beach break in Sidi-Rbat (a natural reserve), to be checked with a small swell and S wind. A hot spot for bird watching.

Un beach break à Sidi-Rbat dans une réserve naturelle, à checker quand c'est petit et que le vent souffle du sud. Un endroit idéaPl pour mater les oiseaux aussi.

Sidi Moussa d'Aglou

Another gentle beach with pumping waves in a small S swell. Beware of nets when getting in and out.

Un autre beach break sympa avec de bonnes vagues par petit swell. Attention aux filets de pêcheurs quand vous sortez ou entrez dans l'eau.

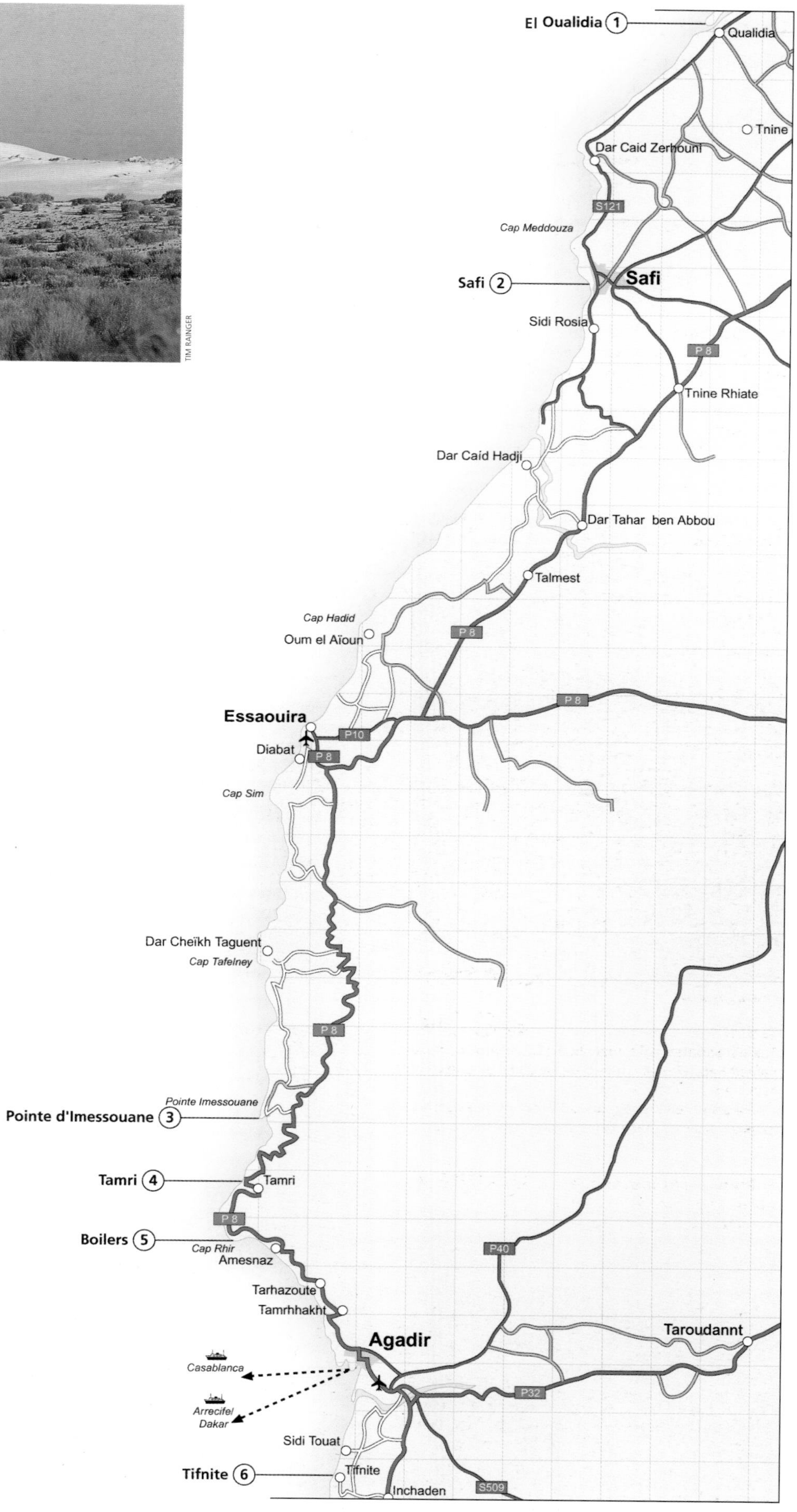

El Oualidia (1)
Qualidia
Tnine
Dar Caid Zerhouni
S121
Cap Meddouza
Safi (2)
Safi
Sidi Rosia
P 8
Tnine Rhiate
Dar Caïd Hadji
Dar Tahar ben Abbou
Talmest
Cap Hadid
Oum el Aïoun
P 8
P 8
Essaouira
P10
Diabat
P 8
Cap Sim
Dar Cheïkh Taguent
Cap Tafelney
P 8
Pointe Imessouane
Pointe d'Imessouane (3)
Tamri (4)
Tamri
P 8
Boilers (5)
Cap Rhir
Amesnaz
P40
Tarhazoute
Tamrhhakht
Agadir
Taroudannt
Casablanca
Arrecife/
Dakar
P32
Sidi Touat
Tifnite (6)
Tifnite
Inchaden
S509

Central Morocco
Tarhazoute

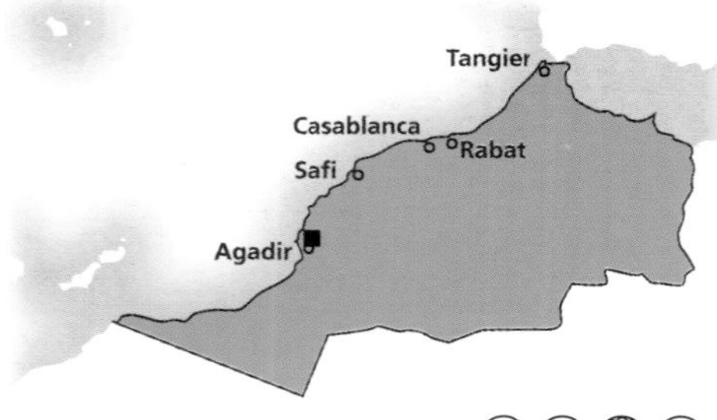

1. Killer Point

Named after the killer whales that sometimes cruise around, 'Killers' is the most consistent Tarhazoute spot because it sucks all available swell. It breaks a long way from shore and is always bigger than it looks. In small swells, at low tide, the peak in front of the cliff has a short left (heading straight into some rocky caves) and a sectioning right. As the swell increases, the take-off area moves S and a powerful, workable right can peel for 400m (360yd). The inside fires at high tide as it's fully protected from north winds. Take the long paddle out rather than use the slippery cliff top track unless you're a chamoix.

Ainsi nommé parce que des orques épaulards se promènent de temps en temps(!). La vague démarre en face d'un gros rocher, puis on arrive à l'inside qui est la meilleure partie. Se surfe jusqu'à très gros. Abrité des vents de nord. Attention aux cavernes en face des vagues. Le chemin peut être glissant.

2. La Source

Found on the inside of Mystery Point, this wave is best on small days only. Fresh water bubbles up from onshore rock formations and here you can rinse your face and wetsuit. It's best on an incoming tide with a medium swell.

Sur l'inside de Mystery Point. Seulement quand c'est petit. De l'eau douce jaillit de rochers sur la plage où on peut se rincer et la combard par la même occasion. Meilleur à marée montante par houle moyenne.

3. Mysteries

A sucky wave with small take-off area that's best on a medium sized swell. Only breaks when the sand combines with the shallow reef to produce deceptively long rights. Low tide exposes the reef but mid tide normally sees the odd barrel.

Une vague qui suce à max avec une zone de take-off restreinte. Mieux avec une houle de taille moyenne. Les routards squattent là au-dessus de la falaise, en camping sauvage jusqu'à récemment. Les locaux ont commencé à venir demander 5 dirhams pour chaque nuit. Il vaut mieux être en nombre parce que la police ne viendra pas vous aider si elle sait que vous êtes là.

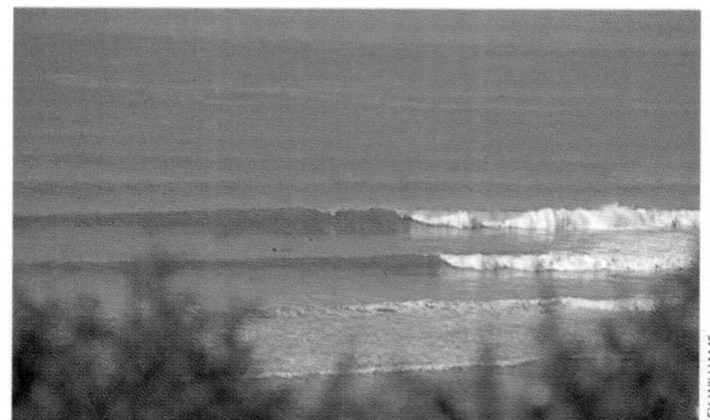
Mysteries

ALEX WILLIAMS

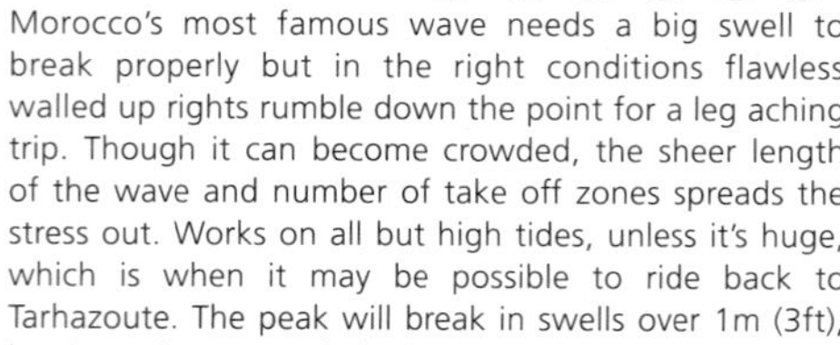
Tarhazoute from the north

TIM RAINGER

4. Anka Point

Morocco's most famous wave needs a big swell to break properly but in the right conditions flawless walled up rights rumble down the point for a leg aching trip. Though it can become crowded, the sheer length of the wave and number of take off zones spreads the stress out. Works on all but high tides, unless it's huge, which is when it may be possible to ride back to Tarhazoute. The peak will break in swells over 1m (3ft), but it's a short, crowded ride when it is small.

La vague la plus célèbre du Maroc qui nécessite un gros swell pour marcher. Même si y'a pas mal de monde, l'ambiance n'est pas trop tendue à l'eau. Ramez depuis la plage au nord (long mais sûr) quand c'est petit ou jetez-vous de l'avancée rocheuse mais attention au timing avec les séries. Au retour, revenez par la plage ou surfez le plus loin possible jusqu'à la plage au sud. A marée haute, ça peut être difficile de monter sur les rochers, y'a déjà eu des planches de cassées entre les rochers.

5. Hash Point

A S-facing beach in the village of Tarhazoute. It's so named after the surfers who smoke too much and can't be bothered to walk to Ankas.

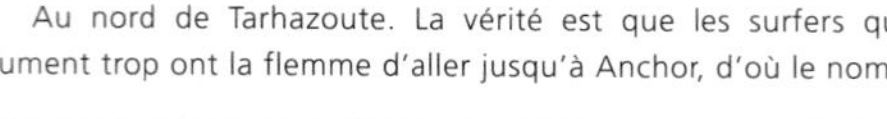

Au nord de Tarhazoute. La vérité est que les surfers qui fument trop ont la flemme d'aller jusqu'à Anchor, d'où le nom!

6. Panorama's

A fast and round wave breaks in front of Panorama's Bar in the village of Tarhazoute.

Une vague ronde et rapide qui casse en face du bar/restaurant Panorama à Tarhazoute.

8. Devil's rock

A tubey left worth checking, 2km (1.2 mi) S of Banana Beach.

Une gauche tubulaire qu'il faut checker, à 2kms au sud de Banana Beach.

7. Banana Beach

A beach on the mouth of a dried-up river at the village of Tamrhakht, which has waves between 1.5-2m (4-6 ft). It closes out at low tide and bigger swells.

Plage à l'embouchure de la rivière à sec à Tamrhakht. Une vague amusante de 1m à 1,5m. Ferme à marée basse et par grosse houle.

Anka Point

ALEX WILLIAMS

Killer Point

ALEX WILLIAMS

La Source

RHIGEZZA

The Canary Islands

The 'Hawaii of the Atlantic' is the term most commonly used by surfers to describe the Canary Islands. Open ocean swells from three directions unload on volcanic reefs and points with power comparable to just about anywhere in the world. As with Hawaii the air and water temperature changes little all year round. Hot sunny days on the beach and surfing in a shortie are some of the enticing aspects of this mandatory Atlantic island experience.

Les Isles Canaries

Souvent considéré par les surfers comme le " Hawaii de l'Atlantique", cet achipel volcanique émerge de l'océan pour recevoir les swells de toutes les directions. Ces houles terminent leur course sur une grande variété de récifs et de pointes de lave, avec une puissance comparable à toutes les bonnes destinations surf. Se rôtir au soleil et surfer en shorty sont parmi les innombrables attraits du surf canarien.

Long, powerful and consistent.
Morro Negro, Lanzarote

ERIC CHAUCHE

Introduction

The People

The earliest inhabitants of these islands are believed to be the aboriginal Guanches – but how they got there is open to debate. The most popular theory is that they were descended from the Berbers of north-west Africa. History has left us little of the Guanches due to the ravages of the colonisation process. In the 13th and 14th centuries Portuguese, French, Genoese and Majorcan navigators visited the islands and at first were welcomed. Things began to change in 1402, and after about a hundred years of bloody warring, the Guanches were virtually wiped out: the Spanish had colonised the islands.

Population: 1.6 million
Area: 7,770 sqkm/3,000 sqmi
Time: GMT + 1
Language: Spanish
Currency: Peseta (ptas)

SPARROW
Man eating raw squid

Over the years the Canaries established themselves as a major staging post between Europe and the Americas – Columbus sailed from Gran Canaria on his voyage of discovery to America in 1492. Cargo and passengers were plagued by pirates from many countries including the English, the Dutch and the Moors.

Since then, tourists have been the major invading force. English, German, Scandinavian, French and Spanish people flock to the islands on various package deals, especially in winter. They come for the sun, sea and surf and to stay in purpose-built towns such as Playa del Inglés or Playa de las Américas that offer package deals to hell.

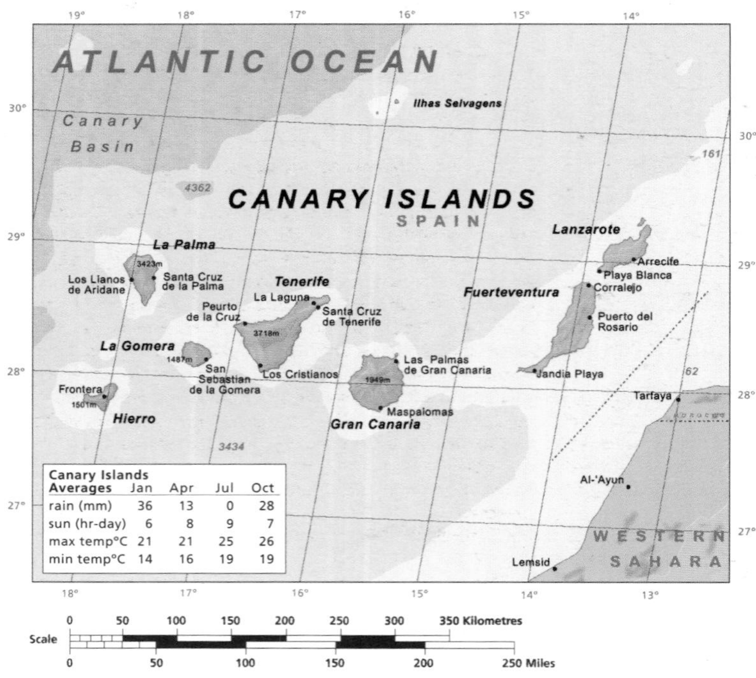

Canary Islands Averages	Jan	Apr	Jul	Oct
rain (mm)	36	13	0	28
sun (hr-day)	6	8	9	7
max temp°C	21	21	25	26
min temp°C	14	16	19	19

Canary Islands: Physical Geography

SPARROW
Two lunar landscapes

The Land

The Canaries are a volcanic chain of seven main islands lying at a latitude of 28 degrees north. Only 95 kilometres (55 miles) separates the Canary Islands from Africa, however that's where the similarities stop. Made up of extinct volcanic cones that rise out of the ocean floor, the highest point on the Canaries is the lofty snow-capped peak of Pico de Teide (3,718m/12,195ft) on Tenerife. There is a definite east-west split when it comes to vegetation: the western islands provide a moister climate for plants and cultivation than the barren, arid interiors of Fueteventura and Lanzarote. It is on these two islands that fire and water have conspired to create a landscape that can only be likened to the surface of the moon. Erosion has hardly had time to work on the landscape and only a few hardy plants survive on the barely-cooled lava.

The Climate

The Romans dubbed the Canary Islands the 'fortunate islands' due to the mild, consistent climate influenced mostly by the Atlantic Ocean. Temperatures range from 18°C to 24°C (70°F to 80°F) in winter and 24°C to 32°C (80°F to 90°F) in summer. Rainfall is low, especially on Lanzarote and Fuerteventura. Prevailing winds are from the north east to north west. These winds are occasionally interrupted by the dust-laden 'sirocco', a hot wind coming directly from the Sahara. The sirocco is not loved by tourists but is welcomed by surfers and windsurfers for the offshore conditions it brings to the islands' west-facing breaks. Constant breeze keeps the air feeling fresh even on the hottest days. The sun's intensity can go unnoticed, particularly in the water, cooled by the Canarian current.

MIKE SEARLE
North Shore Fuerteventura

Introduction

La population

On suppose que les premiers habitants de ces îles furent les aborigènes Guanches, mais le moyen qu'ils utilisèrent pour les coloniser reste à déterminer. On les prétend descendants des berbères d'Afrique du Nord. Les ravages de la colonisation ont effacé presque toutes les traces des Guanches. Au 13e et 14e siècles, les navigateurs portugais, génois, français et majorcains firent étape dans l'archipel où ils étaient, au départ, bien accueillis. Mais les Espagnols ont définitivement colonisé ces îles en 1402, après environ un siècle de batailles sanglantes.

Durant les siècles qui suivirent, les Canaries se sont établis comme base avancée vers les Amériques. Christophe Colomb est d'ailleurs parti de Gran Canaria pour sa quête du Nouveau Monde en 1492, tandis que cargos ou navires de passagers étaient souvent rançonnés par les pirates anglais, hollandais ou maures.

Depuis, les touristes sont la seule invasion qu'aient à subir les îles. Anglais, Allemands, Français, Scandinaves et Espagnols profitent des promos touristiques de l'hiver. Ils débarquent à la recherche du soleil et de la mer et sont parqués dans des complexes construits pour l'occasion tels Playa del Inglès ou Playa las Americas.

Le pays

Situé à 28° de latitude nord, l'archipel canarien est composé de sept îles. Seulement 95 km les séparent du continent africain, mais les similitudes s'arrêtent là. Le point culminant des volcans éteints qui forment l'archipel est Pico de Teide et ses neiges éternelles, qui culmine à 3718m sur l'île de Ténérife. On note un fort clivage entre les climats des îles de l'est et de l'ouest. Les premières sont plus humides, et favorables à la végétation est aux cultures, en opposition au climat arride et sec de Fuerteventura et Lanzarote. C'est sur ces deux îles que le feu et l'eau se sont liés pour créer ces paysages que l'on ne .retrouvera que sur la lune. L'érosion est à ses débuts et peu de plantes survivent sur la lave écrasée par le soleil.

Le climat

Les Romains avaient surnommé les Canaries les " îles fortunées", pour décrire le climat doux et temperé d'influence océanique. 18° à 24° en hiver, contre 24°à 32° en été pour les températures. Le taux de précipitations est minime, spécialement à Lanzarote et Fuerteventura. Les vents dominants sont de secteur Nord-Est ou Nord-ouest. Ceux-ci sont parfois interrompus par des "coups de Sirocco ", vent chaud et chargé de poussière, en provenance directe du Sahara. Les touristes détestent le Sirocco, mais les surfers et les funboarders le bénissent, pour les conditions offshore des spots des côtes ouest. En général, les vents rafraîchissent les journées les plus chaudes et la violence du soleil peut passer inaperçue, surtout dans l'eau qui est refroidie par le courant des Canaries.

Surf Culture

History

PETER CADE
The accommodation at La Fitania before the hotels were built, 1980

Americans get the credit for being the first surfers in the Canaries. They were on Gran Canaria in 1970 and soon after published an article in *Surfer Magazine*. The Las Palmas area, particularly Confital, was soon playing host to many nationalities, led by Aussies like Jack McCoy who came with a crew in 1972. Mainland Spain quickly followed suit, lured by stories of an Hawaiian-like climate and waves. Raul Dordal, one of the early Basque surfers realised the surf potential in the early 70s and eventually transplanted to Tenerife, becoming integral to the Canaries' scene. Tenerife was the next island to be surfed, at Puerta De La Cruz, then around Bajamar, and finally, the southern areas around Playa de las Américas. This natural progression east eventually led to the discoveries of the modern Meccas Lanzarote and Fuertaventura. La Santa has become the surf media's focus in the Canaries, but all the small islands in the chain now play host to a growing posse of international travellers. Windsurfing also made its home in the islands during the 80s boom period, which led to Fuerteventura becoming entrenched on the world competition circuit. Equipment is now widely available in main towns although locally produced boards are still difficult to come by.

The Ocean Environment

Overview

PETER CADE

Water pollution problems are rare in the Canaries, due to low population, very little heavy industry, and the cleansing properties of the Canarian current. On Lanzarote and Fuerteventura, apart from a few isolated instances, the main surf zones have squeaky clean water. Reports of sluicing oil and petrol holding tanks, then allowing the run off to go into the harbour at Puerta del Rosario, has very little impact on surfers. Hotel complexes are required to treat their own sewerage. First it settles, then they use the water for irrigation, and finally the solids are deposited inland. Correlejo is getting a new town sewerage system, which is identical to the one used by the hotels. With far larger populations, Gran Canaria and Tenerife have greater problems. These two islands also suffer from destruction of surfing 'habitat' through construction of breakwalls and groynes in an attempt to provide nice safe swimming havens for the package holiday hordes. The environmental action group, ADES, has sadly disbanded, leaving the way clear for proposed developments. The existance of 46 waves is still threatened. However, the current government stance is not to continue any coastal development involving artificial beaches or sea walls. This policy may change at any time, making the stay of execution brief for the list of threatened waves.

PETER CADE
Carwyn Williams' first surf trip to Tenerife, aged 17

On Localism

Crowds will always be a talking point here. On Gran Canaria and Tenerife the problems have led to a heavy 'locals only' attitude, which although partially understandable should never have come to the point where it is now. Rip-offs and aggro are an ugly, unnecessary side of surfing, detrimental to the activity in every way. Some of the reasons for this are the vast numbers of surf hungry foreigners who have not shown enough respect to the locals to whom these breaks are home. A change from both sides is the only hope of being able to go to these places as friends rather than enemies. Lanzarote is not as bad, although crowding is quickly becoming worse, particularly at La Santa, where a large contingency of local surfers and bodyboarders control the line up at Village Lefts (The Slab). Being such a wave rich area, it is advisable to search around for less crowded conditions. One way to beat the crowds is to rise early, as the locals are particularly fond of sleeping in. Fuerteventura is the youngest and least populated island in the chain. The local surfers are more relaxed than on other islands, however this will change if visitors are overzealous and greedy in their wave selection. The right-hand point of Lobos is one example of a growing problem, with crowds swarming here from both Fuerteventura and Lanzarote by the boat load. A tight take-off zone exacerbates the situation. The locals will only be cool if the visitors act likewise.

Specificités du littoral

En bref

Les problèmes de pollution de l'eau sont rares aux Canaries, car la population est minime, l'industrie lourde est confidentielle et le courant des Canaries balaye tout. A Lanzarote et Fuerteventura, les spots principaux sont plutôt propres, à quelques exceptions près. Le dégazage des pétroliers et le déversement d'eaux usées dans le port de Puerta del Rosario affectent peu les surfers. Les complexes hôteliers doivent traiter eux-mêmes leurs eaux usées par décantation. L'eau récupérée est utilisée pour l'irrigation tandis que les solides sont déposés à l'interieur des terres. Corralejo vient d'être doté d'un nouveau système d'épuration, sur le même principe de retour à la terre. Gran Canaria et Ténérife sont confrontés à de plus graves problèmes, liés à une population plus dense. Ces deux îles ont perdu de nombreux écosystèmes marins par la construction de digues, destinées à crée de véritables piscines pour que les hordes de touristes puissent nager en sécurité. Le Groupe d'Action Environnemental A.D.E.S. à malheureusement disparu, laissant au moins 46 spots à la merci nombreuses propositions de développement immobilier. Toutefois, la position du gouvernement actuel n'est pas de poursuivre le développement de la côte au moyen de digues et de plages artificielles. Cette politique peut, hélas, changer, et replacer de nombreux spots sur la liste des condamnés.

Le localisme

La foule est parfois un vrai problème. A Gran Canaria et à Ténérife, la situation à créé une ambiance trés " locals only ". Cet état de fait, compréhensible et parfois excusable est indéfendable dans ses excès. L'agressivité et le vandalisme sont sont un aspect inutile et moche du surf, dégradant à tous points de vue pour le sport. Une des raisons réside dans le manque de respect qu'ont pu témoigner certains visiteurs envers les locaux. Un effort des deux cotés est indispensable afin de pouvoir débarquer en ami et non en ennemi. A Lanzarote la situation est moins sombre, bien que la surpopulation approche à La Santa, où un bataillon de surfers et de bodyboarders locaux contrôlent le line-up à la Gauche du Village. Il y a plein de vagues ailleurs, on conseillera donc de rester à l'écart de ces endroits surpeuplés. Le seul moyen d'éviter la foule sur certains spots est de se lever tôt, les locaux n'étant pas tès matinaux. Fuerteventura est la plus récente et la moins peuplée des îles Canaries. Les locaux sont plus relax qu'ailleurs, mais cela peut changer si les visiteurs sont trop gourmands dans leurs choix de vagues. La pointe de droites de Lobos illustre bien ce problème, quand les hordes de surfers débarquent de Fuerte et de Lanzarote par bateau entier. Une zone de take-off trés précise envenime la situation. Les locaux seront cools si les visiteurs le sont, et le meilleur moyen d'éviter les embrouilles est de trouver une de ces vagues désertes qui fait encore la magie de ces îles.

Lanzarote

Pablo Postigo, El Quemao

Where to go

Surf Areas

In this chapter you'll find detailed information on four of the islands. Lanzarote and Fuerteventura are unquestionably better surf destinations than Tenerife and Gran Canaria, but all the islands are popular and they all receive good waves.

For at least a decade, **Lanzarote** has been one of the hottest spots in Europe to find powerful, consistent surf. The best waves are found in the north half of the island with both coasts hosting classic reefs offering good surf in an array of conditions. Swells from the west and north produce waves on the west coast and north swells will also strike the east coast. South swells (most common in summer) can produce good waves around the south and east coasts, although it is the winter north-westerly swells that have built Lanzarote's reputation amongst the surfing community world-wide.

Virtually without exception the best spots are shallow, lava reefs. Surf of up to 5m (15ft) has been ridden and this occurs with some frequency. Big boards are as common as broken boards. The majority of foreign surfers are English, with a complement of French, Spanish, Kiwis, Australians, Americans, Scandinavians and Germans. There is a strong local surfing population that includes a high proportion of bodyboarders, who keep largely to themselves. While the spirit of localism is understandably strong here, it hasn't yet led to the behaviour seen on other islands.

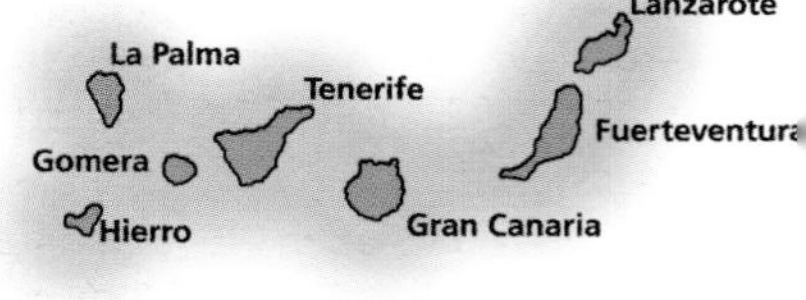

The area from **Playa de Famara to La Santa** must rate as one of the best surf locations in Europe. It picks up all north and west swells and offers a variety of breaks facing in numerous directions. Famara is a good beach for beginners, curving through 90 degrees, thus providing a range of wave sizes and wind directions. The west coast undoubtedly holds some rarely ridden spots, which require boats, long walks or a 4WD.

You can find accommodation at Famara, in La Santa village, and also at the monstrous sports complex that sits just north of the village on the point overlooking Morro Negro.

Ou aller

Les zones de surf

Dans ce chapître, l'information est donnée pour 4 îles. Lanzarote et Fuerteventura sont indiscutablement les meilleures destinations pour surfer que Tenerife et Gran Canaria bien que toutes ces îles soient connues et reçoivent de bonnes vagues.

Pendant au moins dix ans, ça a été un des endroits les plus convoités d'Europe pour trouver des vagues puissantes et consistantes. Les meilleures vagues de l'île se trouvent au nord dont les deux côtes abritent de super reefs donnant de bonnes conditions dans pas mal de conditions. Les houles de nord et d'ouest donnent des vagues sur la côte ouest et sur les îles. Les houles de nord atteignent la côte est. Les houles de sud, surtout en été, peuvent donner de bonnes vagues sur les côtes Est et Sud, bien que ce soit les swells hivernaux de nord et d'ouest qui ont construit la réputation de Lanzarote dans la communauté du surf dans le monde.

Presque sans exception, les meilleurs spots sont sur de la lave avec peu d'eau. On peut surfer jusqu'à 5 mètres et ça arrive plus souvent qu'on ne pense. On y voit souvent des grandes planches, de même que des planches cassées. La majorité des étrangers sont anglais aidés par les néo-zélandais, les australiens, les américains, les Scandinaves et les allemands. Parmi les locaux qui sont nombreux, on trouve de plus en plus de bodyboarders, qui restent vraiment entre eux. Alors que l'esprit de localisme est naturellement fort ici, ça n'a pas mené au comportement qu'on a pu observer sur les autres îles.

La portion de côte entre **La Santa et le nord de Playa Famara** est sans aucun doute une des meilleures d'Europe. Une variété de spots prend tous les swells de nord et d'ouest. Famara est bon pour les débutants car ce beach-break tourne à 90° et offre donc le choix en taille de vagues et en direction de vent. Mis à part les nombreux récifs accessibles de cette région, la côte ouest réserve une variété de récifs peu surfés à qui sait les trouver. Tous les moyens sont bons, voire necessaires : bateau, marche, 4x4 et de toute façons une bonne dose de volonté.

On pourra se loger à Famara, au village de La Santa, ou dans l'énorme complexe sportif au nord de la pointe qui domine Morro Negro.

Fuerteventura est la seconde île de l'archipel en superficie. Connue sous le nom de " Isla de la Soledad ", l'ile de la Solitude, possède plus de plages que toute autre île. Les côte nord et ouest ainsi que l'île Lobos sont les plus surfées. Les côtes sud et est sont plus prisées par les funboarders et les baigneurs des voyages organisés. Moins de swell en hiver, mais les solides vents on-shore de l'été peuvent lever de sérieuses vagues.

La côte nord: une piste cabossée longe sur 20km les récifs de lave qui prennent tous les swells de nord. La plupart des surfers

Fuerteventura

Derecha at Hierro, also known as 'The Bubble'

SPARROW

Fuerteventura is the second largest island in the Canary group. It is commonly known as *isla de soledad* (islands of the sun) and has more sandy beaches than the other islands. The north and west coasts, along with Lobos Island, are the main areas with a concentration of lava reefs. The east and south shores are more popular among the windsurfing community and package holiday swimmers, and although they receive less swell in winter, the summer onshores can kick up mast high waves on occasion.

The North Coast A pot-hole ridden nightmare of a track runs for 20km (12mi) along the north coast beside volcanic reefs which pick up all north swell. Corralejo is where most surfers stay and there are good bars, excellent seafood restaurants, supermarkets, patisseries, cafés and surf shops. It's an easy place to look after yourself and most of a surfer's needs can be found fairly cheaply.

The West Coast receives masses of swell but access is extremely restricted. Between Cotillo and Punta del Tigre miles of reefs and sandy beaches form a coastline that has little protection from Atlantic waves. Because of its desolate nature and wild seas, only a few fishing villages punctuate its length. Roads to the coast are few and even 4WD vehicles experience difficulties.

The Jandia Peninsula also picks up swell and there is still tremendous undiscovered potential in the south of the island. The sandy beaches that line its eastern shores are beautiful if a little empty, but the water is turquoise blue and crowds are not commonplace around most of the surf spots – the best waves break miles from most tourist activity. Sotavento is the most popular activity centre and can be a good place to base yourself.

Gran Canaria

Confital

JAKUE ANDIKOETXEA

Gran Canaria has a roughly circular shape with great potential for surf under many different swell and wind conditions. The north coast picks up the most swell and is easily the most popular area on the island. All the surf shops on Gran Canaria lie in Las Palmas as do the majority of surfers. Gran Canaria, like Tenerife, is not as favourable for travelling surfers as Lanzarote or Fuerteventura due to heavier crowds and localism problems. The best waves on the island are harder to enjoy due to these factors. The north coast is the most populated, but the west coast receives epic swell. Good waves can definitely be had on Gran Canaria and there are some uncrowded surf spots not marked on the map that are easy enough to find. These are the places that a travelling surfer must seek out if they are to fully enjoy Gran Canaria's surf.

There are two main areas to find waves on **Tenerife** – firstly on the south west coast from Playa de las Américas to Los Gigantes, approximately 25km (15mi) to the north and secondly along the north coast up to Playa de los Troches. Main roads service these areas and they are also the scene of intense urbanisation. Playa de las Américas is one of the ugliest examples of the tourist fungus mutating and although the northern coast of Tenerife is beautiful it is also the most heavily populated region in the group.

Tenerife

Punta Blanca – K16

PETER CADE

When to go

Canaries Averages	Jan	Apr	Jul	Oct
water °C	19	18	21	22
wetsuit				

September to April is the best season when consistent swells and good weather come at an affordable price. Many surfers and windsurfers hole up here for two or three months of the year before heading back home for spring surf. Water temperatures vary little throughout the year, remaining at a respectable 18°C (60°F) in winter and 22°C (70°F) in summer. A short suit will keep you comfortable much of the year although most people surf in a steamer in winter.

élisent domicile à Corralejo, connu pour ses bars sympas, d'excellents restos de poissons, supermarchés, patisseries, cafés et même des surf-shops. La côte ouest est bombardée de swell, mais l'accès est limité. Entre Cotillo et Punta del Tigre se déroulent des kilomètres de plages et de reefs qui recoivent de plein fouet la puissance de l'Atlantique. A cause du caractère sauvage et isolé de cette côte, seulement quelques villages de pêcheurs la ponctue. Les routes d'accès à la côte sont rares, et mêmes les 4x4 ont du mal.

la côte ouest reçoit énormément de swell mais son accés est extrêmement limité. Entre Cotillo et Punta del Tigre, des kilomètres de reefs et de plages forment un littoral trés peu protégé des vagues de l'Atlantique. A cause de la désolation ambiante et ses eaux agitées, peu de villages de pêcheurs jalonnent cette côte. Les routes y sont rares et même les 4x4 ont du mal à passer.

La peninsule de Jandia est aussi bien exposée aux houles et il existe encore un potentiel incroyable au sud de l'île. Les plages de sable qui bordent le rivage oriental sont superbes mais un peu vides; l'eau y est bleu turquoise et c'est carrément rare d'être trop nombreux autour des spots. Les meilleures vagues cassent à des kilomètres de toute activité touristique. Sotavento en est un peu le centre; c'est un camp de base assez pratique.

La forme quasi-circulaire de **Gran Canaria** permet un choix de côtes avec du surf dans des conditions différentes. La côte nord qui chope le plus de houle est la zone la plus connue pour surfer. Tous les surf shops de l'île sont sur Las Palmas tout comme la plupart des surfers. Gran Canaria, comme Tenerife, n'est pas aussi adéquat pour les surfers étrangers que Lanzarote ou Fuerteventura à cause du monde et des problèmes de localisme. A cause de ça, il est difficile d'apprécier les meilleures vagues de l'île situées sur la côte nord. Sans aucun doute, la côte orientale reçoit super bien la houle avec de spots peu fréquentés qui ne sont pas marqués sur la carte. Si vous allez sur Gran Canaria, vous pourrez y trouver de bons spots, qui sont ceux que le tripper recherche pour profiter pleinement des vagues qu'offre l'île.

Tenerife Il existe deux zones principales où l'on peut trouver des vagues ici. D'une part sur la côte sud-ouest de Playa de las Américas jusqu'à los Gigantes environ 25kms au nord; et d'autre part le long de la côte nord jusqu'à Playa de los Troches. Des routes nationales desservent ces zones qui sont, par ailleurs, largement urbanisées. Playa de las Américas est un des exemples les plus moches d'une mutation à vocation touristique, et bien que la côte nord de Tenerife soit d'une beauté unique, c'est également la plus fortement peuplée de la région.

Quand aller

L'hiver est toujours la meilleure saison où houles consistantes et climat agréable sont à un prix très abordable. Pas mal de surfers et de windsurfers se calent ici 2 à 3 mois de l'année avant de revenir pour le printemps. La température de l'eau varie très peu tout au long de l'année, oscillant autour de 18 C en hiver et 22 C en été.

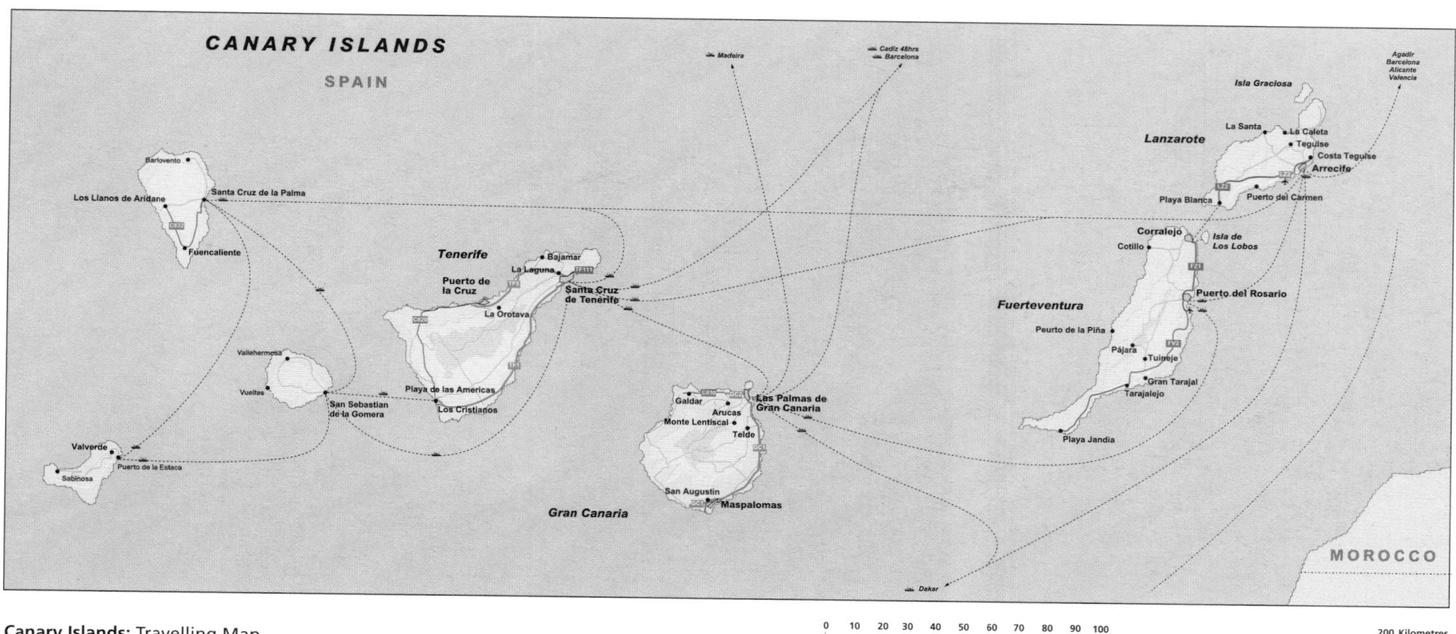

Canary Islands: Travelling Map

Scale 0 10 20 30 40 50 60 70 80 90 100 200 Kilometres; 0 10 20 30 40 50 60 70 80 90 100 Miles

Travel

Air

Fuerteventura: Iberia (28) 85 08 02
Lanzarote: Flight Information (28) 81 14 50

Ferries

Transmediterránea: (28) 44 64 99
Spanish mainland to Canaries and respective inter-island services
Lineas Fred Olsen
Fuerteventura: (28) 53 50 90
Lanzarote: (28) 51 72 66
Every two hours between Lanzarote and Fuerteventura, with a free bus service to and from the ferry terminal
Naviera Armas – *Inter island services*
Gran Canaria (28) 22 72 82
Tenerife (22) 28 90 12
Lanzarote (28) 51 79 12
Fuerteventura (28) 86 70 80

Buses

Gran Canaria: (28) 36 86 35
Tenerife: (22) 21 81 22

Rental

Hertz:
Gran Canaria (28) 57 95 77
Fuerteventura (28) 86 62 59
Opel Corsa 4,650 ptas per day, includes tax, insurance and unlimited mileage and can be taken to any other island. Local deals can work out a lot cheaper, so shop around.

Other Info

Tourist Information

Tourist Information Telephone Service
Turespaña 901 300 600

Tourist Offices

Gran Canaria: (28) 36 22 22
Lanzarote: (28) 51 77 94
Tenerife (22) 38 60 00
Fuerteventura: (28) 86 62 35

For more info, see Spain Travelling p176–177

Travelling

Getting There

By air Scheduled flights leave from a number of European cities bound for the Canaries on Spain's national airline, Iberia. There are international airports on Gran Canaria, Tenerife, Lanzarote and Fuerteventura. The cheapest way of getting there is via charter flights which take the plethora of package tourists at fares way below the scheduled flight price. All flights to the Canaries attract a charge for surfboards between £15 and £35 (return) for charters and even more on Iberia.

By sea The Canaries are serviced by a 'Transmed' car/passenger ferry that leaves Spain from Cádiz and takes approximately 39 hours. It is expensive, but works out well for longer duration trips in a campervan.There are also inter-island vehicle and passenger ferries and jetfoils between all the main islands but it's crucial to make a reservation in advance.

Getting Around

By car Renting a car is just about obligatory but prices can vary considerably. Cheap rusty rattlers are the norm, but a 4WD will almost double the rental rate. Europeans will find their national drivers license OK, others are advised that an international license is required.

By public transport Both Lanzarote and Fuerteventura have an adequate bus service. For long distances there are fast buses with limited stops, marked Expres or Directo. On some routes, surf boards are not allowed on the bus.

Accommodation Camping at some of the remote beaches is the cheapest way to stay, but this is not encouraged by the authorities and can have unpleasant endings. Car security is a problem – rip-offs are a common occurrence. Basic apartment block and self-catering accommodation is widely available outside of peak holiday times and is often most competitive as part of a package deal.

Infos voyage

Y aller

En avion La compagnie aérienne nationale espagnole Iberia propose des vols réguliers depuis la plupart des grandes villes d'Europe. Gran Cananaria, Lanzarote, Ténérife et Fuerteventura ont chacune un aéroport international. Le moyen le plus économique de s'y rendre est peut-être depuis Londres où les compagnies de charters se livrent un guerre des prix pour attirer les touristes. Le passage des planches vous coûtera entre 150 et 400 francs, surtout sur Iberia.

En Bateau Les Canaries sont déservies par les car-ferries " Trans-Med ". Comptez 39h de traversée depuis Cadix. Le prix du passage est plutôt cher, mais vaut le coup pour un long séjour ou si vous voyagez en minibus. Les ferries et les bateaux-jet inter-îles sont trés efficaces, mais n'oubliez pas de reserver.

Se deplacer

En Voiture Louer une voiture est une nécessité, mais les prix varient considérablement. Des voitures pas chères et un peu rouillées sont de mise, mais un 4x4 peut doubler le prix de la location. Les permis de conduire européens sont acceptés. Pour les autres, pensez à l'extention internationale.

Avec les transports en commun.
Lanzarote et Fuerteventura ont un bon service de bus. Pour les longues distances, prennez les bus marqués Express ou Directo, qui s'arrêtent moins. Attention, les planches ne sont pas admises sur certains parcours.

Se loger Si le camping reste le moyen le plus économique de se loger sur certaines plages, il n'est pas conseillé par les autorités, et ça peut mal finir. Le braquage de voitures est également très courant. Si vous évitez la haute saison touristique, vous disposerez d'une offre étendue d'appartements de de bungalows.

PHIL HOLDEN

Fuerteventura north track

Lanzarote

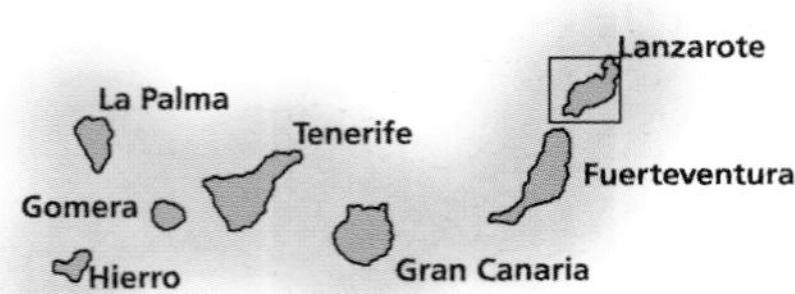

1. Playa de Janubio

The southern-most known surf location on the W coast has 1km (830yd) of black sand beach in front of the salt flats. Waves break on the beach and on reefs at the N end of the bay.

Le spot référencé le plus au sud de la côte ouest, 1 km de plage de sable noir en face de marais salants. Les vagues cassent sur la plage et sur du reef au nord de la baie.

2. El Golfo

The outside reefs here can produce tubey rights and they're surfed less frequently than the other breaks on the island. Check them out from town.

Les reefs au large d'El Golfo peuvent donner des droites tubulaires. Ils sont surfé moins fréquemment que les autres breaks de l'île. Visible depuis la ville.

3. Playa de la Cantería

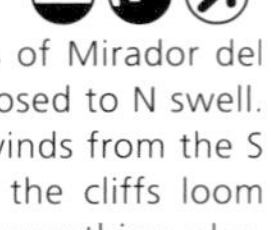

About 500m (1,500ft) below the cliffs of Mirador del Rio, there's a good left reef break, exposed to N swell. It receives maximum protection from winds from the S or W. The location is breathtaking – the cliffs loom straight out of the ocean, dwarfing everything else. The wave works best at high tide.

1500 mètres au-dessous des falaises du Mirador del Rio, il y a une bonne gauche de reef, exposée aux swells de nord. Elle reçoit une protection maximale des vents de sud ou d'ouest. L'endroit est à couper le souffle-les falaises surgissent droitde l'océan, minimisant tout le reste. Meilleur à marée haute.

4. Jameos del Agua

The N most site in a string of left-hand reefs and points, located E of the car park at Jameos del Agua. The waves work in a N swell with a wind from SW to NW, while S swells break here in summer with accompanying N winds. The two peaks can either connect or close out depending on conditions. Wave-jumpers love the outside reef.

Le plus au nord d'une tripotée de gauches de reefs et de points. Elles cassent par houle de nord avce un vent de SO à NO. Les houles de sud cassent ici en été, accompagnés par les alizés de nord. Les deux pics peuvent ou connecter ou fermer selon les conditions. le reef outside est un must pour les sauteurs de vagues en windsurf. Situé au nord du parking à Jameos del Agua.

THE GILL

Jameos del Agua

ERIC CHAUCHE

Arrieta

5. Punta Usaje

A shallow left point breaks close to the shore, accessed by a dirt track 500m (400yd) from the car park at Jameos del Agua. This wave works only on a big N swell and is best from mid to high tide.

Une gauche avec peu de fond, 500m au sud de Jameos del Agua, qui casse prés du bord. Ca casse seulement par grosse houle de nord, de préférence de mi-marée à marée haute. Un chemin terreux mène au spot depuis le parking de Jameos.

6. Punta de Mujeres

Right and left reef break, S of the village that works in N and S swells. It faces ESE and is best in a W or NW wind at high tide.

Un spot de droites et de gauches, juste au sud du village, qui casse par houle de nord et sud. Exposé est/sud-est, mieux par vent d'ouest/nord-ouest à marée haute.

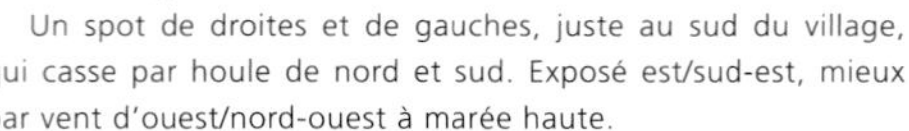

7. Arrieta

There's a few reefs facing ESE at the town of Arrieta that are all sucky, shallow and very dangerous.

Une poignée de reefs exposés est/sud-est sur Arrieta, qui suce tous invariablement, avec peu d'eau et un réel danger.

8. Playa de la Garita

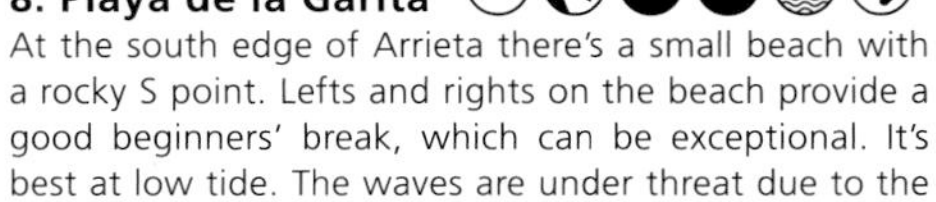

At the south edge of Arrieta there's a small beach with a rocky S point. Lefts and rights on the beach provide a good beginners' break, which can be exceptional. It's best at low tide. The waves are under threat due to the construction of a pier and beach front/promenade area.

Dans la partie sud d'Arrieta se trouve une petite plage avec une gauche de reef. Aussi des pics faciles pour les débutants qui peuvent être nets. De préférence à marée basse. Les vagues y sont menacées à cause de la construction d'une jetée sur le front de mer.

ERIC CHAUCHE

El Golfo

Isla Graciosa

Covering an area of 42sqkm (35sqmi), Graciosa is populated by approximately 800 people who rely on fishing and increasingly tourism for their livelihood. The coastline has many deserted white sandy beaches and around these beaches unridden reefs await adventurers. The main town is Caleta del Sebo where the ferry arrives from Orzola.

Graciosa couvre une zone de 42kms, avec environ 800 habitants qui vivent de la pêche et de plus en plus du tourisme. Le littoral a pas mal de plages de sable blanc vierges truffés de reefs insurfés qui appellent à l'aventure. La ville principale est Caleta del Sabo où le ferry arrive d'Orzola.

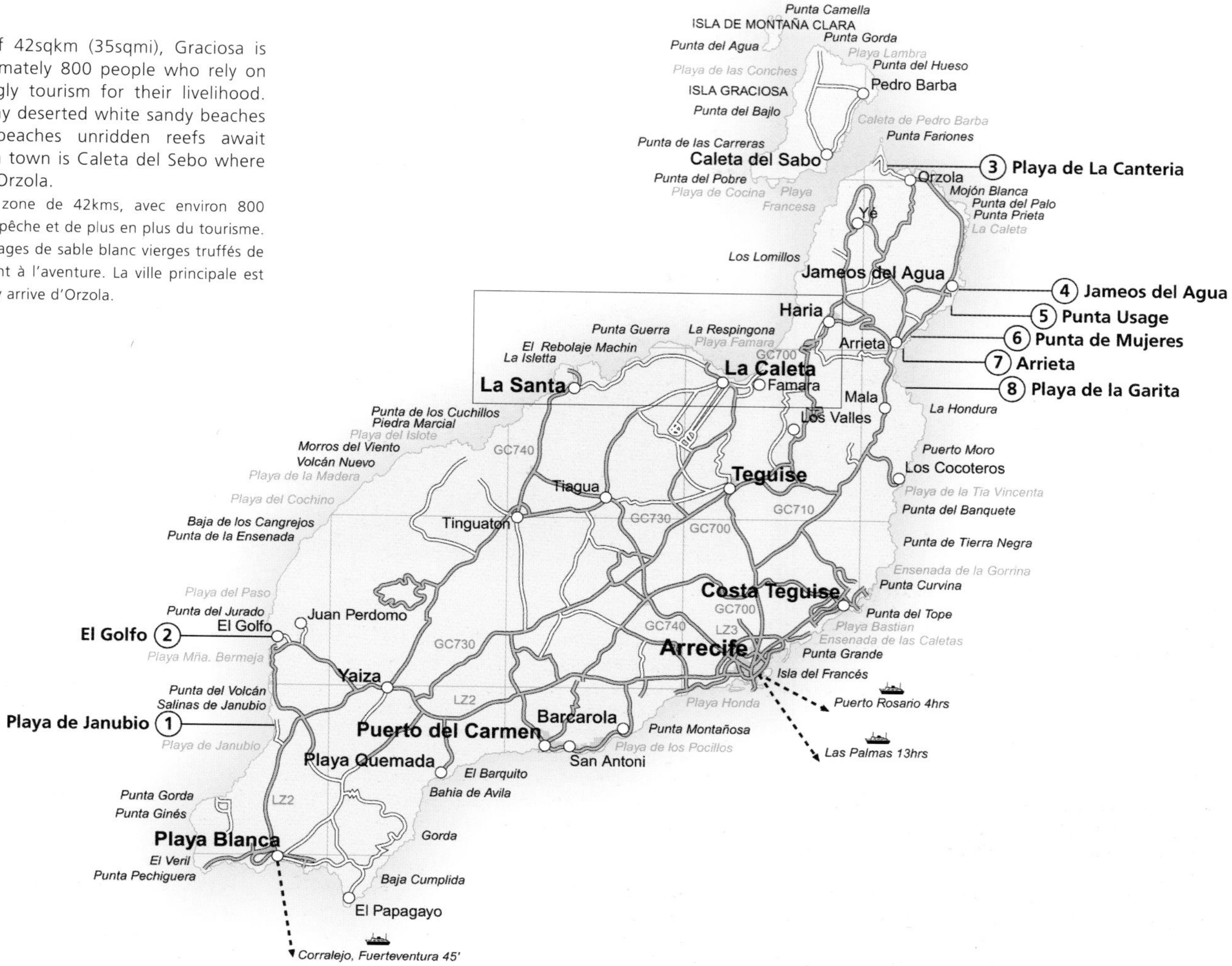

F. MUNOZ

The East Coast

Lanzarote
La Santa to Playa de Famara

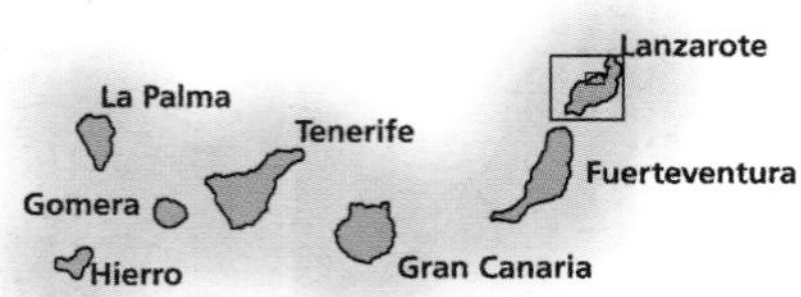

1. El Quemao

A short, sucky left breaking close to the shore in front of the village of La Santa. Optimum swell comes from the W to NW with accompanying S to E winds. The break is visible from many vantage points in town. To get there from the village of La Santa, take a walk to the harbour.

Une gauche courte qui suce cassant prés de la Santa. Le swell idéal vient d'O/NO avec des vents de sud et d'est. Le spot est visible de pas mal de points saillants dans le village. Depuis le village, marchez jusqu'au port.

2. The Slab

This is a thick-lipped beast that breaks over exposed rock at low tide, but as the water covers it, the reef turns on the goods. The lefts are fast, sucky and consistent, the right off the peak, which is always shorter, is just as good. It collects all swell and is often the only wave working on the island. The break is visible from the main road. It is not unusual for locals to order you out of the water.

Un gros barrel avec une lèvre épaisse qui casse sur des caillasses qui émergent à marée basse. Quand la marée recouvre le reef, ça envoie encore le pâté. Rapide, ultra-creux et consistant. Récupère toutes les houles en étant souvent le seul spot qui marche sur l'île quand le vent vient du nord et que les autres spots de la côte ouest sont on-shore. Une droite qui est toujours plus courte et donc rarement surfée. Parfaitement matable depuis la route.

MIKE SEARLE

El Quemao

3. Morro Negro

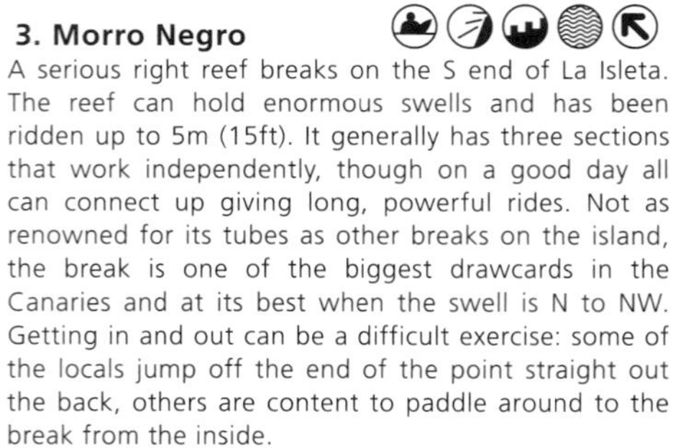

A serious right reef breaks on the S end of La Isleta. The reef can hold enormous swells and has been ridden up to 5m (15ft). It generally has three sections that work independently, though on a good day all can connect up giving long, powerful rides. Not as renowned for its tubes as other breaks on the island, the break is one of the biggest drawcards in the Canaries and at its best when the swell is N to NW. Getting in and out can be a difficult exercise: some of the locals jump off the end of the point straight out the back, others are content to paddle around to the break from the inside.

Une droite qui fait pas rire casse au sud de la Isleta. Le eef peut tenir jusqu'à gros puisqu'a été surfé jusqu'à 5m. Souvent 3 sections qui marchent indépendamment bien que sur les bons jours, elles peuvent connecter et donner des vagues longues et puissantes. Pas aussi réputé pour ses tubes que les voisines mais considérée comme un des atouts de l'île, de préférence quand la houle vient de N/NO. Se mettre à l'eau et sortir peut être un exercice difficile, certains locaux se jettent à l'eau du bout de la pointe direct au line-up, d'autres se contentent de ramer depuis l'inside.

ALEX WILLIAMS

Morro Negro

4. Boca del Abajo

   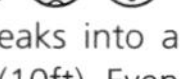

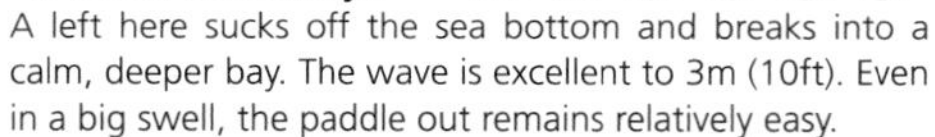

A left here sucks off the sea bottom and breaks into a calm, deeper bay. The wave is excellent to 3m (10ft). Even in a big swell, the paddle out remains relatively easy.

Une gauche qui aspire depuis le fond et qui casse dans une baie calme, plus profonde. La vague est géniale jusqu'à 3m et même quand c'est gros, la rame reste relativement facile.

5. Caleta de Cabello

A left located on the W side of the bay, breaking in shallow water. It's best on a N or NW swell at high tide.

Une gauche située à l'ouest de la baie, qui casse à fleur d'eau. Meilleur par houle de nord à nord-ouest à marée haute.

6. Ghost Town

A spectacular peak breaks in the bay to the right of the town of Caballo when other breaks are 2m (6ft). This has a reputation as one of the Canaries' foremost big wave breaks.

Un pic ahurrissant qui casse dans la baie à droite de la ville de Caballo quand les autres spots font plus de 2m. Considéré comme un des spots de gros proéminents des Canaries.

7. Outside Reef

A bombora reportedly breaks (we've no confirmed accounts of anyone surfing it) 500m (400yd) out to sea when the swell is max N and over 4m (12ft). It could be the big wave of the Canaries or it could be a myth.

Un reef à 500 mètres au large quand la houle vient trés au nord, à partir de 4m. On a aucune confirmation de savoir qui a surfé là, pas grand monde à vrai dire. Ca pourrait être le Waïmea des Canaries comme une hallu complète.

F. MUÑOZ

Caleta de Cabello

8. San Juan

A killer left and a shorter, less consistent right. Offshores are S to SW: a valuable backstop when La Santa is has cross-shore wind. San Juan is a powerful wave that can have swell when other breaks are too small to surf.

Une gauche de folie et une droite plus courte et moins régulière. L'off-shore est au S/SO- une alternative intéressante quand la Santa est cross-shore. San Juan ne manque pas de puissance quand les autres spots sont trop petits pour surfer.

9. La Caleta de Famara

Another shallow reef produces more dredgy lefts best surfed between 1-3m (3-9ft). Paddle out from the breakwater. It's best at high tide.

Un autre reef craignos qui envoie encore des gauches assassines, plus surfables entre 1 et 3m. Ramez depuis la jetée. Meilleur à marée haute.

10. Playa de Famara

Excellent beach wave without intense crowd scenes. Generally the N is bigger, but to get there you have to drive up the side of the mountain range (which shelters it from the NE winds), before descending to the coast. One of Lanzarote's best wave-sailing spots, especially in sirocco conditions.

Super beach break sans les tensions de la Chine. Généralement, le nord est plus gros mais pour y aller, il faut rouler en haut du flanc de la montagne (qui abrite le spot des vents de NE) avant de redescendre sur la côte. Un des meilleurs spots de windsurf, surtout avec le Sirocco.

11. Las Bajas

Located at the N end of the bay is a reef that breaks 200m (180yd) to the SW of rocks called Las Bajas. It's a long paddle out to sea, but worth it if conditions are right. The break is visible from the road N of the beach. It's a dangerous wave, not for beginners.

Situé au nord de la baie, ce reef qui déroule environ 200m au sud ouest de ces rochers appelés Las Bajas. Il faut aller loin au large mais ca vaut le coup de rame quand les conditions sont bonnes. On peut mater depuis la route au nord de la plage. C'est dangereux, débutants s'abstenir.

Philippe Chevalier, San Juan

ERIC CHAUCHÉ

Playa de Famara

WPR

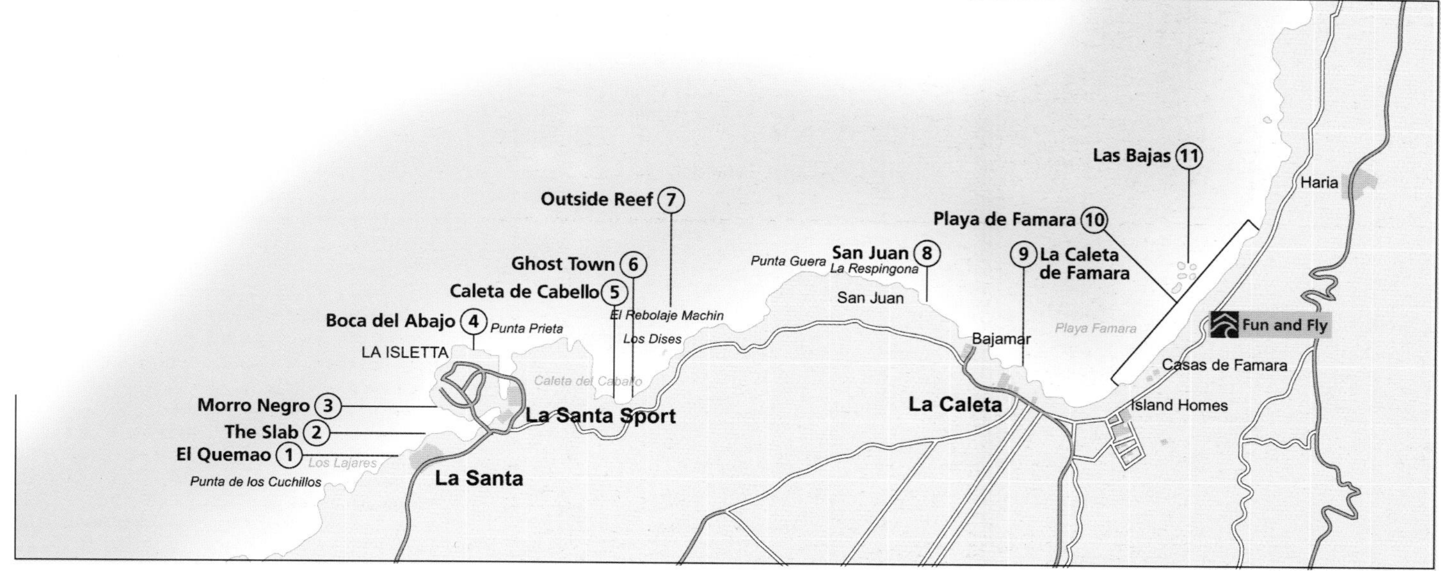

Fuerteventura

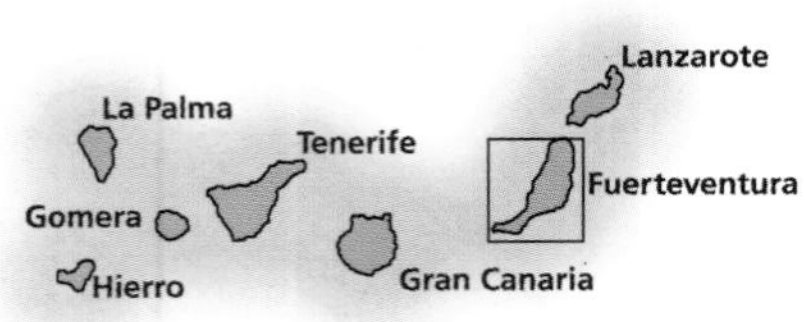

1. Spew Pits/Las Lagunas 

A reef that has its name for a reason! Super hollow spitting barrels. A popular spot, located N of the harbour in Cotillo, which gets busy when the N shore is small. If the sirocco is on, winds will blow E for long periods of time, and that's offshore!

Un reef qui n'a pas volé son nom (le pic qui crache)! Un pic connu qui devient encombré quand c'est petit sur la côte nord. Si le Sirocco souffle alors les vents d'est seront réguliers, ça signifie offshore! Au nord du port c'est Cotillo.

2. Cotillo (South Beach)  

At the S end of this dusty, Mexican-style village is a long sandy beach. The seabed has a distinctive ledge that causes the waves to jack up in virtually the same place whatever the tide state or swell size. It's a popular wave-jumping spot and at the N end there's protection from N winds.

A l'extrémité est de ce village poussiéreux, style Mexique, commence une longue vague de sable. Le littoral a un angle particulier qui font lever les vagues presque au même endroit quelles que soient la marée ou la houle. Encore un spot de prédilection pour windsurfers, du côté nord, c'est protégé des vents de nord.

PHIL HOLDEN

Playa de Esquinzo

3. Playa de Esquinzo   

This is relatively hard to find and consequently crowd-free. The break receives a lot of swell and works best at high tide. Esquinzo is signposted off the main road N of La Oliva: from there the road leads through the desert following an unmarked road with many unmarked turn-offs. If you don't end up here, you could well end up somewhere better. Good luck!

Ce spot est relativement difficile a trouver et donc libre de monde. Le break recois beaucoup de houle et il fonctione le mieux a haute maree. Esquinzo est signe de la route principale aux Nord de la Olivia: de la, la route traverse le desert souivant un chemin non-indique avec beaucoup de detour aussi non-indique . Ci vous y arrivees pas a trouver Esquinzo vous pourrez vous retrouver a un meuillier spot. Bonne chance!

4. Playa de Pared 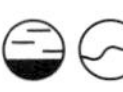  

A black sand beach here picks up loads of swell, breaks on any tide from 0.5m to 3m (2-8ft). Rips are strong along this part of the coast so take extra care. Parking along the beach.

Une plage de sable noir trés bien exposée avec des vagues à n'imorte quelle marée de 30 cms à 3m. Les surfers et windsurfers se sont plutôt rares au sud de l'île et cette zone peu explorée a un potentiel phénoménal. Les courants le long de cette route sont forts, méfiance! Se garer prés de la plage.

5. Cofete

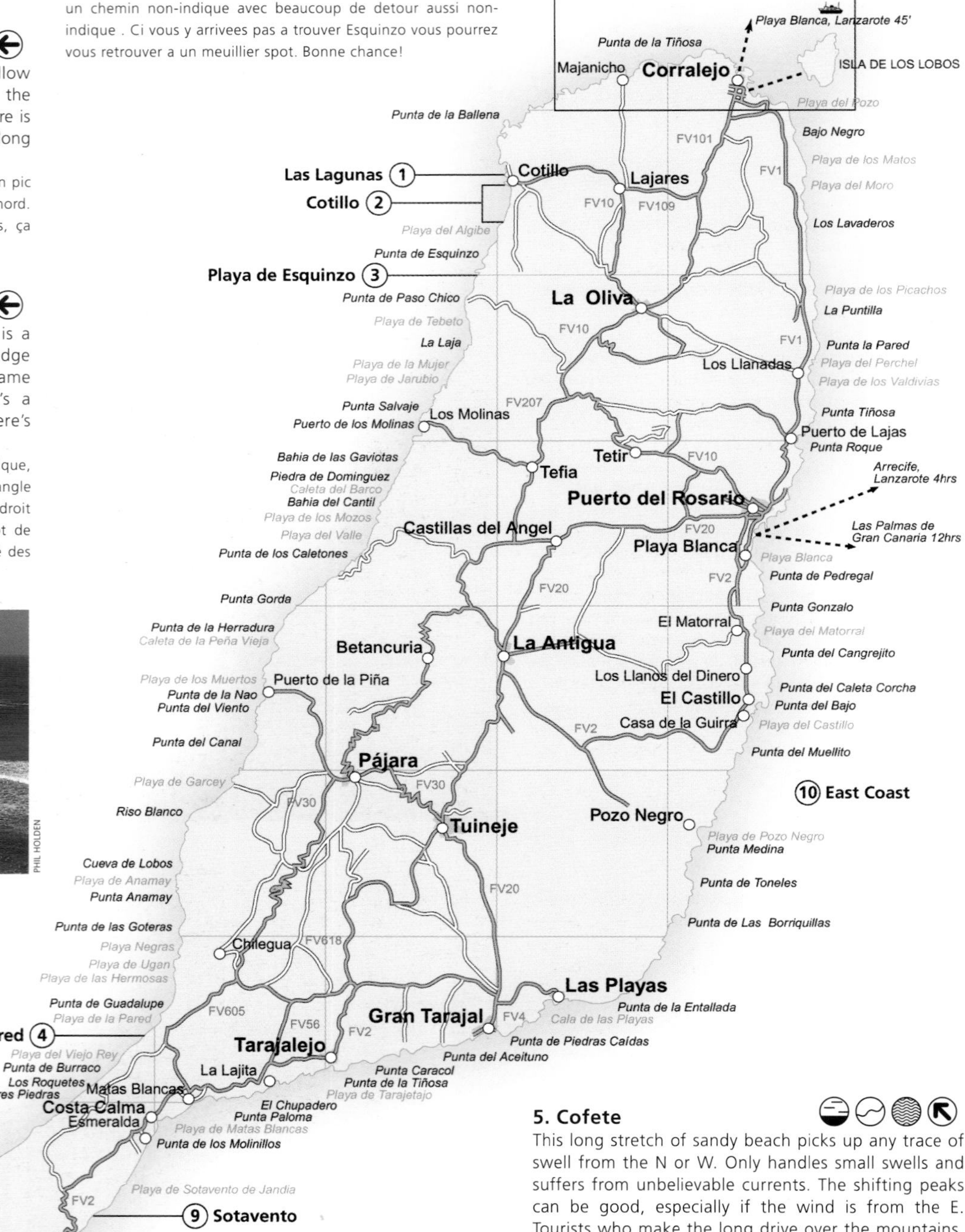

This long stretch of sandy beach picks up any trace of swell from the N or W. Only handles small swells and suffers from unbelievable currents. The shifting peaks can be good, especially if the wind is from the E. Tourists who make the long drive over the mountains, sometimes don't make it back, as the currents have claimed a few swimmers recently.

Cette longue plage sablee attire toute trace de houle du Nord ou Ouest. Peux seulement tenir petite houle et souffre d'un courant incroyable. Les pics bougeants peuvent etre marron, especialment ci le vent vient de l'Est. Les tourists qui font la longue traversee de la montaigne, de temps en temps y reviennent pas pars ce que les courrants on reclame quelque nageurs recement.

6. Punta del Tigre

Swell comes out of deep water and breaks with speed and power over a shallow lava reef. It's rarely surfed due to its remoteness, but worth a look if there's a S swell running.

La houle arrive en eau profonde et forme une vague rapide et puissante sur un reef de lave à fleur d'eau. rarement surfé à cause de son isolement, amis vaut le coup d'oeil quand ça rentre.

7. Las Salinas

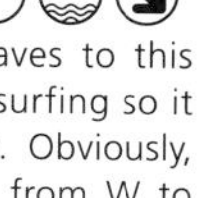

Faces south but a NE swell can just get in to this sharp, shallow right-hander. Stays hollow through all tides, but the volcanic reef can be really punishing at low tide. S swell and N winds will get it pumping.

Fait face aux Sud mais une houle du NE peux juste entree dans ce droitier peux pronfand. Reste creux dans toutes marees, mais le reef volcanique peux punir a maree base. Houle du Sud et vent du Nord ca pette.

8. Cruz Roja

S swell or a strong N/NE wind, brings waves to this area which is more famous for speed windsurfing so it can become crowded out with windy-rigs. Obviously, the wind gets strong, but if it's anywhere from W to NE, cross-offshore conditions will clean up the swell. Almost exclusively rights, which work only on low tide.

Houle du Sud ou grand N/NE aportes des vagues a cette edroit plus connu pour windsurf a vitesse. Bien evidament le vent peut etre fort, mais ci il vient de direction Ouest ou NE, les conditions offshore/croise devrais netoyer la houle. Deviens rame de peoples a voile. Presque seulement des droitiers, qui fonctionnes seulement a maree bas.

9. Sotavento

One of the world's most famous windsurfing beaches with gusts above Force Five on an average 23-25 days a month! Beware of strong offshore winds unless you're planning a trip to South America. On big tides a lagoon is created by the main hotel, which would be perfect for speed-sailing apart from the crowds that such a good spot attracts.

Une des plages de windsurf les plus connues dans le monde, avec des vents de Force 5 en moyenne de 23 à 25 jours par mois. Attention aux venst off-shore à décorner les boeufs à moins que vous ne vouliez aller en Amerique du sud. Pendant les grandes marées (pleine et nouvelle lunes), un lagon se forme prés de l'hotel, ce qui est parfait pour faire de la vitesse, sauf que tout le monde est attiré par ce spot.

10. The East Coast

The extensive sand dunes that run S of Corralejo are a nature reserve and the coast has become a popular windsurfing centre. The seas can be calm here but a big N or S swell creates all sorts of possibilities. Facilities are available.

Les méga-dunes de sable qui s'étendent au sud de Corralejo sont des réserves naturelles alors que la côte s'est convertie en parc à windsurfers. Normalement, la mer y est calme c'est pourquoi on ne surfe que par giga-houle de nord ou par houle de sud. Plein de services à disposition.

DAN HAYLOCK

North of Puerto de Rosario

ROY MAJOR

Las Lagunas (Spew Pits)

PETER CADE

North end of Cotillo Beach

THE GILL

Way down south

Fuerteventura
The North Coast

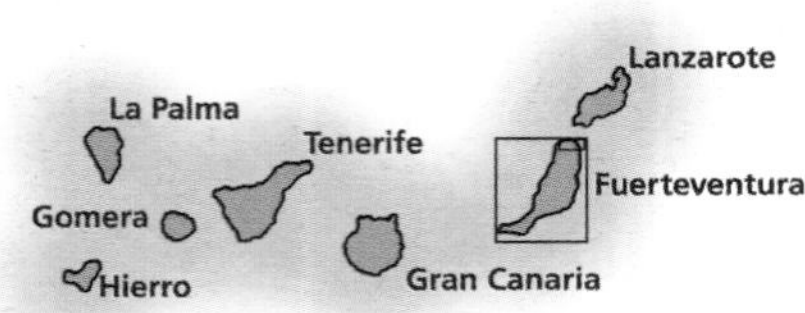

Hierro – spots 2-4
1. Derecha de los Alemanes

There are some quality rights to be found in the W of the bay referred to as Hierro. The crowds often don't travel this far along the N track. Optimum conditions here are a N or NW swell of any size (it can hold a swell) and a S wind.

Dans la même baie que Yarro. Encore des bonnes droites mais les gens ont tendance à ne pas aller aussi loin sur le chemin. Des conditions optima ici par n'importe quelle houle de N/NO (tient la taille) et un vent de sud.

2. Izquierda

Not as tubey as the right, but it's still an excellent wave with great walls for manoeuvres. This picks up a lot of swell giving fun rides even when it's small. It can also get crowded.

Pas aussi tubulaire que la droite mais c'est également une vague top avec des bons murs pour les manoeuvres. Chope pas mal de houle et même quand c'est petit ça vaut le coup. Du monde aussi.

CHRIS POWER

Izquierda

3. Derecha (The Bubble)

Also known as 'The Bubble', but refered to by locals as 'The Right', this is one of the most consistent waves on the N shore. It breaks on the reef at the eastern fringe of the bay, located about 1km (830yd) west of Majanicho. This is a right of exceptional quality, which tubes mercilessly on a typically sharp and shallow volcanic reef. There is also a less critical left. The most popular – and safer – times are mid to high tide, but it can get too crowded. Small circular shelters have been set up in front of the break.

Une des vagues les plus consistantes de la côte nord casse sur du récif sur la limite orientale de la baie. Une droite dont les tubes sont d'une qualité exceptionnelle en cassant sans pitié sur de la lave coupante. Mieux vaut éviter la marée basse. Il peut y avoir pas mal de monde. Environ 1km à l'ouest de Majanicho. Des petits abris ont été construits sous une carcasse de van VW.

PHIL HOLDEN

A typical North Coast set up with Lanzarote in the background

4. Majanicho

About halfway along the car-battering N track lies a ramshackled fishing village. The bay, which the village has been built around, can provide right reef/point waves. They remain surfable up to a good size, but even if it isn't big, watch out! It can be a dangerous place to wipe out.

A peu prés à mi-chemin de la route défoncée qui va vers le nord se trouve un petit village de pêche délabré. La baie sur laquelle le village a été construit peut avoir des droites de point sur du reef. Ca tient une taille respectable mais quand c'est gros, **attention**, c'est pas l'endroit idéal pour tomber.

5. Mejillones

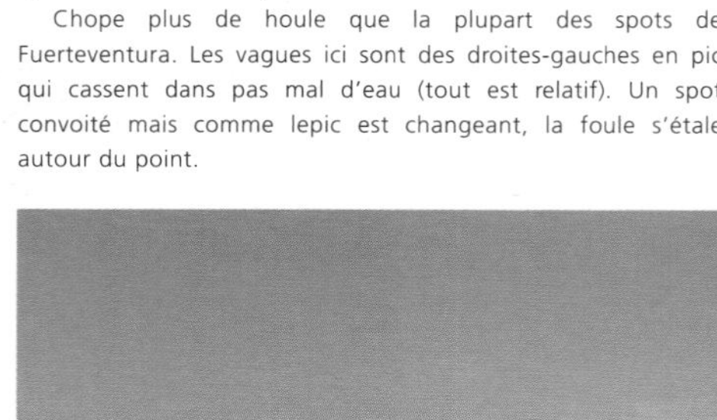

This break picks up more swell than most of Fuerteventura's spots. Peaky rights and lefts break in relatively deep water (for Fuerteventura). It's a popular spot, but because the peaks shift, the crowds are spread around the point.

Chope plus de houle que la plupart des spots de Fuerteventura. Les vagues ici sont des droites-gauches en pic qui cassent dans pas mal d'eau (tout est relatif). Un spot convoité mais comme lepic est changeant, la foule s'étale autour du point.

6. Suicides/Suicidios

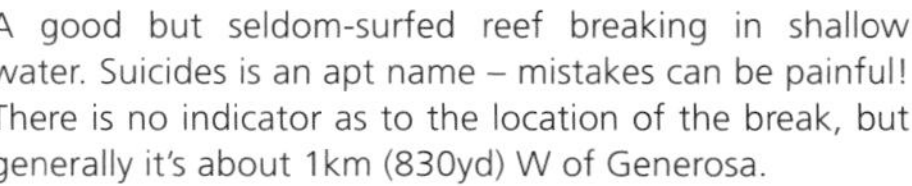

A good but seldom-surfed reef breaking in shallow water. Suicides is an apt name – mistakes can be painful! There is no indicator as to the location of the break, but generally it's about 1km (830yd) W of Generosa.

Un reef rarement surfé qui casse dans peu d'eau. Suicides signifie en clair que chaque erreur peut être douloureuse. Il n'y a aucun panneau pour indiquer le spot. Environ 1km à l'ouest de Generosa.

7. Generosa

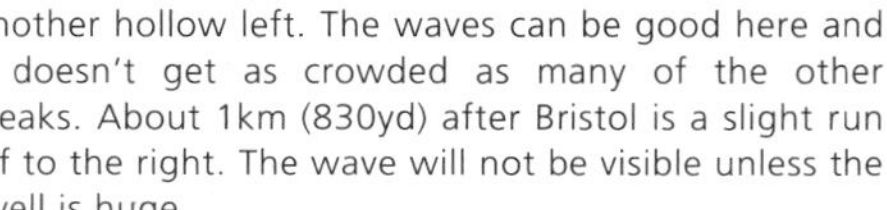

Another hollow left. The waves can be good here and it doesn't get as crowded as many of the other breaks. About 1km (830yd) after Bristol is a slight run off to the right. The wave will not be visible unless the swell is huge.

Une autre gauche creuse. Les vagues peuvent être bonnes ici et y'a moins de monde que sur les autres spots. A peu prés 1km de Shooting Gallery, un sentier descend sur la droite. La vague sera invisible à moins que ce soit énorme.

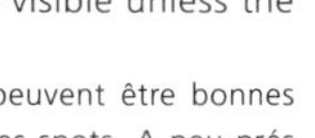

M. SEARLE

Generosa

8. Bristol/Shooting Gallery

A left reef facing NE. Low tide at Bristol is hollow, shallow and fast, the higher the tide, the easier it gets. At high tide Shooting Gallery breaks on the inside. A popular wave-jumping and bodyboarding spot that can become crowded.

Une gauche de reef exposée nord-est. La marée basse y est creuse, sans profondeur et rapide. Plus la marée est haute, plus ça devient facile. Plein de windsurfers et de bodyboards pour gâcher la vague.

9. El Muelle/Harbour Wall 

Behind the harbour wall in Corralejo lies this deservedly popular left; low tide is best. Many of the locals learnt to surf at this break due to its proximity to Corralejo, give the grommies their space!

Derrière le mur à Corralejo, une gauche convoitée qui le mérite. Plein de locaux ont commencé à surfer sur ce break parce que c'est proche de Corralejo. Mieux à marée basse.

10. Bajo del Medio/Rocky Pt 

One of Fuerteventura's most popular spots. When the breaks further N start to close out, Rocky Point suffers from crowding from both surfers and wave-jumpers.

Un des spots les plus fréquentés de Fuerteventura. Quand les spots plus au nord commencent à fermer alors Rcoky Point commence à saturer de surfers et windsurfers à la fois.

PHIL HOLDEN

El Muelle

11. Los Lobos   

A small volcanic island (6.5 sqkm/2.55sqmi), Los Lobos is named after the seals who used to feed in the fish-rich waters that surround it. With a N or NW swell and S or E winds, it can provide 400m (360yd) rides with fast walling sections and clean tubes. On a big day, swell can be seen from Fuerteventura as it powers its way around the island. Camping permits are required to camp on the island.

Los Lobos est une petite île volcanique (6,5 km2) ainsi nommée quand les phoques (loups de mer) se nourrissaient dans les eaux poissonneuses qui l'entourent. Avec une houle de N/NO et des vents de sud et d'est, on peut trouver une vague de 400m avec de bons murs et des tubes sympas. Qaund ça rentre gros, la vague est clairement visible de Fuerteventura pendant qu'elle tourne avec puissnace autour de l'île.

ALEX WILLIAMS

Bajo del Medio – also known as Rocky Point

PHIL HOLDEN

Ian Thomson tucks in out of the wind at Lobos

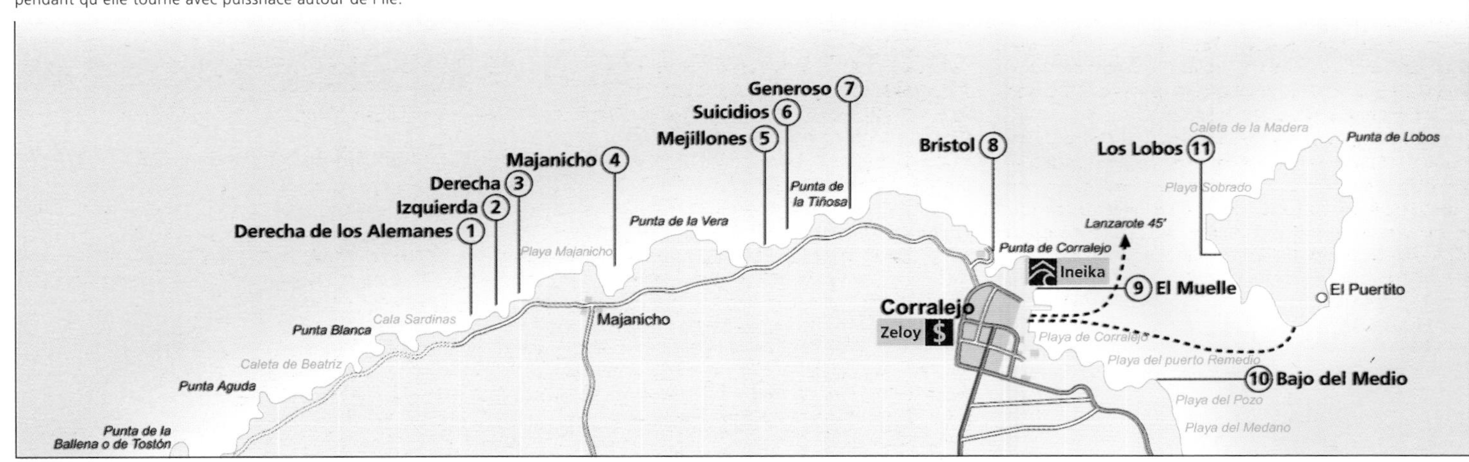

Gran Canaria

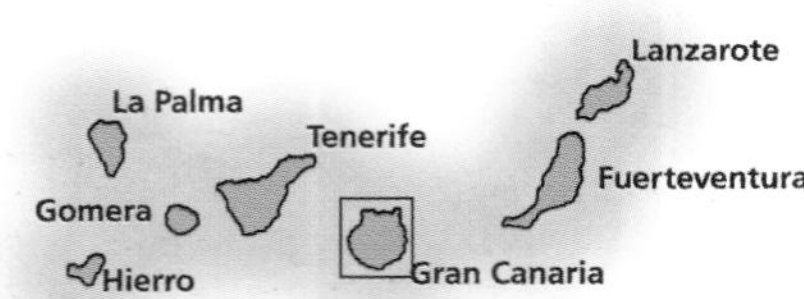

1. Bocabarranco

A consistent spot best at high tide. The water becomes polluted with sewage.

Un spot consistant meilleur à marée haute mais pollué par les égoûts.

2. El Agujero

This is a short and hollow peak popular with locals from Galdar, 300m (200yd) from Bocabarranco.

Un pic creux et puissant qu'apprécient les locaux de Galdar. Juste à 300m de Bocabarranca.

3. La Guancha

A right-hander breaking into open sea that's short, tubey and dangerous as it's surrounded by cliffs. It has the same access as Bocabarranco.

Une droite qui casse au large: courte, tubulaire et dangereuse parce qu'entourée de falaises. Même accés que Bocabarranco.

4. Vagabundo

Various sand-bottom peaks work all year round but are especially good in the summer months.

Plusieurs pics de beach-break qui marchent toute l'année mais surtout en été.

5. El Circo

There are two breaks here: the first is a right and left peak with a very quick and hollow take-off that breaks at high tide, while the second is left-hander that's not as hollow but is longer and works at low tide. Both are located behind the restaurant Los Pescaditos, which is responsible for contaminating the water with its waste. Be warned of the presence of sharks.

Deux spots ici. Le premier est un pic avec un take-off des deux côtés, creux et rapide à marée haute. A marée basse, y'a une gauche moins creuse mais plus longue. Située derrrière le resto 'Los Pescaditos' dont les déchets polluent le spot. Sachez qu'il y a des squales qui patrouillent.

6. El Paso

A great break situated some 300m (200yd) out to sea. It's the only wave on the island that can be surfed when the swell reaches 4m (12ft).

Un super break à environ 300m en mer, le seul vrai spot de gros qui se surfe même au dessus de 3-4 mètres.

7. El Roque

Breaks in front of a big rock and has a fast take off, followed by a slower section. The wave works only in the summer months.

Casse en face d'un gros rocher avec un take-off rapide, suivi d'une section plus lente. Marche pendant les mois d'été.

La Cicer

SIMON MCCOMB

8. Las Piscinas

A long tubing right. Access is the same as El Roque.

Une droite longue et tubulaire. L'accés est le même que pour El Roque.

9. Boquines

This is a wide bay with rocky reef breaks at both ends. On the E end is a right-hander, giving long rides best at mid tide. The wave on the W side of the bay may be shorter but can be fun due to the radical take-off.

Une large baie avec des breaks de reef aux deux extrémités. A l'est, c'est une droite plutôt longue meilleure à mi-marée. La vague à l'ouest est plus courte mais plus tecnhique avec un take-off radical.

10. El Comedor

Powerful wave popular with San Andrés locals.

Une vague puissante bien connue des locaux de San Andres.

11. Quintanilla

Located near the dance hall Quintanilla, this wave can have perfect long rides when it's on.

Peut avoir un déferlement parfait quand ça marche. Situé à côté de la boîte 'Quintanilla'.

12. El Lloret (La Lloreta)

Good waves are found in this spot, but so are the crowds, although the atmosphere is reasonably friendly.

C'est bon sauf si ça souffle side-shore. Du monde mais l'ambiance reste relativement amicale.

13. La Cicer

One of Europe's most popular bodyboarders' breaks with three named areas: Los Muellitos lies at the W end of the beach, next to the breakwater and has a rock bottom with fast and tubey waves; El Bufo is in the middle of the beach with good sand-bottom waves; and El Piti Point has a sand and rock bottom with longer waves than El Bufo (but they break with less power). It's located on the W side of Playa Las Canteras.

Un des vagues d'Europe les plus célèbres pour le bodyboard qui comprend trois pics. Los Muellitos qui se trouve à l'ouest de la baie, prés de la digue casse sur du caillou avec de bons tubes. Ensuite, El Bufo, au milieu de la baie est un bon beach-break de sable. Enfin, El Piti Point sur fond mixte est une plus longue vague qu'El Bufo mais casse moins puissamment. Situé à l'ouest de la Playa de Canteras.

14. La Barra

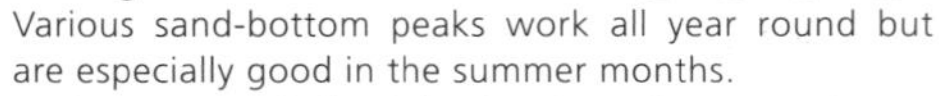

This is an picturesque set-up with a fine golden sand beach, a turquoise lagoon and a lava reef handily positioned 500m (400yd) from shore. Although not a big wave venue, it's also popular with boogieboard crew.

Superbe endroit avec une plage dorée de sable fin, un lagon turquoise et un reef de lave idéalement placé à 500m du bord. Pas vraiment un spot de grosses vagues et bien apprécié des boogies.

15. Confital

Probably the first spot to be surfed in the Canaries, Confital is famous for two things: great waves and heavy localism. The main attraction is a right reef considered to be one of the best waves in the Canaries. A sucky take-off is followed by some clean barrels that are best caught at full tide. Do not leave a vehicle here unattended.

On connaît Confital pour deus choses:une super vague et un localisme gravissime. Le sujet de discorde est cette droite de reef qui est des meilleures vagues des Canaries. Un take-off qui suce est suivi par des tubes secs, meilleurs à marée haute. Ne pas laissez sa caisse sans surveillance.

Confital

J. AMEZAGA

16. Playa Ojo de Garza

Only works on big N swells: it's not a great place. Waves break just by the airport so as you fly in, take a swell check.

Ne marche que par grosse houle de nord. Pas un endroit transcendant mais les vagues cassent tout prés de l'aéroport ce qui est pratique à checker quand on arrive par avion.

Confital

17. Arinaga   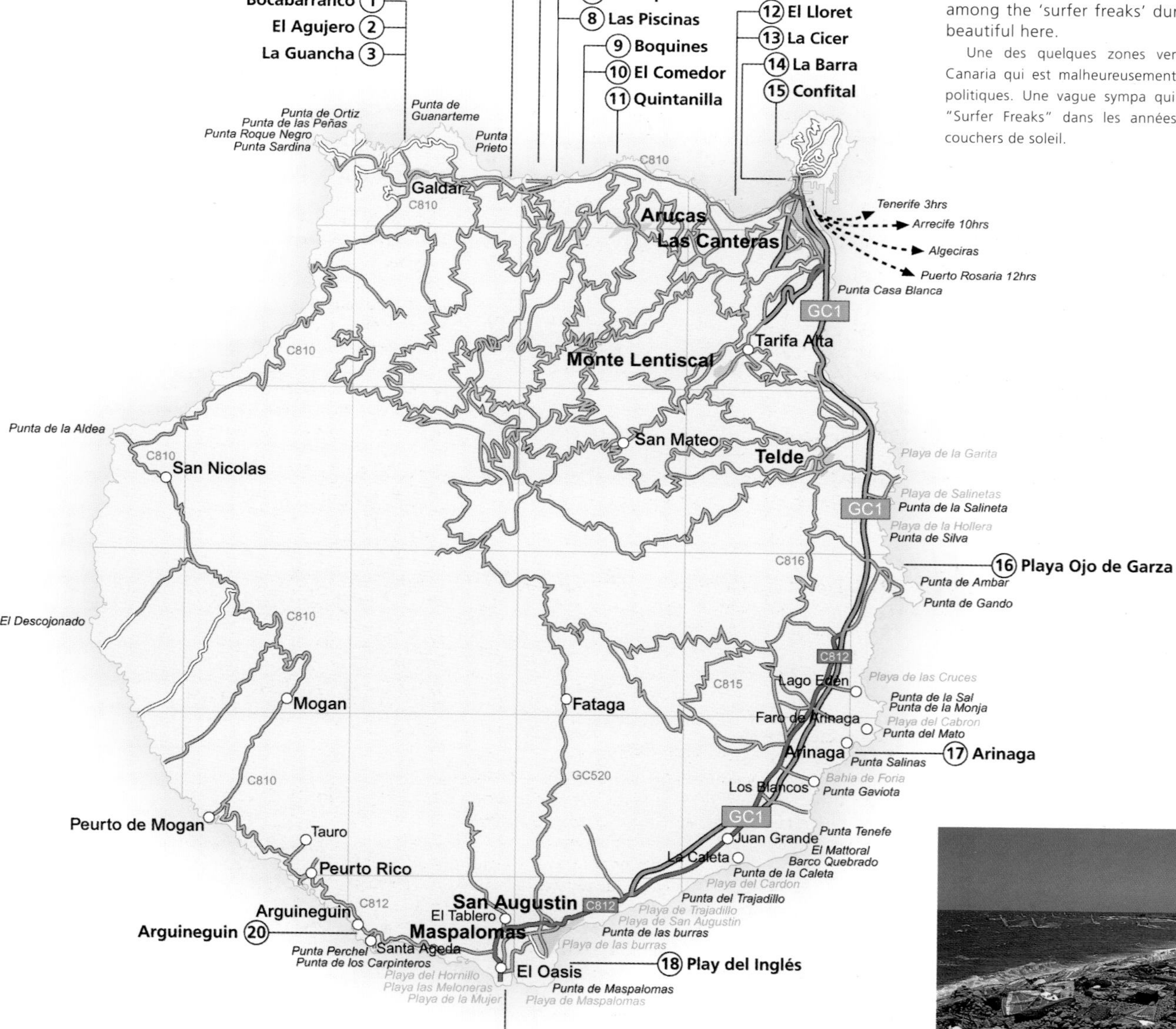  

A very fast wave that's both hollow and short, Arinaga's break is often offshore and makes it the most esteemed ride on the E coast.

Une vague trés rapide qui est à la fois creuse et courte. La fait qu'il y ait souvent off-shore ici la rend le spot le plus apprécié de la côte est.

18. Playa del Inglés 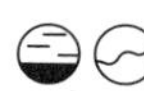 

Another concrete city built for the tourist industry, which has rare clean swells or onshore choppy waves.

Une autre barrière de béton pour touristes. Les houles propres y sont rares car on y trouve plus souvent des mioses immondes, plus propices pour sauter les vagues en windsurf.

19. Maspalomas   

Various peaks break here either side of the lighthouse. As a consequence, it's one of the most popular S spots.

Divers pics qui cassent des deux côtés du phare. Un de spots les plus populaires dans le sud.

20. Arguineguin  

One of the few green areas left in the SW of Gran Canaria is in danger due to decisions by political leaders. It boasts a fun wave that was very popular among the 'surfer freaks' during the 70s. Sunsets are beautiful here.

Une des quelques zones vertes au sud-ouest de Gran Canaria qui est malheureusement menacée par des décisions politiques. Une vague sympa qui était souvent surfé par les "Surfer Freaks" dans les années 70. N'y manquez pas les couchers de soleil.

Bocabarranco (1)
El Agujero (2)
La Guancha (3)
Vagabundos (4)
El Circo (5)
(6) El Paso
(7) El Roque
(8) Las Piscinas
(9) Boquines
(10) El Comedor
(11) Quintanilla
(12) El Lloret
(13) La Cicer
(14) La Barra
(15) Confital
(16) Playa Ojo de Garza
(17) Arinaga
(18) Play del Inglés
(19) Maspalomas
Arguineguin (20)

Punta de Ortiz
Punta de las Peñas
Punta Roque Negro
Punta Sardina
Punta de Guanarteme
Punta Prieto
C810
Galdar
Arucas
Las Canteras
Tenerife 3hrs
Arrecife 10hrs
Algeciras
Puerto Rosaria 12hrs
Punta Casa Blanca
GC1
Tarifa Alta
Monte Lentiscal
San Mateo
Telde
Punta de la Aldea
San Nicolas
Playa de la Garita
Playa de Salinetas
Punta de la Salineta
Playa de la Hollera
Punta de Silva
C816
Punta de Ambar
Punta de Gando
El Descojonado
C812
C815
Lago Eden
Playa de las Cruces
Punta de la Sal
Punta de la Monja
Mogan
Fataga
Faro de Arinaga
Playa del Cabron
Punta del Mato
Arinaga
Punta Salinas
GC520
Bahia de Foria
Los Blancos
Punta Gaviota
Peurto de Mogan
Tauro
Juan Grande
Punta Tenefe
El Mattoral
Barco Quebrado
La Caleta
Punta de la Caleta
Playa del Cardon
Peurto Rico
Punta del Trajadillo
Playa de Trajadillo
Playa de San Augustin
San Augustin
El Tablero
Arguineguin
Maspalomas
Punta de las burras
Playa de las burras
Punta Perchel
Santa Ageda
Punta de los Carpinteros
Playa del Hornillo
Playa las Meloneras
Playa de la Mujer
El Oasis
Punta de Maspalomas
Playa de Maspalomas

Windsurfing contest

Tenerife

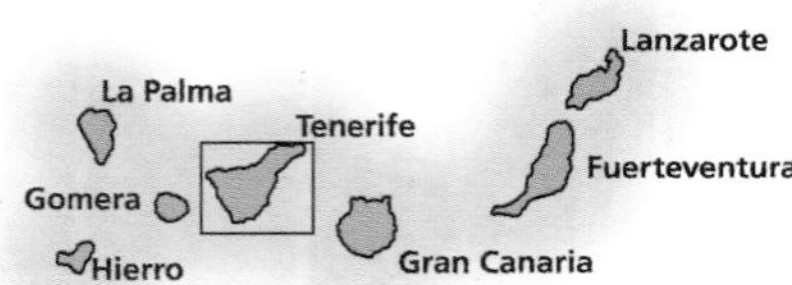

1. El Confital

Best in spring and summer, this is a tubey left that holds a S-SE-SW swell and will break up to 2m (6ft).

La gauche la plus tubulaire de Tenerife. Exige une houle de sud/sud-est/sud-ouest et fonctionnera jusqu'à 2m. Les meilleures périodes sont le printemps et l'été.

2. Las Galletas

The left is the better ride than the right break, although its length has been shortened considerably due to the construction of a pier. It needs a S-SE-SW swell and is best at low tide up to 2m (6ft).

La gauche est la meilleure, bien qu' elle soit bien moins longue depuis qu'on y a construit une digue. A besoin d'une houle de sud/sud-est/sud-ouest et est meilleure à marée basse jusqu'à 2m.

3. La Fitenia

Meaning 'The Desert' La Fitenia is one of the best waves in Tenerife, but will disappear due to proposed construction! There's lefts and rights with the rights being a better ride. Swells come in from S-SE-SW and give waves up to 3m (9ft).

Une des meilleures vagues du sud de Tenerife qui va disparaître en raison d'un programme de construction! Une gauche et une droite avec une préférence pour la droite. Nécessite un swell sud/sud-est/sud-ouest avec des vagues jusqu'à 3m.

4. El Conquistador

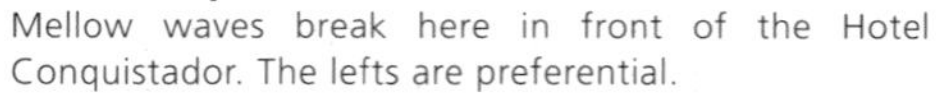

Mellow waves break here in front of the Hotel Conquistador. The lefts are preferential.

Vagues tranquilles devant l'hotel Conquistador. Les gauches sont meilleures.

5. La Derecha del Cartel

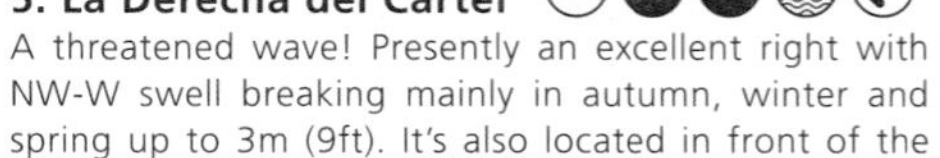

A threatened wave! Presently an excellent right with NW-W swell breaking mainly in autumn, winter and spring up to 3m (9ft). It's also located in front of the Hotel Conquistador and is best at mid tide.

Vague menacée! Excellente droite avec un swell de nord-ouest/ouest, marchant essentiellement en automne, hiver et printemps jusqu'à 3m. Située devant l'hotel Conquistador.

PETER CADE

THE GILL

Bajamar

6. La Izquierda/Spanish Left

Undoubtedly the best and most famous wave of Tenerife. This long tubey left fires with a NW-W swell up to 3m (9ft). Many foreigners come to surf this wave and you can see it in front of the main drag at Playa de las Américas.

Vague menacée! Certainement la plus belle et la plus célèbre vague de Tenerife. Une longue gauche qui tube avec une houle de nord-ouest/ouest jusqu'à 3m. Beaucoup d'étrangers viennent surfer cette vague... vous pouvez la voir devant le ponton principal de Las Américas.

PETER CADE

La Izquierda/Spanish Left

7. Punta Blanca – K16

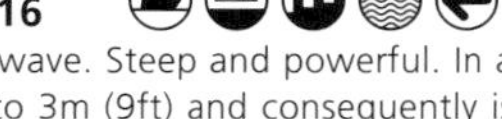

A short and intense left wave. Steep and powerful. In a NW swell it reaches up to 3m (9ft) and consequently is popular with foreigners. A less reliable right to the N.

Vague menacée! Une gauche, courte et intense en raison de la pente et de la puissance de la vague. Une houle de nord-ouest jusqu'à 3 m. Pas mal d'étrangers sur ce spot fréquenté. Les autres vagues des environs sont également menacées.

8. La Caleta

A right and left both threatened by construction! A N-NW swell up to 3m (9ft) gives waves all year round. Both waves are hazardous.

La gauche et la droite sont toutes deux menacées par une construction! Un swell de nord/nord-ouest jusqu'à 3m avec des vagues toute l'année. Les deux vagues sont quelque peu dangereuses.

9. Playa del Sorocco

Powerful sand and rock bottom waves come with a N swell up to 3m (9ft). This is a popular break with waves all year round.

Rompiente sobre arena y rocas. Aguanta tres metros con mar del Norte. Es bastanta frecuentada ya que funciona todo el año.

PETER CADE

The rights at K16

10. El Charco

Threatened by construction of swimming pools. A big long left for experienced surfers only as the NW swell brings in waves up to 4m (12ft). It's primo in autumn and winter.

Menacée par la construction de piscines! Une grosse gauche et longue réservée aux bons surfeurs. Une houle de nord-ouest jusqu'à 4m. Meilleures saisons: automne et hiver.

11. Fuera de la Bajeta

Another threatened wave. A very good long right-hander that needs a N-NW swell to hold good size. Winter sees it peaking.

Vague menacée! Une très bonne droite et longue. A besoin d'un swell de nord/nord-ouest et tient bien la houle. Meilleure en hiver.

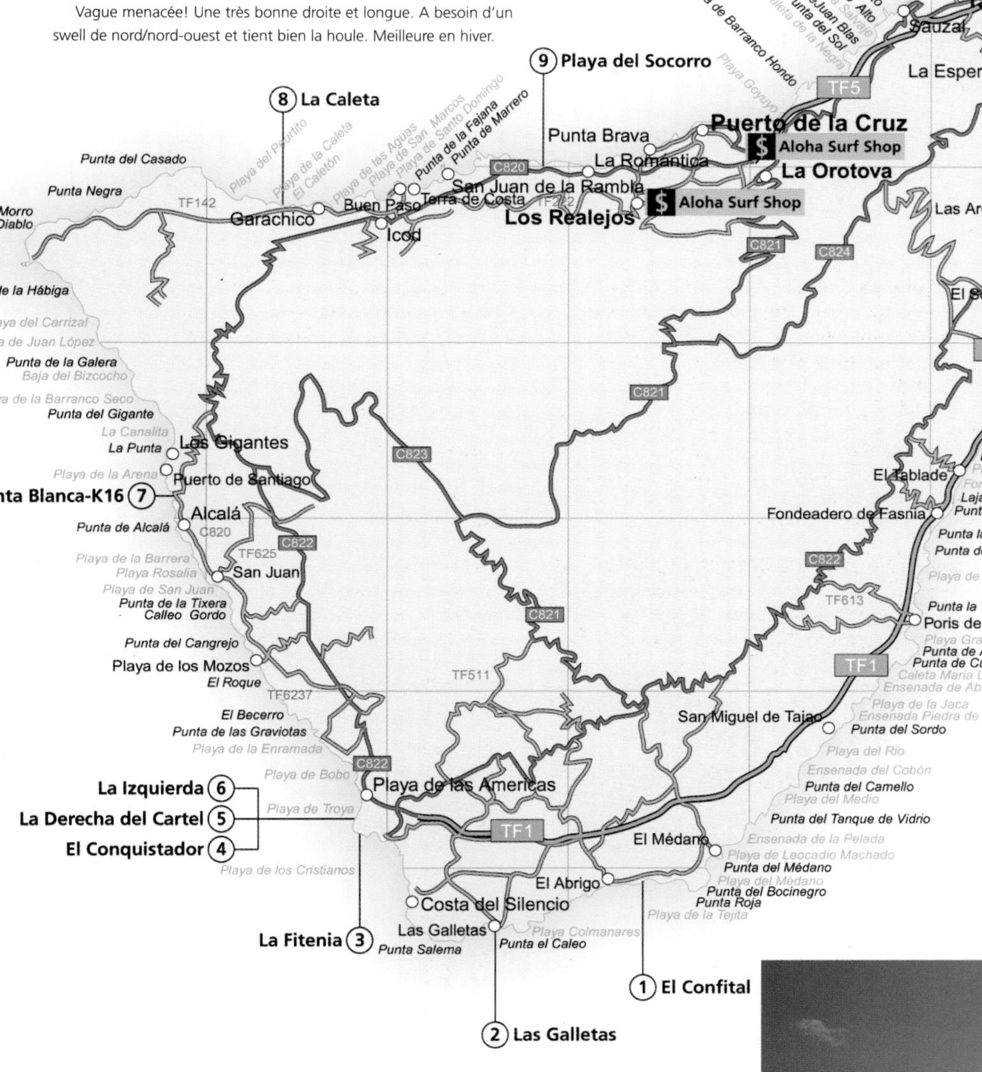

14. Igueste de San Andrés

A good long tubey left with long walls that is born out of a NE to SE swell on all tides. High tide brings in the best waves that break over smooth rocks and sand. It's at its prime in winter when it reaches up to 2.5m (7.5ft).

Bonne gauche tubulaire et longue formant de longs murs. Bien que meilleure à marée haute, elle marche avec n'importe quelle marée par swell de nord-est/nord/sud-est. Elle pète sur des rochers lisses et du sable. Meilleure en hiver jusqu'à 2,5 m.

12. Los dos Hermanos

Set in a spectacular bay, this wave has powerful rights and lefts. Big and tubey – N-NE-NW sees swell up to 4m (12ft) – it's popular with more experienced surfers.

Droite et gauches puissantes à l'intérieur d'une baie impressionnante. Gros, tubulaire et fréquenté avec pas mal de bons surfeurs. Swell de nord/nord-est/nord-ouest jusqu'à 4m. Meilleur en hiver.

13. La Derecha de Almáciga

A right-hander that's good for beginners and works on any swell all year round.

Cette droite, bonne pour les débutants, marche avec n'importe quel swell tout au long de l'année.

TIM RAINGER, LP

Los dos Hermanos

The Azores

The Azores appear from space as a handful of black and green stones flung into the middle of the vast Atlantic. In centuries past, sailors used to refer to this chain as 'the disappearing isles' because of the huge ocean swells that would obscure them from view. They wink unceasingly at seasoned surf travellers who can instantly appreciate their insane possibilities, yet they remain an enigma even for those who've ridden waves on their lava-fringed shores. Richly Portuguese, each of the nine specks exhibit an immense local variety and together have retained their integrity as a hard-core and relatively unknown destination.

Les Açores

Vues de l'espace, les Açores ressemblent à une poignée de cailloux noirs et verts, jettés au milieu de l'Atlantique. Ces îles attirent sans cesse les surfers voyageurs qui savent apprecier leur potentiel. Mais les Açores savent toujours garder une part de mystère, même envers ceux qui ont surfé ses rivages de lave. Sans perdre le caractère hard-core et sauvage de cette destination surf, chacune des neuf îles portugaises réserve au voyageur sa palette de couleurs et d'expériences aussi locales que variées.

Swell lines bending into one of the many stretches of lightly surfed coastline

ALEX WILLIAMS

Introduction

The People

The islands were discovered and mapped by an Arab navigator named Sherif Mohammed al Adresi, who made a series of extraordinary Atlantic voyages around 1220. Alone in a vast sea of nothingness, he sailed west into the setting sun, pushing the boundaries of the known world, motivated by a thirst for knowledge. Others followed. In 1427 the Portuguese rediscovered and claimed the islands. The Azores have since been Portugal's main staging post for cross-Atlantic travel, reaching their strategic peak during the reign of the Portuguese empire. Over time, the seafaring tradition has stayed. Sailors come and go but a rich and unique culture remains. Now a part of metropolitan Portugal, the islands constitute three of its 22 districts, with a greater autonomy than those on the mainland.

Population: 237,795
Area: 2,355 sqkm/909sqmi
Time: GMT –1 (summer GMT)
Language: Portuguese
Currency: Escudos (Esc)

TIM RAINGER

The Land

A massive sub-sea volcanic chain runs the entire length of the Atlantic from Iceland almost to Antarctica. The Azores archipelago represents the highest peaks of the mid-Atlantic ridge. Nine main islands make up the group which sits in mid-ocean, some 1,200km (750 miles) west of Lisbon. Similar to Madeira, Portugal's other north Atlantic island group, much of the land subsides steeply into the sea. Owing to its humid climate, vegetation is rife.

The Climate

The islands' climates are influenced by the Atlantic's enveloping presence. The Azores' 'mid-Atlantic high' is a consistent area of high pressure centred in this region that contributes to its variable winds. Air temperatures, as on the Canaries, are moderated by the surrounding sea and vary between 12°C (55°F) in winter and 25°C (75°F) in summer with the humidity often ranging between 75% to 90%. Swell comes from all directions, though it is often of short duration due to the islands' proximity to the weather systems which bring it. Frontal systems regularly accompany the waves, unlike the Canaries, which lie further south. Rain is usually a daily occurrence.

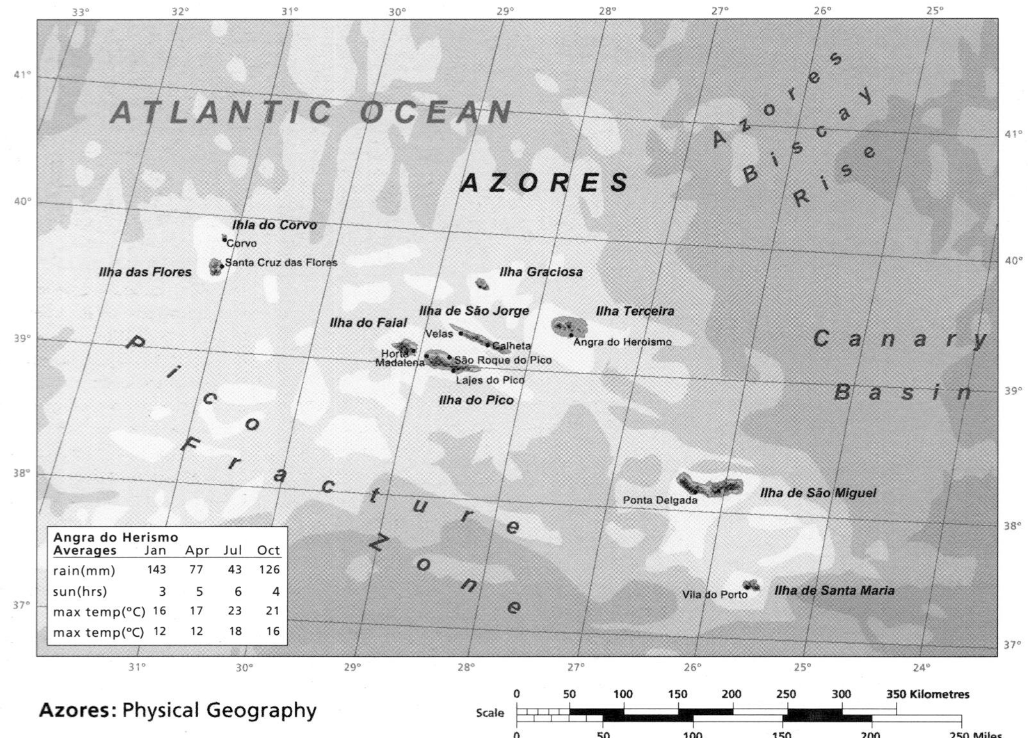

Angra do Herismo Averages	Jan	Apr	Jul	Oct
rain(mm)	143	77	43	126
sun(hrs)	3	5	6	4
max temp(°C)	16	17	23	21
max temp(°C)	12	12	18	16

Azores: Physical Geography

Introduction

La Population

C'est un jeune navigateur arabe, Shérif Mohamed Al Adresi, qui découvrît ces îles et établit la première carte en 1220, à l'occasion d'une série de voyages étonnants en Atlantique. D'autres ont suivi, et les portugais en prirent possession en 1427. L'archipel a eu depuis un rôle stratégique déterminant, comme étape avant la traversée, notamment au règne de l'Empire Portugais. L'archipel fait aujourd'hui partie intégrante du Portugal, et compte 3 des 22 départements du pays, avec toutefois une plus grande autonomie. La tradition maritime a survécu, les navigateurs vont et viennent, mais perdure une culture riche et unique.

TIM RAINGER

Le Pays

De l'Islande à l'Antarctique, une grande chaîne volcanique parcoure le fond de l'Atlantique. Les Açores représentent le point culminant connu sous le nom de la crête du Moyen-Atlantique. L'archipel est formé par neuf îles principales, regroupées au milieu de l'océan, à 1200 km à l'ouest de Lisbonne. Tout comme Madère, le second archipel portugais en Atlantique nord, ces îles offrent une côte très escarpée, qui plonge dans l'océan. Les paysages sont oujours verdoyants grâce à un climat très humide qui rend la végétation luxuriante.

La Meteo

Le climat insulaire est, de toute évidence, sous influence océanique. Le fameux Anticyclone des Açores est à l'origine des vents dominants d'ouest et du nord. Les températures sont douces toute l'année, entre 12° l'hiver et 25° l'été, avec un taux d'humidité constant entre 75% et 90%. Les swells viennent de toutes les directions, mais sont généralement de courte durée, à cause de la proximité des depressions. Contrairement aux Canaries, plus au sud, la présence de vagues est souvent synonyme de précipitations, et il pleut presque tous les jours.

ALEX WILLIAMS

Surf Culture

History

The Azores receive an abundance of swell and as a consequence homemade boards were reportedly being ridden by the early 60s. However, little contact was made with foreign surfers until the early 70s when a group of US Air Force personnel got wise to the potential surrounding them. The word has spread – but not that far, yet. Since all roads lead to Lisbon, Portuguese surfers are the most common visitors though a growing number of adventurous Kiwis, Aussies, Americans and European nationals have also ridden waves on this dramatic and verdant island group.

Today

There are first generation surfers on all the main islands. São Miguel and Terceira are the nuclei, but even on those islands, boards, wetsuits and gear are difficult to obtain, mainly coming courtesy of travellers or via the daily contact with Lisbon. Bodyboards are commonly ridden by the groms, however, some of the older stand-up surfers charge. The number of visiting surf travellers still remains minimal due to a combination of factors, not the least being the price of air tickets.

The Ten Commandments of The Company of Runners of Open Sea Waves

1. Respect the act of riding waves as both a spiritual and sporting activity.
2. Protect existing waves against phenomenon that could deteriorate their quality.
3. Keep searching for new spots; create new waves where possible.
4. Defend ceaselessly freedom of access to all waves, wherever they break.
5. Reduce potentially dangerous situations when the line up is crowded.
6. Ignore any initiatives, by nature reactionary, commercial, egocentric, chauvinistic, aggressive and vulgar, which lead to the destruction or alteration of the pleasures of this simple lifestyle.
7. The only worthy fulfilment is one, done day after day, in the search for perfection.
8. The only wave that counts is the one caught at the peak.
9. The only trophy to envy is natural, pure joy.
10. Play the role allocated to you by destiny. Immerse yourself in a dangerous life and in so doing, save it.

ALEX WILLIAMS

Culture Surf

Historique

Les Açores ont toujours été bénies par le swell, d'où l'apparition des premières planches dans les années 60. Il y a eu peu d'échanges avec l'étranger jusqu'aux années 70, et c'est un groupe de l'US Air Force qui fît connaître le potentiel de ces îles. L'information a circulé, mais sans excès. Comme tout passe par Lisbonne, les visiteurs portugais sont les plus assidus. Ils sont suivi par un nombre croissant de néo-zélandais, d'australiens, d'américains et d'européens, tous sensibles à la qualité des vagues de cette côte sauvage.

Aujourd'hui

Chaque île a sa population de jeunes surfers. Sào Miguel et Terceira furent les premières à être surfées, mais même sur ces îles, planches, combis et autres matos sont durs à trouver. L'approvisionnement est assuré par les visiteurs, ou par le contact journalier avec Lisbonne. Le bodyboard a la cote, notamment chez les jeunes, mais certains des surfers les plus agés assurent. Le nombre de surfers à visiter ces îles reste encore minime pour une quantité de raisons, le prix des billets d'avion n'étant pas des moindre.

ALEX WILLIAMS

Angro do Heroismo, Terceira

Ilha do Corvo
Ilha das Flores
Ilha Graciosa
Ilha de São Jorge
Ilha Terceira
Ilha do Faial
Ilha do Pico
Ilha de São Miguel
Ilha de Santa Maria

Where to go

Surf Areas

Each island has a limited number of surf spots due to the steep landscape. With few quality beach breaks, the prevailing reef formations are, without exception, shallow and dangerous. The points can offer deeper water waves but entry to many of the best spots can be difficult thanks to constant erosion and landslides caused by frequent rain and sheer terrain. Snapped boards and reef rubbings are very common.

Faial It's dubbed the 'Azure' isle because of its magnificent hydrangeas in every shade of blue. Horta, the capital, boasts a rivetting history of naval battles and political struggles, and remains the sailing capital of the group, with constant traffic in sail craft flying all flags. There's a couple of good left points and beaches, which the small local surf community enjoy.

ALEX WILLIAMS

Corvo The most westerly island is unserviced by the airline and though reputed to have some waves, we've no firm info.

Flores As the name implies, a glorious island that was, until 1933, a French missile base. No locals and little information exists on surf spots, though there may be one or two. Getting and staying there is a mission in itself.

Pico Lightly populated but full of culture, Pico is also home to Portugal's highest mountain (of the same name), which rises to 2351m (7771ft) and is snow-capped in winter. A few spots exist, but are some distance apart.

ALEX WILLIAMS

You have to walk for an hour to get to this one, but only the locals will tell you where ...

São Jorge Long, thin and incredibly steep, São Jorge is a sparsely populated island with a history of earthquakes and cataclysm. There's only a couple of spots, one accessible by road. Very few accommodation options are near the surf. which makes it a strictly hard-core 'walk in with all you need and camp' destination. Rain, strong winds and huge landslides are a slightly deterring factor.

Graciosa The graceful isle is a quiet rural haven with chequered fields, gently sloping wooded hills and small vineyards. It's a tranquil island with one or two heavy spots.

Terceira The most densely populated, historically rich and cosmopolitan of the group. The beautiful capital, Angra do Heroísmo, is a world heritage town which was the largest fort in the old Portuguese empire. It's now equipped with all modern facilities including world-class restaurants and a busy nightlife. There's three or four good surf spots, once again a long way apart.

ALEX WILLIAMS

The north coast of São Miguel

São Miguel The biggest island also houses the largest town, Ponta Delgada. Points of interest include large, decent beaches on both north and south coasts, as well as a selection of reefs and points. Other attractions include nightlife and the thermal hot pools at Furnas. The group's largest surf population comfortably share the waves.

Santa Maria The earliest settled and most south east of the islands was inhabited by a handful of pioneers and their families from the Algarve. Vila do Porto, the island's capital, is the oldest town on the Azores.

When to go

The Azores Averages	Jan	Apr	Jul	Oct
water °C	16	16	19	19
wetsuit				

Calling the best time to visit the Azores is a tricky one. They can get awesome waves at any time of the year from all directions including northerlies, westerlies (Atlantic lows) and southerlies (summer hurricanes). It really depends on what you're looking for. Big waves are obviously a winter phenomena in the North Atlantic, but good conditions can occur at any time, especially autumn and spring. Summers are balmy but it's also when the waves are small, inconsistent, busy and expensive.

Ou Aller

Les Espaces de Surf

Faial Cette île est surnommée l'île d'Azur à cause des magnifiques cascades qui prennent tous les tons de bleus. La capitale, Horta, est bien connue des navigateurs de tous pays, comme escale au milieu de l'Atlantique, et pour son histoire chargée de batailles navales. La petite communauté locale de surfers profite de quelques point-breaks en gauches et de quelques plages.

Corvo La plus à l'ouest, non desservie par les avions de liaison, aurait des vagues, mais nous n'avons pas d'informations précises.

Flores Une très belle île, comme son, nom l'indique, qui fut base militaire française jusqu'en 1933. Pas ou peu de surfers locaux ni d'infos sur les spots.

Pico Peu peuplée mais riche en culture. Quelques spots, assez éloignées les uns des autres.

São Jorge Longue, étroite, et très escarpée, Sao Jorge est peu peuplée et son histoire est marquée de cataclysmes et de tremblements de terre. Aucune possibilité d'hébergement à proximité. C'est une destination hard-core, où le camping est de rigueur. Prévoir tout, car il n'y a rien sur place. La pluie, les vents violents et les glissements de terrain peuvent en décourager certains, mais la récompense est à la hauteur.

Graciosa L'île gracieuse est tranquille, rurale, parsemée de champs et de vignes qui courrent le long des collines. Une île paisible qui offre toutefois un ou deux spots plutôt costauds.

Terciera Riche en histoire, cette îles est la plus peuplée et la plus cosmopolite de l'archipel. La capitale, Angra de Heroismo, est une ville superbe, construite sur le site du plus grand fort de l'ancien Empire Portugais. Si ses murs recellent des trésors du passé, c'est aujourd'hui une ville contemporaine où rien ne manque, des grands restaurants à la vie nocturne. Trois ou quatre bons spots de surf, assez éloignés les uns des autres.

São Miguel La plus grande île, et le plus grande ville, Ponta Delgada. A noter de grandes plages sur les côtes nord et sud, et un choix de récifs et de point breaks. Ne pas manquer la vie nocturne, et les sources d'eau chaude à Furnas. La plus large population de surfers de l'archipel, mais la foule n'est pas un problème.

Santa Maria Située à l'extrême sud-est, cette île fut la première à être habitée. Vila do Porto est la ville la plus ancienne de l'archipel.

Quand s'y Rendre

Difficile de répondre à cette question. Un méga swell est toujours possible toute l'année, et de toutes directions, nord, ouest (dépressions atlantiques), et sud (cyclones d'été). Tout dépend de ce que vous recherchez. Les grosses vagues sont monnaie courante dans l'Atlantique nord, mais de bonnes conditions sont possibles à tout moment, surtout en automne et au printemps. Les été sont doux, mais aussi petits et inconsistents, et les déplacements sont plus chers et encombrés.

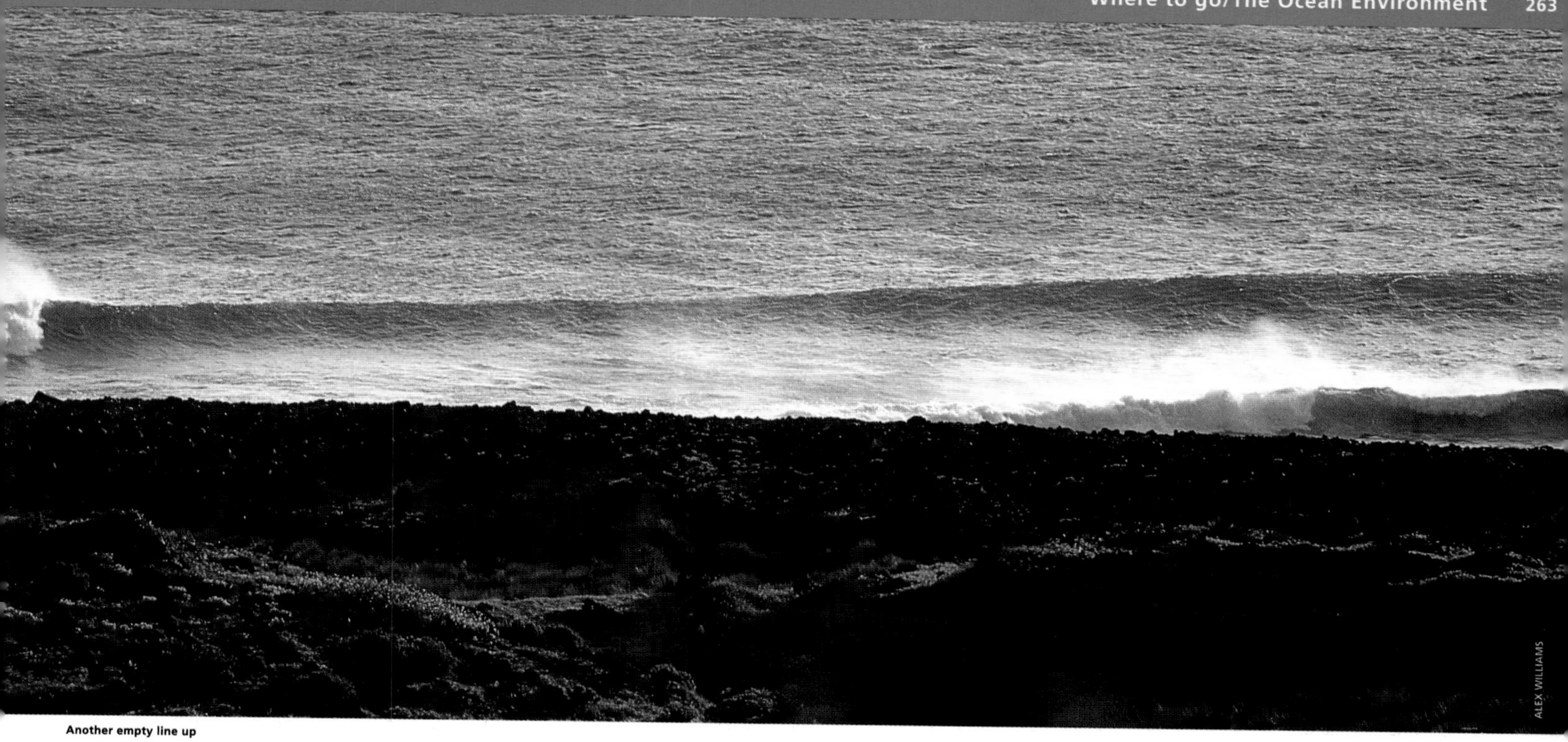

ALEX WILLIAMS

Another empty line up

The Ocean Environment

Water Temperatures

The water is cool in winter and warm in summer. The sea is filled with weird marine life, including some of the planet's largest species of shark and squid. Great whites are populous, but with only one death in 20 years, it's unlikely you'll get dragged back into the food chain.

Water Quality

The seas that surround the group are crystalline, though instances of localised run off, littering and degradation through irresponsible development are apparent. São Miguel's larger towns have an appreciable environmental impact as do some of the smaller towns of the north coast. The glorious Praia Vittoria on the island of Terceira was destroyed by an oversized port construction financed by the US military. A mile of good beach peaks as well as a world-class reef break disappeared and typically it was the surf community who spearheaded the protest movement in opposition to the developers.

On Localism

That catastrophic loss seems to have catalysed an intense ecological and social awareness among the locals of Terceira in particular. They are an individualistic bunch who fully appreciate what they have and who are working hard to protect it, both from the destructive forces inherent in 20th-century growth and the negative influences of a deteriorating international surf ethic. They have discussed the issues that surround modern surf travel in a reasonable way, and have formed a vehicle for realising their aspirations for the future of wave riding on these islands. Their society exists in a loose format and includes most of the active surfers on the island. They made their points clearly when they met us, and we have not named the spots showed to us on any of the islands out of respect for their wishes.

The situation is mirrored on all the islands in the group. There are only a few breaks on each island and there are already enough surfers on each island ready and waiting to surf most of the waves on offer. So, if you come with an open mind and relaxed attitude, you'll be welcome. If you want to get the best surf, you'll need the locals' help. If you're humble you'll get it. If not, you won't. Simple.

It's impossible to arrive with surfboards unnoticed and once here you can't escape the consequences of your behaviour. It's time to be cool: no trash, no pissing in public, no bad-ass driving. No aggro to the local surfers and farmers. When surfing, don't drop-in. Be friendly. Respect the family vibe. We had an incredible trip, so could you.

ALEX WILLIAMS

Terceira crew

TIM RAINGER

The one that got away – Deadly Princess

L'Environs Ocean

Faune Marine

L'eau est fraîche en hiver et chaude en été. On compte parmi les résidents locaux la plus grande population de requins et de calmars. Le Grand Blanc est largement représenté, mais avec un mort en vingt ans, il y a peu de chance qu'il vous rappelle votre place dans la chaîne alimentaire.

Qualite de l'eau

Les eaux de l'archipel sont cristallines, même si parfois des rejets, décharges et autres dégradations trahissent des comportements irresponsables.Les grandes villes de Sào Miguel, et les petites villes de la côte nord ont un impact certain sur l'environnement. La superbe plage Praia Vittoria a été massacrée par la construction d'un port démesuré, financée par l'armée américaine. Le désastre a englouti 1,5 km de beach break et un reef de classe mondiale. Comme c'est souvent le cas, la communauté surf locale a porté le flambeau de la protestation qui s'est opposé aux promoteurs.

Localisme

La perte de ces spots a éveillé une conscience écologique parmi les locaux, notamment à Terceira. C'est un groupe d'individus à part, conscients de la qualité de leur patrimoine, et motivé pour la préserver des aspects négatifs de la modernisation et du localisme. A titre de prévention, les locaux ont formé un groupe, qui débat de ce qu'implique les trips surf d'aujourd'hui, et de ce que sera le surf de demain dans l'archipel. Sans être très structuré, le regroupement des "Coureurs de vagues venues du large" rassemble tous les surfers de l'île. Nous les avons rencontré et leur message a été clair. Ainsi, conformément à leur souhait, nous n'avons nommé aucun des spots sur aucune des iles de l'archipel.

Le shéma est le même sur chacune des îles. Premièrement : quelques spots seulement par île. Deuxièment : Il y a déjà suffisament de surfers qui attendent de pouvoir surfer ces quelques spots. Alors, où que vous alliez, en étant relax et ouvert d'esprit, vous serez les bienvenus. Et si vous recherchez les meilleures vagues, vous aurez besoin des locaux. Avec humilité, vous gagnerez. Sans elle, vous perdrez. Tout simplement. D'ailleurs, impossible d'arriver incognito avec des planches, et une fois sur place, vous recolterez ce que vous semerez. Pensez-y : ne rien jeter, ne pas pisser en public, ne pas conduire comme un fou. Respectez les surfers autant que les paysans. Soyez sympas et soyez attentifs à leur esprit de famille. En surfant, bien sur pas de taxe. Notre séjour fut inoubliable, pourquoi pas le vôtre ?

TIM RAINGER

Travelling

Getting There

By air All flights from within Europe depart from Lisbon and the price of a return ticket is about £160 at the time of writing. Inter-island flights run daily between the islands all year round, however, surfboards present difficulties for the small cargo holds on the planes, especially in winter. The airline is the transport and communications mainstay of the economy and due to local needs, boards are considered dispensable and are packed last on the plane. This can mean they don't get on for a few days – you might be lucky and you might not too!

ERIC CHAUCHE

By sea There are no ferries from Portugal to the Azores, but transport between the islands is possible by sea. The ferries, which are cheaper, run at a reduced timetable during the winter (when you need them most), with occasional cancellations due to bad weather.

Getting Around

By car A car is a must but rentals, though widely available, aren't cheap.

By public transport São Miguel, Terceira, Graciosa, Pico and Faial have an extensive system of public buses. It is advisable to get to the bus stop in good time, as the drivers keep very tight schedules. If you want to be picked up by a passing bus, you must give a clear hand signal, even when waiting at a bus stop.

ALEX WILLIAMS

Accommodation It is not a bucket-shop destination with facilities on a large scale, nor will it ever be. With few *dormidas* and *pensiones*, accommodation is limited but reasonably priced. There are no official campgrounds to speak of, but it's possible on some of the less populated islands. A room in a small guesthouse ranges from 10-15,000 Esc, whereas a room in an inn would set you back around 18,000 Esc. These prices vary considerably according to season and quality.

Food The Azores rate among the most satisfying places in Europe to eat fresh fish, local bread, cheeses and wines. There are loads of good restaurants on the main islands which serve a varied mix of tasty food. Supermarkets are good and generally cheap.

Infos Voyage

Comment s'y rendre

Par avion Tous les vols d'Europe continentale passent par Lisbonne, et il vous coûtera environ 1500 francs pour un passage aller-retour. Les vols inter-îles sont journaliers toute l'année, mais la prise en charge des planches peut poser des problèmes, surtout en hiver. Le transport aérien étant le premier vecteur de liaison, les planches sont considérées comme accessoires, et chargées à bord au dernier moment ! Si la demande est forte, vos planches peuvent rester à terre quelques jours, mais avec un peu de chance, çà passera !

Par Mer Il n'y a pas de ferry du Portugal aux Açores, mais la liaison inter-îles est possible. C'est un moyen économique de se déplacer, mais il y en a moins en hiver (le moment où on en a besoin), et le mauvais temps provoque certaines annulations.

Se Deplacer

En Voiture Une fois sur place, il faut pouvoir se déplacer, mais les locations sont chères. Le taxi est une solution moins onéreuse.

En Transporten Commun Sào Miguel, Terceira, Graciosa, Pico et Faial ont un excellent réseau d'autobus. Il est conseillé d'arriver à l'heure aux arrêts, les chauffeurs étant très ponctuels. Pour qu'il s'arrête, à un arrêt ou sur son parcours, n'oubliez pas de faire un signe bien visible de la main.

Se Loger Les Açores n'étant pas une grande destination touristique, la capacité d'accueil et le choix proposé sont limités. Les quelques pensions de famille et chambres d'hôtes sont à des prix abordables. Une chambre d'hôte vous coûtera entre 10 000 et 15 000 escudos et une chambre d'hotel sera plutot dans les 18 000. Ces prix varient beaucoup suivant la saison et la qualité de l'offre. Il n'y a pas de campings tels que nous les connaissons, mais c'est une solution envisageable sur les îles moins fréquentées.

Se nourrir Les Acores sont connues pour ître un des meilleurs endroits en Europe pour manger du poisson frais, du pain artisanal, du fromage et déguster les vins locaux. Plein de bons restaurants sur les plus grosses Óles servent une cuisine variée faite d aliments frais, on trouve également des formules snack tout fait convenables dans tous les bars. Les supermarchés proposent de bons produits et sont généralement bon marché.

TIM RAINGER

Azores: Travelling Map

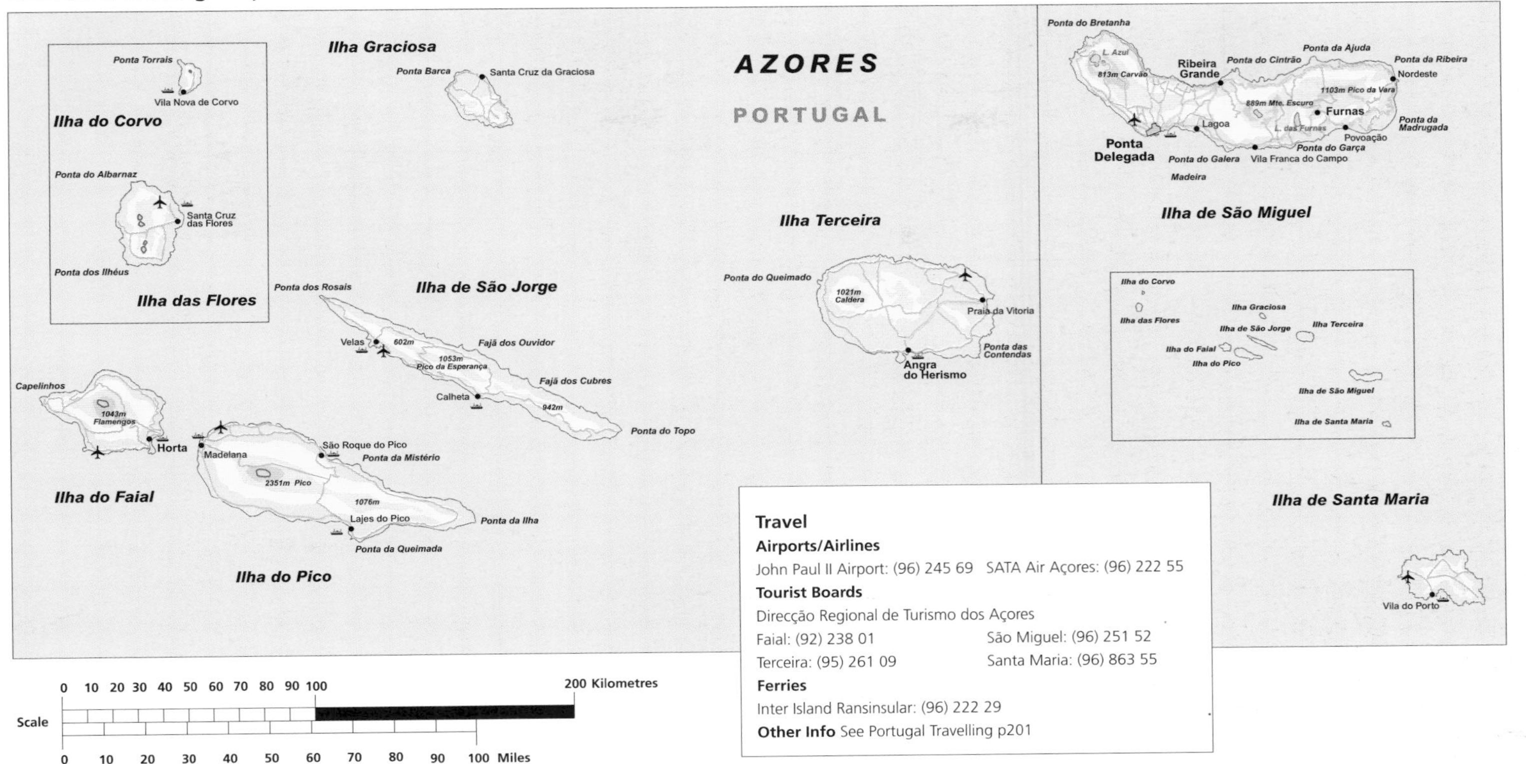

Travel

Airports/Airlines

John Paul II Airport: (96) 245 69 SATA Air Açores: (96) 222 55

Tourist Boards

Direcção Regional de Turismo dos Açores

Faial: (92) 238 01 São Miguel: (96) 251 52

Terceira: (95) 261 09 Santa Maria: (96) 863 55

Ferries

Inter Island Ransinsular: (96) 222 29

Other Info See Portugal Travelling p201

Gabe Davies dispenses with the remnants of a small spring swell

ALEX WILLIAMS

Monster rights like this have been winding down her steep coasts for thousands of years

ALEX WILLIAMS

Madeira

If your idea of wintertime fun is clawing your way into pitching mountains of the rawest Atlantic juice, dust off your rhino-chaser and book a ticket to Madeira. The island has recently exploded into the European psyche after years of constant rumours about epic big waves. *Surfer Magazine* turned the lights on with its Jardim do Mar story, syndicated across the world's surf media. Most aware Europeans immediately knew where it was, though few had ventured there. Those that had been came back with the same consistent comment: 'It's either huge or it's flat!' So the old North Shore mantra seems entirely apt here: go big or go home!

Madére

Si votre trip de l'hiver idéal consiste à chevaucher des montagnes d'eau de la puissance atlantique la plus pure, sortez votre plus grand gun du placard et résevez un billet pour Madère. L'île vient de se révéler aux chasseurs de vagues de tous poils après des années de rumeurs comme quoi les vagues étaient juteuses. *Surfer Mag* a mis un coup de projecteur avec un sujet remarquable sur Jardim do Mar, qui parcourut le monde entier. Les Européens un peu géographes n'eurent pas de mal à localiser l'endroit, mais peu se décidèrent à y aller. Ceux qui en sont revenus formulent toujours ce même commentaire: 'Soit c'est énorme, soit c'est flat!' Ce qui nous rappelle la vieille devise du North Shore hawaiien: surfez bien ou surfez rien!

Introduction

The People

Madeira was uninhabited until 1419 when it was discovered by João Gonçalves Zarco and Teixeira, two captains on a Portuguese expedition sent by Prince Henry the Navigator. Today the islands constitute one of Portugal's 22 national administrative districts, but are largely self governed. The economy depends mostly on the export of handicrafts, bananas, sugar and the famed Madeira wine, a brew fortified with cane sugar that gives it a distinctive smoky taste. Tourism is increasingly important.

Population: 273,000
Capital: Funchal
Language: Portuguese
Area: 769sqkm/307sqmi
Currency: Escudos

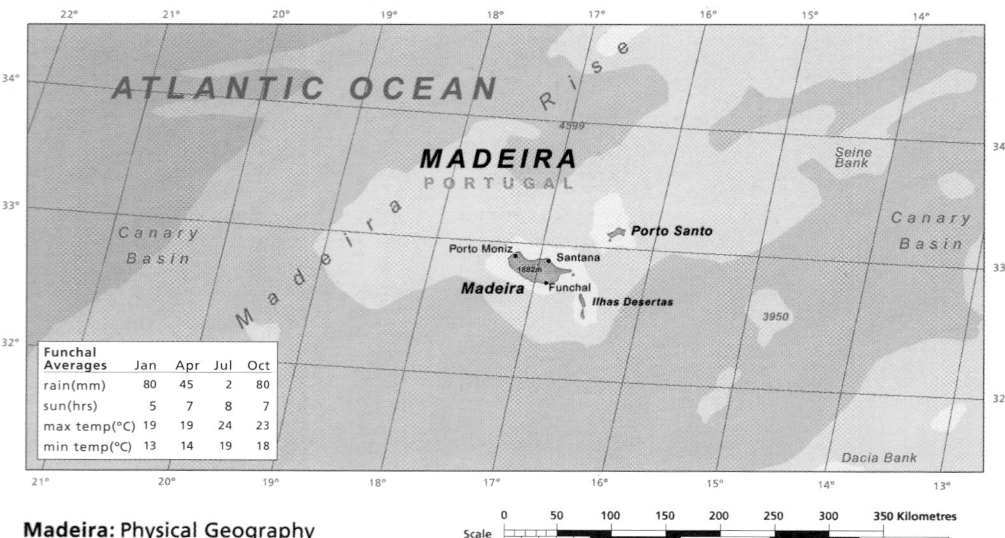

Funchal Averages	Jan	Apr	Jul	Oct
rain(mm)	80	45	2	80
sun(hrs)	5	7	8	7
max temp(°C)	19	19	24	23
min temp(°C)	13	14	19	18

Madeira: Physical Geography

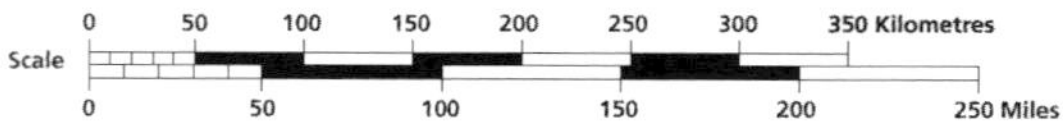

ERIC CHAUCHE

ALEX WILLIAMS

The Land

Two main islands and seven uninhabited islets thrust their vertical peaks skyward out of the Atlantic, 1000 kilometres (600 miles) west of Sagres and make up Portugal's better known Atlantic archipelago. All volcanic in origin, the islands share similarities with the Azores. The island of Madeira is steep and mountainous, slashed by deep valleys and there's little flat land except on the south coast around the capital, Funchal. Porto Santo to the northeast is smaller and flatter, with a tiny population.

The Climate

Madeira experiences a maritime climate with water warmed by the Gulf stream and air freshened by variable to inconsistent north/north-east tradewinds. The north coast is wetter with an annual rainfall around 1500 to 3000mm (60 to 120 inches), while in both winter and summer, periods of high pressure, the north coast can experience foggy patches.

Introduction

Le pays

Deux îles principales et 7 ilôts inhabités dirigent leurs pics vertigineux vers le ciel au beau milieu de l'Atlantique, à 500 km à l'ouest de Casablanca, formant l'archipel portugais le plus célèbre.

D'origine volcanique, ces îles présentent beaucoup de similitudes avec les Açores. L'île de Madère est escarpée et montagneuse, avec des vallées profondes. Les plateaux sont rares : autour de Funchal et au nord-ouest du centre de l'île. Porto Santo au nord-est est plus petit et plat avec une micro population.

Les gens

Madère fut inhabité jusqu'au 15ème siècle, où elle fut découverte et déclarée portugaise par João Gonzales Zarco lors d'une expédition financée par le Prince Henry le Navigateur. L'ile constitue aujourd'hui une des 22 régions du pays mais elle jouit d'une grande autonomie. Son économie dépend principalement de l'exportation de son artisanat, de bananes, de sucre, de bois et du vin, dont le goût fumé vient du sucre de canne. Le tourisme de luxe d'antan passe à un écotourisme moins élitiste.

Le climat

En tant qu'archipel baigné par l'Atlantique, le climat est océanique subtropical avec des eaux réchauffées par le Gulf Stream et un air refroidi par les alizés irréguliers de nord/nord-est. La côte nord est très humide avec des précipitations variant de 1,5m sur la côte à 3m sur les hauteurs. Même en été, les bancs de brouillards y sont fréquents. Le sud jouit d'un ensoleillement exemplaire.

Surf Culture

Madeira's surf population is the least developed of the Macronesian islands. There are only about 10 hardcore surfriders and 20 beginners in total. Visiting surfers have been coming since the 70s and since *Surfer Mag* published shots of Evan Slater and crew charging monster rights, there has been a recent flood of interest. The existence of seriously big winter waves has resulted in the 'Billabong Challenge', where since 1996, Billabong has flown eight top Portuguese surfers to the island during a month long waiting period from January to February. The results have been spectacularly screened on TV in Portugal and in local surfing magazines.

As the word has been kept low key for decades and because Madeira is relatively expensive and as yet unchartered, travelling surfers are still thin on the ground. Most of them are Portuguese, British and US east coasters willing and able to deal with the punishment and still charge. If you don't regularly ride a gun, don't even think about it.

Culture Surf

La population de surfers est la moins développée de toute la Macaronésie. Il existe environ une dizaine de surfers motivés auxquels on peut ajouter une vingtaine de débutants ou bodyboarders qui vivent généralement à Funchal. Les surfers étrangers viennent là depuis les années 70 mais le déclic s'est produit depuis que Surfer Mag a publié les photos d 'Evan Slater et Ross Williams chargeant d'énormes droites. Cette réalité de grosses vagues d'hiver s'est affirmée avec l'organisation du Billabong Challenge. Depuis 1996, Billabong Portugal a acheminé 8 des meilleurs surfers de grosses vagues portugais pour s 'affronter dans les meilleures conditions possibles sur une Waiting Period de près de 2 mois en hiver. La couverture médiatique a été époustouflante sur la télé portugaise.

Le fait qu'il y ait de bonnes grosses vagues à Madère est longtemps resté sous silence. Comme les vols charters ont tardé à faire baisser le prix du billet d'avion, Madère a vu passer très peu de surfers. La plupart d'entre eux sont Portugais, Français et surtout Américains de la Côte Est, habitués de spots de grosses vagues, qui viennent là avec des méga-guns attendre les gros swells.

Where to go

Surf Areas

The north coast appears to be more consistent with a majority of lefts but it's generally more rainy and foggy. If you don't mind a bit of precipitation and a rather lifeless atmosphere, the best place to stay along this coast is São Vicente.

While the north coast receives more swell, the south west of the island has an orientation that lends consistency to the waves, especially in winter when north-east trade winds blow offshore on this shoreline.

Jardim do Mar rates as the best surfzone with three different quality rights and a relaxing atmosphere. It's a lovely village of 300 people with enough going on to keep you sane while sitting through flat periods. There's a good, cheap restaurant (Tar-Mar), a lively bar (Joe's), numerous cashpoints, a brand new hotel that's very clean (three stars) and not too expensive. There are also plenty of families who'll put you up for 1,000–1,500Esc per night. The main break is right in front of the village.

The next spot north is Ponta Pequena: by foot it involves a 45-minute walk on rolling boulders and down high cliffs. It takes another 30 minutes to reach Paúl do Mar. A tunnel is presently being dug under the cliff so that Paúl and Jardim will be linked by a five, instead of 40-minute, drive. When the surf's big, these two places are dangerous. Paúl do Mar is the most consistent wave of the bunch, but the village is not as friendly towards foreigners.

Jardim do Mar

ERIC CHAUCHE

JOÃO VALENTE

Ou Aller

Les Espace de surf

Madeira Averages	Jan	Apr	Jul	Oct
water °C	17	17	21	21
wetsuit				

Bien que la côte nord reçoive plus de houle, le meilleur plan est de se caler à Jardim Do Mar, au sud-ouest de l'île. La côte est orientée ouest-sud-ouest avec une consistance de surf quasi équivalente au nord, surtout en hiver. Jardim est un village plein de charme avec 300 habitants et ce qu'il faut pour attendre : un bon resto pas trop cher(Tar-Mar), un bar vivant (Joe's), des checkpoints en pagaille (bancs), un hôtel tout neuf plutôt class (3 étoiles) et des familles prêtes à vous loger pour 1000 à 1500 esc par jour. On accède à la droite de Ponta Pequena après 45 minutes de marche sur des rochers à flanc de falaises. Paul do Mar est jouable en 1 heure et quart mais bien galère avec 2 passages chauds surtout à marée haute et par grosse houle. A noter qu'un tunnel de 2 km commence à être percé et reliera Jardim à Paul en l'an 2000 ! Paul do Mar est la vague la plus consistante mais le village est plus austère. L'autre solution est San Vincente sur la côte nord qui est souvent pluvieuse et sombre sans vraiment d'âme. Il faudra aller à Seixal ou Porto da Cruz pour retrouver une ambiance de village.

ERIC CHAUCHE

Above: Woo tucking under the lip Below: Morning light

ALEX WILLIAMS

Above: Jardim do Mar surf zone Below: Even Carwyn gets the blues

ALEX WILLIAMS

The Ocean Environment

ALEX WILLIAMS

About as mellow as it gets

Introduction
Madeira is a big wave destination of the highest pedigree, but the island generally just catches the heart of a swell. As a consequence swells surge and die out extremely quickly. The hyper-jagged landscape means the sea bottom gets very deep, very fast thus the waves have a Hawaiian intensity that should never be underestimated. Like the Azores, some of the best surfzones exist where eroded cliffs have created *faja*, flat platforms of accumulated rocks and boulders with submerged rocks often appearing in the wave face. Beaches, like small wave spots, are almost non-existent, although Machico and Prainha Beach are exceptions. Getting in and out is always heavy when it's overhead: be ready for some nervous over-the-shoulder glances as you paddle towards the foaming rocks – be patient. Booties are a lifesaver when escaping the clutches of the grinding shore break. Locals have been rumoured to launch ropes at Jardim do Mar to trail surfers ashore in big swells, evidence of its extremely perilous nature. Urchins are rare and the shoreline rocks are smooth but slippery.

Water Quality
There are few major problems except around the capital, which has some environmental impact on the sea. Remember your place in the ecosystem and bring a good trash ethic when you come.

On Localism
Except when deep lows launch head high-plus swell, the number of surfable waves are limited, so crowds will be a problem in the long term. To date a friendly spirit of wave sharing between visitors and locals prevails. This isn't an island for pretenders.

ALEX WILLIAMS

Further Information

Tourist Information
Madeira Tourist Office
Funchal: (91) 229 057

Living
Hotel (single-budget range)
3000-5000
Fuel (Diesel-low): 113
Fuel(Super-low): 169

Other Info See Portugal Travelling p201

Travelling

Getting There
By air Every year 500,000 visitors from Portugal, Great Britain and France fly SATA Air Açores or TAP Air Portugal on conference or family-orientated holidays. Flights are either direct or via Lisbon. These are supplemented by a wide range of direct charter flights covering many other major European cities. There are regular shuttle air services between Lisbon and Funchal, and also between Funchal and Porto Santo.

Getting Around
By car You really need a car to access Madeira's surf potential,consequently you'll almost spend as much time driving as surfing. The breathtaking scenery, which includes mountain peaks in the clouds, terraced fields (*poios*), sheer cliffs and waterfalls on the roads, is a total nature show. Reaching spots is like reaching a ski resort: you make hundreds of turns up and down but there is no snow and the goal is not to ride down the slopes, but though spectacular, winding, narrow roads become tiring. The locals drive very slowly: 40km/h (26m/h) is a good average and you won't hit 50km/h (32m/h) without taking radical risks. Traffic is limited to tourists, taxis and pick-up trucks in most parts of the island except on Sundays. Crossing the mountain inland is always a better bet than driving around the coasts, however, motoring around the cliffs on the north coast will be a highlight of your trip. Cars are easy to hire and relatively inexpensive. Galp and Shell gas stations are plentiful.
By public transport There are public bus services from Funchal to nearby destinations, but travel to other parts of the island is best organised by car.

Spécificités du littoral

Introduction
Le surf peut être massif mais la houle s'active aussi vite qu'elle se désactive parce que l'île ne capte que le coeur du swell. La côte ultra-escarpée creuse des profondeurs d'eau effrayantes autour des spots. Comme aux Açores, les meilleurs spots se situent sur des parties affaissées de la côte, les "Fajas", ces plateformes de rochers et galets qui rentrent en pente légère dans l'océan. Avis, on trouve souvent des rochers émergés dans le déferlement de la vague. Les plages sont quasi-inexistantes, Machico et Prainha étant les deux exceptions. Par conséquent, les petites houles donnent rarement des vagues surfables car trop en shorebreak. Rentrer dans l'eau et en sortir devient une épreuve de patience quand ça rentre gros. Préparez-vous à attendre pour ramer comme un furieux au-dessus de la mousse et entre les rochers pendant l'accalmie. Porter des chaussons permet d'accélérer le mouvement dans le shorebreak de galets. Le bruit du roulement des galets devient tonitruant. On raconte que les locaux ont déjà jeté des cordes à Jardim do Mar pour ramener des surfers au bord. Les oursins sont rares mais certains caillasses sont couverts d'une algue très glissante : attention aux chevilles!

Infos Voyage

Y aller
En avion Chaque année 500.000 visiteurs du Portugal, de Grande-Bretagne et de France volent sur SATA Air Açores ou la TAP dont la plupart pour du tourisme d'affaires ou des vacances en famille. Les vols réguliers sont parfois directs mais souvent via Lisbonne. Des vols charters sont affrétés depuis la plupart des capitales européennes. Un service de navettes entre Lisbonne et Funchal et Porto Santo.

Se déplacer
Par la route Comme il faut osciller inlassablement entre la côte nord et la côte sud pour checker les spots, vous passerez plus de temps sur la route que sur les vagues. Cela signifie donc qu'il faut louer une voiture pour être le plus vite possible au meilleur spot et pour découvrir les autres attraits de l'île. Attention, les routes sineuses sont lentes et éprouvantes. La circulation sur les routes secondaires se limite souvent aux voitures de loc', aux taxis jaunes et aux pick-ups sauf le dimanche où ça roule de partout. Traverser l'île de part en part fait gagner du temps par rapport à la route côtière. Cependant, on ne se lasse pas de l'itinéraire des falaises de la côte nord.

Ireland

Great Outdoors
Chatham Street, Dublin, Ireland
Tel : +353 (0) 1 679 4293 Fax : +353 (0) 1 679 4554
E-mail : greatod@indigo.ie
Surf, snowboard and travel equipment, clothing for learners to legends, for weekend breaks to world-wide trips. All the main brands all the time.

Causeway Coast

Troggs surf shop
88 Main Street, Portrush, Co. Antrim, N. Ireland BT56 8AW
Tel : (01265) 825476 Fax : (01265) 823923
Ireland's largest surf shop. All major brands in stock. Managed by Andy Hill, 6 times Irish National Surfing Champion. Board and wetsuit hire, surf coaching. Budget surf hostel accommodation available
Also at : 20 The Diamond, Portstewart, Co Antrim
Tel : (01265) 833361 Swell line : (0839) 337770

Donegal Bay

The Strand
Strandhill
Co. Sligo
Ireland
Restaurant Tel: 071 68641
Bar Tel: 071 68140
Fax 071 68593

Find Yourself meandering betweenKnocknarea Mountain and the Great Atlantic Ocean, youll be close to The Strand! You'll love the food, the drink, and as for the craic? Well, you'll just have to visit! Music 7 nights a week during Summer Season, also Sunday afternoon music session. All musicians welcomed.

The Surfers Bar
Rossnowlagh
Co Donegal

County Clare

Lahinch surf shop
Old Promenade, Lahinch, Co Clare, Ireland
Tel : + 353 (0) 65 708 1543 Fax : + 353 (0) 708 1684
E-mail : bear@iol.ie
Ireland's first surf shop, open Saturday, Sunday and Bank Holidays all year. Open 6 days/week March to end of October. Sales and Rentals.

Southern Ireland

Attitude Surf 'n' Skate
On the Beach, Tramore, Co. Waterford, Ireland
Tel : +353 (0) 51 386022 Fax : +353 (0) 51 381423
Hardcore surf shop. Quality wetsuits, accessories & leisure-wear. For Pro. advice ask Billy - 20 years surfing experience.

Dingle

Jamie Knox
Windsurfing/Surfing/School and Hire/Shop and Accommodation.
Maharees, Castlegregory, Co Kerry
Tel (00 353) 066 39411
Fax (00 353) 0066 39011
e-mail: jamieknox@tinet.le

Surfing lessons-All levels. Beginners Windsurfing-Guaranteed to get you windsurfing in one hour. Improver and Advanced windsurfing lessons. Experienced one to one tuition. Course designed for you. ISA and RYA Recognised.

Scotland

Clan
45 Hyndland Street, Partick, Glasgow G11 5QF
Tel/Fax : (0141) 339 6523
Premier surfing equipment for colder oceans, skate hardware for Glasgow streets and snowboard gear for the Scottish Highlands and beyond. The real deal.

Moray Firth

E.S.P & She.S.P
5-7 Moss Street, Elgin, Scotland IV30 1LU
Tel/Fax : (01343) 550129
Boarding since 1992. Surf-Snow-Skate-Wake. Nigel Semmens world-class surfboards. Snugg custom made wetsuits. The freshest labels in streetwear and accessories for your lifestyle. Advice-service-repairs.

East Coast

Granite Reef Boardriders
41 Justice Street, Aberdeen AB11 5SH
Tel/Fax : (01224) 621193
E-mail : g.forbes@virgin.net
Street. Mountain. Ocean. Large stocks of surfboards, snowboards & skateboards. Wetsuits from Sola, Tiki, Rip Curl, Billabong, Quiksilver. Clothing and accessories by all major brands. Learn to surf, fully qualified BSA approved school.

Momentum surf shop
22 Bruntsfield Place, Edinburgh EH10 4HN
Tel/Fax : (0131) 229 6665

Canarian Dreams
10 Colworth Avenue, Falmouth, Cornwall TR11 4AD
Tel/Fax : (01326) 317506
E-mail : steve@canariandreams.demon.co.uk
Web : www.canariandreams.demon.co.uk

England

The Low Pressure Shop
23 Kensington Park Road
Notting Hill Gate
London W11 2EU
LOW PRESSURE
Tel/Fax 0171 792 3134

London's authentic Surf and Snow shop, owned and run by commited riders. New & second hand. Sales and Rentals. Huge stock list. No Bullshit.
10.00am - 6.00pm Mon - Sat
11.00am - 5.00pm Sun
For full travel service call 0181 960 1916.

Hi-Life
299/301 High Street, Dorking, Surrey RH4 1RE
Tel : (01306) 881910
Surrey's surf shop. Monday-Saturday 10am-5.30pm, Friday 10am-7pm. Custom boards to order. Wetsuits, accessories, videos, mags. Large range of exclusive surfwear. Also snowboards and skateboards, surfboards new and second hand, 10 minutes from the M25 Junction 9.

Surfboards:
shortboards, longboards, minimals
Wetsuits:
Bodyboards:
Clothing:
Skateboards:
In-lines:
Hire facilities:

Stockists of all major brands

4 Pavilion Terrace
Scarborough England
tel/fax +44(0)1723 500467
Phone for a free surf check
e-mail:secretspotsurfshop@btinternet.com

Wave Games
13 Upper High Street, Taunton, Somerset TA1 3PZ
Tel/Fax : (01823) 251729

North Yorkshire and Humberside

Cool Classics surf shop
No.1 Museum Terrace, Scarborough
North Yorkshire YO11 2HB
Tel : (01723) 503762 Fax : (01482) 860906
Web : www.coolclassics.co.uk (inc. e-mail)

South Coast

Torquay Windsurf Centre, Sail Repairs and Windsurfing School
55 Victoria Road, Ellacombe, Torquay TQ1 1HX
Tel : (01803) 212411 Fax : (01803) 329850

Freeride surf shop
32 Haven Road, Canford Cliffs, Poole, Dorset BH13
Tel : (01202) 708555 Fax : (01202) 70943
E-Mail : fcwatersports@btinternet.com
Web : www.btinternet.com/~fcwatersports
Surfboards: Stewart, Hobie, Phil Edwards, Spyder, CHP, Fluid Juice, Freeride custom and s/hand always available. Bodyboards: CustomX, Morey, Mike Stewart. Accessories: FCS, Balin, K. Grip. Clothing: Quiksilver, Billabong, Rip Curl, Mambo etc.

Bournemouth Surfing Centre
127 Belle Vue Road, Southbourne, Bournemouth, Dorset BH6 3DJ
Tel : (01202) 433544 Fax : (01202) 434344
Web : www.bournemouth-surfing.co.uk
Bournemouth's longest established surf shop. Surfboards, bodyboards, wetsuits, clothing by Nigel Semmens, Manta, Morey, Gul, O'Neill, Rip Curl, Billabong, Quiksilver, Reef, Headworx, Animal. Clifftop location. Very freindly staff. Open all year.
Swell line : (01202) 434344

Crazywater
402 Lymington Road, Highcliffe, Dorset BH23 5HE
Tel : (01425) 275111 Fax : (01202) 434344
Web : www.bournemouth-surfing.co.uk
200m from Clifftop. Terrific new shop with styling from the old days. Hundreds of wetsuits, bodyboards, surboards and clothing by O'Neill, Gul, Rip Curl, Quiksilver, Billabong, Oxbow, Animal, Saltrock, Reef, Headworx.

Hythe Marina Watersports
12 Shamrock way, Hythe Marina Village, Hythe, Southampton SO45 6DY
Tel : (01703) 843290
Web : www.yell.co.uk/sites/hythe-watersports/

Surf Shack
7 Widmore Road, Bromley, Kent BR1 1RL
Tel : (0181) 460 5453 Fax : (0181) 460 5399
Surf Shack
13 Market Buildings, Maidstone, Kent ME74 1HP
Tel : (01622) 661997 Fax : (01622) 690689

Channel Islands - Guernsey

Nautifun
L'Islet Crossroads, St. Sampson's, Guernsey
Tel : (01481) 46690 Fax : (01481) 43282

Channel Islands - Jersey

Seaflight surf shop
St Peter, Jersey
Tel : (01534) 483118
Real surf shop, specialising in classic and modern long-boards, Aussi wetsuits, leisure wear, custom surfboards, bodyboards, plus repairs, insurance and surf stories.

South Devon and Cornwall

Big Wednesday surf shop
26 Church Street, Falmouth TR11 3EG
Tel/Fax : (01326) 211159
Leading West Cornwall stockist of surfboards, bodyboards, wetsuits, surf leisurewear and footwear

Harbour Sports
Fore Street, Exeter; Barbican, Plymouth; Harbour, Paignton
Tel : (01803) 550180 Fax : (01803) 558084
E-mail : surf@harbour.co.uk
Web : www.harbour.co.uk

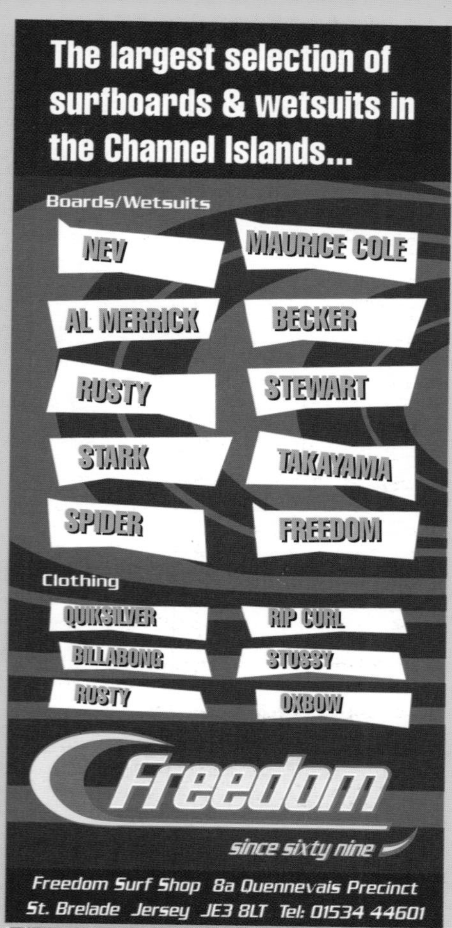

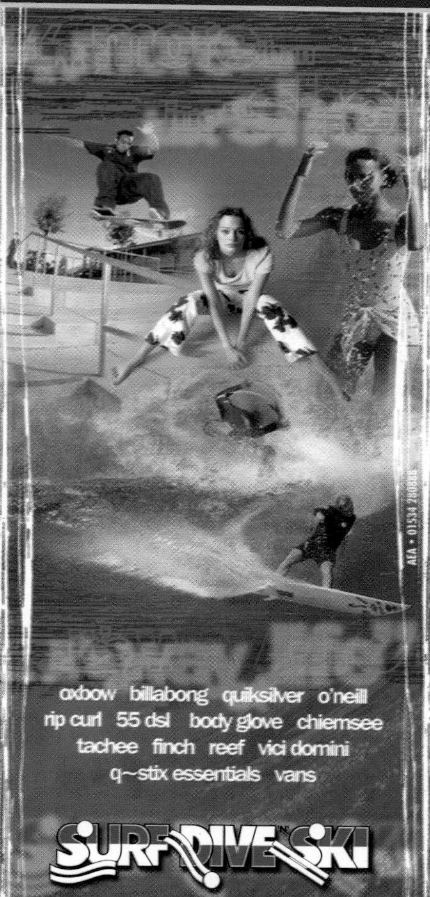

West Cornwall

Europe's Finest
SURFBOARDS
BEACH BEAT.
LINDEN.
NAT YOUNG.
KINGSLEY.
shapes by CHOPS
at
Laminations
FULL DELIVERY SERVICE
WHEAL KITTY. St AGNES. CORNWALL.
TEL:01872 552574 FAX:01872 553918

Main store in centre of town behind Boots.
Open every day for sales, surf checks & mail order.
Just call on 01288 354956

Belle Vue Lane, Bude, Cornwall EX23 8BR

always there ...

Aggie surf shop
5 Peterville Square, St. Agnes, Cornwall
Tel : (01872) 553818 Fax : (01872) 553918
E-mail : lam2574@aol.com
The Sennen Surfing Centre and surf school
4 Trevilley Farm Cottages, Sennen, Lands End, Penzance, Cornwall TR19 7AH
Tel : (01736) 871458 Fax : (01736) 365091

Whitesands lodge, guest house and backpackers
Sennen, Cornwall TR19 7AR
Tel/Fax : (01736) 871776
E-mail : whitsan@global.co.uk
Dorm beds, bed and breakfast, camping, self catering, cafe/restaurant, bar, TV/video lounge. Nor curfew - close to beach - open all year - great atmosphere

Newquay

Burning Ambitions

11 Cliff Road Newquay Cornwall
Great Britain TR7 2NE
Tel: 01637 850 848
Fax: 01637 850 870

The Fistral Beach Hotel
Esplanade Road, Pentire, Newquay, Cornwall TR7 1QA
Tel : (01637) 873044/850626 Fax : (01637) 850626

Newquay Backpackers International
69-73 Tower Road, Newquay, Cornwall
Tel/Fax : (01637) 879366
Cornwall's premier surf hostel: Great atmosphere, clean comfortable surroundings, close to all beaches & nightlife, hot showers, surfboard/wetsuit storage, large kitchen, TV/Satellite/video/music lounge, no curfew, free pick-ups
Web : www.backpackers.co.uk (inc. e-mail)

Fistral Backpackers
18 Headland Road, Newquay, Cornwall TR7 1HN
Tel : (01637) 873146

OCEAN MAGIC SURF SHOP

Surfboards by: Nigel Semmens, Ocean Magic, Al Merrick, Maurice Cole, Nev and Insight.
Main dealers for: Rip Curl mens and ladies clothing, wetsuits, watches, wallets, bags and accessories.
Clothing by: Ocean Magic.
Accessories by: Balin, Pro Surf, On a Mission, Rhino.
Sunglasses by: DSO and Legend.

1973 – 1998
25 YEARS OF SURFING EXCELLENCE

11 Cliff Road, Newquay, Cornwall TR7 2NE
Tel: 01637 850071

North Shore
36 Fore Street, Newquay, Cornwall TR7 1LP
Tel : (01637) 850620 Fax : (01637) 851968
Men's and women's wear by; Quicksilver, Billabong, Mambo, O'Neill, Airwalk, Vans, Aloha, Headworx, Oxbow. Shoes by; Vans, Airwalk, O'Neill, Simple, Reef, Globe, DC's. Large range of surfing equipment and accessories.

Smile surf shop
28 Fore Street, Newquay, Cornwall TR7 1LN
Tel : (01637) 873389 Fax : (01637) 877454

Rick's
8 Springfield Road, Newquay, Cornwall TR7 1RT
Tel : (01637) 851143
Clean and comfortable accommodation for surfers and travellers. Centrally located in Newquay and just two minutes walk to the surf. No curfews. Accommodation from £5.00 per night/£25 per week

Dolphin School of Surf
Horizon Court, Porth, Newquay, Cornwall TR7 3ND
Tel : (01637) 873707 Fax : (01637) 859099
E-mail : jp@dolphinsurfinghq.demon.co.uk
Web : www.dolphinsurf.co.uk

North Cornwall

Fluid Juice surf shop and factory
The Old Airfield, St. Merryn, Padstow, Cornwall PL28 8PU
Tel : (01841) 520928 Fax : (01841) 532478

North Devon

Le Sport surf shops
60 High Street, Barnstable, also at Croyde and Woolacombe
Tel : (01271) 379675 Fax : (01271) 323123
Swell line: 066 066 2661 - 50p/minute

The Bay surf shop
Barton Road, Woolacombe, North Devon EX34 7BA
Tel/Fax : (01271) 870961
E-mail : dhastilow@aol.com
The biggest surf shop on the North Devon coast! Massive selection of boards, bodyboards and accessories. Wetsuits by Gul and O'Neill. All top clothing brands stocked and - our staff surf!

Croyde Bay Surf Designs
7 Moor Lane, Croyde Bay, North Devon EX33 1NR
Tel/Fax : (01271) 890453 or 0700 4 SURFING
Hire specialists - Swells softboards, Freebirds, Wave-tecs, Gulfstream customs!! HB bodyboards, Octoblades. Summer, warm winter titanium wetsuits, boots, gloves, hats. Groups welcome (open W/E's only in winter). Talk to us!

Redwood surf shop
4 Bridge House, Hobbs Hill, Croyde, North Devon EX33 1LX
Tel/Fax : (01271) 890999
Web : www.redwoodsurfshop.co.uk
Redwood is owned by former English and British Champion Richard Carter with over 20 years surfing experience. Richard is available to advise surfers of any standard. Open all year. Hire always available.

Second Skin surf shop and workshop
26 Caen Street, Braunton, North Devon EX33 1AA
Tel : (01271) 812195 workshop Tel/Fax : (01271) 813300
Established 1975. Superb quality custom surfsuits handmade by Andy Schollick. Plus 100 world class surfboards, plus Oxbow - Stussy - Freshjive - Volcom - SMP - Gotcha - T & C - OP - Tahchee - Headworx - O'Neill etc. Phone for brochure.

Saltrock surf shack
24 Saunton Road, Braunton, North Devon EX33 1HB
Tel/Fax : (01271) 815619
E-mail/Web : t.b.c.
Saltrock's factory shop, run privately by Roy and Marcus selling the whole range of Saltrock clothing, accessories and seconds. Also authorised dealers for Oakley, Fanatic and many more brands.

Chapter surf shop
12 South Street, Braunton, North Devon EX33 2AA
Tel/Fax : (01271) 814517
Since 1975, run by surfers for surfers.

Wales

North Wales

Funsport
1 Beach Terrace, Rhosneigr LL64 5QB
Tel/Fax : (01407) 810899
West Coast surf shop
Lon Pen Cei, Abersoch, Gwynedd LL53 7AP
Tel : (01758) 713067 Fax : (01758) 713465
E-mail : surf@westcoastsurf.demon.co.uk
Abersoch Watersports
The Bridge, Abersoch, Gwynedd LL53 7DY
Tel : (01758) 712483 inc. mail order, Fax : (01758) 713714
E-mail : abersochwatersports@btinternet.com
Abersoch surf shop
"The first and the best"
Lon Pont Morgan, Abersoch, LL53 7HP
Tel/Fax : (01758) 712365
E-mail : surfshop@boardphoto.com

Pembrokeshire

Seaweed surf shop
The Green Room, Wilton House, Quay Street, Haverfordwest SA61 1BG
Tel/Fax : (01437) 760774
Haven Sports
Marine Road, Broadhaven, Haverfordwest, Pembrokeshire SA62 3JR
Tel/Fax : (01437) 781354
E-mail : havensports@netwales.co.uk
Web : www.boards.co.uk/shops/haven/htm

Ma Simes Surf Hut
Cross Square, St. Davids, Dyfed SA62 6SL
Tel/Fax : (01437) 720433
With over 30 years of world-wide surfing experience, we believe that Ma Simes Surf Hut is West Wales' premier surf shop. As Ma says, "it probably stocks the worlds most exclusive surfing equipment at Europe's best prices". For surf checks, sales, hire and repairs, call us.

The Gower

Hot Dog surf shop
26 Pennard Road, Kittle, Gower SA3 3JS
Tel : 01792 234073
Dave Friar surf shop
1 Tivoli Walk, Mumbles, Swansea SA3 4EE
Tel : (01792) 368861 Fax : (01792) 362277

Gower Boardriders
52b Plymouth Street, Swansea SA1 3QQ
Tel/Fax : (01792) 459555
Big Drop surf shop
1 St. David's Square, St. David's Centre, Swansea SA1 3LG
Tel : (01792) 480481 Fax : (01792) 480482

Severn Estuary

Freelap Surfboards
Unit 9, South Cornelly Trading Estate, Nr. Porthcawl, South Wales CF33 4RE
Tel : (01656) 744691 day (01639) 898932 evening
Black Rock surf shop

CARDIFF - 27, CASTLE ARCADE
01222 342068
SWANSEA - 4, PICTON ARCADE
01792 654169
EVERYTHING YOU NEED TO GO

25 New Road, Porthcawl, Mid Glamorgan CF36 5DL
Tel : (01656) 782220
Windsurfer's World/B.S.B. Snowboarding
68 West Street, Old Market, Bristol BS2 0BL
Tel : (0117) 955 0779 Fax : (0117) 941 1744

North Sea Nations

Surfsentrum
Madlaveien 10, 4008 Stavanger, Norway
Tel : (51) 531122 Fax : (51) 528550
E-mail : surf@telepost.no
Outback Sports-wear
Strandstraße 19, 25980 Westerland/Sylt, Germany
Tel : (04651) 1673 Fax : (04651) 24045
Germany's real surf shop
Dark Blue surf shop
Klostergade 8, 3000 Helsingør, Denmark
Tel : (4921) 0346 Fax : (4921) 4046
Windsurfing Klitmøller
Ørhagevej 119, Klitmøller, 7700 Thisted, Denmark
Tel : (9797) 5656 Fax : (9797) 5611
Danish Surfing Association
Ruskor 53,10, 2610 Rødovre, Denmark
Tel/Fax : (3647) 4090

van den Berg Windsurfing
Kernweg 1, HN 80, 1627 LC Hoorn, Nederland
Tel : (022) 921913 Fax : (022) 9211203
E-mail : vandenberghoorn@tref.nl
Web : www.vandenberg-surf.nl
REM Surfing
Passage 14, 2042 KU Zandvoort, Nederland
Tel : (023) 5718600 Fax : (023) 578600
Web : www.remsurfing.com
Spare Time California Sports and Clothing
Rijnstraat 205, 1079 HE Amsterdam, Nederland
Tel : (020) 6460807 Fax : (020) 6611521
E-mail : info@sparetime.nl
Web : www.sparetime.nl

House of Lifestyle, XXX
Overtoom 338, 1054 JE Amsterdam, Nederland
Tel/Fax : (020) 6890345
E-mail : hol.xxx@wxs.nl
We are an Amsterdam based surf shop producing local 'Concha Custom Surfboards'. The pro shop in Holland

Hart Beach shop
Vissershavenweg 55b, 2583 DL Scheveningen, Nederland
Tel : (070) 3545583 Fax : (070) 3514556
Web : www.hartbeach.nl
Surf shop since 1968. Open seven days, always 50+ boards in stock. School, rental, repair, wetsuits, fashion etc. Major brands including Rusty, Quiksilver, Billabong, O'Neill, Pipe Dream, Hobie, T & C, Robert August, Blue Hawaii, Nev.

Uli Scherb · Martin Storck
Beckstraße 54 · 64287 Darmstadt

Phone: ++49 (0)6151- 45727
Fax: ++49 (0)6151-425052
e-mail: info@wavetours.com
http//:www.wavetours.com
Germany

DWV anerkannte Schule

Go Klap surf shop
Dr Lelykade 44, (2nd Harbour) 2583 CM Scheveningen, Nederland
Tel : (070) 3548679 Fax : (070) 3588194
The far out oldest surfshop in Holland. Surfboards, bodyboards, waveski's, sailboards, wetsuits, skates, surf and streetwear etc. Also rental and surf check!!

Windsurfing Renesse
De Zoom 15, 4325 BG Renesse, Nederland
Tel/Fax : (0111) 462702
Pro surf and fashion shop. Wind-surf-body and skimboards, second hand, hire and repairs, world-wide surfing holidays : "Surf and travel agency". Clothing, wetsuits, accessories etc... Test-centre + shop on the beach, Rooms for rent!!

Vertriels Hautzel
Maastrichterstr.36
50672 Köln
Germany
Tel: 0221 525280
Fax: 0221 525290

Distributors of: Billabong, Atlantis, Simple and the Low Pressure Guides

Sportshop Domburg
Weststraat 2a, 4357 BM Domburg, Nederland
Tel : (0118) 586012 Fax : (0118) 586013
E-mail : jansan@zeelandnet.nl
Web : www.uitsite.nl (action sports)
Surfer's Paradise surf club
Strand, 8301 Knokke-Heist, België
Tel : (050) 615960 Fax : (050) 628587
E-mail : frank.vanleenhove@pophost.eunet.be
Web : www.netgate.be/surfersparadise
Beachcam : www.surfersparadise.be
Oostend Surfing
Troonstraat 49, 8400 Oostende, België
Tel : (059) 505818
Blue Marine
Kaai 13, 8620 Nieuwpoort, België
Tel : (058) 238523

Wim Van Cleynenbreugel
Bunsbeekstraat 9
3012 Wilsele
België
Distributors of: Semente Boards and Clothing and the Low Pressure Guides

Rip Curl Scandinavia
Ryesgade 56 b, kld.tv
2100 KBH
Danemark
Phone:45 35 34 33 04
Fax: 45 35 34 33 09
E. mail: Flojo@post6.tele.dk
Distributors of: Rip Curl and the Low Pressure Guides

La Manche

Chattanooga surf shop
53-71, avenue Bosquet, 75007 Paris
Tel (01) 4551 7665 Fax : (01) 4753 0150
Depuis 1978. 2 min de la Tour Eiffel. Métro : école militaire. Du lundi au samedi. 10h30-19h30. Tout l'équipement pour le surf, le bodyboard, le skate et le snow. Catalogue VPC sur demande. Se habla español. English spoken.

France

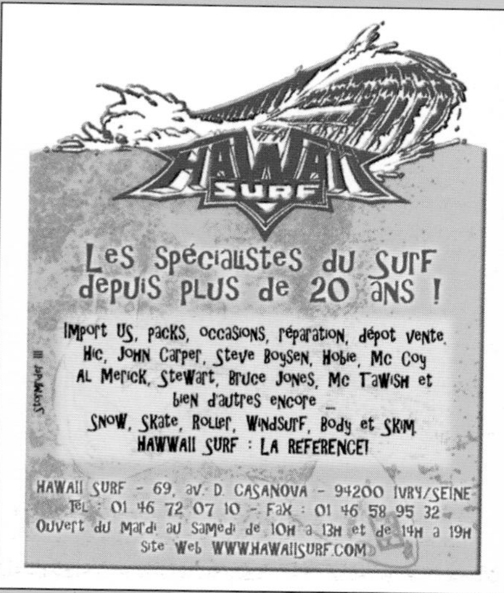

Shark Island surf shop
66, rue d' Ecosse, 76200 Dieppe, Tel/fax : (02) 3540 0590

Bretagne Nord

Magic Surf
39, rue Branda, 29200 Brest
Tel : (02) 9844 9588 Fax : (02) 9843 1206

Kana Beach surf shop
10, Place de la Liberté, 29000 Brest
Tel : (02) 9838 3164, Fax : (02) 9843 6731
Ouvert toute l'année du mardi au samedi 10h-12h/14h-19h
Longboards et shortboards Kana + toute la collection Kana Beach. Matos surf/ skate : K-Grip, OAM, Powell, Plan B, Indy…90 modèles de shoes.
Services : réparations, OSR : (08) 3668 1360

Bretagne Sud

Atlantic surf shop
Route de la Torche, 29120 Plomeur
Tel : (02) 9858 7487, Fax : (02) 9858 7069
Swell line : (08) 3668 4064
Dezert Point surf shop
5bis, Place de Locronan, 29000 Quimper
Tel/fax : (02) 9853 5960

Authentic surf shop
48, Av du général de Gaulle, 56170 Quiberon
Tel : (02) 9750 0193 Fax : (02) 9750 0987

Action Line
Centre commercial de la plage, 56520 Guidel
Tel : (02) 9705 9300 Fax : (02) 9705 9752
Ouvert tous les jours, toute l'année, sauf le dimanche en hiver. 10h-12h / 14h-19h. Un shaper de renom à disposition pour tous types de planches. Conseils, réparations, locations tous azimuts (wind, roller, kayak). We won't laugh at your french but we speak english.
OSR : (08) 3668 1360

Vendeé

Pointbreak surf shop
8, quai des greniers, 85800 St-Gilles Croix de Vie
Tel/fax : (02) 5155 0808 Swell line : (08) 3668 4064

Bahia surf shop
42, rue des Remparts. Le Remblai, 85100 Les Sables d'Olonne
Tel/fax : (02) 5121 2199 Swell line : (08) 3668 4064

Seatime surf shop
13, Promenade Georges Clémenceau
85100 Les Sables d'Olonne Tel / fax: (02) 5132 8905
Face à l'océan. Ouvert toute l'année. Grand choix de marques (Rosaleen), conseils techniques (Cedric), location et cours de surf&bodyboard. OSR : (08) 3668 1360

Charente

Le Palmier surf shop
14, rue du Pertuis Breton, 85360 La Tranche / Mer
Tel / fax : (02) 5127 4590

Matos/sport connexion shop
Tous la glisse depuis 1981, 17410 St-Martin de Ré
Tel /fax : (05) 4609 1148

Island surf shop
4, rue de la Bouline, 17310 St-Pierre d'Oléron
Tel : (05) 4647 3798, Fax : (05) 4647 3967

Vent d'ouest surf shop
142, rue Gambetta
17200 Royan
Tel : (05) 4639 8654
Fax : (05) 4639 4814
Au dessus du port. Ouvert toute l'année, tous les jours sauf le lundi en hiver. 9h30-12h30 / 14h30-19h30. Ecole Surf Academy d'avril à Septembre. English spoken.
Swell line : (08) 3668 4064

Gironde

Surfer's
23, rue des Remparts, 33000 Bordeaux
Tel : (05) 5644 0022 Fax : (05) 5652 7683

Pacific Island
15, Allées Pierre Ortal, 33680 Lacanau Océan
Tel/fax : (05) 5603 2706
Rue principale. Ouvert tous les jours d'avril à octobre. Conseils avisés de Thierry Fernandez, champion d'Europe, pour tous types de planches. Surfwear de grandes marques et nombreux accessoires techniques.

Maison de la Glisse
Bd de la Plage, 33680 Lacanau Océan
Tel : (05) 5626 3884, Fax : (04) 5626 3885

Tutti Frutti surf shop
42, Bd de la plage, 33950 Cap Ferret
Tel : (05) 5660 6178 Fax : (05) 5603 7232
Swell line : (08) 3668 4064

Landes

Blue Hawaii surf shop
321, Bd d'Arcachon, 40600 Biscarrosse plage
Tel : (05) 5878 2811 Swell line : (08) 3668 4064

Maa surf shop
3, Centre commercial, 40660 Moliets & Maa
Tel/fax : (05) 5848 5569

Wishbone surf shop
Res Rivages. BP 42, 40480 Vieux-Boucau
Tel/Fax : (05) 5848 3070
Sur le promenoir du lac. Ouvert en saison tous les jours d'avril à septembre. Tout le matos de la glisse en vente et en location. Réparations, cours et stages de surf.
Swell line : (08) 3668 4064

Hossegor

La Vigie surf shop
1, place de Castille, 40510 Seignosse-le-Penon
Tel : (05) 5843 3070 Fax : (05) 5843 3956

Biarritz

Espaces Neige & Vagues
Residence Itsasoan
64210 GUETHARY
Tel/Fax 05 5954 8178

Barland shapes & O'neill wetsuit
32, Allées Paulmy, 64100 Bayonne
Tel : (05) 5959 0240 Fax : (05) 5925 5005

Stark Shapes
7, Allées de Foix, 64600 Anglet
Tel/Fax : (05) 5963 9478

Auberge de Jeunesse d'Anglet, 19 rue des Vignes, 64600 Anglet Tel : (05) 5958 7000 Fax : (05) 5958 7007
Hébergment en chambres et en camping. A 500m des plages, ouvert toute l'année. Formules pour tous budgets. Ecole et stage de surf. Pub ecossais le soir : ambiance assurée !

Le Point d'or. Face a l'ocean.
Hos' Oyat Surf shop & école de surf Magic Glisse depuis 1986. Ouvert de mai à octobre.
tel/fax 05 5843 9290.

Hebergement - cours - Tarifs - reservations
RENSEIGNEMENTS MATAHARI Surf Shop : 2, rue Jules Ferry
33680 LACANAU OCEAN Tel/Fax : 05.56.03.13.01

Seaside surf shop & school
Chambre d'Amour
64600 Anglet
Tel : (05) 5903 0191
Fax (05) 5903 3098
Swell line : (08) 3668 4064

Boardrider surf shop
Casino Municipal, 64200 Biarritz
Tel : (05) 5922 0312 Fax : (02) 5924 3244
Tous les jours toute l'année de 9h30 à 19h30 en face de la Grande Plage. Toute la collection Quiksilver. Jeff Hakman surf school. English spoken, se habla español.
Swell line: (08) 3668 4064

Barland surf shop
60, Av Edouard VII, 64200 Biarritz
Tel : (05) 5924 4220

Auberge de
Jeunesse de Biarritz, 8 rue Chiquito de Cambo
64200 Biarritz
Tel : (05) 5941 7600 Fax : (05) 5941 7607
Au carrefour de l'océan et des Pyrénées, en plein Pays Basque. Hébergement moderne et adapté à l'accueil des surfers, sur l'un des meilleurs spots d'Europe.

Méditerranée

Neptune surf shop
Villa Bianca . Avenue Foch, 34250 Palavas
Tel : (04) 6768 1960 Fax : (04) 6768 1880
Swell line : (08) 3668 4064

Welcome 264 surf shop
92, Place de Bonnegrâce, 83140 Six-Fours-Les-Plages
Tel/fax : (04) 9407 5226

Manipura shapes
Extension Plein Sud. Av de la Pétanque, 13600 La Ciotat
Tel/fax : (04) 4283 5519 Swell line : (08) 3668 4064

Planete Glisse surf shop
Bat. A 15, av Ilaires, 83890 Le Lavandou
Tel : (04) 9471 1650 Fax : (04) 9464 7285
Swell line : (08) 3668 4064

Massilia surf shop
2, rue Dieudé, 13006 Marseille
Tel /fax: (04) 9154 3060
Près de la préfecture. Ouvert tous les jours (sauf lundi en hiver), toute l'année. 9h30-19h30. Planches Nev, Aloha. Réparation et location tous types de planches. Infos pour le surfclub de la Sardine. Rayon snowboard.

Mac Millan surf shop
La Gare SNCF, 13960, Sausset-Les-Pins
Tel : (04) 4244 7800 Fax : (04) 4244 7544
La gare la plus surf de Méditerranée ouverte toute l'année, tous les jours sauf le lundi matin. Atelier de shape top juste à côté : custom et shortboards. Le shaper vous écoute. Réparations. Ride the train, ride the waves !
OSR : (08) 3668 1360

Pukas surf shops
- Nafarroa Kalea 4, 20800 Zarautz
  Tel : (943) 835821 Fax : (943) 134149
- C/Mayor 5, 20003 San Sebastian
  Tel : (943) 427228 Fax : (943) 428369
  E-mail : pukas@facilnet.es (both shops)
  Web : www.pukas-surf.com

Pukas surf schools

PUKAS Surf Eskola

- Zarautz Beach
  (on the beach front
  "in the paseo")
  Tel : (970) 422036
- Zurriola Beach, San Sebastian
  (at the right side of the beach)
  Tel : (943) 580163
  Web : www.pukas-surf.com

Pukas board factory and surfwear wholesale
- Olatu S.A., Apartado 60, 20180 Oyarzun
  Tel : (943) 493258/493258
  Fax : (943) 491571
  E-mail : olatu@facilnet.es
  Web : www.pukas-surf.com

Spain

Styling Surf, Snow, Ski, Sport
Pza. Campuzano, Bilbao
Tel : (944) 416150
Centro Comercial, Artea-Leioa
Tel : (944) 601416 Fax : (944) 601422

Mundaka Surf Shop
Txorrokopunta 8, Mundaka 48360, Bizkaia
Tel : (946) 876721 Fax : (946) 877845
E-mail : mundsurf@jet.es
Surf shop established since 1985 in Europe's famous left-hander. Surfboard factory experienced in making boards for waves from Italy to Canaries, Surf school operative in summer. Rental service. Open 7 days.

La Tribu Rock Bar
C/ La Costa 4, 39180 Noja - Cantabria
Tel : (919) 249973

Surf and Rock
C/ Cordeleria 15, 15003 A Coruna
Tel : (981) 224828 Fax : (981) 701512

Spot surf store
C/Ponzos 54; C/Maria 176, 15404 Ferrol
Tel : (981) 354364 Tel/Fax : (981) 370672

Portugal

Semente Factory and Shop
Tel : (061) 864630/63552 Fax : (061) 864630
Rabo da Raposa, 2640 Ribamar
Quality boards, wetsuits, accessories, clothing, repairs, advice, vibes. Portugese - English - Spanish - French.

The Surf Experience
The Town House, 42 Rua do Castello Dos Governadores, 8600 Lagos, Algarve
Tel/Fax : (82) 761943
The Country Villa, PO Box 621, 8600 Lagos, Algarve
Tel : (082) 760964 Fax : (082) 767288
or Low Pressure Travel, Tel : +44 (0) 181 960 1916
Based at Lagos on the south west tip of Portugal, and accessing some of the best waves and most beautiful beaches in Europe. Accommodation either at the legendary Town House in the centre of Lagos, or full luxury at The Country Villa. Both locations include full 4WD transport to south and west coast breaks, airport transfers and breakfast plus a generous lunch on the beach. Full quiver of quality boards and rubber available to hire.

Morocco

Fun & Fly/Dynamic Loisirs
A Tamghart, Fun & Fly vous propose un Surf Camp dans une jolie et typique maison d'hôtes dominant les spots de surf. Excellente cuisine. Gestion français. Ecole de surf (avec encadrement français) ouverte d'octobre à avril.
In Tamghart, Fun & Fly offers a Surf Camp in a pretty typical guest house upon a hill overlooking famous surf spots (qualified instructors), open from October to April.
Information
55 bd de l'Embouchure, 31200 Toulouse, France
Tel : +33 (0) 562 72 46 05
Fax : +33 (0) 561 13 00 03
E-mail : info@fun-and-fly.com

Canaries

Fun & Fly/La Santa Surf (Lanzarote)
A La Santa, Fun and Fly vous propose un large choix d'hébergements/studios appartements proche des meilleurs spots de la côte nord. La Santa Surf School est ouverte toute l'année (pour tous niveaux).
In La Santa, Fun and Fly features a range of accommodation close to all the North Shore famous surf spots. The La Santa Surf School is open all year round (all levels).
Information
55 bd de l'Embouchure, 31200 Toulouse, France
Tel : +33 (0) 562 72 46 05
Fax : +33 (0) 561 13 00 03
E-mail : info@fun-and-fly.com

Ineika surf camp and surf school
35660 Corralejo, Fuerteventura
Tel/Fax : (928) 535744 ; Germany Tel : +89 (0) 4314403
E - Mail : Ineikafun@aol.com
or Low Pressure Travel
Tel/Fax +44 (0) 181 960 1916
On the north tip of Fuerteventura, close to north coast hot spots and famous Lobos rights. Cruise the lunar landscape to lava reefs, long sandy beaches or take the boat to Lobos long before the first ferry. Surf school or 4WD to 20 of the best breaks.

Aloha surf shops
C/ St Domingo 12, 38400 Puerto de la Cruz, Tenerife
Tel : (922) 380005
C/ Imeldo Seris 17, 38003 St Cruz de Tenerife, Tenerife
Tel : (922) 242206
C/ San Agustin 23, 38410 Los Realejos, Tenerife
Tel : (922) 354269
Aloha Surf Shop was established in 1980 as the first surf shop in the Canaries. In the year 2000 it will be our 20th anniversary on the road servicing lovers of the fine sport of surfing, and we want to take this opportunity to thank all our clients for their support.

Wave Tours
Beckstr. 54, Darmstadt 64287, Germany
Tel : +49 (0) 6151 45725 Fax : +49 (0) 425052
E-mail : info@wavetours.com
Web : www.wavetours.com
Surf camps in France, Portugal and Fuertaventura

the snowboard GUIDE
europe
THE snowboard GUIDE
NORTH AMERICA
THE STORMRIDER GUIDE
EUROPE
A LOW PRESSURE PUBLICATION
THE STORMRIDER GUIDE
NORTH AMERICA
A LOW PRESSURE PUBLICATION